Y0-AWH-422

Donated by
Donna Rook
to The Heartland Institute
2016

2006 Index of Economic Freedom

MARC A. MILES, Ph.D., is Director of the Center for International Trade and Economics (CITE) at The Heritage Foundation.

KIM R. HOLMES, Ph.D., is Vice President, Foreign and Defense Policy Studies, and Director, Kathryn and Shelby Cullom Davis Institute for International Studies at The Heritage Foundation .

MARY ANASTASIA O'GRADY is Editor of the "Americas" column and Senior Editorial Page Writer at *The Wall Street Journal.*

EDWIN J. FEULNER, Ph.D., is President of The Heritage Foundation.

William W. Beach is John M. Olin Senior Fellow in Economics and Director of the Center for Data Analysis at The Heritage Foundation.

Pauline Dixon, Ph.D., is International Research Coordinator of the E.G. West Centre in the School of Education, University of Newcastle, United Kingdom.

Ana Isabel Eiras is Senior Policy Analyst in International Economics in the Center for International Trade and Economics (CITE) at The Heritage Foundation. She is also Editor of the Spanish-language edition of the *Index of Economic Freedom.*

Paul A. Gigot is Editor of *The Wall Street Journal* Editorial Page.

Michael Gonzalez is Editorial Page Editor of the *Asian Wall Street Journal.*

Anthony B. Kim is Research Associate in the Center for International Trade and Economics (CITE) at The Heritage Foundation.

Barun Mitra is Director of the Liberty Institute, an independent public policy research organization in New Delhi, India.

Brett D. Schaefer is Jay Kingham Fellow in the Margaret Thatcher Center for Freedom at The Heritage Foundation.

James Tooley, Ph.D., is Director of the E.G. West Centre in the School of Education, University of Newcastle, United Kingdom.

As this year's edition of the *Index* was being prepared for press, our colleague Mary O'Grady was awarded the prestigious Bastiat Prize in Journalism.

Established and run by International Policy Network (IPN), the Bastiat Prize celebrates journalists whose writing cleverly and wittily promotes the institutions of free society, emulating the 19th century French philosopher Frédéric Bastiat.

The judges certainly chose well. Our warmest congratulations to Mary on this richly deserved honor.

—Kim R. Holmes and Marc A. Miles

2006 Index of Economic Freedom

Marc A. Miles, Ph.D.

Kim R. Holmes, Ph.D.

Mary Anastasia O'Grady

with Ana Isabel Eiras, Brett D. Schaefer, and Anthony B. Kim

The Heritage Foundation   THE WALL STREET JOURNAL.

Copyright © 2006 by The Heritage Foundation and Dow Jones & Company, Inc.

The Heritage Foundation
214 Massachusetts Avenue, NE
Washington, DC 20002
(202) 546-4400
heritage.org

The Wall Street Journal
Dow Jones & Company, Inc.
200 Liberty Street
New York, NY 10281
(212) 416-2000
www.wsj.com

Cover images by photos.com, gettyimages.com, and istockpro.com
Cover design by Rick Harrigan
ISBN: 0-89195-271-3
ISSN: 1095-7308

Table of Contents

Foreword

The big economic story of the past year has been the paradox of high energy prices coexisting with strong growth. Despite oil prices reaching $70 a barrel, the global economy continued its post-bubble and post–September 11 expansion, growing a remarkable 5.1 percent in 2004 and continuing at a more than 4 percent pace in 2005, according to the International Monetary Fund. The explanation for this seeming contradiction can be found in the trends illuminated over the past dozen years in this *Index of Economic Freedom.*

As he prepares to depart after 18 years as Federal Reserve Chairman, Alan Greenspan has been touting the virtues of America's economic "flexibility." Among other things, he cites financial derivatives that allow banks to diversify their risk, as well as open labor markets that allow companies to hire—and, crucially, fire—workers more easily. If you read between the lines, what Mr. Greenspan is describing are the practical benefits of economic liberty. Free-market policies allow economies to absorb financial and other shocks more quickly and with less long-term pain.

Nowhere is this more evident than in the United States, which continued to drive the world economy despite critics who often sound as if American policies are the problem. For two years following the 2003 tax cuts, the U.S. grew at an average and relatively consistent rate of about 4 percent. At this writing, Hurricane Katrina seemed likely to break that streak, but the economy had enough momentum before the storm that a recession was improbable. Thanks to its "flexibility," the U.S. is about twice as energy-efficient today as it was during the energy crisis of the 1970s. So while $70 oil acts like a tax, it hasn't been as damaging as it would have been in the past.

The world has also received a lift from the Communist countries that have come in from the socialist cold. China's growth gets the most media attention, but the contribution from the nations of Central Europe has also been notable. The Baltic States, the Slovak Republic, Slovenia, and Poland have all climbed sharply up the freedom ranks, earning the prosperity that comes with sound policies.

These countries have even begun to set

the world's policy agenda by their adoption of the flat tax. First promoted in America by Milton Friedman, the flat tax has now been adopted in some form by at least 11 European countries. More are interested, including once-socialist Greece. As capital has poured into flat-tax countries, this innovation has created tax-policy competition that other European Union countries can't ignore. Even Germany and France, so wedded to their welfare state model, have had to consider reducing their tax rates.

It's worth noting, by the way, that this kind of policy competition is exactly what was predicted by Robert Mundell, the Nobel-winning economist, and former *Wall Street Journal* Editor Robert Bartley when they advocated the adoption of the euro. Once politicians were no longer able to inflate their way out of their fiscal burdens, they would have no choice but to confront their bad policies. Whether the formerly Communist nations of Eastern Europe can rescue the slow-growth, high-unemployment welfare states of Western Europe is a drama to watch in the coming years.

The main threats to the global expansion are policy errors. In the U.S., the risks include a modest inflation revival caused by the Fed's monetary accommodation in 2003 and 2004. It's hard to know how far the Fed will have to tighten money to prevent any larger inflation breakout, but you can bet Chairman Greenspan will not want to leave his successor with an inflation prob-

lem. He's set to depart in January, and the financial markets will quickly test the new appointee's anti-inflation bona fides.

Another storm cloud is trade tension, especially between the U.S. and China. After the evidence of the past 50 years, you'd think the case for open trade was beyond dispute. But the same American political forces that fretted about Japan in the 1980s have now turned their blame on China. The Bush Administration bent to these forces by imposing quotas on textiles and, more ominously, has so far been unwilling to make a full-throated defense of free trade. The Central American Free Trade Agreement passed Congress by a whisker, and then only because the Administration declined to veto a spendthrift highway bill in return. A successful conclusion to the Doha Round of multilateral trade talks would be a welcome antidote to this growing protectionist drift.

The terrorism threat also remains, though even here the world seems to be adjusting. The 2005 bombings in London and Bali did little economic damage, in contrast to the shock of September 11. This, too, is a tribute to the adaptability of a world economy that has slowly but surely come to understand the practical necessity of free markets.

Paul A. Gigot
Editorial Page Editor
The Wall Street Journal
November 2005

Preface

Every person, no matter how poor or how rich, has a dream. Some dream of someday owning a huge business. Others dream of owning a home, traveling, sending their children to a good school, buying a car, or just having food on the table every day. Still others dream of a professional career. At the same time, people have skills that they can use to work, save, and achieve their dreams. In some countries, achieving these dreams is easier than in others. At the heart of our *Index of Economic Freedom* is the assessment of how difficult it is to achieve those dreams because of the obstacles that ordinary people face in different parts of the world in trying to fulfill their life goals.

Economic freedom is necessary for people to prosper. By reducing obstacles, it creates a framework within which people can choose how to use their time, skills, and resources: a framework in which innovation is welcomed and economic growth is enhanced. Simply put, around the world, countries with a higher degree of and strong commitment to economic freedom enjoy a higher standard of living.

The *Index of Economic Freedom* has docu-mented this relationship over 12 years of research and analysis of economic policies in 161 countries. Published jointly by The Heritage Foundation and *The Wall Street Journal*, the *Index* has presented a portrait of economic freedom around the world and established a benchmark by which to gauge a country's prospects for economic success. Tracing the path to economic prosperity, the annual *Index* continues to serve a wide and diverse audience of students, teachers, policymakers, business leaders, investors, and the media.

The *Index* identifies the strong complementarities among the 10 key ingredients of economic freedom such as low tax rates, tariffs, regulation, and government intervention, as well as strong property rights, open capital markets, and monetary stability. As previous editions have shown, increased economic freedom in one factor amplifies economic freedom in another. Likewise, a decline of freedom in one area makes it harder to take advantage of economic freedom in another.

In this 12th edition, we find once again that economic freedom is crucial to development and sustained prosperity in our integrated global market. A commitment to open markets is essential if a country wants to stay competitive and respond positively to constant changes in the global economy. Repressed markets create rigid conditions that doom countries to falling behind innovations elsewhere.

The *2006 Index of Economic Freedom* shows that economic freedom continues to advance around the world, with more people enjoying the benefits of its expansion. Every region except North Africa and the Middle East has significant net gains in this year's edition. North America and Europe experience the greatest regional net gain. While economic freedom declines in only 10 economies, the level improves in 33 countries. Austria, Armenia, Cyprus, and the Czech Republic are among those countries most strongly embracing more economic freedom. Thus, this region remains the freest, with six of the top 10 ranked countries.

Sub-Saharan Africa, Asia and the Pacific, and Latin America and the Caribbean have net gains of 13, 10, and five countries, respectively. Yet persistent obstacles to achieving greater economic freedom still remain in North Africa and the Middle East, which have three more countries with declining rather than rising freedom.

The *2006 Index* contains three stories that focus on the effects of economic repression on the life of ordinary people. In India, convoluted regulations condemn the lives of millions of people to perpetual poverty by pushing them to live and work in the informal market. Yet the Indian people find a way to minimize the impact of these restrictions. In Nigeria, the quality of public schools is so wretched that people living on less than a dollar a day pay a small fee to give their children better education through unsanctioned, privately run schools. The same behavior can be found in five other very poor cities in Asia and Africa. In China, a private network of small lenders is providing the emerging private sector with loans that debt-burdened state banks cannot provide. It is clear from these stories that people will always strive to find a way to advance their individual freedom. It is also clear that governments could and should encourage their efforts.

The message from this year's *Index* is unmistakable: Improving and maintaining economic freedom is the only reliable way to generate a positive cycle of economic growth and prosperity in this era of increasing globalization. Shortsighted economic measures or repeated government intervention run the risk of interrupting this positive cycle and, in the worst case, replacing it with a vicious cycle of repression and poverty. The key is commitment and an understanding of the rewards that commitment can bring.

Edwin J. Feulner, Ph.D., President
The Heritage Foundation
November 2005

Acknowledgments

We wish to express our grateful appreciation to the many individuals, especially those at The Heritage Foundation, who have made such valuable contributions to this 12th annual edition of the *Index of Economic Freedom*.

The primary responsibility for producing the *Index* was borne by The Heritage Foundation's Center for International Trade and Economics (CITE). Ana Isabel Eiras, Brett Schaefer, and Anthony Kim did an excellent job in grading the countries this year. Anthony also assumed the responsibility of coordinating the complex process by which the *Index* is produced and authored the statistical summary that accompanies each country write-up. Gail Garnett provided outstanding production support for all aspects of this project.

Other divisions of The Heritage Foundation also made their usual valuable contributions. In the Douglas and Sarah Allison Center for Foreign Policy Studies, a division of the Kathryn and Shelby Cullom Davis Institute for International Studies, Ariel Cohen, John Hulsman, Stephen Johnson, James Phillips, and Will Schirano wrote introductory paragraphs and provided their expertise. We are especially grateful for the many insightful contributions that Helle C. Dale, Director of the Douglas and Sarah Allison Center for Foreign Policy Studies, made to the content of this year's *Index*. Yvette Campos and Marla Graves provided valuable production support, in addition to which Marla did the initial editing of the 161 country introductions.

In the Asian Studies Center, Director Peter Brookes, Dana Dillon, Balbina Hwang, and John Tkacik, Jr., wrote introductions and provided assistance, and Allison Goodman provided valuable production support. We are particularly grateful to William Beach, Director of the Center for Data Analysis, for his continued support and for his contributions to Chapter 5. We thank Todd Gaziano, Senior Fellow in Legal Studies, for his perceptive comments on the property rights factor in the United States. His superb insights once again added depth to our understanding of legal changes in the United States, clarified relevant issues, and helped us to focus on those issues in a global perspective. In the Information Technology Department, invaluable help was provided by Vice President of Information Technology Michael Spiller, Genevieve Grimes, Joanna Yu, and Michael Smith. We are grateful for their professionalism.

We are also grateful to Ted Morgan, Director of Online Communications, and his staff for placing the entire *Index* on the Heritage Web site (*www.heritage.org/index/*). They also did an excellent job of developing a searchable database that helps researchers identify key trends over the 12-year history of the *Index*.

Once again, we wish to express our deep appreciation for the work of Senior Editor Richard Odermatt, who was responsible for final review of the entire text, and Senior Copy Editor William T. Poole, who continues to bear the primary responsibility for editing the entire book. Each year, their professionalism, commitment to the project, and attention to detail continue to play a major part in making the *Index* a reality.

In Publishing Services, Director Jonathan Larsen, Elizabeth Brewer, and Rick Harrigan were responsible for the extensive design and layout that make this 12th edition the most readable and accessible yet published, as well as for developing the regional and country maps and formatting the charts and tables, and Therese Pennefather coordinated the entire production process. We also thank Rebecca Hagelin, Vice President of Communications and Marketing, for her insightful contributions to the book.

Countless individuals serving with various accounting firms, businesses, research organizations, U.S. government agencies, foreign embassies, and other organizations cooperated by providing us with the data used in the *Index*. Their assistance is much appreciated. Barbara Weinschelbaum did a superb job of proofreading the English-language *Index*, crosschecking facts and figures; and the invaluable efforts of Heritage interns Frank Caliva, John Goodman, Patrick Rooney, and Mark Williams made the specialists' in-depth analysis possible. We wish them all the best in their new ventures.

As always, we acknowledge our enduring debt both to Heritage Trustee Ambassador J. William Middendorf II, for originally encouraging us to undertake such a study of global economic freedom, and to the many other people within Heritage who continue to lend their expertise to our effort as they have in past years.

Finally, we would like to express our appreciation to the many people who, year after year, have either praised or criticized the *Index of Economic Freedom* so enthusiastically. The support and encouragement of people in all parts of the world continue to serve as a major source of inspiration for The Heritage Foundation and *The Wall Street Journal* in their ongoing collaboration on this important work. We hope this year's effort once again matches the expectations of our supporters, as well as the thoughtful critics who so often have provided the insights that enable us to continue to improve the *Index*.

Marc A. Miles, Ph.D.
Kim R. Holmes, Ph.D.
Mary Anastasia O'Grady
November 2005

What's New in the 2006 *Index?*

Every year, the editors of the *Index* evaluate the publication and consider ways to improve the product. Years have seen dramatic changes in the layout of the *Index*, resulting in a more user-friendly and informative publication. Both the 2000 *Index* and the 2004 *Index* introduced changes in methodology for the monetary policy, fiscal burden of government, and government intervention in the economy factors to enhance the robustness of those factors in capturing economic freedom. The 2001 *Index* saw the publication of a Spanish-language edition in cooperation with several Latin American think tanks. That same edition was the first to suspend countries from grading due to insufficient or inapplicable data.

As with previous years, the 2006 *Index* incorporates improvements in the publication and changes in the world's landscape.

- **Revised methodology for the trade policy factor.** The editors were pleased when the *Index* trade policy factor was chosen by the United States Millennium Challenge Corporation as one of its 16 indicators for determining eligibility for development

grants. The MCC chose the *Index* based on its breadth of coverage and transparency. However, the MCC expressed frustration over the five-point grading scale, which resulted in clumping of countries, making differentiation among MCC candidate countries difficult. To assist the MCC, the editors hired an independent expert to analyze the existing scale and prevailing trade barriers in order to devise a scale with a wider distribution (finer differences between countries). Aside from the wider grading scale, the methodology is unchanged. The trade policy score is based on a country's weighted average tariff rate—weighted by imports from the country's trading partners. The higher the rate, the worse (or higher) the score. If there is ample evidence of non-tariff barriers and/or corruption, a country's score based solely on tariff rates receives an additional point (representing decreased economic freedom).

- **Incorporation of 10 new countries into the European Union.** For the first time since publication of the *Index* began, there has been a major political shift by a group of

Revised Trade Policy Grading Scale

Score	Levels of Protectionism	Criteria
1	Very low	Weighted average tariff rate less than or equal to 2.5 percent.
1.5	Low	Weighted average tariff rate greater than 2.5 percent but less than or equal to 5 percent.
2	Low	Weighted average tariff rate greater than 5 percent but less than or equal to 7.5 percent.
2.5	Moderate	Weighted average tariff rate greater than 7.5 percent but less than or equal to 10 percent.
3	Moderate	Weighted average tariff rate greater than 10 percent but less than or equal to 12.5 percent.
3.5	High	Weighted average tariff rate greater than 12.5 percent but less than or equal to 15 percent.
4	High	Weighted average tariff rate greater than 15 percent but less than or equal to 17.5 percent.
4.5	Very high	Weighted average tariff rate greater than 17.5 percent but less than or equal to 20 percent.
5	Very high	Weighted average tariff rate greater than 20 percent.

countries that significantly affects their treatment in the *Index*. When Cyprus, the Czech Republic, Estonia, Hungary, Latvia, Lithuania, Malta, Poland, Slovakia, and Slovenia joined the European Union in May 2004, they agreed to adopt EU policies in trade, regulation, agriculture, monetary policy, and fiscal policy that related directly to factors graded by the *Index*. Implementation of these policies, however—even for long-standing EU members—has been uneven, and not all of these commitments currently affect *Index* scoring. One area in which implementation of EU accession commitments occurred quickly is trade policy. Therefore, the trade policy scores for the 10 new EU countries are based on EU-wide trade policy. Bulgaria and Romania will receive similar treatment if they join the EU as expected in 2007. If EU policies involving other factors become binding, they also could affect future scoring.

- **Angola and Burundi graded for the first time since 2000.** As suggested by the regional experts, in 2000, the editors reviewed evidence that data from some countries were unreliable or did not accurately reflect the situation in much of the country. After review, grading was suspended for four countries: Angola, Burundi, the Democratic Republic of Congo, and Sudan. Iraq and Serbia and Montenegro, respectively, were suspended in the 2003 and 2004 editions of the *Index*. For the 2006 *Index*, the editors determined that the situation in Angola and Burundi had improved enough for grading to be resumed. The decision was slightly delayed to assure the graders that the newly acquired stability was not fleeting and that there would be a couple of years' worth of data upon which to base grading. It is at least somewhat encouraging that both Angola and Burundi have improved their economic freedom from "repressed" when last graded in 2000 to "mostly unfree."

A paramount concern of the editors is that the *Index* remains a useful tool for researchers and a consistent barometer of economic freedom over time. For example, where appropriate, each edition of the *Index* retroactively applies any change in methodology and reports these revised scores in the historical country rankings on pages 13-16. Revised scores of individual factors for all years are available for download at *heritage.org*.

Executive Summary

Marc A. Miles, Ph.D., Kim R. Holmes, Ph.D., and Mary Anastasia O'Grady

With the publication of this edition, The Heritage Foundation/Wall Street Journal *Index of Economic Freedom* marks its 12th anniversary. The idea of producing a user-friendly "index of economic freedom" as a tool for policymakers and investors was first discussed at The Heritage Foundation in the late 1980s. The goal then, as it is today, was to develop a systematic, empirical measurement of economic freedom in countries throughout the world. To this end, the decision was made to establish a set of objective economic criteria that, since the inaugural 1995 edition, have been used to study and grade various countries for the annual publication of the *Index of Economic Freedom*.

The *Index*, however, is more than just a dataset based on empirical study; it is a careful theoretical analysis of the factors that most influence the institutional setting of economic growth. Moreover, although there are many theories about the origins and causes of economic development, the findings of this study are straightforward: The countries with the most economic freedom also have higher rates of long-term economic growth and are more prosperous than are those with less economic freedom.

The *2006 Index of Economic Freedom* measures 161 countries against a list of 50 independent variables divided into 10 broad factors of economic freedom. Low scores are more desirable. The higher the score on a factor, the greater the level of government interference in the economy and the less economic freedom a country enjoys.

These 50 variables are grouped into the following categories:

- Trade policy,
- Fiscal burden of government,
- Government intervention in the economy,
- Monetary policy,
- Capital flows and foreign investment,
- Banking and finance,
- Wages and prices,
- Property rights,
- Regulation, and
- Informal market activity.

Chapter 5 explains these factors in detail. Taken together, they offer an empirical depiction of a country's level of economic freedom. A systematic analysis of these factors continues to demonstrate that countries

Table 1:
Index of Economic Freedom: Performance Over the Past 10 Years

Year	Average Score	Median Score	Country Representative of Median
2006	2.98	3.04	Nicaragua
2005	3.02	3.08	Guyana
2004	3.03	3.08	Guyana
2003	3.04	3.09	Argentina/Saudi Arabia
2002	3.10	3.16	Djibouti/Saudi Arabia
2001	3.11	3.13	Qatar
2000	3.20	3.19	Cambodia/Ecuador
1999	3.21	3.18	Cambodia/Mongolia
1998	3.23	3.18	Gabon
1997	3.20	3.23	Colombia/Fiji

Source: Marc A. Miles, Kim R. Holmes, and Mary Anastasia O'Grady, *2006 Index of Economic Freedom* (Washington, D.C.: The Heritage Foundation and Dow Jones & Company, Inc., 2006), at *www.heritage.org/index*.

with the highest levels of economic freedom also have the highest living standards.

WORLDWIDE PATTERNS

This year, economic freedom has advanced throughout the world: The scores of 99 countries are better, the scores of 51 are worse, and the scores of five are unchanged. In addition, two countries suspended from grading in the 2005 *Index* were graded this year. Of the 157 countries numerically graded in the 2006 *Index*, 20 are classified as "free," 52 as "mostly free," 73 as "mostly unfree," and 12 as "repressed." Four countries (the Democratic Republic of Congo, Iraq, Serbia and Montenegro, and Sudan) were suspended from grading because of questions about the accuracy of the data reported by the country or about whether the data truly reflect economic circumstances for most of the country.[1] For two other countries (Angola and Burundi), the data were deemed reliable enough to make grading possible for the first time since their suspension from grading in the 2001 *Index*.

Over the past 10 years of the *Index*,[2] there has been a definite trend toward economic freedom. For the first time, the average *Index* score of 2.98 now classifies as "mostly free" although the median score of 3.04 remains "mostly unfree." The average score and the median score, respectively, have improved 0.22 point and 0.19 point since the 1997 *Index*. (See Table 1.)

What do these improvements mean? Studies in previous editions of the *Index* confirm the tangible benefits of living in freer societies. Not only is a higher level of economic freedom clearly associated with a higher level of per capita gross domestic product (GDP), but GDP growth rates also increase as a country's economic freedom score improves.

Figure 1 illustrates that economically free countries tend to have higher per capita incomes than less free countries. Citizens of countries that are classified as "mostly unfree" or "repressed" earn almost 70 percent less than citizens of "mostly free" countries. In addition, the citizens of "free" countries enjoy a per capita income that is more than twice as high as their counterparts in "mostly free" countries. This demonstrates the core importance of economic freedom: Economic freedom makes life more livable for individual people.

Figure 2 ranks the graded countries according to their improvement in economic freedom between 1997 and 2006. The countries represented in the left-hand bar were most improved, and those in the right-hand bar were least improved or actually declined. Average growth rates across the nine years of changes were then computed for the countries in each bar or group. As Figure 2 illustrates, countries that improved their economic freedom the most experienced the highest average economic growth. The lesson? Countries that committed to improving economic freedom enjoy the most progress toward prosperity.

- Table 2 shows that while scores in most regions have improved since the 1997 *Index*, progress has not been uniform. The North America–Europe region has demonstrated a strong, consistent trend toward greater economic freedom over the past 10 editions of the *Index*. The average score for the region has improved by 0.39 point since the 1997 *Index*, while the median score has improved by 0.3 point. The countries that represent the median score for North America and Europe—Portugal and Spain—are very competitive and rank among the world's top 33 freest countries in the 2006 *Index*, demonstrating that the region is head and shoulders above others in terms of economic freedom.

- Economic freedom in Latin America and the Caribbean has stagnated. Over the past 10 years of the *Index*, the average score has improved by an unimpressive 0.09 point, largely as a result of minor improvements by some of the region's least free economies plus improvement by Chile—the region's sole "free" economy. The median score for the region has worsened by 0.03 point—not a dramatic decline but nevertheless indicative of the overall stagnation of economic freedom in the region since the 1997 *Index*. The countries that are representative of the median score for Latin America and the Caribbean in the 2006 *Index*—Guatemala and Nicaragua—are poised between "mostly free" and "mostly unfree."

- As with Latin America and the Caribbean, there have been mixed trends in North Africa and the Middle East over the past 10 years of the *Index*. While the average score for the region has improved by 0.09 point since the 1997 *Index*, the median score has declined by 0.04 point. This illustrates progress toward economic freedom by the region's least free countries (although the

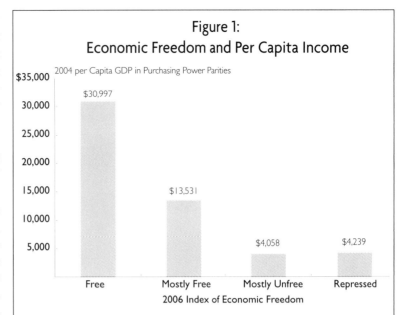

**Figure 1:
Economic Freedom and Per Capita Income**

2004 per Capita GDP in Purchasing Power Parities

Free: $30,997
Mostly Free: $13,531
Mostly Unfree: $4,058
Repressed: $4,239

2006 Index of Economic Freedom

Sources: World Bank, *World Development Indicators Online*, available by subscription at *www.worldbank.org/data*; Central Intelligence Agency, *The World Factbook 2005*, available at *www.cia.gov/cia/publications/factbook/index.html*; Marc A. Miles, Kim R. Holmes, and Mary Anastasia O'Grady, *2006 Index of Economic Freedom* (Washington, D.C.: The Heritage Foundation and Dow Jones & Company, Inc., 2006), at *www.heritage.org/index*.

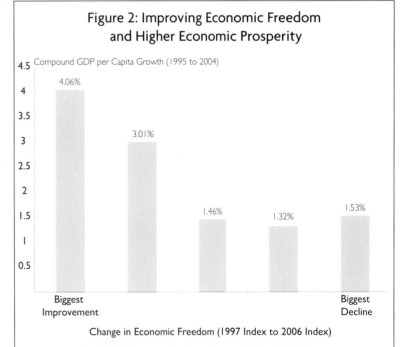

**Figure 2: Improving Economic Freedom
and Higher Economic Prosperity**

Compound GDP per Capita Growth (1995 to 2004)

Biggest Improvement: 4.06%
3.01%
1.46%
1.32%
Biggest Decline: 1.53%

Change in Economic Freedom (1997 Index to 2006 Index)

Sources: World Bank, *World Development Indicators Online*, available by subscription at *www.worldbank.org/data*; Central Intelligence Agency, *The World Factbook 2005*, available at *www.cia.gov/cia/publications/factbook/index.html*; Marc A. Miles, Kim R. Holmes, and Mary Anastasia O'Grady, *2006 Index of Economic Freedom* (Washington, D.C.: The Heritage Foundation and Dow Jones & Company, Inc., 2006), at *www.heritage.org/index*.

suspension of Iraq since the 2003 *Index* has contributed to a better average) but a retreat on the part of the freer economies. Indeed, with Bahrain's decline in economic freedom, the region no longer has

Table 2: Regional Performance Over the Past 10 Years

North America and Europe

Year	Average Score	Median Score	Country Representative of Median
2006	2.39	2.31	Portugal/Spain
2005	2.46	2.34	Spain
2004	2.54	2.42	Latvia/Portugal
2003	2.60	2.4	Portugal
2002	2.67	2.46	Spain
2001	2.64	2.49	Latvia
2000	2.72	2.56	Spain
1999	2.77	2.66	Cyprus
1998	2.79	2.64	Cyprus
1997	2.78	2.61	Spain

Latin America and the Caribbean

Year	Average Score	Median Score	Country Representative of Median
2006	3.02	3.03	Guatemala/Nicaragua
2005	3.06	2.99	Nicaragua/Guyana
2004	3.05	3.04	Guyana
2003	3.01	3.04	Brazil
2002	3.03	2.98	Colombia
2001	3.01	2.92	Guatemala/Jamaica
2000	3.01	2.88	Guatemala
1999	3.04	2.96	Jamaica
1998	3.04	2.98	Guatemala/Costa Rica
1997	3.11	3.00	Barbados

North Africa and the Middle East

Year	Average Score	Median Score	Country Representative of Median
2006	3.23	3.04	Qatar
2005	3.20	3.10	Lebanon
2004	3.14	2.94	Tunisia
2003	3.11	2.96	Morocco
2002	3.27	3.06	Algeria
2001	3.29	3.06	Tunisia/Qatar
2000	3.33	3.09	Lebanon
1999	3.31	3.04	Lebanon
1998	3.33	3.03	Morocco
1997	3.32	3.00	Saudi Arabia

Sub-Saharan Africa

Year	Average Score	Median Score	Country Representative of Median
2006	3.35	3.32	Zambia
2005	3.36	3.37	Guinea/Gabon
2004	3.36	3.34	Mozambique/Ghana
2003	3.41	3.38	Mozambique
2002	3.44	3.39	Lesotho
2001	3.48	3.41	Gabon/Lesotho
2000	3.66	3.63	Cape Verde/Ethiopia
1999	3.65	3.61	Burkina Faso
1998	3.68	3.69	Cape Verde/Lesotho
1997	3.69	3.69	Zimbabwe

Table 2: Regional Performance Over the Past 10 Years (continued)

Asia and the Pacific

Year	Average Score	Median Score	Country Representative of Median
2006	3.18	3.28	Philippines/Pakistan
2005	3.25	3.39	Azerbaijan
2004	3.26	3.38	Pakistan/Kyrgyz Republic
2003	3.25	3.45	Pakistan
2002	3.28	3.49	Fiji/Indonesia/Pakistan
2001	3.32	3.53	China
2000	3.33	3.47	China
1999	3.31	3.36	Fiji
1998	3.31	3.3	Cambodia/Pakistan
1997	3.18	3.23	Fiji

Source: Marc A. Miles, Kim R. Holmes, and Mary Anastasia O'Grady, *2006 Index of Economic Freedom* (Washington, D.C.: The Heritage Foundation and Dow Jones & Company, Inc., 2006), at www.heritage.org/index.

a "free" economy. However, it does have two "repressed" economies. The country that represents the median score for North Africa and the Middle East in the 2006 *Index* is Qatar, a "mostly unfree" economy with heavy government intervention but some aspects of economic freedom.

- No region has made greater strides in economic freedom than sub-Saharan Africa. Both the average and median scores for the region have improved dramatically from the 1997 *Index* at 0.34 point and 0.37 point, respectively. In fact, the region improved over 2005 despite the fact that Angola and Burundi were graded for the first time since 2001. The Democratic Republic of Congo and Sudan remain suspended. Regrettably, these admirable gains have been from relatively low levels of economic freedom, and sub-Saharan Africa remains the world's least free region. This relative lack of economic freedom is illustrated by the region's median country—Zambia—which is ranked in the lowest third of countries in the 2006 *Index*.

- Despite containing the two freest economies in the *Index*, the Asia–Pacific region is the only one in which neither the average nor the median scores have improved over the past 10 years. The average score for the region is the same as it was in the 1997 *Index*, and the median score is 0.05 point worse. Both of the median score countries for Asia and the Pacific in the 2006 *Index*—

the Philippines and Pakistan—are in the lower half of the overall rankings.

These long-term trends are, in most cases, echoed in the 2006 *Index*, as demonstrated in the regional breakdown.

NORTH AMERICA AND EUROPE

North America and Europe continues to be the world's most economically free region in the 2006 *Index*, with seven of the world's 11 freest countries and 15 of the world's "free" economies. Of the countries in this region, 33 exhibited an increase in economic freedom while only 10 experienced a decline in economic freedom.

Improvements in economic freedom by Austria, Germany, and Cyprus led these countries to be ranked as "free" in the 2006 *Index*. Although both Austria and Cyprus had previously been ranked as "free," this is the first time Germany has achieved this ranking. The change reflects small improvements in Germany's trade policy and fiscal burden factors. Notable is the fact that the United States climbed back into the top 10 economies, moving up three spots from its 2005 ranking of 12th into a tie for ninth with Australia and New Zealand.

The most improved country in this region is Romania, followed closely by Armenia, Georgia, and Turkey. Romania improved by 0.39 point this year, making it the world's second most improved country. (See Table

Table 4: Score Changes in 10 New EU Members' Trade Policy Factor

Country	Trade Score Before Joining the EU	Trade Score After Joining the EU	Score Change
Estonia	1	2	1 point worse
Latvia	2	2	0
Lithuania	2	2	0
Slovenia	2	2	0
Czech Republic	2.5	2	0.5 point better
Malta	2.5	2	0.5 point better
Poland	2.5	2	0.5 point better
Cyprus	3	2	1 point better
Hungary	3	2	1 point better
Slovakia	3	2	1 point better

Source: Marc A. Miles, Kim R. Holmes, and Mary Anastasia O'Grady, *2006 Index of Economic Freedom* (Washington, D.C.: The Heritage Foundation and Dow Jones & Company, Inc., 2006), at *www.heritage.org/index*.

3.) Armenia and Georgia improved by 0.32 point and 0.31 point, respectively. Turkey also improved 0.3 point based on improved scores in trade policy, fiscal burden of government, monetary policy, and banking and finance. All four ranked among the 10 most improved economies in the 2006 *Index*. While Romania remains "mostly unfree," it is moving strongly toward greater freedom. Improvements in Georgia vaulted that country into the ranks of the "mostly free" for the first time. Armenia now ranks among the 30 freest economies.

Belarus continues as the least free country in the region, and declines in its fiscal burden and informal market scores led to its return to the ranks of "repressed" economies. Belarus has made little progress on economic reform and market liberalization, and its overall economy is impeded by Soviet-era anti-market policies.

Ireland surpassed Luxembourg as the freest country in the region in the 2006 *Index*, based on improvement in its fiscal burden score and sustained low inflation. Ireland eagerly welcomes foreign investors and remains a favored destination for both U.S. and European investment. With a GDP per capita that has grown to over $40,058, Ireland is a prime example of the fruits of economic freedom. Estonia fell to the fifth freest country in the region as a result of adopting the European Union's more restrictive trade policy upon its accession to the EU. Iceland

Table 3: Top 10 Improved

Countries	Score Change
Pakistan	0.40
Romania	0.39
Kyrgyz Republic	0.35
Suriname	0.33
Armenia	0.32
Turkmenistan	0.32
Georgia	0.31
Turkey	0.30
Tajikistan	0.29
Kazakhstan	0.26

Source: Marc A. Miles, Kim R. Holmes, and Mary Anastasia O'Grady, *2006 Index of Economic Freedom* (Washington, D.C.: The Heritage Foundation and Dow Jones & Company, Inc., 2006), at *www.heritage.org/index*.

continued to improve and is now tied with the United Kingdom for the world's fifth freest economy.

The accession of Cyprus, the Czech Republic, Estonia, Hungary, Latvia, Lithuania, Malta, Poland, Slovakia, and Slovenia to the European Union in May 2004 resulted in policy changes that affected their scores in the 2006 *Index*. As part of their accession, these countries agreed to adopt EU policies in trade, agriculture, regulation, monetary policy, and fiscal policy. While implementation of these policies has been uneven, with few caveats, they have all adopted EU policies on trade. Therefore, the trade policy scores for the 10 new EU countries

Table 5: Top 10 Worsened

Countries	Score Change
Iran	-0.30
Italy	-0.22
Guinea	-0.22
Bolivia	-0.21
United Arab Emirates	-0.20
Oman	-0.20
Equatorial Guinea	-0.16
Sri Lanka	-0.16
Egypt	-0.16
El Salvador	-0.15
Nicaragua	-0.15

Source: Marc A. Miles, Kim R. Holmes, and Mary Anastasia O'Grady, *2006 Index of Economic Freedom* (Washington, D.C.: The Heritage Foundation and Dow Jones & Company, Inc., 2006), at *www.heritage.org/index*.

now conform to the EU-wide trade policy in this year's *Index*. As a result, scores for most of the new EU countries improved. Only Estonia's trade policy score declined. (See Table 4.)

LATIN AMERICA AND THE CARIBBEAN

Economic freedom in Latin America and the Caribbean improved marginally, with 15 countries improving and 10 countries becoming less free. Central to the region's lack of progress are the three repressed economies (Cuba, Venezuela, and Haiti). Of the 10 countries with the world's largest declines in economic freedom, three are Latin American: Bolivia, El Salvador, and Nicaragua. (See Table 5.) Bolivia's improved fiscal burden of government score was more than offset by declines in its trade policy, monetary policy, and foreign investment scores. It was fourth among countries seeing the biggest decline in economic freedom in the 2006 *Index*. El Salvador, although still ranked as "mostly free," has fallen behind Barbados and the Bahamas in terms of economic freedom. Nicaragua's decline resulted in its falling from "mostly free" to "mostly unfree."

Despite remaining a "repressed" economy, Cuba slightly improved its ranking in the 2006 *Index* due to improved monetary policy and informal market scores. Cuba is one of the world's 12 "repressed" econo-

mies and needs to improve in nearly every factor to experience improvements in economic growth. Cuba's significant non-tariff barriers, high taxes, numerous state-owned companies, barriers to investment, high level of restrictions in banking and finance, weak protection of property rights, and government-set wages and prices ensure that its economic promise will continue to languish.

Haiti is a case study of how inept, corrupt governance can destroy an economy. Haiti improved slightly in economic freedom in the 2006 *Index* but remains "repressed." Although its trade policy score improved, its fiscal burden of government score declined. Notably, Suriname was among the most improved countries in the 2006 *Index*, but it still remains among the bottom fifth of all countries in terms of economic freedom.

Chile is the only free economy in Latin America and the Caribbean and is the economic star of the region, a poster child for how to prosper through economic freedom. Notably, the government has vigorously pursued free trade agreements and has liberalized capital markets. However, it must guard against political pressures to reverse free-market policies. Although Chile experienced only a small decline in economic freedom, with other countries improving, this decline was sufficient for Chile to fall to 14th in the overall ranking.

NORTH AFRICA AND THE MIDDLE EAST

North Africa and the Middle East have experienced a net decline in economic freedom since last year. The scores of seven countries in this region have improved, while those of 10 are worse.

Despite a slightly worse score this year, Bahrain remains the region's most economically free country. It is one of the most advanced economies in the Persian Gulf. Bahrain maintains a pro-business environment with an excellent banking and finance system, low regulation, and low barriers to foreign investment. Yet it receives over 80 percent of its revenues from state-owned enterprises, mostly oil and gas, demonstrating an unhealthy level of government intervention in the economy.

Israel remains the region's second freest economy. Israel's overall score is slightly improved due to a better score in trade policy. Despite steady improvements in economic freedom over the past decade, terrorist attacks have depressed the tourism industry, discouraged foreign investment, and led to reduced growth.

Both Libya and Iran remain "repressed" and need significant improvement in all factors. However, the two countries seem to be moving in opposite directions. Once one of the more advanced in the Middle East, Iran's economy is now characterized by heavy regulation, high unemployment, inflation, corruption, and government intervention. Liberalization remains hamstrung by opposition from entrenched bureaucrats in state agencies and by Islamic hard-liners opposed to reform. Declines in Iran's trade policy and capital flows and foreign investment scores in the 2006 *Index* more than offset improvements in recent years, and Iran earned its lowest economic freedom score since the 2002 *Index*.

Libya is still a "repressed" economy and is characterized by state-dominated industry, heavy regulation, and trade protectionism. However, for the second straight year, it was the region's most improved economy, with better scores in fiscal burden of government, capital flows and foreign investment, and banking and finance.

SUB-SAHARAN AFRICA

Sub-Saharan Africa joins North Africa and the Middle East as one of only two regions without a "free" economy. At the same time, it differs from North Africa and the Middle East in that its overall level of economic freedom continues to improve, with 25 countries' economic freedom scores improving and 12 countries' scores declining.

These improvements, however, are from very low levels of economic freedom, and sub-Saharan Africa remains the world's least economically free region. The country that represents the median score for sub-Saharan Africa—Zambia—ranks 111th in the 2006 *Index*. Over three-quarters of the region's countries—33 out of 40 graded in the 2006 *Index*—remain "mostly unfree."

Benin was the region's most improved country, followed closely by Tanzania and Botswana. A small decline in Benin's fiscal burden of government score was offset by improvements in its trade policy, informal market, and government intervention scores. Similarly, Tanzania's fiscal burden of government score is worse this year, but its trade policy and capital flows and foreign investment scores improved. Botswana solidified its position as the region's freest country and serves as an example of the positive impact that economic policy can have on development. Botswana's market-led economy has had one of the world's highest average growth rates over the past several decades. Its improved fiscal burden of government and government intervention scores vaulted Botswana into the ranks of the world's 30 freest countries.

A notable change is the fact that Angola and Burundi have been graded for the first time since the 2000 *Index*. These countries were suspended when *Index* editors determined that the policies being evaluated were not applicable to large portions of the country. Thankfully, the situation has improved in Angola and Burundi to the point where grading was deemed appropriate. While both countries were "repressed" economies when last graded, both have improved markedly and are "mostly unfree" in the 2006 *Index*. Regrettably, the situations in the Democratic Republic of Congo and Sudan have not improved enough to merit grading.

Guinea declined more than any other country in the region. An improvement in Guinea's fiscal burden of government score was more than offset by declines in its trade policy, monetary policy, and banking and finance scores. Equatorial Guinea followed Guinea with the second biggest decline in economic freedom, with worse scores in fiscal burden of government and government intervention.

Even though its score improved marginally, Zimbabwe continues to be the least free country in the region and one of two "repressed" economies in the region. Not surprisingly, Zimbabwe's economy is in shambles. Disastrous economic policies, including expropriation of land and businesses, excessive government spending, inflationary monetary policy, and government-sanctioned violence, have discouraged foreign investment, hindered economic production, and led to extremely high unemployment. With a decline in its government intervention score, Nigeria joins Zimbabwe as sub-Saharan Africa's second "repressed" economy.

ASIA–PACIFIC

On net, the scores of the Asia–Pacific region are better for 10 countries, with scores for 19 countries improved and scores for nine countries worse this year. However, the region is one of contrasts. Although nearly half of its countries are ranked "mostly unfree," the region contains four of the world's 11 freest economies, including the two freest (Hong Kong and Singapore). Additionally, Pakistan, the Kyrgyz Republic, Turkmenistan, and Kazakhstan are among the world's 10 most improved countries, albeit from relatively low levels of economic freedom. However, the region also has four of the world's most repressed economies in Turkmenistan, Laos, Burma, and North Korea.

Once again, Hong Kong is the poster economy for economic freedom around the world. With a duty-free port, simple procedures for starting businesses, minimal capital controls, and a transparent, fair rule of law, Hong Kong has earned its place as a trading and financial hub. Likewise, as the world's second freest country, Singapore is a standard bearer in free trade policy, strong property rights, monetary policy, and foreign investment. The two economies have long been rivals for the world's freest economy, and the competition continued in the 2006 *Index*, with Singapore's fiscal burden of government score improving slightly while Hong Kong improved its fiscal burden of government and government intervention scores.

The Asia–Pacific region is also home to more "repressed" economies than any other region. North Korea remains the least free country, both in the region and in the world. It earns the worst score on every factor and has nowhere to go but up—if it should ever choose to do so. The region's other repressed economies are Laos, Turkmenistan, and Burma (Myanmar). Notably, Uzbekistan and Tajikistan climbed up into the ranks of the "mostly unfree" economies and are no longer considered "repressed" economies. Laos and Turkmenistan are poised to follow them after improved scores this year.

COUNTRY TREND TABLES

Table 3 (page 6) lists the countries whose scores have improved the most since publication of the 2005 edition of the *Index*. Unlike last year, most of the countries improved from rather poor scores. Countries with low levels of economic freedom have the potential for great improvement but historically have struggled to maintain that progress. These countries should strive to avoid recidivism if they wish to improve their prospects for economic growth and development.

Pakistan, which saw the second largest decline in economic freedom in the 2005 *Index*, is the most improved country based on improved trade policy, government intervention, capital flows and foreign investment, banking and finance, and wages and prices scores. Romania, the second most improved country, improved its score in four factors: fiscal burden of government, government intervention, monetary policy, and capital flows and foreign investment. Georgia and the Kyrgyz Republic improved and made the jump to the "mostly free" ranks. Tajikistan moved from "repressed" into the "mostly unfree" category.

Table 5 (page 7) lists the countries experiencing the greatest decline in economic freedom during the past year. Iran's overall level of economic freedom fell the most. Its trade policy and capital flows and foreign investment scores declined. As a result, Iran is now the world's second most repressed economy.

Italy experienced the second largest decline in economic freedom. While its fiscal burden of government score is better this year, its banking and finance, property rights, and informal market scores all declined.

Oman and Nicaragua—sixth and tied for tenth, respectively—experienced significant declines in economic freedom that saw them fall from the ranks of the "mostly free" economies. Nicaragua's capital flows and foreign investment score improved, but its trade

Table 6: Top 10 Improved Over Index History	
Countries	Score Change
Bosnia and Herzegovina	1.60
Armenia	1.48
Slovenia	1.38
Lithuania	1.31
Malta	1.28
Azerbaijan	1.27
Rwanda	1.07
Botswana	1.04
Nicaragua	1.03
Poland	1.02

Source: Marc A. Miles, Kim R. Holmes, and Mary Anastasia O'Grady, *2006 Index of Economic Freedom* (Washington, D.C.: The Heritage Foundation and Dow Jones & Company, Inc., 2006), at *www.heritage.org/index*.

Table 7: Top 10 Declined Over Index History	
Countries	Score Change
Venezuela	-0.94
Nigeria	-0.63
Malaysia	-0.48
United Arab Emirates	-0.48
Thailand	-0.45
Argentina	-0.45
Belarus	-0.41
Bahrain	-0.41
Paraguay	-0.32
Tunisia	-0.32

Source: Marc A. Miles, Kim R. Holmes, and Mary Anastasia O'Grady, *2006 Index of Economic Freedom* (Washington, D.C.: The Heritage Foundation and Dow Jones & Company, Inc., 2006), at *www.heritage.org/index*.

policy, fiscal burden of government, and monetary policy scores worsened; Oman's trade policy and informal market scores both declined. Both of these countries are now classified as "mostly unfree" economies.

Table 6 enumerates the countries that have made the largest overall improvement over the entire history of the *Index* (since 1995 where possible; otherwise, since the first time it was scored in the *Index*). Bosnia and Herzegovina remains the most improved with a score change of 1.6 points since it was first graded in the 1998 *Index*. With its strong improvement in the 2006 *Index*, Armenia is now the second most improved country over the history of the *Index*, improving by 1.48 points. Slovenia and Lithuania are the third and fourth most improved, respectively. Botswana also makes the list as a testament to its persistent improvement over time.

Table 7 shows the countries that have exhibited the greatest decline in economic freedom over the entire history of the *Index*. Venezuela has declined the most over the 12 years of the *Index*. President Hugo Chávez has demonstrated little understanding of his country's long-standing, dire need for economic freedom. Nigeria ranks second on this list with a net decline of 0.63 in its overall score. Malaysia is tied with the United Arab Emirates as the countries experiencing the third largest decline in economic freedom since first being graded in the *Index*.

An interesting trend over the life of the *Index* has been the adoption by Eastern European countries of "flat taxes"—whereby governments apply only one tax rate on all income earned—instead of progressively higher tax rates. Indeed, many of these countries extend the flat rate to corporate income taxes as well. (See Table 8.)

GLOBAL FREE TRADE ALLIANCE

In the 2001 edition of the *Index*, three Heritage analysts proposed a plan for a global free trade alliance (GFTA).[3] Further analysis of the issue was presented in the 2005 *Index*.[4] This year, 11 countries qualify, and 20 are in the "near-miss" category, falling short in only one factor by 1 point.[5]

The qualifying countries, based on *2006 Index of Economic Freedom* data, are Botswana, Cyprus, Denmark, Estonia, Finland, Hong Kong, Ireland, Luxembourg, Singapore, the United Kingdom, and the United States. Other than Cyprus, all of these countries qualified last year as well.

Among the near-miss countries are examples that range from Switzerland to Bahrain. Regulation continues to be the most common reason for a near miss. Malta's trade policy score improved this year, moving the country into the near-miss category, but barriers to foreign investment still keep it from qualifying.

Of the 20 near-miss countries, 14 fail to qualify because of their regulation scores;

Table 8: Eastern Europe Embraces the Flat Tax

Country	Flat Tax Rate	Year of Flat Tax Adoption
Estonia	24 percent on Personal Income	1994
Lithuania	33 percent on Personal Income	1994
Latvia	25 percent on Personal Income	1995
Russia	13 percent on Personal Income	2001
Serbia	10 percent on both Personal and Corporate Income	2003
Slovakia	**19 percent on both Personal and Corporate Income**	**2003**
Ukraine	13 percent on Personal Income	2003
Albania	23 percent on Corporate Income	2005
Bulgaria	15 percent on Corporate Income	2005
Georgia	12 percent on Personal Income	2005
Montenegro	9 percent on Corporate Income	2005
Romania	16 percent on both Personal and Corporate Income	2005

Note: Bold countries are members of the EU.

Source: Marc A. Miles, Kim R. Holmes, and Mary Anastasia O'Grady, *2006 Index of Economic Freedom* (Washington, D.C.: The Heritage Foundation and Dow Jones & Company, Inc., 2006), at *www.heritage.org/index*.

two (Canada and Malta) do not qualify because of their capital flows and foreign investment scores; three (Australia, Bahrain, and New Zealand) do not qualify because of restrictions on trade; and one (Slovenia) does not qualify because of weak property rights.

Although all trade liberalization during the past year has been accomplished through bilateral free trade agreements, such agreements include only two parties, thereby creating trade diversion for those who are left out. A GFTA would be more comprehensive. While no substitute for a comprehensive World Trade Organization (WTO) agreement, it would seek to advance liberalization while the WTO round is being negotiated.

A GFTA would limit trade diversion by welcoming all those who are truly free traders into the fold. Additionally, a GFTA would motivate other countries to liberalize their markets in order to join.

CRITERIA FOR MEMBERSHIP IN A GLOBAL FREE TRADE ALLIANCE

Market liberalization should be voluntary, and the GFTA would operate under this concept. Membership in the GFTA would be open only to countries that have demonstrated their commitment to free trade and free markets. Specifically, they would have to show their commitment to:

Freedom to Trade. Countries must maintain an open trade policy, with minimal barriers to imports and minimal subsidies to domestic industries. This means an average tariff rate no greater than 7.5 percent as well as few or no non-tariff barriers, which include import quotas or licensing requirements that restrict trade. Countries that generally set low tariff barriers, do not impose excessive non-tariff barriers, and do not put serious impediments in the way of foreign investment demonstrate their fundamental commitment to free trade.

Freedom to Invest. Countries must maintain liberal policies regarding capital flows and investment. Specifically, this means a transparent and open foreign investment code, impartial treatment of foreign investments, and an efficient approval process. Restrictions on foreign investment must be few in number and must not be significant economically.

Freedom to Operate a Business (Low Regulatory Burden). Countries must maintain an open environment for business. Overly burdensome regulations can deter trade and investment. Investors may choose not to enter a country because of the difficulties involved in opening a business or because the cost of doing business in that country is excessive. Countries must maintain simple licensing procedures, apply regulations uniformly, and be nondiscriminatory in their treatment of foreign-owned business.

Secure Property Rights. A country with a

Table 9: Membership in a Global Free Trade Alliance

Qualifying Countries	Countries Next in Line	Policy Blocking Membership
1. Botswana	1. Australia	Trade Policy
2. Cyprus	2. Austria	Regulation
3. Denmark	3. Bahrain	Trade Policy
4. Estonia	4. Belgium	Regulation
5. Finland	5. Canada	Capital Flows & Foreign Investment
6. Hong Kong	6. Chile	Regulation
7. Ireland	7. Czech Republic	Regulation
8. Luxembourg	8. Germany	Regulation
9. Singapore	9. Hungary	Regulation
10. United Kingdom	10. Israel	Regulation
11. United States	11. Japan	Regulation
	12. Malta	Capital Flows & Foreign Investment
	13. Netherlands	Regulation
	14. New Zealand	Trade Policy
	15. Portugal	Regulation
	16. Slovenia	Property Rights
	17. Spain	Regulation
	18. Sweden	Regulation
	19. Switzerland	Regulation
	20. Taiwan	Regulation

Source: Marc A. Miles, Kim R. Holmes, and Mary Anastasia O'Grady, *2006 Index of Economic Freedom* (Washington, D.C.: The Heritage Foundation and Dow Jones & Company, Inc., 2006), at *www.heritage.org/index*.

well-established rule of law protects private property and provides an environment in which business transactions can take place with a degree of certainty. Investors are likely to engage in economic transactions when they know the judicial system protects private property and is not subject to outside influence. Secure property rights help to ensure that efforts to expand trade with a GFTA country can be successful.

Endnotes

1   Data for suspended countries are reviewed annually to ascertain whether the situation has improved. The Democratic Republic of Congo and Sudan were suspended from grading in the 2006 *Index* because civil unrest or anarchy indicated that official government policies did not apply to large portions of the country. Serbia and Montenegro and Iraq were suspended because reliable data were not available.

2   The analysis does not extend to the 1996 and 1995 editions of the *Index* because significantly fewer countries were graded in those years.

3   John C. Hulsman, Gerald P. O'Driscoll, Jr., and Denise H. Froning, "The Free Trade Alliance: A Trade Agenda for the New Global Economy," in Gerald P. O'Driscoll, Jr., Kim R. Holmes, and Melanie Kirkpatrick, *2001 Index of Economic Freedom* (Washington, D.C.: The Heritage Foundation and Dow Jones & Company, Inc., 2001), pp. 33–41.

4   John C. Hulsman, Brett D. Schaefer, and Anthony Kim, "The Benefits of a Global Free Trade Alliance," in Marc A. Miles, Edwin J. Feulner, and Mary Anastasia O'Grady, *2005 Index of Economic Freedom* (Washington, D.C.: The Heritage Foundation and Dow Jones & Company, Inc., 2005), pp. 37–48.

5   See Table 9, "Membership in a Global Free Trade Alliance."

Index of Economic Freedom Rankings *

2006 Rank	Country	2006	2005	2004	2003	2002	2001	2000	1999	1998	1997	1996	1995
							Past Year's Scores						
1	Hong Kong	1.28	1.35	1.34	1.44	1.39	1.29	1.40	1.51	1.40	1.54	1.50	1.51
2	Singapore	1.56	1.60	1.61	1.61	1.69	1.66	1.59	1.54	1.54	1.68	1.63	1.68
3	Ireland	1.58	1.70	1.79	1.73	1.78	1.65	1.86	1.93	1.96	2.19	2.19	2.20
4	Luxembourg	1.60	1.63	1.76	1.68	1.93	1.84	1.89	2.00	2.01	2.01	2.04	n/a
5	Iceland	1.74	1.81	2.05	1.98	2.18	2.16	2.11	2.20	2.20	2.30	n/a	n/a
5	United Kingdom	1.74	1.75	1.84	1.88	1.88	1.83	1.90	1.86	1.90	2.00	1.90	1.80
7	Estonia	1.75	1.65	1.76	1.68	1.73	1.89	2.19	2.29	2.43	2.46	2.44	2.45
8	Denmark	1.78	1.76	1.85	1.71	1.84	2.15	2.34	2.18	2.16	2.03	2.18	n/a
9	Australia	1.84	1.84	1.93	1.95	1.96	1.96	1.95	1.99	2.00	2.24	2.13	2.14
9	New Zealand	1.84	1.75	1.70	1.68	1.73	1.76	1.80	1.76	1.88	1.80	1.79	n/a
9	United States	1.84	1.90	1.85	1.86	1.89	1.78	1.89	1.94	1.94	1.93	1.99	2.04
12	Canada	1.85	1.91	1.98	2.00	1.95	2.06	2.11	2.09	2.14	2.13	2.03	2.05
12	Finland	1.85	1.90	2.00	1.85	1.94	2.09	2.11	2.19	2.09	2.23	2.39	n/a
14	Chile	1.88	1.86	1.91	2.06	1.88	2.03	2.04	2.13	2.10	2.26	2.56	2.60
15	Switzerland	1.89	1.85	1.84	1.88	1.80	1.89	1.91	1.88	1.91	1.91	1.99	n/a
16	Cyprus	1.90	2.13	2.00	2.14	2.18	2.16	2.68	2.66	2.64	2.68	2.69	n/a
16	Netherlands, The	1.90	1.95	2.09	2.00	2.08	1.89	2.08	2.06	2.08	1.93	1.94	n/a
18	Austria	1.95	2.09	2.13	2.08	2.13	2.08	1.98	2.08	2.13	2.03	2.06	2.09
19	Germany	1.96	2.00	2.08	2.03	2.05	2.09	2.29	2.31	2.41	2.20	2.31	2.20
19	Sweden	1.96	1.89	1.95	1.88	1.93	2.08	2.15	2.25	2.29	2.30	2.58	2.68
21	Czech Republic	2.10	2.31	2.39	2.35	2.29	2.10	2.20	2.19	2.48	2.24	2.28	2.33
22	Belgium	2.11	2.13	2.24	2.10	2.15	2.15	2.19	2.11	2.10	2.08	2.11	n/a
23	Lithuania	2.14	2.18	2.19	2.21	2.35	2.53	2.84	2.90	2.98	3.10	3.45	n/a
24	Malta	2.16	2.28	2.46	2.71	2.73	2.84	3.09	3.14	3.15	3.25	3.24	3.44
25	Bahrain	2.23	2.15	2.13	2.09	2.05	1.96	1.93	1.86	1.95	1.85	1.80	1.83
26	Barbados	2.25	2.35	2.41	2.24	2.48	2.59	2.74	2.86	2.63	2.98	3.15	n/a
27	Armenia	2.26	2.58	2.63	2.59	2.78	3.08	3.26	3.45	3.45	3.50	3.74	n/a
27	Bahamas, The	2.26	2.25	2.25	2.15	2.06	2.23	2.23	2.16	2.16	2.05	2.09	2.36
27	Japan	2.26	2.46	2.53	2.36	2.34	2.04	2.06	2.16	2.21	2.16	2.18	2.06
30	Botswana	2.29	2.49	2.55	2.54	2.99	2.95	2.93	2.91	2.90	2.75	3.04	3.33
30	Norway	2.29	2.33	2.35	2.28	2.40	2.44	2.25	2.28	2.28	2.44	2.44	n/a
30	Portugal	2.29	2.44	2.43	2.40	2.35	2.38	2.39	2.36	2.46	2.46	2.65	2.85
33	Spain	2.33	2.34	2.36	2.31	2.46	2.54	2.56	2.46	2.45	2.55	2.78	2.49
34	El Salvador	2.35	2.20	2.24	2.35	2.28	2.21	2.10	2.38	2.61	2.55	2.68	2.89
34	Slovak Republic	2.35	2.43	2.44	2.71	2.81	2.85	3.18	3.38	3.31	3.18	3.13	2.83
36	Israel	2.36	2.41	2.41	2.45	2.55	2.60	2.70	2.68	2.65	2.64	2.81	2.90
37	Taiwan	2.38	2.34	2.48	2.34	2.38	2.23	2.03	2.14	2.29	2.16	2.18	2.21
38	Slovenia	2.41	2.64	2.70	2.86	3.25	3.06	3.20	3.10	3.20	3.50	3.79	n/a
39	Latvia	2.43	2.31	2.41	2.35	2.49	2.49	2.69	2.74	2.84	2.86	3.19	n/a
40	Hungary	2.44	2.40	2.55	2.50	2.23	2.43	2.38	2.89	2.94	3.09	3.03	2.93
41	Poland	2.49	2.59	2.81	2.83	2.65	2.69	2.84	2.83	2.91	3.14	3.29	3.51
42	Italy	2.50	2.28	2.31	2.31	2.33	2.26	2.26	2.29	2.39	2.46	2.61	2.63
42	Trinidad and Tobago	2.50	2.54	2.40	2.54	2.49	2.59	2.43	2.49	2.60	2.63	2.69	n/a
44	France	2.51	2.63	2.68	2.74	2.90	2.54	2.49	2.39	2.39	2.38	2.36	2.35

* A summary of the 2006 factor scores by country can be found in the Appendix (page 412).

Index of Economic Freedom Rankings

Past Year's Scores

2006 Rank	Country	2006	2005	2004	2003	2002	2001	2000	1999	1998	1997	1996	1995
45	Korea, Republic of (South Korea)	2.63	2.64	2.64	2.75	2.54	2.40	2.55	2.43	2.35	2.36	2.54	2.46
46	Cape Verde	2.69	2.84	2.86	3.30	3.25	3.56	3.61	3.76	3.69	3.75	3.55	n/a
46	Costa Rica	2.69	2.76	2.66	2.76	2.73	2.84	2.83	3.00	3.00	3.03	3.00	3.04
46	Uruguay	2.69	2.60	2.55	2.50	2.56	2.35	2.50	2.60	2.59	2.65	2.85	3.03
49	Panama	2.70	2.74	2.83	2.64	2.68	2.58	2.61	2.48	2.50	2.49	2.55	2.70
50	Kuwait	2.74	2.81	2.75	2.58	2.66	2.53	2.50	2.45	2.55	2.44	2.55	n/a
50	South Africa	2.74	2.83	2.79	2.63	2.79	3.00	3.01	2.98	2.88	2.94	3.20	3.23
52	Albania	2.75	2.93	3.10	3.23	3.24	3.48	3.83	3.56	3.58	3.64	3.63	3.53
52	Madagascar	2.75	2.73	3.14	2.85	3.29	3.29	3.39	3.45	3.51	3.49	3.55	3.74
54	Jamaica	2.76	2.76	2.81	2.68	2.96	2.96	2.66	2.96	2.94	2.91	2.94	3.11
55	Belize	2.78	2.71	2.69	2.69	2.74	2.64	2.84	2.76	2.96	2.71	2.74	2.85
55	Croatia	2.78	2.95	3.06	3.06	3.34	3.39	3.54	3.55	3.63	3.56	3.58	n/a
57	Greece	2.80	2.80	2.85	2.79	2.89	2.74	2.74	2.93	2.94	2.86	3.00	3.20
57	Jordan	2.80	2.79	2.78	2.80	2.73	2.80	2.95	2.91	2.94	2.85	3.15	2.95
57	Macedonia	2.80	3.00	3.09	3.18	3.35	n/a	n/a	n/a	n/a	n/a	n/a	n/a
60	Mexico	2.83	2.84	2.90	2.81	2.96	3.05	3.09	3.30	3.41	3.35	3.31	3.05
60	Mongolia	2.83	2.75	2.85	2.96	2.98	3.03	3.06	3.18	3.14	3.28	3.55	3.45
62	Saudi Arabia	2.84	2.99	3.05	3.09	3.16	3.35	3.20	3.16	2.94	3.00	3.00	n/a
63	Peru	2.86	2.83	2.88	2.91	2.88	2.56	2.69	2.61	2.91	3.08	3.01	3.59
64	Bulgaria	2.88	2.74	2.98	3.26	3.28	3.33	3.40	3.44	3.65	3.53	3.50	3.56
65	United Arab Emirates	2.93	2.73	2.65	2.25	2.33	2.21	2.25	2.35	2.30	2.40	2.45	n/a
66	Uganda	2.95	3.00	2.70	2.95	3.15	3.15	3.15	2.64	2.64	2.80	2.94	3.15
67	Bolivia	2.96	2.75	2.64	2.54	2.66	2.31	2.56	2.61	2.61	2.51	2.56	3.16
68	Cambodia	2.98	2.89	2.90	2.73	2.83	3.00	3.19	3.18	3.29	3.68	n/a	n/a
68	Georgia	2.98	3.29	3.14	3.40	3.53	3.63	3.85	3.90	3.83	3.93	3.99	n/a
68	Malaysia	2.98	2.91	3.16	3.14	3.18	3.00	2.81	2.64	2.59	2.80	2.68	2.50
71	Kyrgyz Republic	2.99	3.34	3.41	3.46	3.60	3.75	3.73	3.68	3.95	n/a	n/a	n/a
71	Thailand	2.99	3.03	2.81	2.71	2.51	2.34	2.76	2.58	2.56	2.53	2.53	2.54
73	Lebanon	3.00	3.10	3.13	3.04	3.01	2.70	3.06	3.03	3.06	2.73	2.91	n/a
74	Bosnia and Herzegovina	3.01	3.16	3.30	3.54	3.89	4.09	4.40	4.61	4.61	n/a	n/a	n/a
74	Guatemala	3.01	3.18	3.16	3.01	3.00	2.88	2.91	2.94	2.96	2.94	3.10	3.36
74	Oman	3.01	2.81	2.75	2.70	2.63	2.65	2.93	2.85	2.74	2.79	2.85	2.70
77	Mauritius	3.03	2.90	2.99	2.96	2.95	2.98	2.90	2.73	n/a	n/a	n/a	n/a
78	Qatar	3.04	3.05	2.81	2.78	3.08	3.13	3.13	3.06	n/a	n/a	n/a	n/a
78	Swaziland	3.04	3.11	3.18	3.05	3.21	3.05	3.16	3.06	3.13	3.26	3.35	3.11
80	Nicaragua	3.05	2.90	2.99	3.14	3.23	3.49	3.65	3.65	3.68	3.75	3.65	4.08
81	Brazil	3.08	3.20	3.10	3.06	3.11	3.26	3.46	3.24	3.41	3.33	3.61	3.41
81	Mauritania	3.08	2.98	2.99	3.15	3.46	3.89	4.00	4.00	3.96	4.03	3.88	n/a
83	Moldova	3.10	3.11	3.09	3.13	3.25	3.70	3.30	3.44	3.43	3.60	3.45	4.10
83	Senegal	3.10	3.04	3.05	3.33	3.45	3.33	3.29	3.36	3.46	3.64	3.76	n/a
85	Guyana	3.11	3.08	3.08	3.15	3.23	3.35	3.35	3.30	3.55	3.40	3.38	3.70
85	Namibia	3.11	3.15	2.96	2.70	2.84	2.93	2.98	2.84	2.99	2.80	n/a	n/a
85	Turkey	3.11	3.41	3.39	3.50	3.38	2.93	2.68	2.80	2.66	2.75	2.95	2.95
88	Ivory Coast	3.14	3.26	3.13	3.16	3.00	3.08	3.68	3.73	3.74	3.80	3.83	3.43

Index of Economic Freedom Rankings

Past Year's Scores

2006 Rank	Country	2006	2005	2004	2003	2002	2001	2000	1999	1998	1997	1996	1995
88	Mali	3.14	3.18	3.29	3.20	3.10	3.15	3.08	3.19	3.28	3.45	3.39	3.48
90	Fiji	3.15	3.28	3.06	3.48	3.49	3.50	3.29	3.29	3.23	3.23	3.24	3.49
91	Colombia	3.16	3.21	3.13	3.10	2.99	3.05	3.14	3.09	3.19	3.23	3.10	3.05
92	Romania	3.19	3.58	3.71	3.71	3.78	3.59	3.20	3.20	3.21	3.30	3.40	3.65
92	Sri Lanka	3.19	3.03	3.06	3.05	2.89	2.84	2.91	2.86	2.76	2.61	2.94	3.06
94	Djibouti	3.20	3.30	3.23	3.30	3.16	3.38	3.38	3.28	3.29	3.18	n/a	n/a
94	Kenya	3.20	3.23	3.26	3.21	3.23	3.26	3.05	3.14	3.06	3.31	3.59	3.45
94	Tanzania	3.20	3.41	3.24	3.49	3.51	3.60	3.58	3.41	3.53	3.51	3.73	3.79
97	Morocco	3.21	3.18	2.93	2.96	3.10	2.80	3.05	2.90	3.03	3.05	2.94	3.03
98	Philippines, The	3.23	3.30	3.10	3.00	3.05	3.21	3.00	3.03	2.89	3.06	3.14	3.35
99	Lesotho	3.24	3.41	3.50	3.29	3.39	3.44	3.44	3.48	3.69	3.70	3.73	n/a
99	Tunisia	3.24	3.14	2.94	2.91	2.89	2.99	2.94	2.96	2.90	2.89	2.83	2.93
99	Ukraine	3.24	3.16	3.49	3.59	3.84	3.88	3.75	3.95	3.83	3.78	4.00	4.00
102	Burkina Faso	3.28	3.28	3.28	3.35	3.33	3.45	3.56	3.58	3.75	3.76	3.91	n/a
102	Gabon	3.28	3.40	3.43	3.18	3.33	3.38	3.26	3.09	3.18	3.31	3.63	3.19
102	Honduras	3.28	3.43	3.53	3.24	3.38	3.50	3.51	3.71	3.51	3.58	3.58	3.58
105	Chad	3.29	3.33	3.54	3.59	3.75	3.74	3.95	4.01	4.19	4.24	n/a	n/a
105	Ghana	3.29	3.25	3.35	3.54	3.54	3.24	3.24	3.29	3.29	3.43	3.54	3.54
107	Argentina	3.30	3.49	3.43	3.09	2.63	2.29	2.28	2.23	2.48	2.70	2.58	2.85
107	Ecuador	3.30	3.49	3.60	3.58	3.60	3.56	3.19	3.14	3.15	3.26	3.33	3.39
109	Paraguay	3.31	3.45	3.44	3.40	3.33	3.34	3.06	2.95	3.09	2.96	2.94	2.99
110	Pakistan	3.33	3.73	3.35	3.44	3.49	3.50	3.50	3.50	3.31	3.29	3.26	3.34
111	China, People's Republic of	3.34	3.51	3.59	3.49	3.56	3.55	3.49	3.56	3.69	3.73	3.78	3.78
111	Zambia	3.34	3.45	3.55	3.55	3.35	3.30	2.99	2.96	2.99	2.88	3.08	3.15
113	Kazakhstan	3.35	3.61	3.65	3.50	3.65	3.80	3.95	4.14	4.23	n/a	n/a	n/a
113	Mozambique	3.35	3.29	3.33	3.40	3.20	3.35	3.94	3.95	4.15	4.15	4.06	4.34
115	Niger	3.38	3.48	3.48	3.61	3.74	3.78	4.09	3.91	4.01	4.19	4.20	n/a
116	Dominican Republic	3.39	3.54	3.51	3.29	3.19	3.09	3.08	3.20	3.26	3.24	3.34	3.63
117	Benin	3.40	3.63	3.49	3.56	3.46	3.23	3.21	3.34	3.35	3.44	3.53	n/a
118	Central African Republic	3.41	3.51	3.38	3.28	3.31	n/a	n/a	n/a	n/a	n/a	n/a	n/a
119	Algeria	3.46	3.49	3.26	3.39	3.05	3.45	3.40	3.59	3.64	3.63	3.70	3.68
119	Cameroon	3.46	3.60	3.63	3.54	3.45	3.50	3.73	3.65	3.96	3.95	4.08	3.51
121	India	3.49	3.53	3.53	3.58	3.61	3.91	3.93	3.93	3.83	3.88	3.93	3.93
122	Russia	3.50	3.61	3.51	3.54	3.74	3.84	3.80	3.65	3.54	3.83	3.70	3.60
123	Azerbaijan	3.51	3.43	3.44	3.50	3.58	3.88	4.28	4.24	4.30	4.58	4.78	n/a
123	Gambia, The	3.51	3.45	3.49	3.44	3.29	3.64	3.69	3.55	3.71	3.60	n/a	n/a
125	Nepal	3.53	3.55	3.53	3.63	3.51	3.65	3.79	3.49	3.71	3.89	3.86	n/a
125	Rwanda	3.53	3.54	3.41	3.93	3.78	3.94	4.23	4.29	4.60	4.60	n/a	n/a
127	Guinea	3.55	3.33	3.24	3.26	3.45	3.21	3.34	3.19	3.16	3.39	3.13	3.29
128	Egypt	3.59	3.43	3.33	3.44	3.48	3.53	3.53	3.30	3.26	3.49	3.40	3.69
129	Suriname	3.60	3.93	3.96	4.01	3.98	3.98	3.98	4.08	4.10	4.00	4.10	n/a
130	Malawi	3.63	3.65	3.51	3.63	3.59	3.76	3.84	3.89	3.96	3.86	3.64	3.74
131	Guinea-Bissau	3.65	3.80	3.85	3.90	4.15	4.19	4.40	4.50	n/a	n/a	n/a	n/a
132	Burundi	3.69	n/a	n/a	n/a	n/a	n/a	4.00	4.20	4.38	4.20	n/a	n/a

Index of Economic Freedom Rankings

Past Year's Scores

2006 Rank	Country	2006	2005	2004	2003	2002	2001	2000	1999	1998	1997	1996	1995
133	Ethiopia	3.70	3.73	3.33	3.79	3.70	3.83	3.65	3.68	3.70	3.85	3.80	3.90
134	Indonesia	3.71	3.59	3.76	3.43	3.49	3.65	3.55	3.14	3.00	3.05	3.00	3.53
134	Togo	3.71	3.68	3.78	3.86	3.88	4.00	4.05	4.14	n/a	n/a	n/a	n/a
136	Equatorial Guinea	3.74	3.58	3.69	3.73	4.15	4.13	4.18	4.36	n/a	n/a	n/a	n/a
137	Sierra Leone	3.76	3.78	3.73	3.95	n/a	n/a	4.09	4.01	3.70	3.79	3.65	3.85
137	Tajikistan	3.76	4.05	4.20	4.15	4.14	4.16	4.16	4.15	4.30	n/a	n/a	n/a
139	Angola	3.84	n/a	n/a	n/a	n/a	n/a	4.48	4.50	4.48	4.43	4.38	4.38
139	Yemen	3.84	3.75	3.70	3.73	3.79	3.98	3.94	4.14	4.15	3.90	3.83	3.74
141	Bangladesh	3.88	3.95	3.70	3.69	3.95	4.05	4.04	3.98	3.80	3.76	3.79	3.79
142	Vietnam	3.89	3.83	3.93	3.90	3.98	4.24	4.49	4.48	4.33	4.46	4.50	4.60
143	Congo, Republic of	3.90	3.80	3.90	3.80	3.90	3.95	4.20	4.26	4.71	4.43	4.49	4.00
144	Uzbekistan	3.91	4.05	4.29	4.29	4.34	4.56	4.51	4.59	4.63	n/a	n/a	n/a
145	Syria	3.93	3.90	3.88	3.88	4.11	4.00	4.05	4.04	4.01	4.14	4.15	n/a
146	Nigeria	4.00	3.95	3.90	3.99	3.74	3.49	3.34	3.40	3.40	3.43	3.48	3.38
147	Haiti	4.03	4.09	3.73	3.86	4.13	4.08	4.33	4.26	4.43	4.30	4.59	4.79
148	Turkmenistan	4.04	4.36	4.31	4.21	4.39	4.39	4.40	4.39	4.50	n/a	n/a	n/a
149	Laos	4.08	4.33	4.40	4.68	4.76	4.70	4.80	4.75	4.63	4.65	4.95	4.95
150	Cuba	4.10	4.24	4.13	4.48	4.83	4.83	4.83	4.85	4.90	4.85	4.95	4.95
151	Belarus	4.11	4.04	4.04	4.19	4.16	4.10	4.18	4.19	4.20	3.95	3.45	3.70
152	Libya	4.16	4.40	4.55	4.48	4.60	4.90	4.85	4.95	4.95	4.95	4.95	n/a
152	Venezuela	4.16	4.09	4.23	3.76	3.93	3.78	3.38	3.43	3.48	3.53	3.58	3.23
154	Zimbabwe	4.23	4.36	4.54	4.63	4.44	4.21	4.04	3.89	4.16	3.69	3.79	4.09
155	Burma (Myanmar)	4.46	4.60	4.40	4.35	4.33	4.45	4.28	4.15	4.31	4.33	4.40	n/a
156	Iran	4.51	4.21	4.31	4.30	4.63	4.84	4.69	4.51	4.71	4.80	4.79	n/a
157	Korea, Democratic Republic of (North Korea)	5.00	5.00	5.00	5.00	5.00	5.00	5.00	5.00	5.00	5.00	5.00	5.00
n/a	Congo, (Democratic Republic of)	n/a	n/a	n/a	n/a	n/a	n/a	4.60	4.59	4.29	4.39	4.29	3.89
n/a	Iraq	n/a	n/a	n/a	n/a	5.00	4.90	4.90	4.85	4.85	4.85	4.85	n/a
n/a	Serbia and Montenegro	n/a	n/a	n/a	4.28	4.21	n/a	n/a	n/a	n/a	n/a	n/a	n/a
n/a	Sudan	n/a	n/a	n/a	n/a	n/a	n/a	4.05	4.39	4.29	4.30	4.10	4.30

Asia and the Pacific Index of Economic Freedom Scores (30 Economies)

2006 Rank	Country	2006	2005	2004	2003	2002	2001	2000	1999	1998	1997	1996	1995
						Past Year's Scores							
1	Hong Kong	1.28	1.35	1.34	1.44	1.39	1.29	1.40	1.51	1.40	1.54	1.50	1.51
2	Singapore	1.56	1.60	1.61	1.61	1.69	1.66	1.59	1.54	1.54	1.68	1.63	1.68
9	Australia	1.84	1.84	1.93	1.95	1.96	1.96	1.95	1.99	2.00	2.24	2.13	2.14
9	New Zealand	1.84	1.75	1.70	1.68	1.73	1.76	1.80	1.76	1.88	1.80	1.79	n/a
27	Japan	2.26	2.46	2.53	2.36	2.34	2.04	2.06	2.16	2.21	2.16	2.18	2.06
37	Taiwan	2.38	2.34	2.48	2.34	2.38	2.23	2.03	2.14	2.29	2.16	2.18	2.21
45	Korea, Republic of (South Korea)	2.63	2.64	2.64	2.75	2.54	2.40	2.55	2.43	2.35	2.36	2.54	2.46
60	Mongolia	2.83	2.75	2.85	2.96	2.98	3.03	3.06	3.18	3.14	3.28	3.55	3.45
68	Cambodia	2.98	2.89	2.90	2.73	2.83	3.00	3.19	3.18	3.29	3.68	n/a	n/a
68	Malaysia	2.98	2.91	3.16	3.14	3.18	3.00	2.81	2.64	2.59	2.80	2.68	2.50
71	Kyrgyz Republic	2.99	3.34	3.41	3.46	3.60	3.75	3.73	3.68	3.95	n/a	n/a	n/a
71	Thailand	2.99	3.03	2.81	2.71	2.51	2.34	2.76	2.58	2.56	2.53	2.53	2.54
90	Fiji	3.15	3.28	3.06	3.48	3.49	3.50	3.29	3.29	3.23	3.23	3.24	3.49
92	Sri Lanka	3.19	3.03	3.06	3.05	2.89	2.84	2.91	2.86	2.76	2.61	2.94	3.06
98	Philippines, The	3.23	3.30	3.10	3.00	3.05	3.21	3.00	3.03	2.89	3.06	3.14	3.35
110	Pakistan	3.33	3.73	3.35	3.44	3.49	3.50	3.50	3.50	3.31	3.29	3.26	3.34
111	China, People's Republic of	3.34	3.51	3.59	3.49	3.56	3.55	3.49	3.56	3.69	3.73	3.78	3.78
113	Kazakhstan	3.35	3.61	3.65	3.50	3.65	3.80	3.95	4.14	4.23	n/a	n/a	n/a
121	India	3.49	3.53	3.53	3.58	3.61	3.91	3.93	3.93	3.83	3.88	3.93	3.93
123	Azerbaijan	3.51	3.43	3.44	3.50	3.58	3.88	4.28	4.24	4.30	4.58	4.78	n/a
125	Nepal	3.53	3.55	3.53	3.63	3.51	3.65	3.79	3.49	3.71	3.89	3.86	n/a
134	Indonesia	3.71	3.59	3.76	3.43	3.49	3.65	3.55	3.14	3.00	3.05	3.00	3.53
137	Tajikistan	3.76	4.05	4.20	4.15	4.14	4.16	4.16	4.15	4.30	n/a	n/a	n/a
141	Bangladesh	3.88	3.95	3.70	3.69	3.95	4.05	4.04	3.98	3.80	3.76	3.79	3.79
142	Vietnam	3.89	3.83	3.93	3.90	3.98	4.24	4.49	4.48	4.33	4.46	4.50	4.60
144	Uzbekistan	3.91	4.05	4.29	4.29	4.34	4.56	4.51	4.59	4.63	n/a	n/a	n/a
148	Turkmenistan	4.04	4.36	4.31	4.21	4.39	4.39	4.40	4.39	4.50	n/a	n/a	n/a
149	Laos	4.08	4.33	4.40	4.68	4.76	4.70	4.80	4.75	4.63	4.65	n/a	n/a
155	Burma (Myanmar)	4.46	4.60	4.40	4.35	4.33	4.45	4.28	4.15	4.31	4.33	4.40	n/a
157	Korea, Democratic Republic of (North Korea)	5.00	5.00	5.00	5.00	5.00	5.00	5.00	5.00	5.00	5.00	5.00	5.00

North America and Europe Index of Economic Freedom Scores (45 Economies)

2006 Rank	Country	2006	2005	2004	2003	2002	2001	2000	1999	1998	1997	1996	1995
								Past Year's Scores					
3	Ireland	1.58	1.70	1.79	1.73	1.78	1.65	11.86	1.93	1.96	2.19	2.19	2.20
4	Luxembourg	1.60	1.63	1.76	1.68	1.93	1.84	1.89	2.00	2.01	2.01	2.04	n/a
5	Iceland	1.74	1.81	2.05	1.98	2.18	2.16	2.11	2.20	2.20	2.30	n/a	n/a
5	United Kingdom	1.74	1.75	1.84	1.88	1.88	1.83	1.90	1.86	1.90	2.00	1.90	1.80
7	Estonia	1.75	1.65	1.76	1.68	1.73	1.89	2.19	2.29	2.43	2.46	2.44	2.45
8	Denmark	1.78	1.76	1.85	1.71	1.84	2.15	2.34	2.18	2.16	2.03	2.18	n/a
9	United States	1.84	1.90	1.85	1.86	1.89	1.78	1.89	1.94	1.94	1.93	1.99	2.04
12	Canada	1.85	1.91	1.98	2.00	1.95	2.06	2.11	2.09	2.14	2.13	2.03	2.05
12	Finland	1.85	1.90	2.00	1.85	1.94	2.09	2.11	2.19	2.09	2.23	2.39	n/a
15	Switzerland	1.89	1.85	1.84	1.88	1.80	1.89	1.91	1.88	1.91	1.91	1.99	n/a
16	Cyprus	1.90	2.13	2.00	2.14	2.18	2.16	2.68	2.66	2.64	2.68	2.69	n/a
16	Netherlands, The	1.90	1.95	2.09	2.00	2.08	1.89	2.08	2.06	2.08	1.93	1.94	n/a
18	Austria	1.95	2.09	2.13	2.08	2.13	2.08	1.98	2.08	2.13	2.03	2.06	2.09
19	Germany	1.96	2.00	2.08	2.03	2.05	2.09	2.29	2.31	2.41	2.20	2.31	2.20
19	Sweden	1.96	1.89	1.95	1.88	1.93	2.08	2.15	2.25	2.29	2.30	2.58	2.68
21	Czech Republic	2.10	2.31	2.39	2.35	2.29	2.10	2.20	2.19	2.48	2.24	2.28	2.33
22	Belgium	2.11	2.13	2.24	2.10	2.15	2.15	2.19	2.11	2.10	2.08	2.11	n/a
23	Lithuania	2.14	2.18	2.19	2.21	2.35	2.53	2.84	2.90	2.98	3.10	3.45	n/a
24	Malta	2.16	2.28	2.46	2.71	2.73	2.84	3.09	3.14	3.15	3.25	3.24	3.44
27	Armenia	2.26	2.58	2.63	2.59	2.78	3.08	3.26	3.45	3.45	3.50	3.74	n/a
30	Norway	2.29	2.33	2.35	2.28	2.40	2.44	2.25	2.28	2.28	2.44	2.44	n/a
30	Portugal	2.29	2.44	2.43	2.40	2.35	2.38	2.39	2.36	2.46	2.46	2.65	2.85
33	Spain	2.33	2.34	2.36	2.31	2.46	2.54	2.56	2.46	2.45	2.55	2.78	2.49
34	Slovak Republic	2.35	2.43	2.44	2.71	2.81	2.85	3.18	3.38	3.31	3.18	3.13	2.83
38	Slovenia	2.41	2.64	2.70	2.86	3.25	3.06	3.20	3.10	3.20	3.50	3.79	n/a
39	Latvia	2.43	2.31	2.41	2.35	2.49	2.49	2.69	2.74	2.84	2.86	3.19	n/a
40	Hungary	2.44	2.40	2.55	2.50	2.23	2.43	2.38	2.89	2.94	3.09	3.03	2.93
41	Poland	2.49	2.59	2.81	2.83	2.65	2.69	2.84	2.83	2.91	3.14	3.29	3.51
42	Italy	2.50	2.28	2.31	2.31	2.33	2.26	2.26	2.29	2.39	2.46	2.61	2.63
44	France	2.51	2.63	2.68	2.74	2.90	2.54	2.49	2.39	2.39	2.38	2.36	2.35
52	Albania	2.75	2.93	3.10	3.23	3.24	3.48	3.83	3.56	3.58	3.64	3.63	3.53
55	Croatia	2.78	2.95	3.06	3.06	3.34	3.39	3.54	3.55	3.63	3.56	3.58	n/a
57	Greece	2.80	2.80	2.85	2.79	2.89	2.74	2.74	2.93	2.94	2.86	3.00	3.20
57	Macedonia	2.80	3.00	3.09	3.18	3.35	n/a	n/a	n/a	n/a	n/a	n/a	n/a
60	Mexico	2.83	2.84	2.90	2.81	2.96	3.05	3.09	3.30	3.41	3.35	3.31	3.05
64	Bulgaria	2.88	2.74	2.98	3.26	3.28	3.33	3.40	3.44	3.65	3.53	3.50	3.56
68	Georgia	2.98	3.29	3.14	3.40	3.53	3.63	3.85	3.90	3.83	3.93	3.99	n/a
74	Bosnia and Herzegovina	3.01	3.16	3.30	3.54	3.89	4.09	4.40	4.61	4.61	n/a	n/a	n/a
83	Moldova	3.10	3.11	3.09	3.13	3.25	3.70	3.30	3.44	3.43	3.60	3.45	4.10
85	Turkey	3.11	3.41	3.39	3.50	3.38	2.93	2.68	2.80	2.66	2.75	2.95	2.95
92	Romania	3.19	3.58	3.71	3.71	3.78	3.59	3.20	3.20	3.21	3.30	3.40	3.65
99	Ukraine	3.24	3.16	3.49	3.59	3.84	3.88	3.75	3.95	3.83	3.78	4.00	4.00
122	Russia	3.50	3.61	3.51	3.54	3.74	3.84	3.80	3.65	3.54	3.83	3.70	3.60
151	Belarus	4.11	4.04	4.04	4.19	4.16	4.10	4.18	4.19	4.20	3.95	3.45	3.70
n/a	Serbia and Montenegro	n/a	n/a	n/a	4.28	4.21	n/a	n/a	n/a	n/a	n/a	n/a	n/a

North Africa and the Middle East Index of Economic Freedom Scores (18 Economies)

2006 Rank	Country	2006	Past Year's Scores 2005	2004	2003	2002	2001	2000	1999	1998	1997	1996	1995
25	Bahrain	2.23	2.15	2.13	2.09	2.05	1.96	1.93	1.86	1.95	1.85	1.80	1.83
36	Israel	2.36	2.41	2.41	2.45	2.55	2.60	2.70	2.68	2.65	2.64	2.81	2.90
50	Kuwait	2.74	2.81	2.75	2.58	2.66	2.53	2.50	2.45	2.55	2.44	2.55	n/a
57	Jordan	2.80	2.79	2.78	2.80	2.73	2.80	2.95	2.91	2.94	2.85	3.15	2.95
62	Saudi Arabia	2.84	2.99	3.05	3.09	3.16	3.35	3.20	3.16	2.94	3.00	3.00	n/a
65	United Arab Emirates	2.93	2.73	2.65	2.25	2.33	2.21	2.25	2.35	2.30	2.40	2.45	n/a
73	Lebanon	3.00	3.10	3.13	3.04	3.01	2.70	3.06	3.03	3.06	2.73	2.91	n/a
74	Oman	3.01	2.81	2.75	2.70	2.63	2.65	2.93	2.85	2.74	2.79	2.85	2.70
78	Qatar	3.04	3.05	2.81	2.78	3.08	3.13	3.13	3.06	n/a	n/a	n/a	n/a
97	Morocco	3.21	3.18	2.93	2.96	3.10	2.80	3.05	2.90	3.03	3.05	2.94	3.03
99	Tunisia	3.24	3.14	2.94	2.91	2.89	2.99	2.94	2.96	2.90	2.89	2.83	2.93
119	Algeria	3.46	3.49	3.26	3.39	3.05	3.45	3.40	3.59	3.64	3.63	3.70	3.68
128	Egypt	3.59	3.43	3.33	3.44	3.48	3.53	3.53	3.30	3.26	3.49	3.40	3.69
139	Yemen	3.84	3.75	3.70	3.73	3.79	3.98	3.94	4.14	4.15	3.90	3.83	3.74
145	Syria	3.93	3.90	3.88	3.88	4.11	4.00	4.05	4.04	4.01	4.14	4.15	n/a
152	Libya	4.16	4.40	4.55	4.48	4.60	4.90	4.85	4.95	4.95	4.95	4.95	n/a
156	Iran	4.51	4.21	4.31	4.30	4.63	4.84	4.69	4.51	4.71	4.80	4.79	n/a
n/a	Iraq	n/a	n/a	n/a	n/a	5.00	4.90	4.90	4.85	4.85	4.85	4.85	n/a

Sub-Saharan Africa Index of Economic Freedom Scores (42 Economies)

2006 Rank	Country	2006	2005	2004	2003	2002	2001	2000	1999	1998	1997	1996	1995
							Past Year's Scores						
30	Botswana	2.29	2.49	2.55	2.54	2.99	2.95	2.93	2.91	2.90	2.75	3.04	3.33
46	Cape Verde	2.69	2.84	2.86	3.30	3.25	3.56	3.61	3.76	3.69	3.75	3.55	n/a
50	South Africa	2.74	2.83	2.79	2.63	2.79	3.00	3.01	2.98	2.88	2.94	3.20	3.23
52	Madagascar	2.75	2.73	3.14	2.85	3.29	3.29	3.39	3.45	3.51	3.49	3.55	3.74
66	Uganda	2.95	3.00	2.70	2.95	3.15	3.15	3.15	2.64	2.64	2.80	2.94	3.15
77	Mauritius	3.03	2.90	2.99	2.96	2.95	2.98	2.90	2.73	n/a	n/a	n/a	n/a
78	Swaziland	3.04	3.11	3.18	3.05	3.21	3.05	3.16	3.06	3.13	3.26	3.35	3.11
81	Mauritania	3.08	2.98	2.99	3.15	3.46	3.89	4.00	4.00	3.96	4.03	3.88	n/a
83	Senegal	3.10	3.04	3.05	3.33	3.45	3.33	3.29	3.36	3.46	3.64	3.76	n/a
85	Namibia	3.11	3.15	2.96	2.70	2.84	2.93	2.98	2.84	2.99	2.80	n/a	n/a
88	Ivory Coast	3.14	3.26	3.13	3.16	3.00	3.08	3.68	3.73	3.74	3.80	3.83	3.43
88	Mali	3.14	3.18	3.29	3.20	3.10	3.15	3.08	3.19	3.28	3.45	3.39	3.48
94	Djibouti	3.20	3.30	3.23	3.30	3.16	3.38	3.38	3.28	3.29	3.18	n/a	n/a
94	Kenya	3.20	3.23	3.26	3.21	3.23	3.26	3.05	3.14	3.06	3.31	3.59	3.45
94	Tanzania	3.20	3.41	3.24	3.49	3.51	3.60	3.58	3.41	3.53	3.51	3.73	3.79
99	Lesotho	3.24	3.41	3.50	3.29	3.39	3.44	3.44	3.48	3.69	3.70	3.73	n/a
102	Burkina Faso	3.28	3.28	3.28	3.35	3.33	3.45	3.56	3.58	3.75	3.76	3.91	n/a
102	Gabon	3.28	3.40	3.43	3.18	3.33	3.38	3.26	3.09	3.18	3.31	3.63	3.19
105	Chad	3.29	3.33	3.54	3.59	3.75	3.74	3.95	4.01	4.19	4.24	n/a	n/a
105	Ghana	3.29	3.25	3.35	3.54	3.54	3.24	3.24	3.29	3.29	3.43	3.54	3.54
111	Zambia	3.34	3.45	3.55	3.55	3.35	3.30	2.99	2.96	2.99	2.88	3.08	3.15
113	Mozambique	3.35	3.29	3.33	3.40	3.20	3.35	3.94	3.95	4.15	4.15	4.06	4.34
115	Niger	3.38	3.48	3.48	3.61	3.74	3.78	4.09	3.91	4.01	4.19	4.20	n/a
117	Benin	3.40	3.63	3.49	3.56	3.46	3.23	3.21	3.34	3.35	3.44	3.53	n/a
118	Central African Rep.	3.41	3.51	3.38	3.28	3.31	n/a	n/a	n/a	n/a	n/a	n/a	n/a
119	Cameroon	3.46	3.60	3.63	3.54	3.45	3.50	3.73	3.65	3.96	3.95	4.08	3.51
123	Gambia, The	3.51	3.45	3.49	3.44	3.29	3.64	3.69	3.55	3.71	3.60	n/a	n/a
125	Rwanda	3.53	3.54	3.41	3.93	3.78	3.94	4.23	4.29	4.60	4.60	n/a	n/a
127	Guinea	3.55	3.33	3.24	3.26	3.45	3.21	3.34	3.19	3.16	3.39	3.13	3.29
130	Malawi	3.63	3.65	3.51	3.63	3.59	3.76	3.84	3.89	3.96	3.86	3.64	3.74
131	Guinea-Bissau	3.65	3.80	3.85	3.90	4.15	4.19	4.40	4.50	n/a	n/a	n/a	n/a
132	Burundi	3.69	n/a	n/a	n/a	n/a	n/a	4.00	4.20	4.38	4.20	n/a	n/a
133	Ethiopia	3.70	3.73	3.33	3.79	3.70	3.83	3.65	3.68	3.70	3.85	3.80	3.90
134	Togo	3.71	3.68	3.78	3.86	3.88	4.00	4.05	4.14	n/a	n/a	n/a	n/a
136	Equatorial Guinea	3.74	3.58	3.69	3.73	4.15	4.13	4.18	4.36	n/a	n/a	n/a	n/a
137	Sierra Leone	3.76	3.78	3.73	3.95	n/a	n/a	4.09	4.01	3.70	3.79	3.65	3.85
139	Angola	3.84	n/a	n/a	n/a	n/a	n/a	4.48	4.50	4.48	4.43	4.38	4.38
143	Congo, Republic of	3.90	3.80	3.90	3.80	3.90	3.95	4.20	4.26	4.71	4.43	4.49	4.00
146	Nigeria	4.00	3.95	3.90	3.99	3.74	3.49	3.34	3.40	3.40	3.43	3.48	3.38
154	Zimbabwe	4.23	4.36	4.54	4.63	4.44	4.21	4.04	3.89	4.16	3.69	3.79	4.09
n/a	Congo, Democratic Republic of	n/a	n/a	n/a	n/a	n/a	n/a	4.60	4.59	4.29	4.39	4.29	3.89
n/a	Sudan	n/a	n/a	n/a	n/a	n/a	n/a	4.05	4.39	4.29	4.30	4.10	4.30

Latin America and the Caribbean Index of Economic Freedom Scores (26 Economies)

2006 Rank	Country	2006	Past Year's Scores 2005	2004	2003	2002	2001	2000	1999	1998	1997	1996	1995
14	Chile	1.88	1.86	1.91	2.06	1.88	2.03	2.04	2.13	2.10	2.26	2.56	2.60
26	Barbados	2.25	2.35	2.41	2.24	2.48	2.59	2.74	2.86	2.63	2.98	3.15	n/a
27	Bahamas, The	2.26	2.25	2.25	2.15	2.06	2.23	2.23	2.16	2.16	2.05	2.09	2.36
34	El Salvador	2.35	2.20	2.24	2.35	2.28	2.21	2.10	2.38	2.61	2.55	2.68	2.89
42	Trinidad and Tobago	2.50	2.54	2.40	2.54	2.49	2.59	2.43	2.49	2.60	2.63	2.69	n/a
46	Costa Rica	2.69	2.76	2.66	2.76	2.73	2.84	2.83	3.00	3.00	3.03	3.00	3.04
46	Uruguay	2.69	2.60	2.55	2.50	2.56	2.35	2.50	2.60	2.59	2.65	2.85	3.03
49	Panama	2.70	2.74	2.83	2.64	2.68	2.58	2.61	2.48	2.50	2.49	2.55	2.70
54	Jamaica	2.76	2.76	2.81	2.68	2.96	2.96	2.66	2.96	2.94	2.91	2.94	3.11
55	Belize	2.78	2.71	2.69	2.69	2.74	2.64	2.84	2.76	2.96	2.71	2.74	2.85
63	Peru	2.86	2.83	2.88	2.91	2.88	2.56	2.69	2.61	2.91	3.08	3.01	3.59
67	Bolivia	2.96	2.75	2.64	2.54	2.66	2.31	2.56	2.61	2.61	2.51	2.56	3.16
74	Guatemala	3.01	3.18	3.16	3.01	3.00	2.88	2.91	2.94	2.96	2.94	3.10	3.36
80	Nicaragua	3.05	2.90	2.99	3.14	3.23	3.49	3.65	3.65	3.68	3.75	3.65	4.08
81	Brazil	3.08	3.20	3.10	3.06	3.11	3.26	3.46	3.24	3.41	3.33	3.61	3.41
85	Guyana	3.11	3.08	3.08	3.15	3.23	3.35	3.35	3.30	3.55	3.40	3.38	3.70
91	Colombia	3.16	3.21	3.13	3.10	2.99	3.05	3.14	3.09	3.19	3.23	3.10	3.05
102	Honduras	3.28	3.43	3.53	3.24	3.38	3.50	3.51	3.71	3.51	3.58	3.58	3.58
107	Argentina	3.30	3.49	3.43	3.09	2.63	2.29	2.28	2.23	2.48	2.70	2.58	2.85
107	Ecuador	3.30	3.49	3.60	3.58	3.60	3.56	3.19	3.14	3.15	3.26	3.33	3.39
109	Paraguay	3.31	3.45	3.44	3.40	3.33	3.34	3.06	2.95	3.09	2.96	2.94	2.99
116	Dominican Republic	3.39	3.54	3.51	3.29	3.19	3.09	3.08	3.20	3.26	3.24	3.34	3.63
129	Suriname	3.60	3.93	3.96	4.01	3.98	3.98	3.98	4.08	4.10	4.00	4.10	n/a
147	Haiti	4.03	4.09	3.73	3.86	4.13	4.08	4.33	4.26	4.43	4.30	4.59	4.79
150	Cuba	4.10	4.24	4.13	4.48	4.83	4.83	4.83	4.85	4.90	4.85	4.95	4.95
152	Venezuela	4.16	4.09	4.23	3.76	3.93	3.78	3.38	3.43	3.48	3.53	3.58	3.23

Economic Freedom and Per Capita Income

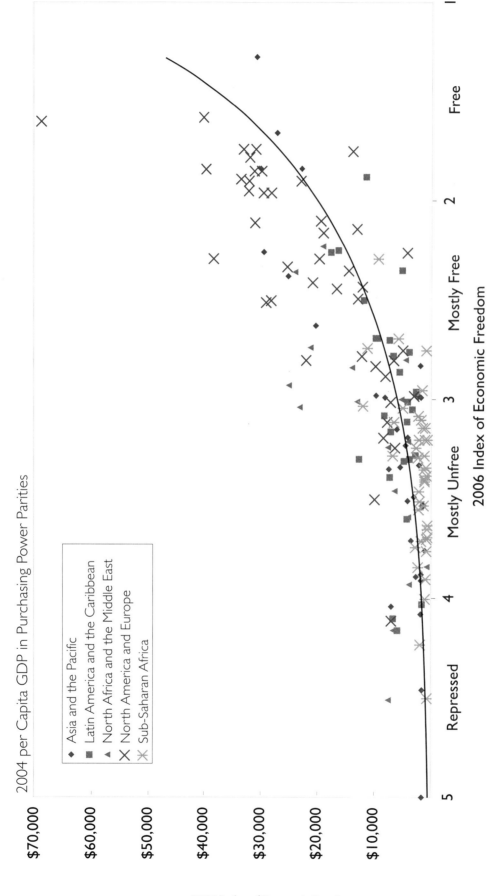

2004 per Capita GDP in Purchasing Power Parities

Legend:
- ♦ Asia and the Pacific
- ■ Latin America and the Caribbean
- ▲ North Africa and the Middle East
- ✕ North America and Europe
- ✳ Sub-Saharan Africa

Y-axis: $70,000 / $60,000 / $50,000 / $40,000 / $30,000 / $20,000 / $10,000

X-axis: 5 Repressed / 4 / Mostly Unfree / 3 / Mostly Free / 2 / Free / 1

2006 Index of Economic Freedom

Sources: World Bank, *World Development Indicators Online*, available by subscription at *www.worldbank.org/data*; Central Intelligence Agency, *The World Factbook 2005*, available at *www.cia.gov/cia/publications/factbook/index.html*, for the following countries: Bahamas, Bahrain, Barbados, Burma, Cuba, Equatorial Guinea, Iraq, Kuwait, North Korea, Libya, Qatar, Suriname, Taiwan, United Arab Emirates, Zimbabwe; Marc A. Miles, Kim R. Holmes, and Mary Anastasia O'Grady, *2006 Index of Economic Freedom* (Washington, D.C.: The Heritage Foundation and Dow Jones & Company, Inc., 2006), at *www.heritage.org/index*.

Chapter 1

Introduction

Marc A. Miles, Ph.D.

Economic freedom is about people. Each day, around the world, people get out of bed, get dressed, and decide how they will spend the day to provide for their families and pursue their dreams. These dreams could be as simple as providing food and a roof over the heads of their family. Or maybe it is something much more extravagant, such as an around-the-world trip. The point is, however, that some governments make it so much easier to achieve these goals than others do.

In an economically free country, individuals can pretty much determine their natural abilities, figure out how best to use them, and go about their business. Not so in an economically unfree country. There people are constantly fighting obstacles, such as corruption, the bureaucratic maze, regulations, or being cut off from opportunities elsewhere in the world.

Faced with the enormous costs in time, money, and effort to overcome these obstacles, some entrepreneurs will simply give up in disgust. Not only does this dash the dreams of the entrepreneur, but it also eliminates all hope for potential employees that entrepreneur might hire.

The good news for the world's people is that hope appears to be growing. Economic freedom is improving, and opportunities are increasing. This year, there are 20 economically "free" economies in the world—an increase of three. Moreover, for the first time, the average economic freedom score in the world has improved from "mostly unfree" to "mostly free."

The importance of this improvement in economic freedom cannot be overestimated. After all, wealth comes from the actions of people, not the actions of government, and the freer people are to direct their efforts to where they are most productive, the greater the wealth created. That is why, of the 10 countries with the highest GDP per capita, six are in the top 10 of the list of freest countries.

To honor this growth in freedom, three of our chapters highlight the efforts of people around the world to overcome the barriers they face.

- In Chapter 2, James Tooley and Pauline Dixon describe their research on how the entrepreneurial talents of people in Africa and Asia have created non–government-

This year, there are 20 economically "free" economies in the world—an increase of three. Moreover, for the first time, the average economic freedom score in the world has improved from "mostly unfree" to "mostly free."

sanctioned private schools that deliver a superior level of education.

- In Chapter 3, Barun Mitra writes of the entrepreneurs in India who have managed to circumvent pervasive restrictions and create markets where there might have been none. Are cheap cars unavailable because of high tariffs? Have one made by the local village mechanic.
- And in Chapter 4, Michael Gonzalez writes about how informal banking institutions in Chinese provinces are providing accessible funding to individuals that the state-run banks cannot serve.

A BETTER MEASURE OF TRADE BARRIERS

Tariff rates vary widely around the world. Until now, we have captured that variation in scoring steps of a single point. However, finer gradations are not only desirable, but also possible. The finer gradations in turn would allow for a wider distribution of scores and, potentially, more precise distinctions among countries. Among the beneficiaries of this wider distribution would be the Millennium Challenge Corporation, which uses Heritage's trade factor in determining whether countries qualify to apply for Millennium Challenge Account aid.

This year, the trade factor scores for previous years were analyzed statistically to determine precisely how to accomplish this goal. The result was a new scoring system that increases in steps of only one-half point. Thus, two countries with the same trade factor score last year might have scores differing by one-half point this year. The country with the slightly lower tariff would now appropriately appear more economically free than the second country.

In order to maintain the usefulness of the *Index* as an aid to research, policy, or investment, the historical trade factor scores for all countries were also converted to this new distribution. However, as before, the presence of non-tariff barriers continues to add a point to (in other words, to downgrade) the score.

We believe that reevaluating our methodology periodically makes the *Index* stronger and more useful. In fact, plans are already

underway to examine two areas for next year's *Index*.

- *First,* the monetary policy factor will be analyzed to determine whether it, too, can be converted to one-half point steps. There is also the question of how to deal appropriately with countries experiencing deflation.
- *Second,* we want to examine how the increased concentration of European Union power in Brussels has affected individual countries. Has there been harmonization of laws concerning labor, the environment, or investment that must be captured in our scoring? It is hoped that next year we will have definitive evidence one way or the other.

NEW MEMBERS OF THE EUROPEAN UNION

In May 2004, 10 countries (Cyprus, the Czech Republic, Estonia, Hungary, Latvia, Lithuania, Malta, Poland, Slovakia, and Slovenia) joined the European Union. Over the ensuing months, each country adopted the EU tariff system. As a result, tariff rates rose in some countries and fell in others, and this is reflected in this year's trade factor scores. As shown in Table 4 of the Executive Summary, Estonia was the only country whose trade factor score was adversely affected by accession to the EU; the other nine countries found their higher tariff rates cut.

Another important development in these countries has been the adoption of flat-rate taxes for individuals and corporations. While countries in the West can only discuss such a policy, Eastern and Central European countries have eagerly adopted it. Under a flat-rate tax, a lower rate of taxation applies equally over all income, whereas the progressive tax system found in most of the West attempts to impose higher rates as incomes rise. Estonia was first in 1994 to adopt a flat tax, with a 26 percent rate.

On January 1, 2004, the Slovak Republic halved its top individual rate to 19 percent as part of its new flat tax rate system. Corporate rates were also lowered to 19 percent, making the Slovak Republic a more attractive place for German and other manufac-

This year, the trade factor scores for previous years were analyzed statistically to determine precisely how to accomplish this goal. The result was a new scoring system that increases in steps of only one-half point.

turers to set up shop. Other former Eastern Bloc countries such as Romania (16 percent), Russia (13 percent), Serbia (10 percent), and Montenegro (9 percent) also have adopted low, flat taxes, setting off a "tax competition" for the lowest rate in this part of the world. Estonia, for example, has had to respond by cutting its flat tax rate from 26 percent to 20 percent in 2006.

This competition is starting to put pressure on Western countries, which should welcome such change. They could learn from the positive experience of these pioneer countries to their east. Perhaps, given the growing competitive pressures, the Western countries should no longer ask what will happen if a flat tax is adopted, but rather what is likely to happen to their economies if they fail to adopt a low, flat tax.

MISGUIDED CRITICISM OF THE *INDEX*

From time to time, people criticize the *Index of Economic Freedom*. We welcome such criticism, for it often opens a useful dialogue and creates opportunities to learn something that helps to make the *Index* even better. However, during the past year, a counterproductive line of criticism has appeared. Specifically, this criticism attacks a straw man that reflects neither the *Index* analysis nor any claim made about the *Index*.

A prime example of this misguided criticism appears in Jeffrey Sachs' recent book *The End of Poverty*. Each year, the *Index* has shown a close correlation between the *level* of economic freedom and the *level* of prosperity. In the past couple of years, we have demonstrated an even closer relationship between *changes* in economic freedom and *growth rates*.

So imagine our surprise when Mr. Sachs attempted to dismiss the *Index* by showing that there is no relationship between the position of a country in the *Index* rankings and its growth rate. A relationship between the *level* of economic freedom and *growth*? Who claimed that to be true? Certainly, we did not.

Chapter 2

The Failures of State Schooling in Developing Countries and the People's Response

James Tooley and Pauline Dixon

Drive across the low highway viaduct toward Victoria Island in the bustling city of Lagos, Nigeria, and you see the shantytown of Makoko, home to an estimated 50,000 people, sprawling out into the black waters below. Wooden huts on stilts stretch out into the lagoon; young men punt and women paddle dug-out canoes down into narrow canals weaving between the raised homes; teenage boys stand on rocks in the water and cast their fishing nets; large wooden boats, some with noisy outboard motors, carry fishermen out to below the highway and into the ocean beyond. Across the top of the shantytown, there is a veneer of drifting smog created by the open fires used for cooking.

It is possibly the last place where you would expect to witness an educational revolution taking place, but that is precisely what is happening. In Makoko—as in other poor communities around the developing world—parents are abandoning public education *en masse*, disturbed by its low quality, and educational entrepreneurs are setting up private schools to cater to this demand. These private schools, it turns out, whatever their appearances might suggest, are of higher quality than the public alternative, achieving higher standards at a fraction of the cost of public education. Their existence provides a neat grassroots solution to the problem that so perplexes development experts: how to achieve universal basic education—the United Nations Millennium Summit development goal of "education for all"—by 2015.

Instead of celebrating this good news story, however, development experts are nonplussed. Whatever the experience so far, they see public education as the only way forward, and private schools for the poor imperil that. But we believe that the people of Makoko are on to something important. It is time the international development experts caught up with them.

EDUCATING MAKOKO

To get to Makoko by road, you turn off Third Mainland Bridge, into the congested Murtal Muhammed Way, and sharply into Makoko Street, easing past the women crowding the streets as they sell tomatoes, peppers, yams, chillies, and crayfish. At the end of this road is the entrance to two parallel

These private schools, it turns out, whatever their appearances might suggest, are of higher quality than the public alternative, achieving higher standards at a fraction of the cost of public education.

and imposing four-storey concrete buildings. These buildings contain three public primary schools, originally church schools nationalized by the state in the 1980s, all on the same site and designed by state officials to serve the whole population of Makoko.

Visiting these three public schools is a dispiriting experience. Because our visit was a scheduled one, the schools had had time to prepare. Even so, in most of the classrooms, the children seemed to be doing very little. In one, the young male teacher was fast asleep at his desk, not aroused even when the children rose to chant noisy greetings to their visitors. In others, the teacher was sitting reading a newspaper or chatting with others outside the door, having written a few simple things on the board, which the class had finished copying.

In one of the three schools, Grade 1 had 95 children present, with three classes combined because of long-term teacher absenteeism. The children were doing nothing. Some were also sleeping. One girl was cleaning the windows. The one teacher was hanging around outside the class door.

No one, certainly not the headmistress, seemed remotely embarrassed by any of this. We asked the children what lesson they were doing. When no one responded, the head teacher bellowed at the pupils to get an answer. "It is a mathematics lesson," she reported pleasantly, without any sense of incongruity, for no child had a single book open.

This one of the three schools alone could accommodate 1,500 children. The headmistress told us that parents left the school *en masse* a few years earlier because of teachers' strikes. Things have improved now, and children have returned, she said, with 500 now enrolled. On the top floor of the stark building, however, there were six empty classrooms, all complete with desks and chairs, waiting for children to return.

"Why don't parents send their children here?" we asked the headmistress. Her explanation was simple: "Parents in the slums don't value education. They're illiterate and ignorant. Some don't even know that education is free here. But most can't be bothered to send their children to school."

When we innocently remarked that we had heard that, perhaps, parents were sending their children to private schools instead, we were greeted with laughter: "They are very poor families living in the slum.... They can't afford private education!"

She is, however, entirely wrong about this. Continue past the three public schools, past where the tarred road ends at a raised speed bump, and enter "Apollo Street," too muddy for a vehicle. Here you need to pick your way carefully, squelching your way from one side of the street to the other, avoiding the worst excesses of the slime and mud and the excrement and piled rubbish. Walk alongside the huts visible from the highway—homes made of flat timbers, supported by narrow slivers of planks sunk into the black waters below—and you come to a pink plastered concrete building with colorful pictures of children's toys and animals and "Ken Ade Private School" emblazoned across the top of the wall.

Ken Ade Private School—not on any official list of schools and so unknown to government—is owned by Mr. Bawo Sabo Elieu Ayeseminikan, known to everyone as "B.S.E." B.S.E. has three sites for his school: The youngest children are housed in a church hall along Apollo Street, learning on wooden benches in front of blackboards; the middle-grade children are in the rented pink building by the water's edge; and the eldest pupils are on B.S.E.'s own land nearby, in a building made of planks nailed to posts that support a tin roof. B.S.E.'s ambition is to accommodate all of his children on that one site and also to open a junior secondary school.

B.S.E. had set up the school on April 16, 1990, starting with only five children in the church hall, with parents paying fees on a daily basis when they could afford to do so. Now he has about 200 children, from Nursery to Primary 6. The fees are about Naira (N) 2,200 ($17) per term, or about $4 per month, but there are 25 children who come for free. "If a child is orphaned, what can I do? I can't send her away," he says.

His motives for setting up the school are a mixture of philanthropy and commerce. Yes, he needed work and saw that there was a demand for school places from parents

Ken Ade Private School—not on any official list of schools and so unknown to government—is owned by Mr. Bawo Sabo Elieu Ayeseminikan, known to everyone as "B.S.E."

disillusioned with the state schools, but his heart also went out to the children in his community and from his church. How could he help them better themselves? True, there were the three public schools at the end of the road, but although they were only about a kilometre from where he set up his school, the distance was a barrier for many parents who did not want their girls walking down the crowded streets where abductors might lurk.

Mainly, however, it was the educational standards in the public school that made parents want an alternative. When they encouraged B.S.E. to set up the school 15 years earlier, parents knew that the teachers were frequently on strike—in fairness to the teachers, protesting about non-payment of their salaries.

We arrange to meet some parents, visiting in their homes on stilts. The parents from the community are all poor, the men usually fishermen and the women trading in fish or selling other goods along Apollo Street. Their maximum earnings might amount to about $50 per month, but many are on lower incomes than that. The parents tell us without hesitation that there is no question of where they send their children if they can afford to do so: to private school. Some have one or two of their children in the private school and one or two others in the public school, and they know well, they tell us, how differently children are treated in each.

One woman said: "We see how children's books never get touched in the public school." Another man ventured: "We pass the public school many days and see the children outside all of the time, doing nothing. But in the private schools, we see them everyday working hard. In the public school, children are abandoned." One handsome young father, who was reading Shakespeare when we approached him outside his home on stilts, said that in the private school, "the teachers are dependable."

Even more remarkably, Ken Ade Private School is not alone in Makoko. In fact, it is one of 30 private primary schools in the shantytown. We know because we sent in a research team made up of graduate students from Nigeria's premier university, the

University of Ibadan, to find as many of the schools as we could. In the 30 private schools found, enrollment was reported to be 3,611, all from the slum itself, while the enrollment in the three public schools was reported to be 1,709, some of them from outside Makoko. Overall, the great majority—at least 68 percent—of all school children in Makoko attend private school.

B.S.E. knows most of the schools and their proprietors, for 26 of them are registered with the Association of Formidable Educational Development (AFED), a federation with which he is actively involved as Makoko chapter coordinator. The federation is only for low-fee private schools, like the ones in Makoko, and others that exist all over Lagos State, including the rural areas.

Why was the AFED formed? In 2000, B.S.E. reports, there was a two-pronged attack to close down private schools like his. On one front, this came from the "posh" private school association, the Association of Proprietors of Private Schools (APPS), that represents schools charging anything from 10 to 100 times what his school charges. APPS complained to the government about the low quality in schools like his, which prompted the government to move to close down the low-fee private schools. "We are still fighting that battle now," B.S.E. says. "We are trying to give the people who are not so rich the privilege of having some decent education."

Working with the AFED, the schools' proprietors fought the closure, and with a change of heart in government, they were neglected for a bit. Then, a few months before our first visit, the government of Lagos again issued an edict saying that they must be closed down. They are fighting this and have been given a stay of execution for six months.

Meanwhile, the association has written to all the kings in Lagos State telling them what the government is threatening, saying that 600,000 children will be pushed out of school and thousands of staff made redundant if what is threatened comes to pass. "When you have a headache," says B.S.E., "the solution is not to cut off the head! If the government has a problem with us, then we can work together to help us improve, not cut us off completely!"

Mainly, however, it was the educational standards in the public school that made parents want an alternative.

In the private schools, unlike in the imposing public schools, the children felt at home. This was especially the case because the teachers were drawn from the community itself and knew all its problems as well as its vibrancy.

We spent a lot of time observing the classes in B.S.E.'s school and in every other private school we visited, usually unannounced. With only an occasional exception, the teachers were teaching when visited; in the rare cases when a teacher was off sick, the head teacher had set out work for the children and was keeping an eye on progress.

A typical teacher is Edamisan. He is 23, has just completed his high school diploma ("A-levels"), and wants to go to university to read economics. He can't afford to do so, so he carries on living where he was brought up in Makoko, teaching and saving his small salary to fund his future career. He says he feels privileged to be a teacher: "When I am teaching, I am also learning. When I'm teaching children that the square on the hypotenuse is equal to the squares on the other two sides, I have to think deeply: Why is that the case? And I find I learn all sorts of new things for myself."

Edamisan is clearly enthusiastic about teaching and engages all the children with him. His commitment and passion make him exactly the sort of teacher you would want to have for yourself or your own children.

Another private school in Makoko is a French medium school, whose proprietor is from the neighboring country of Benin, serving migrant children from the surrounding Francophone countries. This is the largest school in Makoko, with 400 children; it is a two-storey (or "storey," as these buildings are called in Nigeria) wooden building, built on stilts.

The oldest school, Legacy, founded in 1985, is also now housed in a "storey" building, with a plank floor upstairs that creaked and groaned as we walked along and through which we could see the classes below. When we visited at 5:00 pm, a teacher was still teaching upstairs, voluntarily helping the senior children with preparation for their examinations. The proprietor here had started the school by going from door to door, encouraging parents to send their children to school—there being no accessible public school then, and he wanted his community to be literate. Then he started charging 10 kobo (10 hundredths of a Naira, the Nigerian currency, worth less than one

U.S. cent) per day. Later, he worked on making parents pay weekly fees. As his numbers grew, he moved to monthly and then termly fees. He, like everyone else, found it a really difficult job to get the fees from parents; and he, like everyone else, offered free places to many of his most deprived children.

Why do the private school owners act philanthropically in this way? All of the school owners interviewed came out with the same strong message: They all live in the shantytown itself, and they all proclaim the desire to assist children of their community. The school owner at Zico United School started his school in 1998 to "build the leaders of tomorrow." Asked why he gives free places, he said, "Sometimes we have to carry the children along so that they are not a burden on society. Some of the children are very brilliant, and therefore that has to be considered."

A similar story was told by the school owner at St. Mary's Nursery and Primary school. He had started with evening classes in 1996, when students had said, "Uncle, help me with my work." He did not at first charge regular fees, instead asking parents to give whatever they could afford, and conducted his classes in "an outside space." Then, "Two years ago, the parents asked me to start a private school. I live in the community, and I want to help them as well as the less privileged ones.... I give concessionary fees and scholarships for families that have more children."

At the Ministry of Education, senior officials are unsympathetic about these schools. One prominent woman, who drives a brand-new Mercedes, said—with no sense of irony—that poor parents send their children to the private schools as a "fake status symbol." They are "ignoramuses," she said, wanting the symbol of private education but hoodwinked by unscrupulous businessmen. The schools were a threat to educational standards and should all be closed down.

It is true that the school *buildings*—which give outsiders first impressions of the school itself—are of poor quality, but they are no worse than the buildings where people lived. It is true that they did not normally have toilets, but neither do the people's homes—and we also saw that children in the public school urinated in a corner of the schoolyard.

Moreover, in the private schools, unlike in the imposing public schools, the children felt at home. This was especially the case because the teachers were drawn from the community itself and knew all its problems as well as its vibrancy. In the public schools, the teachers often travelled for an hour or more to the school, and most said that they had never actually been inside Makoko itself to see where their charges lived. The more we visited these schools, the more we realized how organic they were: part of the community they served, quite unlike the public schools outside.

FROM MAKOKO TO THE DEVELOPING WORLD

Makoko is one shantytown, one poor community in a developing country, but the same story is repeated elsewhere. Across the developing world, you find people like B.S.E. who have set up schools to serve the poor, charging low fees, affordable to the communities. And you find people like him who offer free places to the poorest of the poor, even though they are running the schools as businesses.

For the past two years or so, we have been conducting research in poor communities like Makoko, elsewhere in Nigeria, and in Ghana, Kenya, and India.[1] In India, Ghana, and Nigeria, we found the *majority* of schoolchildren in the poor areas examined attending private schools.

In the "notified slums" of three zones of Hyderabad's Old City, capital of the state of Andhra Pradesh, India, we found 918 schools, of which only 35 percent were government schools—fewer than the 37 percent of unrecognized private schools. In total, 65 percent of schoolchildren in these low-income areas attended private unaided school.

In the Ga District of Ghana, the low-income suburban and rural area surrounding the capital city of Accra, we found 779 schools in total, of which only 25 percent were government schools; 64 percent of schoolchildren attended private school.

Just as in Makoko, in the "poor" areas of three other local government districts (one rural, two urban) of Lagos State, Nigeria, we found 540 schools, of which 34 percent were government and the largest proportion (43 percent) were private unregistered. We estimated that 75 percent of all schoolchildren were enrolled in private schools, with more children in unregistered schools than in government ones.

In Kenya, we looked at the urban slum of Kibera, reportedly the largest in sub-Saharan Africa, and found 76 private schools serving around 12,000 students. Usefully, our research occurred 10 months or so after the introduction of free primary education in January 2003. Although this was widely credited with massively increasing primary school enrollment—so much so that former U.S. President Bill Clinton told a prime-time ABC television audience that the person he most wanted to meet was President Mwai Kibaki of Kenya, "Because he has abolished school fees," which "would affect more lives than any president had done or would ever do by the end of this year"[2]—our research suggested that the reality was different.

This assessment did not take into account the impact on the private schools serving the slum populations, for the private schools had suffered a huge fall in enrollment since free primary education was introduced, and at least 25 private schools in Kibera had closed altogether. In fact, the number of children lost from private education appeared to be far greater than the additional enrollment in the state schools bordering Kibera. At best, allowing for some exaggeration by the school owners of the numbers of children who had left, we could infer that the additional enrollment was a result of children transferring from private to public schools, not an overall increase in enrollment at all.

Children transferring from the "mushrooming" private to government schools may not seem such a bad thing to some in the development community, given the widespread assumption—shared by the senior official in the Lagos State Ministry of Education reported above—that such private schools are of low quality. But our research explored the relative attainment of students in private and public schools serving poor communities and found that private schools in general had a large achievement advantage.

Our research explored the relative attainment of students in private and public schools serving poor communities and found that private schools in general had a large achievement advantage.

All of this suggests that a great success story is taking place. In particular, because so many children are in unrecognized private schools that do not appear in government statistics, achieving universal basic education—the United Nations Millennium Summit development goal of "education for all" by 2015—may be much easier than is currently believed.

For instance, in Lagos State, the mean math score advantage over government schools was about 15 and 19 percentage points, respectively, more in private registered and unregistered schools, while in English it was 23 and 30 percentage points more. In Hyderabad, similarly, mean scores in mathematics were about 22 and 25 percentage points higher in private unrecognized and recognized schools, respectively, than in government schools. The advantage was even more pronounced for English. When we controlled for all relevant background variables, including family income and education, and for pupil IQ, the achievement advantage remained.

The private schools, including the unregistered ones, we found to be substantially outperforming government schools. Importantly, they spend far less on teachers—a cost which is likely to make up most of school's recurrent expenditure—than do government schools. In general, the average monthly teacher salary in a government school ranges between *three to four times higher* than in an unrecognized private school.

All of this suggests that a great success story is taking place. In particular, because so many children are in unrecognized private schools that do not appear in government statistics, achieving universal basic education—the United Nations Millennium Summit development goal of "education for all" by 2015—may be much easier than is currently believed.

For instance, a recent report from the Lagos State Economic Empowerment and Development Strategy (LASEEDS) estimates that 50 percent of "school aged" children in Lagos State are out of school.[3] Assuming that this figure applies to those in primary schools, we can use the official state figures on enrollment to get the second column of Table 1.

However, if we add in our own estimates of the number of children in private unregistered schools—schools like B.S.E.'s—the total of out-of-school children is sharply reduced to 26 percent of the total school-age children. Bringing 26 percent of children into school may be much easier than bringing 50 percent into school. Nigeria's task of achieving "education for all" may be considerably easier than

Table 1
Lagos State: Official and Estimated Out-of-Primary-School Children

	Official Figures	Authors' Estimates
Government	451,798	451,798
Private registered	737,599	737,599
Private unregistered	0	577,024
Total	1,189,397	1,766,421
Estimated out of school		
	1,189,397	612,373
	(50%)	(26%)
Total school-age children		
	2,378,794	2,378,794

Sources: Authors' census data; Report from Lagos State to the Joint Consultative Committee on Educational Planning (JCCE) Reference Committee on Educational Planning Holding at Owerri, Imo State Between 18th and 23rd April 2004, Ministry of Education, Alausa, Ikeja, Lagos State, 2004, p. 29; Lagos State Economic Empowerment and Development Strategy (LASEEDS) (2005–2007), 2nd Draft, Ministry of Economic Planning, Alausa, Ikeja, Lagos State, 2004, at *www.lagosstate.gov.ng/LASEEDS/LASEEDS%20DOCUMENT.pdf.*

is currently anticipated. These findings—and parallel ones from each of the countries surveyed—are surely good news for the international development community.

TWO PROPOSITIONS IN SEARCH OF A CONCLUSION

Curiously, however, that is not how the international development community sees the "mushrooming" private schools. This is the case even though there is an acute awareness of the failures of public education. The foregoing descriptions of the Makoko public schools fit squarely within how state education is seen by the development experts; indeed, it is a rather more sanguine view than those reported from many other sources.

The failures of public education for the poor are in fact well documented. For instance, the *Oxfam Education Report*, handbook of the international aid agency Oxfam International, notes that "there is no doubting the *appalling standard of provision in public education* across much of the developing world."[4] In parts of sub-Saharan Africa, it is reported that "education scores based on multiple-choice tests are so low that they are almost random, indicating that there is little or no value in attending school. Under these circumstances, it is not difficult to see why many poor households regard spending on [public] education as a bad use of scarce resources."[5]

Nobel Laureate Amartya Sen is equally as up-front about the gross failings of state education for the poor in India in particular. The main factor in making parents not send their children to government schools is reported to be "the discouragement effect" brought on in part by the *abysmal quality* of Indian [state] schools."[6]

One major problem is teacher absenteeism. A major survey of educational provision in four northern Indian states, the *Public Report on Basic Education* ("Probe Report"), produced startling findings on the quality of state schools. When researchers called unannounced on a large random sample of government schools, *in only half* was there any "teaching activity" going on at all! In fully *one-third*, the head teacher was absent.[7] The team reported "several cases of irresponsible teachers keeping a school closed or non-functional for several months at a time; a school where the teacher was drunk…a headteacher who asks the children to do domestic chores, including looking after the baby; several cases of teachers sleeping at school…; a headteacher who came to school once a week…and so on down the line."[8]

Indeed, the Probe Team observed that in the government schools, "generally, teaching activity has been reduced to a minimum, in terms of both time and effort." Importantly, "this pattern is not confined to a minority of irresponsible teachers—it has become a way of life in the profession."[9]

Moreover, it is not just in India that teacher absenteeism is a problem. The UNESCO *EFA Global Monitoring Report 2005*, for instance, reports: "random surveys in many countries confirm that teacher absenteeism remains a persistent problem. The need to hold second jobs, lax professional standards and lack of support by education authorities are common causes."[10]

Add to teacher absenteeism the problem of corruption and bribes within the state systems,[11] the lack of teacher commitment and preparation even when present in the schools,[12] and the misdirection of resources,[13] and it is easy to see why development experts appear to be unanimous about the problems of state education for the poor. In its *World Development Report 2004*, the World Bank calls it "government failure," with "services so defective that their opportunity costs outweigh their benefits for most poor people."[14] ActionAid does not mince its words either: Government basic education "in many of the world's poorest countries" is "a moral outrage, and a gross violation of human rights."[15]

The same development experts, however, argue that the only way forward is more state education, assisted by billions more in international aid. The *World Development Report 2004* concludes that, just because "public provision has often failed to create universally available and effective schooling does not imply that the solution is a radically different approach."[16] Certainly, says the World Bank, making public education work for the poor is a "formidable" challenge that will require changing both the ways in which "foreign aid is transferred" and the ways in which governments operate: "there is *no silver bullet*…. Even if we know what is to be done, it may be difficult to get it done. Despite the urgent needs of the world's poor people, and the many ways services have failed them, quick results will be hard to come by. Many of the changes involve fundamental shifts in power—something that cannot happen overnight. Making services work for poor people *requires patience*."[17]

The experiences of Makoko and all the rest of the places we have researched, however, suggest that the poor are not showing the required patience. The poor are not acquiescing in state failure. They may themselves have found the "silver bullet" that is off the radar as far as the international agencies are concerned. For they are responding to the inadequacies of state education by creating for themselves private schools to serve their needs.

Importantly, it is not the case that this possible way forward is ignored because the international development community

Add to teacher absenteeism the problem of corruption and bribes within the state systems, the lack of teacher commitment and preparation even when present in the schools, and the misdirection of resources, and it is easy to see why development experts appear to be unanimous about the problems of state education for the poor.

is unaware of the existence of the private schools. Quite the contrary. Again, the *Oxfam Education Report* is typical: It states that "the notion that private schools are servicing the needs of a small minority of wealthy parents is misplaced" and that "a lower cost private sector has emerged to meet the demands of poor households." Indeed, there is "a growing market for private education among poor households" and "private education is a far more pervasive fact of life than is often recognised."[18]

Research in the Indian state of Haryana found that private unrecognized schools "are operating practically in every locality of the urban centers as well as in rural areas" and are often located adjacent to a government school.[19] Reporting on evidence from the Indian states of Haryana, Uttar Pradesh, and Rajasthan, researchers noted that "private schools have been expanding rapidly in recent years" and that these "now include a large number of primary schools which charge low fees," in urban as well as rural areas.[20] Serving the poor of Calcutta, there has been a "mushrooming of privately managed unregulated pre-primary and primary schools."[21]

The same phenomenon exists in sub-Saharan Africa. In Uganda and Malawi, for example, private schools have "mushroomed due to the poor quality government primary schools";[22] and in Kenya, "the deteriorating quality of public education…created demand for private alternatives."[23] In sub-Saharan Africa and Asia generally, "the poor and declining quality of public education has led to growing numbers of parents sending their children to non-state schools"; and in southern Asia, "this amounts to a mass exodus."[24]

WHY ARE PRIVATE SCHOOLS NOT PART OF THE SOLUTION?

If there is this mushrooming of private schools, known to the development experts, why are these schools not celebrated as part of the way forward in achieving "education for all"? There seem to be three practical reasons why not.

First, private schools charge fees, thus making them out of reach of the poorest.[25] But why, if these private schools are supe-

rior to government schools, as our research seems to suggest, is this seen as an insurmountable obstacle to extending access to them? For example, creating *targeted* vouchers for the poorest to use at private schools, following the private schools' own lead at offering scholarships, potentially overcomes this objection.

Interestingly, the United Nations Development Programme (UNDP) notes this as a possibility: "To ensure that children from poor families unable to pay school fees are able to attend private schools, governments could finance their education through vouchers."[26] The *Oxfam Education Report* also notes the success of two targeted voucher programs in Colombia and Pakistan, the latter targeted at girls.[27] Neither agency, however, then makes what seems to us the obvious connection in seeing these private schools as a valuable way forward.

The *second* objection questions whether high-quality provision could exist in private schools serving the poor because levels of resourcing are low. The *Oxfam Education Report* notes that, although "there is no doubting the appalling standard of provision in public education systems," there is "little hard evidence to substantiate the view that private schools systematically outperform public schools *with comparable levels of resourcing*."[28] The UNDP makes precisely the same claim.[29]

In reality, the suggestion that poor parents, whose resources are scarce, are frittering away funds on private schools that are worse than the free state alternative is highly implausible. Our research suggests that this objection is simply not valid and that poor parents are not being systematically hoodwinked as the development experts appear to believe.

The *third* objection is oddest of all. It concerns the impact of private provision on state education: If poor parents support private education, this allegedly "carries a real danger of undermining the government schooling system."[30] However, it is not obvious in *practical* terms why this is a viable objection to an increased role for the private sector. If private schools can be made available to all, including to the poorest and most excluded,

In reality, the suggestion that poor parents, whose resources are scarce, are frittering away funds on private schools that are worse than the free state alternative is highly implausible. Our research suggests that this objection is simply not valid and that poor parents are not being systematically hoodwinked as the development experts appear to believe.

through targeted vouchers (first set of objections), and if it can be shown that their quality is higher than the government alternative without pushing up costs (second set of objections), then, from the perspective of the poor, it would seem irrelevant whether this would undermine the state system, providing that education for all was achieved.

None of this discussion, of course, means that nothing could be improved in the private sector's efforts to serve the poor. As noted already, access to private education could be extended even further by building on the initiatives—already undertaken by the private schools themselves—that offer free and reduced-fee seats to the poorest children. Such informal schemes could be extended and replicated by philanthropists and/or the state so that "pupil passports" or vouchers could be targeted at the poorest children (although there may be the danger of additional regulations that could stifle the growth of private schools if they were administered by the state). With these passports or vouchers, many more of the poor could be empowered to attend private unaided schools.

Private school managers themselves also realize that their school infrastructure and facilities can be improved, and many are active in creating private school federations, like the Association of Formidable Educational Development in Makoko, that link school managers in self-help organizations. Such associations in many countries are actively pursuing management, teacher training, and curriculum development and challenging the regulatory regimes imposed by government. They could be supported in their endeavors, perhaps through the creation of a global network of private schools and their associations that would conduct further research and disseminate information about the role of private schools for the poor to opinion leaders and policymakers. Such networks could reward innovation and excellence in the schools and mobilize additional resources to help with improvements.

As an activity parallel to our research in Nigeria and Hyderabad, we have been mobilizing resources for the creation of two revolving loan funds to help private schools improve their facilities. Schools are borrowing up to $1,000 to build new classrooms, equip libraries and laboratories, and improve teacher training. Such loan funds could be extended and replicated to enable more children to access education in an even better, safer, and educationally more conducive environment. Other educational services could also be offered to help the private unaided schools improve and better serve their communities.

In Makoko, as in other poor communities in developing countries, parents do not accept the supposed need for patience until governments and the international development agencies get public education working. They need solutions urgently for their children, and they cannot wait. The mushrooming private schools are part of their solution, not a problem to be dealt with.

And that is surely what they are: a dynamic demonstration of how the entrepreneurial talents of people in Africa and Asia can contribute powerfully to the improvement of education, even for the poor. Private schools for the poor signal the urgent need for a rethink by the international development community.

Private schools are a dynamic demonstration of how the entrepreneurial talents of people in Africa and Asia can contribute powerfully to the improvement of education, even for the poor. Private schools for the poor signal the urgent need for a rethink by the international development community.

Endnotes

1   Also in China but not reported here as the results are still being analyzed. Further details of this research are reported in J. Tooley and P. Dixon, "Private Education Is Good for the Poor: A Study of Private Schools Serving the Poor in Low-Income Countries," Cato Institute, Washington, D.C., 2005, and J. Tooley, "Private Schools for the Poor," *Education Next*, Fall 2005.

2   *The Nation* (Nairobi), November 23, 2004.

3   *Lagos State Economic Empowerment and Development Strategy (LASEEDS) (2005–2007)*, 2nd Draft, Ministry of Economic Planning, Alausa, Ikeja, Lagos State, 2004, at *www.lagosstate. gov.ng/LASEEDS/LASEEDS%20DOCUMENT.pdf*.

4   K. Watkins, *The Oxfam Education Report* (Oxford: Oxfam in Great Britain, 2000), p. 230. Emphasis added.

5   *Ibid.*, p. 106.

6   J. Dreze and A. Sen, *India: Development and Participation*, 2nd Edition (New Delhi and Oxford: Oxford University Press, 2002), p. 158. Emphasis added.

7   The Probe Team, *Public Report on Basic Education in India* (Oxford and New Delhi: Oxford University Press, 1999), p. 47.

8   *Ibid.*, p. 63.

9   *Ibid.*

10 *EFA Global Monitoring Report 2005: Education for All, The Quality Imperative* (Paris: UNESCO Publishing, 2004), p. 18.

11 *World Development Report 2004: Making Services Work for Poor People* (Oxford and New York: World Bank/Oxford University Press, 2003), p. 24.

12 Geetha B. Nambissan, *Educational Deprivation and Primary School Provision: A Study of Providers in the City of Calcutta*, Institute of Development Studies *Working Paper* No. 187, 2003, pp. 25 and 30.

13 *World Development Report 2004: Making Services Work for Poor People*, p. 25, and United Nations Development Programme, *Human Development Report 2003: Millennium Development Goals: A Compact Among Nations to End Human Poverty* (New York and Oxford: Oxford University Press, 2003), p. 93.

14 *World Development Report 2004: Making Services Work for Poor People*, p. 182.

15 Patrick Watt, Policy Advisor, UK Action Team, "Response to World Development Report 2004 Outline," London, ActionAid, January 2003, p. 1.

16 *World Development Report 2004: Making Services Work for Poor People*, p. 113.

17 *Ibid.*, p. 18. Emphasis added.

18 Watkins, *The Oxfam Education Report*, pp. 229–230.

19 Y. Aggarwal, *Public and Private Partnership in Primary Education in India: A Study of Unrecognised Schools in Haryana* (New Delhi: National Institute of Educational Planning and Administration, 2000), p. 20.

20 A. De, M. Majumdar, M. Samson, and C. Noronha, "Private Schools and Universal Elementary Education," in R. Govinda, ed., *India Education Report: A Profile of Basic Education* (Oxford and New Delhi: Oxford University Press, 2002), p. 148.

21 Nambissan, *Educational Deprivation and Primary School Provision*, p. 52.

22 P. Rose, "Is the Non-State Education Sector Serving the Needs of the Poor? Evidence from East and Southern Africa," paper prepared for Department for International Development seminar in preparation for 2004 World Development Report, 2002, p. 6, and P. Rose, "From the Washington to the Post-Washington Consensus: The Influence of International Agendas on Education Policy and Practice in Malawi," *Globalisation, Societies and Education*, Vol. 1, No. 1 (2003), p. 80.

23 A. Baurer, F. Brust, and J. Hybbert, "Entrepreneurship: A Case Study in African Enterprise Growth: Expanding Private Education in Kenya: Mary Okelo and Makini Schools," Columbia Business School, *Chazen Web Journal of International Business*, Fall 2002, p. 3.

24 P. Bennell, *Teacher Motivation and Incentives in Sub-Saharan Africa and Asia* (Brighton: Knowledge and Skills for Development, 2004), p. iv.

25   Watkins, *The Oxfam Education Report*, p. 207; The Probe Team, *Public Report on Basic Education in India*, p. 105; and United Nations Development Programme, *Human Development Report 2003*, p. 115.

26   United Nations Development Programme, *Human Development Report 2003*, p. 115.

27   Watkins, *The Oxfam Education Report*, p. 232.

28   *Ibid.*, p. 230. Emphasis added.

29   United Nations Development Programme, *Human Development Report 2003*, p. 115.

30   The Probe Team, *Public Report on Basic Education in India*, pp. 105–106.

Chapter 3

Grassroots Capitalism Thrives in India

Barun S. Mitra

India, among today's fastest growing economies, averages over 6 percent annual growth. Its potential to emerge as an economic giant is now acknowledged, as is its rise in the arena of information technology (IT). The present debate over outsourcing only emphasizes India's enormous human capital and its ability to compete with the best in the world. We've come a long way.

There is still some distance to be covered, though. India remains a poor country, with a per capita income of around US$550 (around US$3,100 in purchasing power parity). At the same time, however, it is rich in potential—a potential that is fueled by the real stars of the Indian economy, the ordinary Indians who have survived the heavy hand of government that has sought to control almost every aspect of economic activity since the 1950s.

Ingenuity, a spirit of enterprise and innovation, has helped most Indians, particularly those at the bottom of the socioeconomic ladder, survive strangulating economic policies. Being a pluralistic democracy has actually helped to moderate some of these economic policies, allowing people to bend oppressive regulations.

Reinforcing the pluralist democracy is a free press. Notwithstanding the ideological fervor of the intelligentsia and the rhetoric of the political class, there is a point beyond which the government cannot impose rigid economic regulations. Where such regulations are indeed laid down, there is a point beyond which enforcement agencies cannot implement the laws on the ground.

That is the way it has always been. While the dominant political party adopted the doctrine of a "socialistic pattern of development" in the mid-1950s and sought to implement Soviet-style five-year plans, a large part of the Indian economy continued to function virtually outside the scope of the law. Today, 15 years after economic liberalization, experts estimate that 30 percent–40 percent of the Indian economy continues to be in the informal sector. This informal economy reflects India's true economic potential.

SPINNING WHEELS

If the world is impressed with India's success in outsourcing, it would be fascinated by the extraordinary lengths to which entrepreneurs in India have gone to escape

> Ingenuity, a spirit of enterprise and innovation, has helped most Indians, particularly those at the bottom of the socioeconomic ladder, survive strangulating economic policies.

oppressive government regulations in the manufacturing sector.

Almost a century after Henry Ford revealed the economic power of the assembly line, Indian grassroots entrepreneurs have shown that their hand-made automobiles can and do beat the competition from more modern counterparts in rural India.

In the 1930s, India became one of the first countries in the developing world to manufacture automobiles. However, since the 1950s, the automobile has been viewed as a luxury item by Indian policymakers, and the automobile sector has been heavily licensed, controlled, and punitively taxed. The duties on imported vehicles, even second-hand ones, continue to be prohibitive. Indeed, the latest scam in India's automobile sector is the import of luxury cars, supposedly as tourist taxis, which attract significantly less import duty, but actually for use by the rich and powerful.

The automobile sector has seen gradual deregulation over the past two decades, and about a dozen international car manufacturers now operate in India. In a country of one billion and counting, the annual sale of automobiles is around 900,000 vehicles, around three-quarters of them in the small-car segment. Of the 65 million vehicles on Indian roads today, two-thirds are two-wheelers; the rest include cars, buses, and trucks.

India has one of the lowest vehicle densities in the world. Most Indians still cannot afford cars. In addition, the public transport sector is dominated by loss-making public-sector corporations, which are a further burden on the taxpayers. Consequently, there is a tremendous and largely unfulfilled demand for transportation, particularly in rural areas.

Over a third of Indian households do not own any form of private transportation; over 43 percent of people own just a bicycle. Draught animals continue to play a huge role in the transportation sector. The gap between the bullock cart and formal-sector transportation is filled by a unique breed of village mechanics. Having learned the trade of maintaining and repairing various kinds of farm equipment over the past three decades, these mechanics are now in a position to assemble a motorized mini-truck in about two weeks' time. Operating from small workshops, they can assemble a whole vehicle from scratch right under the roadside tree. In many parts of north India, these homemade vehicles are called *jugaad*, slang for "quick fix."

The flourishing auto-parts market in Delhi generally provides used car parts like gearboxes, radiators, wheels, and steering wheels. The mechanics start with an 8–12 horsepower agricultural diesel engine of the sort typically used to drive a water pump or other farm equipment. Then the chassis is welded, the engine is mounted, and the gearbox is connected to power the rear wheels. With a rudimentary bench as seat, the vehicle is ready to chug along at around 20 kilometers an hour, carrying around 25 people. To save on fuel, electric lights and horns are often eliminated. The vehicle costs from US$1,000 to US$2,000. Compare this to the price of a basic small car (800 cubic centimeters), which seats only four and costs about US$5,000.

Out in the countryside, these unorthodox vehicles easily hold their place between bullock and camel carts at one end and regular cars and trucks at the other. Meeting the short-haul needs of small towns and villages within a radius of 50 kilometers, these vehicles ferry children to school, carry produce or farmers and local traders to nearby markets, or carry cows to the local veterinarians.

And now a farmer-turned-innovator has designed an award-winning, low-cost small tractor that is ideally suited for the small land holdings of a typical Indian farmer. He has sought to patent it and would like to send the vehicle for conventional road testing so that he can manufacture it commercially. Unfortunately, he has been unable to raise the money necessary to get the tests done, which could cost quite a bit more than the US$2,000 he has spent on assembling one of his prototypes.

None of these vehicles currently qualifies for registration, and under the law, none can run on public roads. Nevertheless, keeping to the Indian tradition, law enforcement agencies tend to look the other way, since the economic and political costs of actually

Meeting the short-haul needs of small towns and villages within a radius of 50 kilometers, these vehicles ferry children to school, carry produce or farmers and local traders to nearby markets, or carry cows to the local veterinarians.

stopping these vehicles are too high for the government.

VIRTUAL HARDWARE

India's manufacturing revolution extends beyond the low-tech production of home-made vehicles. There is also the Indian IT revolution—a revolution that might not have been possible without the informal-sector technicians who assemble computers.

India's IT services sector is among the fastest-growing in the world. One estimate holds that while IT services revenue increased less than 2 percent from 2000 to 2003 worldwide, India's IT services industry experienced a 22 percent revenue growth, a pace comparable to that of Hong Kong's electronics industry during the 1970s.[1] Over 80 percent of India's IT services is exported.

However, this sector stands on a shallow foundation. The official number of personal computers sold in the country in 1997 was just over 500,000; today, it stands at 3.6 million. The level of PC penetration jumped tenfold between 1997 and 2005 but stands today at barely 12 per 1,000 people. Internet subscriptions are only 6.6 million, although the total number of users stands at over 52 million.[2]

These numbers have to be viewed within the context of Indian reality. Just as in the automobile sector, the success of Indian IT has come about in large measure despite efforts by the government to curb it. Typically, during the 1980s, tariffs on PCs were set at 300 percent to 400 percent, stifling the growth of the hardware sector.

Enter the informal PC assemblers: skilled technicians who maintain and repair the country's small but high-value PCs. By the late 1980s, there was an army of technicians assembling lower-cost PCs for a large number of consumers. Increased demand naturally led to the rise of a huge network of traders who smuggled components into the country, avoiding tariffs. Whole markets developed in major Indian cities that specialized in supplying imported components needed to assemble the PCs.

Even today, 60 percent–70 percent of PCs are assembled by this "grey" market. Typically, an assembled PC sells at 25 percent less than its branded equivalent. Today, when import duties on PCs are down to zero and the hidden tax burden on branded PCs is down to about 10 percent–15 percent, the informal sector continues to hold its ground.

The competitive informal-sector assemblers have ensured that most first-time buyers invariably buy a locally assembled PC. The biggest advantage that the informal-sector assemblers have is their flexibility to assemble a PC tailored to the customer's needs and financial constraints. For almost every major component, they provide a range of options, balancing quality and price. And, of course, they also provide on-site repair options.

Hewlett Packard (HP) is the largest seller of branded PCs in India today, holding 12 percent of market share. Senior executives at companies like HP acknowledge that the informal sector has played an enormous role in expanding the market. By familiarizing their customers with personal computers, the informal assemblers have paved the way for these customers to buy branded computers the second time round.

As noted, however, government policies have generally been inimical to the spread of IT in India. Sabir Bhatia, the Silicon Valley entrepreneur and co-founder of Hotmail, says:

> In my travels around the world, I am often asked a question: "Could you have done Hotmail in India?" And my answer has inevitably been, "No!" Had I attempted to create Hotmail in India, somebody would have come to me claiming that I was taking away the revenues of phone or fax companies![3]

PEOPLE POWER

The major impediments to economic growth in India are in the infrastructure sector, where one finds glaring shortcomings in the state of roads, ports, electricity, and the like. There is also a crying need to improve the social infrastructure, such as the country's education and health facilities.

Per capita consumption of electricity in India is 1/20th of per capita consumption of electricity in the United States. Over half of India's nearly 200 million households do not have electricity. Around 70 percent rely

I am often asked a question, says Hotmail's co-founder: "Could you have done Hotmail in India?" And my answer has inevitably been, "No!" Had I attempted to create Hotmail in India, somebody would have come to me claiming that I was taking away the revenues of phone or fax companies!

on traditional, non-commercial fuel such as firewood, cow-dung cakes, and other agricultural waste to cook their food. Most Indians experience power outages as routine blackouts, either for a few hours every day or for days at a time.

Electricity is still considered a natural monopoly in India. Most of the generation and distribution is controlled by public-sector organizations. Typically, rather than looking at growing demand as a potential business opportunity, these service providers tend to blame consumers for their insatiable appetite. Here too, Indian entrepreneurs, particularly those in the informal sector, have stepped in to answer the demand.

In Delhi, private entrepreneurs provide the electricity needs of consumers. At the top end, many households, housing societies, and whole neighborhoods have installed backup electricity generators to supply the energy when the utility fails.

Officially, private generation of electricity stands at 18 percent, but this captures only installations of over one megawatt. If all the household, commercial, and small industrial installations that have their own power backup are counted, it is between one-fourth and one-third of all power in the country—again, despite all manner of regulations against such generation and taxes on installing and generating private power.

Even more interesting is the local parallel grid being run in many parts of urban India. Shop owners have set up businesses along roads and, without the sanction of the civic administration, collaborate to set up kerosene or diesel generator sets to supply lighting during the evening shopping hours. Typically, an entrepreneur wires 50 to 100 shops or vendors in one neighborhood or at an informal marketplace. The fee charged is usually based on the number of light bulbs that are connected for a certain number of hours each evening. While the cost of electricity is much higher than it would be if it were available from the grid, the vendors have the flexibility to decide whether the benefits of attracting customers during peak shopping hours outweigh the high unit costs.

At the top end, the arrangements are quite sophisticated. Recently, for example,

the government declared as unauthorized a whole upper-income neighborhood in Delhi. This area houses many of the city's rich and powerful; as a result, for all its illegal status, no houses have been demolished. The government, however, does not provide amenities like electricity. Consequently, every house in the area has installed a generator. Over time, service providers have come into the picture, installing larger generation units to power whole blocks. Typically, the cost of electricity in this area is about four times the rate charged by the public utility.

Such examples, covering both the top and bottom ends of the socioeconomic strata of society, provide two lessons: (1) consumers are willing to pay for reliable electricity, and (2), given an opportunity, entrepreneurs can expose the myth of natural monopoly even in sectors as conventional as electricity.

Perhaps the best example of private-sector entrepreneurialism in wiring is cable television. Since the early 1990s, cable TV in India has been dominated by independent private entrepreneurs in almost every urban locality. In 10 years, they connected 30 million urban households—much more than the public-sector telephone companies had managed to connect during the previous 50 years. In fact, India today has the unique distinction of being perhaps the only country in the world where more homes have cable TV than telephones.

Nor are these informal infrastructure services restricted to electricity or cable TV. Urban waste recycling is mostly in the hands of a million men who make a living gathering and sorting waste material. Virtually nothing that can be recycled or reused is left behind. Even in the case of water supply, there is evidence of a flourishing and diverse water market in rural and urban India. Naturally, all of this operates peacefully outside the purview of the law.

MASS EDUCATION

Perhaps the most unrecognized phenomenon in India is the role of the informal sector in providing basic education. Since the 1950s, education has truly been a sacred cow; the role of the state in providing primary, secondary, and higher education has never

Such examples, covering both the top and bottom ends of the socioeconomic strata of society, provide two lessons: (1) consumers are willing to pay for reliable electricity, and (2), given an opportunity, entrepreneurs can expose the myth of natural monopoly even in sectors as conventional as electricity.

been questioned. For instance, in Delhi, to set up a school recognized by the government, almost 40 permissions are required to satisfy the authorities that the education being provided meets the best standard.

The record of public education, however, particularly at the primary level, has been anything but credible. Almost 60 years since India gained its independence from British rule, literacy rates have barely exceeded 60 percent. The number of illiterate Indians today exceeds the total population of the country in 1950. The paradox is even greater when one considers that while some Indians are carving out a niche in the Information Age, many more are deprived of the three R's of education.

The definition of literacy itself has undergone some changes. Just being able to sign one's name is considered adequate to qualify one as functionally literate. While the education bureaucracy and budget have inflated, and while the number of children enrolled at primary levels has reached 95 percent, the number of children slipping through the official education net has remained high. The probability of dropping out increases as the child moves through higher grades.

As can be expected, entrepreneurs have entered education in a big way too. India always had some of the world's best private schools, but what has not been appreciated is the scale of educational service provided by the informal sector. According to some estimates, about 50 percent of the poorest children in urban India are attending private neighborhood schools, some run by charitable organizations and the majority run by local entrepreneurs.

The Indian experience forces one to draw the conclusion that many of the poorest families not only value education, but also are willing to pay for that service. And they have a reason: Independent studies have shown that students in these informal private schools routinely outperform those in government schools.[4]

State-sponsored schooling is virtually free in India. The government provides the books, often the school uniform, and often one meal as part of its effort to induce parents to send their children to schools. On the other hand, numerous surveys have pointed out the serious problems with public schooling in India. Lack of facilities, lack of accountability, teachers' absenteeism, and truancy all constitute part of the problem.

Thus, even when a public school is within easy reach and free, many impoverished parents prefer paying around US$1 to US$2 a month to send their children to informal private schools in their neighborhoods.

Typically, these informal schools are run by families from the community. They will have 50 to 100 students—often students in different grades attending a common class under a common teacher—and are frequently operated in two or three rooms of a house owned by the principal teacher. They may hire local boys and girls who may have completed high school or even have a college degree to act as additional teachers. More often than not, they operate under extreme competition from other educational entrepreneurs in the vicinity, so there is some accountability.

ALL THAT GLITTERS?

The world finds the Indian love affair with gold perplexing. A poor country with an apparent shortage of capital, India is the world's largest consumer of gold. At current market values, gold accounts for 10 percent–15 percent of the Indian household balance sheet. Therefore, while Indian GDP is about 1/20th that of the United States, India's gold consumption is one-and-a-half times that of the U.S. India accounts for a huge 18 percent of the annual global gold demand, while India's share of nominal global GDP is only 1.6 percent.

According to some estimates, Indians hold over 15,000 tons of gold, most of it in private hands. The total value of this gold equals roughly a third of India's approximately US$750 billion GDP. Interestingly, this enormous private asset has been built despite government efforts to persuade people to give up their gold through a series of carrot-and-stick policies.

Last year alone, the demand for gold in India increased by more than 17 percent to about 643 metric tons. Some analysts believe that the growth in demand came from inves-

Even when a public school is within easy reach and free, many impoverished parents prefer paying around US$1 to US$2 a month to send their children to informal private schools in their neighborhoods.

tors in other assets, such as real estate and equities, booking their profits and shifting to gold. It is estimated that about 15 percent of gold is for investment, with the rest being used for jewelry and coins.

This involvement with gold is not new. In the economically challenged 1960s, the government instituted a draconian Gold Control Act in an attempt to discourage people from accumulating a nonproductive asset. Imports of gold were prohibited, and the price differential between domestic and international prices of gold widened. Not surprisingly, from the 1960s to the 1980s, Indians turned gold smuggling into an art form. Smuggling became the theme of countless Bollywood films showing the exotic ways the yellow metal was being brought into the country. In the 1980s, 150 to 200 tons of gold were smuggled annually into India.

As import bans created a vast network of smugglers and illicit dealers, restrictions on gold ownership turned virtually every Indian household into *de facto* violators of the law, and this widespread breach of an unsustainable set of laws corrupted law enforcement agencies. Fortunately, the trade in gold and a wide range of commodities was significantly liberalized in the 1990s. One can only imagine what catastrophic effects such a criminal–corrupt official nexus would have in today's world where terrorists could leverage the existing criminal networks.

Yet, after all the deregulation and liberalized trade, roughly 40–50 metric tons of gold continues to be smuggled into India annually. One corollary of India's insatiable demand for gold has been that jewelry making has become a vast cottage industry. The skills of Indian artisans have attracted the attention of the world. In 2003, gold accounted for 21 percent of India's non-oil imports, and jewelry accounted for 18 percent of total merchandise exports.

Given that the opportunity cost of investing in a nonproductive asset like gold can be huge, why does the average Indian household not replace even part of its gold holdings with financial assets? The answer is that gold provides basic economic security, even to the poor. Two-thirds of the demand comes from rural India, where the formal banking

sector's reach has been very limited.

Additionally, gold has been an attractive asset in the face of inflation, which has often surged well past the rate of return on any financial assets. For the poor Indian who has no access to banking, the easy liquidity of gold, provided by jewelers and pawnshops in the smallest towns, has made it a highly prized asset. In other words, gold often replaces financial services, such as savings and loans, or other investments that are difficult to access.

MONEY TRANSFERS

When people find barriers in their path, they usually find a way to circumvent or reduce the impact of those barriers. This also creates unintended consequences.

The demand for gold in India bumped against one of the world's most restrictive barriers: controls on the foreign exchange market that are intended to stem capital flight. India's huge appetite for gold needed a foreign exchange market. For gold to be brought in, money had to be sent out. So, despite the restrictions, capital flight still characterized the Indian economy until the early 1990s.

This example illustrates one of the biggest paradoxes faced by many poor countries: national economies need productive investment to climb out of endemic poverty, yet economic policies are rarely conducive to attracting investment. Rather than reassessing the wisdom of policy instruments affecting investments, most governments prefer instead to go after the miscreants.

It was in such an economic climate that the informal *hawala* system of international money transfers was born and perfected in the 1960s, particularly in South Asia. In Urdu, a language spoken primarily by the Muslim population in India and Pakistan, hawala means "in the air." In Arabic, it generally translates as "transfer." In other words, hawala is an invisible transfer of money from one country to another.

Hawala also leveraged the gap between the market and official exchange rates that is caused by government restrictions on foreign currency transactions. But hawala is not money laundering. Money laundering is an

As import bans created a vast network of smugglers and illicit dealers, restrictions on gold ownership turned virtually every Indian household into *de facto* violators of the law, and this widespread breach of an unsustainable set of laws corrupted law enforcement agencies.

attempt to camouflage the source of funds by processing them through a number of international transactions, almost always through banking and other formal-sector financial channels, while hawala is based primarily on a private network of dealers operating across countries and continents and working mostly outside the formal banking system.

Initially, it was a response to rigid foreign currency regulations in South Asia and the very high transaction costs of dealing in foreign currency. The rapid, worldwide spread of South Asian expatriate communities that wanted to send money home reinforced the need.

Assume, for instance, that a taxi driver in New York wants to send some money home to his mother. He approaches a hawala agent in his neighborhood, who decides on a simple commission, typically about 0.25 percent, or offers an exchange rate that is 10 percent to 15 percent higher than the official rate. The agent then informs his counterpart in India about the transaction, and the counterpart ensures that the money is delivered within 24 to 48 hours to the mother, usually in cash, since the recipient probably does not have a bank account.

Despite economic liberalization and the spread of communication technologies, a wire transfer from one bank to another takes days. Relying on trust, the network, and using simple codes, the telephone, fax, e-mail, and now SMS text messaging, the hawala system is able to provide faster service at a lower cost. There are about 20 million Indians living abroad, and it is believed that most of them have used the hawala system at some point.

Countering hawala would mean figuring out ways to lower the transaction costs of foreign exchange transfer so that the 90 percent of transactions now taking place through hawala are absorbed into the formal system. For that to happen, however, the formal banking channels must be able to compete with the low-cost hawala network. Even though most hawala transactions involve relatively small amounts, legitimately earned and saved, being sent by ordinary people to their family and friends, the banking sector's ability to provide such low-cost service is hindered by India's high regulatory costs, restrictions on foreign exchange, and resultant low level of competition.

POOR MAN'S BANK

According to the 2001 census, barely 50 percent of urban households and only 30 percent of rural households avail themselves of banking services in India. The paperwork involved in opening a bank account, coupled with low income levels and the fact that most Indians operate in the informal cash economy, mean that maintaining a bank account is not an attractive proposition for most people.

Microfinance is the new mantra for the governments and banks because it provides them a high-visibility scheme, showcasing their intention to deal with poverty. However, very little has been done to make formal-sector banking accessible to the large population in the informal economy. Consequently, the informal sector has improvised to provide its own credit and savings facilities.

For instance, at almost every commercial complex in Delhi, people at the lowest income levels have tried to band together in small groups, led by a reliable coordinator. The members are typically 10 to 100 people working in the vicinity, or people who have known each other for a long time. They agree on various savings schemes in which the members may put in, say, US$1 a week or US$5 a month. The coordinator acts as a mobile bank, carrying the cash in his pocket and ready to disburse a loan on the spot. Every member has the opportunity to withdraw his contribution or to take a loan. The interest rate is determined by the members of the group themselves and is typically 2 percent–5 percent per annum.

Members join these groups for different reasons. Some want to save in a simple and convenient way so that they can buy something that they want, perhaps a TV or a refrigerator. Others join so that they can get a loan to help meet the cost of a child's education or a daughter's marriage. Such independent groups, operating outside the scope of microfinance institutions, are quite common in rural as well as in urban India. Shopkeepers in low-income neighborhoods often provide daily or weekly savings schemes

The banking sector's ability to provide such low-cost service is hindered by India's high regulatory costs, restrictions on foreign exchange, and resultant low level of competition.

to help their clients buy goods from them. Women in villages often join such groups in order to save small amounts, which they can then withdraw in rotation to meet family expenses.

No one actually knows the precise number of such independent schemes operating in India, but they far outnumber the 100,000 or so recognized microfinance schemes. This is another example of grassroots entrepreneurship in the informal sector.

One reason why formal banks have not stepped forward to cater to this segment is that they have not figured out how to lower the cost of processing clients who transact in low amounts of money yet have higher frequency of transaction. This indicates that the level of competition in the banking sector is not high enough to motivate banks to innovate and reach out to new clients. In addition, the banks do not yet have the freedom to charge higher interest rates to compensate for the higher perceived risks associated with informal-sector clients.

GRASSROOTS ENTREPRENEURSHIP

These are only a few examples of the all-pervading spirit of enterprise, particularly among people at the bottom of the economic ladder, in India today. They exhibit an uncanny ability to identify an unmet need and then find a way to supply that demand. Relative lack of formal education and training, or of capital and technology, are not obstacles.

The biggest obstacle faced by Indian grassroots entrepreneurs is the government's attempts to outlaw their businesses or impose regulations. The World Bank's annual "Doing Business 2006" survey, which measures the ease of doing business in a country, ranks India 116th out of 155 countries surveyed. New Zealand leads the rankings, followed by Singapore.[5]

Despite recent economic reforms, starting a formal business in India requires 11 procedures and 71 days (down from 89 last year). In addition:

- Dealing with licenses requires 20 procedures and 270 days;
- Export procedures take 36 days;
- Import procedures take 43 days;

- There are 59 taxes, compliance with which takes about 264 hours; and
- Overall, some 40 procedures and 425 days are required for a contract.

The "rigidity of employment" index, which relates to difficulties in hiring and firing workers, ranks India 62nd on an index of 100—by far the highest in the region. And while starting a business is obviously difficult, closing a business is likely to be even more so. According to this report, bankruptcy procedures take 10 years in India.[6]

Some formal-sector competitors complain that those who are involved in the large informal sector in India have an edge because they avoid paying taxes and do not bear the full cost of economic regulations. On the other hand, the single biggest obstacle to the informal sector is its vulnerability to extortion from law-enforcing agencies. Strictly enforcing some of the regulations would gravely affect some of the poorest sections of society who are engaged in the whole range of informal economic activities. Political upheaval would inevitably follow. Because India is a democracy, its government has to maintain a balancing act.

The other cost that the informal sector has to bear because of its extra-legal status is the inability to raise the capital necessary to expand businesses even if they are competitive and have successful products or services. This inability to capitalize assets, and the consequent underutilization of capital for economic development, has been well researched by Peruvian economist Hernando de Soto in his book *The Mystery of Capital.*[7] A corollary to this problem is the formal sector's difficulty in taking advantage of successful informal-sector players' managerial and technical expertise by integrating them into their operations.

This brief survey provides a glimpse of the culture of entrepreneurship that prevails in India. If these grassroots capitalist entrepreneurs were freed from the shackles of bureaucratic economic regulations, they could well take India to the top of the development ladder. It would not be too far-fetched to suggest that there is hardly any country in the world today where informal-

If these grassroots capitalist entrepreneurs were freed from the shackles of bureaucratic economic regulations, they could well take India to the top of the development ladder.

sector economic activity is as diverse and as widespread as it is in India. This activity is an unrealized potential just waiting to be harnessed.

Endnotes

1 Pratyush Bharati, *India's IT Services Industry: A Comparative Analysis* (Boston: University of Massachusetts, January 2005).

2 *India: Internet Users and Subscribers 1998–2005* (New Delhi: National Association of Software Service Companies, 2005).

3 M. Raja, "Online Businesses Grow in India," *Asia Times*, August 31, 2005, at *www.atimes. com/atimes/South_Asia/GH31Df04.html*.

4 James Tooley, *The Enterprise of Education* (New Delhi: Liberty Institute, 2001).

5 World Bank, *Doing Business 2006*, available at *http://www.doingbusiness.org/*.

6 *Ibid.*

7 Hernando de Soto, *The Mystery of Capital: Why Capitalism Triumphs in the West and Fails Everywhere Else* (New York: Basic Books, 2000).

Chapter 4

Informal Finance: Encouraging the Entrepreneurial Spirit in Post-Mao China

Michael Gonzalez

Kellee Tsai vividly remembers visiting the "Reading Here and Reading There Club," also known popularly as the 3D Club (short for *Dulai, Duqu, Dushu She*), a magazine-reading club in the capital of Henan Province. One room resembled a public library, which was to be expected. It was the other room that was out of place. People were lining up to hand over wads of cash at the deposit windows while armed guards stood by. The place resembled more a bank in a major metropolis—and a very active one at that—than a reading club in a backwater province. That's because it *was* a bank, albeit an illegal one.

The 3D was just a particularly ingenious example of a phenomenon that makes up the very sinews of capitalism in China. Without 3D and the many permutations of what is generically known as "informal finance," China's capitalist revolution would have been stillborn.

This is no hyperbole. Economists estimate that the money taken in as deposits by 3D and other "shadow banks" goes on to finance fully three-fourths of private-sector needs. 3D is also a particularly poignant example of human creativity and of how

freedom seeps into every crevice that government abandons, either because it lacks enforcement capacity or the will to use it.

In China, back-alley banks do most of the intermediation between savers and private businesses. In 2000, only 0.5 percent of loans extended by the state banks went to the private sector. It is estimated that even today, this number is not much larger than 1 percent.

Even when you count lending by the few legal private banks that do exist, such as the Minsheng Banking Corporation—or lending by state-owned enterprises that take in the loans they get from the state banks and then pass them on to put them to better use—informal finance accounts for 75 percent of private-sector finance. Foreign businessmen often complain about the difficulties of getting finance in China. Well, it isn't much easier for the Chinese either.

VARIETIES OF INFORMAL FINANCE

Informal finance takes many forms. The illegal institutions that intermediate between China's millions of savers and hundreds of thousands of small and medium-sized enterprises range from the large and imaginative,

The 3D was just a particularly ingenious example of a phenomenon that makes up the very sinews of capitalism in China. Without 3D and the many permutations of what is generically known as "informal finance," China's capitalist revolution would have been stillborn.

like 3D, to simple associations. They can be groups of family members, neighbors, or friends who pool their cash and then lend it. Borrowers can be members of the associations or enterprises.

These rotating credit associations, which go under the general term of *hui* in Mandarin, can be as small as five to 10 people. They resemble other similar investing groups around the world, from the microfinance lenders in places like Bangladesh to the ladies' quilting clubs in the Midwest whose stock portfolios did so well in the 1990s. The main difference is that they inhabit a grey area of illegality.

Their resourcefulness is legendary. When Ms. Tsai, a finance professor at Johns Hopkins University in Baltimore, asked the 3D manager why there was a need for tellers, he gave her a knowing look and murmured something about the club members needing to "make deposits for their magazines." He added: "The more ambitious ones could make larger deposits, as large as 50,000 RMB. In a good year they could get 20 percent on that deposit."

The second-floor offices revealed the extent of 3D's reach. "I went upstairs with him and it looked like the trading floor at Morgan Stanley, and I know because I used to work at Morgan Stanley," Professor Tsai related to me. "They even had computer screens hooked up to Reuters, Bloomberg and UPI." The finishing touch was a banner hanging outside the premises that proclaimed proudly in giant characters: "the Communist Party of Henan Supports This Club Because It Promotes Spiritual Civilization and Helps Our Literacy Campaign."

The 3D Club does that and more. Private financing is an activity that is still mostly illegal in China almost three decades after Mao's death and little more than a year before China must fulfill its obligations to the World Trade Organization (WTO) and open its banking sector to foreign entities. Only a very few private financial institutions have been allowed to come into being legally. Minsheng remains the best-known example of a legal private bank, though many question the extent to which it is truly private. But the authorities cannot really stomp on the informal institutions that have risen through the cracks because they are essential to the private sector.

The reason is simple enough, though still perverse. State banks—meaning the "Big Four" commercial lenders: Agricultural Bank, China Construction Bank, Industrial and Commercial Bank, and Bank of China—must carry the state-owned enterprises created in the communist era, which in some localities still employ the lion's share of the working population. Many of these companies are already bankrupt, but the state banks sustain their existence, making them the walking dead.

Foreign investors would dearly love to come in and fill the void, acting either as angels that give Chinese entrepreneurs a shot at life early in the process, or in mezzanine investment that provides capital to a company already providing a product downstream, or even as banks. Despite its towering reputation as the place to be, however, China continues to maintain a regulatory steel gossamer that prevents foreign capital from coming into the country. It is still not very clear how China will implement its obligation, made when it became a member of the WTO in 2005, to throw open its banking sector to foreign competition.

INFORMAL FINANCE AS MAINSTAY OF CAPITALISM

Until foreign banks come in and shake up the system, the local informal system will continue to be the mainstay of capitalism. This is the way it has been since time immemorial. Informal banking is organic and has sunk deep roots, with the nearly three decades of Maoism constituting the only hairline fracture in the continuum of China's 5,000-year history. In the ancient past, Buddhist monasteries used to act as pawnshops and to take in deposits as well. The system grew over time, and before Mao and the communists took over, the network was extensive and no longer limited to monasteries. The communists, desiring that the state have a monopoly on all things big and small, finance first and foremost, wiped out the system.

After Mao's death in 1976, and after the

Informal banking is organic and has sunk deep roots, with the nearly three decades of Maoism constituting the only hairline fracture in the continuum of China's 5,000-year history.

end of the convulsions of the Cultural Revolution, China's new rulers decided to take a softer approach. Informal finance was one of the first things to crop up. Of course, China is a vast country, and not every part developed equally. In this way, the informal finance system became living proof of the value of localizing decision-making to the greatest extent possible.

The shadow banks have worked out different arrangements with local authorities, as the example of 3D shows. Today, areas where the communists invested heavily, such as Manchuria in the northeast, make up China's decaying rust belt and have little informal finance activity. Local authorities do not want depositors to have a choice of outlets. On the other hand, provinces or areas where the communists did not want to invest, such as Zhejiang Province, which was seen as sensitive because it is across from Taiwan, have seen a veritable mushrooming of back-alley banks and have thrived, with thousands of private businesses feeding off the illegal banks.

Informal finance cropped up first in regions where local proclivities and peculiarities contributed to its return. In the city of Wenzhou in Zhejiang Province—an area that has perhaps become, more than any other part of China, most closely associated with private finance—it was a combination of bad topography and worse linguistics.

Wenzhou is all mountains and water, so the lack of arable land always meant that its people had to depend on something other than farming. It has always been very difficult to reach, and even today a complicated combination of buses and trains is needed to get there. But as Professor Tsai reminds me, that can be said of thousands of places in China. The arable land of this hardscrabble country is less than 30 percent.

What helped Wenzhou to become even more isolated is that its geographical remoteness also encouraged a dialect that even people nearby cannot understand. The combination forged a people reputed to be among the best at "wheeling and dealing" in all of China.

In 1949, the communists had a very difficult time taking the area. Even during the Cultural Revolution, there were stories of how Wenzhou people who were sent to hard labor in the countryside tried to supplement their income by selling dumplings to their tormentors, the Red Guards. As soon as the dead hand of the state began to be lifted following Mao's death, the city fathers once again allowed freedom to reign. Their attitude, says Professor Tsai, was "we're going to let our enterprises do whatever it takes to get ahead." The city became the first in China to ignore government ceilings on lending.

As with all new experiments, there were problems at first. Some of the shadow banks metastasized into pyramids and Ponzi schemes. Scandals broke out as some people absconded with the nest eggs of many. State authorities in Shanghai also blamed Wenzhou financial entrepreneurs for revving up the Shanghai real estate market in 2003, calling them "wandering ghouls."

Despite these kinks, however, informal finance has generally been very good at regulating itself. The system thrives exactly because it is informal. This self-policing keeps initiative-killing, artificial regulation away. As Wu Jianguan, the owner of a restaurant that specializes in such delicacies as shark's fin soup and large snails and whose business depends on illegal borrowing, told Matthew Forney of *Time* in 2004, "if the bank repossesses my home I have nowhere to live, but I can still do business. But if I fail to repay my friends, I'll never do business in this town again."

Classical liberal philosophers, who have long argued that the case for a "meta-enforcer" (the government) is a weak one, could not ask for a better real-life example to buttress their beliefs. The case against the meta-enforcer is twofold.

First, there is the problem of who regulates the meta-enforcer. In democracies there is an answer, albeit an imperfect one: The voters regulate the meta-enforcer at regular intervals with the ever-present threat of turning out the government. In China, there is no such check. Despite the incredible advances that have been made since the death of Mao, the meta-enforcer gets its legitimacy from the barrel of a gun. Witness Tiananmen Square.

Second, the classical liberal argument is

China is a vast country, and not every part developed equally. In this way, the informal finance system became living proof of the value of localizing decision-making to the greatest extent possible.

that the meta-enforcer is not really needed. Classical liberal thinker Anthony de Jasay sought to prove that people really do have an incentive to behave ethically and will do so without a regulator enforcing anything because there really is no escape. The world is not that big a place. In the Chinese universe, even if you become a stowaway on a boat and steal away to New York, your reputation will catch up with you.

INFORMAL FINANCE AND THE MONEY SUPPLY

Informal finance even damages the case for a monetary authority. Despite the recognition that shadow banks are needed to keep the private sector alive, the central government has seriously considered cracking down on them when it has feared that they will get in the way of central bank authorities' attempts to control the growth of the money supply. But the informal banks are closer to the people and have a much better intuitive sense of what the demand for money is. The supply they create through credit does not outstrip demand.

The interest rates in the curb market come closer to approximating the actual cost of money than do the rates charged by the central People's Bank of China. "China's curb market is remarkably efficient," says Professor Tsai.

One of the main reasons why unregulated rates are closer to the mark is that the "official" market has numerous distortions, "including most obviously, artificially depressed interest rates," says Professor Tsai. "The official banks also have stringent collateral requirements. They won't take your ox or your motorcycle as collateral. The informal financiers will." People who pay 20 percent for a loan, or higher, have fully worked out the likelihood of whether they will be able to pay back the money.

This should put to rest another question about informal finance: whether it is "usurious" or extortionary in any way. We are, after all, talking in some instances about pawnshops and loan sharks. Pawnshops have been, however, one of the earliest intermediators of capital. Whenever a king's favorite (an early form of prime minister)

or a financial official wanted to extend the financial elbow room in his realm, one of the first things he would do would be to send out the signal that pawnshops would be tolerated.

Under Mao, where everything happened in reverse, pawnshops were one of the first institutions to be repressed by the communists, and it later became standard communist propaganda to decry their existence under the Kuomintang: so much so that after the period of reform began and informal finance began to take off, authorities, even local ones, sometimes found it difficult to tolerate pawnshops. Despite their bad reputation, however, pawnshops can be viewed as little banks where a personal possession such as a ring becomes collateral for a small loan. It is not more usurious, parasitical, or predatory than a mortgage on a house; the only difference is in scale.

ENCOURAGING THE ENTREPRENEURIAL SPIRIT

Economists such as Hernando de Soto have rightly put an emphasis on the need to legalize underground activity. And in a sense, the important role that informal finance plays in China shows how dysfunctional the place remains. I prefer to think the glass is half full, however, and see the informal finance phenomenon as proof of how the entrepreneurial spirit of the Chinese people shines through any crack in the great wall of repressive government.

China is often seen as a capitalist powerhouse: too often, in fact. China is doubtlessly a manufacturing phenomenon that churns out billions in exports, but its potential remains shackled by dysfunctional policies left over from its recent communist past.

The dead hand of the state continues to restrain people's economic freedom in China more than it does in France or Germany—countries that are commonly thought of as socialist infernos. The reason China seems to have a more exciting future is perhaps that the government and its writ suffer from a deficit of legitimacy unknown in democracies and that the people are used to bypassing the law.

As the growing phenomenon of infor-

China is a fascinating study in the economic truths advanced by Adam Smith, Frederick Hayek, and Hernando de Soto, illustrating that its recent communist past continues to feed many serious policy distortions.

mal finance reveals, the Chinese are quick to open shop in any nook or cranny abandoned by the state. China is a fascinating study in the economic truths advanced by Adam Smith, Frederick Hayek, and Hernando de Soto, illustrating that its recent communist past continues to feed many serious policy distortions.

Chapter 5

Explaining the Factors of the *Index of Economic Freedom*

William W. Beach and Marc A. Miles, Ph.D.

Since 1995, the *Index of Economic Freedom* has offered the international community an annual in-depth examination of the factors that contribute most directly to economic freedom and prosperity. As the first comprehensive study of economic freedom ever published, the 1995 *Index* defined the method by which economic freedom can be measured in such vastly different places as Hong Kong and North Korea. Since then, other studies have joined the effort, analyzing such issues as trade or government intervention in the economy.[1]

There is overlapping coverage among these indices, but the *Index of Economic Freedom* includes the broadest array of institutional factors determining economic freedom:

- Corruption in the judiciary, customs service, and government bureaucracy;
- Non-tariff barriers to trade, such as import bans and quotas as well as strict labeling and licensing requirements;
- The fiscal burden of government, which encompasses income tax rates, corporate tax rates, and trends in government expenditures as a percent of output;

- The rule of law, efficiency within the judiciary, and the ability to enforce contracts;
- Regulatory burdens on business, including health, safety, and environmental regulation;
- Restrictions on banks regarding financial services, such as selling securities and insurance;
- Labor market regulations, such as established work weeks and mandatory separation pay; and
- Informal market activities, including corruption, smuggling, piracy of intellectual property rights, and the underground provision of labor and other services.

Analyzing economic freedom annually permits the authors of the *Index* to include the most recent information on these factors as it becomes available country by country. Not surprisingly, changes in government policy are occurring at a rapid rate in many less-developed countries. The *Index of Economic Freedom*, because it is published each year, enables readers around the world to see how recent changes in government policy affect economic freedom in any of 161 specific countries. The historical score graph on each country page also permits readers to discriminate among those countries where economic freedom and opportunities are expanding and those where they are not. (This year, numerical grading was suspended for four countries: the Democratic Republic of Congo, Iraq, and Sudan, all of which are in a state of civil unrest or anarchy, and Serbia–Montenegro, for which data necessary to grade the country are not available. Information is provided, however, even for these countries. Grading was resumed for Angola and Burundi, for which grading had been suspended since 2001 due to civil unrest or anarchy.)

MEASURING ECONOMIC FREEDOM

Economic freedom is defined as *the absence of government coercion or constraint on the production, distribution, or consumption of goods and services beyond the extent necessary for citizens to protect and maintain liberty itself.* In other words, people are free to work, produce, consume, and invest in the ways they feel are most productive.

All government action involves coercion. Some minimal coercion is necessary for the citizens of a community or nation to defend themselves, promote the evolution of civil society, and enjoy the fruits of their labor. This Lockean idea was embodied in the U.S. Constitution. For example, citizens are taxed to provide revenue for the protection of person and property as well as for a common defense. Most political theorists also accept that certain goods—what economists call "public goods"—can be supplied most conveniently by government.

When government coercion rises beyond that minimal level, however, it risks trampling on freedom. When it starts interfering in the market beyond the protection of person and property, it risks undermining economic freedom. Exactly where that line is crossed is open to reasoned debate. The goal in the scoring of economic freedom is not to define these extremes—either anarchy or utopia—but to describe the world's economies as they are.

Throughout history, governments have imposed a wide array of constraints on eco-

nomic activity. Many constraints can be measured by assessing their impact on economic choices. Constraining economic choice distorts and diminishes the production, distribution, and consumption of goods and services (including, of course, labor services).[2]

One fact, however, is overridingly true: When governments restrict people, their behavior changes, and probably not for the best. Coercion alters choices that ordinary people make. Economic freedom is diminished, and economic growth suffers.

To measure economic freedom and rate each country, the authors of the *Index* study 50 independent economic variables. These variables fall into 10 broad categories, or factors, of economic freedom:

- Trade policy,
- Fiscal burden of government,
- Government intervention in the economy,
- Monetary policy,
- Capital flows and foreign investment,
- Banking and finance,
- Wages and prices,
- Property rights,
- Regulation, and
- Informal market activity.

A detailed discussion of each of these factors and their component variables follows this overview.

Weighting. In the *Index of Economic Freedom*, all 10 factors are equally important to the level of economic freedom in any country. Thus, to determine a country's overall score, the factors are weighted equally.

This is a common-sense approach. It is also consistent with the purpose of the *Index*: to reflect the economic environment in every country surveyed. The *Index* is not designed to measure how much each factor adds to economic growth; that is ably done in the many empirical studies of economic growth. Rather, the authors of the *Index* identify institutional factors that, taken together, determine the degree to which economies are free to respond to changing world market conditions. It is this institutional environment that allows economies to grow and prosper.

While our approach appeals to common sense, recent research on the determinants of growth indicates that some factors are statistically more important than others. In the 2004 *Index*, Professor Richard Roll illustrated that equally weighting the *Index* factors reveals as true a picture of economic freedom in a country as the best weighting system that statistics can devise.[3] In any event, it is clear that for a country to succeed in achieving long-term growth and economic well-being, it must perform well in *all* 10 factors.

The Grading Scale. Each country receives its overall economic freedom score based on the simple average of the 10 individual factor scores. Each factor is graded according to a unique scale. The scales run from 1 to 5: A score of 1 signifies an economic environment or set of policies that are most conducive to economic freedom, while a score of 5 signifies a set of policies that are least conducive to economic freedom.

In addition, following each factor score is a description—"better," "worse," or "stable"—to indicate, respectively, whether that factor of economic freedom has improved, worsened, or stayed the same compared with the country's score last year.

Finally, the 10 factors are added and averaged, and an overall score is assigned to the country.

The four broad categories of economic freedom in the *Index* are:

- **Free**—countries with an average overall score of 1.99 or less;
- **Mostly Free**—countries with an average overall score of 2.00 to 2.99;
- **Mostly Unfree**—countries with an average overall score of 3.00 to 3.99; and
- **Repressed**—countries with an average overall score of 4.00 or higher.

Previous Scores. The *Index of Economic Freedom* includes a comprehensive listing of 161 countries with their scores for each of the 10 factors. Each country's section also includes a graph of its overall score for each year the country has been graded since 1995. With this history, readers can easily discern whether a country's economic freedom has improved or diminished over time, or simply has become stuck in the mud.

Transparency. To assist the reader, the authors endeavor to make their scoring as transparent as possible. This chapter explains why each factor is an important element of economic freedom, how the five levels of economic freedom are broken down and scored, and what sources of data and information were used for this analysis.

Factor scoring is straightforward and consistent across countries. If a country's banking system received a score of 3, for example, this means that its banking and financial system displays most of the characteristics for level 3, which are spelled out on page 68: The government exercises substantial influence on the financial sector; the government owns or operates some banks; the government influences credit allocation; foreign banks face restrictions that domestic banks do not; financial services face limitations or restrictions; and there are significant barriers to the formation of banks. Similarly, a country receiving a score of 5 in trade policy has the characteristics explained on page 59: The government imposes either an average tariff rate that is greater than 20 percent or a lower tariff coupled with very high non-tariff barriers that, for all practical purposes, close its markets to imports.

Period of Study. For the *2006 Index of Economic Freedom*, the authors generally examined data for the period covering the second half of 2004 through the first half of 2005. To the extent possible, the information considered for each factor was current as of June 30, 2005.

It is important to understand, however, that some factors are based on historical information. For example, the monetary policy factor is a 10-year weighted average rate of inflation from January 1, 1995, to December 31, 2004. Other factors are current for the year in which the *Index* is published. For example, the taxation variable for this *Index* considers tax rates that apply to the taxable year 2005.

Occasionally, because the *Index* is published several months after the cutoff date for evaluation, major economic events occur that cannot be factored into the scores. In the past, such occurrences have been uncommon and isolated to one region of the world. The Asian financial crisis, for example, erupted as the *1998 Index of Economic Freedom* was ready to go to print. As a result, the effects of policy changes in response to that crisis were not considered in that year's scoring; however, they were considered in later editions. In the country write-ups, the authors and editors also note major events that might have a substantial impact on a country's score in the future.

Sources. In evaluating the criteria for each factor, the authors have used a range of authoritative sources. For example, a statement about the level of corruption in a country's customs service may be followed by a supporting quote from a source of demonstrated reliability. There also are innumerable lesser sources of information, including conversations with government officials and visits to Internet sites. These sources are indicated in the narrative where appropriate. It would be unnecessarily cumbersome to cite all the sources used in scoring every single variable of each factor; therefore, unless otherwise noted, the major sources used in preparing the country summaries may be found below, in the introduction to Chapter 6, and in the list of Major Works Cited.

A SUMMARY OF FACTOR VARIABLES

To grade each country's level of economic freedom for the *Index*, the authors examined 50 independent variables. The information collected was analyzed to determine for each of the 10 factors which of the five grade levels most closely resembles that country's environment. Even though all of the variables were studied, not all are given an individual score or specific mention in the text. For example, it is not necessary to mention cases in which corruption in the judiciary is virtually nonexistent; in general, it is necessary to discuss judicial corruption only when it is a documented problem.

In other words, what is most important is accurately grading each of the 10 broad factors of economic freedom, not necessarily each of the 50 variables, of the 157 countries that are scored in this year's edition. Such a system keeps the *Index* to a manageable length. The independent variables used to evaluate each factor are summarized in the callout box within the factor's description.

FACTORS OF ECONOMIC FREEDOM

Factor #1: Trade Policy

 Trade policy is a key factor in measuring economic freedom. The degree to which government hinders access to and the free flow of foreign commerce can have a direct bearing on the ability of individuals to pursue their economic goals.

For example, when a government taxes directly the importation of a product through tariffs, or impedes it through non-tariff barriers, incentives are distorted. Some groups of people in that country will now have an incentive to produce that product instead of another one that they may be better suited to producing. The import limitation reduces opportunities or economic freedom by discouraging individuals from applying their talents and skills in a manner that they know or believe will be better for them. In addition, it limits consumers' choices, thereby also limiting their well-being.

Methodology. The trade policy score is based on a country's weighted average tariff rate—weighted by imports from the country's trading partners. The higher the rate, the worse (or higher) the score. Gathering data on tariffs to make a consistent cross-country comparison can be a challenging task. Unlike data on inflation, for instance, countries do not report their weighted average tariff rate or simple average tariff rate every year; in some cases, the last time a country reported its tariff data could have been as far back as 1993. To preserve consistency in grading the trade policy factor, the authors have decided to use the most recently reported weighted average tariff rate for a country from our primary source. If another reliable source reports more updated information on the country's tariff rate, the authors note this fact and may review the grading of this factor if there is strong evidence that the most recently reported weighted average tariff rate is outdated.

The World Bank produces the world's most comprehensive and consistent information on weighted average applied tariff rates. When the weighted average applied

Factor 1: Trade Policy Grading Scale

Score	Levels of Protectionism	Criteria
1	Very low	Weighted average tariff rate less than or equal to 2.5 percent.
1.5	Low	Weighted average tariff rate greater than 2.5 percent but less than or equal to 5 percent.
2	Low	Weighted average tariff rate greater than 5 percent but less than or equal to 7.5 percent.
2.5	Moderate	Weighted average tariff rate greater than 7.5 percent but less than or equal to 10 percent.
3	Moderate	Weighted average tariff rate greater than 10 percent but less than or equal to 12.5 percent.
3.5	High	Weighted average tariff rate greater than 12.5 percent but less than or equal to 15 percent.
4	High	Weighted average tariff rate greater than 15 percent but less than or equal to 17.5 percent.
4.5	Very high	Weighted average tariff rate greater than 17.5 percent but less than or equal to 20 percent.
5	Very high	Weighted average tariff rate greater than 20 percent.

tariff rate is not available, the authors use the country's average applied tariff rate; and when the country's average applied tariff rate is not available, the authors use the weighted average or the simple average of most favored nation (MFN) tariff rates.[4] If neither applied tariff nor MFN tariff data are available, the authors base their grading on the revenue raised from tariffs and duties as a percentage of total imports of goods. The data for customs revenues and total imports may not be consolidated in just one source. In addition, in the very few cases in which data on duties and customs revenues are not available, the authors use data on international trade taxes instead. In all cases, the authors clarify the type of data used and the different sources for those data in the corresponding write-up for the trade policy factor. Sometimes, when none of this information is available, the authors simply analyze the overall tariff structure and estimate an effective tariff rate.

Tariffs, however, are not the only barriers to trade. Many countries impose import

Variables for Factor #1

- Weighted average tariff rate
- Non-tariff barriers
- Corruption in the customs service

quotas, licensing requirements, and other mandates—known collectively as non-tariff barriers (NTBs)—to restrict imports. The trade analysis also considers corruption within the customs service. This is an important consideration because, even though countries may have low published tariff rates and no official NTBs, their customs officials may be corrupt and may require bribes to allow products to enter their ports. Alternatively, customs officials may steal goods for themselves, creating a cost or barrier to trade.

The circumstances are analyzed and documented whenever possible. If NTBs exist in sufficient quantity, or if there is ample evidence of corruption, a country's score based solely on tariff rates receives an additional

Factor 2: Individual Income Tax Grading Scale

This scale lists a score from 1 through 5. The higher the tax rate, the higher the score.

Score	Tax Rates	Criteria
1	Very low	Top marginal income tax rate less than 10 percent.
1.5	Low	Top marginal income tax rate equal to or greater than 10 percent and less than 20 percent.
2	Low	Top marginal income tax rate equal to or greater than 20 percent and less than 25 percent.
2.5	Moderate	Top marginal income tax rate equal to or greater than 25 percent and less than 30 percent.
3	Moderate	Top marginal income tax rate equal to or greater than 30 percent and less than 35 percent.
3.5	High	Top marginal income tax rate equal to or greater than 35 percent and less than 40 percent.
4	High	Top marginal income tax rate equal to or greater than 40 percent and less than 45 percent.
4.5	Very high	Top marginal income tax rate equal to or greater than 45 percent and less than 50 percent.
5	Very high	Top marginal income tax rate equal to or greater than 50 percent.

point on the scale (representing decreased economic freedom).

Sources. Unless otherwise noted, the authors used the following sources to determine scores for trade policy, in order of priority: World Bank, *World Development Indicators 2005* and *Data on Trade and Import Barriers: Trends in Average Tariff for Developing and Industrial Countries 1981–2003*; World Trade Organization, *Trade Policy Reviews*, 1995 to March 2005; Office of the U.S. Trade Representative, *2005 National Trade Estimate Report on Foreign Trade Barriers*; U.S. Department of Commerce, *Country Commercial Guide*, 2004 and 2005;[5] Economist Intelligence Unit, *Country Report*, *Country Profile*, and *Country Commerce*, 2004–2005 and 2005–2006; and official government publications of each country.

Factor #2: Fiscal Burden of Government

 To measure the fiscal burden a government imposes on its citizens, the authors examined both marginal tax rates and the year-to-year change in the level of government expenditures as a percent of gross domestic product (GDP). The marginal tax rate confronting an individual is in effect a "price" paid for supplying the next economic effort or engagement in an entrepreneurial venture. What remains after the tax is subtracted are the "rewards" of the effort. The higher the price of effort or entrepreneurship, the lower the rewards and the less of it will be undertaken. Higher tax rates interfere with the ability of individuals to pursue their goals in the marketplace.

The year-to-year change in the share of output diverted to government expenditures captures the incremental increase or decrease of the true cost of government in a society. When a government expends money, it acquires resources, diverting them away from potentially more productive private choices and goals. This is true whether the expenditure is to acquire resources for its own purposes (government consumption) or for transfer payments among citizens. As a government increases (decreases) its expen-

Factor 2: Corporate Tax Grading Scale

This scale lists a score from 1 through 5. The higher the tax rate, the higher the score.

Score	Tax Rates	Criteria
1	Very low	Top marginal corporate tax rate less than 15 percent.
1.5	Low	Top marginal corporate tax rate equal to or greater than 15 percent and less than 18 percent.
2	Low	Top marginal corporate tax rate equal to or greater than 18 percent and less than 21 percent.
2.5	Moderate	Top marginal corporate tax rate equal to or greater than 21 percent and less than 24 percent.
3	Moderate	Top marginal corporate tax rate equal to or greater than 24 percent and less than 27 percent.
3.5	High	Top marginal corporate tax rate equal to or greater than 27 percent and less than 30 percent.
4	High	Top marginal corporate tax rate equal to or greater than 30 percent and less than 33 percent.
4.5	Very high	Top marginal corporate tax rate equal to or greater than 33 percent and less than 36 percent.
5	Very high	Top marginal corporate tax rate equal to or greater than 36 percent.

ditures, it necessarily reduces (increases) the level of economic freedom in a society.

The government's need to finance these year-to-year changes in expenditures creates a burden. The choice is whether to tax the public now or in the future. No matter how a given level of government expenditure is financed—by current taxation, or future (debt issuance or money creation), or varying amounts of each—resources are going to be diverted from the private sector. Hence, the expenditures reflect the total fiscal burden.

This perspective underlies Milton Friedman's belief that government expenditures are the most complete measure of a state's burden on the economy. Government expenditures capture the possibility of spending in excess of tax revenues, financed either by increased borrowing or by the printing of money, which imposes further costs on an economy.[6]

Methodology. The score for the fiscal burden of government has three components:

Variables for Factor #2

- Top marginal income tax rate
- Top marginal corporate tax rate
- Year-to-year change in government expenditures as a percent of GDP

the top marginal income tax rate, the top marginal corporate tax rate, and the year-to-year change in government expenditures as a share of GDP. The authors followed several steps in scoring this factor. First, a country's individual income tax score was assigned a score between 1 and 5 based on the top marginal income tax rate. (See text box, "Individual Income Tax Grading Scale.") Second, a country's corporate tax score was assigned a score between 1 and 5 based on the top marginal corporate tax rate. (See text box, "Corporate Tax Grading Scale.") Third, a country was assigned a score between 1 and 5 based on the year-to-year change in government

Factor 2: Change in Government Expenditures Scale

This scale lists a score from 1 through 5. The more the level of government expenditures as a percent of GDP increases, the higher the score.

Score	Year-to-year Change in Government Expenditures as Percent of GDP	Criteria
1	Very high decrease	Equal to or greater than −4 percentage points.
1.5	High decrease	Equal to or greater than −3 percentage points and less than −4 percentage points.
2	Moderate decrease	Equal to or greater than −2 percentage points and less than −3 percentage points.
2.5	Low decrease	Equal to or greater than −1 percentage point and less than −2 percentage points.
3	Very low decrease	Equal to or greater than 0 percentage point and less than −1 percentage point.
3.5	Low increase	Greater than 0 percentage point and less than or equal to 1 percentage point.
4	Moderate increase	Greater than 1 percentage point and less than or equal to 2 percentage points.
4.5	High increase	Greater than 2 percentage points and less than or equal to 3 percentage points.
5	Very high increase	Greater than 3 percentage points.

expenditures as a percent of GDP. (See text box, "Change in Government Expenditures Scale.")

The authors then calculated a weighted average of the three components of the fiscal burden of government factor to arrive at a final score. The top income tax rate was assigned a 25 percent weight, the top corporate tax rate was assigned a 50 percent weight, and the year-to-year change in the share of government expenditures was assigned a 25 percent weight. The authors conducted a statistical analysis of the relationship between the individual components of the fiscal burden factor and the overall level of economic freedom and found that the correlation between the top corporate tax rate and overall economic freedom was about twice as great as the correlation between economic freedom and either the top income tax rate or the year-to-year change in gov-

ernment spending as a share of GDP. Thus, the authors chose to place the double weight on the top corporate tax rate.

Sources. Unless otherwise noted, the authors used the following sources for information on taxation, in order of priority: Ernst & Young, *2005 The Global Executive* and *2005 Worldwide Corporate Tax Guide*; Deloitte, *Country Snapshot*, May 2005, and *Corporate Tax Rates at a Glance*, January 2005; International Monetary Fund, Staff Country Report, *Selected Issues and Statistical Appendix*, 2002 to 2005; investment agencies; and other governmental authorities (i.e., embassy confirmations, treasury/tax authority). Sources other than Ernst & Young are noted in the text.

For information on government expenditures, the authors' primary sources were Organisation for Economic Co-operation and Development data (for member countries); African Development Bank; Interna-

Factor 3: Government Consumption Grading Scale

This scale lists a score from 1 through 5. The higher the level of government consumption as a percent of GDP, the higher the score.

Score	Level of Government Consumption in the Economy	Criteria
1	Very low	Less than or equal to 5 percent of GDP.
2	Low	Greater than 5 percent but less than or equal to 10 percent of GDP.
3	Moderate	Greater than 10 percent but less than or equal to 20 percent of GDP.
4	High	Greater than 20 percent but less than or equal to 40 percent of GDP.
5	Very high	Greater than 40 percent of GDP.

tional Monetary Fund, Staff Country Report, *Selected Issues and Statistical Appendix*, 2002 to 2005; Asian Development Bank, *Development Outlook 2005* and *Key Indicators 2004*; and official government publications of each country and individual contacts from government agencies and multinational organizations such as the IMF and World Bank. Sources other than the OECD and the IMF are noted in the text. It should be noted that the sources at times revise their earlier estimates and issue amended data. Because the authors of the 2006 *Index* have used the most current and reliable data available in grading this factor, the data reported in this edition may vary from the data reported by these sources that were used in earlier editions of the *Index*.

Factor #3: Government Intervention in the Economy

 This factor measures government's direct use of scarce resources for its own purposes and government's control over resources through ownership. The measure comprises both government consumption and government production. Transfer payments (the difference between government expenditure and government consumption), which consist of compulsory exchange of the rights to resources from some people to others, are excluded from this measure.

Variables for Factor #3

- Government consumption as a percentage of the economy
- Government ownership of businesses and industries
- Share of government revenues from state-owned enterprises and government ownership of property
- Economic output produced by the government

Government consumption totals net purchases of goods, services, and structures (for example, bridges and buildings); wages paid to government employees; net purchases of fixed assets; and inventory changes in government enterprises.[7] Government production is described below. The government intervention factor is distinct from government's regulatory role and complements the measure of fiscal burden.[8]

Methodology. Government consumption as a percentage of GDP is evaluated separately from government production. First, the level of government intervention in the economy is determined. The higher the rate of government consumption as a percentage of GDP, the more resources the government is pulling from the private or free market and, therefore, the lower its level of economic freedom and the higher its *Index* score (lower ranking).

Factor 3: Share of Revenues from State-Owned Enterprises and Property

This scale lists a score from 1 through 5. The higher the share of revenues from state-owned enterprises and property as a percent of total government revenues, the higher the score.

Score	Share of Revenues Received from State-Owned Enterprises and Property	Criteria
1	Very low	Less than or equal to 5 percent of government revenues.
2	Low	Greater than 5 percent but less than or equal to 10 percent of government revenues.
3	Moderate	Greater than 10 percent but less than or equal to 20 percent of government revenues.
4	High	Greater than 20 percent but less than or equal to 40 percent of government revenues.
5	Very high	Greater than 40 percent of government revenues.

Governments intervene in the economy not only by consuming scarce resources, but also to engage in business activities that generally could be carried out more efficiently in the private sector. Governments that operate state-owned enterprises crowd out private initiative and investment, and the resultant inefficiency deters economic growth. Economic freedom and the economy suffer. The authors measure the size of the state-owned sector using the share of revenues a country receives from both state-owned enterprises and government-owned property.

Grading employs two tables that assign one score for each level of government consumption as a percentage of GDP and one score for each level of the share of government revenues from state-owned enterprises and property. The two scores are then averaged to obtain the final government intervention score for each country.

The main source for revenues from state-owned enterprises is the International Monetary Fund's *Government Finance Statistics Yearbook*. When these data are not available, the authors rely on the country's economic or finance ministry's Web site, the International Monetary Fund's statistical appendix, or the country's embassy to the United States. When the authors obtain the data on revenues from state-owned enterprises from more than one place, they note this fact in the country's write-up.

For countries in which the share of total revenues from state-owned enterprises and government ownership of property was not available, 1 point was added to the government intervention score (with a variety of sources used in making this judgment) when evidence of many state-owned enterprises was found.

The government intervention factor also examines the state of privatization programs. If a country's state-owned sector is being aggressively privatized, the authors note this fact, which puts into context any statements about the size of the state-owned sector. If the privatization program has stalled, or if one is not in place, the authors note that as well.

Additionally, in a few cases, there is strong reason to doubt either the reported measure of government consumption or the reported share of enterprise income. In these cases, when compelling evidence of heavy government involvement in the economy was found, the authors added 1 or more points to the score (making it worse).[9]

Sources. Unless otherwise noted, the

Factor 4: Monetary Policy Grading Scale

Score	Inflation Rate	Criteria
1	Very low	Weighted rate of inflation less than or equal to 3 percent.
2	Low	Weighted rate of inflation greater than 3 percent but less than or equal to 6 percent.
3	Moderate	Weighted rate of inflation greater than 6 percent but less than or equal to 12 percent.
4	High	Weighted rate of inflation greater than 12 percent but less than or equal to 20 percent.
5	Very high	Weighted rate of inflation greater than 20 percent.

authors used the following sources for information on government intervention in the economy, in order of priority: World Bank, *World Development Indicators 2005* and *Country at a Glance* tables; official government publications of each country; Economist Intelligence Unit, *Country Report* and *Country Profile*, 2004–2005; International Monetary Fund, *Government Finance Statistics April 2005* CD–ROM; Organisation for Economic Co-operation and Development, *OECD Statistics*; United Nations, *National Account Statistics Databases*; and U.S. Department of Commerce, *Country Commercial Guide*, 2003, 2004, and 2005.[10]

Often, data for the share of total revenues from state-owned enterprises and government ownership of property are not readily available. In these cases, the authors look both for data on total revenues from state-owned enterprises and property and for data on total government revenues and then calculate the percentage of total revenues that is attributable to revenues from state-owned enterprises and property.

Factor #4: Monetary Policy

 The value of a country's currency is shaped largely by its monetary policy. With a stable monetary policy, people can rely on market prices for the foreseeable future. Hence, investment, savings, and other longer-term plans are easier to make, and individuals enjoy greater economic freedom. John Maynard Keynes observed about the opposite of stable money that, "by a continuing process of inflation,

Variable for Factor #4

• Weighted average inflation rate from 1995 to 2004

governments can confiscate, secretly and unobserved, an important part of the wealth of their citizens."[11] Inflation not only confiscates wealth, but also distorts pricing, misallocates resources, raises the cost of doing business, and undermines a free society.

There is no singularly accepted theory of the right monetary institutions for a free society. At one time, the gold standard enjoyed widespread support, but this is no longer the case (though some continue to support that system). What characterizes almost all monetary theorists today, however, is support for low or zero inflation. A good way to gauge the influence of monetary policy on economic freedom is to analyze the inflation rate over a period of time.

Methodology. This factor's score is based on a country's weighted average annual rate of inflation from 1995 to 2004. First, the authors weighted inflation rates for each of the past 10 years, giving the year farthest from the present the least weight and the current year the greatest weight. Then they calculated an average of these weighted rates.[12] In some cases, data were not available for all 10 years; for these countries, the authors used as many years of data as were available.[13] The reader should be aware that when governments impose comprehensive price and wage controls, measured inflation probably is distorted.

Sources. Unless otherwise noted, the authors used the following sources for data on monetary policy, in order of priority: International Monetary Fund, *International Financial Statistics On-line*; International Monetary Fund, *2005 World Economic Outlook*, available at *www.imf.org/external/pubs/ft/weo/2005/01/index.htm*; and Economist Intelligence Unit, *Country Report*, 1999 to 2005, and *Country Profile*, 2004–2005.

Factor #5: Capital Flows and Foreign Investment

 Restrictions on foreign investment limit the inflow of capital and thus hamper economic freedom. By contrast, little or no restriction of foreign investment enhances economic freedom because foreign investment provides funds for economic expansion. For this factor, the more restrictions a country imposes on foreign investment, the lower its level of economic freedom and the higher its score.

Methodology. This factor scrutinizes each country's policies toward foreign investment in order to determine its overall investment climate. Questions examined include whether there is a foreign investment code that defines the country's investment laws and procedures; whether the government encourages foreign investment through fair and equitable treatment of investors; whether there are restrictions on access to foreign exchange; whether foreign firms are treated the same as domestic firms under the law; whether the government imposes restrictions on payments, transfers, and capital transactions; and whether specific industries are closed to foreign investment. This analysis helps to develop an overall description of the country's investment climate. The authors then grade each country based on those variables.

Sources. Unless otherwise noted, the authors used the following sources for data on capital flows and foreign investment, in order of priority: International Monetary Fund, *Annual Report on Exchange Arrangements and Exchange Restrictions 2004*; official government publications of each country;

Variables for Factor #5

- Foreign investment code
- Restrictions on foreign ownership of business
- Restrictions on industries and companies open to foreign investors
- Restrictions and performance requirements on foreign companies
- Foreign ownership of land
- Equal treatment under the law for both foreign and domestic companies
- Restrictions on repatriation of earnings
- Restrictions on capital transactions
- Availability of local financing for foreign companies

Economist Intelligence Unit, *Country Commerce, Country Profile*, and *Country Report*, 2004 and 2005; Office of the U.S. Trade Representative, *2005 National Trade Estimate Report on Foreign Trade Barriers*; and U.S. Department of Commerce, *Country Commercial Guide*, 2004 and 2005.[14]

Factor #6: Banking and Finance

 In most countries, banks provide the essential financial services that facilitate economic growth; they lend money to start businesses, purchase homes, and secure credit that is used to buy durable consumer goods, in addition to furnishing a safe place in which individuals can store their earnings. The more banks are controlled by the government, the less free they are to engage in these activities. Hence, heavy bank regulation reduces opportunities and restricts economic freedom; therefore, the more a government restricts its banking sector, the lower its level of economic freedom and the higher its score.

In developed economies, commercial banks are relatively less important because a higher proportion of credit is supplied in organized securities markets. Over the years, the authors have devoted more attention to the non-banking part of the financial services industry (insurance and securities). If the government intervenes in the stock market, it contravenes the choices of millions of individuals. It does so by interfer-

Factor 5: Capital Flows and Foreign Investment Grading Scale

Score	Barriers to Foreign Investment	Criteria
1	Very low	Equal treatment of foreign investment; transparent foreign investment code and professional, efficient bureaucracy; no restrictions on foreign investments with rare exceptions, such as restrictions in sectors related to national security; country has legal guarantees against expropriation of property and permits international arbitrations of disputes; foreign investors may purchase real estate; both residents and non-residents have access to foreign exchange and may conduct international payments, transfers, or capital transactions freely.
2	Low	Equal treatment of foreign investment; transparent foreign investment code, but process may face bureaucratic or other informal impediments; some restrictions on foreign investments through general rules or in a few specified sectors, such as utilities, natural resources, or national security; country has legal guarantees against expropriation of property and permits international arbitration of disputes; foreign investors may purchase real estate; residents and non-residents face few restrictions on access to foreign exchange or their ability to conduct international payments, transfers, or capital transactions.
3	Moderate	Foreign investment is generally encouraged but may not receive equal treatment with domestic investors in all sectors; foreign investment code may be unclear, and the investment process may face some bureaucratic impediments or corruption; country restricts foreign investments through many requirements or in a significant number of sectors; expropriation of property is very unlikely, and country guarantees compensation; foreign investors may face restrictions on their ability to purchase real estate; residents and/or non-residents face some restrictions on access to foreign exchange or their ability to conduct international payments, transfers, or capital transactions.
4	High	Foreign investment is permitted only on a case-by-case basis; foreign investment code is discriminatory, and foreign investment does not receive equal treatment in all sectors; investment process is characterized by significant bureaucratic impediments and corruption; country restricts foreign investments in many sectors; expropriation of property is possible; foreign investors may purchase real estate only on a case-by case basis or only in restricted areas; residents and/or non-residents face strict restrictions on access to foreign exchange, and government imposes many controls on international payments, transfers, or capital transactions.
5	Very high	Foreign investors do not receive equal treatment; foreign investment code is discriminatory, and the approval process is opaque and corruption is widespread; foreign investment is very restricted, and few sectors are open to foreign investment; expropriation of property has occurred in the recent past; foreign investors may not purchase real estate; government controls or prohibits most international payments, transfers, and capital transactions.

Factor 6: Banking and Finance Grading Scale

Score	Restrictions on Banks	Criteria
1	Very low	Government provides financial sector with prudent regulatory supervision by an independent central bank; government may be active in some financial institutions but must comprise a very minor role in terms of total market share; credit allocated on market terms; foreign financial institutions able to operate freely and treated the same as domestic financial institutions; banks may engage in all types of financial services.
2	Low	Limited government involvement in financial sector beyond providing prudent regulatory supervision by an independent central bank; few limits on foreign financial institutions; credit allocated on market terms; government may be active in some financial institutions but must comprise a limited role in terms of total market share; banks may engage in all types of financial services.
3	Moderate	Substantial government influence in financial sector; regulatory supervision of financial institutions may be insufficient; government owns or controls banks that have a significant role in terms of market share; government influences allocation of credit; foreign financial institutions face restrictions; country may maintain some limits on financial services; bank formation may face some barriers.
4	High	Heavy government involvement in financial sector; central bank not independent; regulatory supervision of financial institutions poor; banking system in transition or unstable; government owns or controls most financial institutions; government directs allocation of credit; possible corruption; foreign financial institutions discouraged; bank formation faces significant barriers.
5	Very high	Very heavy government involvement in financial sector; nearly all financial institutions owned or controlled by government; financial institutions in crisis or collapse, or banks operate on primitive basis; nearly all credit controlled by government; most credit extended to state-owned enterprises; corruption widespread; foreign financial institutions prohibited; bank formation virtually nonexistent.

ing with the pricing of capital—the most critical function of a market economy. Equity markets measure, on a continual basis, the expected profits and losses in publicly held companies. This measurement is essential in allocating capital resources to their highest-valued uses and thereby satisfying consumers' most urgent wants.

It should be noted that virtually all countries provide some type of prudential supervision of banks and other financial services. This supervision serves two major purposes: ensuring the safety and soundness of the

Variables for Factor #6

- Government ownership of financial institutions
- Restrictions on the ability of foreign banks to open branches and subsidiaries
- Government influence over the allocation of credit
- Government regulations that inhibit financial activity
- Freedom to offer all types of financial services, securities, and insurance policies

Factor 7: Wages and Prices Grading Scale

Score	Wage and Price Controls	Criteria
1	Very low	Market sets prices of goods and services, and either the country does not have a minimum wage or the evidence indicates that the minimum wage applies to a small portion of the workforce and is therefore not relevant in wage setting.
2	Low	Government controls prices on some goods and services, such as utilities, or influences prices through subsidies in some industries, but such actions do not apply to a significant portion of national output. Government has a minimum wage that applies to a significant portion of the workforce.
3	Moderate	Government controls prices or influences prices through ownership of parastatals or subsidies of goods and services that constitute a significant portion of national output, and/or government-set wages apply to a large portion of the workforce.
4	High	Government determines most prices of goods and services and most wages.
5	Very high	Wages and prices of goods and services are almost completely controlled by the government.

financial system and ensuring that financial services firms meet basic fiduciary responsibilities. Ultimately, this task falls under a government's duty to enforce contracts and protect its citizens against fraud.

The marketplace provides some protection of this sort through such institutions as independent auditors and firms providing information services, and it arguably could take over even more of this oversight responsibility. The key point, however, is that markets demand independent oversight of financial services firms because of the high standards of fiduciary duty required in that industry. Such oversight is distinguished from burdensome government regulation or government ownership of banks, both of which interfere with market provision of financial services to consumers. It is the latter, not the former, that interferes with economic freedom and causes a country's grade on this factor to be better or worse.

Methodology. The banking and finance factor measures the relative openness of a country's banking and financial system. The authors score this factor by determining spe-

cifically whether foreign banks and financial services firms are able to operate freely, how difficult it is to open domestic banks and other financial services firms, how heavily regulated the financial system is, how great the presence of state-owned banks is, whether the government influences the allocation of credit, and whether banks are free to provide customers with insurance and invest in securities (and vice versa). The authors use this analysis to develop a description of the country's financial climate.

Sources. Unless otherwise noted, the authors used the following sources for data on banking and finance, in order of priority: Economist Intelligence Unit, *Country Commerce, Country Profile,* and *Country Report,* 2004 and 2005; official government publications of each country; and U.S. Department of Commerce, *Country Commercial Guide,* 2004 and 2005.[15]

Factor #7: Wages and Prices

 In a free-market economy, prices allocate resources to their highest use. A firm that needs more employ-

Chapter 5

69

ees may signal this need to the market by offering a higher wage; an individual who greatly values a home on the market offers a higher price to purchase it. Prices also act as signals to producers and consumers by conveying information that it otherwise would be prohibitively costly to obtain. For example, increased demand for a good is reflected in the price of the product and is a signal to producers to increase production.

When prices are determined freely, resources go to their most productive use for satisfying consumers. As Nobel Laureate Friedrich A. Hayek put it, "We must look at the price system as…a mechanism for communicating information if we want to understand its real function—a function which, of course, it fulfills less perfectly as prices grow more rigid."[16]

Some governments mandate wage and price controls. By so doing, they inhibit information, restrict economic activity, and curtail economic freedom. Government control can emanate not only from explicit price controls, but also from heavy involvement in the economy, which distorts pricing. Therefore, the more a government intervenes and controls prices and wages, the lower its level of economic freedom and the higher its score.

Methodology. The authors score this factor by the extent to which a government allows the market to set wages and prices. Specifically, this factor looks at which products have prices that are set by the government and whether the government has a minimum wage policy or otherwise influences wages. The factor's scale measures the relative degree of government control over wages and prices. A "very low" score of 1 represents wages and prices that are set almost completely by the market, whereas a "very high" score of 5 means that wages and prices are set almost completely by the government.

Sources. Unless otherwise noted, the authors used the following sources for data on wages and prices, in order of priority: Economist Intelligence Unit, *Country Commerce, Country Profile,* and *Country Report,* 2004 and 2005; official government publications of each country; and U.S. Depart-

Variables for Factor #7

- Minimum wage laws
- Freedom to set prices privately without government influence
- Government price controls
- Extent to which government price controls are used
- Government subsidies to businesses that affect prices

ment of Commerce, *Country Commercial Guide,* and U.S. Department of State, *Country Reports on Human Rights Practices,* 2004 and 2005.[17]

Factor #8: Property Rights

 The ability to accumulate private property is the main motivating force in a market economy, and the rule of law is vital to a fully functioning free-market economy. Secure property rights give citizens the confidence to undertake commercial activities, save their income, and make long-term plans because they know that their income and savings are safe from expropriation. This factor examines the extent to which the government protects private property by enforcing the laws and how safe private property is from expropriation. The less protection private property receives, the lower a country's level of economic freedom and the higher its score.

Methodology. This factor scores the degree to which a country's laws protect private property rights and the degree to which its government enforces those laws. It also assesses the likelihood that private property will be expropriated and analyzes the independence of the judiciary, the existence of corruption within the judiciary, and the ability of individuals and businesses to enforce contracts. The less certain the legal protection of property, the higher a country's score; similarly, the greater the chances of government expropriation of property, the higher a country's score.

Sources. Unless otherwise noted, the authors used the following sources for information on property rights, in order of priority:

Factor 8: Property Rights Grading Scale

Score	Protection of Private Property	Criteria
1	Very high	Private property guaranteed by government; court system efficiently enforces contracts; justice system punishes those who unlawfully confiscate private property; corruption nearly nonexistent, and expropriation highly unlikely.
2	High	Private property guaranteed by government; court system suffers delays and is lax in enforcing contracts; corruption possible but rare; expropriation unlikely.
3	Moderate	Court system inefficient and subject to delays; corruption may be present; judiciary may be influenced by other branches of government; expropriation possible but rare.
4	Low	Property ownership weakly protected; court system inefficient; corruption present; judiciary influenced by other branches of government; expropriation possible.
5	Very low	Private property outlawed or not protected; almost all property belongs to the state; country in such chaos (for example, because of ongoing war) that property protection nonexistent; judiciary so corrupt that property not effectively protected; expropriation frequent.

Variables for Factor #8

- Freedom from government influence over the judicial system
- Commercial code defining contracts
- Sanctioning of foreign arbitration of contract disputes
- Government expropriation of property
- Corruption within the judiciary
- Delays in receiving judicial decisions and/or enforcement
- Legally granted and protected private property

Economist Intelligence Unit, *Country Commerce*, 2004 and 2005, and U.S. Department of Commerce, *Country Commercial Guide*, and U.S. Department of State, *Country Reports on Human Rights Practices*, 2004 and 2005.[18]

Factor #9: Regulation

Regulations and restrictions are in effect a form of taxation that makes it difficult for entrepreneurs to create and/or maintain new businesses. In some countries, government officials frown on any private-sector initiatives; in a few, they even make them illegal. Although many regulations hinder businesses, the most important are associated with licensing new companies and businesses. In some countries, as well as many states in the United States, the procedure for obtaining a business license can be as simple as mailing in a registration form with a minimal fee. In Hong Kong, for example, obtaining a business license requires filling out a single form, which can be completed in a few hours.[19] In other countries, such as India and countries in parts of South America, the process involved in obtaining a business license requires endless trips to government offices and can take a year or more.

Once a business is open, government regulation does not always subside; in some cases, it increases. Interestingly, two countries with the same set of regulations can impose different regulatory burdens. If one of them, for instance, applies its regulations evenly and transparently, it lowers the regu-

Factor 9: Regulation Grading Scale

Score	Levels of Regulation	Criteria
1	Very low	Existing regulations straightforward and applied uniformly to all businesses; regulations not much of a burden for business; corruption nearly nonexistent.
2	Low	Simple licensing procedures; existing regulations relatively straightforward, applied uniformly most of the time, but burdensome in some instances; corruption possible but rare.
3	Moderate	Complicated licensing procedures; regulations impose substantial burden on business; existing regulations may be applied haphazardly and in some instances are not even published by the government; corruption may be present and poses minor burden on businesses.
4	High	Highly complicated licensing procedures; regulations impose heavy burden on business; existing regulations applied haphazardly and in some instances are not even published by the government; corruption present and poses a substantial burden on businesses.
5	Very high	Government-set production quotas and some state planning; government regulations virtually impede creation of new businesses; corruption widespread; regulations applied randomly.

Variables for Factor #9

- Licensing requirements to operate a business
- Ease of obtaining a business license
- Corruption within the bureaucracy
- Labor regulations, such as established workweeks, paid vacations, and parental leave, as well as selected labor regulations
- Environmental, consumer safety, and worker health regulations
- Regulations that impose a burden on business

latory burden because it enables businesses to make long-term plans more easily. If the other applies regulations inconsistently, it raises the regulatory burden on businesses by creating an unpredictable business environment. For example, in some countries, an environmental regulation may be used to shut down one business but not another. Business owners are uncertain about which regulations they must obey. In addition, the existence of excessive regulation can support corruption as confused and harassed business owners attempt to navigate the red tape.

Methodology. This factor measures how easy or difficult it is to open and operate a business. The more regulations are imposed on business, the harder it is to establish one. The factor also examines the degree of corruption in government and whether regulations are applied uniformly to all businesses. Another consideration is whether the country has state planning agencies that set production limits and quotas. The scale establishes a set of conditions for each of the five possible grades. These conditions also include the extent of government corruption, how uniformly regulations are applied, and the extent to which regulations impose a burden on business. A "very low" score of 1 indicates that corruption is virtually nonexistent and regulations are minimal and applied uniformly; a "very high" score of 5 indicates that corruption is widespread, regulations are applied randomly, and the general level of regulation is very high. A country need only meet a majority of the conditions for a particular score to receive that score.

Factor 10: Informal Market Grading Scale
(Countries Not Covered by Transparency International)

Score	Informal Market Activity	Criteria
1	Very low	Country has free-market economy with informal market in such things as drugs and weapons.
2	Low	Country may have some informal market involvement in labor or pirating of intellectual property.
3	Moderate	Country may have some informal market activities in labor, agriculture, and transportation and moderate levels of intellectual property piracy.
4	High	Country may have substantial levels of informal market activity in such areas as labor, pirated intellectual property, and smuggled consumer goods and in such services as transportation, electricity, and telecommunications.
5	Very high	Country's informal market is larger than its formal economy.

Sources. Unless otherwise noted, the authors used the following sources for data on regulation, in order of priority: Economist Intelligence Unit, *Country Commerce* and *Country Report*, 2004 and 2005; official government publications of each country; U.S. Department of Commerce, *Country Commercial Guide*, 2004 and 2005;[20] and Office of the U.S. Trade Representative, *2005 National Trade Estimate Report on Foreign Trade Barriers*.

Factor #10: Informal Market

 At times, the existence of an informal market is positive: There is some ability to engage in entrepreneurship or to obtain scarce goods and services that otherwise would not exist. "In some circumstances," notes Harvard economist Robert Barro, "corruption may be preferable to honest enforcement of bad rules. For example, outcomes may be worse if a regulation that prohibits some useful economic activity is thoroughly enforced rather than circumvented through bribes."[21] Alejandro Chafuen and Eugenio Guzmán, however, point out that "corruption is the cost of obtaining privileges that only the State can 'legally' grant, such as favoritism in taxation, tariffs, subsidies, loans, government con-

Variables for Factor #10

- Smuggling
- Piracy of intellectual property in the informal market
- Agricultural production supplied on the informal market
- Manufacturing supplied on the informal market
- Services supplied on the informal market
- Transportation supplied on the informal market
- Labor supplied on the informal market

tracting, and regulation."[22]

Informal markets are the direct result of some kind of government intervention in the marketplace. An informal market activity is one that the government has taxed heavily, regulated in a burdensome manner, or simply outlawed in the past. This factor captures the effects of government interventions that are not always fully measured elsewhere.

Many societies, of course, outlaw such activities as trafficking in illicit drugs, but others frequently limit individual liberty by outlawing such activities as private transportation and construction services. A government regulation or restriction in one area may create an informal market in another. For example, a country with high barriers to trade may have laws that protect its domestic market and prevent the import of foreign goods, but these barriers create incentives for smuggling and an informal market for the barred products. In addition, governments that do not have strong property rights protection for intellectual property, for example, or that do not enforce existing laws encourage piracy and theft of these products.

For the purposes of this *Index*, the informal market reflects restrictions, taxes, or imperfections in the private market. Hence, the larger the informal market, the lower the country's level of economic freedom; and the more prevalent informal market activities are, the worse the country's score. Conversely, the smaller the informal market, the higher the country's level of economic freedom; and the less prevalent these activities are, the better the country's score.

Methodology. This factor relies on Transparency International's Corruption Perceptions Index (CPI), which measures the level of corruption in 146 countries, to determine the informal market scores of countries that are also listed in the *Index of Economic Freedom*.[23] As the level of corruption increases, the level of informal market activity rises as well. Citizens often engage in corrupt activity, such as bribing an official, so that they can enter the informal market.

Because the CPI is based on a 10-point scale in which 10 equals very little corruption and 1 equals a very corrupt government, it was necessary to transform the CPI to a five-point scale consistent with the other nine factors graded in the *Index*. To do this, the authors regressed the CPI on the informal market *Index of Economic Freedom* score. After estimating the relationship between the two variables, the authors substituted the CPI into the equation to arrive at a number between 1 and 5. They then rounded the numbers to the nearest half point (0.5 point).[24] If 2004 Transparency International data were not available and 2003 or 2002 TI data were available, the authors used the earlier TI data.

For countries that are not covered in the CPI, the informal market score is determined by using the same procedure as in previous years. (See text box, "Informal Market Grading Scale.") This procedure considers the extent to which informal market activities occur. Although information on the size of informal markets in less-developed countries is difficult to obtain, information on the extent of smuggling, piracy of intellectual property, and informal labor can be found. When such information is available, the authors use it to determine the extent of informal market activities. The higher the level of informal market activity, the lower the level of overall economic freedom and the higher a country's score. As newer data become available, it may become possible to document the percentage of informal market activity in a country's overall economy.

Although this factor measures informal market activity in the production, distribution, or consumption of goods and services, it does not measure such things as informal market exchange rates or illegal provision of such "vices" as gambling, narcotics, prostitution, and related activities. Such activities are very difficult to quantify with objectivity.

Sources. Unless otherwise noted, the authors used the following sources for information on informal market activities, in order of priority: Transparency International, *Corruption Perceptions Index*, 2002 and 2004; U.S. Department of Commerce, *Country Commercial Guide*, 2004 and 2005;[25] Economist Intelligence Unit, *Country Commerce*, *Country Profile*, and *Country Report*, 2004 and 2005; Office of the U.S. Trade Representative, *2005 National Trade Estimate Report on Foreign Trade Barriers*; and official government publications of each country.

Endnotes

1. See, for example, James D. Gwartney and Robert A. Lawson with Erik Gartzke, *Economic Freedom of the World, 2005 Annual Report* (Vancouver, Canada: Fraser Institute, 2005), and Richard E. Messick, *World Survey of Economic Freedom: 1995–1996* (New Brunswick, N.J.: Transaction Publishers, 1996).

2. "The property which every man has in his own labour, as it is the original foundation of all other property, so it is the most sacred and inviolable." Adam Smith, *An Inquiry into the Nature and Causes of the Wealth of Nations* (New York: The Modern Library, 1937), pp. 121–122; first published in 1776.

3. Richard Roll, "Weighting the Components of the Index of Economic Freedom," Chapter 3 in Marc A. Miles, Edwin J. Feulner, and Mary Anastasia O'Grady, *2004 Index of Economic Freedom* (Washington, D.C.: The Heritage Foundation and Dow Jones & Company, Inc., 2004).

4. The most favored nation tariff rate is the "normal," non-discriminatory tariff charged on imports of a good. In commercial diplomacy, exporters seek MFN treatment; that is, the promise that they will be treated as well as the most favored exporter. The MFN rule requires that the concession be extended to all other members of the World Trade Organization.

5. The *Country Commercial Guides* are published by the U.S. Commercial Service but are based on data from U.S. embassies, the U.S. Department of State, and the U.S. Department of Commerce. Quotes from these publications are cited in the country write-ups as originating with the U.S. Department of Commerce.

6. Walter Block, ed., *Economic Freedom: Toward a Theory of Measurement* (Vancouver, Canada: Fraser Institute, 1991).

7. U.S. Department of Commerce, Bureau of Economic Analysis, *Survey of Current Business*, March 1998, p. 31.

8. In a few cases, data on government consumption were not available for a country, but data on government expenditures were available, or vice versa. When information on government consumption was not available for the government intervention factor and data on government expenditures were available, the authors used government expenditures as a proxy for government consumption. Similarly, when data on government expenditures were not available for the fiscal burden of government factor and data on government consumption were available, the authors used government consumption as a proxy for government expenditures.

9. The countries for which data correction points were added include Bangladesh, Belarus, Burkina Faso, Burma, China, Cuba, Djibouti, Indonesia, Iran, Macedonia, Malawi, Niger, Syria, Tajikistan, Turkmenistan, and Vietnam.

10. See note 5.

11. John Maynard Keynes, *The Economic Consequences of the Peace* (London: Macmillan and Co., Ltd., 1919), pp. 102–103.

12. The weights were generated using an exponential weighting procedure and are as follows: The most recent year received a weight of 1.0, followed by 0.36788, 0.13534, 0.04979, 0.01832, 0.00674, 0.00248, 0.00091, 0.00034, and 0.00012.

13. In his cross-country study on growth, Robert J. Barro found that relatively recent inflation had the main explanatory power for growth. Robert J. Barro, *Determinants of Economic Growth: A Cross-Country Empirical Study* (Cambridge, Mass.: MIT Press, 1997).

14. See note 5.

15. See note 5.

16. Friedrich A. Hayek, "The Use of Knowledge in Society," in *Individualism and Economic Order* (Chicago: University of Chicago Press, 1948), p. 86.

17. See note 5.

18. See note 5.

19. John Stossel, "Is America Number One?" ABC News, aired September 19, 1999.

20. See note 5.

21. Robert J. Barro, "Rule of Law, Democracy, and Economic Performance," Chapter 2 in Gerald P. O'Driscoll, Jr., Kim R. Holmes, and Melanie Kirkpatrick, *2000 Index of Economic Freedom* (Washington, D.C.: The Heritage Foundation and Dow Jones & Company, Inc., 2000), p. 36.

22. Alejandro A. Chafuen and Eugenio Guzmán, "Economic Freedom and Corruption," Chapter 3 in O'Driscoll, Holmes, and Kirkpatrick, *2000 Index of Economic Freedom*, p. 53.

23. This year, the authors graded the informal market factor using Transparency International's 2002, 2003, and 2004 Corruption Perceptions Index (CPI) reports.

24. The equation that the authors estimated is as follows: informal market = 5.227 − 0.4771*CPI. The authors then substituted the country's CPI score into the equation to arrive at a number between 1 and 5. For example, substituting Denmark's CPI score of 9.5 into the equation yields an informal market score of 0.695 (which rounds up to a score of 1).

25. See note 5.

Chapter 6

The *2006 Index of Economic Freedom:* The Countries

Marc A. Miles, Ph.D., Kim R. Holmes, Ph.D.,
Ana Isabel Eiras, Brett D. Schaefer, and Anthony B. Kim

This chapter is a compilation of 161 countries, each graded in all 10 factors of the *Index of Economic Freedom.* (For this year's edition of the *Index*, numerical grading was suspended for four countries: the Democratic Republic of Congo, Iraq, and Sudan, which are in a state of civil unrest or anarchy, and Serbia–Montenegro, for which data necessary to grade the country are not available. Information is provided, however, even for these countries. On the other hand, grading was resumed for Angola and Burundi, for which grading had been suspended since 2001 due to civil unrest or anarchy.)

Each country is given a score ranging from 1 through 5 for all 10 factors, and these scores are then averaged (using equal weights) to get the country's final *Index of Economic Freedom* score. Countries with a score between 1 and 2 have the freest economies; those with a score around 3 are less free; those with a score near 4 are excessively regulated and will need significant economic reform to achieve sustained increases in economic growth; and those with a score of 5 are the most economically repressed.[1]

In addition to these factor scores and an overall score, each country summary includes a brief introduction describing the country's political and economic background, as well as the principal challenges that it faces, and a statistical profile with the main economic indicators. These statistics and their sources are outlined in detail below.

To assure consistency and reliability for each of the 10 factors on which the countries are graded, every effort has been made to use the same source for each country; when data are unavailable from the primary source, secondary sources are used as indicated in Chapter 5. The information included reflects the most recent data available at the time of publication.

GUIDE TO STATISTICS

Unless otherwise indicated, the data in each country's statistical profile are for 2003 and in constant 2000 U.S. dollars. As of 2006 *Index* production time, data for 2004 were available for 36 countries: Australia, Austria, Belgium, Canada, Chile, the Czech Republic, Denmark, Estonia, Finland, France, Germany, Greece, Hong Kong, Hungary, Iceland, Ireland, Israel, Italy, Japan, Luxembourg, Mexico, the Netherlands, New Zealand, Norway, Poland, Portugal, Singapore, the Slovak Republic, the Republic of Korea, Spain, Sweden, Switzerland, Taiwan, Turkey, the United Kingdom, and the United States. The few cases in which no statistical data were available are indicated by "n/a."

The sources for each country's statistical profile include the following.

Population: 2003 estimate from World Bank, *World Development Indicators Online.* For some countries, the sources are the country's statistical agency and/or central bank and U.S. Central Intelligence Agency, *The World Factbook 2005.*

Total area: Both land and sea area, expressed in square kilometers. From U.S. Central Intelligence Agency, *The World Factbook 2005.*

GDP: Gross domestic product—total production of goods and services—expressed in constant 2000 U.S. dollars. The primary source for GDP data is World Bank, *World Development Indicators Online.* Other sources include Economist Intelligence Unit, *Country Reports,* 2005, and *Country Profiles,* 2003–2004 and 2004–2005; the country's statistical agency; and the country's central bank. For some countries, 2004 GDP estimates were calculated by applying the real 2004 GDP growth rate to real 2003 GDP data in constant 2000 U.S. dollars. The data used in this calculation are from Organisation for Economic Co-operation and Development, *Main Economic Indicators;* Economist Intelligence Unit, *Country Reports,* 2004 and 2005; International Monetary Fund, *World Economic Outlook: Globalization and External Imbalances,* April 2005; the country's statistical agency; and the country's central bank.

GDP growth rate: Annual percentage growth rate of GDP at market prices based on constant local currency. The primary sources for 2003 data are World Bank, *World Development Indicators Online,* and Economist Intelligence Unit, *Country Reports,* 2004 and 2005. Data on 2004 growth rates are from Organisation for Economic Co-operation and Development, *Main Economic Indicators;* the country's statistical agency; the country's central bank; and International Monetary Fund, *World Economic Outlook: Globalization and External Imbalances,* April 2005.

GDP per capita: Gross domestic prod-

uct expressed in constant 2000 U.S. dollars divided by total population. The sources for these data are World Bank, *World Development Indicators Online;* Economist Intelligence Unit, *Country Reports,* 2004 and 2005; Organisation for Economic Co-operation and Development, *Main Economic Indicators;* and the country's statistical agency.

Major exports: The country's four to six principal export products. Data for major exports are from U.S. Central Intelligence Agency, *The World Factbook 2005,* and Economist Intelligence Unit, *Country Reports,* 2004 and 2005, and *Country Profiles,* 2003–2004 and 2004–2005.

Exports of goods and services: The value of all goods and other market services. Included is the value of merchandise, freight, insurance, travel, and other non-factor services. Factor and property income, such as investment income, interest, and labor income, is excluded. Data are in constant 2000 U.S. dollars. Data for 2003 are from World Bank, *World Development Indicators Online,* and Economist Intelligence Unit, *Country Reports,* 2004 and 2005, and *Country Profiles,* 2003–2004 and 2004–2005. Other sources include the country's statistical agency and/or ministry of economy and trade. Data necessary for this calculation are from Economist Intelligence Unit, *Country Reports,* 2004 and 2005; World Bank, *World Development Indicators Online;* and the country's statistical agency.

Major export trading partners: Main destination of exports from each country and percentage of overall exports. From Economist Intelligence Unit, *Country Reports,* 2004 and 2005, and *Country Profiles,* 2003–2004 and 2004–2005.

Major imports: The country's six to eight principal import products. From U.S. Central Intelligence Agency, *The World Factbook 2005,* and Economist Intelligence Unit, *Country Reports,* 2004 and 2005, and *Country Profiles,* 2003–2004 and 2004–2005.

Imports of goods and services: The value of all goods and other market services. Included is the value of merchandise, freight, insurance, travel, and other non-factor services. Factor and property income, such as investment income, interest, and labor income, is excluded. Data are in constant 2000 U.S. dollars. The primary source is World Bank, *World Development Indicators Online*. Other sources include Economist Intelligence Unit, *Country Reports*, 2004 and 2005, and *Country Profiles*, 2003–2004 and 2004–2005; the country's statistical agency; and the country's ministry of economy and trade.

Major import trading partners: Principal countries from which imports originate and percentage of overall imports. From Economist Intelligence Unit, *Country Reports*, 2004 and 2005, and *Country Profiles*, 2003–2004 and 2004–2005.

Foreign direct investment (net): Net inflows of investment to acquire a lasting management interest (10 percent or more of voting stock) in an enterprise operating in an economy other than that of the investor. It is the sum of equity capital, reinvestment of earnings, other long-term capital, and short-term capital as shown in the balance of payments. This series indicates total net; that is, net FDI in the reporting economy (inflows) less net FDI by the reporting economy (outflows). Data are in constant 2000 U.S. dollars. The 2000 GDP deflator was used to convert net FDI from current U.S. dollars to constant 2000 U.S. dollars. Data for 2003 are from World Bank, *World Development Indicators Online*; United Nations Conference on Trade and Development, *World Investment Report*

2004; the country's statistical agency; and the country's central bank. Data for 2004 are from the country's central bank; the country's statistical agency; and Organisation for Economic Co-operation and Development, *Trends and Recent Developments in Foreign Direct Investment*.

TERMS USED IN IMPORT–EXPORT STATISTICS

CARICOM: Caribbean Community and Common Market, consisting of the Bahamas, Barbados, Belize, Guyana, Haiti, Jamaica, Suriname, Trinidad and Tobago, and the Windward and Leeward Islands in the Eastern Caribbean.

CIS: Commonwealth of Independent States, consisting of Azerbaijan, Armenia, Belarus, Georgia, Kazakhstan, Kyrgyz Republic, Moldova, Russia, Tajikistan, Turkmenistan, Uzbekistan, and Ukraine.

EU: European Union, consisting of Austria, Belgium, Cyprus, the Czech Republic, Denmark, Estonia, Finland, France, Germany, Greece, Hungary, Ireland, Italy, Latvia, Lithuania, Luxembourg, Malta, the Netherlands, Poland, Portugal, Slovakia, Slovenia, Spain, Sweden, and the United Kingdom.

SACU: Southern African Customs Union, consisting of Botswana, Lesotho, Namibia, South Africa, and Swaziland.

Endnote

1   For a detailed explanation of the scoring procedure used in this year's *Index*, see Chapter 5.

ALBANIA

Rank: 52

Score: 2.75

Category: Mostly Free

Present & Past Scores

(Best) 1
2
3   3.53 3.63 3.64 3.58 3.56 3.83 3.48 3.24 3.23 3.10 2.93 2.75
4
(Worst) 5
'95 '96 '97 '98 '99 '00 '01 '02 '03 '04 '05 '06

Albania's development has been significantly retarded by political and economic corruption. Since coming to power in July 2002, the socialist government of Fatos Nano has failed to reform the judicial system to any significant degree and has been unsuccessful in fighting corruption and organized crime. Many members of the political elite are allegedly involved in criminal activities, and the Organisation for Economic Co-operation and Development reports that in the private sector, the level of informal activity exceeds the level of formal activity. World Bank data indicate that 77 percent of Albanian companies have bribed officials. Albania remains the only Balkan country that has failed during the past decade to hold a general election that is fully accepted by the international community. The July 2005 general election once again ended in stalemate, with both sides claiming voter fraud. Privatization of large state-owned companies has advanced slowly, although the large Savings Bank of Albania was sold in 2004 and privatization efforts in the insurance, fixed-line telecommunications, and refinery industries are ongoing. Albania remains a major transit route and warehouse for international organized crime, and its government has failed to crack down on human trafficking or the smuggling of heroin and cigarettes. Albania's fiscal burden of government score is 0.3 point better this year, and its government intervention score and banking and finance score are, respectively, 0.5 point and 1 point better. As a result, Albania's overall score is 0.18 point better this year.

QUICK STUDY

SCORES

Trade Policy	4
Fiscal Burden	2.5
Government Intervention	2
Monetary Policy	1
Foreign Investment	2
Banking and Finance	2
Wages and Prices	2
Property Rights	4
Regulation	4
Informal Market	4

Population: 3,169,064

Total area: 28,748 sq. km

GDP: $4.4 billion

GDP growth rate: 6.0%

GDP per capita: $1,392

Major exports: textiles and footwear, tobacco, vegetables, food, beverages, machinery

Exports of goods and services: $1.0 billion

Major export trading partners: Italy 74.9%, Greece 12.8%, Germany 3.4%

Major imports: chemicals, machinery and equipment, minerals, fuels, electricity

Imports of goods and services: $2.2 billion

Major import trading partners: Italy 33.6%, Greece 20.1%, Turkey 6.6%, Germany 5.7%

Foreign direct investment (net): $167 million

2003 Data (in constant 2000 US dollars)

TRADE POLICY
Score: **4**–Stable (high level of protectionism)

According to the World Bank, Albania's weighted average tariff rate in 2001 (the most recent year for which World Bank data are available) was 11.3 percent. (The World Bank has revised the figure for 2001 downward from the 12.4 percent reported in the 2005 *Index*.) According to the U.S. Department of Commerce, "There are no non-tariff barriers in Albanian legislation. However, administrative bureaucracy can delay trade and increase costs." The *Financial Times* reports significant corruption in the customs service. Based on the revised trade factor methodology, Albania's trade policy score is unchanged.

FISCAL BURDEN OF GOVERNMENT
Score—Income Taxation: **3**–Worse (moderate tax rates)
Score—Corporate Taxation: **2.5**–Better (moderate tax rates)
Score—Change in Government Expenditures: **2**–Better (moderate decrease)
Final Score: **2.5**–Better (moderate cost of government)

According to the International Monetary Fund, Albania's top income tax rate is 30 percent, up from the 25 percent reported in the 2005 *Index*. Albania implemented a flat corporate tax rate of 23 percent in January 2005. In 2003, government expenditures as a percentage of GDP fell 2.6 percentage points to 28.5 percent, compared to a 0.5 percentage point decrease in 2002. On net, Albania's fiscal burden of government score is 0.3 point better this year.

GOVERNMENT INTERVENTION IN THE ECONOMY
Score: **2**–Better (low level)

The World Bank reports that the government consumed 8.5 percent of GDP in 2003, down from the 8.6 percent reported in the 2005 *Index*. Also in 2003, based on data from the International

Monetary Fund, Albania received 9.1 percent of its revenues from state-owned enterprises and government ownership of property, down from the 10.8 percent reported in the 2005 *Index*. As a result, Albania's government intervention score is 0.5 point better this year.

MONETARY POLICY
Score: **1**–Stable (very low level of inflation)

From 1995 to 2004, Albania's weighted average annual rate of inflation was 2.37 percent.

CAPITAL FLOWS AND FOREIGN INVESTMENT
Score: **2**–Stable (low barriers)

Foreign and domestic firms are treated equally under the law and are guaranteed safety from expropriation or nationalization. The government does not screen foreign investments, and nearly all sectors of the economy are open to foreign investment. Foreigners may not purchase agricultural land but are permitted to lease agricultural land for up to 99 years. Political instability, crime, corruption, and a thriving informal market continue to discourage foreign investment and undermine the implementation of reform. The International Monetary Fund reports that both residents and non-residents may hold foreign exchange accounts. Payments and transfers exceeding a specified amount require supporting documentation but face no other restrictions. The Bank of Albania monitors and reviews the purchase of capital and money market instruments, outward direct investment, most credit operations, and the purchase of real estate abroad by residents. These transactions must be conducted through entities licensed by the BOA.

BANKING AND FINANCE
Score: **2**–Better (low level of restrictions)

The banking sector remains underdeveloped, and the economy is largely a cash economy. The government privatized the second largest bank, the National Commercial Bank, in June 2000 and the Savings Bank of Albania, which accounted for 80 percent of all deposits, in early 2004. The private sector now controls most banking assets, and the government plans to sell its 40 percent stake in two small banks: Italian–Albanian Bank and United Albanian Bank. In October 2003, the government sold a 39 percent stake in the state-owned insurance company, INSIG. Overall, according to the Economist Intelligence Unit, "the inadequacy of Albania's financial sector has been an important factor inhibiting the development of the economy. Most transactions are carried out in cash, and banking services remain undeveloped; there are few cash dispensers, and payment by credit card is relatively rare." There are 16 commercial banks, of which 14 were foreign-owned at the end of 2004. Based on the withdrawal of the state from the banking sector, Albania's banking and finance score is 1 point better this year.

WAGES AND PRICES
Score: **2**–Stable (low level of intervention)

The Economist Intelligence Unit reports that government subsidies and price setting affect prices for water, education, railway transport, and electricity. A minimum wage applies to all workers over 16 years old.

PROPERTY RIGHTS
Score: **4**–Stable (low level of protection)

Albania's judicial system weakly enforces the law. The *Financial Times* reports that "European criticism focuses on the Socialists' slow progress with judicial reform and measures to crack down on organized crime. In addition, reports the Economist Intelligence Unit, "some [judges] are corrupt and incompetent, having been appointed solely for political reasons." According to the U.S. Department of Commerce, "because of political pressure, intimidation, endemic corruption, bribery, and limited resources, the judiciary was unable to function independently and efficiently." The pace of judicial reform remains very slow.

REGULATION
Score: **4**–Stable (high level)

Albania has made some progress toward streamlining its bureaucracy. According to the U.S. Department of Commerce, however, "Businesses have complained that in some instances bureaucracy and corruption made obtaining a business license a lengthy and/or costly process." In addition, "The regulatory system is not yet fully transparent. Businesses have difficulty obtaining copies of laws and regulations. Laws and regulations are sometimes inconsistent, leading to unreliability of interpretation. Some ministries have recently undertaken campaigns in order to consult with business, civil society and affected groups about issues in proposed laws and regulations." According to the World Bank, the bureaucratic and monetary costs of starting a business, hiring and firing, and registering property in Albania are moderate.

INFORMAL MARKET
Score: **4**–Stable (high level of activity)

Transparency International's 2004 score for Albania is 2.5. Therefore, Albania's informal market score is 4 this year.

ALGERIA

Rank: 119

Score: 3.46

Category: Mostly Unfree

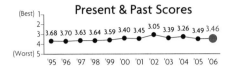

Present & Past Scores

(Best) 1 — 2 — 3 — 4 — (Worst) 5

3.68 3.70 3.63 3.64 3.59 3.40 3.45 3.05 3.39 3.26 3.49 3.46

'95 '96 '97 '98 '99 '00 '01 '02 '03 '04 '05 '06

QUICK STUDY

SCORES

Trade Policy	4
Fiscal Burden	3.6
Government Intervention	4
Monetary Policy	2
Foreign Investment	3
Banking and Finance	4
Wages and Prices	3
Property Rights	4
Regulation	3
Informal Market	4

Population: 31,832,612

Total area: 2,381,740 sq. km

GDP: $60.9 billion

GDP growth rate: 6.8%

GDP per capita: $1,916

Major exports: petroleum, natural gas, and petroleum products

Exports of goods and services: $25.13 billion

Major export trading partners: Italy 19.2%, US 18.7%, France 13.7%, Spain 12.7%

Major imports: capital goods, food and beverages, consumer goods

Imports of goods and services: $14.12 billion

Major import trading partners: France 30.7%, Italy 9.5%, Spain 6.1%, Germany 5.5%

Foreign direct investment (net): $584.6 million

2003 Data (in constant 2000 US dollars)

lgeria gained its independence from France in 1962 and imposed a socialist economic model that retarded economic growth, wasted oil wealth, and exacerbated social, political, and economic problems when oil prices declined in the late 1980s. After the army seized power in January 1992 and cancelled parliamentary elections, Islamic radicals launched a brutal civil war that has claimed more than 100,000 lives. The government gained the upper hand in the late 1990s, and President Abdelaziz Bouteflika negotiated a peace accord with the Islamic Salvation Front, although more radical Islamic groups continue to fight. Bouteflika was re-elected in April 2004 with 83 percent of the vote, largely because of his calls for national reconciliation and improvements in security. His economic reform program, which includes the encouragement of foreign investment, liberalization, and privatization, has been stalled by the military elite, state bureaucrats, and labor unions, which share a vested interest in the current system. Economic prospects have improved as a result of increases in oil production, high dollar oil prices, and growing natural gas exports. Algeria is the world's second largest exporter of natural gas and has the world's fifth largest natural gas reserve and 14th largest oil reserve. Algeria's monetary policy score is 1 point worse this year; however, its trade policy score is 1 point better, and its fiscal burden of government score is 0.3 point better. As a result, Algeria's overall score is 0.03 point better this year.

TRADE POLICY

Score: **4–Better** (high level of protectionism)

According to the World Bank, Algeria's weighted average tariff rate in 2003 (the most recent year for which World Bank data are available) was 12 percent, down from the 15.3 percent for 2002 reported in the 2005 *Index*. Non-tariff barriers take the form of bureaucratic customs clearance procedures. A World Bank survey ranking 51 countries in terms of the number of days required to clear imports through customs identified Algeria as the worst at 23 days. The International Monetary Fund reports that there is corruption in the customs administration. Based on the decreased tariff rate, as well as a revision of the trade factor methodology, Algeria's trade policy score is 1 point better this year.

FISCAL BURDEN OF GOVERNMENT

Score—Income Taxation: **4–Stable** (high tax rates)
Score—Corporate Taxation: **4–Stable** (high tax rates)
Score—Change in Government Expenditures: **2.5–Better** (low decrease)
Final Score: **3.6–Better** (high cost of government)

According to the International Monetary Fund, Algeria's top income tax rate is 40 percent. The top corporate tax rate is 30 percent. In 2003, according to the African Development Bank, government expenditures as a percentage of GDP decreased 1.7 percentage points to 34 percent, compared to a 4.2 percentage point increase in 2002. On net, Algeria's overall fiscal burden of government score is 0.3 point better this year.

GOVERNMENT INTERVENTION IN THE ECONOMY

Score: **4–Stable** (high level)

The World Bank reports that the government consumed 14.1 percent of GDP in 2003. In the same year, based on data from the International Monetary Fund, Algeria received 68.75

percent of its total revenues from state-owned enterprises in the hydrocarbon sector.

MONETARY POLICY
Score: **2**–Worse (low level of inflation)

From 1995 to 2004, Algeria's weighted average annual rate of inflation was 3.14 percent, up from 2.41 percent from 1994 to 2003. As a result, Algeria's monetary policy score is 1 point worse this year.

CAPITAL FLOWS AND FOREIGN INVESTMENT
Score: **3**–Stable (moderate barriers)

In 1993, Algeria revised its investment code to provide equal and nondiscriminatory treatment for all investors. In August 2001, the National Investment Development Agency was created to simplify investment procedures. Foreign ownership of pipelines, however, is prohibited. A 2005 hydrocarbons law made the state-owned energy company Somatrach a purely commercial entity, stripped it of its regulatory functions, and eliminated requirements that foreign firms allow Somatrach a majority stake in any joint venture. Foreign exchange and capital transactions are subject to numerous restrictions. The International Monetary Fund reports that both residents and non-residents may hold foreign exchange accounts, subject to some restrictions. Payments and transfers are subject to various limits, approvals, surrender requirements, and restrictions. According to the IMF, "Capital transfers to any destination abroad are subject to individual approval by the [Bank of Algeria]." Purchase, sale, or issue of capital market securities is permitted through an authorized intermediary.

BANKING AND FINANCE
Score: **4**–Stable (high level of restrictions)

Although a number of foreign banks have a presence in Algeria, the government plays a dominant role in the banking sector. State-owned banks account for over 95 percent of total bank assets. According to the Economist Intelligence Unit, state-owned banks "have tended to lend to loss-making public companies or regime insiders, with little or no credit risk assessments.... [T]he level of non-performing loans continues to be high, damaging banks' solvency and profitability. As a result, credit is expensive and beyond the reach of most private firms and individuals." The EIU reports that an IMF assessment of the banking industry identified as the top priority ending the practice of using the state-owned banks to prop up failing state-owned enterprises with soft loans that are seldom repaid.

WAGES AND PRICES
Score: **3**–Stable (moderate level of intervention)

Although the government has removed some price controls, it still influences prices through subsidies and direct controls on some commodities. According to the Economist Intelligence Unit, a state retail network keeps prices on agricultural goods artificially low. The government establishes a minimum wage.

PROPERTY RIGHTS
Score: **4**–Stable (low level of protection)

The constitution provides for an independent judiciary; according to the U.S. Department of State, however, "Executive branch decrees and influence, interference by the Ministry of the Interior, and inefficiency within the justice system restricted the independence of the judiciary." In addition, "The judicial environment is inefficient and, in fields like the adjudication of intellectual property disputes, suffers from a lack of trained magistrates."

REGULATION
Score: **3**–Stable (moderate level)

According to the World Bank, the cost of starting a business, hiring and firing and registering property in Algeria is high, both in terms of bureaucracy and money. The U.S. Department of Commerce reports that "Algerian commercial law can be complex and technical, with more than 400 legislative and regulatory texts. Many investors consider it blurry and rely on local counsel and agents to ensure that all procedures and rules are followed." Lack of transparent rules also affects businesses. According to the Economist Intelligence Unit, "The shadowy military elite have an enormous influence on political and economic decisions, but remain accountable only to themselves" and "can influence the bureaucracy and the judiciary, resulting in a situation where only businessmen that are connected can prosper." In the first quarter of 2005, the government approved a new hydrocarbon law, which, according to the EIU, will "[strip] away the regulatory functions of the state energy company, Somatrach, and [remove] its right to an automatic majority stake in any oil or gas discovery by a foreign operator." The law provides for the creation of other agencies to regulate tariffs and access to infrastructure.

INFORMAL MARKET
Score: **4**–Stable (high level of activity)

Transparency International's 2004 score for Algeria is 2.7. Therefore, Algeria's informal market score is 4 this year.

ANGOLA

Rank: 139

Score: 3.84

Category: Mostly Unfree

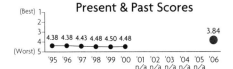

Present & Past Scores

(Best) 1
2
3
4
(Worst) 5

4.38 4.38 4.43 4.48 4.50 4.48   3.84

'95 '96 '97 '98 '99 '00 '01 '02 '03 '04 '05 '06
                      n/a n/a n/a n/a n/a

QUICK STUDY

SCORES

Trade Policy	3.5
Fiscal Burden	2.9
Government Intervention	4.5
Monetary Policy	5
Foreign Investment	4
Banking and Finance	3
Wages and Prices	3
Property Rights	4
Regulation	4
Informal Market	4.5

Population: 13,522,112

Total area: 1,246,700 sq. km

GDP: $11 billion

GDP growth rate: 4.5%

GDP per capita: $814

Major exports: crude oil, diamonds, timber, cotton, coffee, refined petroleum products

Exports of goods and services: $6.3 billion

Major export trading partners: US 47.4%, China 23.2%, France 7.3%

Major imports: electrical equipment and machinery, medicines, food, textiles

Imports of goods and services: $5.7 billion

Major import trading partners: Portugal 17.9%, South Africa 12.2%, US 12.0%, France 6.4%, Brazil 5.7%

Foreign direct investment (net): $1.3 billion

2003 Data (in constant 2000 US dollars)

The 27-year civil war between the National Union for the Total Independence of Angola (UNITA) and the ruling Popular Movement for the Liberation of Angola (MPLA) ended in 2002. Since then, the country has worked to repair and improve the devastated telecommunications, transportation, and energy infrastructure that remains a drag on economic activity. The economy has also been hindered by high, albeit declining, inflation and fiscal deficits caused by enormous off-budget expenditures. The International Monetary Fund has insisted that the government increase budget transparency, but progress has been very slow, particularly with regard to oil revenues. Corruption and patronage remain pervasive. Angola is one of the world's poorest nations, despite extensive oil and gas resources, diamonds, hydroelectric potential, and rich agricultural land. Oil remains the primary driver of the economy, and economic growth has been strong since the end of the conflict due to increased production and higher oil prices. The first elections since 1992 are tentatively scheduled for 2006–2007, and the MPLA is expected to continue its political dominance. The increasing availability of reliable data after several years of peace has made it possible to grade Angola for the first time since 2000.

TRADE POLICY
Score: **3.5**–Stable (high level of protectionism)

According to the World Bank, Angola's weighted average tariff rate in 2002 (the most recent year for which World Bank data are available) was 8.5 percent. According to the U.S. Trade Representative, "Administration of Angola's customs department has improved…. [T]he average port clearance time has fallen from several months to less than two weeks." However, the USTR also reports that import licenses are required for many goods and that specific authorization from various government ministries is required for a broad range of goods, from pharmaceuticals, radios, plants, and postal stamps to fireworks.

FISCAL BURDEN OF GOVERNMENT
Score—Income Taxation: **1.5**–Stable (low tax rates)
Score—Corporate Taxation: **4.5**–Stable (very high tax rates)
Score—Change in Government Expenditures: **1**–Stable (very high decrease)
Final Score: **2.9**–Stable (moderate cost of government)

Angola's top income tax rate is 15 percent. The top corporate tax rate is 35 percent. In 2003, according to the African Development Bank, government expenditures as a percentage of GDP decreased by 5.1 percentage points to 44.7 percent, compared to a 3.5 percentage point increase in 2002.

GOVERNMENT INTERVENTION IN THE ECONOMY
Score: **4.5**–Stable (very high level)

According to the World Bank, the government consumed 29.7 percent of GDP in 2003. In the same year, based on data from the International Monetary Fund, Angola received 75.1 percent of its total revenues from state-owned enterprises and government ownership of property in the oil sector.

MONETARY POLICY
Score: **5**–Stable (very high level of inflation)

Between 1995 and 2004, Angola's weighted average annual rate of inflation was 70.7 percent.

CAPITAL FLOWS AND FOREIGN INVESTMENT
Score: **4**–Stable (high barriers)

Angola's Law on Private Investment (Law 11/03), which replaces the 1994 Foreign Investment Law, provides equal treatment to foreign investors, simplifies investment regulations, and lowers the required investment. According to the U.S. Trade Representative, however, "the new investment law is vague on profit repatriation and includes weak legal safeguards to protect foreign investors. The law also does not allow for international arbitration and requires that any investment dispute be handled in Angolan courts." Foreign investments over $100,000 require government approval. Foreign investment in defense, internal public order, state security, certain banking activities, and the administration of ports and airports is not explicitly prohibited, reports the USTR, but is "assumed to be off-limits." Furthermore, "Obtaining the proper permits and business license to operate in Angola is time-consuming and adds to the cost of investing." The International Monetary Fund reports that capital and money market transactions, real estate transactions, and personal capital movements are subject to strict controls. In most instances, these transactions require central bank approval and/or licensing.

BANKING AND FINANCE
Score: **3**–Stable (moderate level of restrictions)

Angola's rapidly growing banking sector consists of seven commercial banks (four foreign-owned banks, two state-owned banks, and one local private bank); one investment bank (partially state-owned); one small agricultural bank; one small-business fund (partially state-owned); and two representative offices of foreign banks. Foreign banks have been present since 1992. State-owned banks retain substantial influence. However, foreign banks are increasingly competitive and the biggest commercial bank in Angola is a fully owned subsidiary of Portugal's Banco BPI. "Because state and state-affiliated companies enjoy privileged access to loans, often at concessionary rates," reports the U.S. Department of Commerce, "there has been a high rate of bankruptcy. Currently, the banking sector's non-performing loan rate is 5 to 7 percent."

WAGES AND PRICES
Score: **3**–Stable (moderate level of intervention)

The government continues to set, control, or manipulate wage rates and prices in almost all sectors of the economy. According to the Economist Intelligence Unit, "tight control over diamond marketing allows the state diamond marketing company, Sodiam, to force producers to accept below-market prices." The U.S. Department of Commerce reports that a minimum wage is indexed to the rate of inflation.

PROPERTY RIGHTS
Score: **4**–Stable (low level of protection)

The Economist Intelligence Unit reports that one of the greatest risks to business is that the rule of law "cannot be guaranteed through the local justice system and political interference means that foreign business should not expect a level playing field for their operations." According to the U.S. Department of Commerce, "Angola's legal and judicial system suffers from lack of capacity and is not efficient in handling commercial disputes. Legal fees are high, and most businesses avoid taking disputes to court. However, in July 2003, the National Assembly approved the Voluntary Arbitration Law (VAL) to provide a general legal framework for non-judicial arbitration of disputes, except for cases expressly excluded by the law. The VAL awaits official promulgation and is not yet in effect."

REGULATION
Score: **4**–Stable (high level)

According to the World Bank, the cost of starting a business, hiring and firing, and registering property in Angola is very high in terms of both bureaucracy and money. Government regulations are a severe hindrance. "Traditionally," reports the U.S. Department of Commerce, "the regulatory system has been complex, vague, and inconsistently enforced. In many sectors, no effective regulatory system exists due to lack of capacity." In addition, "Petty corruption is a problem due to low civil service salaries and a proliferation of bureaucracy and regulations.... Complicated procedures and long bureaucratic delays sometimes tempt investors to seek quicker service and approval by paying gratuities and facilitation fees."

INFORMAL MARKET
Score: **4.5**–Stable (very high level of activity)

Transparency International's 2004 score for Angola is 2. Therefore, Angola's informal market score is 4.5 this year.

ARGENTINA

Rank: 107

Score: 3.30

Category: Mostly Unfree

Present & Past Scores

(Best) 1
2
3
4
(Worst) 5

2.85 2.58 2.70 2.48 2.23 2.28 2.29 2.63 3.09 3.43 3.49 3.30

'95 '96 '97 '98 '99 '00 '01 '02 '03 '04 '05 '06

QUICK STUDY

SCORES

Trade Policy	3
Fiscal Burden	4
Government Intervention	2
Monetary Policy	3
Foreign Investment	3
Banking and Finance	4
Wages and Prices	3
Property Rights	4
Regulation	3
Informal Market	4

Population: 36,771,840

Total area: 2,766,890 sq. km

GDP: $263.5 billion

GDP growth rate: 8.8%

GDP per capita: $7,165

Major exports: oil seeds and fruits, mineral oils and fuels, cereals, vehicles, vegetable oils

Exports of goods and services: $34.7 billion

Major export trading partners: Brazil 15.8%, Chile 12.0%, US 10.6%, China 8.4%, Spain 4.7%

Major imports: boilers, machines and mechanical equipment, electrical machinery, vehicles, organic chemicals, plastic materials

Imports of goods and services: $19.4 billion

Major import trading partners: Brazil 34.0%, US 16.4%, Germany 5.6%, China 5.2%

Foreign direct investment (net): –$279 million

2003 Data (in constant 2000 US dollars)

After the 2001 crisis that drove a president from office and produced a series of transitional chief executives, new elections brought Nestor Kirchner to power in May 2003. Since then, the state's role in the economy has expanded, primarily through price fixing in some industries and the creation of a state-owned airline and a state-owned energy company. The government is also looking at the possibility of creating a state-owned oil company. An exchange offer for Argentina's $81 billion defaulted debt was completed in May 2005, with 76 percent of bondholders accepting the restructuring. The settlement with the other 24 percent of bondholders was still unresolved as this book was being readied for printing. High GDP growth in the past few years was mostly a result of emergence from deep crisis, high commodity prices, and a debt moratorium, not the government's economic policies. Overall, rather than move with the worldwide tide of opening markets, Argentina's government continues to support price controls, financial restrictions, weak currency, and gross violations of property rights. Argentina's fiscal burden of government score is 0.1 point worse this year, but its trade policy and monetary policy scores are 1 point better. As a result, Argentina's overall score is 0.19 point better this year.

TRADE POLICY
Score: **3–Better** (moderate level of protectionism)

As a member of the Southern Cone Common Market (MERCOSUR), Argentina adheres to a common external tariff that ranges from zero to 25 percent. According to the World Bank, Argentina's weighted average tariff rate in 2004 was 6.3 percent, down from the 11.9 percent for 2002 reported in the 2005 *Index*. Argentina has adopted a number of policies designed to constrain trade, including minimum import prices, quotas, requirements for import permits, phytosanitary rules, anti-dumping investigations, and "other practices to inhibit imports and protect domestic industry," according to the U.S. Department of Commerce. Customs corruption also acts as a non-tariff barrier. Based on the lower tariff rate, as well as a revision of the trade factor methodology, Argentina's trade policy score is 1 point better this year.

FISCAL BURDEN OF GOVERNMENT
Score—Income Taxation: **3.5–Stable** (high tax rates)
Score—Corporate Taxation: **4.5–Stable** (very high tax rates)
Score—Change in Government Expenditures: **3.5–Worse** (low increase)
Final Score: **4–Worse** (high cost of government)

According to Deloitte, Argentina's top income tax rate is 35 percent. The top corporate tax rate is also 35 percent. In 2004, according to the Economist Intelligence Unit, government expenditures as a share of GDP increased by 1 percentage point to 20.1 percent, compared to the 2.9 percentage point decrease in 2003. On net, Argentina's fiscal burden of government score is 0.1 point worse this year.

GOVERNMENT INTERVENTION IN THE ECONOMY
Score: **2–Stable** (low level)

According to the Ministry of Economy and Production, the government consumed 11.1 percent of GDP in 2004. In the same year, based on data from the same source, Argentina received

1.76 percent of its total revenues from state-owned enterprises and government ownership of property.

MONETARY POLICY
Score: **3**–Better (moderate level of inflation)

From 1995 to 2004, Argentina's weighted average annual rate of inflation was 8.08 percent, down from 14.39 percent from 1994 to 2003. As a result, Argentina's monetary policy score is 1 point better this year.

CAPITAL FLOWS AND FOREIGN INVESTMENT
Score: **3**–Stable (moderate barriers)

Argentina's rules and regulations on foreign investment and capital flows are unclear, irregularly enforced, and frequently changed. According to the U.S. Department of Commerce, "Legal uncertainties continue concerning creditor, contract and property rights, and frequent and unpredictable regulatory changes have diminished the attractiveness of some sectors for foreign investors." Most local companies may be wholly owned by foreign investors. Foreign investment is prohibited in a few sectors, including shipbuilding, fishing, border-area real estate, and nuclear power generation. A law passed in June 2003 restricts foreign investment in "cultural goods" such as media and Internet companies to 30 percent unless the foreign investor's country allows greater than 30 percent foreign ownership of its cultural goods. In December 2001, Argentina defaulted on more than $81 billion in government debt—the fifth default in its history. After lengthy negotiations, 76 percent of bondholders accepted a debt restructuring that was worth approximately 35 cents on the dollar. The International Monetary Fund reports that Argentina maintains significant restrictions on capital flows and investment.

BANKING AND FINANCE
Score: **4**–Stable (high level of restrictions)

Although Argentina's banking system is showing signs of recovery, it was devastated by the 2001 economic crisis. The sector, after losing 16 billion pesos in 2002 and 4 billion pesos in 2003, is in an improved financial position and has returned to pre-crisis liquidity levels. Non-performing loans, caused by the economic crisis and the 2002 government ban on asset foreclosures, continue to be a significant problem, and lending remains depressed. Informal financial activity is common. In February 2002, the government converted all dollar deposits at a rate of 1.4 pesos per dollar when the floating exchange rate was around 2 pesos per dollar. Even then, depositors did not have full access to their funds. Banks also have been facing court challenges by depositors demanding the full value of their dollar deposits. Aside from the economic crisis, the government remains heavily involved in the banking sector. The Economist Intelligence Unit reports that the government has 100 percent ownership in four banks, including the country's largest bank, Banco de la Nación.

WAGES AND PRICES
Score: **3**–Stable (moderate level of intervention)

The government imposes price controls on certain products. According to the Economist Intelligence Unit, "The government continues to control prices only in the areas of urban transport; local telephone services; electricity, water and gas distribution at the retail level; and tolls on highways and rivers. However, the specter of rising inflation has resulted in tacit agreements to keep prices stable. The government has signed such agreements with dairy producers, petrol retailers and some pharmaceutical companies." The government also has updated the punishments it can assess on private companies for such practices as "(1) increasing prices for reasons not associated with cost structure; (2) generating profits beyond what the government deems proper...(7) selling goods similar to those with price caps, but that are not regulated." The government mandates a minimum wage.

PROPERTY RIGHTS
Score: **4**–Stable (low level of protection)

In 2001, the government violated contracts with most utility providers, forced several banks to convert their assets into devalued pesos, and defaulted on thousands of domestic and foreign bondholders with virtually no punishment from the courts. According to the Economist Intelligence Unit, "The judiciary suffers from long-standing organizational problems. Traditionally, the power of the executive has undermined its independence and credibility." In addition, reports *The Economist*, "Argentine courts are notoriously slow, inefficient, secretive and corrupt." Another important violation of property rights involves "piquetes," a new form of protest in which the protestors take over private business, causing extensive losses with no effective punishment by either the police or the government.

REGULATION
Score: **3**–Stable (moderate level)

Frequent changes in the regulatory framework after the 2001 crisis have increased investor insecurity. According to the U.S. Department of Commerce, "Businesses in Argentina—foreign and domestic alike—still face problems involving inconsistent application of regulations, fraud and corruption." The labor market remains rigid. The Economist Intelligence Unit reports that severance costs, pension payments, mandatory contributions to a union-run health plan, mandatory holidays and overtime, and payroll taxes are among the highest barriers to creating jobs. According to the World Bank, the cost of starting a business, hiring and firing, and registering property is very high in terms of both time and money.

INFORMAL MARKET
Score: **4**–Stable (high level of activity)

Transparency International's 2004 score for Argentina is 2.5. Therefore, Argentina's informal market score is 4 this year.

ARMENIA

Rank: 27

Score: 2.26

Category: Mostly Free

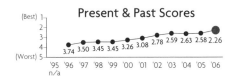

Present & Past Scores

(Best) 1
2
3
4
(Worst) 5

3.74 3.50 3.45 3.45 3.26 3.08 2.78 2.59 2.63 2.58 2.26

'95 '96 '97 '98 '99 '00 '01 '02 '03 '04 '05 '06
n/a

QUICK STUDY

SCORES

Trade Policy	2
Fiscal Burden	2.1
Government Intervention	2
Monetary Policy	2
Foreign Investment	1
Banking and Finance	1
Wages and Prices	2
Property Rights	3
Regulation	4
Informal Market	3.5

Population: 3,055,630

Total area: 29,800 sq. km

GDP: $2.7 billion

GDP growth rate: 13.9%

GDP per capita: $884

Major exports: mineral products, diamonds, copper ore, scrap metal, machinery and equipment

Exports of goods and services: $867 million

Major export trading partners: Belgium 18.0%, UK 16.6%, Israel 15.6%, Russia 12.0%, US 6.2%

Major imports: natural gas, petroleum, mineral products, prepared foodstuffs

Imports of goods and services: $1.4 billion

Major import trading partners: Belgium 11.6%, Russia 11.6%, Israel 11.4%, US 9.5%

Foreign direct investment (net): $147 million

2003 Data (in constant 2000 US dollars)

President Robert Kocharian has a majority in the National Assembly, but there are frictions within the ruling coalition. After allegations of ballot rigging in the 2003 presidential and legislative elections, the government developed election code amendments in cooperation with the Organization for Security and Cooperation in Europe. Economic and fiscal policies and a poverty-reduction strategy developed in cooperation with the World Bank and the International Monetary Fund continue to guide economic decision-making. Pressure from tax authorities and introduction of a 1 percent gross-receipts tax have increased tax collections, but government spending on wages and social benefits has also risen. The banking sector improved in 2004, posting a solid profit after years of losses, defending the currency against flight to dollars, and consolidating commercial banks. Resolution of the Nagorno–Karabakh border dispute may have been helped by an April 2005 meeting of Armenian and Azerbaijani foreign ministers. Turkey is seeking to establish diplomatic relations and has proposed a joint commission to probe the mass killings of Armenians in the last years of the Ottoman Empire—the cause of a rift that has lasted for nearly a century. As of June 30, 2005, Armenia was negotiating with the U.S. for Millennium Challenge Account assistance. Armenia's fiscal burden of government score is 0.2 point better this year; in addition, its government intervention and informal market scores are 0.5 point better, and its foreign investment and wages and prices scores are 1 point better. As a result, Armenia's overall score is 0.32 point better this year.

TRADE POLICY
Score: **2**–Stable (low level of protectionism)

According to the World Bank, Armenia's weighted average tariff rate in 2001 (the most recent year for which World Bank data are available) was 2.2 percent. (The World Bank has revised the figure for 2001 downward from the 2.5 percent reported in the 2005 *Index*.) The U.S. Department of Commerce reports that "improper implementation of the Customs Code remains a barrier to trade. According to a recent study by the World Bank in partnership with the Armenian Ministry of Trade and Economic Development, more than half of medium-sized companies engaged in foreign trade operations described customs administration as a major obstacle to doing business." The Economist Intelligence Unit reports that non-tariff restrictions on imports are limited to weapons, pharmaceuticals, and agricultural chemicals and that such restrictions on exports are limited to nuclear-related products, military goods, medicines, live animals and plants, and textiles destined for the European Union. Based on the revised trade factor methodology, Armenia's trade policy score is unchanged.

FISCAL BURDEN OF GOVERNMENT
Score—Income Taxation: **2**–Stable (low tax rates)
Score—Corporate Taxation: **2**–Stable (low tax rates)
Score—Change in Government Expenditures: **2.5**–Better (low decrease)
Final Score: **2.1**–Better (low cost of government)

The Embassy of Armenia reports that Armenia's top income tax rate is 20 percent. The top corporate tax rate is 20 percent. In 2004, based on data from the Ministry of Finance and Economy, government expenditures as a share of GDP decreased 1.6 percentage points to 17.6 percent, compared to a 0.2 percentage point decrease in 2003. On net, Armenia's fiscal burden of government score is 0.2 point better this year.

GOVERNMENT INTERVENTION IN THE ECONOMY
Score: **2**–Better (low level)

The World Bank reports that the government consumed 10.3 percent of GDP in 2003. In the same year, based on data from the International Monetary Fund, Armenia received 4.43 percent of its total revenues from state-owned enterprises and government ownership of property, down from the 5.7 percent reported in the 2005 *Index*. As a result, Armenia's government intervention score is 0.5 point better this year.

MONETARY POLICY
Score: **2**–Stable (low level of inflation)

Between 1995 and 2004, Armenia's weighted average annual rate of inflation was 5.71 percent.

CAPITAL FLOWS AND FOREIGN INVESTMENT
Score: **1**–Better (very low barriers)

Armenia offers equal official treatment to foreign investors, who have the same right to establish businesses as native Armenians in nearly all sectors of the economy. The government continues to restrict ownership of land by foreigners, although they may lease it. The International Monetary Fund reports that there are no restrictions or controls on the holding of foreign exchange accounts, invisible transactions, or current transfers and no repatriation requirements. Based on evidence of openness, Armenia's capital flows and foreign investment score is 1 point better this year.

BANKING AND FINANCE
Score: **1**–Stable (very low level of restrictions)

The central bank adopted a reform and consolidation program in 1994 after several banks had collapsed. The banking system is improving as supervision increases, regulation becomes more efficient, and minimum capital requirements are increased. The Economist Intelligence Unit reports that all banks now adhere to international accounting standards. Under the revised rules and standards, many banks have closed or merged; the number of banks fell from 58 in 1994 to 20 as of December 2004, and further consolidation was expected to occur after a new minimum capital requirement was implemented in July 2005. However, banks remain hindered by the difficulty in debt recovery that is caused by a weak judicial system. Foreign banks are permitted to operate and command a significant portion of banking capital. The Ministry of Finance and Economy, which regulates the insurance industry, allows the presence of foreign insurance companies. The last state-owned bank, Armsberbank, was sold in September 2001.

WAGES AND PRICES
Score: **2**–Better (low level of intervention)

According to the U.S. Department of Commerce, "Prices are largely determined by supply and demand." However, the state continues to control prices for energy and natural gas. At the beginning of 2004, the government raised the minimum wage. The Department of Commerce reports that the government sets the price of the dollar. Based on new information regarding the government's control of prices, Armenia's wages and prices score is 1 point better this year.

PROPERTY RIGHTS
Score: **3**–Stable (moderate level of protection)

The judiciary is weak and subject to influence from the Executive. According to the Economist Intelligence Unit, "A further consideration [for investors] is the underdeveloped and corrupt judiciary, which is a substantial impediment to the enforcement of contractual rights and obligations, thereby keeping business risk high." The U.S. Department of Commerce reports that "Disputes to which the Armenian government is not a party may be brought before an Armenian or any other competent court, as provided for by law or by agreement of the parties. There is a special Economic Court that hears commercial disputes."

REGULATION
Score: **4**–Stable (high level)

Regulations are applied haphazardly. According to the Economist Intelligence Unit, the business environment is risky "because of weak implementation of the country's otherwise favourable business legislation, but also because of the corruption that stems from the excessive role of the state in the economy." In addition, "a high level of corruption…results in firms directing activity underground in order to reduce their vulnerability to extortion by government officials." The U.S. Department of Commerce reports that "bribery is widespread and is the most common form of corruption…."

INFORMAL MARKET
Score: **3.5**–Better (high level of activity)

Transparency International's 2004 score for Armenia is 3.1. Therefore, Armenia's informal market score is 3.5 this year— 0.5 point better than last year.

AUSTRALIA

Rank: 9

Score: 1.84

Category: Free

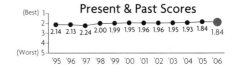
Present & Past Scores

(Best) 1
2
3
4
(Worst) 5

2.14 2.13 2.24 2.00 1.99 1.95 1.96 1.96 1.95 1.93 1.84 **1.84**

'95 '96 '97 '98 '99 '00 '01 '02 '03 '04 '05 '06

QUICK STUDY

SCORES

Trade Policy	2.5
Fiscal Burden	3.9
Government Intervention	2
Monetary Policy	1
Foreign Investment	2
Banking and Finance	1
Wages and Prices	2
Property Rights	1
Regulation	2
Informal Market	1

Population: 20,200,000

Total area: 7,713,000 sq. km

GDP: $446.5 billion

GDP growth rate: 3.6%

GDP per capita: $22,103

Major exports: coal, gold, meat, crude petroleum, iron ore, aluminum, machinery, financial services, insurance, travel services

Exports of goods and services: $120.3 billion

Major export trading partners: Japan 18.9%, China 9.3%, US 8.1%, South Korea 7.8%

Major imports: passenger motor vehicles, aircraft and parts, computers, medicaments, travel services, financial services, insurance

Imports of goods and services: $103.3 billion

Major import trading partners: US 14.5%, China 12.7%, Japan 11.8%, Germany 5.8%

Foreign direct investment (net): $25.5 billion

2004 Data (in constant 2000 US dollars)

With a highly developed and sophisticated economy, Australia has enjoyed almost 14 years of uninterrupted economic growth—the longest sustained expansion in its history. Prime Minister John Howard became the second longest-serving prime minister (after Sir Robert Menzies) in Australian history when his conservative coalition achieved victory in the October 2004 general election. Howard had been subject to considerable criticism based on Australia's role in Iraq, but the state of the country's economy was enough to assure his fourth term. Australia's public debt remains at around 18 percent of GDP—the lowest in the developed world—and its unemployment is close to a 20-year low at 5.6 percent. According to *The Economist*, this stunning performance stems to a significant degree from "sound monetary and fiscal policies and from structural reforms." Deregulation, more flexible labor practices, and lower trade barriers have increased productivity. Driven largely by a services sector that accounts for about 70 percent of GDP, Australia has transformed itself into an internationally competitive exporter of technologies, services, and high value–added manufactured goods. The U.S.–Australia Free Trade Agreement went into effect in January 2005. Australia's overall score is unchanged this year.

TRADE POLICY
Score: **2.5**–Stable (moderate level of protectionism)

According to the World Bank, Australia's weighted average tariff rate in 2004 was 3.8 percent, down from the 3.9 percent for 2002 reported in the 2005 *Index*. The U.S. Trade Representative reports that non-tariff barriers include "extremely stringent…sanitary and phytosanitary (SPS) measures, resulting in restrictions and prohibitions on imports of many agricultural products." Tariff-rate quotas are applied to some cheese items and tobacco. Based on the revised trade factor methodology, Australia's trade policy score is unchanged.

FISCAL BURDEN OF GOVERNMENT
Score—Income Taxation: **4.5**–Stable (very high tax rates)
Score—Corporate Taxation: **4**–Stable (high tax rates)
Score—Change in Government Expenditures: **3**–Stable (very low decrease)
Final Score: **3.9**–Stable (high cost of government)

According to Deloitte, Australia's top income tax rate is 47 percent. The top corporate tax rate is 30 percent. In 2004, government expenditures as a share of GDP decreased 0.6 percentage point to 35.5 percent, compared to a 0.3 percentage point decrease in 2003.

GOVERNMENT INTERVENTION IN THE ECONOMY
Score: **2**–Stable (low level)

Data from the Australian Bureau of Statistics indicate that the government consumed 18.6 percent of GDP in 2004. In fiscal year 2004 (July 2003 to June 2004), based on data from Australia's Treasury Department, the government received 2.93 percent of its total revenues from state-owned enterprises and government ownership of property.

MONETARY POLICY
Score: **1**–Stable (very low level of inflation)

From 1995 to 2004, Australia's weighted average annual rate of inflation was 2.58 percent.

 ## CAPITAL FLOWS AND FOREIGN INVESTMENT
Score: **2**–Stable (low barriers)

Australia's economy is open to foreign investment, and foreign investors receive national treatment. The Foreign Investment Review Board requires notification of some proposed investment. The International Monetary Fund reports that proposals to start new businesses with an investment of A$10 million must also receive prior authorization. The government accepts most of these proposals routinely, although it may reject them if the investment is determined not to be consistent with the country's "national interest," national security, or economic development concerns. While no sector is completely closed, foreign investment in media, banking, airlines, airports, shipping, urban and residential real estate, and telecommunications is subject to limitations. Foreign investors with investments greater than A$50 million, involving acquisition of 15 percent for a single firm or 40 percent for two or more unrelated foreign interests in an Australian business, must have prior authorization.

 ## BANKING AND FINANCE
Score: **1**–Stable (very low level of restrictions)

Australia has a modern, competitive financial system. Banks are relatively free of government control, and foreign banks may be licensed as branches or subsidiaries and may offer a full range of banking operations. The Australian embassy reports that as of June 2005, there were 14 domestic and 10 foreign bank subsidiaries operating in Australia. There were also 27 foreign bank branches, 14 building societies, and 168 credit unions. There are no government-owned banks. The government has focused on streamlining and reforming financial-sector regulation and does not affect the allocation of credit.

 ## WAGES AND PRICES
Score: **2**–Stable (low level of intervention)

The market determines most wages and almost all prices. There are no national price controls on goods, but states retain the power to impose their own price controls. According to the Economist Intelligence Unit, "There are several price regulating laws—for example, on price-capping in telecommunications." In addition, reports the U.S. Department of Commerce, "The national regulator, the Australian Competition and Consumer Commission...has the power...to investigate, vet or monitor the prices charged by businesses. The Price Surveillance Act gives the Australian Competition and Consumer Commission...power to examine the prices of selected goods and services to promote competitive pricing wherever possible and restrain price rises in markets where competition is less than effective."

 ## PROPERTY RIGHTS
Score: **1**–Stable (very high level of protection)

Property rights are well protected. According to the Economist Intelligence Unit, "Contractual agreements...are protected by the rule of law and the independence of the judiciary...although backlogs in the court lists can delay cases coming for trial for several years.... [A]buse of political influence is extremely rare." Government expropriation is highly unlikely.

 ## REGULATION
Score: **2**–Stable (low level)

According to the World Bank, the cost of starting a business, hiring and firing, and registering property is low in terms of both time and money. However, environmental regulations, generated primarily by the states, may not be uniformly applied. "The civil service is also of excellent quality," reports the Economist Intelligence Unit. "There is no entrenched institutional corruption in the bureaucracy, and abuse of political influence is extremely rare." In addition, "In areas of the economy dominated by small businesses, the government favors self-regulation with 'light-handed' intervention by government.... If [the government] is convinced that self regulation is not working, it has the power under the Trade Practices Act to declare the code of conduct mandatory." Labor laws are somewhat burdensome. An Office of Regulation Review monitors new and existing regulations to determine the costs they would impose on business. The level of corruption is very low.

 ## INFORMAL MARKET
Score: **1**–Stable (very low level of activity)

Transparency International's 2004 score for Australia is 8.8. Therefore, Australia's informal market score is 1 this year.

> If Australia were to improve its trade policy score, it would qualify for the Global Free Trade Alliance.

AUSTRIA

Rank: 18

Score: 1.95

Category: Free

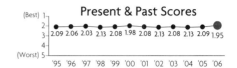

Present & Past Scores

(Best) 1
2
3
4
(Worst) 5

2.09 2.06 2.03 2.13 2.08 1.98 2.08 2.13 2.08 2.13 2.09 1.95

'95 '96 '97 '98 '99 '00 '01 '02 '03 '04 '05 '06

QUICK STUDY

SCORES

Trade Policy	2
Fiscal Burden	3.5
Government Intervention	2
Monetary Policy	1
Foreign Investment	2
Banking and Finance	2
Wages and Prices	2
Property Rights	1
Regulation	3
Informal Market	1

Population: 8,200,000

Total area: 83,858 sq. km

GDP: $203 billion

GDP growth rate: 2.0%

GDP per capita: $24,756

Major exports: machinery, consumer goods, chemical products, food, drink and tobacco, paper, travel services, financial services, insurance

Exports of goods and services: $107.7 billion

Major export trading partners: Germany 32.1%, Italy 8.6%, US 6.0%, Switzerland 4.5%

Major imports: transport equipment, consumer goods, raw materials, financial services, insurance, travel services

Imports of goods and services: $106.9 billion

Major import trading partners: Germany 42.6%, Italy 6.8%, France 4.0%, US 3.3%

Foreign direct investment (net): –$2.3 billion

2004 Data (in constant 2000 US dollars)

During the past decade, the government of Austria has relinquished control of formerly nationalized oil and gas, steel, and engineering companies and has deregulated telecommunications and electricity, yet foreign investors continue to face rigidities, barriers to market entry, and elaborate regulations. For example, in October 2004, the government shied away from promises to privatize Telekom Austria. This, following a failure to partially privatize the postal service, left the government's policy in tatters. People's Party Chancellor Wolfgang Schuessel, however, has accelerated the pace of market reform. A major tax reform initiative, simplifying both wage and income taxes, was enacted in May 2004. Corporate tax rates were reduced from 34 percent to 25 percent, which is among the lowest rates in Western Europe. Parliamentary elections led to reconfiguration of the fragile governing coalition in February 2003. Since then, support for the People's Party's coalition partner, the far-right Freedom Party, has declined, leading to a split in the Freedom Party, with a small group of party members remaining in government. Such an outcome would seem to vindicate the chancellor's controversial decision to go into government with the Freedom Party. In 2004, GDP grew by 2 percent—a higher rate than was experienced by Austria's economically moribund German neighbor. Austria's fiscal burden of government score is 0.9 point better this year, and its informal market score is 0.5 point better. As a result, its overall score is 0.14 point better this year, causing Austria to be classified as a "free" country.

TRADE POLICY
Score: **2**–Stable (low level of protectionism)

Austria's trade policy is the same as the policies of other members of the European Union. In 2003, according to the World Bank, the common EU weighted average tariff rate was 1.3 percent, down from the 2.4 percent for 2002 reported in the 2005 *Index*. According to the U.S. Department of Commerce, "The most important tariff quotas for manufactured goods are on chemicals and electronics. Both are administered on a first-come, first-served licensing basis." The EU requires quotas for many goods, especially agricultural products. Based on the revised trade factor methodology, Austria's trade policy score is unchanged.

FISCAL BURDEN OF GOVERNMENT
Score—Income Taxation: **5**–Stable (very high tax rates)
Score—Corporate Taxation: **3**–Better (moderate tax rates)
Score—Change in Government Expenditures: **3**–Better (very low decrease)
Final Score: **3.5**–Better (high cost of government)

According to Deloitte, Austria's top income tax rate is 50 percent. The top corporate tax rate is 25 percent, down from 34 percent. In 2004, government expenditures as a share of GDP decreased 0.2 percentage point to 50.6 percent, compared to a 0.2 percentage point increase in 2003. On net, Austria's fiscal burden of government score is 0.9 point better this year.

GOVERNMENT INTERVENTION IN THE ECONOMY
Score: **2**–Stable (low level)

According to the Austrian National Bank, the government consumed 17.8 percent of GDP in 2004. In the same year, based on data from the Austrian Federal Finance Agency, Austria received 3.2 percent of its total revenues from state-owned enterprises and government ownership of property.

MONETARY POLICY
Score: **1**–Stable (very low level of inflation)

Austria is a member of the euro zone. From 1995 to 2004, Austria's weighted average annual rate of inflation was 1.89 percent.

CAPITAL FLOWS AND FOREIGN INVESTMENT
Score: **2**–Stable (low barriers)

Austria welcomes most foreign direct investment and does not officially discriminate against foreign investors. According to the U.S. Department of Commerce, "There are no formal sectoral or geographic restrictions on foreign investment." Foreign investment is forbidden in arms and explosives, as well as industries in which the state has a monopoly (casinos, printing of banknotes, and minting coins). The International Monetary Fund reports that restrictions exist for non-residents in the auditing and legal professions, transportation, and electric power generation. There are no controls or requirements on current transfers, access to foreign exchange, or repatriation of profits. Although the national government no longer imposes restrictions on foreign purchases of land, the International Monetary Fund reports that real estate transactions are subject to approval by local authorities.

BANKING AND FINANCE
Score: **2**–Stable (low level of restrictions)

Austrian banks offer services ranging from credit to finance, and the government permits savings banks to perform commercial banking functions, including the brokering of securities and mutual funds. According to the Economist Intelligence Unit, there were 895 banks as of June 2004, but most of these were small institutions targeting farming businesses. The EIU confirms that foreign banks have a significant presence: "In 2002, 27 percent of all assets and 29 percent of all liabilities were of foreign origin." Although Austrian political parties have historically maintained close ties with the large banks, modernization and liberalization of the financial sector has reduced this relationship. "In January 2001, Bank Austria merged with the Bavarian HypoVereinsbank (HVB), creating Europe's third-largest banking group (dominated by the German partner)," reports the EIU. "This marked the end of political influence over a large part of Austria's financial sector."

WAGES AND PRICES
Score: **2**–Stable (low level of intervention)

Prices are determined primarily by the market, although the government heavily subsidizes rail travel. The government also affects agricultural prices through its participation in the Common Agricultural Policy, which heavily subsidizes agricultural goods. Austria does not maintain a minimum wage; minimum wages are determined by annual collective bargaining agreements between employers and employee trade unions.

PROPERTY RIGHTS
Score: **1**–Stable (very high level of protection)

Property is very secure in Austria. The Economist Intelligence Unit reports that "contractual agreements are very secure, and the protection of both private property and intellectual property [is] well established."

REGULATION
Score: **3**–Stable (moderate level)

Austria's regulatory system is characterized in some sectors by complexity and slow bureaucratic procedures. EU membership adds regulations that are burdensome and not always transparent. "The Austrian government has made progress in streamlining its complex and time consuming regulatory environment," reports the U.S. Department of Commerce. "In general, the time for obtaining all necessary permits has been reduced to about three months, except for large projects requiring an environmental impact assessment." According to the World Bank, the cost of starting a business, hiring and firing workers, and registering property is moderate in terms of both time and money. However, according to the Austrian Trade Commission, businesses need to file a separate application for a license and registration in the commercial register. The Economist Intelligence Unit reports that "Austria's per-employee cost of fringe benefits is high, at around 100% of base salary"—one of the highest in the European Union.

INFORMAL MARKET
Score: **1**–Better (very low level of activity)

Transparency International's 2004 score for Austria is 8.4. Therefore, Austria's informal market score is 1 this year—0.5 point better than last year.

> If Austria were to improve its regulation score, it would qualify for the Global Free Trade Alliance.

AZERBAIJAN

Rank: 123

Score: 3.51

Category: Mostly Unfree

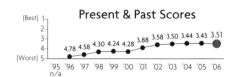

Present & Past Scores

(Best) 1
2
3
4
(Worst) 5

4.78 4.58 4.30 4.24 4.28 3.88 3.58 3.50 3.44 3.43 3.51

'95 '96 '97 '98 '99 '00 '01 '02 '03 '04 '05 '06
n/a

QUICK STUDY

SCORES

Trade Policy	3
Fiscal Burden	3.6
Government Intervention	3
Monetary Policy	2
Foreign Investment	4
Banking and Finance	4
Wages and Prices	3
Property Rights	4
Regulation	4
Informal Market	4.5

Population: 8,233,000

Total area: 86,600 sq. km

GDP: $7.1 billion

GDP growth rate: 11.2%

GDP per capita: $865

Major exports: oil and gas, machinery and equipment, cotton, textiles, foodstuffs

Exports of goods and services: $2.9 billion

Major export trading partners: Italy 34.1%, Czech Republic 12.3%, Germany 10.3%, France 8.1%, Turkey 5.8%

Major imports: machinery and equipment, oil products, foodstuffs, metals, chemicals

Imports of goods and services: $4.7 billion

Major import trading partners: Russia 15.5%, Turkey 12.0%, UK 8.7%, Germany 8.1%, US 4.6%

Foreign direct investment (net): $2.2 billion

2003 Data (in constant 2000 US dollars)

Ilham Aliyev, son of former President Heydar Aliyev, has followed in his father's footsteps. After winning what many viewed as an unfair presidential election in October 2003, he began to dismiss government ministers and crack down on the opposition. Because Azerbaijan is a major oil exporter, foreign direct investment in the energy and related industries has been strong. Rising oil revenues have given the government budget a solid surplus, and the reserves of the State Oil Fund, set up in 1999, have increased to $950 million. At the same time, government spending, mainly on health care and education, has risen as part of Azerbaijan's commitment to the International Monetary Fund's poverty reduction and growth plan. According to the World Bank, Azerbaijan is one of the leaders among the Commonwealth of Independent States in privatization of land. Preoccupation with the oil industry, however, has diverted state attention from non–oil-sector development and slowed down judicial and legal reforms. Rising oil exports should provide a steady cash flow and generate strong economic growth. There is also ongoing discussion regarding construction of an American military base in Azerbaijan—a move that could engender opposition from both Russia and Iran. Azerbaijan's trade policy score is 0.5 point better this year; however, its fiscal burden of government score is 0.3 point worse, and its monetary policy score is 1 point worse. As a result, Azerbaijan's overall score is 0.08 point worse this year.

 TRADE POLICY
Score: **3–Better** (moderate level of protectionism)

According to the World Bank, Azerbaijan's weighted average tariff rate in 2002 (the most recent year for which World Bank data are available) was 6.2 percent, down from the 7.9 percent for 2001 reported in the 2005 *Index*, based on International Monetary Fund data. "Non-tariff barriers," reports the U.S. Department of Commerce, "include a weak and unpredictable legal regime, arbitrary customs administration, clear conflicts of interest in regulatory/commercial matters, and corruption. The [government's] inadequate IPR protections amount to a trade barrier. Alcoholic beverages and tobacco products are subject to both quantitative restrictions and import licenses." Based on the lower tariff rate, as well as a revision of the trade factor methodology, Azerbaijan's trade policy score is 0.5 point better this year.

 FISCAL BURDEN OF GOVERNMENT
Score—Income Taxation: **3.5–Stable** (high tax rates)
Score—Corporate Taxation: **3–Better** (moderate tax rates)
Score—Change in Government Expenditures: **5–Worse** (very high increase)
Final Score: **3.6–Worse** (high cost of government)

The Ministry of Taxes reports that Azerbaijan's top income tax rate is 35 percent. The top corporate tax rate is 24 percent, down from 25 percent. According to the Asian Development Bank, government expenditures as a share of GDP increased by 6.4 percentage points to 27.2 percent in 2003, compared to a 0.7 percentage point increase in 2002. On net, Azerbaijan's fiscal burden of government score is 0.3 point worse this year.

 GOVERNMENT INTERVENTION IN THE ECONOMY
Score: **3–Stable** (moderate level)

According to the World Bank, the government consumed 11.7 percent of GDP in 2003. In

95

2004, based on data from the Ministry of Finance, Azerbaijan received 10.75 percent of its total revenues from state-owned enterprises and government ownership of property.

MONETARY POLICY
Score: 2–Worse (low level of inflation)

From 1995 to 2004, Azerbaijan's weighted average annual rate of inflation was 5.94 percent, up from 2.36 percent from 1994 to 2003. As a result, Azerbaijan's monetary policy score is 1 point worse this year.

CAPITAL FLOWS AND FOREIGN INVESTMENT
Score: 4–Stable (high barriers)

The government officially welcomes foreign investment, but according to the U.S. Department of Commerce, "government bureaucracy, weak legal institutions, and predatory behavior by politically connected monopoly interests have severely hindered investment outside of the energy sector." The government prohibits investments in national security and defense sectors and restricts investment in government-controlled sectors like energy, mobile telephony, and oil and gas. The International Monetary Fund reports that the Azerbaijan National Bank regulates most foreign exchange transactions and foreign exchange accounts. Payments and transfers are subject to documentation requirements and quantitative limits. The central bank must authorize most capital transactions. Direct investment abroad by residents, including real estate transactions, requires central bank approval.

BANKING AND FINANCE
Score: 4–Stable (high level of restrictions)

Azerbaijan's banking system, which consists of 44 banks, including two state-owned banks, is weak, inefficient, and burdened by non-performing loans. Most transactions in the economy are conducted in cash. The U.S. Department of Commerce reports that "lack of credit is a key constraint to the development of private business in Azerbaijan…. Outside of the donor-backed credit lines, there is essentially no bank credit exceeding 12–18 months." The central bank raised minimum capital requirements, but most commercial banks do not meet this standard. According to the Economist Intelligence Unit, "The sector is dominated by two state-owned banks—United Universal Bank (UUB) and International Bank of Azerbaijan (IBA)—which together account for over half of the banking sector's total assets." The International Monetary Fund reports that plans to sell the government stake in IBA have been delayed. "[T]he financial sector is marginal in terms of financing the economy and tends to lend at very high interest rates," reports the EIU. "Some reform of the banking sector may even lead to a temporary shrinkage in the size of the financial sector as non-viable banks are closed by authorities." Foreign banks have a minimal presence.

WAGES AND PRICES
Score: 3–Stable (moderate level of intervention)

The government sets some prices and keeps others artificially low through subsidies. "A major economic policy issue," reports the Economist Intelligence Unit, "is that domestic energy prices are distorted and payment is difficult to enforce. Although the government unified the domestic and export wholesale prices of oil and natural gas in 2003, the retail price remains extremely low…." The government sets the nationwide administrative minimum wage by decree and, according to the EIU, also heavily subsidizes the agricultural industry.

PROPERTY RIGHTS
Score: 4–Stable (low level of protection)

The legal system does not provide sufficient protection for private property. "As in most post-Soviet republics," reports the Economist Intelligence Unit, "the judiciary is the least developed branch of the government. Judicial and police corruption is widespread…." According to the U.S. Department of Commerce, "Corruption appears most pervasive in the regulatory, tax and dispute settlement systems. Problems in the quality, reliability and transparency of governance, as well as abuse of the regulatory system and poor contract enforcement, significantly impede the ability of many companies to do business in Azerbaijan…. [P]olitically connected businesses appear to have benefited from government regulatory and other decisions to achieve effective control over several lucrative sectors of the economy."

REGULATION
Score: 4–Stable (high level)

The procedure for establishing a business is complicated. The U.S. Department of Commerce reports that "Azerbaijan remains a difficult place to do business given arbitrary tax and customs administration, a weak court system, monopolistic regulation of the market, and corruption." In addition, "The lack of transparent policies and effective laws to establish clear rules and foster competition are particularly serious impediments to investment…. Information on decisions implementing laws and regulations is frequently difficult or impossible to obtain. Ready access to government rules and regulations is an impediment to doing business…. Corruption is a significant deterrent to investment in Azerbaijan."

INFORMAL MARKET
Score: 4.5–Stable (very high level of activity)

Transparency International's 2004 score for Azerbaijan is 1.9. Therefore, Azerbaijan's informal market score is 4.5 this year.

THE BAHAMAS

Rank: 27
Score: 2.26
Category: Mostly Free

Present & Past Scores

(Best) 1
2
3
4
(Worst) 5

2.36 2.09 2.05 2.16 2.16 2.23 2.23 2.06 2.15 2.25 2.25 2.26

'95 '96 '97 '98 '99 '00 '01 '02 '03 '04 '05 '06

QUICK STUDY

SCORES

Trade Policy	5
Fiscal Burden	1.6
Government Intervention	2
Monetary Policy	1
Foreign Investment	3
Banking and Finance	2
Wages and Prices	3
Property Rights	1
Regulation	2
Informal Market	2

Population: 317,413

Total area: 13,940 sq. km

GDP: $5.1 billion

GDP growth rate: 1.9%

GDP per capita: $16,067

Major exports: mineral products, chemicals, rum, vegetables, pharmaceuticals, travel services, transportation, financial and insurance services

Exports of goods and services: $600 million

Major export trading partners: US 34.7%, Spain 10.5%, Germany 7.7%, France 7.6%

Major imports: machinery, manufactured goods, mineral fuels, chemicals, food and live animals, transportation, financial and insurance services

Imports of goods and services: $1.53 billion

Major import trading partners: US 20.8%, South Korea 17.4%, Italy 11.4%, France 9.1%, Brazil 7.5%

Foreign direct investment (net): $136.8 million

2003 Data (in constant 2000 US dollars)

The Bahamas is a small, prosperous nation of islands located 45 miles off the U.S. Atlantic coast. It achieved independence within the British Commonwealth in 1973, and its stable, democratic government and absence of corporate and personal taxes continue to provide a welcoming haven for international commerce and tourism. Banking accounts for 15 percent of GDP, and more than 300 banks and trust companies are licensed to do business. However, stronger money-laundering laws and enforcement of business regulations during the past decade have caused some foreign businesses to leave. The government depends on high tariffs for income. Thus, the Free Trade Area of the Americas and proposed Caribbean Single Market and Economy, which would establish a single market and economy among the 15 English-speaking Caribbean states, would make it necessary to finance government operations by other means. Tourism, which accounts for 60 percent of GDP, has recovered from its initial contraction after the September 11, 2001, attacks on the United States and remains heavily dependent on the strength of the U.S. economy. The Bahamas' fiscal burden of government score is 0.1 point worse this year. As a result, its overall score is 0.01 point worse this year.

 TRADE POLICY
Score: **5**–Stable (very high level of protectionism)

According to the World Bank, the Bahamas' average tariff rate in 2003 (the most recent year for which World Bank data are available) was 34 percent. The U.S. Department of Commerce reports that the government "charges a seven percent 'stamp tax' on most imports. Higher stamp taxes are charged on some duty free goods, including tourist items such as china, crystal, wristwatches, clocks, jewelry, table linens, leather goods, perfume, wine and liquor." The government also restricts imports of some agricultural goods through import permits. Based on the revised trade factor methodology, the Bahamas' trade policy score is unchanged.

 FISCAL BURDEN OF GOVERNMENT
Score—Income Taxation: **1**–Stable (very low tax rates)
Score—Corporate Taxation: **1**–Stable (very low tax rates)
Score—Change in Government Expenditures: **3.5**–Worse (low increase)
Final Score: **1.6**–Worse (low cost of government)

The Bahamas has no income tax, no corporate income tax, no capital gains tax, no inheritance tax, and no value-added tax. In 2003, according to data from the Central Bank of The Bahamas, government expenditures as a share of GDP increased 0.8 percentage point to 20.7 percent, compared to a 0.5 percentage point decrease in 2002. On net, the Bahamas' fiscal burden of government score is 0.1 point worse this year.

 GOVERNMENT INTERVENTION IN THE ECONOMY
Score: **2**–Stable (low level)

According to the Central Bank of The Bahamas, the government consumed 11.3 percent of GDP in 2004. In fiscal year 2003–2004, based on data from the Ministry of Finance, the Bahamas received 4.94 percent of its revenues from state-owned enterprises and government ownership of property.

MONETARY POLICY
Score: **1**–Stable (very low level of inflation)

From 1995 to 2004, the Bahamas' weighted average annual rate of inflation was 1.55 percent.

CAPITAL FLOWS AND FOREIGN INVESTMENT
Score: **3**–Stable (moderate barriers)

The Bahamian government restricts foreign investment in a number of sectors. According to the U.S. Department of Commerce, "Reserved businesses include: wholesale and retail operations; commission agencies engaged in the import/export trade; real estate and domestic property management agencies; domestic newspaper and magazine publication; domestic advertising and public relations firms; nightclubs and some restaurants (except specialty, gourmet and ethnic restaurants and restaurants operating in a hotel, resort complex or tourist attraction); security services; domestic distribution and building supplies; construction companies (except for special structures for which international expertise is required); personal cosmetics/beauty establishments, shallow water scalefish; crustacean, mollusk and sponge fishing operations; auto and appliance service operations, and public transportation." The International Monetary Fund reports that all outward capital transfers and inward transfers by non-residents require exchange control approval and that foreign direct investment must be approved by the central bank. "Capital investment into the Bahamas remains subject to exchange controls," reports the U.S. Department of Commerce, "but as a practical matter these controls have not been known to inhibit repatriation of approved investment capital." Foreigners purchasing real estate for commercial purposes or purchasing more than five acres must obtain a permit from the Investments Board.

BANKING AND FINANCE
Score: **2**–Stable (low level of restrictions)

The financial sector is extremely open to foreigners. Financial services account for 15 percent of GDP and follow tourism as the second largest sector of the economy. The government remains involved in the financial sector through ownership of the Bahamas Mortgage Corporation and the Bahamas Development Bank, which primarily provides financing for commercial, industrial, and agricultural development projects. In an effort to secure its removal from the Organisation for Economic Co-operation and Development's list of jurisdictions with a non-cooperative record on money laundering, the Bahamas passed a package of legislation to tighten controls on such activity. The new legislation imposes extra regulatory costs on the financial sector but does not constrain financial services. The U.S. Department of Commerce reports that 270 banks and trust companies were licensed as of September 2004, down from 415 in 1999. The contraction is a result of stricter regulation and supervision, intended to comply with international Financial Action Task Force and OECD standards, that

has led the government to suspend licenses for a large number of banks that could not show proof of an actual physical presence. The FATF, an intergovernmental body designed to combat money laundering and made up of 31 countries and territories, the European Commission, and the Gulf Cooperation Council, removed the Bahamas from its list of jurisdictions with a non-cooperative record on money laundering in June 2001.

WAGES AND PRICES
Score: **3**–Stable (moderate level of intervention)

According to the central bank, the government monitors and controls prices of "breadbasket items, drugs, gasoline & diesel oil, liquefied petroleum gas (cooking gas), motor vehicles, motor vehicles parts & accessories." A minimum wage for all non-salaried public-sector workers was established in 1996, and legislation establishing a minimum wage for the private sector was passed in 2002.

PROPERTY RIGHTS
Score: **1**–Stable (very high level of protection)

The Bahamas has an efficient legal system based on English common law. According to the U.S. Department of Commerce, "The judiciary is independent, and conducts generally fair, public trials with the ultimate right to appeal judicial decisions to the Privy Council in London." However, "the Bahamian judicial process tends to be much slower than the norm in the United States and the [U.S.] Embassy has received occasional reports of malfeasance on the part of court officials."

REGULATION
Score: **2**–Stable (low level)

The Bahamian government generally follows a hands-off approach to business, but the U.S. Department of Commerce reports that "discretionary issuance of business licenses can result in a lack of transparency in decisions to authorize or to renew the authority of a business.... Obtaining required permits, especially immigration permits, can take an inordinate length of time." Labor laws can be burdensome, especially for domestic business. According to the U.S. Department of State, "allegations of improper conduct on the part of Government officials surface regularly...."

INFORMAL MARKET
Score: **2**–Stable (low level of activity)

Piracy of software, music, and videos is a problem. According to the U.S Department of Commerce, "existing copyright laws are widely ignored, resulting in widespread piracy of videos and music recordings and broadcasts, most of which remain in The Bahamas." The Economist Intelligence Unit reports that illegal drug trafficking and money laundering are also significant.

BAHRAIN

Rank: 25

Score: 2.23

Category: Mostly Free

Present & Past Scores

(Best) 1
2
3
4
(Worst) 5

1.83 1.80 1.85 1.95 1.86 1.93 1.96 2.05 2.09 2.13 2.15 **2.23**

'95 '96 '97 '98 '99 '00 '01 '02 '03 '04 '05 '06

Since gaining its independence from Great Britain in 1971, Bahrain has developed one of the Persian Gulf region's most progressive political systems and most advanced economies. Oil replaced pearl fishing as the leading source of income in the 1930s, and oil production and refining provide about 60 percent of export revenues and 30 percent of GDP. The government has sought to diversify the economy to reduce dependence on Bahrain's declining oil reserves and to encourage foreign investment. Because of its relatively cosmopolitan outlook, modern economy, favorable regulatory structure, and excellent communications and transportation infrastructure, many multinational firms doing business in the Persian Gulf are based in Bahrain. Sheikh Hamad bin Isa al-Khalifa has adopted a conciliatory policy toward the political opposition and the traditionally disaffected Shi'a community, which makes up roughly two-thirds of the population. In 2002, a new constitution declared him king, transforming Bahrain from an absolute monarchy into a constitutional monarchy, and Bahrain held its first parliamentary elections in over 30 years and gave women the right to vote. The United States signed a Trade and Investment Framework Agreement with Bahrain in June 2002, and the two countries signed a Free Trade Agreement in September 2004. Bahrain's fiscal burden of government score is 0.7 point better this year, and its government intervention score is 0.5 point better; however, its monetary policy and property rights scores are 1 point worse. As a result, Bahrain's overall score is 0.08 point worse this year.

QUICK STUDY

SCORES

Trade Policy	3.5
Fiscal Burden	1.3
Government Intervention	4
Monetary Policy	2
Foreign Investment	2
Banking and Finance	1
Wages and Prices	2
Property Rights	2
Regulation	2
Informal Market	2.5

Population: 711,662

Total area: 620 sq. km

GDP: $7.6 billion

GDP growth rate: 3.5%

GDP per capita: $10,889

Major exports: petroleum and petroleum products, base metals, textiles, travel services, transportation

Exports of goods and services: $6.2 billion

Major export trading partners: US 3.6%, South Korea 2.2%, Saudi Arabia 1.9%

Major imports: machinery and appliances, mineral products, chemicals, crude oil

Imports of goods and services: $4.9 billion

Major import trading partners: Saudi Arabia 30.6%, US 11.4%, Japan 7.8%, UK 5.7%, Germany 5.4%

Foreign direct investment (net): −$211.7 million

2003 Data (in constant 2000 US dollars)

TRADE POLICY
Score: **3.5**–Stable (high level of protectionism)

The World Trade Organization reports that Bahrain's average applied MFN tariff rate in 2000 (the most recent year for which WTO data are available) was 7.7 percent. According to the WTO, "Bahrain maintains non-tariff measures in the form of import and export prohibitions and licences for a limited number of products, mainly for health and security reasons…. [The] discrepancy between legislation and practice potentially reduces transparency and predictability in Bahrain's trade regime and may increase the scope for administrative discretion, particularly at the border." Based on the revised trade factor methodology, Bahrain's trade policy score is unchanged.

FISCAL BURDEN OF GOVERNMENT
Score—Income Taxation: **1**–Stable (very low tax rates)
Score—Corporate Taxation: **1**–Stable (very low tax rates)
Score—Change in Government Expenditures: **2**–Better (moderate decrease)
Final Score: **1.3**–Better (very low cost of government)

Bahrain imposes no taxes on income or corporate profits. In 2003, based on data from the Ministry of Finance and Economy and the International Monetary Fund, government expenditures as a percentage of GDP decreased 2.6 percentage points to 29.9 percent, compared to a 4.5 percentage point increase in 2002. On net, Bahrain's fiscal burden of government score is 0.7 point better this year.

GOVERNMENT INTERVENTION IN THE ECONOMY
Score: **4**–Better (high level)

The World Bank reports that the government consumed 19.7 percent of GDP in 2003, down from the 20.1 percent reported in the 2005 *Index*. As a result, Bahrain's government intervention score is 0.5 point better this year. In the same year, based on data from the Directorate of Economic Planning, Bahrain received 81.7 percent of its total revenues (the largest portion being oil and gas revenues) from state-owned enterprises and government ownership of property.

MONETARY POLICY
Score: 2–Worse (low level of inflation)

From 1995 to 2004, based on data from the International Monetary Fund's *2005 World Economic Outlook*, Bahrain's weighted average annual rate of inflation was 3.34 percent, up from the 0.04 percent from 1994 to 2003 reported in the 2005 *Index*. As a result, Bahrain's monetary policy score is 1 point worse this year.

CAPITAL FLOWS AND FOREIGN INVESTMENT
Score: 2–Stable (low barriers)

Foreign investment is welcome, but the government maintains some barriers. According to the U.S. Department of Commerce, "the government seeks to encourage investment in sectors that are export oriented and which do not compete with established local enterprises. In general, the Bahraini government does not license companies wishing to compete with existing government-owned or parastatal companies, or which would be a danger to public health or other aspects of the general welfare.... All significant investments, whether by Bahraini or foreign firms, must go through a lengthy and complicated government approval process." Gulf Cooperation Council nationals may own 100 percent of shares of domestic enterprises. Non-GCC nationals are restricted to 49 percent ownership of most companies, but Bahrain now permits 100 percent foreign ownership of new industrial entities and representative branches or offices. According to the International Monetary Fund, except for GCC nationals, non-residents are generally prohibited from purchasing land except in designated locations, generally tourist areas.

BANKING AND FINANCE
Score: 1–Stable (very low level of restrictions)

There are few restrictions on new banks. Foreign banks are welcome. As of December 2003, there were 357 financial institutions in Bahrain, according to the EIU, including 25 commercial banks, mostly foreign. According to the U.S. Department of Commerce, "In 2004, Bahrain's Central Bank issued seventeen new licenses—one investment bank, four offshore banking units, one full commercial bank, two investment advisory brokers, two financial services ancillary service providers, three representative offices, one money exchange unit, and three Islamic banking and financial institutions." The U.S. Department of State reports that "The Bahrain Stock Exchange (BSE) allows GCC firms and GCC persons to own up to 100 percent of listed companies. Non-GCC firms/persons may own up to 49 percent of listed companies. The Minister announced that within three years non-GCC nationals would be offered

up to 100 percent ownership." The requirement that foreign insurance brokers and loss adjusters have local partners has been lifted.

WAGES AND PRICES
Score: 2–Stable (low level of intervention)

The market sets most wages and prices, but the government's monopoly in water provision and petrol retailing effectively allows it to set prices in these sectors. The government also sets the prices of electricity. The United Nations reports that "a large proportion of the population benefit[s] from government subsidies." According to the International Monetary Fund, the government is considering the introduction of a minimum wage.

PROPERTY RIGHTS
Score: 2–Worse (high level of protection)

Property is secure, and expropriation is unlikely. According to the Economist Intelligence Unit, the king is the "ultimate arbiter" and has the power to "appoint judges, the chairmanship of the Higher Judicial Council and the right to appoint the seven members of a new constitutional court sanctioned to ensure the constitutionality of laws. He also has the right to amend the constitution." Nevertheless, "the Bahraini legal system has a good reputation, and foreign firms have been able to resolve disputes satisfactorily through the local courts. There are no prohibitions on the use of international arbitration to safeguard contracts." Upon more detailed analysis, and based on the fact that the judiciary is not fully independent from the king, Bahrain's property rights score is 1 point worse this year.

REGULATION
Score: 2–Stable (low level)

Bahrain's process for establishing a business is relatively straightforward. The Economist Intelligence Unit reports that the "Bahraini commercial law system has a relatively good reputation...." However, according to the U.S. Department of Commerce, "Bureaucratic procedures can create significant stumbling blocks." Labor laws restrict the hiring of foreign workers. Despite the anticorruption laws, there is occasional high-level corruption in contract bidding and the management of successful investments. Overall, reports the U.S. Department of Commerce, "petty corruption is rare in Bahrain. The bureaucracy is sometimes inefficient but it is honest."

INFORMAL MARKET
Score: 2.5–Stable (moderate level of activity)

Transparency International's 2004 score for Bahrain is 5.8. Therefore, Bahrain's informal market score is 2.5 this year.

If Bahrain were to improve its trade policy score, it would qualify for the Global Free Trade Alliance.

BANGLADESH

Rank: 141

Score: 3.88

Category: Mostly Unfree

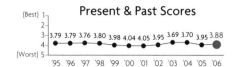

Present & Past Scores

(Best) 1 —
2 —
3 — 3.79 3.79 3.76 3.80 3.98 4.04 4.05 3.95 3.69 3.70 3.95 3.88
4 —
(Worst) 5 —
'95 '96 '97 '98 '99 '00 '01 '02 '03 '04 '05 '06

QUICK STUDY

SCORES

Trade Policy	5
Fiscal Burden	3.3
Government Intervention	4
Monetary Policy	2
Foreign Investment	4
Banking and Finance	4
Wages and Prices	3
Property Rights	4
Regulation	5
Informal Market	4.5

Population: 138,066,368

Total area: 144,000 sq. km

GDP: $54.6 billion

GDP growth rate: 5.3%

GDP per capita: $395

Major exports: garments, fisheries products, leather

Exports of goods and services: $7.91 billion

Major export trading partners: US 23.9%, Germany 13.6%, UK 9.7%, France 5.9%

Major imports: textiles and yarn, petroleum and petroleum products, machinery and transport equipment

Imports of goods and services: $9.6 billion

Major import trading partners: India 15.4%, China 11.3%, Singapore 10.8%, Japan 5.9%, Hong Kong 4.5%

Foreign direct investment (net): $106.5 million

2003 Data (in constant 2000 US dollars)

The People's Republic of Bangladesh is a poor, mostly rural river delta, subject to natural disasters and home to 135 million people. Democracy continues to progress, albeit slowly. Voters unseated the Bangladesh National Party (BNP) in favor of the Awami League (AL) in the 1996 elections. The BNP returned to power in the 2001 elections, but the AL is expected to win the elections scheduled for October 2006. Overall, weak rule of law—manifesting itself in some of the world's worst official corruption, civil crime, and political violence—continues to burden Bangladesh's democracy, and the government's simplistic policy solutions have made the situation worse. Government officials attempted to boost law enforcement by involving the military, which formed the Rapid Action Battalion, attacking suspected criminals and inflicting numerous abuses (including extra-judicial murder, torture, and disappearances) but not measurably reducing crime or corruption. The chaos of a lawless society has added to other problems keeping economic growth to roughly 5 percent annually, substantially below the 8 percent needed for appreciable development. Until the government addresses Bangladesh's many structural weaknesses, there is little reason for optimism about the country's future. Bangladesh's government intervention score is 0.5 point worse this year; however, its fiscal burden of government score is 0.2 point better, and its banking and finance score is 1 point better. As a result, Bangladesh's overall score is 0.07 point better this year.

TRADE POLICY

Score: **5**–Stable (very high level of protectionism)

According to the World Bank, Bangladesh's weighted average tariff rate in 2004 was 15.9 percent. Bangladesh imposes a number of prohibitions and restrictions on imports, and corruption also serves as a non-tariff barrier. The U.S. Department of Commerce reports that "business people consider Bangladesh Customs to be…a thoroughly corrupt organization in which officials routinely exert their power to influence the tariff value of imports and to expedite or delay import and export processing at the ports." Based on the revised trade factor methodology, Bangladesh's trade policy score is unchanged.

FISCAL BURDEN OF GOVERNMENT

Score—Income Taxation: **2.5**–Stable (moderate tax rates)
Score—Corporate Taxation: **4**–Stable (high tax rates)
Score—Change in Government Expenditures: **2.5**–Better (low decrease)
Final Score: **3.3**–Better (moderate cost of government)

Bangladesh's top income tax rate is 25 percent. The top corporate tax rate is 30 percent. In 2003, according to the Asian Development Bank, government expenditures as a share of GDP decreased 1.1 percentage points to 13.7 percent, compared to a 0.8 percentage point increase in 2002. On net, Bangladesh's fiscal burden of government score is 0.2 point better this year.

GOVERNMENT INTERVENTION IN THE ECONOMY

Score: **4**–Worse (high level)

The World Bank reports that the government of Bangladesh consumed 5.3 percent of GDP in 2003, up from the 5 percent reported in the 2005 *Index*. In fiscal year 2004–2005, based on data from the central bank, Bangladesh received 7.34 percent of its total revenues from state-owned enterprises and government ownership of property. According to the Economist Intelligence Unit, however, "The government employs around one-third of those in formal sector employment, either directly in the civil service or through state owned enterprises (SOEs)." The World Bank also reports that state-owned enterprises "accounted for over 25.0% of total fixed capital formation" in 2000. Because the state's presence in the economy is so extensive, 2 points have been added to Bangladesh's government intervention score: 1 point for the inaccuracy of the consumption statistic and another point for the inaccuracy of the figure for revenues from state owned enterprises. Based on the increase in government consumption, Bangladesh's government intervention score is 0.5 point worse this year.

MONETARY POLICY
Score: **2**–Stable (low level of inflation)

From 1995 to 2004, Bangladesh's weighted average annual rate of inflation was 3.73 percent.

CAPITAL FLOWS AND FOREIGN INVESTMENT
Score: **4**–Stable (high barriers)

Foreign investors receive national treatment and are allowed full ownership in most sectors. The International Monetary Fund reports that most capital transactions are controlled or prohibited and that foreign investments, with the exception of investments in the industrial sector, require approval. According to the U.S. Department of Commerce, "Foreigners often find that ministries require unnecessary licenses and permissions. Added to these difficulties are such problems as corruption, labor militancy, an uncertain law and order situation, poor infrastructure, inadequate commercial laws and courts, inconsistent respect for contract sanctity, and policy instability (i.e., policies being altered at the behest of special interests, and decisions taken by previous governments being overturned when a new government comes to power)." Non-resident companies are subject to a higher corporate tax rate (37.5 percent) than are publicly traded companies (30 percent).

BANKING AND FINANCE
Score: **4**–Better (high level of restrictions)

Bangladesh has a small, underdeveloped financial services sector. According to the Economist Intelligence Unit, "State-owned banks—known as nationalised commercial banks, or NCBs—dominate the financial sector. Given that the government is the owner, regulator and major customer of the NCBs, there has been ample opportunity for mismanagement and political interference.... [T]he banking sector remains hampered by poor credit discipline, an archaic loan recovery system, corruption, inefficiency, overstaffing and unionisation." The four NCBs jointly accounted for nearly 60 percent of total deposits in mid-2003. Lending by the NCBs is directed by the government, and lending to state-owned enterprises has contributed to a high level of non-performing loans. Bangladesh

had 28 private banks and 12 foreign banks operating in 2004. Banks, insurance companies, and financial institutions are taxed at a higher rate (45 percent) than are other corporations (30 percent). Two nationalized companies dominate the insurance sector, although private competition is permitted. Based on evidence of private-sector banking, Bangladesh's banking and finance score is 1 point better this year.

WAGES AND PRICES
Score: **3**–Stable (moderate level of intervention)

"Other than a few essential pharmaceutical products and petroleum products," reports the U.S. Department of Commerce, "the [government of Bangladesh] does not impose price controls. Market pricing prevails." However, it sets the prices of goods and services provided by the approximately 76 state-owned enterprises. Bangladesh has no minimum wage, and private-sector employers ignore wages set by the Wage Commission.

PROPERTY RIGHTS
Score: **4**–Stable (low level of protection)

The constitution provides for an independent judiciary. According to the U.S. Department of Commerce, "A fundamental impediment to investment in Bangladesh is a weak and slow legal system in which the enforceability of contracts is uncertain.... It is widely acknowledged that in the lower courts, where cases are first brought, corruption is a serious problem. Nevertheless, the highest levels of the judiciary, including the Supreme Court, have retained a reputation for fairness and competence.... This has meant that at least at the appellate level, the outcome of commercial cases is usually determined on merit."

REGULATION
Score: **5**–Stable (very high level)

Transparency International reports that corruption is a very serious problem. According to the U.S. Department of Commerce, "Policy and regulations in Bangladesh are often not clear, consistent, or publicized.... Businesses must always turn to civil servants to get action, yet may not receive any, even with the support of higher political levels. Unhelpful treatment of businesses by some [government] officials, coupled with other negatives in the investment climate, raise start-up and operational costs, add to risk, and tend to counteract the [government's] praiseworthy investment incentives."

INFORMAL MARKET
Score: **4.5**–Stable (very high level of activity)

Transparency International's 2004 score for Bangladesh is 1.5. Therefore, Bangladesh's informal market score is 4.5 this year.

BARBADOS

Rank: 26

Score: 2.25

Category: Mostly Free

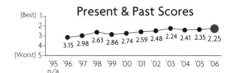

Present & Past Scores

(Best) 1–
2–
3–
4–
(Worst) 5–

3.15 2.98 2.63 2.86 2.74 2.59 2.48 2.24 2.41 2.35 2.25

'95 '96 '97 '98 '99 '00 '01 '02 '03 '04 '05 '06
n/a

The Barbados Labor Party, which has governed the former British colony since 1994, continues to have strong support in Parliament. The Economist Intelligence Unit reports that the economy grew by an estimated 3.4 percent in 2004, led by tourism, which remains the country's most important economic sector. The government's main policy goals include reduction of the fiscal deficit, reduction of income tax rates, and promotion of export-oriented businesses. The heavily subsidized sugar industry, although diminishing in importance, remains an important employer and exporter. Barbados's offshore financial sector, though smaller than others in the Caribbean, makes a significant contribution to the economy and is generally well-regulated. Barbados's government intervention score is 0.5 point worse this year; however, its fiscal burden of government score is 1 point better, and its informal market score is 0.5 point better. As a result, Barbados's overall score is 0.1 point better this year.

TRADE POLICY
Score: **4**–Stable (high level of protectionism)

The World Trade Organization reports that, as an Organization of Eastern Caribbean States member of the Caribbean Community and Common Market (CARICOM) trade bloc, Barbados permits imports from other CARICOM members duty free but applies import duties on third countries of up to 35 percent for industrial products and up to 40 percent for agricultural goods. The World Bank reports that Barbados's average tariff rate in 2003 (the most recent year for which World Bank data are available) was 16.5 percent. According to the U.S. Department of Commerce, "Barbados requires that importers obtain permits, licenses or permission from the relevant authorities for specified products prior to importation." Based on the revised trade factor methodology, Barbados's trade policy score is unchanged.

FISCAL BURDEN OF GOVERNMENT
Score—Income Taxation: **3.5**–Better (high tax rates)
Score—Corporate Taxation: **4**–Better (high tax rates)
Score—Change in Government Expenditures: **2.5**–Better (low decrease)
Final Score: **3.5**–Better (high cost of government)

According to the Economist Intelligence Unit, Barbados has a top income tax rate of 37.5 percent, down from the 40 percent reported in the 2005 *Index*. The top corporate tax rate is 30 percent, down from 36 percent. In 2003, based on data from the Central Bank of Barbados, government expenditures as a share of GDP decreased 1.2 percentage points to 37.1 percent, compared to a 2.6 percentage point increase in 2002. On net, Barbados's fiscal burden of government score is 1 point better this year.

GOVERNMENT INTERVENTION IN THE ECONOMY
Score: **2.5**–Worse (moderate level)

According to the Central Bank of Barbados, the government consumed 24.4 percent of GDP in 2003, up from the 16.7 percent reported in the 2005 *Index*. As a result, Barbados's government intervention score is 0.5 point worse this year. In fiscal year 2003–2004, based on data from the central bank, Barbados received 4.94 percent of its total revenues from state-owned enterprises and government ownership of property.

QUICK STUDY

SCORES

Trade Policy	4
Fiscal Burden	3.5
Government Intervention	2.5
Monetary Policy	1
Foreign Investment	3
Banking and Finance	2
Wages and Prices	2
Property Rights	1
Regulation	2
Informal Market	1.5

Population: 270,584

Total area: 430 sq. km

GDP: $2.5 billion

GDP growth rate: 1.3%

GDP per capita: $9,256

Major exports: chemicals, electrical components, food and beverages, sugar, travel services, financial services, insurance services

Exports of goods and services: $1.25 billion

Major export trading partners: US 18.7%, Trinidad and Tobago 14.7%, UK 14.2%, Jamaica 8.0%

Major imports: consumer goods, machinery, foodstuffs, construction materials, fuel, insurance services

Imports of goods and services: $1.4 billion

Major import trading partners: US 37.7%, Trinidad and Tobago 19.7%, UK 6.2%

Foreign direct investment (net): $113.3 million

2003 Data (in constant 2000 US dollars)

MONETARY POLICY
Score: **1**–Stable (very low level of inflation)

From 1994 to 2003, Barbados's weighted average annual rate of inflation was 1.40 percent.

CAPITAL FLOWS AND FOREIGN INVESTMENT
Score: **3**–Stable (moderate barriers)

Barbados permits 100 percent foreign ownership of enterprises and treats domestic and foreign firms equally. However, according to the U.S. Department of Commerce, "Performance requirements and expectations are central to the administration of certain foreign direct investments. Local officials will more likely approve licenses if they believe the investment will create jobs, increase exports and foreign exchange earnings, and increase economic activity in Barbados…. Foreign investors must finance their investments from external sources or from income that the investment generates. When a foreign investment generates significant employment or other tangible benefits for the country, the authorities may allow the company to borrow locally for working capital." The same source reports that export performance requirements exist for some foreign investments. The International Monetary Fund reports that central bank approval is required for both residents and non-residents to hold foreign exchange accounts. Transactions in foreign currency and current transfers are restricted by quantitative limits. Exchange control approval is required for direct investment and real estate purchases, and the central bank must approve all credit operations.

BANKING AND FINANCE
Score: **2**–Stable (low level of restrictions)

The commercial banking system consists of the formerly state-owned Barbados National Bank, two Canadian banks, and two regional banks. The government affects the allocation of credit. "The Government has intervened in recent years in the local credit market to raise or lower interest rates, limit the volumes of funds available for borrowing, and borrow on the local market," reports the U.S. Department of Commerce, and "Financing using domestically generated funds is generally available only to Barbadians or permanent residents of Barbados." Legislation passed in 1998 tightened the controls against money laundering and prevented Barbados from being identified in 2000 by the Financial Action Task Force as a "non-co-operative jurisdiction." In January 2002, Barbados was removed from the Organisation for Economic Co-operation and Development's list of countries with harmful tax policies and thereby avoided sanctions. This has not curtailed offshore banking, however. According to the Economist Intelligence Unit, "There were 327 new licenses issued for companies to operate in the offshore financial sector in January–November 2004, up from 298 in the year-earlier period."

WAGES AND PRICES
Score: **2**–Stable (low level of intervention)

The market sets most wages and prices. According to the U.S. Department of Commerce, "While the government generally refrains from imposing price controls, certain basic items are controlled." Items that are subject to price controls include basic food items and fuel. The government establishes legally enforced minimum wages for specified categories of workers, but only household domestics and shop assistants are subject to a formal minimum wage.

PROPERTY RIGHTS
Score: **1**–Stable (very high level of protection)

Private property is well-protected in Barbados. The country's legal tradition is based on British common law. "The highest court of appeal is currently the Privy Council in London," reports the U.S. Department of Commerce, "although the new Caribbean Court of Justice may soon replace the Privy Council as the highest court of appeal for CARICOM nations." According to the same source, "By Caribbean standards, the police and court systems are efficient and unbiased, and the government operates in an essentially transparent manner."

REGULATION
Score: **2**–Stable (low level)

The process for establishing a business in Barbados is simple. According to the U.S. Department of Commerce, "Barbados uses transparent policies and effective laws to foster competition and establish clear rules for foreign and domestic investors in the areas of tax, labor, environment, health and safety…. The Ministry of Industry and International Business administers the Companies Act and other statutes dealing with company affairs. The Companies Act is modeled on the Canada Business Corporations Act, and creates flexibility and simplicity for the incorporation and operation of companies in Barbados." Corruption is not regarded as a major problem.

INFORMAL MARKET
Score: **1.5**–Better (low level of activity)

Transparency International's 2004 score for Barbados is 7.3. Therefore, Barbados's informal market score is 1.5 this year—0.5 point better than last year.

BELARUS

Rank: 151

Score: 4.11

Category: Repressed

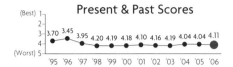

Present & Past Scores

(Best) 1
2
3 3.70 3.45 3.95 4.20 4.19 4.18 4.10 4.16 4.19 4.04 4.04 4.11
4
5
(Worst)
'95 '96 '97 '98 '99 '00 '01 '02 '03 '04 '05 '06

B elarus is both one of the most repressed countries of the former Soviet Union and the one that has retained the closest political and economic ties with Russia. President Alexander Lukashenko, whose authoritarian regime has ruled since 1994, remains firmly in control. In October 2004, a referendum was passed ending presidential term limits, thereby allowing Lukashenko to run again in September 2006 for another five-year term and remain in office indefinitely. The same month, parliamentary elections were held, with opposition candidates prevented from running in many districts and pro-Lukashenko candidates winning every seat. Under Lukashenko's dictatorship, there has been little progress on structural economic reform and market liberalization. Roughly 80 percent of all industry remains in state hands, the industrial base has become obsolete, and more than 40 percent of industrial enterprises work at a loss. Extensive budget subsidies are required to maintain the agriculture sector, which is dominated by Soviet-era collective farms. Arrests and disappearances of opposition leaders and the absence of freedom of expression, coupled with gross economic mismanagement, inhibit foreign investment, and outdated distribution systems unnecessarily constrain exports. Belarus's fiscal burden of government score is 0.2 point worse, and its informal market score is 0.5 point worse. As a result, Belarus's overall score is 0.07 point worse this year.

QUICK STUDY

SCORES
Trade Policy	3.5
Fiscal Burden	3.6
Government Intervention	3.5
Monetary Policy	5
Foreign Investment	4
Banking and Finance	4
Wages and Prices	5
Property Rights	4
Regulation	5
Informal Market	3.5

Population: 9,880,963

Total area: 207,600 sq. km

GDP: $14.9 billion

GDP growth rate: 6.8%

GDP per capita: $1,513

Major exports: machinery and equipment, mineral products, chemicals, textiles, metals

Exports of goods and services: $11.4 billion

Major export trading partners: Russia 49.1%, UK 9.4%, Poland 4.4%, Germany 4.2%

Major imports: mineral products, foodstuffs, metals, chemicals, machinery and equipment

Imports of goods and services: $11.4 billion

Major import trading partners: Russia 65.8%, Germany 7.1%, Ukraine 3.1%

Foreign direct investment (net): $159.4 million

2003 Data (in constant 2000 US dollars

TRADE POLICY
Score: **3.5**–Stable (high level of protectionism)

The World Bank reports that Belarus's weighted average tariff rate in 2002 (the most recent year for which World Bank data are available) was 8.9 percent. (The World Bank has revised the figure for 2002 upward from the 8 percent reported in the 2005 *Index*.) According to the Economist Intelligence Unit, "Belarus has followed active policies of import suppression and export promotion." The International Monetary Fund reports extensive use of licensing and quotas. Based on the revised trade factor methodology, Belarus's trade policy score is unchanged.

FISCAL BURDEN OF GOVERNMENT
Score—Income Taxation: **3**–Stable (moderate tax rates)
Score—Corporate Taxation: **4**–Stable (high tax rates)
Score—Change in Government Expenditures: **3.5**–Worse (low increase)
Final Score: **3.6**–Worse (high cost of government)

The Embassy of Belarus reports that Belarus's top income tax rate is 30 percent. The top corporate income tax rate is also 30 percent. In 2003, according to the International Monetary Fund, government expenditures as a share of GDP increased 0.8 percentage point to 47.2 percent, compared to a 0.4 percentage point decline in 2002. On net, Belarus's fiscal burden of government score is 0.2 point worse this year.

GOVERNMENT INTERVENTION IN THE ECONOMY
Score: **3.5**–Stable (high level)

The World Bank reports that the government consumed 21.4 percent of GDP in 2003. In the same year, based on data from the International Monetary Fund, Belarus received 4.91 percent of its total revenues from state-owned enterprises and government ownership of property. According to the Economist Intelligence Unit, however, "The president, Alyaksandar

Lukashenka, pursues a policy of pervasive state involvement in the economy.… [T]he Lukashenka administration bases its economic policy on consistent support and preservation of large and obsolete state-controlled enterprises." In addition, "95% of the country's industrial output [is] still derived from large state-owned or state-controlled enterprises." Based on the apparent unreliability of the revenue figure, 1 point has been added to Belarus's government intervention score.

 MONETARY POLICY
Score: **5**–Stable (very high level of inflation)

From 1995 to 2004, Belarus's weighted average annual rate of inflation was 27.04 percent.

 CAPITAL FLOWS AND FOREIGN INVESTMENT
Score: **4**–Stable (high barriers)

The International Monetary Fund reports that there are significant restrictions on capital transactions, that foreign investment must be registered with the Minsk City Executive Committee, and that financial institutions must register with the National Bank of Belarus. With the exception of insurance organizations and banks, the proportion of a foreign investor's share is not restricted. However, anti-Western sentiment, an inefficient bureaucracy, corruption, a concerted resistance to the private sector, and resistance to privatization all serve to hinder foreign investment. According to the Economist Intelligence Unit, "Even enterprises in which the government owns less than a majority stake are still technically subject to state intervention. The latter can be exercised through a 'golden share' rule, which gives the government majority voting rights in decision-making, even if it owns only a small number of shares. In March 2004 [the president] extended the golden share rule to include even those enterprises in which the government had no ownership claim at all." The government does not permit foreigners to own land. Natural resources, waters, forests, and land are owned exclusively by the state, although 99-year-use agreements are permitted.

 BANKING AND FINANCE
Score: **4**–Stable (high level of restrictions)

According to government information, as of March 2005, there were 32 banks in Belarus, including 27 banks with some foreign capital. Although the government has issued licenses to a number of private banks and has relinquished some of its holdings in state-owned banks, it continues to exert enormous control over the banking sector. According to the Economist Intelligence Unit, the Central National Bank of Belarus "has been reduced to a conduit for the government's economic policy." In addition, "commercial banks, although nominally independent, have also frequently been pressurised by the government into providing loss-making loans to selected industries and purchasing government-issued securities. Although the government has assured the IMF that it would end this practice, pressure on commercial banks to finance the agricultural sector has continued."

 WAGES AND PRICES
Score: **5**–Stable (very high level of intervention)

The Economist Intelligence Unit reports that the government subsidizes many basic goods and services, including housing and utilities; intervenes directly in agricultural markets; controls most of the economy through state-owned enterprises; otherwise influences prices through its credit policies and purchasing practices; and "retains tight control over the partly privatised retail sector through price regulation.…" The government mandates a monthly minimum wage and determines wages in the private sector. According to the EIU, "Enterprises have been under intense pressure from the authorities to raise wages at a rate well in excess of any improvements in productivity."

 PROPERTY RIGHTS
Score: **4**–Stable (low level of protection)

The legal system does not fully protect private property, and the inefficient court system does not consistently enforce contracts. "Since November 1996," reports the Economist Intelligence Unit, "the judiciary on the whole has proved neither independent nor objective by international standards. Independent lawyers were barred from practising in 1997."

 REGULATION
Score: **5**–Stable (very high level)

According to the Economist Intelligence Unit, "The authorities discourage private enterprise through a combination of high taxes, excessive government regulations, and a deliberately anti-business climate. This has led small and medium-sized private enterprises to concentrate in retail and catering, where relatively low sunk costs prevent excessively high losses in the event of official harassment." In addition, "The administration's lack of progress on political and judicial reforms has further dampened investors' interest.…" Transparency International reports that corruption in the bureaucracy is very high.

 INFORMAL MARKET
Score: **3.5**–Worse (high level of activity)

Transparency International's 2004 score for Belarus is 3.3. Therefore, Belarus's informal market score is 3.5 this year—0.5 point worse than last year.

BELGIUM

Rank: 22

Score: 2.11

Category: Mostly Free

Present & Past Scores

(Best) 1
2
2.11 2.08 2.10 2.11 2.19 2.15 2.15 2.10 2.24 2.13 2.11
3
4
(Worst) 5
'95 '96 '97 '98 '99 '00 '01 '02 '03 '04 '05 '06
n/a

QUICK STUDY

SCORES

Trade Policy	2
Fiscal Burden	4.1
Government Intervention	2.5
Monetary Policy	1
Foreign Investment	1
Banking and Finance	2
Wages and Prices	3
Property Rights	1
Regulation	3
Informal Market	1.5

Population: 10,400,000

Total area: 30,510 sq. km

GDP: $241.4 billion

GDP growth rate: 2.7%

GDP per capita: $23,211

Major exports: chemicals, machinery and equipment, transport equipment, transportation, travel services, financial services, computer services and information

Exports of goods and services: $204.3 billion

Major export trading partners: Germany 17.5%, France 17.4%, Netherlands 12.9%, UK 8.6%

Major imports: machinery, chemicals, transport equipment, travel services, financial services, insurance services

Imports of goods and services: $200.2 billion

Major import trading partners: France 19.9%, Germany 16.6%, Netherlands 13.7%, UK 7.8%, US 5.5%

Foreign direct investment (net): $15.2 billion

2004 Data (in constant 2000 US dollars)

Belgium has one of the world's highest total tax burdens. Government spending amounted to 49.4 percent of GDP in 2004, and the social transfer system remains one of the world's most extensive and expensive; on average, one working-age adult supports slightly more than one benefit recipient. Prime Minister Guy Verhofstadt has concentrated on targeted cuts in income tax and social security contributions to achieve his goal of increased job creation, and the program has met with relative success in Western European terms. GDP increased by 2.7 percent in 2004, with unemployment at 7.8 percent. Another principal fiscal policy objective is budgetary consolidation. Public debt remains staggeringly high (95.9 percent of GDP in 2004) despite years of steady decline. Labor laws remain highly complex, particularly in terms of employment, health, and safety regulations, and lawmakers frequently add to the already onerous European Union labor regulations. Belgium is still run on a largely corporatist basis, with the business federation and unions negotiating a national collective bargaining agreement every other year. Belgium's fiscal burden of government score is 0.2 point better this year. As a result, its overall score is 0.02 point better this year.

TRADE POLICY
Score: **2**–Stable (low level of protectionism)

As a member of the European Union, according to the World Bank, Belgium was subject to a common EU weighted average external tariff of 1.3 percent in 2003, down from the 2.4 percent for 2002 reported in the 2005 *Index*. The EU restricts or has quotas for many goods, especially agricultural products. Based on the revised trade factor methodology, Belgium's trade policy score is unchanged.

FISCAL BURDEN OF GOVERNMENT
Score—Income Taxation: **5**–Stable (very high tax rates)
Score—Corporate Taxation: **4.5**–Stable (very high tax rates)
Score—Change in Government Expenditures: **2.5**–Better (low decrease)
Final Score: **4.1**–Better (high cost of government)

According to Deloitte, Belgium's top income tax rate is 50 percent. The top corporate tax rate is 34 percent. (The corporate tax rate is composed of a 33 percent tax rate and a 3 percent surcharge.) In 2004, government expenditures as a share of GDP fell 1.6 percentage points to 49.4 percent, compared to a 0.8 percentage point decrease in 2003. On net, Belgium's fiscal burden of government score is 0.2 point better this year.

GOVERNMENT INTERVENTION IN THE ECONOMY
Score: **2.5**–Stable (moderate level)

The National Bank of Belgium reports that the government consumed 22.6 percent of GDP in 2004. In the same year, based on data from Statistics Belgium, Belgium received 4.9 percent of its total revenues from state-owned enterprises and government ownership of property.

MONETARY POLICY
Score: **1**–Stable (very low level of inflation)

Belgium is a member of the euro zone. From 1995 to 2004, Belgium's weighted average annual rate of inflation was 1.95 percent.

 CAPITAL FLOWS AND FOREIGN INVESTMENT
Score: **1**–Stable (very low barriers)

Belgium has an attractive foreign investment climate. There are few restrictions on foreign investment that do not also apply to domestic investment. Authorization is required for investment in Belgian flag vessels operated by shipping companies that do not have their main offices in Belgium. There are some restrictions on non–European Union investment in public works as required under EU regulations. There are no restrictions on the purchasing of real estate, repatriation of profit, or transfer of capital.

 BANKING AND FINANCE
Score: **2**–Stable (low level of restrictions)

Belgium's domestic banking system has undergone privatization in the past few years and is now almost all privately owned. There are 66 banks, including 12 branches of foreign banks. There is government oversight, but foreign banks are allowed to operate and are subject to relatively few restrictions. According to the U.S. Department of Commerce, "Belgium has in place policies to facilitate the free flow of financial resources. Credit is allocated at market rates and is available sufficiently to foreign and domestic investors without discrimination." Belgian law distinguishes between foreign banks coming from a country that is part of the European Economic Area (EEA) and those coming from another country. Credit institutions and other issuers of financial instruments that are authorized to conduct banking activities in another EEA country do not need to seek authorization from the Banking and Finance Commission, but institutions outside the EEA may face greater scrutiny or reporting requirements. The U.S. Department of Commerce reports that financial institutions "are subject to simplified notification procedures if they are from another European Union country because they are governed by their home-country legislation and by mutual-recognition procedures." The government affects the allocation of credit; according to the Economist Intelligence Unit, "An interest-rate subsidy may be available from regional authorities on medium- and long-term borrowing."

 WAGES AND PRICES
Score: **3**–Stable (moderate level of intervention)

The market determines most wages and prices. The Economist Intelligence Unit reports that "companies with an annual turnover of 7,436,805.74 [euros] or more must notify the Federal Public Service Economy of any price increase or decrease…. [T]he principle that prices must be 'normal' is still enshrined in legislation and can be enforced in the courts to prevent price gouging." In addition, "Permission is sometimes necessary to put a new product on the market or to increase a price…. The sectors affected are those where there is a deemed monopoly or an explicit social character (water, electricity and gas distribution; waste handling; homes for the elderly, medicines and implantable medical devices; certain cars; compulsory insurance; fire insurance; petroleum products; taxi transport; cable television; and certain types of bread)." The government affects agricultural prices through its participation in the Common Agricultural Policy, which heavily subsidizes agricultural goods. Belgium maintains a minimum wage.

 PROPERTY RIGHTS
Score: **1**–Stable (very high level of protection)

Property is well protected. The Economist Intelligence Unit reports that "contractual agreements are secure in Belgium. The country's laws are codified, and the quality of the Belgian judiciary and civil service is high, though the process is often slow."

 REGULATION
Score: **3**–Stable (moderate level)

Regulations are moderately burdensome, especially for small and medium-size enterprises. According to the Economist Intelligence Unit, investors find that "Belgium's high labour costs are sustainable only for high-value-added processes." According to the World Bank, the cost of starting a business, hiring and firing, and registering property in Belgium is moderate in terms of both bureaucracy and money. The EIU reports that "part-time and temporary work has increased significantly. But rigidities in the system are still a major bar to hiring and firing…." In addition, "Listed companies are [now] expected to comply with a new corporate-governance code drawn up by the Euronext exchange—the Belgian enterprise federation and the financial services regulator—or explain why they have different governance rules."

 INFORMAL MARKET
Score: **1.5**–Stable (low level of activity)

Transparency International's 2004 score for Belgium is 7.5. Therefore, Belgium's informal market score is 1.5 this year.

> If Belgium were to improve its regulation score, it would qualify for the Global Free Trade Alliance.

BELIZE

Rank: 55

Score: 2.78

Category: Mostly Free

Present & Past Scores

(Best) 1
2
3
4
(Worst) 5

2.85 2.74 2.71 2.96 2.76 2.84 2.64 2.74 2.69 2.69 2.71 2.78

'95 '96 '97 '98 '99 '00 '01 '02 '03 '04 '05 '06

Prime Minister Said Musa and his People's United Party continue to enjoy a parliamentary majority, although public confidence in both seems to be declining. This decrease in popularity could affect the government's plans to implement reforms and cut public spending. The International Monetary Fund has pressed the government to narrow its fiscal deficit by increasing various taxes. Belize's economy grew in 2003 by an estimated 9.4 percent. Tourism accounts for about one-half of the economy, but agriculture is also an important sector. Sugar has traditionally been the largest export, but the government is fostering export diversification into other products, including shrimp, citrus, bananas, papayas, and soybeans. The U.S. Department of State has expressed concerns about an increase in drug trafficking through Belize and about the country's vulnerability to money laundering. Belize's fiscal burden of government score is 0.2 point worse this year, and its informal market score is 0.5 point worse. As a result, Belize's overall score is 0.07 point worse this year.

TRADE POLICY
Score: **4.5**–Stable (very high level of protectionism)

As a member of the Caribbean Community and Common Market (CARICOM) trade bloc, Belize has a common external tariff rate that ranges from 0 percent to 20 percent. According to the World Bank, Belize's average tariff rate in 2001 (the most recent year for which reliable data are available) was 13.3 percent. The U.S. Department of Commerce reports that a number of products are subject to quotas and import licenses. Based on the revised trade factor methodology, Belize's trade policy score is unchanged.

FISCAL BURDEN OF GOVERNMENT
Score—Income Taxation: **2.5**–Stable (moderate tax rates)
Score—Corporate Taxation: **3**–Stable (moderate tax rates)
Score—Change in Government Expenditures: **2.5**–Worse (low decrease)
Final Score: **2.8**–Worse (moderate cost of government)

According to the Economist Intelligence Unit, Belize's top income tax rate is 25 percent. Deloitte reports that Belize's top corporate income tax rate is also 25 percent. In 2003, according to the International Monetary Fund, government expenditures as a share of GDP decreased 1.4 percentage points to 30.8 percent, compared to a 2.6 percentage point decrease in 2002. On net, Belize's fiscal burden of government score is 0.2 point worse this year.

GOVERNMENT INTERVENTION IN THE ECONOMY
Score: **2**–Stable (low level)

Data from Belize's Central Statistics Office indicate that the government consumed 14.5 percent of GDP in 2003. In fiscal year 2003–2004, according to Belize's Central Bank, Belize received 0.71 percent of its total revenues from state-owned enterprises and government ownership of property.

MONETARY POLICY
Score: **1**–Stable (very low level of inflation)

From 1995 to 2004, Belize's weighted average annual rate of inflation was 2.54 percent.

QUICK STUDY

SCORES
Trade Policy	4.5
Fiscal Burden	2.8
Government Intervention	2
Monetary Policy	1
Foreign Investment	3
Banking and Finance	3
Wages and Prices	2
Property Rights	3
Regulation	3
Informal Market	3.5

Population: 273,700

Total area: 22,966 sq. km

GDP: $995 million

GDP growth rate: 9.4%

GDP per capita: $3,635

Major exports: sugar, marine products, garments, wood

Exports of goods and services: $532.7 million

Major export trading partners: US 38.9%, UK 24.9%, France 3.8%

Major imports: manufactured goods, food, beverages and tobaccos, machinery and transportation equipment

Imports of goods and services: $669 million

Major import trading partners: US 41.4%, Mexico 12.2%, UK 5.9%, Cuba 5.5%, Japan 5.5%

Foreign direct investment (net): $35.8 million

2003 Data (in constant 2000 US dollars)

CAPITAL FLOWS AND FOREIGN INVESTMENT
Score: **3**–Stable (moderate barriers)

Belize generally is open to foreign investment and allows 100 percent foreign ownership, but a number of sectors—commercial fishing within the barrier reef, merchandising, sugarcane farming, real estate and insurance, internal transportation, some tourism activities, accounting and legal services, entertainment, beauty salons, and restaurants and bars—require special licenses that non-citizens may not acquire. According to the International Monetary Fund, both residents and non-residents may hold foreign exchange accounts subject to government approval. The central bank rations its foreign exchange for invisible payments on an ad hoc basis, controls some payments, and requires that repatriation be made through an authorized dealer. All capital transactions must be approved by the central bank.

BANKING AND FINANCE
Score: **3**–Stable (moderate level of restrictions)

Belize has four commercial banks, of which three are subsidiaries of foreign commercial banks; two state-controlled lending institutions, the Development Finance Corporation (DFC) and Small Farmers and Business Bank; and some small credit unions. It also has a growing offshore banking community. The government significantly affects the allocation of credit. According to the Economist Intelligence Unit, "An increase in the DFC's on-lending activities since the late 1990s has led to a sharp increase in its foreign liabilities…. At the same time, there was a worrying rise in the non-performing loan ratio, to 35% of total loans in 2004. During that year, government transfers to the DFC were equivalent to 2% of GDP to fund credit expansion, with a further 6% to refinance external liabilities…. A November 2004 decision to liquidate the DFC, in line with recommendations from the Inter-American Development Bank (IDB), was not carried out." Belize has agreed to increase its transparency and exchange information on tax matters with Organisation for Economic Co-operation and Development countries to avoid countermeasures and sanctions. The International Financial Services Act, passed in 1999, promotes offshore financial services, and the government offers extensive banking confidentiality.

WAGES AND PRICES
Score: **2**–Stable (low level of intervention)

The market sets most wages and prices, but the U.S. Department of Commerce reports that the prices of some basic commodities such as rice, flour, beans, sugar, bread, butane gas, and fuel are subject to controls. The government also controls the retail price of electricity. Belize maintains a two-tiered minimum wage, with workers in agriculture and the export sector having a slightly lower minimum wage than other sectors.

PROPERTY RIGHTS
Score: **3**–Stable (moderate level of protection)

The constitution provides for an independent judiciary, which in practice is subject to political influence. According to the U.S. Department of State, "the judicial system is constrained by a severe lack of trained personnel, and police officers often act as prosecutors in the magistrate's courts." The result is lengthy trial backlogs. Expropriation is possible.

REGULATION
Score: **3**–Stable (moderate level)

Belize's regulatory regime is not always transparent. The U.S. Department of Commerce reports that "laws and regulations on tax, labor, customs, and health and safety do not significantly distort or impede the efficient mobilization and allocation of investment capital. However, a few investors have found a lack of transparency in the administration of some Belizean laws and procedures, such as compulsory acquisition of land, investment incentive programs and import licenses." According to the same source, "laws against bribery are rarely enforced." Some labor benefits are required by law. There is a minimum wage.

INFORMAL MARKET
Score: **3.5**–Worse (high level of activity)

Transparency International's 2004 score for Belize is 3.8. Therefore, Belize's informal market score is 3.5 this year—0.5 point worse than last year.

BENIN

Rank: 117

Score: 3.40

Category: Mostly Unfree

Present & Past Scores

(Best) 1
2
3
4
(Worst) 5

3.53 3.44 3.35 3.34 3.21 3.23 3.46 3.56 3.49 3.63 3.40

'95 '96 '97 '98 '99 '00 '01 '02 '03 '04 '05 '06
n/a

QUICK STUDY

SCORES

Trade Policy 4.5
Fiscal Burden 4.5
Government Intervention 2.5
Monetary Policy 1
Foreign Investment 4
Banking and Finance 3
Wages and Prices 3
Property Rights 4
Regulation 4
Informal Market 3.5

Population: 6,720,250

Total area: 112,620 sq. km

GDP: $2.6 billion

GDP growth rate: 4.8%

GDP per capita: $392

Major exports: textiles, cotton, cocoa, petroleum

Exports of goods and services: $384.1 million

Major export trading partners: China 22.3%, India 16.1%, Thailand 7.2%, Ghana 6.1%

Major imports: foodstuffs, tobacco, petroleum products

Imports of goods and services: $709 million

Major import trading partners: China 28.8%, France 14.5%, UK 4.6%, Ivory Coast 4.5%

Foreign direct investment (net): $45.3 million

2003 Data (in constant 2000 US dollars)

After a succession of military leaders following independence, Benin has become one of Africa's more stable and democratic countries. President Mathieu Kérékou seized power in 1972 and then moved slowly toward democracy, abiding by his defeat in 1991 and re-winning the presidency in 1996 and 2001. He has hinted that he will end his effort to amend the constitution to permit a third term and will step down in 2006. The most recent presidential and parliamentary elections were judged to have been free and fair. Benin's economy is mixed, with services providing half of GDP. Most of the population engages in agriculture, with cotton and textiles the primary exports. Trade with Nigeria, particularly the re-export of value-added products, is very important to Benin's economy. Economic reform has contributed to annual economic growth averaging nearly 5 percent since the early 1990s. Benin must still privatize key utilities and the state-controlled cotton industry and increase transparency, and the 2006 presidential and 2007 legislative elections are likely to affect promised reform of civil service pay and the pace of privatization. The judiciary is more independent than in previous years but remains inefficient and subject to corruption and interference from the executive branch. Benin's fiscal burden of government score is 0.2 point worse this year; however its trade policy and informal market scores are 0.5 point better, and its government intervention score is 1.5 points better. As a result, Benin's overall score is 0.23 point better this year.

 TRADE POLICY
Score: **4.5**–Better (very high level of protectionism)

Benin is a member of the West African Economic and Monetary Union (WAEMU), which imposes a common external tariff with four rates: 0 percent, 5 percent, 10 percent, and 20 percent. According to the World Bank, Benin's weighted average tariff rate in 2004 was 12.7 percent, down from the 15.5 percent reported in the 2005 *Index*. The U.S. Department of Commerce reports that "an inefficient, corrupt customs process still makes the importation of goods by sea, air or land costly and time consuming." The World Trade Organization notes that Benin restricts imports of some goods to authorized companies and applies selected import bans. Based on the lower tariff rate, as well as a revision of the trade factor methodology, Benin's trade policy score is 0.5 point better this year.

 FISCAL BURDEN OF GOVERNMENT
Score—Income Taxation: **4**–Better (high tax rates)
Score—Corporate Taxation: **5**–Worse (very high tax rates)
Score—Change in Government Expenditures: **4**–Worse (moderate increase)
Final Score: **4.5**–Worse (very high cost of government)

The International Monetary Fund reports that Benin's top income tax rate is 40 percent, down from the 60 percent reported in the 2005 *Index*. According to Deloitte, the corporate tax rate is 38 percent, up from the 35 percent reported in the 2005 *Index*. In 2003, according to the African Development Bank, government expenditures as a share of GDP increased 1.5 percentage points to 21.1 percent, compared to a 0.7 percentage point decrease in 2002. On net, Benin's fiscal burden of government score is 0.2 point worse this year.

GOVERNMENT INTERVENTION IN THE ECONOMY
Score: 2.5–Better (moderate level)

The World Bank reports that the government consumed 13.9 percent of GDP in 2003. In the same year, based on data from the International Monetary Fund, Benin received 5.5 percent of its total revenues from state-owned enterprises and government ownership of property. Based on the availability of new data for revenues from state-owned enterprises, Benin's government intervention score is 1.5 points better this year.

MONETARY POLICY
Score: 1–Stable (very low level of inflation)

As a member of the WAEMU, Benin uses the CFA franc, pegged to the euro. From 1995 to 2004, Benin's weighted average annual rate of inflation was 1.27 percent.

CAPITAL FLOWS AND FOREIGN INVESTMENT
Score: 4–Stable (high barriers)

The U.S. Department of Commerce reports that foreign investors still must contend with inefficient bureaucracies that are subject to corruption. "Many investors complain that the investment code is difficult to implement in practice, however, because of an inefficient and corrupt bureaucracy…. Foreign businessmen complain that establishing a business requires numerous bribes…." In addition, "Many labor laws…remain holdovers from the Marxist era and serve as impediments to private enterprise, despite revamping the labor code in 1998." The government requires part-Beninese ownership of any privatized company. The International Monetary Fund reports that foreign exchange accounts must be authorized by the government and the Central Bank of West African States, or BCEAO. Many capital transactions, including direct investment, are subject to reporting requirements and approval by the government and the BCEAO. There are no controls on the purchase of land by non-residents, except for investments in enterprises, branches, or corporations.

BANKING AND FINANCE
Score: 3–Stable (moderate level of restrictions)

The BCEAO, a central bank common to the eight members of the WAEMU, governs Benin's banking system. The eight BCEAO member countries use the CFA franc, pegged to the euro. The state banking system collapsed in the late 1980s, and the Economist Intelligence Unit reports that the banking sector is now predominantly private. The government continues to own only a minority share in one bank (Continental Bank) and is trying to sell that stake. The International Monetary Fund reports that, as of November 2004, there were "eight commercial banks (which account for about 90 percent of the total financial sector assets), two leasing companies, eight insurance companies, and over 100 formal microfinance institutions." Foreign ownership in banking and insurance is prominent. According to the U.S. Department of Commerce, "Credit is allocated on market terms and foreign investors can get credit on the local market. However, legal, regulatory and accounting systems are often unwieldy. Some observers claim the banking industry is not subject to effective mandatory regulation and most banks are not managed in a transparent fashion." All banks are required to meet a minimum capital adequacy ratio, and supervision of the banking system has been strengthened.

WAGES AND PRICES
Score: 3–Stable (moderate level of intervention)

The government sets some prices; heavily subsidizes the cotton sector, which accounts for about 40 percent of GDP, particularly when the world price for cotton declines; and sets wages for a number of occupations administratively.

PROPERTY RIGHTS
Score: 4–Stable (low level of protection)

Benin's justice system is weak and subject to corruption. The U.S. Department of Commerce reports that there is no separate commercial court system, and the "backlog of civil cases often results in a wait of two or more years before matters proceed to trial…." According to the Economist Intelligence Unit, "Endemic corruption in public administration clouds the business environment and acts as a major disincentive to investment…. The judiciary is also prey to temptation—more than one-half of the country's magistrates were involved in a financial scandal that came to light in 2001."

REGULATION
Score: 4–Stable (high level)

The U.S. Department of Commerce reports that "bureaucratic procedures are insufficiently streamlined and are rarely transparent in practice…. [There is] an excess of paperwork and counter-signings by various ministries. These obstacles work against the 'processing office' (one-stop-shop)," which is aimed at simplifying the investment process, and foster corruption. Many labor laws from the Marxist era still create obstacles to private enterprise. The Economist Intelligence Unit reports that corruption is a serious obstacle to doing business in Benin.

INFORMAL MARKET
Score: 3.5–Better (high level of activity)

Transparency International's 2004 score for Benin is 3.2. Therefore, Benin's informal market score is 3.5 this year—0.5 point better than last year.

BOLIVIA

Rank: 67

Score: 2.96

Category: Mostly Free

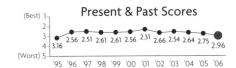

Present & Past Scores

(Best) 1
2
3
4
(Worst) 5

3.16 2.56 2.51 2.61 2.61 2.56 2.31 2.66 2.54 2.64 2.75 2.96

'95 '96 '97 '98 '99 '00 '01 '02 '03 '04 '05 '06

QUICK STUDY

SCORES

Trade Policy	3
Fiscal Burden	2.6
Government Intervention	2
Monetary Policy	2
Foreign Investment	4
Banking and Finance	2
Wages and Prices	2
Property Rights	4
Regulation	4
Informal Market	4

Population: 8,814,158

Total area: 1,098,580 sq. km

GDP: $8.9 billion

GDP growth rate: 2.5%

GDP per capita: $1,017

Major exports: natural gas, processed soya, zinc, gold

Exports of goods and services: $2 billion

Major export trading partners: Brazil 35.7%, Venezuela 13.3%, Colombia 12.4%, US 12.0%

Major imports: raw materials and semi-manufactures, consumer goods, petroleum, foodstuffs

Imports of goods and services: $2.3 billion

Major import trading partners: Brazil 25.9%, Argentina 17.4%, US 13.1%, Chile 10.1%

Foreign direct investment (net): $148.6 million

2003 Data (in constant 2000 US dollars)

Politics in Bolivia has become the art of division, not addition. During the 1990s, market-oriented reforms brought growth and stability, but they did not fundamentally change the government's centralized nature or fully open the economy. The turning point came in October 2003, when violent mobs forced President Gonzalo Sánchez de Lozada from office. His successor, Carlos Mesa-Gisbert, has managed to hang onto power by a thread. A 2004 referendum partly re-nationalized Bolivia's hydrocarbon industries, but indigenous leaders like Movement Toward Socialism congressman Evo Morales are agitating for total state ownership. As a result, citizens in gas-producing districts like Santa Cruz and Tarija would like autonomy from the rest of Bolivia, whose government they view as irresponsible and responding to fear. In March 2005, indigenous groups led by radical activists blocked roads leading into the highland capital of La Paz, threatening gas and food supplies. In May 2005, lawmakers passed a new hydrocarbons measure that levied a 32 percent tax on top of an existing 18 percent royalty on oil and gas production. It also forced 12 foreign energy companies to renegotiate exploration and production contracts. Growth in GDP could shrink substantially as foreign oil and gas companies invest elsewhere. Bolivia's fiscal burden of government score is 0.4 point better this year; however its trade policy score is 0.5 point worse, and its monetary policy and foreign investment scores are 1 point worse. As a result, Bolivia's overall score is 0.21 point worse this year.

TRADE POLICY
Score: **3**–Worse (moderate level of protectionism)

According to the World Bank, Bolivia's weighted average tariff rate in 2004 was 5.3 percent, down from the 8.8 percent reported in the 2005 *Index*. The U.S. Department of Commerce reports, however, that "Bolivian import charges, including domestic taxes (most of which are creditable) and fees, range from 30 to 45 percent, making the effective cost of imports considerably higher than the stated zero to 10 percent tariff." Based on new evidence of non-tariff barriers, as well as a revision of the trade factor methodology, Bolivia's trade policy score is 0.5 point worse this year.

FISCAL BURDEN OF GOVERNMENT
Score—Income Taxation: **1.5**–Stable (low tax rates)
Score—Corporate Taxation: **3**–Stable (moderate tax rates)
Score—Change in Government Expenditures: **3**–Better (very low decrease)
Final Score: **2.6**–Better (moderate cost of government)

Bolivia's income tax rate is 13 percent. The corporate tax rate is 25 percent. In 2003, based on data from the Central Bank of Bolivia, government expenditures as a share of GDP decreased 0.7 percentage point to 32.6 percent, compared to a 2.3 percentage point increase in 2002. On net, Bolivia's fiscal burden of government score is 0.4 point better this year.

GOVERNMENT INTERVENTION IN THE ECONOMY
Score: **2**–Stable (low level)

The World Bank reports that the government consumed 16.6 percent of GDP in 2003. In 2004, based on data from the International Monetary Fund, Bolivia received 1.29 percent of its total revenues from state-owned enterprises and government ownership of property.

MONETARY POLICY
Score: **2**–Worse (low level of inflation)

From 1995 to 2004, Bolivia's weighted average annual rate of inflation was 3.79 percent, up from 2.68 percent from 1994 to 2003. As a result, Bolivia's monetary policy score is 1 point worse this year.

 CAPITAL FLOWS AND FOREIGN INVESTMENT
Score: **4**–Worse (high barriers)

Bolivia encourages foreign investment. The 1990 Investment Law and other legislation establish guarantees of equal treatment of foreign companies, repatriation of profits, currency convertibility, and the right to international arbitration. A new hydrocarbons law sharply increases taxes on oil and gas companies and abrogates current operating contracts. The legislation follows growing hostility to foreign investment by radical elements who have organized repeated strikes urging increased state control of the economy. Still, red tape and bureaucratic obstacles remain. According to the U.S. Department of Commerce, "Public sector corruption also remains a major challenge, with firms sometimes asked for bribes by public officials to speed up bureaucratic procedures or to avoid unpleasant, adverse actions." The same source reports that "investments often do not receive the full protection offered by law due to sometimes inconsistent and arbitrary decisions by regulators, an easily corrupted and influenced judicial system that can deny legal due process, and arbitrarily unfavorable interpretations of laws and regulations by government officials." The International Monetary Fund reports that both residents and non-residents may hold foreign exchange accounts; there are no restrictions or controls on payments, transactions, transfers, purchase of real estate, access to foreign exchange, or repatriation of profits. Based on the confiscatory revision of the hydrocarbons law, Bolivia's capital flows and foreign investment score is 1 point worse this year.

 BANKING AND FINANCE
Score: **2**–Stable (low level of restrictions)

New laws reformed Bolivia's banking system in 1993 and 1995, clarifying the legality of factoring, leasing, and foreign currency hedging; permitting banks to hold foreign currency accounts; increasing reserve requirements; and prohibiting insider lending. Government-owned banks no longer exist. The Economist Intelligence Unit reports that in 2004, Bolivia had nine domestic banks, three foreign banks, and 45 non-bank financial institutions. The banking sector is open to foreign investment. According to the EIU, "Most local banks now have some degree of foreign participation.... The three wholly foreign banking operations have a presence in some larger cities; they mainly engage in corporate lending." The EIU also reports that "The economic downturn of 1999–2001, combined with stricter reporting requirements and tougher conditions imposed on new lending, led to a sharp rise in non-performing loans.... Levels of bad debt have begun to fall, but remain at historic highs."

 WAGES AND PRICES
Score: **2**–Stable (low level of intervention)

There are few price controls. The U.S. Department of Commerce reports that "Bolivia enjoys an open market, with the Government of Bolivia imposing price controls only on petroleum products, the price of which is set by the Superintendent of Hydrocarbons. Municipal governments set prices of some basic goods, such as bread, meat, and vegetables." Bolivia has a minimum wage.

 PROPERTY RIGHTS
Score: **4**–Stable (low level of protection)

Legal protection of private property in Bolivia is weak. The U.S. Department of Commerce warns that "Property and contractual rights may be enforced in Bolivian courts, but the legal process is time-consuming at best and at worst subject to political influences and pervasive corruption. For that reason, the National Chamber of Commerce—with assistance from USAID—has established a local Arbitration Tribunal. The Investment Law provides that investors may submit their differences to arbitration in accordance with the constitution and international norms."

 REGULATION
Score: **4**–Stable (high level)

"Although some bureaucratic procedures have been reduced," reports the U.S. Department of Commerce, "plenty of red tape and archaic policies remain at all levels of the Bolivian Government. The last two administrations worked to 'de-bureaucratize' the government, with modest success at best. Public sector corruption also remains a major challenge." According to the Economist Intelligence Unit, "Repeated cases of corruption and influence peddling by top officials continue to emerge." In May 2005, reports the EIU, the government passed a controversial Hydrocarbons law, levying "a non-deductible 32% tax on energy operators, in addition to the 18% royalty they already pay."

 INFORMAL MARKET
Score: **4**–Stable (high level of activity)

Transparency International's 2004 score for Bolivia is 2.2. Therefore, Bolivia's informal market score is 4 this year.

BOSNIA AND HERZEGOVINA

Rank: 74

Score: 3.01

Category: Mostly Unfree

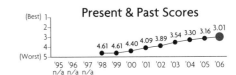

Present & Past Scores

(Best) 1
2
3
4
(Worst) 5

4.61 4.61 4.40 4.09 3.89 3.54 3.30 3.16 3.01

'95 '96 '97 '98 '99 '00 '01 '02 '03 '04 '05 '06
n/a n/a n/a

Despite billions of dollars in assistance since 1995, Bosnia and Herzegovina has yet to enjoy significant economic recovery. Rule of law remains virtually nonexistent, and local courts are subject to substantial political interference and lack the resources to prosecute complex crimes. The 2002 elections brought to power state and entity-level governments dominated by the three nationalist parties, leaving little likelihood of political stability. Most of the older political parties in all three ethnic communities—Serbian, Croatian, and Muslim—are linked to organized crime. For example, the Bosnian Croat member of the three-man presidency, Dragan Covic, has been indicted on charges of fraud and bribery. Problems like intrusive bureaucracy, costly registration procedures, and an overly large role for the state (government expenditures amounted to 46.9 percent of GDP in 2003) remain unaddressed. In 2003, unemployment was 42 percent. Signs of marginal revival include growing trade across inter-entity boundaries, GDP growth of 2.7 percent in 2003, and a record $359.4 million of foreign direct investment. Bosnia's reliance on the international community is coming to an end, and the International Monetary Fund foresees a sharp drop in international aid in coming years. Bosnia and Herzegovina's trade policy score is 0.5 point better this year, and its foreign investment score is 1 point better. As a result, Bosnia and Herzegovina's overall score is 0.15 point better this year.

TRADE POLICY
Score: **2.5**–Better (moderate level of protectionism)

The World Bank reports that Bosnia and Herzegovina's weighted average tariff rate in 2001 was 4.9 percent. (The World Bank has revised the figure for 2001 downward from the 6.6 percent reported in the 2005 *Index*.) According to the Economist Intelligence Unit, "The state-level government announced that it was reinstating customs tariffs, at previous 2003 levels, on a range of agricultural goods imported from Croatia and Serbia and Montenegro. The tariffs, which had been zero-rated, were increased to between 7% and 40% of import value." The EIU also notes that the government often takes a mercantilist approach to trade by supporting key export sectors with subsidies and trade protection. Based on the lower tariff rate, as well as a revision of the trade factor methodology, Bosnia and Herzegovina's trade policy score is 0.5 point better this year.

FISCAL BURDEN OF GOVERNMENT
Score—Income Taxation: **1**–Stable (very low tax rates)
Score—Corporate Taxation: **4**–Stable (high tax rates)
Score—Change in Government Expenditures: **1.5**–Stable (high decrease)
Final Score: **2.6**–Stable (moderate cost of government)

According to the Foreign Investment Promotion Agency of Bosnia and Herzegovina, the top income tax rate is 5 percent. According to Deloitte, the top corporate tax rate is 30 percent. The European Bank for Reconstruction and Development reports that government expenditures as a share of GDP decreased more in 2003 (3.5 percentage points to 46.9 percent) than they did in 2002 (3.1 percentage points).

QUICK STUDY

SCORES

Trade Policy	2.5
Fiscal Burden	2.6
Government Intervention	2.5
Monetary Policy	1
Foreign Investment	3
Banking and Finance	2
Wages and Prices	3
Property Rights	5
Regulation	5
Informal Market	3.5

Population: 4,139,835

Total area: 51,129 sq. km

GDP: $5.1 billion

GDP growth rate: 2.7%

GDP per capita: $1,225

Major exports: manufactured goods, clothing, wood products, base metals

Exports of goods and services: $1.5 billion

Major export trading partners: Italy 28.7%, Croatia 18.2%, Germany 17.1%, Austria 9.2%

Major imports: machinery and transport equipment, fuel, chemicals, foodstuffs

Imports of goods and services: $2.9 billion

Major import trading partners: Croatia 24.4%, Slovenia 14.7%, Germany 13.6%, Italy 12.1%

Foreign direct investment (net): $359.4 million

2003 Data (in constant 2000 US dollars)

GOVERNMENT INTERVENTION IN THE ECONOMY
Score: **2.5**–Stable (moderate level)

According to the World Bank, the government consumed 22.3 percent of GDP in 2003. In 2004, based on data from the International Monetary Fund, Bosnia and Herzegovina received 3.48 percent of its total revenues from state-owned enterprises and government ownership of property.

 MONETARY POLICY
Score: **1**–Stable (very low level of inflation)

Bosnia has a currency board system pegging its marka to the euro. From 1995 to 2004, based on data from the International Monetary Fund's *2005 World Economic Outlook*, Bosnia and Herzegovina's weighted average annual rate of inflation was 0.84 percent.

 CAPITAL FLOWS AND FOREIGN INVESTMENT
Score: **3**–Better (moderate barriers)

The government of Bosnia and Herzegovina grants national treatment to foreign investors, protects investors from changes in laws pertaining to foreign investment, and protects investments against expropriation and nationalization of assets except in special circumstances and only with due compensation. The International Monetary Fund reports few restrictions on capital transaction and foreign exchange accounts. There are no restrictions on the types of business activities that are open to foreign investment, with the exception of armaments and public information, in which foreign control is limited to 49 percent. A privatization law passed by the lower and upper houses of the Federation parliament would prohibit the sale of state-owned companies to foreign-owned companies unless they were majority owned by the private sector. The U.S. Department of Commerce reports that "foreign investors continue to face a number of serious obstacles, including a complex legal and regulatory framework, non-transparent business procedures, and weak judicial structures." Based on evidence of relatively few formal restrictions on foreign investment, Bosnia and Herzegovina's capital flows and foreign investment score is 1 point better this year.

 BANKING AND FINANCE
Score: **2**–Stable (low level of restrictions)

Bosnia and Herzegovina's banking sector has been improving. "With a growing number of foreign banks present in the country," reports the U.S. Department of Commerce, "competition is strong and banks are starting to offer an extended product range (credit cards, consumer loans, mortgages).... Small and medium size enterprises still experience difficulties obtaining long-term credit. Inadequate secured transaction regulations and an inefficient court system make collateral foreclosure difficult and increase the cost of capital." According to the Central Bank of Bosnia and Herzegovina, as of March 2004, there

were 37 banks in Bosnia and Herzegovina (27 in the Bosnian–Croatian Federation and 10 in Bosnian–Serb Republic), and private capital in the banking sector accounted for 92 percent of total capital, including 72 percent accounted for by foreign banks; however, the government continues to have an ownership stake in a number of banks, including majority ownership in a few banks, "mostly those with special functions."

 WAGES AND PRICES
Score: **3**–Stable (moderate level of intervention)

"Although the markets generally determine prices," reports the U.S. Department of Commerce, "certain goods and services are still subject to government control (electricity, gas, telecom services). The government has the ability to influence pricing policy at companies under its direct or indirect control." The government mandates a minimum wage.

 PROPERTY RIGHTS
Score: **5**–Stable (very low level of protection)

The U.S. Department of Commerce reports that "Bosnia and Herzegovina's judicial system...does not yet adequately cover commercial activities. There are no commercial courts...and no efficient way to resolve commercial disputes. Contract and property rights, in practice, are almost unenforceable.... [J]udges typically seek bribes or are subject to influence by public officials. Even when there is a positive decision from the court, there may be no way to enforce a judgment. Further discouraging complaints, the plaintiff must pay a high upfront tax on civil suits."

 REGULATION
Score: **5**–Stable (very high level)

Bosnia and Herzegovina's regulatory environment is burdensome and not transparent. According to the U.S. Department of Commerce, "Establishing a business in Bosnia can be an extremely burdensome and time-consuming process for investors. In the Federation, there are 14 different administrative approvals needed for registration.... The myriad of state, entity and municipal administrations creates a heavily bureaucratic system lacking transparency. This is particularly problematic for investors." In addition, "The business registration and licensing process is particularly vulnerable to corruption.... Domestic and international entrepreneurs often are forced to pay bribes to obtain necessary business licenses, or simply to expedite the approval process."

 INFORMAL MARKET
Score: **3.5**–Stable (high level of activity)

Transparency International's 2004 score for Bosnia and Herzegovina is 3.1. Therefore, Bosnia and Herzegovina's informal market score is 3.5 this year.

BOTSWANA

Rank: 30

Score: 2.29

Category: Mostly Free

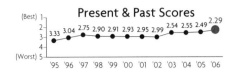

Present & Past Scores

(Best) 1
2
3
4
(Worst) 5

3.33 3.04 2.75 2.90 2.91 2.93 2.95 2.99 2.54 2.55 2.49 2.29

'95 '96 '97 '98 '99 '00 '01 '02 '03 '04 '05 '06

Botswana has Africa's oldest continuous, multiparty democratic system of government, dating back to independence in 1966. Elections are routinely free and fair. The country's market-led economy, rated Africa's freest in the 2005 *Index*, encourages private enterprise and has enjoyed one of the world's highest average growth rates during the past four decades. Despite ongoing difficulties in restraining government spending, Botswana retains an investment-grade rating from both Moody's and Standard and Poor's that places it on par with, or above, countries like Israel and South Africa. Botswana is among the world's biggest diamond producers; diamonds remain the source of over 75 percent of export income, 50 percent of government revenue, and one-third of GDP despite efforts to diversify the economy through lower tax rates, the elimination of exchange controls, and other foreign investment incentives. HIV/AIDS threatens the country's economic future: Estimates indicate that up to one-third of Botswana's adults are infected. The economy has also been hurt by instability in Zimbabwe that has led large numbers of illegal immigrants to flee that country. As a landlocked country with a small population, Botswana depends on its neighbors and is an advocate for regional integration and free trade. Botswana's fiscal burden of government score is 0.5 point better this year, and its government intervention score is 1.5 points better. As a result, Botswana's overall score is 0.20 point better this year.

TRADE POLICY
Score: **1.5**–Stable (low level of protectionism)

Botswana is part of the Southern African Customs Union (SACU) with South Africa, Lesotho, Swaziland, and Namibia. The World Bank reports that in 2001 (the most recent year for which World Bank data are available), the SACU had a weighted average common external tariff rate of 3.6 percent. According to the U.S. Department of Commerce, "There are very few tariff or non-tariff barriers to trade with Botswana, apart from restrictions on licensing for some business operations, which are reserved for [Botswana] companies." Based on the revised trade factor methodology, Botswana's trade policy score is unchanged.

FISCAL BURDEN OF GOVERNMENT
Score—Income Taxation: **2.5**–Stable (moderate tax rates)
Score—Corporate Taxation: **3**–Stable (moderate tax rates)
Score—Change in Government Expenditures: **3**–Better (very low decrease)
Final Score: **2.9**–Better (moderate cost of government)

Botswana has one of Southern Africa's lower tax burdens. According to the International Monetary Fund, the top income tax rate is 25 percent. The top corporate tax rate is also 25 percent. In 2003, reports the African Development Bank, government expenditures as a share of GDP fell 0.5 percentage point to 44.5 percent, compared to a 3 percentage point increase in 2002. On net, Botswana's fiscal burden of government score is 0.5 point better this year.

GOVERNMENT INTERVENTION IN THE ECONOMY
Score: **3**–Better (moderate high level)

According to the World Bank, the government consumed 35.5 percent of GDP in 2003. During the period from April 2003–March 2004, based on data from the Bank of Botswana, Botswana received 6.9 percent of its total revenues from state-owned enterprises and government

QUICK STUDY

SCORES
Trade Policy	1.5
Fiscal Burden	2.9
Government Intervention	3
Monetary Policy	3
Foreign Investment	2
Banking and Finance	2
Wages and Prices	2
Property Rights	2
Regulation	2
Informal Market	2.5

Population: 1,722,468

Total area: 600,370 sq. km

GDP: $6.1 billion

GDP growth rate: 5.4%

GDP per capita: $3,532

Major exports: copper and nickel, diamonds, textiles, meat products

Exports of goods and services: $2.8 billion

Major export trading partners: UK 66.5%, SACU 10.4%, Zimbabwe 2.4% (2001)

Major imports: machinery and transport equipment, textiles, petroleum products

Imports of goods and services: $2 billion

Major import trading partners: SACU 76.6%, Zimbabwe 3.9%, UK 2.7% (2001)

Foreign direct investment (net): $43.7 million

2003 Data (in constant 2000 US dollars)

ownership of property. Based on revised data on revenues from state-owned enterprises, Botswana's government intervention score is 1.5 point better this year.

 MONETARY POLICY
Score: **3**–Stable (moderate level of inflation)

From 1995 to 2004, Botswana's weighted average annual rate of inflation was 7.57 percent.

 CAPITAL FLOWS AND FOREIGN INVESTMENT
Score: **2**–Stable (low barriers)

Botswana is encouraging foreign investment, particularly in the non-mining sector. According to the U.S. Department of Commerce, the government has "abolished all exchange controls...has undertaken largely successful efforts to combat crime, including corruption, and to improve the delivery of the judicial system...[and] has instituted low corporate tax rates, the increasingly speedy processing of applications for business ventures, a stable macroeconomic environment, and a commitment to transparency." The International Monetary Fund reports no restrictions on capital transactions of foreign exchange accounts. "[F]oreign investors have access to credit on the local market.... Botswana banks may lend to non-resident controlled companies and other non-resident owned business entities in Botswana without specific approval from the Bank of Botswana. In fact, foreign investors generally enjoy much better access to credit than local firms," notes the U.S. Department of Commerce. "With the elimination of exchange controls, foreign investors may now participate in this bond market." The government restricts foreign investment in some areas reserved for Botswana citizens, including butchery and produce, petrol filling stations, bars and liquor stores, supermarkets, and retail. The U.S. Department of Commerce reports that "there is a brief list of enterprises reserved for ownership by citizens and a minimum value for foreign investment in a number of industries, but these restrictions are not a meaningful impediment to serious foreign investment."

 BANKING AND FINANCE
Score: **2**–Stable (low level of restrictions)

Botswana's banking system is competitive and advanced. There are five commercial banks, and all are foreign owned (two British, two South African, and one Indian). The government is involved in the banking sector through several financial parastatals—Botswana Development Corporation, the Citizen Entrepreneur Development Agency, the Botswana Building Society, and the National Development Bank. The insurance sector and the stock market have been growing strongly in recent years. There are no barriers to foreign banks, no restrictions on credit or interest rates, and no evidence of government influence on private banks. According to the U.S. Department of Commerce, "[T]he abolition of exchange controls has allowed the further development of Botswana's financial markets through the creation of new portfolio invest-

ment options.... The country's policies facilitate the free flow of financial resources. Credit is available on market terms."

 WAGES AND PRICES
Score: **2**–Stable (low level of intervention)

Price controls have been eliminated, but the government exerts some influence over the price of livestock and agricultural goods. Local farmers receive extensive government relief in drought years—in some cases, to such an extent that profits increase during drought, according to the Economist Intelligence Unit, which reports that "Cattle farmers receive significant financial support and generous tax treatment." The minimum daily wage, determined by the Cabinet with advice from government, labor, and private-sector representatives, was extended to domestic workers in 2002.

 PROPERTY RIGHTS
Score: **2**–Stable (high level of protection)

The constitution provides for an independent judiciary, and the government respects this provision in practice. According to the U.S. Department of State, "The Botswana constitution provides for a judiciary, which is independent of both the executive and legislative authorities.... The legal system is sufficient to conduct secure commercial dealings." However, "the judicial system did not [always] provide timely fair trials due to a serious and increasing backlog of cases."

 REGULATION
Score: **2**–Stable (low level)

Regulation is transparent and evenly applied. The U.S. Department of Commerce reports that the "government adheres to transparent policies and maintains effective laws to foster competition and establishes clear rules for operation." In addition, "Business licenses are issued following a routine review of proposed commercial activities, which is carried out in a transparent and non-discriminatory manner." The government has made some efforts to make it easier for small businesses to open and operate, creating a one-stop shop for investors to avoid unnecessary bureaucratic steps to start a new business. According to the U.S. Department of Commerce, "Investors with experience in other developing nations describe the lack of obstruction or interference by government as among the country's most important assets."

 INFORMAL MARKET
Score: **2.5**–Stable (moderate level of activity)

Transparency International's 2004 score for Botswana is 6. Therefore, Botswana's informal market score is 2.5 this year.

> Botswana qualifies for the Global Free Trade Alliance.

BRAZIL

Rank: 81

Score: 3.08

Category: Mostly Unfree

Present & Past Scores

(Best) 1
2
3
4
(Worst) 5

3.41 3.61 3.33 3.41 3.24 3.46 3.26 3.11 3.06 3.10 3.20 3.08

'95 '96 '97 '98 '99 '00 '01 '02 '03 '04 '05 '06

QUICK STUDY

SCORES

Trade Policy	3.5
Fiscal Burden	2.8
Government Intervention	4
Monetary Policy	3
Foreign Investment	3
Banking and Finance	3
Wages and Prices	2
Property Rights	3
Regulation	3
Informal Market	3.5

Population: 176,596,256

Total area: 8,511,965 sq. km

GDP: $619.9 billion

GDP growth rate: −0.2%

GDP per capita: $3,510

Major exports: transport equipment and parts, soybeans, coffee, oils

Exports of goods and services: $87.9 billion

Major export trading partners: US 22.9%, Argentina 6.2%, China 6.2%, Netherlands 5.8 %, Germany 4.3%

Major imports: machinery and electrical equipment, chemical products, oil

Imports of goods and services: $63.8 billion

Major import trading partners: US 20.1%, Argentina 9.6%, Germany 8.7%, Japan 5.2%

Foreign direct investment (net): $9.3 billion

2003 Data (in constant 2000 US dollars)

Despite reforms implemented under former President Fernando Henrique Cardoso, Brazil's economy—the largest in Latin America—is still burdened with structural problems that undermine prospects for long-term growth. Luiz Inacio "Lula" da Silva, who became president on a predominantly leftist platform, further undermined growth by voluntarily raising the fiscal surplus target established by the International Monetary Fund. The surpluses have been generated primarily by distortionary taxes on financial transactions, further burdening the productive sector. In March 2005, Brazil decided not to renew an agreement with the International Monetary Fund, but it continues to follow the previously agreed-upon IMF framework, including an onerous tax regime designed to quiet fiscal hawks, a floating exchange rate, and inflation targeting. The government has secured congressional approval for limited pension reform. However, there still exist many other serious obstacles to long-term investment and economic growth, including a convoluted tax system, barriers to foreign investment in some sectors, government management of most of the oil and electricity sector and a significant part of the banking system, a weak judiciary, and a complicated regulatory maze. Brazil's fiscal burden of government score is 0.2 point better this year, and its monetary policy score is 1 point better. As a result, Brazil's overall score is 0.12 point better this year.

 TRADE POLICY
Score: **3.5**–Stable (high level of protectionism)

As a member of the Southern Cone Common Market (MERCOSUR), Brazil adheres to a common external tariff that ranges from zero to 25 percent. The World Bank reports that Brazil's weighted average tariff rate in 2004 was 8 percent, down from the 9.9 percent reported for 2002 in the 2005 *Index*. According to the U.S. Department of Commerce, importing "can still be burdensome…. [T]he average customs clearance time in Brazil was the slowest in the [Western] Hemisphere." The government places controls on certain imports. Based on the revised trade factor methodology, Brazil's trade policy score is unchanged.

 FISCAL BURDEN OF GOVERNMENT
Score—Income Taxation: **2.5**–Stable (moderate tax rates)
Score—Corporate Taxation: **3**–Stable (moderate tax rates)
Score—Change in Government Expenditures: **2.5**–Better (low decrease)
Final Score: **2.8**–Better (moderate cost of government)

Brazil's top income tax rate is 27.5 percent. The top corporate tax rate is 25 percent (a 15 percent tax rate and a 10 percentage point surcharge). In 2004, based on data from the National Treasury, government expenditures as a share of GDP decreased 1 percentage point to 30.7 percent, compared to a 0.9 percentage point decrease in 2003. On net, Brazil's fiscal burden of government score is 0.2 point better this year.

 GOVERNMENT INTERVENTION IN THE ECONOMY
Score: **4**–Stable (high level)

Based on data from the Economist Intelligence Unit, the government consumed 18.4 percent of GDP in 2004. The government remains a significant presence in the economy. The EIU reports that the government owns Petrobras, the oil giant; Eletrobras, the state energy company that

119

controls a number of generation companies; Banco do Brasil, the largest retail bank in Latin America; and a national development bank.

MONETARY POLICY
Score: **3**–Better (moderate level of inflation)

From 1995 to 2004, Brazil's weighted average annual rate of inflation was 8.65 percent, down from the 12.34 percent from 1994 to 2003 reported in the 2005 *Index*. As a result, Brazil's monetary policy score is 1 point better this year.

CAPITAL FLOWS AND FOREIGN INVESTMENT
Score: **3**–Stable (moderate barriers)

Foreign capital may enter Brazil freely and receives national treatment. "Setting up new companies is relatively complex, although the Ministry of Development has signaled its desire to simplify this process," according to the U.S. Department of Commerce, but "Restrictions remain on foreign investment in a limited number of sectors: nuclear energy, health services, media, rural property, fishing, mail and telegraph, aviation, and aerospace." Foreigners are allowed to take part in the ongoing privatization process. Foreign ownership of rural land and land adjacent to national borders is prohibited. The International Monetary Fund reports that there are limited restrictions on foreign exchange accounts, as well as legal restrictions prohibiting foreign participation in certain economic activities, and that the central bank must approve outward direct investment in some cases, including transfers and remittances, where the central bank has broad administrative discretion.

BANKING AND FINANCE
Score: **3**–Stable (moderate level of restrictions)

Brazil's highly developed and efficient banking system is the largest in South America and offers a wide range of financial services. As of September 2004, reports the Economist Intelligence Unit, the top 10 domestic banks held nearly 60 percent of total banking assets. Five of Brazil's top 10 banks were foreign-owned at the end of 2004, and foreign banks held about 24 percent of total banking assets as of October 2004. Although the number of state-owned banks has fallen in recent years, the government's presence is still significant. According to the EIU, "Article 52 of Title IX of the 1988 constitution allows for the privatization of state banks.... [M]ost state banks have been sold to foreign and domestic institutions, although two public sector federal banks still account for almost half of the banking system's total assets.... At the federal level, the government maintains a host of financial institutions that carry out certain functions, such as subsidizing mortgages and engaging in development banking for particular industries and specific regions of the country."

WAGES AND PRICES
Score: **2**–Stable (low level of intervention)

The market determines most prices in Brazil, with some exceptions. According to the Economist Intelligence Unit, "Some public goods and services supplied by state-owned enterprises or by local governments remain under government control. Although many public services and infrastructure investments...were either privatized or transferred to private management through public concessions, the federal government still oversees tariffs and prices through regulatory agencies for these sectors." A mandated minimum wage is adjusted by the government each year.

PROPERTY RIGHTS
Score: **3**–Stable (moderate level of protection)

"Contracts in Brazil are generally considered secured," reports the Economist Intelligence Unit, "although it is important to specify the jurisdiction for any disputes...." According to the U.S. Department of State, "The judiciary...is inefficient, subject to political and economic influence, and plagued by problems relating to lack of resources and training of officials." Judicial decisions can take years, and "decisions of the Supreme Federal Tribunal are not automatically binding on lower courts, leading to more appeals than would otherwise occur."

REGULATION
Score: **3**–Stable (moderate level)

Brazil's regulatory structure is burdensome and not entirely transparent. "A study by Brazil's small-business association," reports *The Wall Street Journal*, "found that 70% of entrepreneurs who try to open a business legally never conclude a process that requires about 100 different documents." According to the Economist Intelligence Unit, "Congress approved new legislation to regulate bankruptcies in July 2004. The new law, similar to Chapter 11 rules in the United States, will reduce filing time and give creditors some priority when restructuring and collecting on business debts." The labor market is highly rigid. *The Wall Street Journal* reports that "benefits mandated by the labor legislation double the nation's overall labor cost." The U.S. Department of Commerce characterizes corruption as "a persistent problem." Lax enforcement of existing laws against corruption is part of this problem.

INFORMAL MARKET
Score: **3.5**–Stable (high level of activity)

Transparency International's 2004 score for Brazil is 3.9. Therefore, Brazil's informal market score is 3.5 this year.

BULGARIA

Rank: 64
Score: 2.88
Category: Mostly Free

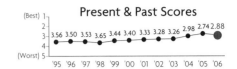
Present & Past Scores

(Best) 1
2
3
4
(Worst) 5

3.56 3.50 3.53 3.65 3.44 3.40 3.33 3.28 3.26 2.98 2.74 2.88

'95 '96 '97 '98 '99 '00 '01 '02 '03 '04 '05 '06

QUICK STUDY

SCORES

Trade Policy	3.5
Fiscal Burden	2.3
Government Intervention	2.5
Monetary Policy	3
Foreign Investment	2
Banking and Finance	2
Wages and Prices	2
Property Rights	4
Regulation	4
Informal Market	3.5

Population: 7,975,000

Total area: 110,910 sq. km

GDP: $14.35 billion

GDP growth rate: 4.3%

GDP per capita: $1,835

Major exports: machinery and transport equipment, textiles, clothing and footwear, base metals, mineral fuels

Exports of goods and services: $8.9 billion

Major export trading partners: Italy 14.1%, Germany 10.9%, Greece 10.5%, Turkey 9.2%

Major imports: machinery and transport equipment, mineral fuels, chemicals, plastics

Imports of goods and services: $10.6 billion

Major import trading partners: Germany 14.4%, Russia 12.6%, Italy 10.3%, France 5.7%

Foreign direct investment (net): $1.3 billion

2003 Data (in constant 2000 US dollars)

Bulgaria signed the European Union's accession treaty in April 2005, and its domestic and economic policies are driven by the anticipation of joining the EU in 2007. Although Prime Minister Simeon Saxe-Coburg-Gotha's coalition government survived the loss of its majority in 2004, the increasingly popular center–left Bulgarian Socialist Party was able to claim victory in the parliamentary elections of July 2005. Economic policy continues to focus on commitments to International Monetary Fund guidelines and EU entry requirements. Tax revenues and government spending increased during the past year. Despite tensions about the privatization of certain key industries, the government has progressed significantly in its economic reforms. Notwithstanding a dramatic increase in the foreign ownership of land, the legal system remains largely ineffective, allowing organized crime and corruption to hamper investment. Although necessary legal changes are unlikely until the next round of parliamentary elections, the new parliament will face greater pressure from the EU to proceed more vigorously with legal reforms. Bulgaria's fiscal burden of government score is 0.1 point better this year, and its foreign investment score is 1 point better; however, its trade policy and monetary policy scores are, respectively, 1.5 points and 1 point worse. As a result, Bulgaria's overall score is 0.14 point worse this year.

TRADE POLICY
Score: **3.5–Worse** (high level of protectionism)

According to the World Bank, Bulgaria's weighted average tariff rate in 2004 was 9.6 percent, up from the 1.5 percent for 2002 reported in the 2005 *Index*, based on data from Bulgaria's Ministry of Finance. The main non-tariff barriers are customs regulations and policies that the U.S. Department of Commerce characterizes as "cumbersome, arbitrary and inconsistent." The most common problems are "excessive documentation requirements, slow processing of shipments, and corruption." Due to the increased tariff rate, as well as a revision of the trade factor methodology, Bulgaria's trade policy score is 1.5 points worse this year.

FISCAL BURDEN OF GOVERNMENT
Score—Income Taxation: **2–Better** (low tax rates)
Score—Corporate Taxation: **1.5–Better** (low tax rates)
Score—Change in Government Expenditures: **4–Worse** (moderate increase)
Final Score: **2.3–Better** (low cost of government)

According to Deloitte, Bulgaria's top income tax rate is 24 percent, down from the 29 percent reported in the 2005 *Index*. Bulgaria implemented a flat corporate tax rate of 15 percent in January 2005, down from the 19.5 percent reported in the 2005 *Index*. In 2003, based on data from the Bulgarian National Bank, government expenditures as a share of GDP increased 1.5 percentage points to 40.9 percent, compared to a 1 percentage point decline in 2002. On net, Bulgaria's fiscal burden of government score is 0.1 point better this year.

GOVERNMENT INTERVENTION IN THE ECONOMY
Score: **2.5–Stable** (moderate level)

The World Bank reports that the government consumed 19 percent of GDP in 2003. In 2004, based on data from the Ministry of Finance, Bulgaria received 8.96 percent of its total revenues from state-owned enterprises and government ownership of property.

121

MONETARY POLICY
Score: 3–Worse (moderate level of inflation)

Bulgaria has a currency board system pegging its lev to the euro. From 1995 to 2004, Bulgaria's weighted average annual rate of inflation was 6.04 percent, up from the 5.53 percent from 1994 to 2003 reported in the 2005 *Index*. As a result, Bulgaria's monetary policy score is 1 point worse this year.

CAPITAL FLOWS AND FOREIGN INVESTMENT
Score: 2–Better (low barriers)

The law mandates equal treatment for foreign and domestic investors. Bulgaria requires approval for majority foreign ownership in certain activities, including armament companies, banking and insurance, development and exploration of natural resources, and real estate purchases in certain geographical areas. The U.S. Department of Commerce reports that the "Problems most often encountered by foreign investors in Bulgaria are: government bureaucracy; poor infrastructure; frequent changes in the legal framework; low domestic purchasing power; a protracted privatization process; and corruption. In addition, a weak judicial system limits investor confidence in the courts' ability to enforce ownership and shareholders rights, contracts, and intellectual property rights." According to the Economist Intelligence Unit, "Petty corruption is also a problem for foreign companies operating in Bulgaria." The International Monetary Fund reports that residents may hold foreign exchange accounts subject to some restrictions; non-residents may hold foreign exchange accounts without restriction. Prior registration with the central bank is required for few capital transactions. Bulgaria's parliament changed the constitution to permit foreign ownership of land, provided the owners are from European Union countries or countries with an international agreement permitting such purchases, and the U.S. Department of Commerce reports that "foreign-owned companies registered in Bulgaria are considered to be Bulgarian persons…[and] may acquire land." Based on relatively low barriers to foreign investment, Bulgaria's capital flows and foreign investment score is 1 point better this year.

BANKING AND FINANCE
Score: 2–Stable (low level of restrictions)

Bulgaria's banking system has undergone major reform since the 1997 introduction of the currency board and stronger supervision and tighter prudential rules for the banking sector. With the possibility of bailouts eliminated under the currency board, banks have had to focus on sound banking practices. According to the U.S. Department of Commerce, "Approximately 50 percent of bank assets are concentrated in three banks: Bulbank, State Saving Bank (DSK), and United Bulgarian Bank (UBB). Bulgaria has completed the privatization of its state-owned banks, attracting some strong foreign banks as strategic investors." There are 35 commercial banks, six of which are foreign branches, and foreign banks account for approximately 73 percent of total banking capital. The insurance sector has been open to foreign firms since 1997. "Despite the imposition of increasingly severe restrictions in 2004," reports the Economist Intelligence Unit, "bank lending has continued to expand rapidly, leading to concerns that it could cause a further increase in the current-account deficit. Several commercial banks dramatically increased their lending in March 2005, in order to reduce the impact of the central bank's new lending restrictions, which came into force at the beginning of April. This increases the chances that the central bank will impose direct controls on individual banks." Imposition of controls could affect Bulgaria's banking and finance score in future editions of the *Index*.

WAGES AND PRICES
Score: 2–Stable (low level of intervention)

The market determines most wages and prices, but the state controls some prices through state-owned utilities, and the U.S. Department of Commerce reports that the government subsidizes some sectors of the economy, including health, education, energy, and railroads. Bulgaria maintains a minimum wage.

PROPERTY RIGHTS
Score: 4–Stable (low level of protection)

Bulgaria's constitution provides for an independent judiciary, but the U.S. Department of Commerce reports that "ineffective rule of law, especially in the judicial system, limits investor confidence in the ability of the courts to enforce contracts, ownership and shareholders rights, and intellectual property rights." The *Financial Times* reports that "attempts to make judges more accountable are hampered by the protection afforded to senior members of the judiciary under the constitution." According to the U.S. Department of Commerce, corruption in the judiciary "remains a serious problem."

REGULATION
Score: 4–Stable (high level)

The U.S. Department of Commerce reports that "an abundance of licensing and regulatory regimes, their sometimes arbitrary interpretation and enforcement by the bureaucracy, and the incentives thus created for corruption, have long been seen as an impediment to investment." According to the Economist Intelligence Unit, labor laws are still rigid, and the government made the registration of labor contracts compulsory in 2003. The EIU also reports that "corruption remains a problem in the state bureaucracy" and is a serious impediment to business opportunities.

INFORMAL MARKET
Score: 3.5–Stable (high level of activity)

Transparency International's 2004 score for Bulgaria is 4.1. Therefore, Bulgaria's informal market score is 3.5 this year.

BURKINA FASO

Rank: 102

Score: 3.28

Category: Mostly Unfree

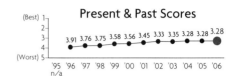

QUICK STUDY

SCORES

Trade Policy	4
Fiscal Burden	3.8
Government Intervention	3
Monetary Policy	1
Foreign Investment	3
Banking and Finance	3
Wages and Prices	3
Property Rights	4
Regulation	4
Informal Market	4

Population: 12,109,229

Total area: 274,200 sq. km

GDP: $3.1 billion

GDP growth rate: 6.5%

GDP per capita: $253

Major exports: cotton, livestock, gold

Exports of goods and services: $300.1 million

Major export trading partners: Singapore 13.3%, China 12.0%, Thailand 8.0%, Italy 6.4%, Ghana 5.5%

Major imports: petroleum goods, foodstuffs, capital goods

Imports of goods and services: $1 billion

Major import trading partners: France 30.7%, Ivory Coast 14.4%, Togo 8.8%, Belgium 4.9%

Foreign direct investment (net): $9.9 million

2003 Data (in constant 2000 US dollars)

Burkina Faso is a poor country even by African standards. Despite frequent droughts, the economy remains heavily agrarian, with over 80 percent of the population engaged in subsistence agriculture. Blaise Compaore seized power in a 1987 coup but has since overseen a transition to multiparty democracy. He was elected president in 1991, was re-elected in 1998, and was expected to win a third term in November 2005 despite a constitutional limit of two presidential terms. The government has used its influence to manipulate the judiciary. Violence in the Ivory Coast has disrupted trade, forcing landlocked Burkina Faso to send goods through alternate routes and cope with as many as 600,000 Burkinabé that have fled the Ivory Coast, and relations between the two nations will remain poor unless the peace process yields significant progress. Particularly in the western part of the nation, economic life continues to be affected by stability in the Ivory Coast. Even after qualifying for debt relief under the International Monetary Fund and World Bank Heavily Indebted Poor Country initiative, Burkina Faso remains significantly indebted and dependent on foreign assistance. Burkina Faso's overall score is unchanged this year.

TRADE POLICY
Score: **4**–Stable (high level of protectionism)

Burkina Faso is a member of the West African Economic and Monetary Union (WAEMU), which imposes a common external tariff with four rates: 0 percent, 5 percent, 10 percent, and 20 percent. According to the World Bank, Burkina Faso's weighted average tariff rate in 2004 was 11.4 percent. The World Trade Organization reports that non-tariff barriers take the form of supplementary taxes on imports, targeted import bans, licenses, and other non-tariff barriers. Corruption is an increasing problem. Based on the revised trade factor methodology, Burkina Faso's trade policy score is unchanged.

FISCAL BURDEN OF GOVERNMENT
Score—Income Taxation: **3**–Stable (moderate tax rates)
Score—Corporate Taxation: **4.5**–Stable (very high tax rates)
Score—Change in Government Expenditures: **3**–Stable (very low decrease)
Final Score: **3.8**–Stable (high cost of government)

The International Monetary Fund reports that Burkina Faso's top income tax rate is 30 percent. According to Deloitte, the top corporate tax rate is 35 percent. In 2003, according to the African Development Bank, government expenditures as a percentage of GDP decreased by 0.7 percentage point to 20.6 percent, compared to a 0.8 percentage point decrease in 2002.

GOVERNMENT INTERVENTION IN THE ECONOMY
Score: **3**–Stable (moderate level)

The World Bank reports that the government consumed 12.8 percent of GDP in 2003. In 2004, based on data from the Ministry of Economy and Finance, Burkina Faso received 3.74 percent of its total revenues from state-owned enterprises and government ownership of property. Despite its privatization program, the government remains active in the economy. By 2004, according to the Economist Intelligence Unit, the government still had not privatized the Office National des Télecommunications (ONATEL); the electricity provider (SONABEL); the hydro-carbons company (SONABHY); the Office National de l'Eau (ONEA); the Centre National

123

d'Équipement Agricole (CNEA); and the Ouagadougou and Bobo–Dioulasso airports. The EIU reports that the government also partly owns SOFITEX, the public-sector cotton enterprise. This has significant implications because more than 80 percent of the population depends on subsistence agriculture and cotton exports. Based on the apparent unreliability of the figure for revenues from state-owned enterprises, 1 point has been added to Burkina Faso's government intervention score.

MONETARY POLICY
Score: **1**–Stable (very low level of inflation)

As a member of the West African Economic and Monetary Union, Burkina Faso uses the CFA franc, pegged to the euro. From 1995 to 2004, Burkina Faso's weighted average annual rate of inflation was 0.57 percent.

CAPITAL FLOWS AND FOREIGN INVESTMENT
Score: **3**–Stable (moderate barriers)

There are few official restrictions on investment, and the investment code guarantees equal treatment of foreign and domestic investors. However, the Ministry of Industry, Commerce, and Mines must approve new investment, according to the U.S. Department of Commerce. Foreign investors are also hindered by poor infrastructure, a weak legal system, and growing corruption. The International Monetary Fund reports that residents may hold foreign exchange accounts with permission of the government and the Central Bank of West African States, or BCEAO. Payments and transfers over a specified amount require supporting documents, and proceeds from non-WEAMU countries must be surrendered to an authorized dealer. All capital investments abroad by residents require government approval, as do most commercial and financial credits.

BANKING AND FINANCE
Score: **3**–Stable (moderate level of restrictions)

The BCEAO, a central bank common to the eight members of the WEAMU, governs Burkina Faso's banking system. The eight member countries use the CFA franc, issued by the BCEAO and pegged to the euro. In the past, the government has been known for heavily regulating and controlling the banking system through its direct ownership of many of the country's banks, but the banking system has undergone restructuring and has been subject to more stringent supervision since the early 1990s. According to the Economist Intelligence Unit, "the government has adopted the principle of limiting state participation in the banking sector to a maximum of 25%. Of the three original commercial banks, the Banque internationale du Bukina Faso completed its reform programme; the Banque nationale de développement du Burkina was liquidated; and the Banque pour le financement du commerce et de l'industrie du Burkina (BFCIB) was privatized. Following an earlier merger with two other banks, the government sold 34% of its shares in BFCIB to local private investors in 1997, and the following year sold another 51 per-

cent to foreign investors." With the addition of several new private commercial banks, there were eight banks as of January 2004. The EIU adds that banking supervision is improving as a result of reforms introduced by the BCEAO, and the International Monetary Fund reports that all banks met minimum capital requirements as of June 2004.

WAGES AND PRICES
Score: **3**–Stable (moderate level of intervention)

The government has eliminated many price controls, although it still works with representatives from the cotton producers' associations and SOFITEX, the cotton parastatal, to determine the price of cotton, which is Burkina Faso's largest export crop. The large public sector continues to influence some prices. Burkina Faso's labor code establishes a monthly minimum wage.

PROPERTY RIGHTS
Score: **4**–Stable (low level of protection)

Burkina Faso's judicial system is weak. Villagers have their own customary or traditional courts. "The Constitution provides for an independent judiciary," reports the U.S. Department of State, but the "President has extensive appointment and other judicial powers. The Constitution stipulates that the Head of State…can nominate and remove high-ranked magistrates and can examine the performance of individual magistrates. Systemic weaknesses in the justice system include removability of judges, outdated legal codes, an insufficient number of courts, a lack of financial and human resources, and excessive legal costs."

REGULATION
Score: **4**–Stable (high level)

Establishing a business in Burkina Faso can be difficult. According to the Economist Intelligence Unit, principal donor countries are "increasingly vocal in expressing concern about…signs of growing corruption within the public administration." *The Economist* reports that labor laws are very rigid. For example, "night and weekend work are forbidden, and the minimum wage is 82% of the average value added worker. To sack someone, an employer must first re-train him, place him in another job and pay him a lump sum equivalent to 18 months' wages." According to the Embassy of Burkina Faso, the government has implemented a one-stop system to register businesses in an attempt to reduce the bureaucracy, but its impact has yet to be seen.

INFORMAL MARKET
Score: **4**–Stable (high level of activity)

Transparency International's 2000 score for Burkina Faso was 3. Therefore, Burkina Faso's informal market score is 4 this year.

BURMA (MYANMAR)

Rank: 155

Score: 4.46

Category: Repressed

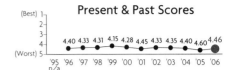

Present & Past Scores

(Best) 1
2
3
4
(Worst) 5

4.40 4.33 4.31 4.15 4.28 4.45 4.33 4.35 4.40 4.60 4.46

'95 '96 '97 '98 '99 '00 '01 '02 '03 '04 '05 '06
n/a

Burma's ruling military junta, the State Peace and Development Council (SPDC), remains an international pariah. In an effort to gain credibility for the current regime, the SPDC proposed a "road map" for democracy, but its refusal to include the National League for Democracy (NLD), Burma's major opposition party, nullified the effort. In 2005, elected representatives from Cambodia, Indonesia, Malaysia, the Philippines, Singapore, and Thailand launched an ASEAN interparliamentary caucus on Myanmar to advance democracy in Burma. Attempts by the international community to impose serious economic sanctions on Burma were largely offset by investment from China and India. Despite these efforts of the world's democracies to influence the junta, pervasive corruption, nonexistent rule of law, arbitrary policymaking, and tight restrictions on imports and exports all make Burma an unattractive investment destination and have severely restrained economic growth. Additionally, Burma's lawless frontiers are home to ethnic and political insurgents, drug smugglers, and drug-financed armies, all of which pose a security nightmare for the region. Burma's fiscal burden of government score is 0.6 point worse this year; however, its government intervention and monetary policy scores are 1 point better. As a result, Burma's overall score is 0.14 point better this year.

QUICK STUDY

SCORES

Trade Policy	5
Fiscal Burden	3.6
Government Intervention	3.5
Monetary Policy	4
Foreign Investment	5
Banking and Finance	5
Wages and Prices	4
Property Rights	5
Regulation	5
Informal Market	4.5

Population: 49,362,500

Total area: 678,500 sq. km

GDP: $7.6 billion

GDP growth rate: −2.0%

GDP per capita: $154

Major exports: clothing, gas, pulses and beans, teak and other hardwoods, fish products

Exports of goods and services: $2 billion

Major export trading partners: Thailand 30.1%, India 12.9%, US 9.8%, China 5.6%

Major imports: machinery and transport equipment, base metals, crude oil, electrical machinery

Imports of goods and services: $2.3 billion

Major import trading partners: China 31.0%, Singapore 22.2%, Thailand 15.0%, Japan 4.3%

Foreign direct investment (net): $120.8 million

2003 Data (in constant 2000 US dollars)

TRADE POLICY
Score: 5–Stable (very high level of protectionism)

The World Bank reports that Burma's weighted average tariff rate in 2003 was 3.9 percent, down from the 4.55 percent for 2002 reported in the 2005 *Index*, based on United Nations data. Data from the Economist Intelligence Unit and the International Monetary Fund, however, indicate an estimated average tariff rate of 37 percent in 2002 (based on customs and other import duties as a percent of total imports). Based on the range of tariffs and Burma's protection of domestic parastatals, the 37 percent estimate seems to be a more accurate measure than 3.9 percent. The U.S. Department of Commerce reports that Burma continues to require "difficult-to-obtain and restrictive permits" and imposes restrictive trade policies designed to protect "crony" companies and state-owned enterprises. Customs corruption is common. Based on the revised trade factor methodology, Burma's trade policy score is unchanged.

FISCAL BURDEN OF GOVERNMENT
Score—Income Taxation: 3–Stable (moderate tax rates)
Score—Corporate Taxation: 4–Stable (high tax rates)
Score—Change in Government Expenditures: 3.5–Worse (low increase)
Final Score: 3.6–Worse (high cost of government)

Burma's top income tax rate is 30 percent. The top corporate tax rate is also 30 percent. In 2003, according to the Asian Development Bank, government expenditures as a percentage of GDP increased by 0.9 percentage point to 9.5 percent, compared to a 1.9 percentage point decrease in 2002. On net, Burma's fiscal burden of government score is 0.6 point worse this year.

GOVERNMENT INTERVENTION IN THE ECONOMY
Score: 3.5–Better (high level)

Data from the Economist Intelligence Unit indicate that the government consumed 3.7 percent of GDP in 2003. According to the International Monetary Fund, in 2000 (the most recent year for which data are available), Burma received 30.63 percent of its total revenues from state-owned enterprises and government ownership of property. However, the EIU reports that the country's economic statistics are unreliable and that "The state totally dominates some sectors, including mining and power, and state-owned firms have an important role in transport, trade and manufacturing. The military is heavily involved in business in many sectors, such as gems and logging.... The government accounts for the largest share of all domestic credit (76% in 2003) and also controls exports of many key commodities." Based on the apparent unreliability of reported figures for government consumption, 1 point has been added to Burma's government intervention score. As a result, Burma's government intervention score is 1 point better this year.

MONETARY POLICY
Score: **4–Better** (high level of inflation)

From 1995 to 2004, based on data from the International Monetary Fund's *2005 World Economic Outlook*, Burma's weighted average annual rate of inflation was 17.67 percent, down from the 39.50 percent from 1994 to 2003 reported in the 2005 *Index*. As a result, Burma's monetary policy score is 1 point better this year.

CAPITAL FLOWS AND FOREIGN INVESTMENT
Score: **5–Stable** (very high barriers)

Foreign investment is highly restricted. Since February 2002, the government has not issued new business permits or renewed existing permits for foreign firms. According to the U.S. Department of Commerce, "This decision has disrupted the business of many foreign investors, and forced closure of several foreign manufacturing firms." The International Monetary Fund reports that the government restricts foreign exchange accounts and current transfers and controls all capital transactions. Foreign firms are prohibited from owning land, but it may be leased from the government. "Foreign direct investment (FDI) is a vital source of capital for cash-strapped Myanmar," reports the Economist Intelligence Unit, "but international sanctions and consumer boycotts, combined with the junta's own mismanagement of the economy, have driven away many large-scale investors."

BANKING AND FINANCE
Score: **5–Stable** (very high level of restrictions)

Burma's banking sector is subject to government intervention. The private banking sector crashed in February 2003. "Though a few of the smaller private banks resumed their operations in 2004," reports the U.S. Department of Commerce, "government instructions and internal bank policies have made it impossible for the largest private banks to take in new deposits or to extend new loans, and weekly withdrawals are capped." There are five state-owned commercial banks. The Economist Intelligence Unit reports that the central bank

provides 60 percent of all credit, that the government relies on the central bank to meet its spending requirement, and that central bank claims on the government increased 36.8 percent year on year at the end of 2004. The EIU further reports that the government revoked the licenses of "two of Myanmar's largest private banks, Asia Wealth Bank and Myanmar Mayflower Bank, for violating the country's banking laws." Concerns remain over money laundering.

WAGES AND PRICES
Score: **4–Stable** (high level of intervention)

The government directly controls some prices. According to the U.S. Department of Commerce, "The [government] sets prices below market value for some staple products produced or imported by the government (such as gasoline, cooking oil, propane, soap, etc.). However the amount of such products made available to customers is rationed, and often the purveyors of these products sell their stocks on the black market for a much higher price." The government's extensive involvement in the economy also affects prices. A minimum wage applies to government employees and the employees of a few traditional industries.

PROPERTY RIGHTS
Score: **5–Stable** (very low level of protection)

Private property is not protected in Burma. According to the U.S. Department of Commerce, "Private and foreign companies are at a disadvantage in disputes with governmental and quasi-governmental organizations.... However, as the...military regime controls all the courts, foreign investors who have had conflicts with the local government, or even had their business illegally expropriated, have had little luck getting compensation." The U.S. Department of State reports that "Pervasive corruption further serves to undermine the impartiality of the justice system."

REGULATION
Score: **5–Stable** (very high level)

Regulations lack transparency and are applied unevenly. "Corruption and cronyism are serious and widespread problems throughout all levels of the government, the military, the bureaucracy and business communities," reports the Economist Intelligence Unit. "The distorted economic climate... means that tax evasion, money-laundering, smuggling and other forms of corruption are widespread." According to the U.S. Department of Commerce, "Policy shifts also tend to be ad hoc, capricious and inconsistent, while regulatory changes are often arbitrary and unpublished."

INFORMAL MARKET
Score: **4.5–Stable** (very high level of activity)

Transparency International's 2004 score for Burma is 1.7. Therefore, Burma's informal market score is 4.5 this year.

BURUNDI

Rank: 132

Score: 3.69

Category: Mostly Unfree

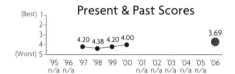

Present & Past Scores

(Best) 1
2
3 — 4.20 4.38 4.20 4.00   3.69
4
(Worst) 5

'95 '96 '97 '98 '99 '00 '01 '02 '03 '04 '05 '06
n/a n/a   n/a n/a n/a n/a n/a

QUICK STUDY

SCORES

Trade Policy	4.5
Fiscal Burden	4.4
Government Intervention	2
Monetary Policy	3
Foreign Investment	3
Banking and Finance	4
Wages and Prices	4
Property Rights	4
Regulation	4
Informal Market	4

Population: 7,205,982

Total area: 27,830 sq. km

GDP: $722 million

GDP growth rate: −1.2%

GDP per capita: $100

Major exports: coffee and tea, sugar, manufactures, hides

Exports of goods and services: $87 million

Major export trading partners: Switzerland 32.0%, UK 16.4%, Rwanda 5.7%, Netherlands 4.3%

Major imports: capital goods, food, consumer goods

Imports of goods and services: $187 million

Major import trading partners: Kenya 14.4%, Tanzania 11.7%, Uganda 5.9%, Zambia 5.2%

Foreign direct investment (net): n/a

2003 Data (in constant 2000 US dollars)

Since gaining its independence in 1961, Burundi has experienced frequent instability. Tensions between the Tutsi minority and Hutu majority incited the 1993 civil war, which resulted in over 300,000 deaths and an estimated 1.2 million refugees. After extensive negotiations, a transitional government was established in November 2001, with power shared between the Tutsi and Hutu factions, but Hutu rebel groups remained active. The security situation improved markedly when the rebel National Council for Defense of Democracy–Forces for the Defense of Democracy joined with the transitional government in 2003. A U.N. disarmament program has been established. Hutu Domitien Ndayizeye succeeded Tutsi Pierre Buyoya, who had seized power in a 1996 coup, as head of government in 2003. The judiciary remains corrupt and subject to political manipulation. Agriculture accounts for nearly 50 percent of GDP, and a majority of the population engages in subsistence agriculture. The public sector dominates the formal economy, and many prices remain controlled, although the government has promised to liberalize the coffee sector and follow through with promised privatization. The increasing availability of reliable data after several years of peace has made it possible to grade Burundi for the first time since 2000.

TRADE POLICY
Score: **4.5**–Stable (very high level of protectionism)

According to the World Bank, Burundi's weighted average tariff rate in 2002 (the most recent year for which World Bank data are available) was 14.5 percent, down from the simple average tariff rate of 23.5 percent reported in the 2005 *Index*. The Economist Intelligence Unit notes that the main anti-corruption non-governmental organization reported corruption in the customs and excise administration. The World Trade Organization reports that Burundi has removed most quantitative restrictions on imports but continues to apply numerous fees and taxes on imports beyond tariffs.

FISCAL BURDEN OF GOVERNMENT
Score—Income Taxation: **3.5**–Stable (high tax rates)
Score—Corporate Taxation: **4.5**–Stable (very high tax rates)
Score—Change in Government Expenditures: **5**–Stable (very high increase)
Final Score: **4.4**–Stable (high cost of government)

The International Monetary Fund reports that Burundi's top income tax rate is 35 percent. The top corporate tax rate is also 35 percent. In 2003, according to the African Development Bank, government expenditures as a share of GDP increased 9.4 percentage points to 35.3 percent, compared to a 1.3 percentage point decrease in 2002.

GOVERNMENT INTERVENTION IN THE ECONOMY
Score: **2**–Stable (low level)

The World Bank reports that the government consumed 8.5 percent of GDP in 2003. In the same year, based on data from the World Bank, Burundi received 8.76 percent of its total revenues from state-owned enterprises and government ownership of property.

MONETARY POLICY
Score: **3**–Stable (moderate level of inflation)

From 1995 to 2004, Burundi's weighted average annual rate of inflation was 8.84 percent.

CAPITAL FLOWS AND FOREIGN INVESTMENT
Score: **3**–Stable (moderate barriers)

The government treats domestic and foreign firms equally and actively seeks investment, but political instability continues to hinder foreign investment. "Burundi has never been a significant destination for foreign direct investment (FDI)," reports the Economist Intelligence Unit, "and its already low levels of FDI have declined even further because of war and sanctions." The International Monetary Fund reports that residents may hold foreign exchange accounts, but documentation must be submitted to the central bank, withdrawals over set limits require supporting documentation, and central bank approval is required to hold them abroad. Non-residents may hold foreign exchange accounts and withdraw funds up to a set limit upon presentation of documentation. Most capital transactions, including credit operations, direct investment, and personal capital movements, are subject to restrictions or authorization requirements. According to the World Trade Organization, "Import substitution is one of the objectives of the Investment Code."

BANKING AND FINANCE
Score: **4**–Stable (high level of restrictions)

The banking system is severely underdeveloped and subject to government influence, but the share of private capital is increasing. According to the Economist Intelligence Unit, "There are seven commercial banks in Burundi, all of which have been heavily involved in lending to the government. During late 2003 and early 2004 there was an injection of private capital into the commercial banking sector, which significantly altered the balance between private and public ownership in three banks." The Banque Burundaise pour le Commerce et l'Investissement, the Burundi Commercial Bank, and the Banque Populaire all now have a majority of private capital.

WAGES AND PRICES
Score: **4**–Stable (high level of intervention)

Wages and prices in Burundi are affected by a large public sector, import substitution policies, and government subsidies, particularly for agriculture. The government affects prices through its state-run monopolies in the telecommunications and cotton sectors and, according to the International Monetary Fund, directly influences the price of coffee. The government mandates a number of minimum wages based on location and skill.

PROPERTY RIGHTS
Score: **4**–Stable (low level of protection)

Private property is subject to government expropriation and armed banditry. According to the Economist Intelligence Unit, "in practice judges, who are appointed by the government, have generally proved to be strongly influenced by political pressure. Judicial personnel are predominantly Tutsi.... The judiciary has proved especially ineffective in dealing with politically charged cases, such as the earlier coups and human rights abuses by members of the armed forces."

REGULATION
Score: **4**–Stable (high level)

Burundi's continuing instability and massive, corrupt bureaucracy make it difficult to establish a business. "Civil conflict and the international sanctions from 1996 to 1999, including a cut-off in non-humanitarian assistance, resulted in a siege approach to economic management," reports the Economist Intelligence Unit. "This included rationing foreign exchange, imposing an overvalued exchange rate for official imports and financing the fiscal deficit through monetary growth and borrowings from the Banque de la Republique du Burundi (the central bank). Economic distortions have provided fertile ground for corruption." The large number of state-owned enterprises is another impediment to the establishment of businesses.

INFORMAL MARKET
Score: **4**–Stable (high level of activity)

Burundi has an active informal market, which is larger than its formal market. According to the Economist Intelligence Unit, "War, instability, and the imposition of sanctions have resulted in an increasing portion of external trade being unrecorded, and total crossborder trade is larger than indicated by official statistics."

CAMBODIA

Rank: 68

Score: 2.98

Category: Mostly Free

Present & Past Scores

(Best) 1
2
3   3.68 3.29 3.18 3.19 3.00 2.83 2.73 2.90 2.89 2.98
4
(Worst) 5

'95 '96 '97 '98 '99 '00 '01 '02 '03 '04 '05 '06
n/a n/a

QUICK STUDY

SCORES

Trade Policy	4
Fiscal Burden	2.3
Government Intervention	2.5
Monetary Policy	1
Foreign Investment	3
Banking and Finance	2
Wages and Prices	2
Property Rights	4
Regulation	4
Informal Market	5

Population: 13,403,644

Total area: 181,040 sq. km

GDP: $4.2 billion

GDP growth rate: 5.2%

GDP per capita: $313

Major exports: garments, fisheries products, rubber, timber

Exports of goods and services: $2.9 billion

Major export trading partners: US 58.2%, Germany 10.2%, UK 7.2%

Major imports: petroleum products, construction materials, vehicles and motorcycles, clothing

Imports of goods and services: $3.3 billion

Major import trading partners: Thailand 26.3%, Hong Kong 14.3%, Singapore 11.7%, China 11.2%, South Korea 4.0%

Foreign direct investment (net): $72.9 million

2003 Data (in constant 2000 US dollars)

After more than a year of uncertainty, the Cambodian People's Party (CPP) and the National United Front for an Independent, Neutral, Peaceful and Co-operative Cambodia, with 26 and 73 seats in the National Assembly, respectively, formed a government that is likely to survive until the next election in July 2008. The CPP dominates the coalition in the National Assembly, the security forces, the judiciary, and the civil service. The Sam Rainsy Party is a vocal opposition party but, with only 24 of the National Assembly's 123 seats, is incapable of challenging the CPP's power; its founder, Sam Rainsy, has been stripped of his parliamentary immunity from prosecution and faces trial for defamation. Beginning in 1999, the government was charged with implementing a detailed Governance Action Plan (GAP) that is monitored by the donor community. However, the GAP's products are meaningless documents verifying Cambodia's compliance, resulting in no substantive change in governance problems. The only positive sign in the country's economic development is provided by the garment industry, which survived the end of the global quota system on fabrics. Cambodia's fiscal burden of government score is 0.1 point better this year; however, its informal market score is 1 point worse. As a result, Cambodia's overall score is 0.09 point worse this year.

TRADE POLICY
Score: **4**–Stable (high level of protectionism)

According to the World Bank, Cambodia's weighted average tariff rate in 2001 (the most recent year for which World Bank data are available) was 15.8 percent, down from the 16.5 percent reported in the 2005 *Index*. According to the U.S. Department of Commerce, "The Cambodian government has…eliminated most non-tariff barriers to trade. Import licenses are required for firearms and pharmaceuticals. Export licenses are required for antiquities, rubber, and timber. Garment exports require certificates of origin (CO) from the Ministry of Commerce. As of January 2000, Cambodia amended its regulations to allow foreign investors to own import and export businesses." Based on the revised trade factor methodology, Cambodia's trade policy score is unchanged.

FISCAL BURDEN OF GOVERNMENT
Score—Income Taxation: **2**–Stable (low tax rates)
Score—Corporate Taxation: **2**–Stable (low tax rates)
Score—Change in Government Expenditures: **3**–Better (very low decrease)
Final Score: **2.3**–Better (low cost of government)

According to the International Monetary Fund, Cambodia's top income tax rate is 20 percent. Deloitte reports that the top corporate income tax rate also is 20 percent. In 2003, according to the Asian Development Bank, government expenditures as a share of GDP declined 0.5 percentage point to 17.4 percent, compared to a 1.6 percentage point increase in 2002. On net, Cambodia's fiscal burden of government score is 0.1 point better this year.

GOVERNMENT INTERVENTION IN THE ECONOMY
Score: **2.5**–Stable (moderate level)

The World Bank reports that the government consumed 6.5 percent of GDP in 2003. In the same year, based on data from the International Monetary Fund, Cambodia received 14.28 percent of its total revenues from state-owned enterprises and government ownership of property.

129

MONETARY POLICY
Score: **1**–Stable (very low level of inflation)

From 1995 to 2004, Cambodia's weighted average annual rate of inflation was 2.98 percent.

CAPITAL FLOWS AND FOREIGN INVESTMENT
Score: **3**–Stable (moderate barriers)

"Current legislation encourages investment, whether domestic or foreign, in a range of sectors including export-oriented projects, tourism, agro-industry, infrastructure, energy and mining," reports the Economist Intelligence Unit. "Restrictions on foreign investment apply in law, accountancy, and certain areas of transport, construction and foreign trade." The EIU also says that political instability, red tape, high utility costs, and corruption are deterrents to foreign investment. According to the U.S. Department of Commerce, "An August 1999 sub-decree created some restrictions on foreign investment: publishing, printing, and broadcasting activities are limited to 49% foreign equity, and there must be an unspecified amount of local equity in gemstone exploitation, brick making, rice mills, wood and stone carving manufacture, and silk weaving. The government recently issued a sub-decree restricting foreign ownership of hospitals and clinics and forbidding the employment of non-Cambodian doctors in any speciality in which the Ministry of Health considers there to be an adequate number of Cambodian practitioners." The International Monetary Fund reports that there are no restrictions or controls on the holding of foreign exchange accounts by either residents or non-residents. Non-residents may not own land, and the government still must approve foreign direct investment.

BANKING AND FINANCE
Score: **2**–Stable (low level of restrictions)

Cambodia's banking system remains underdeveloped. Steps taken to modernize the sector include restricting the National Bank of Cambodia (NBC), which used to operate as a commercial bank as well as the central bank, to a regulatory role supervising commercial banks, printing currency, and controlling foreign exchange and introducing stricter standards over private banking through the 1999 Financial Institutions law. "In December 2000," reports the U.S. Department of Commerce, "the NBC publicly announced that at least ten nonviable banks had been liquidated. As a result of the recent banking restructuring process, as of April 2004, the number of banks was reduced from 31 to 17." According to the Economist Intelligence Unit, the financial system includes 12 private commercial banks and two state owned banks. The government has liberalized interest rates, established reserve requirements, capped total exposure allowed to any one individual or client, and capped bank positions in foreign currency as a percent of the bank's net worth.

WAGES AND PRICES
Score: **2**–Stable (low level of intervention)

The market determines most prices. According to the United

Nations and the International Chamber of Commerce, "Cambodia takes a liberal stance with respect to competition and price setting…. There are hardly any government monopolies and the government does not interfere directly with the prices of commercial goods or services." The Labor Law establishes a minimum wage based on recommendations from the Labor Advisory Committee. The minimum wage can vary regionally but applies only to the garment and footwear industries.

PROPERTY RIGHTS
Score: **4**–Stable (low level of protection)

Cambodia's legal system does not protect private property effectively and contains many gaps in company law, bankruptcy, and arbitration. "There is a lack of real separation in government," reports the Economist Intelligence Unit, "with the executive branch commonly dominating the legislature and the judiciary…. Judges are highly vulnerable to political pressure." According to the U.S. Department of Commerce, "there are frequent problems with inconsistent judicial rulings as well as outright corruption." The Land Titling system is not fully functional; most property owners do not have documentation to prove their ownership.

REGULATION
Score: **4**–Stable (high level)

The regulatory system is opaque. "Numerous issues of transparency in the regulatory regime arise…from the lack of legislation and the weakness of key institutions," reports the U.S. Department of Commerce. "Investors often complain that the decisions of Cambodian regulatory agencies are inconsistent, irrational, or corrupt. The Cambodian government is still in the process of drafting laws and regulations that establish the framework for the market economy. A Company Law and commercial arbitration law have yet to be approved by the National Assembly. Other important business-related laws such as bankruptcy, arbitration, e-commerce and personal property leasing laws are in draft only." The World Bank reports that the cost of starting a business, hiring and firing, and registering property is high in terms of both bureaucracy and money. According to the United Nations and the International Chamber of Commerce, "Bureaucratic delays are commonplace and corruption is a rampant problem." Labor laws are very rigid.

INFORMAL MARKET
Score: **5**–Worse (very high level of activity)

Cambodia's informal sector "accounts for over 80% of GDP and close to 90% of employment outside the public sector," reports the Asian Development Bank, and "it has been estimated that more than 90% of enterprises in Cambodia are small (fewer than 100 employees) and operate entirely in the informal sector." Based on the availability of more current information, Cambodia's informal market score is 1 point worse this year.

CAMEROON

Rank: 119

Score: 3.46

Category: Mostly Unfree

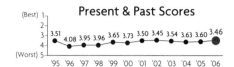

Present & Past Scores

(Best) 1
2
3 3.51 4.08 3.95 3.96 3.65 3.73 3.50 3.45 3.54 3.63 3.60 3.46
4
(Worst) 5
'95 '96 '97 '98 '99 '00 '01 '02 '03 '04 '05 '06

QUICK STUDY

SCORES

Trade Policy	5
Fiscal Burden	4.1
Government Intervention	3.5
Monetary Policy	1
Foreign Investment	3
Banking and Finance	3
Wages and Prices	3
Property Rights	4
Regulation	4
Informal Market	4

Population: 16,087,472

Total area: 475,440 sq. km

GDP: $10.2 billion

GDP growth rate: 4.7%

GDP per capita: $634

Major exports: crude oil, coffee, cocoa, cotton, timber

Exports of goods and services: $2.9 billion

Major export trading partners: Spain 21.9%, Italy 13.5%, France 10.9%, Netherlands 10.6%, US 7.5%

Major imports: fuel, manufactures, machines and electrical equipment, transport equipment

Imports of goods and services: $2.8 billion

Major import trading partners: France 21.9%, Nigeria 9.5%, US 5.7%, Germany 4.3%

Foreign direct investment (net): $200 million

2003 Data (in constant 2000 US dollars)

Although Cameroon is a multi-party democracy, the same party has retained power for decades. Past elections, including the 2004 presidential contest in which President Paul Biya won re-election, have been marred by unfair practices. Biya, who has been in office since 1982, is empowered to control legislation and rule by decree and has used this power to extend his term in office and change the constitution. The ruling party's long domination has encouraged corruption and cronyism. A majority of the population is rural, and agriculture accounts for one-quarter of GDP. Significant government intervention in the economy, widespread state ownership of key utilities and industries, heavy regulation, and high taxes hinder foreign investment and economic growth. Corruption is widespread in the government and the judiciary. Cameroon's debt rating has been downgraded, based on deterioration in the country's fiscal position. The government's short-term economic priority is a new arrangement with the International Monetary Fund that will pave the way for debt relief under the Heavily Indebted Poor Country initiative. The government continues to resist pressure to constrain budgets or trim its unwieldy size. Economic growth, however, has been aided by high oil prices. Cameroon's fiscal burden of government score is 0.1 point worse this year; however, its banking and finance score is 1 point better, and its informal market score is 0.5 point better. As a result, Cameroon's overall score is 0.14 point better this year.

TRADE POLICY
Score: **5**–Stable (very high level of protectionism)

Cameroon is a member of the Central African Economic and Monetary Community (CEMAC). According to the World Bank, Cameroon's weighted average tariff rate in 2002 (the most recent year for which World Bank data are available) was 15.1 percent. (The World Bank has revised the figure for 2002 downward from the 15.8 percent reported in the 2005 *Index.*) Non-tariff barriers include surcharges on certain imports and the prohibition of others, according to the U.S. Department of Commerce, which also reports that "the Cameroon government has tried to speed customs clearance, [but] customs fraud is still a major problem and protracted negotiations with customs officers over the value of imported goods are common." Based on the revised trade factor methodology, Cameroon's trade policy score is unchanged.

FISCAL BURDEN OF GOVERNMENT
Score—Income Taxation: **3.5**–Stable (high tax rates)
Score—Corporate Taxation: **5**–Stable (very high tax rates)
Score—Change in Government Expenditures: **3**–Worse (very low decrease)
Final Score: **4.1**–Worse (high cost of government)

The International Monetary Fund reports that Cameroon's top income tax rate is 38.5 percent. The top corporate tax rate is also 38.5 percent. In 2003, according to the African Development Bank, government expenditures as a share of GDP decreased by 0.8 percentage point to 15.3 percent, compared to a 2.5 percentage point decrease in 2002. On net, Cameroon's fiscal burden of government score is 0.1 point worse this year.

GOVERNMENT INTERVENTION IN THE ECONOMY
Score: **3.5**–Stable (high level)

The World Bank reports that the government consumed 12 percent of GDP in 2003. In the same year, based on data from the International Monetary Fund, Cameroon received 21.37 percent of its revenue just from its state-owned oil companies.

MONETARY POLICY
Score: **1**–Stable (very low level of inflation)

As a member of the Central African Economic and Monetary Community, Cameroon uses the CFA franc, pegged to the euro. From 1995 to 2004, based on data from the International Monetary Fund's *2005 World Economic Outlook*, Cameroon's weighted average annual rate of inflation was 0.99 percent.

CAPITAL FLOWS AND FOREIGN INVESTMENT
Score: **3**–Stable (moderate barriers)

In March 2002, Cameroon passed an investment charter to update the 1990 foreign investment code. The new investment charter is expected to improve the difficult investment environment, under which it was complicated and costly to enforce contracts, protect private property, or secure fair, timely court hearings. The U.S. Department of Commerce reports, however, that the 1990 Investment Code, "which, though attractive on paper, suffered from arbitrary application by government officials and courts…will be in effect until 2007 due to delays in the drafting of the enabling legislation and regulations necessary to implement the more liberal [2002] Investment Charter." The International Monetary Fund reports that some transfers are subject to requirements, controls, and authorization. Residents may open foreign exchange accounts with prior approval of the central bank and the Ministry of Finance and Budget. Most capital transactions, including foreign borrowing, foreign direct investment, and foreign securities, are subject to controls and generally require approval of or declaration to the government.

BANKING AND FINANCE
Score: **3**–Better (moderate level of restrictions)

The government has adopted reforms to restructure the banking system through liberalization and an improved supervisory framework. In January 2000, the state sold the last majority government-owned bank to Banques Populaires Group of France. New private banks have been established since 2000, and the sector now includes 10 commercial banks. However, banking assets are very concentrated, with three banks accounting for over 60 percent of deposits and lending. "Despite the relative soundness of the banking sector, large areas of the economy have little access to loans," reports the Economist Intelligence Unit. "Cameroonian businessmen complain that banks prefer lending to affiliates and subsidiaries of foreign companies…. The reluctance of banks to lend is mainly attributed to outdated bankruptcy laws that heavily favour debtors. The banks are also unhappy with the judiciary, which they accuse of colluding with unscrupulous individuals and corrupt lawyers to abuse the legal right in Cameroon to seize debtors' assets." The government-owned Postal Savings Bank became insolvent in 2004. It is not known whether the govern-

ment intends to separate the banking services from the national postal system. While the government remains involved, the banking system is largely private. On net, Cameroon's banking and finance score is 1 point better this year.

WAGES AND PRICES
Score: **3**–Stable (moderate level of intervention)

The government lifted most price controls in 1994. According to the U.S. Department of Commerce, the government still controls the price of "strategic goods and services," including electricity, water, public transportation and roads, telecommunications, cooking gas, pharmaceuticals, and portside activities (such as stevedoring). The government also controls prices for cotton—a major agricultural product and export—through its monopoly on the marketing, collection, and supply of inputs and fertilizer. By law, the Ministry of Labor sets a single minimum wage that applies to all sectors of the economy.

PROPERTY RIGHTS
Score: **4**–Stable (low level of protection)

Corruption and an uncertain legal environment can result in the confiscation of private property. "Corruption in the judiciary is pervasive," reports the Economist Intelligence Unit; "users of the courts would rather bribe judges and magistrates than pay for legal representation." According to the U.S. Department of Commerce, "some foreign companies have alleged that judgments against them were obtained fraudulently or as the result of frivolous lawsuits. The enforcement of judicial decisions is also slow and fraught with administrative and legal bottlenecks." In April 2004, the National Assembly established the Constitutional Council, which should improve both general governance and efforts to fight corruption.

REGULATION
Score: **4**–Stable (high level)

Existing regulations are applied unevenly and impose a substantial burden on businesses. According to the U.S. Department of Commerce, "Potential investors should be aware that…obtaining government approvals after incorporation in Cameroon can be a lengthy process involving a series of government ministries." In addition, foreign and domestic firms "complain at times about onerous new tax audits and government efforts to compel companies to compromise on tax assessments, including blocking company bank accounts for temporary periods." The African Development Bank reports that, "despite the establishment of anti-corruption committees within ministries and some arrests and prosecutions, government services still suffer from widespread corruption."

INFORMAL MARKET
Score: **4**–Better (high level of activity)

Transparency International's 2004 score for Cameroon is 2.1. Therefore, Cameroon's informal market score is 4 this year—0.5 point better than last year.

CANADA

Rank: 12

Score: 1.85

Category: Free

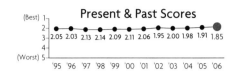
QUICK STUDY

SCORES

Trade Policy	2
Fiscal Burden	2.5
Government Intervention	2
Monetary Policy	1
Foreign Investment	3
Banking and Finance	2
Wages and Prices	2
Property Rights	1
Regulation	2
Informal Market	1

Population: 32,147,000

Total area: 9,976,140 sq. km

GDP: $789.8 billion

GDP growth rate: 3.0%

GDP per capita: $24,568

Major exports: forest products, automobile products, machinery, energy products, agricultural products, travel services, insurance services, computer services and information, transportation

Exports of goods and services: $318.4 billion

Major export trading partners: US 84.5%, Japan 2.0%, UK 1.9%, China 1.6%, Mexico 0.7%

Major imports: machinery, automobile products, travel services, financial services, insurance services

Imports of goods and services: $275 billion

Major import trading partners: US 58.8%, China 6.8%, Japan 3.8%, Mexico 3.8%, UK 2.7%

Foreign direct investment (net): –$38 billion

2004 Data (in constant 2000 US dollars)

I n December 2003, longtime Finance Minister Paul Martin became prime minister of a minority Liberal government. Under Martin and his predecessor, Jean Chrétien, the government balanced its budget for eight straight years, largely through decreases in federal spending. The level of government debt dropped from 64 percent of GDP in 1993 to 40 percent in 2003. The U.S. economic boom coincided with Canada's rapid growth during the 1990s. The United States is Canada's largest trading partner, and the U.S.–Canadian economic relationship is the world's largest such bilateral relationship. Martin intends to use healthy federal finances to cut taxes—the corporate tax rate is scheduled to decrease from 22.1 percent in 2008 to 19 percent in 2010—and send rebates to the provincial governments to prop up Canada's health care system. However, further liberalization is unlikely; Martin's minority government is weak, and he needs the support of the left-leaning New Democratic Party to stay in power. Canada has one of the Organisation for Economic Co-operation and Development's most restrictive foreign ownership policies, particularly in telecommunications, publishing, broadcasting, aviation, mining, and fishing. In 2004, the Canadian economy grew by 3 percent. Canada's fiscal burden of government score is 0.1 point better this year, and its government intervention score is 0.5 point better. As a result, Canada's overall score is 0.06 point better this year.

TRADE POLICY
Score: **2**–Stable (low level of protectionism)

The World Bank reports that Canada's weighted average tariff rate in 2003 (the most recent year for which World Bank data are available) was 0.9 percent, down from the 1.1 percent reported in the 2005 *Index*. According to the European Market Access Database, Canada maintains tariff rate quotas on agricultural imports. The U.S. Department of Commerce reports that "Canada still maintains some non-tariff barriers of concern at both the federal and provincial levels, impeding access to the Canadian market…. Canada closely restricts imports of certain domestic 'supply managed' agricultural products such as dairy products, eggs and poultry through the use of [tariff rate quotas]." Based on the revised trade factor methodology, Canada's trade policy score is unchanged.

FISCAL BURDEN OF GOVERNMENT
Score—Income Taxation: **2.5**–Stable (moderate tax rates)
Score—Corporate Taxation: **2.5**–Stable (moderate tax rates)
Score—Change in Government Expenditures: **2.5**–Better (low decrease)
Final Score: **2.5**–Better (moderate cost of government)

According to Deloitte, Canada's top income tax rate is 29 percent. The top corporate tax rate is 22.1 percent. Government expenditures as a share of GDP decreased more in 2004 (down 1.1 percentage points to 39.4 percent) than they did in 2003 (0.4 percentage point). On net, Canada's fiscal burden of government score is 0.1 point better this year.

GOVERNMENT INTERVENTION IN THE ECONOMY
Score: **2**–Better (low level)

According to the Ministry of Finance, the government consumed 19.3 percent of GDP in 2004. In 2003, according to the International Monetary Fund's Government Financial Statistics

133

CD–ROM, Canada received 3.47 percent of its total revenues from state-owned enterprises and government ownership of property, down from the 6.29 percent reported in the 2005 *Index*. As a result, Canada's government intervention score is 0.5 point better this year.

MONETARY POLICY
Score: **1**–Stable (very low level of inflation)

From 1995 to 2004, Canada's weighted average annual rate of inflation was 2.12 percent.

CAPITAL FLOWS AND FOREIGN INVESTMENT
Score: **3**–Stable (moderate barriers)

The government regulates foreign investment. "Governments exercise control over several business sectors through regulation or ownership restrictions, and sometimes the two are combined," reports the Economist Intelligence Unit. "A federal agency, Investment Canada, must approve direct foreign investments, whether through a new venture or an acquisition. Few applications are totally rejected." Restricted sectors include broadcasting and telecommunications, newspapers, energy monopolies, book publishing, filmmaking and distribution, banking and insurance, and air transport. The International Monetary Fund reports that the government reviews direct investment over specified amounts when the investment would result in the acquisition or control of Canadian business. Lower thresholds apply to investments from non–World Trade Organization members or any investment in cultural industries, financial services, transportation services, or uranium production. There are no restrictions on current transfers, repatriation of profits, purchase of real estate, or access to foreign exchange.

BANKING AND FINANCE
Score: **2**–Stable (low level of restrictions)

Canada has a private financial system with some restrictions. The Economist Intelligence Unit reports that "Parliament passed revisions to financial-services legislation in mid-June 2001 that establish a process for reviewing mergers among Canadian banks. But the revisions also raise permitted levels of ownership by any single investor from 10% to 20% of voting shares and 30% of non-voting shares, subject to a 'fit and proper' test. These larger investments permit strategic alliances with domestic or foreign companies…. The government now allows foreign banks to have full-service and lending branches." The government owns the Business Development Bank, which makes loans to the small and medium enterprise sector and acts as a "lender of the last resort" to companies unable to secure financing through private markets, and the Alberta Treasury Branches, which serves as a financial services provider to small business and agri-industry in Alberta. According to the Department of Finance, "foreign banks wishing to operate in Canada are permitted to have the same range of investments as Canadian banks." Foreign banks may establish more than one branch and own more than one bank. Of the

68 banks operating in Canada as of June 2005, 19 were Canadian-owned and 49 were foreign-owned. Six domestic banks account for some 90 percent of banking assets.

WAGES AND PRICES
Score: **2**–Stable (low level of intervention)

The market sets most prices. "There are no broad controls on prices for goods and services in Canada," reports the Economist Intelligence Unit, "although private companies that operate monopoly services, such as telephones and cable television, are subject to price regulation…. State-owned monopolies, such as the provincial power utilities, submit rates for approval by the government." Additional price controls cover poultry, eggs, dairy, wheat, rail revenues for grain traffic, seaway pricing, pharmaceuticals and telecommunications. The government also subsidizes agriculture. Provinces have jurisdiction over price controls on energy, and provinces or territories set minimum wages.

PROPERTY RIGHTS
Score: **1**–Stable (very high level of protection)

Private property is well-protected in Canada. The judiciary is independent, and the Economist Intelligence Unit reports that "judges and civil servants are generally honest, and bribery and other forms of corruption are rare."

REGULATION
Score: **2**–Stable (low level)

It is relatively easy to establish a business in Canada. According to the U.S. Department of Commerce, "While paperwork and recording requirements may seem onerous, most [business people] find that, with a little experience, they can master the required documentation. In addition, for small exporters, there are many freight forwarders, and similar service providers, who can handle the formalities." To reduce the level of bureaucracy, both information on the administrative procedure to open a business and the necessary forms are available online. One-stop Web sites for business registration at the provincial level are also available. The regulatory system is thorough but essentially transparent. Regulations differ from province to province, as well as from one municipality to the next, as is typical in a federal system.

INFORMAL MARKET
Score: **1**–Stable (very low level of activity)

Transparency International's 2004 score for Canada is 8.5. Therefore, Canada's informal market score is 1 this year.

> If Canada were to improve its foreign investment score, it would qualify for the Global Free Trade Alliance.

CAPE VERDE

Rank: 46

Score: 2.69

Category: Mostly Free

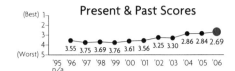

Present & Past Scores

(Best) 1
2
3
4
(Worst) 5

3.55 3.75 3.69 3.76 3.61 3.56 3.25 3.30 2.86 2.84 2.69

'95 '96 '97 '98 '99 '00 '01 '02 '03 '04 '05 '06
n/a

QUICK STUDY

SCORES

Trade Polcy	5
Fiscal Burden	2.9
Government Intervention	2
Monetary Policy	1
Foreign Investment	3
Banking and Finance	3
Wages and Prices	2
Property Rights	2
Regulation	2
Informal Market	4

Population: 469,000

Total area: 4,033 sq. km

GDP: $605 million

GDP growth rate: 5.0%

GDP per capita: $1,290

Major exports: fish products, fuel, clothing and footwear

Exports of goods and services: $193.7 million

Major export trading partners: Portugal 31.5%, France 26.0%, US 18.5%, UK 17.0%

Major imports: fuels, food, and industrial products

Imports of goods and services: $413 million

Major import trading partners: Portugal 46.3%, Netherlands 8.9%, France 4.1%

Foreign direct investment (net): $12.1 million

2003 Data (in constant 2000 US dollars)

Cape Verde is a multi-party parliamentary democracy whose most recent presidential election, held in 2001, was judged free and fair despite President Pedro Verona Rodrigues Pires's very narrow victory. Cape Verde has close economic and political ties to Portugal and the European Union and is seeking EU associate status. The currency is pegged to the euro, which the government is considering adopting officially. Economically driven emigration is common, and remittances from abroad are an important contribution to GDP. Cape Verde has been a model of reform through economic liberalization, good governance, and judicious public investment. Its market-based economy has yielded impressive economic growth in recent years and has earned it middle-income status—high by sub-Saharan African standards. Yet the government remains a recipient of foreign aid. Cape Verde has few natural resources, frequent droughts, and serious water shortages and can produce only 15 percent of its food. The economy is dominated by services, which accounted for 73 percent of GDP in 2004; agriculture and fishing employ much of the population but account for only 11 percent of GDP. In 2005, Cape Verde signed a $110 million compact for development grants from the U.S. Millennium Challenge Account. Cape Verde's fiscal burden of government score is 0.5 point better this year, and its property rights score is 1 point better. As a result, Cape Verde's overall score is 0.15 point better this year.

TRADE POLICY
Score: 5–Stable (very high level of protectionism)

According to the World Bank, Cape Verde's average tariff rate in 2003 (the most recent year for which World Bank data are available) was 24.4 percent, down from the 31 percent for 2002 reported in the 2005 *Index*, based on World Bank data. The U.S. Department of Commerce reports that "imports…are subject to a general customs service tax of 7 percent and a consumption tax on non-priority goods, ranging from 5 percent to up to 60 percent for hard liquor." In addition, "Pharmaceuticals may only be imported by public institutions." Based on the revised trade factor methodology, Cape Verde's trade policy score is unchanged.

FISCAL BURDEN OF GOVERNMENT
Score—Income Taxation: 2–Stable (low tax rates)
Score—Corporate Taxation: 4–Stable (high tax rates)
Score—Change in Government Expenditures: 1.5–Better (high decrease)
Final Score: 2.9–Better (moderate cost of government)

The Embassy of Cape Verde reports that Cape Verde's top income tax rate is 24 percent. The top corporate tax rate is 30 percent. In 2003, according to the African Development Bank, government expenditures as a share of GDP decreased 3.5 percentage points to 29.6 percent, compared to a 0.8 percentage point increase in 2002. On net, Cape Verde's fiscal burden of government score is 0.5 point better this year.

GOVERNMENT INTERVENTION IN THE ECONOMY
Score: 2–Stable (low level)

The World Bank reports that the government consumed 12.6 percent of GDP in 2003. In the same year, based on data from the central bank, Cape Verde received 2.17 percent of its total revenues from state-owned enterprises and government ownership of property.

135

MONETARY POLICY
Score: **1**–Stable (very low level of inflation)

Cape Verde's escudo is pegged to the euro. From 1995 to 2004, Cape Verde's weighted average annual rate of inflation was –0.65 percent.

CAPITAL FLOWS AND FOREIGN INVESTMENT
Score: **3**–Stable (moderate barriers)

Cape Verde is committed to integration into the global economy, and the government encourages foreign investment, particularly in tourism, fishing, light manufacturing, communications, and transportation. The U.S. Department of Commerce reports that Cape Verde has simplified its foreign investment process and has opened privatization to foreign investors, although the government reserves shares for Cape Verdean investors and encourages joint ventures with local investors. All sectors of the economy are now open. The International Monetary Fund reports that both residents and non-residents may hold foreign exchange accounts, subject to government approval and regulations. Most payments and transfers are subject to controls. Real estate transactions require central bank approval. While most capital transactions are permitted, most are also subject to advance approval by the central bank.

BANKING AND FINANCE
Score: **3**–Stable (moderate level of restrictions)

Cape Verde's banking system is overseen by the central bank, which gained greater autonomy following July 1999 constitutional reforms and a banking law passed in May 2002. According to the Economist Intelligence Unit, "The law has allowed the [central bank] to set interest rates freely [and] has eliminated central bank financing of the budget deficit…. At the same time, the law has strengthened the [Bank of Cape Verde's] supervision of the financial sector, partly to promote financial intermediation, but also to prevent money-laundering activities." The EIU reports that the financial sector consists of five commercial banks, including three foreign banks (two Portuguese banks and one West African bank). The government privatized the Banco Comercial do Atlântico and the Caixa Económica de Cabo Verde in 1999–2000 but remains active in the banking sector through the Fundo de Solidariendade Nacional, which is the principal savings institution and channels public investment, and the Instituto Caboverdiano de Solidariendade, which handles international aid.

WAGES AND PRICES
Score: **2**–Stable (low level of intervention)

The market determines most prices, but the government still maintains price controls on certain products, such as fuel prices, and influences prices through subsidies to the remaining state-owned enterprises (maritime transport, the national airline, fish freezing and storage, a port manager, a shipyard, and a pharmaceutical). There is no private-sector minimum wage, but most private-sector wages are linked to those of equivalent civil servants.

PROPERTY RIGHTS
Score: **2**–Better (high level of protection)

Private property is fairly well protected in Cape Verde. "The Constitution provides for an independent judiciary," reports the U.S. Department of State, "and the government generally respected this provision in practice. However, the judiciary was understaffed and inefficient." In addition, "The judiciary generally provided due process; however the right to an expeditious trial was constrained by a seriously overburdened and understaffed judicial system. A backlog of cases routinely leads to trial delays of 6 months or more." Based on new evidence that the judiciary is functioning more effectively, Cape Verde's property rights score is 1 point better this year.

REGULATION
Score: **2**–Stable (low level)

Government efforts to streamline the cumbersome bureaucracy and increase transparency have made it easier to establish a business. According to the U.S. Department of Commerce, "Bureaucratic procedures have been simplified in a number of cases…. The Center for Tourism, Investment and Export Promotion, PROMEX, has become a one-stop shop for external investors. In general, external investment operations are subject to prior authorization from the minister in charge of economic affairs. An application is submitted to PROMEX, and within thirty days the investor should get a reply. If government action is not forthcoming, within 30 days, approval is automatic." Regulations are applied evenly in most cases.

INFORMAL MARKET
Score: **4**–Stable (high level of activity)

Cape Verde has a widespread informal market. According to the International Monetary Fund, "In urban areas, informal activities are the main way out for many families, as indicated by the surge in the informal economy." In addition, "it is estimated that informal employment accounts for about 40% of total employment."

CENTRAL AFRICAN REPUBLIC

Rank: 118

Score: 3.41

Category: Mostly Unfree

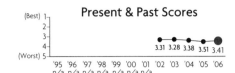

Present & Past Scores

(Best) 1—
2—
3—
4— 3.31 3.28 3.38 3.51 3.41
(Worst) 5—

'95 '96 '97 '98 '99 '00 '01 '02 '03 '04 '05 '06
n/a n/a n/a n/a n/a n/a n/a

T

he Central African Republic has been plagued by political instability, including successive military regimes, since gaining its independence in 1960. A civilian government established in 1993 was overthrown in March 2003 after a six-month rebellion led by former Armed Forces Chief of Staff General Francois Bozize. Bozize appointed a transitional government comprising elements of all political parties, including that of deposed President Ange-Felix Patasse. A new constitution, approved through a national vote, took effect in December 2004. Despite violating his pledge not to run, Bozize won the presidency in the 2005 election. Most of the population is engaged in subsistence farming. Political instability has undermined the economy; pockets of lawlessness persist, and looting and banditry have kept many farmers from their fields. Investors who have been waiting for the election results before returning could help to boost economic growth. Diamonds are a major export, but smuggling is endemic. Because the Central African Republic is landlocked, goods must be transported through other countries. Misappropriation of public funds and corruption remain problems. Government institutions are functioning poorly, and state finances are often conducted informally. The Central African Republic's capital flows and foreign investment score is 1 point worse this year; however, its government intervention and monetary policy scores are each 1 point better. As a result, the Central African Republic's overall score is 0.1 point better this year.

QUICK STUDY

SCORES

Trade Policy	5
Fiscal Burden	4.1
Government Intervention	3
Monetary Policy	1
Foreign Investment	3
Banking and Finance	3
Wages and Prices	3
Property Rights	4
Regulation	4
Informal Market	4

Population: 3,880,847

Total area: 622,984 sq. km

GDP: $889 million

GDP growth rate: −7.3%

GDP per capita: $229

Major exports: diamonds, cotton, coffee, timber

Exports of goods and services: $292.7 million

Major export trading partners: Belgium 42.0%, Italy 10.4%, Spain 9.8%, France 7.6%

Major imports: food, textiles, petroleum products, machinery, electrical equipment

Imports of goods and services: $366.3 million

Major import trading partners: France 27.4%, Cameroon 9.6%, US 5.4%

Foreign direct investment (net): $3.4 million

2003 Data (in constant 2000 US dollars)

TRADE POLICY
Score: **5**–Stable (very high level of protectionism)

The Central African Republic is a member of the Central African Economic and Monetary Community (CEMAC). The World Bank reports that the Central African Republic's weighted average tariff rate in 2002 was 17.9 percent. (The World Bank has revised the figure for 2002 downward from the 20 percent reported in the 2005 *Index*.) According to the International Monetary Fund, "discriminatory practices are applied against imports from third countries by attributing imported goods to categories for which a higher duty rate applies…. Customs fraud is still a major problem…and protracted negotiations with customs officials are reported to be common." Based on the revised trade factor methodology, the Central African Republic's trade policy score is unchanged.

FISCAL BURDEN OF GOVERNMENT
Score—Income Taxation: **5**–Stable (very high tax rates)
Score—Corporate Taxation: **5**–Worse (very high tax rates)
Score—Change in Government Expenditures: **1.5**–Better (high decrease)
Final Score: **4.1**–Stable (high cost of government)

The International Monetary Fund reports that the Central African Republic's top income tax rate is 50 percent. According to Deloitte, the top corporate tax rate is 40 percent, up from the 20 percent reported in the 2005 *Index*. In 2003, according to the African Development Bank, government expenditures as a share of GDP decreased by 3 percentage points to 12.9 percent, compared to a 2.7 percentage point increase in 2002.

GOVERNMENT INTERVENTION IN THE ECONOMY
Score: **3**–Better (moderate level)

The World Bank reports that the government consumed 13.1 percent of GDP in 2003. In the same year, based on data from Banque des Etats de L'Afrique Central, the Central African Republic received 11.62 percent of its total revenues from state-owned enterprises and government ownership of property. Based on newly available data for revenues from state-owned enterprises, the Central African Republic's government intervention score is 1 point better this year.

 MONETARY POLICY
Score: **1**–Better (very low level of inflation)

As a member of the Central African Economic and Monetary Community, the Central African Republic uses the CFA franc, pegged to the euro. From 1995 to 2004, the Central African Republic's weighted average annual rate of inflation was 0.11 percent, down from the 3.48 percent from 1994 to 2003 reported in the 2005 *Index*. As a result, the Central African Republic's monetary policy score is 1 point better this year.

 CAPITAL FLOWS AND FOREIGN INVESTMENT
Score: **3**–Worse (moderate barriers)

"Political instability, high transport costs and the small domestic market have limited foreign investment and access to commercial lending and capital markets," according to the Economist Intelligence Unit. "Most investors are currently staying away until incidences of banditry and extortion are reduced and the government establishes business-friendly credentials." Exchange controls hinder capital transfers and transactions. The International Monetary Fund reports that residents may hold foreign exchange accounts. Transfers and payments to countries other than France, Monaco, members of the West African Economic and Monetary Union (WAEMU), members of the CEMAC, and Comoros are subject to government approval and some reporting requirements. Sale or issue of capital market securities and commercial credits requires government approval. All capital transactions and transfers to countries other than France, Monaco, members of the WAEMU, members of the CEMAC, and Comoros require exchange control approval and are restricted. Based on increased evidence of controls, the Central African Republic's capital flows and foreign investment score is 1 point worse this year.

 BANKING AND FINANCE
Score: **3**–Stable (moderate level of restrictions)

The banking and finance sector is underdeveloped. The Economist Intelligence Unit reports that banking "performance... has been undermined by the accumulation of dubious debts, in particular by the state, and the non-realisation of promised credits." The government uses the banking sector as a source of financing for government expenditures. According to the

EIU, "The IMF reported that in 2003 salaries alone accounted for 90% of the budgetary income, with the result that arrears have mounted, or have been made good with advances on taxes owed by enterprises or through borrowing from domestic banks." There are three commercial banks in the Central African Republic. The government has privatized the two largest banks, Banque Internationale pour le Centrafrique and Commercial Bank Centrafrique, but still partially owns the Banque Populaire Marocco-Centrafricaine. Credit is allocated on market terms, and foreigners have access to credit on the local market, although it is limited by the banking sector's small size.

 WAGES AND PRICES
Score: **3**–Stable (moderate level of intervention)

The government still influences prices, both through its state-owned companies and through subsidies, and directly controls some prices. It controls the price of cotton through the cotton parastatal, Sococa. The Minister of Labor has the authority to set the minimum wage by decree. The minimum wage varies by sector and type of work.

 PROPERTY RIGHTS
Score: **4**–Stable (low level of protection)

Protection of property rights is weak. According to the U.S. Department of State, "the suspended Constitution provides for an independent judiciary; however, the judiciary remained subject to executive interference. Judges are appointed by the President. The courts barely functioned due to inefficient administration of the courts, a shortage of trained personnel, growing salary arrears, and a lack of material resources."

 REGULATION
Score: **4**–Stable (high level)

The state maintains a considerable presence, partly through parastatals, in such important sectors as telecommunications and cotton, the main cash crop. The Economist Intelligence Unit reports that corruption is a problem, partly because payment of civil servants' salaries is several months delayed. According to the U.S. Department of Commerce, "Setting up a business...requires voluminous paperwork and approvals from the ministries of commerce, finance and justice."

 INFORMAL MARKET
Score: **4**–Stable (high level of activity)

Informal market activity, especially diamond smuggling, is extensive. According to the Economist Intelligence Unit, "it is estimated that at least two-thirds of diamond production is traditionally smuggled out of the country." Smuggling of arms also takes place. A significant part of the population is employed in the informal economy.

CHAD

Rank: 105

Score: 3.29

Category: Mostly Unfree

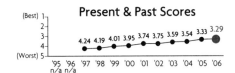

Present & Past Scores

(Best) 1
2
3
4
(Worst) 5

4.24 4.19 4.01 3.95 3.74 3.75 3.59 3.54 3.33 3.29

'95 '96 '97 '98 '99 '00 '01 '02 '03 '04 '05 '06
n/a n/a

QUICK STUDY

SCORES

Trade Policy	4.5
Fiscal Burden	4.9
Government Intervention	2
Monetary Policy	1
Foreign Investment	3
Banking and Finance	3
Wages and Prices	2
Property Rights	4
Regulation	4
Informal Market	4.5

Population: 8,581,741

Total area: 1,284,200 sq. km

GDP: $1.9 billion

GDP growth rate: 11.3%

GDP per capita: $218

Major exports: cotton, livestock, meat

Exports of goods and services: $336.7 million

Major export trading partners: US 24.1%, Germany 16.0%, Portugal 15.0%, France 6.2%

Major imports: petroleum products, foodstuffs, textiles, machinery

Imports of goods and services: $1.5 billion

Major import trading partners: France 28.5%, US 20.4%, Cameroon 14.5%, Netherlands 4.5%

Foreign direct investment (net): $789.3 million

2003 Data (in constant 2000 US dollars)

Idriss Deby, who seized power in a 1990 rebellion and was elected president of Chad in 2001 amid widespread allegations of fraud and vote rigging, has concentrated power in the hands of his supporters, particularly members of his ethnic group. Instability has had a negative impact on the economy. Chad's northern and eastern regions have seen frequent unrest, and refugees and militia groups from neighboring Sudan have contributed to the instability. Deby secured passage of a 2005 referendum to remove the two-term presidential limit and permit him to run for re-election in 2006. Approximately 80 percent of the workforce is employed in subsistence agriculture, herding, and fishing. Corruption and anti-market policies continue to hurt the economy, and the lack of effective legal, administrative, and judicial reform discourages investment outside of the oil sector. In July 2003, Chad began to export oil through a pipeline from the Doba oilfields to the coast via Cameroon. In 2004, the government received its first share of oil royalties, which resulted in real GDP growth of over 30 percent. Expanded budget resources from oil revenues are earmarked for health, education, agriculture, and infrastructure, but lack of government transparency creates opportunities for corruption. Chad's fiscal burden of government score is 0.1 point worse this year; however, its informal market score is 0.5 point better. As a result, Chad's overall score is 0.04 point better this year.

TRADE POLICY
Score: **4.5**–Stable (very high level of protectionism)

Chad is a member of the Central African Economic and Monetary Community (CEMAC). In 2002, according to the World Bank, Chad's weighted average tariff rate was 14 percent. (The World Bank has revised the figure for 2002 downward from the 14.2 percent reported in the 2005 *Index*.) The U.S. Department of Commerce reports "pervasive problems of smuggling and corruption in the customs department." The International Monetary Fund reports that bureaucracy and red tape impede trade. Based on the revised trade factor methodology, Chad's trade policy score is unchanged.

FISCAL BURDEN OF GOVERNMENT
Score—Income Taxation: **5**–Stable (very high tax rates)
Score—Corporate Taxation: **5**–Stable (very high tax rates)
Score—Change in Government Expenditures: **4.5**–Worse (high increase)
Final Score: **4.9**–Worse (very high cost of government)

The International Monetary Fund reports that Chad's top income tax rate is 65 percent. According to Deloitte, the top corporate tax is 45 percent, up from the 40 percent reported in the 2005 *Index*. In 2003, according to the African Development Bank, government expenditures as a share of GDP increased 2.1 percentage points to 22.2 percent, compared to a 1.3 percentage point decrease in 2002. On net, Chad's fiscal burden of government score is 0.1 point worse this year.

GOVERNMENT INTERVENTION IN THE ECONOMY
Score: **2**–Stable (low level)

The World Bank reports that the government consumed 7.8 percent of GDP in 2003. In the same year, based on data from the International Monetary Fund, Chad received 5.51 percent of its total revenues from state-owned enterprises and government ownership of property.

MONETARY POLICY
Score: **1**–Stable (very low level of inflation)

As a member of the Central African Economic and Monetary Community, Chad uses the CFA franc, pegged to the euro. From 1995 to 2004, based on data from the International Monetary Fund's *2005 World Economic Outlook*, Chad's weighted average annual rate of inflation was –2.60 percent.

CAPITAL FLOWS AND FOREIGN INVESTMENT
Score: **3**–Stable (moderate barriers)

Chad places no limits on foreign ownership and provides equal treatment to foreign investors. "There are no explicit screening mechanisms to discriminate against foreign investors," reports the U.S. Department of Commerce, "but companies seeking to invest and operate in Chad must satisfy several bureaucratic requirements, including a review and approval by the Ministry of Commerce. While these procedures can be slow, approvals are routinely granted without discrimination against foreign firms." Foreign investments in cotton, electricity, and telecommunications are restricted to protect state-owned enterprises; it is expected, however, that these sectors will be privatized. According to the U.S. Department of Commerce, "constraints [on investment] include: limited infrastructure, chronic energy shortages, high energy costs, a scarcity of skilled labor, a high tax burden and corruption." The International Monetary Fund reports that both residents and non-residents may hold foreign exchange accounts with government approval. Capital transactions, payments, and transfers to France, Monaco, members of the CEMAC, members of the West African Economic and Monetary Union, and Comoros are permitted freely. Capital transactions, including direct investment, payments, and transfers to other countries, are often subject to exchange controls, quantitative limits, and government approval.

BANKING AND FINANCE
Score: **3**–Stable (moderate level of restrictions)

Privatization of the banking sector was completed in 1999, and there were five commercial banks operating in 2004. According to the U.S. Department of Commerce, "Chad's banking system is believed to be sound, but it is limited in size and in the services available. A limited number of financial instruments are available…. [A]ll major banks have undergone internal reforms to reduce the volume of bad debt and improve lending practices. Credit is available from commercial banks on market terms, which are expensive…." The Economist Intelligence Unit reports that most domestic credit is lent to the cotton parastatal, Coton Tchad. According to the International Monetary Fund, "At end-September 2004, nonperforming loans rose to 22 percent of total credit…mainly because of overdue payments from public enterprises." The private

sector has little confidence in the banking system. "Demand for retail banking is small," reports the EIU, "as any Chadian resident with significant funds tends to place them with the [central bank] or outside the country. Chad's history of instability has impaired confidence in financial institutions and led to reliance on informal services."

WAGES AND PRICES
Score: **2**–Stable (low level of intervention)

Most prices have been liberalized, although the government influences prices of important products like cotton through its parastatals. Chad's labor code requires the government to set minimum wages.

PROPERTY RIGHTS
Score: **4**–Stable (low level of protection)

Protection of private property is weak. According to the U.S. Department of Commerce, "There is a widespread perception that the courts should be avoided at all costs, so most disputes are settled privately…. As an OHADA [Organisation pour l'Harmonisation en Afrique du Droit des Affaires] signatory, Chad is subject to several uniform acts covering securities, establishment of commercial companies, general commercial law, recovery procedures, arbitration procedures and bankruptcy procedures." In addition, "Chad's judiciary is easily influenced by the executive branch. Magistrates are appointed by presidential decree with no legislative oversight, hence the careers of magistrates, judges, clerks, and other judicial agents depend on the Presidency and the Ministry of Justice. Despite some clauses of the constitution, which guarantee the independence of the judiciary, some observers believe it is more accurate to say that the judiciary has a certain authority but not independent judicial power."

REGULATION
Score: **4**–Stable (high level)

Chad's massive and corrupt government bureaucracy makes it hard to establish a business. "While government policies themselves do not hinder approval," reports the U.S. Department of Commerce, "bureaucratic procedures are often cumbersome or slow. Clear rules exist on paper but they are not always followed…. Restrictive labor laws also discourage investment." In addition, "Corruption exists in all levels of government and in many different ministries."

INFORMAL MARKET
Score: **4.5**–Better (very high level of activity)

Transparency International's 2004 score for Chad is 1.7. Therefore, Chad's informal market score is 4.5 this year—0.5 point better than last year.

CHILE

Rank: 14

Score: 1.88

Category: Free

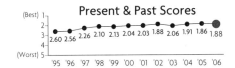
QUICK STUDY

SCORES

Trade Policy	1.5
Fiscal Burden	2.3
Government Intervention	2.5
Monetary Policy	1
Foreign Investment	2
Banking and Finance	2
Wages and Prices	2
Property Rights	1
Regulation	3
Informal Market	1.5

Population: 16,023,000

Total area: 756,950 sq. km

GDP: $94.1 billion

GDP growth rate: 6.1%

GDP per capita: $5,872

Major exports: copper, fresh fruit, wine, paper and printing

Exports of goods and services: $26.8 billion

Major export trading partners: US 16.5%, Japan 10.7%, China 8.8%, Mexico 4.8%

Major imports: consumer goods, chemicals, motor vehicles, fuels, heavy industrial machinery

Imports of goods and services: $22.6 billion

Major import trading partners: Argentina 19.4%, US 13.0%, Brazil 10.4%, China 6.6%

Foreign direct investment (net): $6.3 billion

2004 Data (in constant 2000 US dollars)

The Chilean economy grew significantly in 2004, partly as a result of Chile's increasing integration with the rest of the world. After a free trade agreement with the United States went into effect in January 2004, trade volume between Chile and the United States grew beyond projections, adding to the dynamism of the Chilean economy. Due to Argentina's unpredictable energy policies, one of Chile's most important problems is a shortage of natural gas, which is imported primarily from Argentina. With less gas, Chilean industries are forced to resort to oil and must consequently pay higher international prices. As a result of this crisis, the government is working to modify Chilean law to increase incentives for investment in the gas sector, particularly investment in the use of liquid gas imported from other countries. The government recently passed a law to charge a royalty on total sales by mining exploration companies. Chile's fiscal burden of government score is 0.3 point better this year; however, its government intervention score is 0.5 point worse. As a result, Chile's overall score is 0.02 point worse this year.

TRADE POLICY
Score: **1.5**–Stable (low level of protectionism)

According to the World Bank, Chile's weighted average tariff rate in 2004 was 3.7 percent, up from the 2.9 percent for 2003 reported in the 2005 *Index*. The U.S. Department of Commerce reports that "Chile generally has few barriers to imports." However, there are a few restrictions on agricultural products and processed food. Based on the revised trade factor methodology, Chile's trade policy score is unchanged.

FISCAL BURDEN OF GOVERNMENT
Score—Income Taxation: **4**–Stable (high tax rates)
Score—Corporate Taxation: **1.5**–Stable (low tax rates)
Score—Change in Government Expenditures: **2**–Better (moderate decrease)
Final Score: **2.3**–Better (low cost of government)

According to Deloitte, Chile's top income tax rate is 40 percent. The top corporate income tax rate is 17 percent. In 2004, according to the Economist Intelligence Unit, government expenditures as a share of GDP decreased 2.1 percentage points to 20.4 percent, compared to a 0.4 percentage point decrease in 2003. On net, Chile's fiscal burden of government score is 0.3 point better this year.

GOVERNMENT INTERVENTION IN THE ECONOMY
Score: **2.5**–Worse (moderate level)

Data from the central bank indicate that the government consumed 10.6 percent of GDP in 2004. In 2003, according to the International Monetary Fund's Government Financial Statistics CD–ROM, Chile received 6.95 percent of its total revenues from state-owned enterprises and government ownership of property, up from the 3.48 percent reported in the 2005 *Index*. As a result, Chile's government intervention score is 0.5 point worse this year.

MONETARY POLICY
Score: **1**–Stable (very low level of inflation)

From 1995 to 2004, Chile's weighted average annual rate of inflation was 1.72 percent.

CAPITAL FLOWS AND FOREIGN INVESTMENT
Score: **2**–Stable (low barriers)

Chile's investment regime is transparent and easy to navigate. The general principle of the foreign investment regime is one of non-discrimination between local and foreign individuals and companies, and companies seeking repatriation of capital or profits are guaranteed access to foreign exchange at the best market rate. "There are a few restrictions on foreign ownership of local enterprises and joint ventures, except for those engaged in the petroleum industry, uranium mining and other specialty mineral resources, communication, shipping and fishing," reports the Economist Intelligence Unit. "Continued liberalisation has made Chile an increasingly attractive destination for both direct and portfolio investment. In recent years the authorities lifted all remaining exchange controls, eliminated the minimum stay period on foreign investments, eased procedures for placements in the local capital markets, and passed landmark reforms of corporate governance and the activities of financial companies." The International Monetary Fund reports that both residents and non-residents may hold foreign exchange accounts. There are no controls on current transfers and capital transactions, but some regulations and other requirements apply. Direct investment is not controlled, and foreign investors may own real estate.

BANKING AND FINANCE
Score: **2**–Stable (low level of restrictions)

"The Chilean banking system remains solid," reports the Economist Intelligence Unit. "Prudent management and strong capitalisation have kept the sector well insulated from domestic turbulence...as well as from regional crises." The number of banks dropped from 32 in 1997 to 26 in September 2004, and foreign banks are increasingly involved in Chile, with 13 foreign banks controlling 43 percent of total bank assets in July 2004. According to the U.S. Department of Commerce, "There is one state-owned bank, Banco Estado, which is the nation's second largest. Private banks manage most corporate business. Six large, high volume banks control roughly 68 percent of the market." The 1997 banking law continued the gradual liberalization of the mid-1990s by allowing banks to open branches abroad and to enter the insurance and foreign investment funds businesses domestically. The EIU reports that the central bank "modified its Compendium of Financial Norms in October 2000, substantially widening the range of foreign-currency operations banks may offer by including domestic savings accounts and overdrafts, domestic credits, and trading in foreign-currency instruments issued by local residents." Other laws have been passed in subsequent years to streamline and regularize capital and credit markets.

WAGES AND PRICES
Score: **2**–Stable (low level of intervention)

The market determines most prices. According to the Economist Intelligence Unit, "Controlled prices exist only in sectors dominated by natural monopolies, including water, electricity and fixed-line telephony. Separate regulatory agencies and regulatory regimes cover each of these services." In addition, "Major agricultural products such as cooking oils, sugar and wheat are covered by a system of price bands to encourage local production. These price bands vary with changes in international market prices; they are normally announced mid-year to help farmers decide what to sow.... [T]hey are Chile's exception to the rule of free-market prices." Chile maintains a minimum wage that is subject to adjustment annually.

PROPERTY RIGHTS
Score: **1**–Stable (very high level of protection)

Private property is well protected. The Economist Intelligence Unit reports that "contractual agreements in Chile are probably the most secure in Latin America, and the local public administration is generally honest."

REGULATION
Score: **3**–Stable (moderate level)

The U.S. Department of Commerce reports that Chile's regulatory system is generally transparent and expeditious. Government regulation, however, can be burdensome in some areas. According to the U.S. Trade Representative, "the most heavily regulated areas of the Chilean economy are utilities, the banking sector, securities markets and pension funds. Other regulations tend to be focused on labor, environment and health standards." Labor laws are somewhat rigid, harming mostly small and medium-size businesses, which tend to be labor-intensive and employ most of the population. Corruption exists in the bureaucracy, but only on a small scale.

INFORMAL MARKET
Score: **1.5**–Stable (low level of activity)

Transparency International's 2004 score for Chile is 7.4. Therefore, Chile's informal market score is 1.5 this year.

> If Chile were to improve its regulation score, it would qualify for the Global Free Trade Alliance.

CHINA, PEOPLE'S REPUBLIC OF

Rank: 111

Score: 3.34

Category: Mostly Unfree

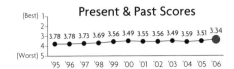

Present & Past Scores

(Best) 1
2
3
4
(Worst) 5

3.78 3.78 3.73 3.69 3.56 3.49 3.55 3.56 3.49 3.59 3.51 3.34

'95 '96 '97 '98 '99 '00 '01 '02 '03 '04 '05 '06

QUICK STUDY

SCORES

Trade Policy   3
Fiscal Burden   3.9
Government Intervention   3
Monetary Policy   1
Foreign Investment   4
Banking and Finance   4
Wages and Prices   3
Property Rights   4
Regulation   4
Informal Market   3.5

Population: 1,299,800,000

Total area: 9,596,960 sq. km

GDP: $1.5 trillion

GDP growth rate: 9.5%

GDP per capita: $1,179

Major exports: machinery and equipment, textiles and clothing, footwear, sporting goods, mineral fuels

Exports of goods and services: $502.8 billion

Major export trading partners: US 21.1%, EU 18.1%, Hong Kong 17.0%, Japan 12.4%

Major imports: machinery and equipment, mineral fuels, plastics, iron and steel, chemicals, crude oil and fuels

Imports of goods and services: $441.8 billion

Major import trading partners: Japan 16.8%, EU 12.5%, Taiwan 11.5%

Foreign direct investment (net): $53.1 billion

2004 Data (in constant 2000 US dollars)

In 2005, China emerged as the world's third-largest trading nation. Its 2004 current account surplus jumped 50 percent to $68.7 billion—more than 10 percent of total exports. The Chinese government reports that 2004 GDP growth continued at a robust rate of 9.5 percent. Beijing moved to cool the economy with cutbacks of construction machinery and investment-related imports and by exporting surplus domestic production of chemicals and metals. Foreign direct investment inflows rose 13.32 percent to $60.63 billion in 2004. Stepped-up complaints of China's failure to address intellectual property crimes and other grievances, as well as pressure from U.S. protectionists, generated a groundswell of sentiment in Congress to sanction China for trade transgressions. In late 2004, China's septuagenarian leader Jiang Zemin finally passed the baton to his sexagenarian successor Hu Jintao, but this "transition" did not ease the machinery of political repression, much less presage political reforms. Through 2004 and 2005, even domestic observers of China's political scene bemoaned tighter controls on speech and expression, particularly via the Internet, and complained that President Hu had sold out to party hard-liners. China's trade policy score is 1.5 points better this year, and its fiscal burden of government score is 0.2 point better. As a result, China's overall score is 0.17 point better this year.

TRADE POLICY
Score: **3–Better** (moderate level of protectionism)

According to the World Bank, China's weighted average tariff rate in 2004 was 6 percent, down from the 12.8 percent for 2001 reported in the 2005 *Index*. According to the Economist Intelligence Unit, "China has begun trimming its non-tariff import barriers" but continues to utilize quotas and licensing and "retains regulatory control over imports via commodity inspection, registration requirements and quarantine rules." Based on the lower tariff rate, as well as a revision of the trade factor methodology, China's trade policy score is 1.5 points better this year.

FISCAL BURDEN OF GOVERNMENT
Score—Income Taxation: **4.5–Stable** (very high tax rates)
Score—Corporate Taxation: **4–Stable** (high tax rates)
Score—Change in Government Expenditures: **3–Better** (very low decrease)
Final Score: **3.9–Better** (high cost of government)

China's top income tax rate is 45 percent. The top corporate tax rate is 30 percent. In 2003, according to the Economist Intelligence Unit, government expenditures as a share of GDP remained unchanged at 21.6 percent, compared to a 1.5 percentage point increase in 2002. On net, China's fiscal burden of government score is 0.2 point better this year.

GOVERNMENT INTERVENTION IN THE ECONOMY
Score: **3–Stable** (moderate level)

The World Bank reports that the government consumed 12.6 percent of GDP in 2003. In 2002, according to the International Monetary Fund, China reported receiving 4.31 percent of its total revenues from state-owned enterprises and government ownership of property. According to the U.S. Department of Commerce, however, the government retains much of the apparatus of a planned economy and owns major corporations in the energy, banking, telecommunications, steel, car manufacturing, food, and home appliances sectors. The *Financial Times* reports that "China's 150,000 state-owned enterprises...still employ more than 50m[illion] workers." Based on the apparent unreliability of reported figures for total revenues, 1 point has been added to China's government intervention score.

MONETARY POLICY
Score: **1**–Stable (very low level of inflation)

From 1995 to 2004, China's weighted average annual rate of inflation was 2.68 percent.

CAPITAL FLOWS AND FOREIGN INVESTMENT
Score: **4**–Stable (high barriers)

According to the U.S. Trade Representative, "General barriers to investment that plague China include a lack of transparency, inconsistently enforced laws and regulations, weak [intellectual property rights] protection, corruption and an unreliable legal system incapable of protecting the sanctity of contracts." The Economist Intelligence Unit reports that "China welcomes foreign investment and is bound under World Trade Organisation rules to open its industries further to foreign businesses, but it does not wish to see its control over important 'strategic' sectors of its economy slip into foreign hands. Partly with this in mind, on July 25th 2004, China announced a significant structural change to its FDI regime...that allowed foreign investment only in specific, government-designated sectors." Foreign investment regulations that took effect on April 1, 2002, requiring various Chinese bureaucracies to regularly update a Foreign Investment Catalogue for the government to use as a guide in approving foreign investment projects remain in effect. In June 2004, the government opened the retail and distribution sector to 100 percent foreign-owned companies. The People's Bank of China regulates the flow of foreign exchange into and out of the country, and the government intervenes and controls foreign investment in the stock market. The International Monetary Fund reports extensive controls, government approval requirements, and quantitative limits on foreign exchange, current transfers, and capital transactions. Direct investment is subject to government approval, as are real estate transactions.

BANKING AND FINANCE
Score: **4**–Stable (high level of restrictions)

The Economist Intelligence Unit reports that over 35,000 financial institutions were operating in China as of 2004. However, the dominant banking institutions remain four state-owned banks, which accounted for 55 percent of total banking assets and deposits as of March 2004. According to *The Economist*, "Most capital is...provided by banks, and the most important banks are still owned by the state. Some of their customers bid for capital at the prevailing rate of interest. Others, the least enterprising and best connected, hustle for it, by pulling strings or calling in favours. But perhaps two-thirds of the banks' loans serve to prop up state-owned

enterprises." *The Wall Street Journal* reported on June 2, 2005, that the "financial system is plagued by bad debts, lack of transparency, corruption and other abuses." The government has injected vast sums into the four major banks to reduce bad loans. According to the U.S. Department of Commerce, "Authoritative estimates of the total stock of bad debt in China's financial system range from 25 to 75 percent of the country's annual gross domestic product." Although the government is relaxing controls on interest rates, the central bank affects the allocation of credit by setting interest rates on deposits and loans. "China's banking sector remains almost entirely state owned, either directly or through state-owned companies...[but the] financial sector is evolving more quickly to a market-oriented system now that the country is a member of the World Trade Organisation," reports the EIU. "Foreign banks are gradually being allowed greater scope for their investments in both permissible business areas and geographical scope." Foreign groups are limited to minority stakes in Chinese banks. In December 2004, the government loosened restrictions to permit foreign insurers to operate throughout the country, changing previous rules restricting their activity to a few major cities, and permitted foreign brokers to own up to 51 percent of joint ventures.

WAGES AND PRICES
Score: **3**–Stable (moderate level of intervention)

"In general," reports the Economist Intelligence Unit, "prices remain controlled only for goods and services deemed essential, such as foodstuffs and tobacco.... Coal, which accounts for three-fourths of China's energy consumption, has been one of the most important commodities under price controls.... Price controls generally apply at the ex-factory level, in the form of subsidies to state-owned enterprises to let them produce and sell goods to wholesalers and retailers at artificially low prices." China does not have a national mandatory minimum wage, but the Labor Law allows local governments to determine their own minimum wages.

PROPERTY RIGHTS
Score: **4**–Stable (low level of protection)

China's judicial system is weak. The Economist Intelligence Unit reports that "many [foreign firms] prefer arbitration because of concerns about the speed and impartiality of the courts. A related concern for foreign companies is the weak tradition of consistent implementation of court rulings...." According to the U.S. Department of Commerce, "Enforcement of arbitral awards is sporadic. Sometimes, even when a foreign company wins in arbitration in China, the local court may delay or fail to enforce the decision. Even when the courts do attempt to enforce a decision, local officials often ignore court decisions with impunity." The EIU reports that corruption extends to the courts. In 2004, according to *The Wall Street Journal*, China introduced a constitutional amendment establishing that a citizen's private property is inviolable. Enforcement of this amendment has yet to be tested.

REGULATION
Score: **4**–Stable (high level)

The U.S. Department of Commerce reports that "China's legal and regulatory system lacks transparency and consistent enforcement despite the promulgation of thousands of regulations, opinions, and notices affecting...investment.... Foreign investors continue to rank the inconsistent and arbitrary enforcement of regulations and the lack of transparency as two major problems in China's investment climate." Corruption is widespread. According to the Economist Intelligence Unit, "Foreign companies investing in China tend to encounter rather different forms of organized dishonesty.... [M]unicipal officials have often given their approval to foreign-invested projects after their children have been granted places in schools abroad...."

INFORMAL MARKET
Score: **3.5**–Stable (high level of activity)

Transparency International's 2004 score for China is 3.4. Therefore, China's informal market score is 3.5 this year.

COLOMBIA

Rank: 91

Score: 3.16

Category: Mostly Unfree

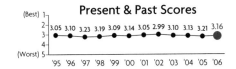

Present & Past Scores

(Best) 1
2
3 3.05 3.10 3.23 3.19 3.09 3.14 3.05 2.99 3.10 3.13 3.21 3.16
4
(Worst) 5
'95 '96 '97 '98 '99 '00 '01 '02 '03 '04 '05 '06

QUICK STUDY

SCORES

Trade Policy	3.5
Fiscal Burden	4.1
Government Intervention	3.5
Monetary Policy	3
Foreign Investment	3
Banking and Finance	2
Wages and Prices	2
Property Rights	4
Regulation	3
Informal Market	3.5

Population: 44,584,000

Total area: 1,138,910 sq. km

GDP: $89.9 billion

GDP growth rate: 3.9%

GDP per capita: $2,017

Major exports: oil, coal, coffee, apparel

Exports of goods and services: $18.6 billion

Major export trading partners: US 47.1%, Ecuador 5.9%, Venezuela 5.3%

Major imports: consumer goods, transportation equipment, chemicals

Imports of goods and services: $19 billion

Major import trading partners: US 29.6%, Brazil 5.5%, Mexico 5.4%, Venezuela 5.2%, Japan 4.6%

Foreign direct investment (net): $789.6 million

2003 Data (in constant 2000 US dollars)

Despite troubles in surrounding countries, Colombia continues to make strides toward providing a more secure environment in which democracy and markets can flourish. Thanks to President Alvaro Uribe Velez's Democratic Security strategy, Colombians have resumed traveling by car throughout much of the countryside and hotels are enjoying higher occupancy rates. More numerous and professional armed forces and police have brought pressure to bear on the country's three illegal armed groups (the Colombian Revolutionary Armed Forces, National Liberation Army, and United Self-Defense Forces), driving the Marxist rebels further into rural hideouts and the paramilitary self-defense forces into disarmament negotiations. Cocaine and heroin seizures have increased 43 percent and 72 percent, respectively. From 2003 to 2004, homicides declined by 13 percent, kidnappings decreased by 42 percent, terrorist attacks dropped from 1,125 to 657, and irregular combatant demobilizations surged by 29 percent. Legitimate exports rose by 24 percent, and the GDP growth rate for 2004 was 4 percent. Justice reforms implemented in 2005, such as oral public trials, are relieving serious backlogs in criminal cases and cutting crime rates in Bogotá and nearby cities where courts have been built. Colombia's trade policy score is 0.5 point better this year. As a result, its overall score is 0.05 point better this year.

TRADE POLICY
Score: **3.5**–Better (high level of protectionism)

According to the World Bank, Colombia's weighted average tariff rate in 2004 was 9.6 percent, down from the 10.1 percent for 2002 reported in the 2005 *Index*. The U.S. Trade Representative reports that some commodities are protected by a "price band" system, tariff rate quotas on some agricultural products, import licenses, and cumbersome customs procedures. Based on the lower tariff rate, as well as a revision of the trade factor methodology, Colombia's trade policy score is 0.5 point better this year.

FISCAL BURDEN OF GOVERNMENT
Score—Income Taxation: **3.5**–Stable (high tax rates)
Score—Corporate Taxation: **5**–Stable (very high tax rates)
Score—Change in Government Expenditures: **3**–Stable (very low decrease)
Final Score: **4.1**–Stable (high cost of government)

Deloitte reports that Colombia's top income tax rate is 38.5 percent. The top corporate tax rate is also 38.5 percent. In 2003, according to the International Monetary Fund, government expenditures as a share of GDP decreased by 0.3 percentage point to 20.5 percent, compared to a 0.1 percentage point increase in 2002.

GOVERNMENT INTERVENTION IN THE ECONOMY
Score: **3.5**–Stable (high level)

Based on data from the World Bank, the government consumed 21.3 percent of GDP in 2003. In the same year, according to the International Monetary Fund, Colombia received 12.99 percent of its total revenues from state-owned enterprises and government ownership of property.

MONETARY POLICY
Score: **3**–Stable (moderate level of inflation)

From 1995 to 2004, Colombia's weighted average annual rate of inflation was 6.38 percent.

CAPITAL FLOWS AND FOREIGN INVESTMENT
Score: **3**–Stable (moderate barriers)

Colombia has an open foreign investment regime and permits 100 percent investment in most sectors of the economy. According to the U.S. Trade Representative, "Colombian law requires that foreign investments be accorded national treatment. One hundred percent foreign ownership is permitted in most sectors of the Colombian economy; exceptions include activities related to national security and the disposal of hazardous waste. Investment screening has been largely eliminated, and the registration mechanisms that still exist are generally mere formalities and non-discriminatory." Foreign investment in television network and programming companies is capped at 40 percent. Aside from formal restrictions, reports the U.S. Department of Commerce, "the largest obstacle to greater openness to foreign investment in the country is the high level of legal instability. Excess regulations and constant changes to the rules affect the country's competitiveness to attract investment, resulting in additional operation costs for foreign firms." A one-year minimum stay for portfolio foreign investment was enacted in December 2004. The International Monetary Fund reports that residents who work in certain internationally related companies may hold foreign exchange accounts. Payments and transfers must be registered with the central bank and may be subject to approval and quantitative limits. All foreign investment must be registered with the central bank.

BANKING AND FINANCE
Score: **2**–Stable (low level of restrictions)

The Colombian financial sector is still recovering from the 1998–1999 crisis. Reforms permitting universal banking have facilitated mergers and consolidation. Foreign banks have complete access to credit and the entire financial system, and the private sector directs almost all credit. Domestic banks may sell securities, insurance policies, and investment services, and domestic and foreign banks are treated as equals. The Economist Intelligence Unit reports that the two largest financial conglomerates, Grupo Sarmiento Angulo and Grupo Empresarial Antioqueno, account for 44 percent of total financial sector assets and that there were "57 private financial institutions operating in Colombia" as of May 2005: "28 commercial banks (including five mortgage banks, four of which are state-owned; eleven domestic-owned; and eight foreign-owned); four [finance companies]; and 25 [commercial financing companies] (including ten specialized in leasing). There are six official institutions." Foreign banks accounted for 17.8 percent of total bank assets at the end of 2004. The government is in the process of privatizing its state-owned banks. According to the U.S. Department of Commerce, "While the Colombian Government still directs credit to some areas (nota-

bly agriculture), credit is, for the most part, allocated by the private financial market."

WAGES AND PRICES
Score: **2**–Stable (low level of intervention)

The market sets most prices. However, according to the Economist Intelligence Unit, the government controls the prices of "ground- and air-transport fares, a few pharmaceutical products, petroleum derivatives, natural gas, some petrochemicals, public utility services, residential rents, schoolbooks and school tuition. To avoid speculation, the agriculture ministry may also intervene temporarily to freeze the prices of basic foodstuffs through agreements with regional wholesalers." The government sets a uniform minimum wage.

PROPERTY RIGHTS
Score: **4**–Stable (low level of protection)

"Although the Supreme Court is held in high regard," reports the Economist Intelligence Unit, "the lower levels of the Judiciary and civil service are susceptible to corruption and intimidation.... Nevertheless, business contracts are generally respected. The legislature approved the Reform to the Prosecutor-General's Office in 2004, which will shift the present criminal system to a US-style prosecutorial system. This system was first implemented in Bogotá in January 2005 and should speed up the criminal justice system and reduce impunity." According to the U.S. Department of Commerce, "Foreign investors find the arbitration process in Colombia complex and dilatory, especially with regard to enforcement of awards." Terrorism in some areas of the country is a serious impediment to investment.

REGULATION
Score: **3**–Stable (moderate level)

The U.S. Department of Commerce reports that "government bureaucracy still constitutes a barrier...for both local and foreign companies." According to the Economist Intelligence Unit, however, "The present administration has had some modest success in further reducing the state's presence in the economy by merging and restructuring state firms and simplifying procedures to eliminate red tape." The U.S. Trade Representative reports that some sectors, including legal services, insurance, distribution services, advertising, and data processing, need further deregulation. Labor laws are somewhat rigid. Statutory fringe benefits include vacation days, end-of-the-year bonuses, paid holidays, social security, and health insurance. The U.S. Department of Commerce reports that bureaucratic corruption remains a problem despite the anti-corruption efforts of different administrations.

INFORMAL MARKET
Score: **3.5**–Stable (high level of activity)

Transparency International's 2004 score for Colombia is 3.8. Therefore, Colombia's informal market score is 3.5 this year.

CONGO, DEMOCRATIC REPUBLIC OF (FORMERLY ZAIRE)

Rank: Suspended

Score: n/a

Category: n/a

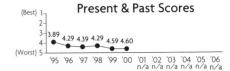

Present & Past Scores

(Best) 1
2
3 — 3.89 4.29 4.39 4.29 4.59 4.60
4
(Worst) 5
'95 '96 '97 '98 '99 '00 '01 '02 '03 '04 '05 '06
                              n/a n/a n/a n/a n/a n/a

QUICK STUDY

SCORES

Trade Policy	n/a
Fiscal Burden	n/a
Government Intervention	n/a
Monetary Policy	n/a
Foreign Investment	n/a
Banking and Finance	n/a
Wages and Prices	n/a
Property Rights	n/a
Regulation	n/a
Informal Market	n/a

Population: 53,153,360

Total area: 2,345,410 sq. km

GDP: $4.61 billion

GDP growth rate: 5.6%

GDP per capita: $87

Major exports: diamonds, crude oil, copper, coffee

Exports of goods (fob): $1.4 billion (2002)

Major export trading partners: Belgium 54.9%, US 15.3%, Zimbabwe 11.1%, Finland 4.8%

Major imports: fuels, machinery and mining equipment, foodstuffs

Imports of goods (fob): $933 million (2002)

Major import trading partners: South Africa 17.1%, Belgium 14.9%, France 12.7%, Germany 6.8%

Foreign direct investment (net): $149.1 million

2003 Data (in constant 2000 US dollars)

With a large population and abundant resources, the Democratic Republic of Congo has the potential for significant economic growth, but continuous violence has undermined its economic and political integrity. A 1997 rebellion led by Laurent Kabila overthrew the government of Mobutu Sese Seko. Shortly thereafter, Kabila was challenged by rebels backed by Rwanda and Uganda, and troops from Angola, Namibia, and Zimbabwe intervened to support Kabila. After Kabila's 2001 assassination, his son Joseph assumed power. Major parties to the conflict established a transitional government in 2003. A new constitution was adopted in May 2005, and the first elections in 40 years were scheduled for late 2005 or early 2006. However, even though major fighting has ended, much of the Democratic Republic of Congo is only nominally under government control, and instability continues, especially in the eastern part of the country. Economic activity is largely informal, barter transactions are common, and corruption remains endemic. Most people are engaged in subsistence agriculture. The infrastructure is in disrepair and practically nonexistent in many parts of the country, although foreign assistance has helped to establish cellular telephone service and initiate road and rail repair. Limited economic liberalization has helped to stabilize the economy and set the stage for economic growth.

TRADE POLICY
Score: Not Graded

According to the World Bank, the Democratic Republic of Congo's weighted average tariff rate in 2003 was 12.6 percent. (The World Bank provided a weighted average tariff rate for 2003, which was used to replace the average tariff rate of 15.6 percent reported in the 2005 *Index*.) The U.S. Department of Commerce reports that "most of the country's trade barriers result from complex regulations, a multiplicity of administrative agencies, and a frequent lack of professionalism and control by officials responsible for their enforcement."

FISCAL BURDEN OF GOVERNMENT
Score—Income Taxation: Not Graded
Score—Corporate Taxation: Not Graded
Score—Change in Government Expenditures: Not Graded
Final Score: Not Graded

The International Monetary Fund reports that the Democratic Republic of Congo's top income tax rate is 50 percent. According to Deloitte, the top corporate tax rate is 40 percent. In 2003, according to the African Development Bank, government expenditures as a share of GDP increased 3.2 percentage points to 13.6 percent, compared to a 2.5 percentage point increase in 2002.

GOVERNMENT INTERVENTION IN THE ECONOMY
Score: Not Graded

The African Development Bank reports that in 2003 (the most recent year for which data are available), the government consumed 5.8 percent of GDP. In the same year, based on data from the International Monetary Fund, the Democratic Republic of Congo received 9.5 percent of its total revenues from state-owned enterprises and government ownership of property. According to the U.S. Department of Commerce, "Much of the government's revenue is kept 'off-book,' and not included in published statistics on revenue and expenditure. Further, published budget figures do not include credit purchases by the government, which were extensive and out of control."

MONETARY POLICY
Score: Not Graded

From 1995 to 2004, based on data from the International Monetary Fund's *2005 World Economic Outlook*, the Democratic Republic of Congo's weighted average rate of inflation was 26.77 percent.

CAPITAL FLOWS AND FOREIGN INVESTMENT
Score: Not Graded

War, economic and political instability, corruption, and anti-market policy decisions have deterred foreign investment in the Democratic Republic of Congo. According to the Economist Intelligence Unit, "The political and economic climate...is not favourable to foreign investment because of pervasive official corruption and the inefficiency of poorly functioning government institutions. The execution of routine transactions through official bodies is fraught with difficulty, and the justice system cannot guarantee the rule of law and the enforcement of contracts. Owing to political interference and the cartel behaviour of local firms, foreign business cannot expect a level playing-field for their operations." Foreign direct investment has increased since the transition government was established and progress has been made in restoring peace, but it still lags behind potential levels, although the EIU reports that "corporate taxes and investment codes are being revised in order to liberalise the domestic business environment and attract foreign investment." Exchange controls have been removed. The International Monetary Fund reports that there are no restrictions on foreign exchange accounts for the credit or debit of international transactions for either residents or non-residents. Direct investment must be licensed.

BANKING AND FINANCE
Score: Not Graded

The banking system is unstable, and the banks that remain in operation are hampered by unpredictable monetary policy and unrecoverable loans. "The financial sector," reports the Economist Intelligence Unit, "has suffered from the chaotic political and economic conditions in the country: hyperinflation, currency distortions, war and political instability, frequent policy changes, and a lack of companies with properly audited accounts or collateral. As a result, many of the banks have accumulated unrecoverable loans. In such risky conditions, loan credit has entirely ceased except for short-term trade finance." Commercial banks are mostly subsidiaries of foreign banks. The state owns 40 percent of an investment bank. According to the EIU, "The central bank has announced that of three public and six private banks that have been

declared insolvent seven are [to] be restructured and two are to be liquidated."

WAGES AND PRICES
Score: Not Graded

In 2001, the U.S. Department of Commerce reported that "the government began enforcing price control laws [during 1999], creating a Commission on Economic Crimes.... Prices are nominally under the control of the Ministry of Economy and an interministerial consultative price commission. But enforcement is inconsistent." There is no new information about the state of price setting in the country. The Economist Intelligence Unit reports that the government has liberalized fuel prices. The government has a minimum wage policy.

PROPERTY RIGHTS
Score: Not Graded

Private property is not secure. According to the Economist Intelligence Unit, local conflicts are common, and fighting, banditry, and human rights abuses threaten property rights and deter economic activity. The U.S. Department of State reports that "courts are marked by a high degree of corruption, public administration is not yet reliable, and both expatriates and nationals are subject to selective application of a complex legal code." BBC News reports that the government has no control over large parts of the country.

REGULATION
Score: Not Graded

The regulatory environment significantly undermines economic activity. In 2001, the U.S. Department of Commerce reported that "Congo has never been able to provide a well-defined, stable, and transparent legal or regulatory framework for the orderly conduct of business and protection of investment. The country's laws and regulations have never been codified.... Combined with the micro-interventionism of the overmanned and underpaid Congolese administration, this has long been a major impediment to both foreign and domestic investment.... Existing tax, labor, and safety regulations are not onerous in themselves, but impose major burdens because they can be capriciously applied and there are no rapid and impartial adjudication mechanisms for relief." There is no new available information about the regulatory environment.

INFORMAL MARKET
Score: Not Graded

Transparency International's 2004 score for the Democratic Republic of Congo is 2. Therefore, the Democratic Republic of Congo's informal market score would have been 4.5 this year, if grading were not suspended.

CONGO, REPUBLIC OF

Rank: 143

Score: 3.90

Category: Mostly Unfree

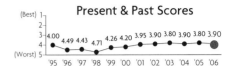

Present & Past Scores

(Best) 1
2
3 4.00 4.49 4.43 4.71 4.26 4.20 3.95 3.90 3.80 3.90 3.80 3.90
4
(Worst) 5
'95 '96 '97 '98 '99 '00 '01 '02 '03 '04 '05 '06

QUICK STUDY

SCORES

Trade Policy	5
Fiscal Burden	4
Government Intervention	4
Monetary Policy	1
Foreign Investment	4
Banking and Finance	4
Wages and Prices	3
Property Rights	5
Regulation	5
Informal Market	4

Population: 3,757,263

Total area: 342, 000 sq. km

GDP: $3.5 billion

GDP growth rate: 2.7%

GDP per capita: $943

Major exports: petroleum, timber, sugar, cocoa

Exports of goods and services: $2.8 billion

Major export trading partners: China 26.9%, US 15.1%, South Korea 12.2%

Major imports: petroleum products, construction materials

Imports of goods and services: $2.2 billion

Major import trading partners: France 21.9%, US 6.7%, Italy 6.2%, China 5.1%, India 5.0%, Belgium 4.6%

Foreign direct investment (net): $365.1 million

2003 Data (in constant 2000 US dollars)

Congo's President Denis Sassou-Nguesso seized power in 1997 and was formally elected in a 2002 election characterized by irregularities. Sassou-Nguesso's party and its allies also won the 2002 legislative elections and control a commanding majority of a parliament in which the opposition holds only 12 of 137 seats. Although demobilization and disarmament continue, pursuant to the 2003 peace accord between the government and the rebels, instability persists and armed groups remain active. The government is moving from a state-run economy to a more market-oriented system, but progress has been slow, and the country remains plagued by corruption and inefficient state-owned enterprises. The government has improved financial transparency in the oil sector and has promised further reforms to increase accountability and disclosure of government finances in order to secure assistance from the International Monetary Fund. The peace agreement has improved stability and helped to spur economic growth. High oil prices have also stimulated growth in the economy, which is heavily dependent on oil. Non-oil exports comprise less than 20 percent of total exports. Congo's fiscal burden of government score is 1 point better this year; however, its property rights and regulation scores are each 1 point worse. As a result, Congo's overall score is 0.1 point worse this year.

TRADE POLICY
Score: **5**–Stable (very high level of protectionism)

Congo is a member of the Central African Economic and Monetary Community (CEMAC). In 2002, according to the World Bank, Congo's weighted average tariff rate was 17.8 percent. (The World Bank has revised the figure for 2002 downward from the 18 percent reported in the 2005 *Index*.) The most significant non-tariff barriers include import licenses, red tape, an inefficient customs service, and corruption. Based on the revised trade factor methodology, Congo's trade policy score is unchanged.

FISCAL BURDEN OF GOVERNMENT
Score—Income Taxation: **5**–Stable (very high tax rates)
Score—Corporate Taxation: **5**–Stable (very high tax rates)
Score—Change in Government Expenditures: **1**–Better (very high decrease)
Final Score: **4**–Better (high cost of government)

Congo's top income tax rate is 50 percent. The top corporate tax rate is 38 percent. In 2003, according to the African Development Bank, government expenditures as a share of GDP decreased 5.8 percentage points to 29.7 percent, compared to a 3.9 percentage point increase in 2002. On net, the Republic of Congo's fiscal burden of government score is 1 point better this year.

GOVERNMENT INTERVENTION IN THE ECONOMY
Score: **4**–Stable (high level)

The World Bank reports that the government consumed 17 percent of GDP in 2003. In the same year, according to the International Monetary Fund, Congo received 42.63 percent of its total revenues from state-owned enterprises and government ownership of property.

MONETARY POLICY
Score: **1**–Stable (very low level of inflation)

As a member of the Central African Economic and Monetary Community, the Republic of Congo uses the CFA franc, pegged to the euro. From 1995 to 2004, Congo's weighted average annual rate of inflation was 1.76 percent.

 ## CAPITAL FLOWS AND FOREIGN INVESTMENT
Score: **4**–Stable (high barriers)

Political instability has discouraged foreign investment beyond the oil sector and forestry, although privatization has attracted some interest. "In November 2003," reports the Economist Intelligence Unit, "Congo's Senate adopted a draft bill—still to be endorsed by the government—that aims to attract foreign investors. The bill streamlines procedures for awarding licenses and limits the state's equity share in mining companies' investments to 10%, down from 35% at present." According to the International Monetary Fund, "Investments of over CFAF 100 million…require the approval of the [Ministry of Economy, Finance, and Budget] within 30 days, unless they involve the creation of a mixed public/private-ownership enterprise." The IMF reports that residents may not hold foreign exchange accounts but that companies can hold foreign exchange accounts with special approval. Non-residents may hold foreign exchange accounts subject to government approval. Payments and transfers to countries other than France, Monaco, members of the CEMAC, members of the West African Economic and Monetary Union (WAEMU), and Comoros are subject to documentation requirements. Capital transactions to countries other than France, Monaco, members of the CEMAC, members of the WAEMU, and Comoros require exchange control approval and are restricted.

 ## BANKING AND FINANCE
Score: **4**–Stable (high level of restrictions)

Congo's central bank, as it is for five other countries of the Central African region of the franc zone, is the Central Bank of West African States, or BCEAO. According to the Economist Intelligence Unit, "The banking sector was devastated by the civil conflicts of the 1990s, which left it with a host of bad debts. As highlighted by the IMF the banks now earn most of their revenue from charges and transaction fees, which are extremely high. Credit is generally not available…. [T]he IMF's concerns about the sector confirm that these banks, which are now in foreign hands, are having great trouble in cleaning up their balance sheets and returning to profitability…. Although all banks have now been privatised, three of them have inadequate capital bases and a fourth is judged to be in critical condition." The International Monetary Fund reports that the government prohibits lending in CFA francs to non-residents unless special permission is granted by the Ministry of Economy, Finance, and Budget.

 ## WAGES AND PRICES
Score: **3**–Stable (moderate level of intervention)

The government influences prices through state-owned companies in rail transport, river ports and transports, telecommunications, electricity, and water utilities. According to the Economist Intelligence Unit, "Public service and parastatal companies have traditionally been the foundation of formal-sector activity in Brazzaville." The labor code stipulates a monthly minimum wage.

 ## PROPERTY RIGHTS
Score: **5**–Worse (very low level of protection)

The war in the late 1990s reduced the country to chaos. According to the U.S. Department of State, "The Constitution provides for an independent judiciary; however, in practice the judiciary continues to be corrupt, overburdened, under financed, and subject both to political influence and bribery. Lack of resources continues to be a severe problem; almost nothing remains of judicial records, case decisions, and law books following the looting during the civil wars of the late 1990s." The Economist Intelligence Unit reports that the "other main security risks to business in Congo are the lack of clarity in regulation, and slow and poorly functioning government institutions on which investors may depend for routine matters. Security of contracts and the enforcement of justice cannot be guaranteed through the slow-moving justice system." Based on increasing evidence of the weakness of property rights protection, the Republic of Congo's property rights score is 1 point worse this year.

 ## REGULATION
Score: **5**–Worse (very high level)

The Economist Intelligence Unit reports that corruption remains a considerable problem. According to the EIU, "The 1997 war seriously damaged Brazzaville's substantial retailing sector, including shops, cafés, restaurants, western-style supermarkets and other services…. Since December 1999 many businesses in Brazzaville have reopened, but the sector is far from its pre-war level of activity and has been disrupted by the renewed fighting in 2002 and the still unresolved insurgency in Pool. The private-sector business association, Unicongo, is an active participant in economic debate. A large proportion of commercial activity in smaller towns and in Brazzaville's rambling shanty quarters is informal and is therefore little regulated or recorded." Global Edge cites the high costs of labor, energy, raw materials, and transportation and a restrictive labor law as factors discouraging investment. Based on new evidence of the regulatory environment, the Republic of Congo's regulation score is 1 point worse this year.

 ## INFORMAL MARKET
Score: **4**–Stable (high level of activity)

Transparency International's 2004 score for Congo is 2.3. Therefore, Congo's informal market score is 4 this year.

COSTA RICA

Rank: 46

Score: 2.69

Category: Mostly Free

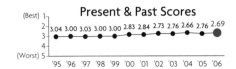
QUICK STUDY

SCORES

Trade Policy	2.5
Fiscal Burden	3.4
Government Intervention	2
Monetary Policy	3
Foreign Investment	2
Banking and Finance	3
Wages and Prices	2
Property Rights	3
Regulation	3
Informal Market	3

Population: 4,004,680

Total area: 51,100 sq. km

GDP: $17.6 billion

GDP growth rate: 6.5%

GDP per capita: $4,410

Major exports: coffee, bananas, sugar, textiles, industrial and manufactured goods

Exports of goods and services: $8.2 billion

Major export trading partners: US 14.2%, Guatemala 3.0%, Nicaragua 2.7%

Major imports: raw materials, consumer goods, capital goods

Imports of goods and services: $7.9 billion

Major import trading partners: US 23.2%, Mexico 4.7%, Venezuela 3.2%

Foreign direct investment (net): $509.7 million

2003 Data (in constant 2000 US dollars)

Costa Rica, one of Latin America's oldest and most stable democracies, has been plagued by corruption scandals involving presidents and political appointees during the past year. Current president Abel Pacheco allegedly accepted substantial campaign donations from the French telecommunications firm Alcatel and Taiwanese donors, and former President Miguel Angel Rodríguez was accused of receiving a kickback from Alcatel after it won a lucrative contract to install cellular phone lines. (Political parties are not supposed to receive foreign funding, but the law is unclear about individual politicians.) Newly installed as Secretary General of the Organization of American States, Rodríguez was forced to resign in October 2004. With corruption dominating the news, neither the executive branch nor Congress showed the political will to advance a fiscal reform package—on hold since 2003—or to approve the DR–CAFTA trade agreement before ratification by the United States. The "fiscal reform" package increases tax rates and extends taxation from territorial to global income. Students and labor unions have intensified their protests against tepid market-oriented economic policies, such as privatization of some public services. Meanwhile, the growing traffic in arms and drugs between South and North America is taxing the capacity of Costa Rica's security forces. Costa Rica's trade policy score is 0.5 point better this year, and its fiscal burden of government score is 0.2 point better. As a result, Costa Rica's overall score is 0.07 point better this year.

TRADE POLICY
Score: **2.5**–Better (moderate level of protectionism)

According to the World Bank, Costa Rica's weighted average tariff rate in 2004 was 3.8 percent, down from the 5.8 percent reported in the 2005 *Index*. The U.S. Trade Representative reports that "establishment of an electronic 'one-stop' import and export window, and other recent improvements, have significantly reduced the time required for customs processing in Costa Rica. Nonetheless, procedures remain complex and bureaucratic. Sanitary and phytosanitary (SPS) requirements can often be cumbersome and lengthy." Based on the lower tariff rate, as well as a revision of the trade factor methodology, Costa Rica's trade policy score is 0.5 point better this year.

FISCAL BURDEN OF GOVERNMENT
Score—Income Taxation: **2.5**–Stable (moderate tax rates)
Score—Corporate Taxation: **4**–Stable (high tax rates)
Score—Change in Government Expenditures: **3**–Better (very low decrease)
Final Score: **3.4**–Better (moderate cost of government)

Deloitte reports that Costa Rica's top income tax rate is 25 percent. The top corporate income tax rate is 30 percent. In 2003, according to the International Monetary Fund, government expenditures as a share of GDP decreased 0.9 percentage point to 21.7 percent, compared to a 1.3 percentage point increase in 2002. On net, Costa Rica's fiscal burden of government score is 0.2 point better this year.

GOVERNMENT INTERVENTION IN THE ECONOMY
Score: **2**–Stable (low level)

The World Bank reports that the government consumed 14.5 percent of GDP in 2003. In the

same year, according to the International Monetary Fund's Government Financial Statistics CD–ROM, Costa Rica received 3.7 percent of its total revenues from state-owned enterprises and government ownership of property.

MONETARY POLICY
Score: **3**–Stable (moderate level of inflation)

From 1995 to 2004, Costa Rica's weighted average annual rate of inflation was 11.32 percent.

CAPITAL FLOWS AND FOREIGN INVESTMENT
Score: **2**–Stable (low barriers)

Costa Rica offers one of Central America's better investment climates, and foreign investors are treated the same as domestic investors. According to the U.S. Department of Commerce, "Costa Rica has a generally open international trade and investment regime, with the exception of a few sectors that are reserved for state companies." State monopolies constrain some investment opportunities, and the constitution provides guarantees of government control of some sectors, including "insurance, telecommunications and the extraction, refining and importing of hydrocarbons and radioactive materials," reports the Economist Intelligence Unit. In the past, the government has expropriated some land owned by foreign investors. There are no controls on capital flows, but reporting requirements are mandatory for some transactions. The International Monetary Fund reports that there are no restrictions or controls on the holding of foreign exchange accounts by either residents or non-residents. Foreign investors may acquire real estate.

BANKING AND FINANCE
Score: **3**–Stable (moderate level of restrictions)

According to the Economist Intelligence Unit, "Financial markets in Costa Rica...remain small, divided and weakly developed." Although there are other state-owned financial institutions, three large state-owned banks dominate the banking sector and accounted for 49 percent of total banking assets in 2004. There are 30 private banks and 57 foreign banks recognized in Costa Rica, reports the EIU, but private-sector banks accounted for less than 30 percent of total banking assets. The government affects the allocation of credit. According to the U.S. Department of Commerce, "Credit is allocated on market terms, although the state-owned banks are sometimes obliged to act as development banks for activities deemed to be of public interest."

WAGES AND PRICES
Score: **2**–Stable (low level of intervention)

The market determines most prices. According to the Economist Intelligence Unit, however, "The Public Services Regulatory Authority (Autoridad Reguladora de Servicios Públicos) applies price controls to services it considers essential, such as energy, petroleum, telecommunications services and water provision. An adjustment to fuel prices generally affects all prices in the economy." Costa Rica's constitution provides for a minimum wage, which is set by a tripartite council representing government, business, and labor.

PROPERTY RIGHTS
Score: **3**–Stable (moderate level of protection)

"Although the judiciary is sometimes slow and complicated," reports the Economist Intelligence Unit, "it is considered honest and independent. Contracts are generally upheld and investments are secure. Nevertheless, a legal complaint filed over a contract takes an average of 550 days to resolve...." According to the U.S. Department of Commerce, "Litigation can be long and costly. The legal system is significantly backlogged, and civil suits take over five years on average from start to finish.... The process to resolve squatter cases through the courts can be especially cumbersome. The legal owner of land is at a disadvantage in a system that quickly recognizes rights acquired by squatters, especially when the disputed land is rural and is not being actively worked. Also, civil archives recording land title are at times incomplete or contradictory."

REGULATION
Score: **3**–Stable (moderate level)

According to the U.S. Department of Commerce, "Costa Rican laws, regulations and practices are generally transparent and foster competition, except in monopoly sectors where competition is explicitly excluded.... Environmental regulations and the Costa Rican organization that reviews environmental impact statements have caused problems for investors resulting in delays for completing projects.... Bureaucratic procedures are frequently long, involved and discouraging to new investors." The government has created an on-line investor manual and one-stop windows to ease the regulatory burden. It also requires private companies to grant vacations, a substantial holiday bonus, overtime, and social insurance. The U.S. Department of Commerce reports that some businesses have complained of corruption in the administration of public tenders. Entrepreneurs in the tourism sector identify municipal-level corruption as a problem.

INFORMAL MARKET
Score: **3**–Stable (moderate level of activity)

Transparency International's 2004 score for Costa Rica is 4.9. Therefore, Costa Rica's informal market score is 3 this year.

CROATIA

Rank: 55

Score: 2.78

Category: Mostly Free

Present & Past Scores

(Best) 1
2
3
4
(Worst) 5

3.58 3.56 3.63 3.55 3.54 3.39 3.34 3.06 3.06 2.95 2.78

'95 '96 '97 '98 '99 '00 '01 '02 '03 '04 '05 '06
n/a

Parliamentary elections in November 2003 brought the nationalist Croatian Democratic Union (HDZ) back to power. Prime Minister Ivo Sanader has pledged to transform the HDZ into another European Christian Democratic Party and to repudiate its ultra-nationalist past; he also has had some success in expelling more extreme nationalists from the party. However, in March 2005, because of failure to turn Ante Gotovina—a Croatian general accused of war crimes—over to the International Criminal Tribunal for the Former Yugoslavia, Croatia's strenuous efforts to begin accession talks with the European Union were put on hold. This is regrettable because, although Croatia remains a country in economic transition, its recent efforts at reform have met with some success. GDP grew at a rate of 3.7 percent in 2004, two-thirds of the economy has been privatized, and 90 percent of banking assets is privately owned. Organized crime is less prevalent in Croatia than in other Balkan countries. Other problems remain to be resolved, and the EU rightly sees judicial reform as the central long-term challenge to meeting its membership criteria. Croatia must decrease political influence over the courts and improve their institutional capacity to tackle the country's massive case backlog, a reform scheduled for mid-2006. Croatia's trade policy, fiscal burden of government, and government intervention scores are, respectively, 1 point, 0.2 point, and 0.5 point better this year. As a result, its overall score is 0.17 point better this year.

QUICK STUDY

SCORES

Trade Policy	2.5
Fiscal Burden	2.8
Government Intervention	2
Monetary Policy	1
Foreign Investment	3
Banking and Finance	2
Wages and Prices	3
Property Rights	4
Regulation	4
Informal Market	3.5

Population: 4,444,653

Total area: 56,542 sq. km

GDP: $21.1 billion

GDP growth rate: 4.3%

GDP per capita: $4,751

Major exports: machines and transport equipment, chemicals, mineral fuels and lubricants, food

Exports of goods and services: $10.5 billion

Major export trading partners: Italy 26.1%, Bosnia and Herzegovina 14.6%, Germany 12.0%, Slovenia 8.3%, Austria 7.9%

Major imports: machines and transport equipment, mineral fuels and lubricants, chemicals

Imports of goods and services: $12.8 billion

Major import trading partners: Italy 17.9%, Germany 15.6%, Slovenia 7.4%, Russia 4.7%

Foreign direct investment (net): $1.6 billion

2003 Data (in constant 2000 US dollars)

TRADE POLICY
Score: **2.5**–Better (moderate level of protectionism)

According to the World Bank, Croatia's weighted average tariff rate in 2004 was 3.3 percent, down from the 9.8 percent for 2001 reported in the 2005 *Index*. Non-tariff barriers include strict testing and certification requirements for some imports and corruption in customs. Based on the lower tariff rate, as well as a revision of the trade factor methodology, Croatia's trade policy score is 1 point better this year.

FISCAL BURDEN OF GOVERNMENT
Score—Income Taxation: **4.5**–Stable (very high tax rates)
Score—Corporate Taxation: **2**–Stable (low tax rates)
Score—Change in Government Expenditures: **2.5**–Better (low decrease)
Final Score: **2.8**–Better (moderate cost of government)

Deloitte reports that Croatia's top income tax rate is 45 percent. The top corporate tax rate is 20 percent. In 2004, according to the International Monetary Fund, government expenditures as a share of GDP decreased 1.1 percentage points to 51.6 percent, compared to a 1.3 percentage point increase in 2003. As a result, Croatia's fiscal burden of government score is 0.2 point better this year.

GOVERNMENT INTERVENTION IN THE ECONOMY
Score: **2**–Better (low level)

Based on data from Croatia's Central Bureau of Statistics, the government consumed 19.9 percent of GDP in 2004, down from the 21.25 percent reported in the 2005 *Index*. As a result, Croatia's government intervention score is 0.5 point better this year. In 2003, based on data from the Economist Intelligence Unit, Croatia received 2.52 percent of its total revenues from state-owned enterprises and government ownership of property.

MONETARY POLICY
Score: 1–Stable (very low level of inflation)

From 1995 to 2004, Croatia's weighted average annual rate of inflation was 2.77 percent.

CAPITAL FLOWS AND FOREIGN INVESTMENT
Score: 3–Stable (moderate barriers)

Foreign investors have the same rights and status as domestic investors and may invest in nearly every sector of the economy, but unofficial barriers persist. "While foreign investors enjoy equality under the law with domestic investors," reports the U.S. Department of Commerce, "in practice foreign investors often face difficulties. These problems are a result of institutional weaknesses in government bodies, and in some cases, corruption. Red tape presents difficulties to foreign and domestic investors alike.... [L]ack of transparency in government decision-making often leads to allegations of conflict of interest or bad decisions.... Some local governments have occasionally been openly hostile to foreign investment." According to the International Monetary Fund, foreigners may purchase real estate only with permission from the government. The IMF also reports that both residents and non-residents are allowed to hold foreign exchange accounts, but numerous limitations exist, and government approval is required in certain instances. Some capital transactions, such as inward portfolio investment, are subject to limitations and conditions set by the Ministry of Finance.

BANKING AND FINANCE
Score: 2–Stable (low level of restrictions)

The European Bank for Reconstruction and Development reports that Croatia's "banking sector is 91 per cent foreign-owned, stable, and competitive." According to the Economist Intelligence Unit, "The privatization and sale of the large majority of the banking sector to well-capitalised foreign banks in 2001 and 2002 induced rapid growth in consumer credit." The government owns the Croatian Bank for Reconstruction and Development, but the World Bank reports that approximately 90 percent of banking assets is privately owned. Two large commercial banks, Zagrebacka Banka and Privredna Banka Zagrab, hold nearly half of total bank assets. The central bank adopted regulations in 2004 to constrain the rapid growth of foreign banks' foreign currency borrowing to finance profitable lending in Croatia. A law passed in 2001 brought banking regulations more closely into harmonization with European Union standards—for example, by raising capital adequacy requirements. "The industry has seen significant consolidation in the past several years," reports the EIU. "The number of banks fell from 60 at end-1998 to 45 by mid-2003, and to 40 by mid-2004."

WAGES AND PRICES
Score: 3–Stable (moderate level of intervention)

According to the Economist Intelligence Unit, "The government retains control over prices of a range of goods and services, including logs, some forms of transportation, and most public utilities. Energy and telecommunications prices are directly administered not by the government but by independent regulatory bodies. The share of administered prices in the retail price index was just under 23% in 2003, the fourth consecutive year in which that share had increased." The government also financially subsidizes small businesses through the Croatian Agency for Small Businesses (HAMAG).

PROPERTY RIGHTS
Score: 4–Stable (low level of protection)

The court system is cumbersome and inefficient. According to the U.S. Department of Commerce, "Huge case backlogs mean that business disputes can go unresolved for years; some investors have chosen to insist that contract arbitration take place outside of Croatia. The Government of Croatia has made a commitment to reinvigorate its efforts to reform the judiciary, but much remains to be done." The same source reports that the government's "anti-corruption plan also involves reform of the judiciary, one of the areas most in need of reform, according to the prime minister."

REGULATION
Score: 4–Stable (high level)

Croatia's bureaucracy remains entrenched, and red tape abounds. The Economist Intelligence Unit reports that the government has implemented two programs to promote the creation of small businesses. However, these efforts have not produced as much investment as expected since, according to the U.S. Department of Commerce, "bureaucracy remains onerous, as high costs to start new businesses, burdensome administrative regulations, and occasional monopolistic or oligopolistic situations challenge new entrepreneurs." The EIU cites high wage costs and "restrictive labour laws" as impediments to business activity and reports that "corruption...seems to be a [great] source of worry for foreign businesses. Often, gratuities are requested to speed up the process...."

INFORMAL MARKET
Score: 3.5–Stable (high level of activity)

Transparency International's 2004 score for Croatia is 3.5. Therefore, Croatia's informal market score is 3.5 this year.

CUBA

Rank: 150

Score: 4.10

Category: Repressed

Present & Past Scores

(Best) 1—
2—
3—
4— 4.95 4.95 4.85 4.90 4.85 4.83 4.83 4.83 4.48 4.13 4.24 4.10
(Worst) 5—
'95 '96 '97 '98 '99 '00 '01 '02 '03 '04 '05 '06

C uba has a totalitarian government, a state-directed command economy, a captive labor force, and few exports to balance trade accounts. Fidel Castro's government consistently restricts basic human rights, such as freedom of expression, and maintains harsh prison conditions. Little independent data on the economy are available, and per capita GDP does not reflect actual individual income. State salaries average $15 to $20 per month in Cuban pesos, and personal needs are satisfied under a state rationing system. Cuba is chronically dependent on credit accounts that rotate from country to country. Typical imports are food, fuel, clothing, and machinery. Exports include nickel, cigars, and state-sponsored labor, for which the government charges many times what it pays in state salaries. Lacking investment, Cuba's sugar industry is no longer viable: The island has become a net importer. Venezuela now supplies up to 80,000 barrels of oil per day on generous credit terms, although Cuba produces small amounts of poor-quality sulfurous crude on its own. Venezuelan assistance has also enabled Cuba to retreat on limited liberal reforms such as allowing self-employment in careers like snack vending and bicycle repair. Cuba's fiscal burden of government score is 0.1 point worse this year, and its regulation score is 1 point worse; however, its monetary policy score is 1 point better, and its informal market score is 1.5 points better. As a result, Cuba's overall score is 0.14 point better this year.

QUICK STUDY

SCORES

Trade Policy	3.5
Fiscal Burden	4.5
Government Intervention	4.5
Monetary Policy	1
Foreign Investment	4
Banking and Finance	5
Wages and Prices	5
Property Rights	5
Regulation	5
Informal Market	3.5

Population: 11,326,000

Total area: 110,860 sq. km

GDP: $28.5 billion

GDP growth rate: 2.9%

GDP per capita: $2,516

Major exports: seafood, nickel, tobacco, sugar, citrus, coffee

Exports of goods (fob): $2.1 billion

Major export trading partners: Netherlands 21.6%, Canada 17.4%, Russia 10.6%, Spain 8.6%, China 7.1%

Major imports: machinery and equipment, chemical products, food, consumer goods

Imports of goods (fob): $4.9 billion

Major import trading partners: Spain 16.9%, Venezuela 12.7%, Italy 8.6%, US 8.5%, China 7.7%

Foreign direct investment (net): $2.8 million

2003 Data (in constant 2000 US dollars)

TRADE POLICY
Score: **3.5**–Stable (high level of protectionism)

According to the World Bank, Cuba's weighted average tariff rate in 2004 was 9.9 percent, up from the 9.4 percent reported in the 2005 *Index*. The Economist Intelligence Unit reports that "new procedures for the allocation of hard currency and centralizing of imports…have resulted in delays and bottlenecks." Corruption in customs is common. Based on the revised trade factor methodology, Cuba's trade policy score is unchanged.

FISCAL BURDEN OF GOVERNMENT
Score—Income Taxation: **5**–Stable (very high tax rates)
Score—Corporate Taxation: **4.5**–Worse (very high tax rates)
Score—Change in Government Expenditures: **4**–Better (moderate increase)
Final Score: **4.5**–Worse (very high cost of government)

According to information from the Pi Management Association, Cuba's top income tax rate is 50 percent. Deloitte reports that Cuba's top corporate tax rate is 35 percent, up from the 30 percent reported in the 2005 *Index*. In 2003, according to the Economist Intelligence Unit, government expenditures as a share of GDP increased by 2 percentage points to 58 percent, compared to a 2.7 percentage point increase in 2002. On net, Cuba's fiscal burden of government score is 0.1 point worse this year.

GOVERNMENT INTERVENTION IN THE ECONOMY
Score: **4.5**–Stable (very high level)

Based on United Nations data, the government consumed 34.9 percent of GDP in 2003. In 2001, based on data from the Economist Intelligence Unit, Cuba received 11.05 percent of its total revenues from state-owned enterprises and government ownership of property. (No new information about revenues from state-owned enterprises is available.) The state, however,

157

produces most economic output and employs most of the labor force. The industrial and services sectors are largely dominated by the state, which, according to the EIU, also employs 73.2 percent of the labor force. Based on the apparent unreliability of reported total revenue figures, 1 point has been added to Cuba's government intervention score.

MONETARY POLICY
Score: **1–Better** (very low level of inflation)

From 1995 to 2004, based on data from the Economist Intelligence Unit, Cuba's weighted average annual rate of inflation was 1.37 percent, down from the 4.21 percent reported in the 2005 *Index*. As a result, Cuba's monetary policy score is 1 point better this year.

CAPITAL FLOWS AND FOREIGN INVESTMENT
Score: **4–Stable** (high barriers)

The government maintains exchange controls. The Economist Intelligence Unit reports that, officially, "all sectors are open to foreign capital except defence, public health and education." In practice, however, all investments must be approved by the government, and licensing is required for all businesses. Cuba has been reversing limited liberalization of foreign investment. According to the EIU, "Alongside the centralisation of fiscal management and control of hard currency, a series of decisions over the past year has confirmed that some of the liberalising reforms of the 1990s—particularly the expansion of self-employment, the creation of free trade zones, and the opening to foreign business—are being rolled back." The EIU notes that the government has revised the terms for business licenses to include "social objectives" and has erected other deterrents to investment, such as delaying payments from Cuban enterprises, imposing onerous regulations, and increasing operating costs. Cuba has loosened restrictions to permit investment commitments and credit lines from China and Venezuela.

BANKING AND FINANCE
Score: **5–Stable** (very high level of restrictions)

The government passed a law in 2003 under which transactions between Cuban enterprises must be carried out in peso convertibles rather than U.S. dollars. "In January 2005," reports the Economist Intelligence Unit, "the rules changed once more to give the Central Bank closer control of the use of both hard currency and pesos convertibles, with all such deposits required to be held at the Central Bank and the authorities' approval required for transactions." Over a dozen foreign banks have opened representative offices, but they cannot operate freely. Some changes also have been introduced in the insurance sector, among them the introduction of new insurance products, but the government controls this sector as well. According to the EIU, "banking modernization is proceeding at a cautious pace and the state retains control."

WAGES AND PRICES
Score: **5–Stable** (very high level of intervention)

The price mechanism is highly complex. The government sets most prices, but in the retail sector, for example, the Economist Intelligence Unit reports that there are six markets: "US dollar and peso, state and private, legal and illegal." In the sectors where prices are freer, such as food production, prices "remain severely distorted by the dual exchange rate system as well as by state restrictions on the scope of markets and fixing of prices elsewhere."

PROPERTY RIGHTS
Score: **5–Stable** (very low level of protection)

Private ownership of land and productive capital by Cuban citizens is limited to farming and self-employment. According to the U.S. Department of State, "The Constitution…explicitly subordinates the courts to the ANPP [National Assembly of People's Power] and the Council of State, which is headed by Fidel Castro. The ANPP and its lower level counterparts choose all judges…. The law and trial practices do not meet international standards for fair public trials."

REGULATION
Score: **5–Worse** (high level)

Cuba's government regulates the entire economy. Private entrepreneurship exists, but on a very small scale. According to *The Economist*, "Cuba, out of necessity, has allowed capitalism into its socialist system. But it then keeps capitalism down…with a mass of complex and sometimes contradictory rules and regulations. Just when [investors] find out how things work, the rules change again." In addition, "except for food service operations…assistants and employees are not permitted…. [P]rivate taxis are barred from picking up passengers at tourist hotels or airports…. [T]eachers may not work as private tutors." Based on the evidence that formal private entrepreneurship is only minimally accepted and suffocated with *ad hoc* regulations, Cuba's regulation score is 1 point worse this year.

INFORMAL MARKET
Score: **3.5–Better** (high level of activity)

Transparency International's 2004 score for Cuba is 3.7. Therefore, Cuba's informal market score is 3.5 this year—1.5 points better than last year.

CYPRUS

Rank: 16

Score: 1.90

Category: Free

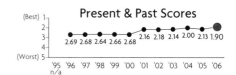

Present & Past Scores
(Best) 1-
2-
3- 2.69 2.68 2.64 2.66 2.68 2.16 2.18 2.14 2.00 2.13 1.90
4-
(Worst) 5-
'95 '96 '97 '98 '99 '00 '01 '02 '03 '04 '05 '06
n/a

QUICK STUDY

SCORES

Trade Policy	2
Fiscal Burden	2.5
Government Intervention	2
Monetary Policy	1
Foreign Investment	2
Banking and Finance	2
Wages and Prices	2
Property Rights	1
Regulation	2
Informal Market	2.5

Population: 769,954

Total area: 9,250 sq. km

GDP: $9.73 billion

GDP growth rate: 4.0%

GDP per capita: $12,647

Major exports: pharmaceuticals, clothing, potatoes, citrus, cigarettes, travel services, transportation

Exports of goods and services: $6.5 billion

Major export trading partners: UK 32.1%, Greece 9.2%, Lebanon 3.4%

Major imports: consumer goods, fuels and lubricants, chemicals, transport equipment, insurance services

Imports of goods and services: $6.9 billion

Major import trading partners: Greece 12.0%, Italy 9.8%, UK 8.3%, Germany 7.5%, France 5.1%

Foreign direct investment (net): $456.8 million

2003 Data (in constant 2000 US dollars)

After U.N. Secretary General Kofi Annan's reconciliation plan was rejected in April 2004, with 76 percent of Greek Cypriots voting not to accept a deal to forge the island into a unitary (if decentralized) state, the Greek portion of Cyprus joined the European Union as talks deadlocked. The Greek Cypriot government did not veto the start of EU accession talks with Turkey, but peace now seems far off. The desire to meet EU requirements has helped to liberalize the economy. Even after EU accession, Greek Cypriot fiscal policy has focused on consolidating the budget to prepare for entry into the Economic and Monetary Union, the central bank has sped the liberalization of capital flows, and government control of the economy has declined to around 25 percent. Under President Tassos Papadopoulos's coalition government, whose allies include the nominally communist Akel party, GDP grew by 3.5 percent in 2004, although the government deficit of 4.2 percent exceeded target. The government, somewhat in thrall to trade union support, is unlikely to privatize remaining state-owned companies such as airports, power utilities, or the Cyprus Telecoms Authority. Cyprus's fiscal burden of government score is 0.7 point worse this year; however, its trade policy, monetary policy, and capital flows and foreign investment scores are all 1 point better. As a result, its overall score is 0.23 point better this year, causing Cyprus to be classified as a "free" country.

TRADE POLICY
Score: **2**–Better (low level of protectionism)

Cyprus adopted the trade policies of the European Union when it joined the EU in May 2004. The common EU weighted average external tariff was 1.3 percent in 2003, based on World Bank data. In the 2005 *Index,* based on World Bank data, Cyprus had a tariff of 5.73 percent. According to the World Trade Organization and the U.S. Trade Representative, the EU imposes non-tariff trade barriers through a complex regulatory system and export subsidies. Based on its adoption of EU trade policies, and on the revised trade factor methodology, Cyprus's trade policy score is 1 point better this year.

FISCAL BURDEN OF GOVERNMENT
Score—Income Taxation: **3**–Stable (moderate tax rates)
Score—Corporate Taxation: **1**–Better (very low tax rates)
Score—Change in Government Expenditures: **5**–Worse (very high increase)
Final Score: **2.5**–Worse (moderate cost of government)

According to Deloitte, Cyprus's top income tax rate is 30 percent. The top corporate tax rate is 10 percent, down from the 15 percent reported in the 2005 *Index*. In 2003, according to the International Monetary Fund, government expenditures as a share of GDP increased by 3.8 percentage points to 41.5 percent, compared to the 1.4 percentage point increase in 2003. On net, Cyprus's fiscal burden of government score is 0.7 point worse this year.

GOVERNMENT INTERVENTION IN THE ECONOMY
Score: **2**–Stable (low level)

Data from the United Nations indicate that the government consumed 19.1 percent of GDP in 2003. In 2004, according to the Ministry of Finance, Cyprus received 2.28 percent of its total revenues from state-owned enterprises and government ownership of property.

MONETARY POLICY
Score: **1**–Better (very low level of inflation)

From 1995 to 2004, Cyprus's weighted average annual rate of inflation was 2.77 percent, down from 3.60 percent from 1994 to 2003. As a result, Cyprus's monetary policy score is 1 point better this year.

CAPITAL FLOWS AND FOREIGN INVESTMENT
Score: **2**–Better (low barriers)

In January 2000, Cyprus liberalized all foreign direct investment controls on local businesses for residents of the European Union, who may now own 100 percent of local companies and any company listed on the Cyprus Stock Exchange. The U.S. Department of Commerce reports that on October 1, 2004, the government of Cyprus "lifted most capital restrictions and limits on foreign equity participation/ownership, thereby granting national treatment to foreign investors. Non-EU investors (both natural and legal persons) may now invest freely in Cyprus in most sectors, either directly or indirectly." There is no longer a mandatory screening process for foreign investment, and no authorization is necessary beyond that required of domestic investment. The U.S. Department of Commerce reports that the only remaining exceptions involve the acquisition of property and investments in tertiary education and mass media. According to the International Monetary Fund, the purchase of real estate abroad by residents is permitted, subject to some limitations, and non-resident purchase of real estate is subject to approval. Some payments, current transfers, and capital transactions are subject to central bank approval or restrictions. On net, Cyprus's capital flows and foreign investment score is 1 point better this year.

BANKING AND FINANCE
Score: **2**–Stable (low level of restrictions)

The Economist Intelligence Unit reports that there are 12 banks incorporated in Cyprus, as well as two foreign branches and 29 offshore banks. In addition, over 350 credit societies, co-operative savings banks, and other credit institutions account for 32 percent of total deposits. According to the Embassy of Cyprus, there are two state-owned banks. The January 2000 liberalization of foreign investment permits non-residents to own up to 50 percent of a Cypriot bank, up from 15 percent, but acquisition of more than 10 percent requires central bank approval. Interest rates were liberalized as of January 1, 2001, and are now set by the market. Effective January 2001, the government lifted restrictions on foreign-currency–denominated lending for more than two years for residents. The government also increased transparency of bank charges in January 2001. In compliance with European Union requirements, Cyprus's central bank was granted full independence. According to the EIU, "Business services, like financial services, in the past benefited from a favourable offshore regime, which led many companies to move to Cyprus…. Growth in this sector is likely to slow in future, as the preferential treatment for offshore

companies will be fully abolished by 2005, and anti-money laundering regulations are now much tighter."

WAGES AND PRICES
Score: **2**–Stable (low level of intervention)

The market sets most prices. According to the U.S. Department of Commerce, the government controls the prices of "pharmaceuticals for the private health sector, including for nonprescription, over-the-counter medicines," as well as some means of transportation, like taxis. The Economist Intelligence Unit reports that the government liberalized gas prices on May 24, 2004, but retains the right to intervene in this sector. The government mandates a minimum wage.

PROPERTY RIGHTS
Score: **1**–Stable (very high level of protection)

Private property in Cyprus is well protected. "Effective means are available for enforcing property and contractual rights," reports the U.S. Department of Commerce. According to the Economist Intelligence Unit, "By constitution, the civil judiciary, including the Supreme Court (which carries out the functions of a constitutional court, a high court of appeal and an administrative court), is independent from government interference. De facto, some meddling does seem to take place, but the judiciary has nevertheless caused several embarrassing defeats for the government."

REGULATION
Score: **2**–Stable (low level)

It is relatively easy to establish a business in Cyprus, especially since the government streamlined regulations before joining the European Union in 2004. According to the U.S. Department of Commerce, "Existing procedures and regulations affecting business…are sufficiently transparent and applied in practice without bias…." The Embassy of Cyprus reports that opening a new business "usually takes a month on average but through the acceleration procedure introduced the last few years…the time is reduced to 4–7 days." The U.S. Embassy in Cyprus "is not aware of any U.S. firms identifying corruption as an obstacle to foreign direct investment in Cyprus."

INFORMAL MARKET
Score: **2.5**–Stable (moderate level of activity)

Transparency International's 2004 score for Cyprus is 5.4. Therefore, Cyprus's informal market score is 2.5 this year.

Cyprus qualifies for the Global Free Trade Alliance.

CZECH REPUBLIC

Rank: 21

Score: 2.10

Category: Mostly Free

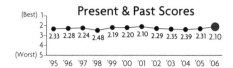

Present & Past Scores

(Best) 1 — 2 — 3 — 4 — (Worst) 5

2.33 2.28 2.24 2.48 2.19 2.20 2.10 2.29 2.35 2.39 2.31 2.10

'95 '96 '97 '98 '99 '00 '01 '02 '03 '04 '05 '06

QUICK STUDY

SCORES

Trade Policy	2
Fiscal Burden	2.5
Government Intervention	2.5
Monetary Policy	1
Foreign Investment	2
Banking and Finance	1
Wages and Prices	2
Property Rights	2
Regulation	3
Informal Market	3

Population: 10,206,923

Total area: 78,866 sq. km

GDP: $62.6 billion

GDP growth rate: 4.0%

GDP per capita: $6,133

Major exports: machinery and equipment, chemicals, raw materials and fuels

Exports of goods and services: $43.8 billion

Major export trading partners: Germany 37.1%, Slovakia 8.0%, Austria 6.3%, Poland 4.8%, France 4.7%

Major imports: machinery and transport equipment, raw materials and fuels, chemicals

Imports of goods and services: $48 billion

Major import trading partners: Germany 32.6%, Italy 5.3%, China 5.2%, Slovakia 5.2%, France 4.9%

Foreign direct investment (net): $3.6 billion

2004 Data (in constant 2000 US dollars)

The Czech Republic's coalition government has survived a political crisis despite a poor performance by the ruling Social Democrats in the Senate and a scandal surrounding Prime Minister Stanislav Gross's personal finances, which forced him to resign in April 2005. Despite the scandal, the new prime minister-designate was determined to lead the fractious center–left coalition until 2006. Economically, the Czech Republic appears to be on much sturdier ground. Substantive reforms in a number of key areas have helped to expand the economy and increase 2004 budget revenues. Privatization seems to be on track. Major sales of the telecommunications and coal industries were scheduled for 2005. Exports are booming, and the inflows of foreign direct investment are growing. According to the Economist Intelligence Unit, the Czech Republic's membership in the European Union will continue to produce an "increasingly stable and predictable legal environment," which further improves the country's economic promise. The Czech Republic's trade policy and informal market scores are both 0.5 point better this year, and its fiscal burden of government score is 1.1 points better. As a result, the Czech Republic's overall score is 0.21 point better this year.

TRADE POLICY
Score: 2–Better (low level of protectionism)

The Czech Republic adopted the trade policies of the European Union when it joined the EU in May 2004. The common EU weighted average external tariff was 7.3 percent in 2003, based on World Bank data. In the 2005 *Index*, based on World Bank data, the Czech Republic had a tariff of 4.1 percent. According to the World Trade Organization and the U.S. Trade Representative, the EU imposes non-tariff trade barriers through a complex regulatory system and export subsidies. Based on its adoption of EU trade policies, and on the revised trade factor methodology, the Czech Republic's trade policy score is 0.5 point better this year.

FISCAL BURDEN OF GOVERNMENT
Score—Income Taxation: 3–Stable (moderate tax rates)
Score—Corporate Taxation: 3–Better (moderate tax rates)
Score—Change in Government Expenditures: 1–Better (very high decrease)
Final Score: 2.5–Better (moderate cost of government)

According to Deloitte, the Czech Republic's top income tax rate is 32 percent. In January 2005, the top corporate tax rate was cut to 26 percent from 28 percent. In 2004, government expenditures as a share of GDP decreased by 7.3 percentage points to 45.9 percent, compared to a 6.3 percentage point increase in 2003. On net, the Czech Republic's fiscal burden of government score is 1.1 points better this year.

GOVERNMENT INTERVENTION IN THE ECONOMY
Score: 2.5–Stable (moderate level)

Data from the central bank indicate that the government consumed 22.7 percent of GDP in 2004. In 2003, according to the International Monetary Fund, the Czech Republic received 2.53 percent of its total revenues from state-owned enterprises and government ownership of property.

MONETARY POLICY
Score: 1–Stable (very low level of inflation)

Between 1995 and 2004, the Czech Republic's weighted average annual rate of inflation was 2.19 percent.

CAPITAL FLOWS AND FOREIGN INVESTMENT
Score: 2–Stable (low barriers)

According to the Economist Intelligence Unit, "Foreigners are generally accorded the same economic rights and responsibilities as Czech nationals. In accordance with the commercial code, foreigners are freely permitted to establish new joint ventures and participate in existing enterprises, with as much as 100% foreign ownership in both cases…. However, the government deems strategic industries (such as defence) of vital importance to national security, and thus places them off-limits." Foreign private individuals are not allowed to purchase land, but branches or offices of foreign companies can buy local real estate, with the exception of farmland or woodland. The Czech Republic has opened its privatization program to foreign investors, and the U.S. Department of Commerce reports that "most major state-owned companies have been privatized with foreign participation." The International Monetary Fund reports no restrictions on payments or current transfers, and both residents and non-residents may hold foreign exchange accounts. Prior authorization is required for issuance of debt securities and money market securities. There are restrictions on foreign direct investment in the air transport sector. The U.S. Department of Commerce reports that a lack of transparency in the government procurement process is an obstacle to foreign tenders for government contracts.

BANKING AND FINANCE
Score: 1–Stable (very low level of restrictions)

Following the 1990s banking crises and subsequent privatization, the government has no stake in the banking sector, and foreign owners now control 90 percent of Czech banking assets. According to the Economist Intelligence Unit, "Most of the largest banks are now owned and operated by large Western European financial groups from France, Belgium, Germany and Austria. Through these and other acquisitions, foreign firms have come to dominate the local markets for banking, brokerage, insurance, pension-fund management and other financial services." Subject to approval by the central bank, a foreign bank may establish a wholly owned bank, buy into an existing bank, or open a branch. The Economist Intelligence Unit reports that there were 35 banks, 26 of which were partially or wholly foreign-owned, at the end of 2004. Another 18 banks were in liquidation or bankruptcy proceedings. The Czech Republic's "universal" banking license allows nearly all banks to operate anywhere in the country and in all types of banking activities. The sector remains burdened by a weak bankruptcy framework and a backlog of bankruptcy claims.

WAGES AND PRICES
Score: 2–Stable (low level of intervention)

The market sets most wages and prices, but the Economist Intelligence Unit reports that the government effectively controls the prices of energy, some raw materials, domestic rents, and rail and bus transport, and sets maximum prices on mail and telecommunications services. Potentially, under the Price Law (Law 526/1990), which has been in effect since January 1991, the government has broad power to fix prices and to set minimum or maximum prices for any commercial transaction for any period. The government mandates a minimum wage.

PROPERTY RIGHTS
Score: 2–Stable (high level of protection)

Private property is well-protected. The Economist Intelligence Unit reports that "contractual agreements are generally secure in the Czech Republic." According to the U.S. Department of Commerce, however, "The judiciary is independent, but decisions may vary from court to court. Commercial disputes, particularly those related to bankruptcy proceedings, can drag on for years. Companies' registration is in the hands of the courts and is sometimes slow and overly complicated."

REGULATION
Score: 3–Stable (moderate level)

Red tape and bureaucratic corruption are still big problems. According to the U.S. Department of Commerce, "bureaucracy and unnecessary red tape remain sources of complaints by both domestic and foreign investors. Delays and allegations of corruption are common, especially in the process of registering companies and changes to corporate structure, and are of particular concern to foreign companies operating in the Czech Republic." The Economist Intelligence Unit reports that "firms must meet myriad local standards on health, hygiene, ventilation, and utilities use, among others." In addition, "to establish a company or change a registration, bundles of documents stamped by notaries have to be submitted to a special judge at a regional court." As a result, companies are almost forced to hire lawyers and bribe officials to complete the process.

INFORMAL MARKET
Score: 3–Better (moderate level of activity)

Transparency International's 2004 score for the Czech Republic is 4.2. Therefore, the Czech Republic's informal market score is 3 this year—0.5 point better than last year.

> If Czech Republic were to improve its regulation score, it would qualify for the Global Free Trade Alliance.

DENMARK

Rank: 8

Score: 1.78

Category: Free

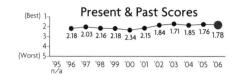

Present & Past Scores

(Best) 1
2
3
4
(Worst) 5

2.18 2.03 2.16 2.18 2.34 2.15 1.84 1.71 1.85 1.76 1.78

'95 '96 '97 '98 '99 '00 '01 '02 '03 '04 '05 '06
n/a

D enmark enjoys one of the world's highest standards of living. The private sector is marked by many small and medium-sized companies. According to *The Economist*, "Firms with less than 50 employees account for about half of total employment, and only 12 percent of the labor force work in companies with more than 500 employees." Like most of its European counterparts, Denmark also has a large welfare state, which includes free public education, lifelong health care coverage, and subsidized care for children and the elderly. Because Danes appear to see Anders Fogh Rasmussen as the best guarantor of this large welfare system, his center–right coalition won another victory in the February 2005 general election. Along with restraining taxes, addressing the costs and benefits of Denmark's comprehensive social welfare system is one of the key issues on the current political agenda. The 30 percent corporate tax rate was cut to 28 percent. Denmark's fiscal burden of government is 0.2 point worse this year. As a result, its overall score is 0.02 point worse this year.

TRADE POLICY
Score: **2**–Stable (low level of protectionism)

As a member of the European Union, Denmark was subject to a common EU weighted average external tariff of 1.3 percent in 2003, down from the 2.4 percent for 2002 reported in the 2005 *Index*, based on World Bank data. According to the World Trade Organization and the U.S. Trade Representative, the EU imposes non-tariff trade barriers through a complex regulatory system and export subsidies. The U.S. Department of Commerce reports that "marking and labeling requirements for products sold in Denmark are numerous and vary from product to product." Based on the revised trade factor methodology, Denmark's trade policy score is unchanged.

FISCAL BURDEN OF GOVERNMENT
Score—Income Taxation: **5**–Worse (very high tax rates)
Score—Corporate Taxation: **3.5**–Better (high tax rates)
Score—Change in Government Expenditures: **3**–Better (very low decrease)
Final Score: **3.8**–Worse (high cost of government)

The Embassy of Denmark reports that Denmark's top income tax rate is 59 percent, up from the 26.5 percent incorrectly reported in the 2005 *Index*. The top corporate tax rate was cut to 28 percent from 30 percent. In 2004, government expenditures as a share of GDP decreased 0.1 percentage point to 56.3 percent, compared to a 0.2 percentage point increase in 2003. On net, Denmark's fiscal burden of government score is 0.2 point worse this year.

GOVERNMENT INTERVENTION IN THE ECONOMY
Score: **3**–Stable (moderate level)

Based on Statistics Denmark data, the government consumed 26.5 percent of GDP in 2004. In the same year, based on data from the central bank, Denmark received 5.43 percent of its revenues from state-owned enterprises and government ownership of property.

QUICK STUDY

SCORES
Trade Policy	2
Fiscal Burden	3.8
Government Intervention	3
Monetary Policy	1
Foreign Investment	2
Banking and Finance	1
Wages and Prices	2
Property Rights	1
Regulation	1
Informal Market	1

Population: 5,397,640

Total area: 43,094 sq. km

GDP: $166.4 billion

GDP growth rate: 2.0%

GDP per capita: $30,828

Major exports: manufactured goods, dairy products, furniture, meat and meat products, fuels, ships, transportation, travel services

Exports of goods and services: $92.1 billion

Major export trading partners: Germany 18.0%, Sweden 13.3%, UK 8.7%, US 5.7%, Norway 5.4%

Major imports: transport equipment, capital goods, intermediate goods

Imports of goods and services: $78.2 billion

Major import trading partners: Germany 22.2%, Sweden 13.4%, UK 6.1%, Netherlands 6.0%, France 4.8%

Foreign direct investment (net): –$324 million

2004 Data (in constant 2000 US dollars)

163

MONETARY POLICY
Score: **1**–Stable (very low level of inflation)

From 1995 to 2004, Denmark's weighted average annual rate of inflation was 1.55 percent.

CAPITAL FLOWS AND FOREIGN INVESTMENT
Score: **2**–Stable (low barriers)

Foreign investors, including those from outside the European Union, are subject to the same laws as domestic investors. According to the Economist Intelligence Unit, "The central and the regional governments encourage foreign investment on a national-treatment basis. As a general rule, foreign direct investment in Denmark may take place without restrictions or pre-screening. Ownership restrictions apply to only a few sectors." The International Monetary Fund reports that non-residents may not purchase real estate unless the person formerly resided in Denmark for at least five years, is an EU national working in Denmark, or is a non-EU national with a valid residence or business permit. There are no restrictions on capital transfers. Limitations on foreign ownership apply for hydrocarbon exploration, arms production, aircraft, and ships registered in the Danish International Ships Register.

BANKING AND FINANCE
Score: **1**–Stable (very low level of restrictions)

Denmark's banking system is open to foreign competition, and the central bank is independent. The same rules apply to commercial and savings banks, and banks may provide services in a wide variety of areas, including mortgage financing, stock trading, leasing, factoring, investment, real estate, and insurance. Denmark had 548 financial institutions in 2003, including 176 banks, according to the Danish Financial Supervisory Authority. The Danish embassy reports that there are no state-owned banks. Eighteen foreign banks operate in Denmark. The largest bank (Danske Bank) accounted for a 47.8 percent market share in 2003. According to the Economist Intelligence Unit, "Supervision of Denmark's entire financial services industry—banks, mortgage credit institutions, securities firms and insurance companies—is in the hands of a single regulator, Finanstilsynet. Supervision standards are derived from EU legislation."

WAGES AND PRICES
Score: **2**–Stable (low level of intervention)

The market sets wages and most prices. According to the Economist Intelligence Unit, "The government retains the power to intervene with price controls in an emergency—such as during a period of accelerating inflation…. Otherwise, none apply." The government affects agricultural prices through Denmark's participation in the European Union's Common Agricultural Policy, a program that heavily subsidizes agricultural goods. There is an established minimum wage.

PROPERTY RIGHTS
Score: **1**–Stable (very high level of protection)

The judiciary is independent and, in general, both fair and efficient. According to the U.S. Department of Commerce, "The legal system is independent of the government and is based on a centuries-old legal tradition. It includes written and consistently applied commercial and bankruptcy laws, and secured interests in property are recognized and enforced."

REGULATION
Score: **1**–Stable (very low level)

Establishing a business is a simple process, and many forms and submissions can be done on the Internet. Regulations are applied evenly and efficiently in most cases. According to the International Institute for Management Development, Denmark has one of the most flexible labor laws in Europe (including Ireland), surpassed only by the United States. The U.S. Department of Commerce reports that "Denmark applies high standards with regard to environment, health and safety, and labor…. Bureaucratic procedures appear streamlined and transparent, and corruption is generally unknown." Corruption in the bureaucracy is almost nonexistent.

INFORMAL MARKET
Score: **1**–Stable (very low level of activity)

Transparency International's 2004 score for Denmark is 9.5. Therefore, Denmark's informal market score is 1 this year.

> Denmark qualifies for the Global Free Trade Alliance.

DJIBOUTI

Rank: 94

Score: 3.20

Category: Mostly Unfree

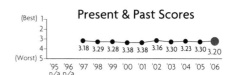

Present & Past Scores

(Best) 1
2
3
4
(Worst) 5

3.18 3.29 3.28 3.38 3.38 3.16 3.30 3.23 3.30 3.20

'95 '96 '97 '98 '99 '00 '01 '02 '03 '04 '05 '06
n/a n/a

QUICK STUDY

SCORES

Trade Policy	5
Fiscal Burden	3.5
Government Intervention	3.5
Monetary Policy	1
Foreign Investment	3
Banking and Finance	2
Wages and Prices	2
Property Rights	4
Regulation	4
Informal Market	4

Population: 705,480

Total area: 22,000 sq. km

GDP: $598 million

GDP growth rate: 3.5%

GDP per capita: $848

Major exports: coffee, hides and skins

Exports of goods (fob): $89 million

Major export trading partners: Yemen 22.5%, Ethiopia 5.0%

Major imports: machinery, petroleum products, food and beverages

Imports of goods (fob): $338 million

Major import trading partners: Saudi Arabia 18.6%, Ethiopia 10.3%, China 8.8%, India 8.6%, US 4.6%

Foreign direct investment (net): $10.8 million

2003 Data (in constant 2000 US dollars)

Djibouti has been ruled by the People's Rally for Progress party since gaining its independence in 1977. President Ismael Omar Guelleh, first elected in 1999, was re-elected in 2005 when opposition parties failed to put forth a candidate. Guelleh's party also won all 65 seats in the 2003 legislative elections, albeit amid allegations of fraud. Djibouti has few natural resources, and its service-based economy is centered on port facilities, the railway, and military bases at which both France and the United States have a significant troop presence. Spain and Germany also maintain troops in Djibouti. The port and transport sector accounts for one-third of GDP. Ethiopia is an important economic partner, being responsible for some 85 percent of goods moving through the port of Djibouti after another major transshipment client moved its business to Yemen. Nomadic subsistence is the primary occupation for those living outside the capital city (also called Djibouti). The government has dragged its feet on implementing reforms under the International Monetary Fund program, which included a new investment code, tax and banking reform, and fiscal transparency. It also remains reluctant to reduce either the bloated civil service or corruption. Djibouti's banking and finance score is 1 point better this year. As a result, its overall score is 0.1 point better this year.

TRADE POLICY
Score: **5**–Stable (very high level of protectionism)

The International Monetary Fund reports that Djibouti's average tariff rate in 2002 was 21 percent. According to the Economist Intelligence Unit, much trade with neighboring countries is informal. Based on the revised trade factor methodology, Djibouti's trade policy score is unchanged.

FISCAL BURDEN OF GOVERNMENT
Score—Income Taxation: **3**–Stable (moderate tax rates)
Score—Corporate Taxation: **3**–Stable (moderate tax rates)
Score—Change in Government Expenditures: **5**–Stable (very high increase)
Final Score: **3.5**–Stable (high cost of government)

The International Monetary Fund reports that Djibouti's top income tax rate is 30 percent. According to Deloitte, the top corporate tax rate is 25 percent. In 2003, according to the African Development Bank, government expenditures as a share of GDP increased 3.6 percentage points to 36.5 percent, compared to a 3.2 percentage point increase in 2002.

GOVERNMENT INTERVENTION IN THE ECONOMY
Score: **3.5**–Stable (high level)

Based on United Nations data, the government consumed 26.6 percent of GDP in 2003. In 2002, according to the International Monetary Fund, Djibouti received 1.88 percent of its total revenues from state-owned enterprises and government ownership of property. However, much of Djibouti's GDP is produced by the state. The Economist Intelligence Unit reports that the government owns "all the principal public utilities: water; electricity; postal services and telecommunications; and the railway (owned jointly with Ethiopia) and port." Two pharmaceutical factories and dairy products plants are also state-owned, and the EIU reports that the government employs most of the labor force. Based on the level of state-owned enterprise, 1 point has been added to Djibouti's government intervention score.

MONETARY POLICY
Score: **1–Stable** (very low level of inflation)

Djibouti has a currency board system pegging its franc to the U.S. dollar. From 1995 to 2004, Djibouti's weighted average annual rate of inflation was 2.51 percent.

CAPITAL FLOWS AND FOREIGN INVESTMENT
Score: **3–Stable** (moderate barriers)

"The government of Djibouti welcomes all foreign direct investment," according to the U.S. Department of Commerce. "Djibouti has no major laws that would discourage incoming foreign investment. In principle there is no screening of investment or other discriminatory mechanisms. That said, certain sectors, most notably public utilities, are state owned and some parts are not currently open to investors." Investment is inhibited also by numerous administrative difficulties. "Access to licenses and approvals is complicated not so much by law as by administrative procedures," reports the U.S. Department of Commerce. These procedures take the form of a "circular dependency" by which "the Finance Ministry will issue a license only if an investor possesses an approved investor visa, while the Interior Ministry will only issue an investor visa to a licensed business." The International Monetary Fund reports that both residents and non-residents may hold foreign exchange accounts, and there are no restrictions on payments or transfers. However, the IMF does report that Djibouti imposes controls on all credit transactions between residents and non-residents.

BANKING AND FINANCE
Score: **2–Better** (low level of restrictions)

Little formal economic activity occurs outside of the capital city of Djibouti. "The banking sector is dominated by foreign-owned banks, two of which are owned by French commercial banks, Banque pour le commerce et l'industrie-Mer Rouge, in which Banque nationale de Paris has a 51% stake, and Bank Indosuez-Mer Rouge, owned by Groupe Indosuez of France. These two banks account for about 95 percent of deposits and issue more than 85% of credit. In addition, Commercial Bank of Ethiopia operates in the country, but, with non-performing loans amounting to US$16.7m in early 2004, the bank is on the verge of shutting down its Djibouti branch after more than 40 years of operation." The government has a stake in the Banque pour le Commerce et l'Industrie-Mer Rouge. Commercial banks generally provide only short-term financing and lending. The central bank is stepping up its supervision of existing financial institutions, and a law against money laundering was passed in 2002. A Development Fund for Djibouti was authorized by the government in 2001 to provide loans for rural development and the tourism, agriculture, and fishing industries, but it has not yet become operational. Based on evidence that the banking sector is predominantly private, Djibouti's banking and finance score is 1 point better this year.

WAGES AND PRICES
Score: **2–Stable** (low level of intervention)

The market sets wages and prices for most products, but the government sets the prices of utilities through state-owned companies in the electricity, water, and telecommunications sectors, as well as postal services, the railway, port services, pharmaceutical factories, and dairy products plants. Djibouti maintains a minimum wage.

PROPERTY RIGHTS
Score: **4–Stable** (low level of protection)

Private property rights are weakly protected. The courts are frequently overburdened, and the enforcement of contracts can be time-consuming and cumbersome. The Economist Intelligence Unit reports that "political manipulation has undermined the credibility of the judicial system. Effective power resides in the diverse branches of the security services, controlled by the presidency, and the political culture is dominated by personal and clan patronage." According to the U.S. Department of Commerce, "Djibouti does have written commercial and bankruptcy laws, but they are not applied consistently." In addition, "While there are laws against corruption, they are rarely enforced, in part because most people prefer to deal with corruption issues on their own rather than involve complicated legal mechanisms."

REGULATION
Score: **4–Stable** (high level)

Djibouti's regulations are both cumbersome and significantly burdensome. According to the Economist Intelligence Unit, "Djibouti's economy is characterised by a lack of flexibility, high levels of regulation and labour protection." The U.S. Agency for International Development reports that "the most recurrent problem mentioned by investors in almost every stage of the investment start-up process is the lack of procedural transparency. There are few formal, written guidelines. The success of many applications and requests hinges on the approval of the Minister responsible for the particular portfolio.... [T]he company registration process is dispersed across several agencies with little or no coordination among them; moreover, there are numerous duplicative requirements among these agencies."

INFORMAL MARKET
Score: **4–Stable** (high level of activity)

Most economic activity still occurs informally. According to the United Nations, "The economy of Djibouti is dual and characterized by an important informal sector.... It is estimated that more than 80 percent of enterprises are within the informal and semi-informal sector, including a large number of informal micro-enterprises, which play a key role in the economy of the country."

DOMINICAN REPUBLIC

Rank: 116

Score: 3.39

Category: Mostly Unfree

Present & Past Scores

(Best) 1–
2–
3–
4–
(Worst) 5–

3.63 3.34 3.24 3.26 3.20 3.08 3.09 3.19 3.29 3.51 3.54 3.39

'95 '96 '97 '98 '99 '00 '01 '02 '03 '04 '05 '06

The Dominican Republic is a country on the mend following a 2003 banking scandal under former President Hipólito Mejía, when inflation spiked to 63 percent and GDP contracted by 0.4 percent. Since then, President Leonel Fernández has improved banking supervision, cut government spending, and introduced tax reforms. During 2004, the Dominican Republic posted a modest 2 percent growth rate. Many challenges remain, however. One is the continuous flow of undocumented Haitians seeking refuge and employment as their country tries to get back on its feet. Another is an inefficient legal system in which a lack of resources and personnel keeps rule-of-law reforms from expediting judicial processes. Additionally, a deteriorated electrical distribution system, partly sustained by subsidies, is subject to frequent outages that hurt industry and tourism. Finally, the end of global quotas on apparel exports might allow China to increase its share of sales to the United States, cutting into exports from the Dominican Republic. The DR–CAFTA agreement could help the Dominican Republic to overcome such changes in global markets, but increases in the competitiveness of the economy are required. The Dominican Republic's monetary policy score is 1 point worse this year, and its informal market score is 0.5 point worse; however, its trade policy and fiscal burden of government scores are both 0.5 point better, and its banking and finance score and wages and prices score are both 1 point better. As a result, the Dominican Republic's overall score is 0.15 point better this year.

QUICK STUDY

SCORES

Trade Policy	3.5
Fiscal Burden	2.9
Government Intervention	1.5
Monetary Policy	5
Foreign Investment	3
Banking and Finance	3
Wages and Prices	3
Property Rights	4
Regulation	4
Informal Market	4

Population: 8,738,639

Total area: 48,730 sq. km

GDP: $21.1 billion

GDP growth rate: −0.4%

GDP per capita: $2,413

Major exports: coffee, sugar, tobacco, gold, cocoa

Exports of goods and services: $10.3 billion

Major export trading partners: US 83.7%, Canada 1.6%, Haiti 1.5%

Major imports: cotton and fabrics, chemicals, foodstuffs, petroleum

Imports of goods and services: $11.3 billion

Major import trading partners: US 52.1%, Venezuela 11.9%, Mexico 4.7%

Foreign direct investment (net): $292.4 million

2003 Data (in constant 2000 US dollars)

TRADE POLICY
Score: **3.5**–Better (high level of protectionism)

According to the World Bank, the Dominican Republic's weighted average tariff rate in 2004 was 8.8 percent, down from the 10.1 percent for 2001 reported in the 2005 *Index*. "Entering goods into the Dominican Republic can be a slow and arduous process," reports the U.S. Trade Representative. "Customs Department interpretations often provoke complaints by businesspersons, and arbitrary clearance procedures sometimes delay the importation of merchandise for lengthy periods." Based on the lower tariff rate, as well as a revision of the trade factor methodology, the Dominican Republic's trade policy score is 0.5 point better this year.

FISCAL BURDEN OF GOVERNMENT
Score—Income Taxation: **2.5**–Stable (moderate tax rates)
Score—Corporate Taxation: **3**–Stable (moderate tax rates)
Score—Change in Government Expenditures: **3**–Better (very low decrease)
Final Score: **2.9**–Better (moderate cost of government)

According to the Direccion General de Impuestos Internos, the Dominican Republic's top income tax rate is 25 percent. The top corporate tax rate is also 25 percent. In 2003, according to the Inter-American Development Bank, government expenditures as a share of GDP decreased 0.3 percentage point to 18.2 percent, compared to a 0.6 percentage point decrease in 2002. On net, the Dominican Republic's fiscal burden of government score is 0.5 point better this year.

GOVERNMENT INTERVENTION IN THE ECONOMY
Score: **1.5**–Stable (low level)

The World Bank reports that the government consumed 7 percent of GDP in 2003. In the same year, based on data from the Finance Secretariat, the Dominican Republic received 0.84 percent of its total revenues from state-owned enterprises and government ownership of property.

MONETARY POLICY
Score: 5–Worse (very high level of inflation)

From 1995 to 2004, the Dominican Republic's weighted average annual rate of inflation was 39.78 percent, up from the 19.65 percent from 1994 to 2003 reported in the 2005 *Index*. As a result, the Dominican Republic's monetary policy score is 1 point worse this year.

CAPITAL FLOWS AND FOREIGN INVESTMENT
Score: 3–Stable (moderate barriers)

According to the U.S. Department of Commerce, the Dominican Republic has partially liberalized its foreign investment policy and "welcomes foreign investment. However, some laws exist that apply to specific sectors of the economy (e.g., insurance) that may discriminate between domestic and foreign investments." There is no screening of foreign investment, but investments must be registered with the Central Bank of the Dominican Republic. The International Monetary Fund reports that foreign direct investment is permitted in all sectors except the disposal and storage of toxic, hazardous, or radioactive waste; activities that affect public health or the environment; and activities related to defense and security. According to the U.S. Trade Representative, "Existing Dominican legislation does not contain effective procedures for settling disputes arising from the government's actions. Dominican expropriation standards are not consistent with international law standards, and numerous U.S. investors have had disputes related to expropriated property." The IMF reports that both residents and non-residents may hold foreign exchange accounts. Payments and transfers are subject to documentation requirements. Some capital transactions are subject to approval, documentation, or reporting requirements.

BANKING AND FINANCE
Score: 3–Better (moderate level of restrictions)

Confidence in the Dominican Republic's banking system has been improving since resolution of the banking crisis caused by the March 2003 collapse of Banco Intercontinental (Baninter), the country's second largest bank, due to embezzlement, fraud, and mismanagement. The government bailed out Baninter depositors and two other smaller banks that collapsed in the wake of the Baninter-inspired crisis (estimated to cost over 20 percent of GDP) and moved to improve supervision of the banking system. "Supervision and regulation of the system were found badly wanting in light of the massive banking fraud uncovered in 2003," reports the Economist Intelligence Unit. "Banks are under-capitalised. The reforms centre on measures to strengthen the regulatory framework, including the adoption of consolidated accounting and supervision, and ensuring that all banks comply with the phased implementation of asset valuation and

capital adequacy norms based on international best practices." According to the U.S. Department of Commerce, "There are 14 multi-service banks, 15 development banks, 18 savings and loan associations, 1 mortgage bank, 69 finance companies, 23 loan houses, and 1 national housing bank." Citibank and Scotiabank were the only two foreign-owned banks operating in the Dominican Republic in 2004. Based on improved stability in the financial sector, the Dominican Republic's banking and finance score is 1 point better this year.

WAGES AND PRICES
Score: 3–Better (moderate level of intervention)

The government subsidizes certain agricultural crops and sets the prices of electricity and fuel. According to the Economist Intelligence Unit, it also subsidizes liquefied natural gas, public transportation, electricity, and certain retail food. The government maintains a minimum wage. Based on a reassessment of the available data, the Dominican Republic's wages and prices score is 1 point better this year.

PROPERTY RIGHTS
Score: 4–Stable (low level of protection)

The court system is inefficient, bureaucratic red tape run high, and the government can expropriate property. According to the U.S. Department of Commerce, "A number of…investors have outstanding disputes with the Dominican government concerning expropriated land…. Investors and lenders often do not receive prompt or adequate payment for their losses, and payment has been difficult to obtain even when a Dominican court has ordered compensation…." In addition, despite recent judicial reforms, "Dominican and foreign business leaders have complained of judicial and administrative corruption, and have charged that corruption affects the settlement of business disputes."

REGULATION
Score: 4–Stable (high level)

Regulations are still burdensome. The U.S. Department of Commerce reports that some of the challenges businesses face include "Corruption…in government, in the private sector, and within law enforcement agencies nationwide; Non-transparent government procurement; [and] Government non-compliance with contracts." In addition, "The interpretation of laws and regulations is often arbitrary. This has contributed to an unstable and capricious regulatory environment. Businesses, domestic as well as foreign, complain that the rules of the game are constantly changing."

INFORMAL MARKET
Score: 4–Worse (high level of activity)

Transparency International's 2004 score for the Dominican Republic is 2.9. Therefore, the Dominican Republic's informal market score is 4 this year—0.5 point worse than last year.

ECUADOR

Rank: 107

Score: 3.30

Category: Mostly Unfree

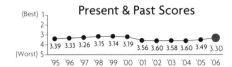

Present & Past Scores

(Best) 1
2
3
4
(Worst) 5

'95 3.39 | '96 3.33 | '97 3.26 | '98 3.15 | '99 3.14 | '00 3.19 | '01 3.56 | '02 3.60 | '03 3.58 | '04 3.60 | '05 3.49 | '06 3.30

QUICK STUDY

SCORES

Trade Policy	3.5
Fiscal Burden	3
Government Intervention	1.5
Monetary Policy	3
Foreign Investment	4
Banking and Finance	3
Wages and Prices	3
Property Rights	4
Regulation	4
Informal Market	4

Population: 13,007,942

Total area: 283,560 sq. km

GDP: $17.8 billion

GDP growth rate: 2.7 %

GDP per capita: $1,368

Major exports: bananas, oil, shrimp

Exports of goods and services: $6.1 billion

Major export trading partners: US 42.4%, Colombia 5.7%, Germany 5.6%

Major imports: raw materials, machinery and equipment, fuel, consumer goods

Imports of goods and services: $6.8 billion

Major import trading partners: US 24.2%, Colombia 13.0%, Venezuela 7.2%, Japan 4.3%

Foreign direct investment (net): $1.5 billion

2003 Data (in constant 2000 US dollars)

Ecuador's democracy has come close to unraveling during the past decade. Abdalá Bucaram, known as El Loco, was elected president in 1996 and dismissed by Congress in 1997 for erratic behavior and corruption. Jamil Mahuad was elected in 1998 and stepped aside in January 2000, following a banking crisis. Labor unions and special-interest groups had protested his proposal to dollarize the economy (make the dollar the legal tender). Mahuad's vice president and successor, Gustavo Noboa, proceeded with dollarization and tamed runaway inflation. In 2002, voters elected as president one of the military participants in Mahuad's early resignation, Army Colonel Lucio Gutierrez Borbua. Surrounding himself with competent advisers and observing fiscal restraint, Gutierrez initially kept Ecuador on a stable path, but leftist supporters eventually deserted his coalition. Thereafter, he fruitlessly sought alliances with other power blocs, including the exiled Bucaram. His term lasted until April 2005, when Congress voted him out of office for exceeding his authority. Vice President Alfredo Palacio assumed the presidency and picked a new cabinet that threatened to roll back a number of Gutierrez's policies. Economy Minister Rafael Correa proposed eliminating an oil stabilization fund used for retiring debt obligations so that the money could be spent on social needs. Ecuador's fiscal burden of government score is 0.1 point worse this year; however, its trade policy and government intervention scores are both 0.5 point better, and its monetary policy score is 1 point better. As a result, Ecuador's overall score is 0.19 point better this year.

TRADE POLICY
Score: **3.5**–Better (high level of protectionism)

The World Bank reports that Ecuador's weighted average tariff rate in 2004 was 9 percent, down from the 10.5 percent in 2002 reported in the 2005 *Index*. According to the U.S. Trade Representative, "Importers must register with the Central Bank through approved banking institutions to obtain an import license. Ecuador requires prior authorization from various government agencies...for importation of most commodities." The government also maintains import bans on several products, and its bureaucratic customs processes "generally add six to eight weeks to shipping times." Based on the lower tariff rate, as well as a revision of the trade factor methodology, Ecuador's trade policy score is 0.5 point better this year.

FISCAL BURDEN OF GOVERNMENT
Score—Income Taxation: **2.5**–Stable (moderate tax rates)
Score—Corporate Taxation: **3**–Stable (moderate tax rates)
Score—Change in Government Expenditures: **3.5**–Worse (low increase)
Final Score: **3**–Worse (moderate cost of government)

According to Deloitte, Ecuador's top income tax rate is 25 percent. The top corporate tax rate is also 25 percent. In 2003, based on data from Ecuador's central bank and the World Bank, government expenditures as a share of GDP increased 0.1 percentage point to 22.7 percent, compared to a 3.5 percentage point decrease in 2002. On net, Ecuador's fiscal burden of government score is 0.1 point worse this year.

GOVERNMENT INTERVENTION IN THE ECONOMY
Score: **1.5**–Better (low level)

The World Bank reports that the government consumed 9.5 percent of GDP in 2003, down

169

from the 10.5 percent reported in the 2005 *Index*. In the same year, based on data from the Ministry of Economy and Finance, Ecuador received 1.64 percent of its total revenues from state-owned enterprises and government ownership of property. As a result, Ecuador's government intervention score is 0.5 point better this year.

MONETARY POLICY
Score: **3**–Better (moderate level of inflation)

Ecuador uses the U.S. dollar as its legal tender. From 1995 to 2004, Ecuador's weighted average annual rate of inflation was 7.25 percent, down from the 14.99 percent from 1994 to 2003 reported in the 2005 *Index*. As a result, Ecuador's monetary policy score is 1 point better this year.

CAPITAL FLOWS AND FOREIGN INVESTMENT
Score: **4**–Stable (high barriers)

Ecuador grants foreign firms national treatment, but numerous official and unofficial barriers impede foreign investment. According to the U.S. Trade Representative, "Under Ecuadorian law, foreign investors are accorded the same rights of establishment as Ecuadorian private investors, may own up to 100 percent of enterprises in most sectors without prior government approval, and face the same tax regime. There are no controls or limits on transfers of profits or capital." However, numerous restrictions apply equally to domestic and foreign investors, including cumbersome labor laws and lack of contract enforcement. The U.S. Department of Commerce reports that "many government officials see foreign investors as targets for exploitation and use regulatory schemes and questionable legal interpretations to either extract money from or refuse to pay foreign investors." The government maintains restrictions in the petroleum exploration and development, mining, domestic fishing, electricity, telecommunications, broadcast media, coastal and border real estate, and national security sectors. The International Monetary Fund reports no restrictions on foreign exchange accounts, direct investment, or current transfers.

BANKING AND FINANCE
Score: **3**–Stable (moderate level of restrictions)

The financial crisis in late 1998 and 1999 led to government default on Brady bonds and Eurobonds in mid-1999, government takeover of most commercial banks, and a freeze on bank deposits. According to the Economist Intelligence Unit, "The state took control of 16 banks in 1998–99; of these, four merged into two banks and 12 have since closed operations. The state controlled 9.7% of national bank assets in September 2004." Only one bank taken over by the government (Pacífico) still operates. The EIU also reports that Ecuador had 24 commercial banks operating in November 2004, including two foreign banks that controlled 3.7 percent of assets. The government has enacted strict regulations governing the banking sector in the wake of the crisis, including higher capital standards, stricter reporting requirements, and prohibitions on lending

by banks to companies or individuals if they are financially tied to the bank through shareholding or management.

WAGES AND PRICES
Score: **3**–Stable (moderate level of intervention)

The government sets some prices. "In general," reports the Economist Intelligence Unit, "the government does not have a policy of fixing prices. However, bananas, coffee, cocoa, pharmaceuticals and fuels are exceptions to the rule." Since coffee, bananas, and cocoa comprise a large portion of the country's output, controls on these products have a significant effect on the economy. The EIU also reports that the government controls prices of telephone services, electricity, pharmaceuticals, and cooking gas and that transportation services are subsidized. The government periodically sets the minimum wage.

PROPERTY RIGHTS
Score: **4**–Stable (low level of protection)

The rule of law is weak and does not adequately protect private property rights. "Lack of rule of law is the most important problem faced by...companies investing in or trading with Ecuador," reports the U.S. Department of Commerce. "The Ecuadorian judicial system is plagued by processing delays, questionable and unpredictable judgments in civil and commercial cases, inconsistent rulings, limited access to the courts, and impunity, particularly in corruption cases…. Ecuador's complex and corruption-riddled legal system hinders the enforcement of property and concession rights." Expropriation is possible. According to the U.S. Department of Commerce, "A number of foreign and local investors have had agricultural land seized by squatter groups over the years."

REGULATION
Score: **4**–Stable (high level)

The Economist Intelligence Unit reports that Ecuador's "civil service is renowned for slowing investment decisions with needless bureaucracy. There have been efforts to reduce size, cost and corruption at higher levels, but the bureaucracy remains complex and much larger than necessary." According to the U.S. Department of Commerce, "Cabinet ministries, parastatals, and regional and municipal governments all impose their own requirements and regulations on commercial activity. A 2001 Price Waterhouse Coopers Survey measured the cost of capital due to the lack of clear, accurate, formal and widely accepted practices…. It was estimated that society-imposed costs such as over regulation, corruption, nuisance lawsuits, and the unpredictable policy framework were equivalent to an additional corporate tax of 31%."

INFORMAL MARKET
Score: **4**–Stable (high level of activity)

Transparency International's 2004 score for Ecuador is 2.4. Therefore, Ecuador's informal market score is 4 this year.

2006 Index of Economic Freedom

EGYPT

Rank: 128

Score: 3.59

Category: Mostly Unfree

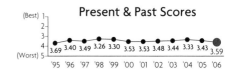

Present & Past Scores

(Best) 1
2
3
4
(Worst) 5

3.69 3.40 3.49 3.26 3.30 3.53 3.53 3.48 3.44 3.33 3.43 3.59

'95 '96 '97 '98 '99 '00 '01 '02 '03 '04 '05 '06

QUICK STUDY

SCORES

Trade Policy	4.5
Fiscal Burden	4.4
Government Intervention	3.5
Monetary Policy	3
Foreign Investment	3
Banking and Finance	4
Wages and Prices	3
Property Rights	3
Regulation	4
Informal Market	3.5

Population: 67,559,040

Total area: 1,001,450 sq. km

GDP: $109.6 billion

GDP growth rate: 3.2%

GDP per capita: $1,622

Major exports: petroleum, cotton yarn and garments, textiles, aluminum

Exports of goods and services: $17.1 billion

Major export trading partners: US 13.4%, Italy 12.3%, UK 8.0%, France 4.6%

Major imports: consumer goods, foodstuffs, machinery and equipment

Imports of goods and services: $20.1 billion

Major import trading partners: US 13.7%, Germany 7.5%, Italy 7.0%, France 6.6%

Foreign direct investment (net): $204.5 million

2003 Data (in constant 2000 US dollars)

Egypt is the most populous Arab country and has long played a leading role in Middle Eastern affairs. President Hosni Mubarak's government has undertaken incremental reforms to renovate the socialist economic system of the 1950s and 1960s. Until recently, however, economic reform took a back seat to social policies such as maintaining the payment of subsidies on food, energy, and other key commodities, and little progress was made in privatizing or streamlining the public sector. Political stability has been enhanced by success in containing the radical Islamic movements that threaten the country with persistent terrorism. Economic reform became a higher priority after the July 2004 appointment of Prime Minister Ahmed Nazif, a technocrat who placed liberal reformers in key policy positions and has pushed through several measures to increase foreign investment and stimulate economic growth led by the private sector. In September 2004, the government lowered duties and simplified customs procedures, proposed income and corporate tax reforms, reduced energy subsidies, and privatized several state-owned enterprises. Revenues from tourism, Egypt's largest source of foreign currency, reached record levels despite terrorist bombings in Taba and Nuweiba in 2004 and in Cairo in 2005. Egypt's fiscal burden of government, government intervention, and monetary policy scores are, respectively, 0.1 point, 0.5 point, and 1 point worse this year. As a result, Egypt's overall score is 0.16 point worse this year.

TRADE POLICY
Score: **4.5**–Stable (very high level of protectionism)

According to the World Bank, Egypt's weighted average tariff rate in 2002 (the most recent year for which World Bank data are available) was 13.7 percent. (The World Bank has revised the figure for 2002 upward from the 13.4 percent reported in the 2005 *Index*.) The U.S. Trade Representative reports that the main non-tariff barriers include mandatory quality control standards, selective import restrictions, burdensome and non-transparent sanitary and phytosanitary measures, and cumbersome customs procedures. Based on the revised trade factor methodology, Egypt's trade policy score is unchanged.

FISCAL BURDEN OF GOVERNMENT
Score—Income Taxation: **4**–Stable (high tax rates)
Score—Corporate Taxation: **5**–Stable (very high tax rates)
Score—Change in Government Expenditures: **3.5**–Worse (low increase)
Final Score: **4.4**–Worse (high cost of government)

Egypt's top income tax rate is 40 percent. The corporate tax rate is also 40 percent. In 2003, according to the Economist Intelligence Unit, government expenditures as a share of GDP increased 0.1 percentage point to 26.8 percent, compared to a 0.1 percentage point decrease in 2002. On net, Egypt's fiscal burden of government score is 0.1 point worse this year.

GOVERNMENT INTERVENTION IN THE ECONOMY
Score: **3.5**–Worse (high level)

The World Bank reports that the government consumed 12.5 percent of GDP in 2003. In the 2003–2004 fiscal year, based on data from the International Monetary Fund, Egypt received 29.04 percent of its total revenues from state-owned enterprises and government ownership

171

of property, up from the 12.02 percent reported in the 2005 *Index*. As a result, Egypt's government intervention score is 0.5 point worse this year.

 MONETARY POLICY
Score: **3**–Worse (moderate level of inflation)

From 1995 to 2004, Egypt's weighted average annual rate of inflation was 8.53 percent, up from the 3.67 percent from 1994 to 2003 reported in the 2005 *Index*. As a result, Egypt's monetary policy score is 1 point worse this year.

 CAPITAL FLOWS AND FOREIGN INVESTMENT
Score: **3**–Stable (moderate barriers)

"Foreign investors may own up to 100 percent of a business within the scope of the [applicable] legislation," reports the U.S. Department of Commerce, "but some projects still require prior approval from relevant ministries. These projects include: investments in the Sinai; all military products and related industries; and tobacco and tobacco products. Law 15 of 1963 prohibits foreign ownership of areas designated as agricultural lands (in the Nile Valley, Delta, and Oases), except for desert reclamation projects." According to the Economist Intelligence Unit, "Official approval is required for all foreign direct investment. In theory, automatic approval should be granted to most investment projects; in practice, all projects must pass through a review process to gain legal status and qualify for incentives." The International Monetary Fund reports that both residents and non-residents may hold foreign exchange accounts. There are no restrictions on payments and transfers. The Capital Market Authority must approve bond issues.

 BANKING AND FINANCE
Score: **4**–Stable (high level of restrictions)

The Economist Intelligence Unit reports that the central bank listed 55 banks operating in 2004, including four public-sector commercial banks and 14 foreign-registered banks that operate under non-commercial foreign branch licenses, and that "[t]he state still dominates banking in Egypt." Four 100 percent state-owned commercial banks—National Bank of Egypt (NBE), Banque Misr, Banque du Caire, and Bank of Alexandria—controlled at least 49 percent of total banking assets and well over half of total bank deposits as of June 2003. According to the U.S. Department of Commerce, "The Central Bank has not issued a new commercial banking license in almost 20 years. In practice, the only way for a new bank, whether foreign or local, to enter the market (except as a representative office) is to purchase an existing bank." Although the law authorizes privatization of state-owned insurance companies and permits 100 percent foreign ownership, four state-owned companies continue to dominate the sector.

 WAGES AND PRICES
Score: **3**–Stable (moderate level of intervention)

According to the Economist Intelligence Unit, the elimination of price controls and subsidies "has been achieved in many sectors, with the notable exceptions of energy (including fuel), transport, medicine, and some basic foods." The government subsidizes bread, wheat, rice, cooking oil, corn syrup, fava beans, lentils, tea, and macaroni, as well as energy and pharmaceuticals. "In general" reports the EIU, "the massive size of the public sector also limits the private sector's ability to set rates."

 PROPERTY RIGHTS
Score: **3**–Stable (moderate level of protection)

The legal code is complex and can create delays. "Many Egyptians view the judiciary as the only institution with some degree of independence from the regime," reports the Economist Intelligence Unit. "The government can circumvent this by using fast-track military courts…. [A] commercial case takes, on average, six years to be decided in Egypt, and appeal procedures can extend court cases beyond 15 years. Nevertheless, local contractual arrangements are generally secure. Islamic law (sharia) is officially the main inspiration for legislation, but the Napoleonic Code exerts a significant influence. Judicial procedures tend to be protracted, costly and subject to political pressure."

 REGULATION
Score: **4**–Stable (high level)

According to the U.S. Department of Commerce, "The streamlining of Egyptian investment procedures and the creation of the Ministry of Investment in July 2004 represent a constructive step toward improving Egypt's business environment. However…[s]ignificant obstacles continue to hinder private sector investment in Egypt, including the often-arbitrary imposition of bureaucratic impediments and the length of time needed to resolve them…. Enforcement of health and safety regulations is uneven and is complicated by a multiplicity of laws, agencies, and opinions. For example, at least four ministries regulate the operation of restaurants. Egypt's accounting standards are still not fully consistent with international norms…." Labor laws are somewhat rigid.

 INFORMAL MARKET
Score: **3.5**–Stable (high level of activity)

Transparency International's 2004 score for Egypt is 3.2. Therefore, Egypt's informal market score is 3.5 this year.

EL SALVADOR

Rank: 34

Score: 2.35

Category: Mostly Free

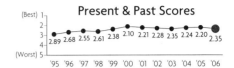

Present & Past Scores

(Best) 1
2
3
4
(Worst) 5

2.89 2.68 2.55 2.61 2.38 2.10 2.21 2.28 2.35 2.24 2.20 2.35

'95 '96 '97 '98 '99 '00 '01 '02 '03 '04 '05 '06

QUICK STUDY

SCORES

Trade Policy	2.5
Fiscal Burden	3
Government Intervention	2
Monetary Policy	2
Foreign Investment	2
Banking and Finance	2
Wages and Prices	2
Property Rights	3
Regulation	2
Informal Market	3

Population: 6,533,215

Total area: 21,040 sq. km

GDP: $13.9 billion

GDP growth rate: 1.8%

GDP per capita: $2,129

Major exports: coffee, sugar, shrimp, textiles, chemicals

Exports of goods and services: $3.9 billion

Major export trading partners: US 67.8%, Guatemala 11.5%, Honduras 5.9%

Major imports: raw materials, consumer goods, capital goods, petroleum, foodstuffs

Imports of goods and services: $6.2 billion

Major import trading partners: US 50.0%, Guatemala 8.0%, Mexico 5.5%

Foreign direct investment (net): $130.1 million

2003 Data (in constant 2000 US dollars)

Despite ongoing security problems caused by gang activity, transnational crime, and kidnappings, El Salvador continues to enjoy stable democratic government, modest economic growth, and declining poverty rates. Like previous governments, the administration of President Elias Antonio Saca views increased trade and private investment, both domestic and foreign, as essential to economic growth. With one of Latin America's most open trade and investment environments, comparing favorably to Chile and Mexico, El Salvador stands to gain considerably under DR–CAFTA: not only assured access to U.S. markets, but also liberalized trade among Central American countries, among which El Salvador is an industrial leader. Low average levels of education in the labor force and an inefficient judicial system are checks on economic growth. As industries begin to supplant agriculture, workers will need to be more literate; and if Salvadoran leaders want to continue attracting foreign investment, the justice system will have to make headway against crime and support commercial arbitration. According to the U.S. Department of Commerce, remittances of $2.1 billion (largely from emigrants sending money back to families) accounted for 14 percent of GDP in 2003; but such a windfall eventually must be replaced by local enterprise. El Salvador's informal market score is 0.5 point better this year; however, its trade policy and government intervention scores are both 0.5 point worse, and its monetary policy score is 1 point worse. As a result, El Salvador's overall score is 0.15 point worse this year.

TRADE POLICY
Score: **2.5**–Worse (moderate level of protectionism)

According to the World Bank, El Salvador's weighted average tariff rate in 2004 was 4.3 percent, down from the 6.1 percent in 2001 reported in the 2005 *Index*. The U.S. Trade Representative reports import quota systems on rice and pork, discriminatory sanitary practices on poultry, and a few other discriminatory applications of standards. Based on evidence of non-tariff barriers, 1 point has been added to El Salvador's trade policy score this year. As a result of this evidence, as well as a revision of the trade factor methodology, El Salvador's trade policy score is 0.5 point worse this year.

FISCAL BURDEN OF GOVERNMENT
Score—Income Taxation: **2.5**–Better (moderate tax rates)
Score—Corporate Taxation: **3**–Stable (moderate tax rates)
Score—Change in Government Expenditures: **3.5**–Worse (low increase)
Final Score: **3**–Stable (moderate cost of government)

El Salvador's top income tax rate is 25 percent, down from the 30 percent reported in the 2005 *Index*. The top corporate tax rate is also 25 percent. In 2003, based on data from the World Bank and El Salvador's central bank, government expenditures as a share of GDP increased 0.5 percentage point to 16.1 percent, compared to the 0.1 percentage point increase in 2002.

GOVERNMENT INTERVENTION IN THE ECONOMY
Score: **2**–Worse (low level)

The World Bank reports that the government consumed 10.7 percent of GDP in 2003, up from the 8.2 percent for 2002 that was reported in the 2005 *Index*. As a result, El Salvador's government intervention score is 0.5 point worse this year. In 2004, based on data from the

173

central bank, El Salvador received 0.3 percent of its total revenues from state-owned enterprises and government ownership of property.

MONETARY POLICY
Score: **2**–Worse (low level of inflation)

El Salvador uses the U.S. dollar as its legal tender. From 1995 to 2004, El Salvador's weighted average annual rate of inflation was 3.62 percent, up from the 2.20 percent from 1994 to 2003 reported in the 2005 *Index*. As a result, El Salvador's monetary policy score is 1 point worse this year.

CAPITAL FLOWS AND FOREIGN INVESTMENT
Score: **2**–Stable (low barriers)

El Salvador maintains an open foreign investment climate. Under the 1999 Investment Law, foreign investors receive equal treatment. Foreign investment has been a central component of El Salvador's privatization program, according to the U.S. Department of Commerce. "Foreign investors may obtain credit in the local financial market under the same conditions as local investors." The International Monetary Fund reports that the government limits foreign direct investment in commerce, industry, certain services, and fishing; investments in railroads, piers, and canals require government approval. There are no controls or requirements on current transfers, access to foreign exchange, or most capital transactions. There are some restrictions on land ownership; foreign persons may purchase land, up to 245 hectares, only if there is a reciprocal arrangement with their home country.

BANKING AND FINANCE
Score: **2**–Stable (low level of restrictions)

According to the U.S. Department of Commerce, "The banking system is sound and in general well managed and supervised…. Under the 1999 Banking Law and amendments made in 2002, foreign banks are afforded national treatment and can offer the same services as Salvadoran banks; they can open branches and buy or invest in Salvadoran financial institutions." Most local and foreign banks are allowed to offer a wide range of financial services, and interest rates and fees are set by the market. Regulations on opening branches of foreign banks are open and transparent. The Monetary Integration Law converted all financial system assets, liabilities, and operations to U.S. dollars on January 1, 2001. The Economist Intelligence Unit reports that El Salvador had 10 domestic commercial banks as of October 2004, one more than in 2003. In addition, "There are two foreign commercial banks and one other foreign bank agency that does not accept public deposits. Two foreign bank agencies, Dresdner Latinamerika and Dresdner Bank (both of Germany), recently left El Salvador. There also are two state banks: Banco Hipotecario de El Salvador and the Banco de Fomento Agropecuario…. [The] top four banks capture over 80% of the banking business in El Salvador."

WAGES AND PRICES
Score: **2**–Stable (low level of intervention)

Most prices are determined by the market. According to the Economist Intelligence Unit, "Only a few essentials are subject to price controls…. The government establishes minimum base prices for other items, such as electricity. Liquid propane gas and public transport rates are controlled, because providers are subsidised through excise taxes on petrol." El Salvador has a minimum wage.

PROPERTY RIGHTS
Score: **3**–Stable (moderate level of protection)

Property rights are moderately protected in El Salvador. According to the U.S. Department of Commerce, "investors have found that seeking resolution of problems through the slow-moving domestic legal system can be costly and unproductive. The course of some cases has shown that the legal system is subject to manipulation by private interests, and final rulings are sometimes not enforced." The Economist Intelligence Unit reports that two of the "main constraints on growth in foreign investment are high crime levels [and] an inefficient judiciary…."

REGULATION
Score: **2**–Stable (low level)

El Salvador has made significant progress in reducing onerous regulations. The U.S. Department of Commerce reports that "the laws and policies of El Salvador are relatively transparent and generally foster competition. Bureaucratic procedures have improved in recent years and are relatively streamlined for…investors." The labor law requires that 90 percent of the labor force at plants and in clerical jobs be composed of Salvadorans, but foreigners may hold professional and technical positions. New business projects must submit environmental impact studies to obtain a license.

INFORMAL MARKET
Score: **3**–Better (moderate level of activity)

Transparency International's 2004 score for El Salvador is 4.2. Therefore, El Salvador's informal market score is 3 this year—0.5 point better than last year.

EQUATORIAL GUINEA

Rank: 136

Score: 3.74

Category: Mostly Unfree

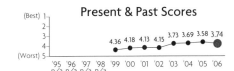

Present & Past Scores

(Best) 1
2
3
4
(Worst) 5

4.36 4.18 4.13 4.15 3.73 3.69 3.58 3.74

'95 '96 '97 '98 '99 '00 '01 '02 '03 '04 '05 '06
n/a n/a n/a n/a

QUICK STUDY

SCORES

Trade Policy	4.5
Fiscal Burden	3.4
Government Intervention	2.5
Monetary Policy	3
Foreign Investment	4
Banking and Finance	3
Wages and Prices	4
Property Rights	4
Regulation	4
Informal Market	5

Population: 494,000

Total area: 28,051 sq. km

GDP: $1.8 billion

GDP growth rate: 14.7%

GDP per capita: $3,716

Major exports: petroleum, coffee, timber, cocoa

Exports of goods (fob): $2.7 billion

Major export trading partners: US 33.2%, Spain 25.4%, China 14.2%

Major imports: manufactured goods and equipment

Imports of goods (fob): $1.3 billion

Major import trading partners: US 30.6%, UK 16.0%, France 15.0%, Spain 8.2%

Foreign direct investment (net): $1.3 billion

2003 Data (in constant 2000 US dollars)

P resident Teodoro Obiang Nguema's sub-clan has controlled Equatorial Guinea since 1968, and Obiang has ruled since seizing power in a 1979 military coup. He was re-elected in 2002 with 97.1 percent of the vote amid charges of massive voter fraud and intimidation, and his Democratic Party of Equatorial Guinea also won the 2004 legislative elections, again criticized by international election experts. The judiciary is subject to political influence. A coup attempt by foreign mercenaries in March 2004 resulted in highly publicized arrests and trials of questionable fairness. Oil and gas dominate the economy and accounted for nearly 90 percent of GDP in 2003. National income has risen sharply in recent years due to increased crude oil production, but this has had little impact on much of the population, most of which is engaged in subsistence farming, hunting, and fishing. The government is characterized by poor fiscal management and a lack of transparency. There are widespread allegations of illicit transfers of oil wealth to government officials. The business environment remains risky because of arbitrary enforcement of law, unclear regulatory rules, and corruption. Equatorial Guinea's fiscal burden of government score is 0.6 point worse this year, and its government intervention score is 1 point worse. As a result, Equatorial Guinea's overall score is 0.16 point worse this year.

TRADE POLICY
Score: **4.5**–Stable (very high level of protectionism)

Equatorial Guinea is a member of the Central African Economic and Monetary Community (CEMAC). The World Bank reports that Equatorial Guinea's weighted average tariff rate in 2002 (the most recent year for which World Bank data are available) was 14 percent. According to the U.S. Department of Commerce, "Customs fraud is endemic in Equatorial Guinea and protracted negotiations with customs officers over the value of imported goods are common." Based on the revised trade factor methodology, Equatorial Guinea's trade policy score is unchanged.

FISCAL BURDEN OF GOVERNMENT
Score—Income Taxation: **3.5**–Worse (moderate tax rates)
Score—Corporate Taxation: **4.5**–Worse (very high tax rates)
Score—Change in Government Expenditures: **1**–Better (very high decrease)
Final Score: **3.4**–Worse (moderate cost of government)

The International Monetary Fund reports that Equatorial Guinea's top income tax rate is 35 percent, up from the 10 percent reported in the 2005 *Index*. The IMF also reports that the top corporate tax rate (as of April 2005) is 35 percent, up from the 25 percent reported in the 2005 *Index*. In 2003, according to the African Development Bank, government expenditures as a share of GDP decreased 4.5 percentage points to 10.5 percent, compared to the 3.2 percentage point increase in 2002. On net, Equatorial Guinea's fiscal burden of government score is 0.6 point worse this year.

GOVERNMENT INTERVENTION IN THE ECONOMY
Score: **2.5**–Worse (moderate level)

The Economist Intelligence Unit reports that the government consumed 11.2 percent of GDP in 2003, up from the 9.2 percent reported in the 2005 *Index*. In the same year, based on data from the International Monetary Fund, Equatorial Guinea received 8.38 percent of its total revenues from state-owned enterprises and government ownership of property in the oil sector, up from the 0.1 percent reported in the 2005 *Index*. Based on the increase in government consumption and revenues from state-owned enterprises, Equatorial Guinea's government intervention score is 1 point worse this year.

 ## MONETARY POLICY
Score: **3**–Stable (moderate level of inflation)

As a member of the Central African Economic and Monetary Community, Equatorial Guinea uses the CFA franc, pegged to the euro. From 1995 to 2004, Equatorial Guinea's weighted average annual rate of inflation was 7.53 percent.

 ## CAPITAL FLOWS AND FOREIGN INVESTMENT
Score: **4**–Stable (high barriers)

Officially, Equatorial Guinea's investment regime is relatively open, but there are many disincentives to foreign investment. The U.S. Department of Commerce reports, "The investment code, while liberal in intent, is extremely bureaucratic in practice and open to manipulation.... Foreign investors are required to pay customs duties as well as income, turnover and business taxes." The same source reports lax enforcement of investment law and corruption as serious impediments to investment. According to the International Monetary Fund, the government has adopted a decision requiring foreign investors to obtain a local partner. The IMF reports that both residents and non-residents may hold foreign exchange accounts, but approval is required for resident accounts held domestically. Capital transactions, payments, and transfers to countries other than France, Monaco, members of the CEMAC, members of the West African Economic and Monetary Union, and Comoros are subject to restrictions.

 ## BANKING AND FINANCE
Score: **3**–Stable (moderate level of restrictions)

The Commission Bancaire de L'Afrique Centrale (COBAC) has acted as Equatorial Guinea's central bank since the country joined the franc zone in 1985. Three banks were operating in 2004, although a fourth bank had its license approved in 2004 and should begin operation in 2005. "The banking system in Equatorial Guinea is broadly sound, with the regional banking supervisory agency (COBAC) rating the three commercial banks well above the average of the members of the Central African Economic and Monetary Union (CEMAC)," reports the International Monetary Fund. "However, compliance with prudential regulations continued to be mixed.... Nonperforming loans as a share of total loans increased to 16 percent in 2004." The government has a minority ownership stake in two of the three banks operating in Equatorial Guinea. According to the U.S. Department of Commerce, "Foreign investors are able to obtain credit on the local market, but usually borrow offshore due to high domestic interest rates."

 ## WAGES AND PRICES
Score: **4**–Stable (high level of intervention)

The government imposed price controls on a number of consumer products, including tinned sardines, meat, powdered milk, sugar, cooking oil, rice, matches, medicines, construction materials, agricultural products, and school books, in 2002. Prices are also affected by state-owned enterprises in the electricity, oil, and telecommunications sectors. No new data on prices are available.

 ## PROPERTY RIGHTS
Score: **4**–Stable (low level of protection)

According to the U.S. Department of Commerce, "Companies...cite lax enforcement of existing laws as a greater impediment than the content of the laws. Senior government officials have extorted money from foreign companies...threatening to take away logging concessions, for example. The investment code, while liberal in intent, is extremely bureaucratic in practice and open to manipulation. The judicial system is open to influence from the administration." Equatorial Guinea is a member of OHADA (Organisation pour l'Harmonisation en Afrique du Droit des Affaires), a regional organization that trains judges and lawyers in commercial law to help reform the enforcement of contracts.

 ## REGULATION
Score: **4**–Stable (high level)

Equatorial Guinea's regulatory structure imposes a great burden on business. The U.S. Department of Commerce reports that "the regulatory system is operating more efficiently, but transparency remains a major problem. Export licensing requirements are still in effect for timber and cocoa and can complicate activities in those sectors.... The investment code... is extremely bureaucratic in practice and open to manipulation." In addition, "Corruption among officials is widespread, and many business deals are concluded under non-transparent circumstances."

 ## INFORMAL MARKET
Score: **5**–Stable (very high level of activity)

Smuggling is extensive, especially in timber and ivory, and illegal logging is widespread. According to the U.S. Department of State, "Equatorial Guinea is a transit and destination country for women and children trafficked for the purpose of sexual exploitation, involuntary domestic servitude, and other forced labor." A large portion of the population works informally. The government offers no protection for intellectual property rights.

ESTONIA

Rank: 7

Score: 1.75

Category: Free

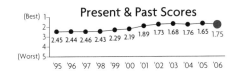

Present & Past Scores

(Best) 1
2
3
4
(Worst) 5

2.45 2.44 2.46 2.43 2.29 2.19 1.89 1.73 1.68 1.76 1.65 1.75

'95 '96 '97 '98 '99 '00 '01 '02 '03 '04 '05 '06

QUICK STUDY

SCORES

Trade Policy 2
Fiscal Burden 2
Government Intervention ... 2
Monetary Policy 1
Foreign Investment 1
Banking and Finance 1
Wages and Prices 2
Property Rights 2
Regulation 2
Informal Market 2.5

Population: 1,351,069

Total area: 45,227 sq. km

GDP: $10.1 billion

GDP growth rate: 6.2%

GDP per capita: $7,475

Major exports: food processing, machinery and equipment,
wood and paper, clothing and
footwear, transportation, travel
services, computer services
and information

**Exports of goods and ser-
vices:** $5.1 billion

**Major export trading part-
ners:** Finland 23.3%, Sweden
15.4%, Germany 8.4%, Latvia
7.8%

Major imports: machinery
and equipment, chemicals,
transport equipment, financial services

**Imports of goods and ser-
vices:** $5.9 billion

**Major import trading part-
ners:** Finland 22.1%, Germany
12.9%, Sweden 9.7%, Russia 9.2%

**Foreign direct investment
(net):** $700.4 million

2004 Data (in constant 2000 US dollars)

Following deepening tensions within the three-party ruling coalition, Minister of Foreign Affairs Kristiina Ojuland was removed for professional misconduct in February 2005. After a "no confidence" vote for Minister of Justice Ken-Marti Vaher, Prime Minister Juhan Parts resigned in March 2005. The new prime minister, Andrus Ansip, is from the right-of-center coalition that had outperformed the presiding centrists with progressive tax-cutting policies. Because of their poor popular ratings, among other considerations, most of the parties do not favor holding parliamentary elections before 2007. These developments, however, are unlikely to spill over into the economy. As a result of significant market reforms, Estonia has strengthened its economy with the most competitive business environment in Central and Eastern Europe. In 2004, Estonia became the most technologically advanced country in the European Union. Already an EU member, it is set to join the Shengen Group (free cross-border movement of people) in 2007, which should further harmonize its economy with the EU. Estonia's trade policy score is 1 point worse this year. As a result, its overall score is 0.1 point worse this year.

TRADE POLICY
Score: **2**–Worse (low level of protectionism)

Estonia adopted the trade policies of the European Union when it joined the EU in May 2004. The common EU weighted average external tariff was 1.3 percent in 2003, based on World Bank data. In the 2005 *Index*, based on World Bank data, Estonia had a tariff of 0.053 percent. According to the World Trade Organization and the U.S. Trade Representative, the EU impos-es non-tariff trade barriers through a complex regulatory system and export subsidies. Based on its adoption of EU trade policies, and on the revised trade factor methodology, Estonia's trade policy score is 1 point worse this year.

FISCAL BURDEN OF GOVERNMENT
Score—Income Taxation: **2**–Better (low tax rates)
Score—Corporate Taxation: **1**–Stable (very low tax rates)
Score—Change in Government Expenditures: **4**–Worse (moderate increase)
Final Score: **2**–Stable (low cost of government)

According to Deloitte, Estonia has reduced its flat income tax rate to 24 percent from 26 percent, and the government intends to reduce it to 20 percent by 2006. The corporate tax on reinvested profits is 0 percent. In 2004, based on data from the central bank, government expenditures as a share of GDP increased 1.9 percentage points to 37.7 percent, compared to a 0.5 percentage point increase in 2003.

GOVERNMENT INTERVENTION IN THE ECONOMY
Score: **2**–Stable (low level)

According to the Statistical Office of Estonia, the government consumed 19 percent of GDP in 2004. In the same year, based on data from the Ministry of Finance, Estonia received 4.42 percent of its total revenues from state-owned enterprises and government ownership of property.

MONETARY POLICY
Score: 1–Stable (very low level of inflation)

Estonia has a currency board system pegging its kroon to the euro. From 1995 to 2004, Estonia's weighted average annual rate of inflation was 2.81 percent.

CAPITAL FLOWS AND FOREIGN INVESTMENT
Score: 1–Stable (very low barriers)

Estonia is open to foreign investment, and foreign investors receive national treatment. The government allows foreigners to invest in all sectors, with requirements restricted to nondiscriminatory regulation and documentation. According to the U.S. Department of Commerce, "Estonia's government does not screen foreign investments. It does, however, establish requirements for certain sectors. These requirements are not intended to restrict foreign ownership but rather to regulate it and establish clear ownership responsibilities." Foreigners may own real estate, although the International Monetary Fund reports that purchases over 10 hectares of agricultural or forest land are subject to government approval. According to the Economist Intelligence Unit, "Estonia's rapid trade and regulatory liberalization and macroeconomic stabilisation have produced a positive environment for foreign investment, reinforced by the country's entry into the EU. The use of international tenders early in the privatisation programme encouraged foreign companies into the economy...." The government requires licenses for investment in banking, mining, gas and water supply or related structures, railroads and transport, energy, and communications networks, but this requirement has not restricted investment and is applied in a routine, nondiscriminatory manner. The IMF reports that residents and non-residents may hold foreign exchange accounts, and payments, transfers, and most capital transactions are not subject to controls. Foreign direct investment rules regarding real estate, aviation, maritime transport, and security service enterprises were harmonized with European Union regulations in 2003 and 2004.

BANKING AND FINANCE
Score: 1–Stable (very low level of restrictions)

Estonia's sound, prudently regulated banking sector is considered the strongest and most developed in the Baltic States. "At the end of 2004," reports the Economist Intelligence Unit, "Estonia had six commercial banks, three foreign bank branches and six representative offices of foreign banks." Its universal banking system allows banks to engage in a wide range of financial activities, including insurance, leasing, and brokerage services. The government welcomes foreign participation in the banking sector, which is dominated by foreign banks. According to the U.S. Department of Commerce, "the Estonian banking system is dominated by two foreign controlled banking groups: Hansapank (Swedbank) and Uhispank (Skandinaviska Enskilda Banken)." Estonia's largest bank in terms of assets and market share, Hansabank, became 100 percent

owned by Sweden's Swedbank in April 2005. The Embassy of Estonia reports that the government does not have a stake in any bank. The U.S. Department of Commerce characterizes Estonia's financial sector as "modern and efficient.... Credit is allocated on market terms and foreign investors are able to obtain credit on the local market."

WAGES AND PRICES
Score: 2–Stable (low level of intervention)

The market determines most wages and prices, but the Embassy of Estonia reports that the government controls the prices of some utilities. Estonia maintains a minimum wage that affects only 5 percent to 6 percent of the workforce. Accession to the European Union has made Estonia eligible to subsidize agricultural prices through the Common Agricultural Policy.

PROPERTY RIGHTS
Score: 2–Stable (high level of protection)

According to the U.S. Department of Commerce, "Estonia's judiciary is independent and insulated from government influence. Property rights and contracts are enforced by the courts. In the past, judicial decisions were occasionally arbitrary and indifferent to the law. Such decisions are increasingly rare." The Economist Intelligence Unit reports that "Estonia has continued to strengthen its judicial procedures since gaining EU membership, including adopting a new code of criminal procedure in 2004."

REGULATION
Score: 2–Stable (low level)

Regulations in Estonia are transparent and evenly applied. The government is increasingly using the Internet to reduce the bureaucracy. According to the U.S. Department of Commerce, "The Government has set out transparent policies and effective laws to foster competition and establish clear 'rules of the game.' However, due to the small size of Estonia's commercial community, instances of favoritism are not uncommon despite the regulations and procedures that are designed to limit it." It takes from two to three weeks, on average, to obtain a permit to start a business, reports the Embassy of Estonia. The U.S. Department of Commerce reports that corruption "has not been a major problem faced by...investors."

INFORMAL MARKET
Score: 2.5–Stable (moderate level of activity)

Transparency International's 2004 score for Estonia is 6. Therefore, Estonia's informal market score is 2.5 this year.

Estonia qualifies for the Global Free Trade Alliance.

ETHIOPIA

Rank: 133

Score: 3.70

Category: Mostly Unfree

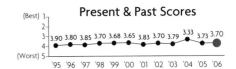

Present & Past Scores

(Best) 1
2
3
4
(Worst) 5

3.90 3.80 3.85 3.70 3.68 3.65 3.83 3.70 3.79 3.33 3.73 3.70

'95 '96 '97 '98 '99 '00 '01 '02 '03 '04 '05 '06

QUICK STUDY

SCORES

Trade Policy	4.5
Fiscal Burden	4
Government Intervention	3.5
Monetary Policy	3
Foreign Investment	3
Banking and Finance	4
Wages and Prices	3
Property Rights	4
Regulation	4
Informal Market	4

Population: 68,613,472

Total area: 1,127,127 sq. km

GDP: $7.0 billion

GDP growth rate: −3.7%

GDP per capita: $102

Major exports: coffee, oil-seeds, leather products

Exports of goods and services: $1.4 billion

Major export trading partners: Djibouti 13.2%, Germany 11.3%, Saudi Arabia 6.9%, Japan 6.7%, Italy 6.4%

Major imports: consumer goods, petroleum and petroleum products, food, motor vehicles

Imports of goods and services: $2.5 billion

Major import trading partners: Saudi Arabia 24.2%, US 17.1%, China 6.4%, Italy 4.1%

Foreign direct investment (net): $33 million

2003 Data (in constant 2000 US dollars)

After decades of dictatorship, Ethiopia is moving toward a federal system of democratic governance. Problems remain, however, as demonstrated by widespread allegations of fraud following the May 2005 parliamentary elections, in which preliminary results showed the incumbent Ethiopian People's Revolutionary Democratic Front retaining a majority. The government response to post-election protests resulted in thousands of arrests and many deaths. Ethiopia's economy is based principally on small farms, with agriculture accounting for nearly half of GDP. More than three-quarters of the population in rural areas is engaged in agriculture. Adverse weather has severe consequences in Ethiopia, which remains reliant on food aid during years with poor harvests. The government continues to promise economic reform, but progress has been slow: Nearly 200 state-owned enterprises have yet to be privatized, corruption is widespread, bureaucracy is burdensome, and much economic activity occurs in the informal sector. In addition, taxation is unevenly enforced, the judiciary is overwhelmed, and key sectors of the economy remain closed to foreign investment. The government has taken some steps toward reforming the civil service, improving infrastructure, and removing regulatory impediments to investment and business establishment. Land-locked Ethiopia depends heavily on Djibouti for access to foreign goods. Ethiopia's government intervention score is 0.5 point worse this year; however, its trade policy score is 0.5 point better, and its fiscal burden of government score is 0.3 point better. As a result, Ethiopia's overall score is 0.03 point better this year.

TRADE POLICY
Score: 4.5–Better (very high level of protectionism)

According to the World Bank, Ethiopia's weighted average tariff rate in 2002 (the most recent year for which World Bank data are available) was 13.5 percent, down from the 16.5 percent in 2001 reported in the 2005 *Index*. According to the U.S. Department of Commerce, "The strict foreign exchange control regime administered by the national bank is still a deterrent to imports." Other non-tariff barriers include import licenses and burdensome regulations and bureaucracy. Based on the lower tariff rate, as well as a revision of the trade factor methodology, Ethiopia's trade policy score is 0.5 point better this year.

FISCAL BURDEN OF GOVERNMENT
Score—Income Taxation: **4–Stable** (high tax rates)
Score—Corporate Taxation: **4–Stable** (high tax rates)
Score—Change in Government Expenditures: **4–Better** (moderate increase)
Final Score: 4–Better (high cost of government)

The International Monetary Fund reports that Ethiopia's top income tax rate is 40 percent. The top corporate tax rate is 30 percent. In 2003, according to the African Development Bank, government expenditures as a share of GDP increased 1.9 percentage points to 35.9 percent, compared to a 3.6 percentage point increase in 2002. On net, Ethiopia's fiscal burden of government score is 0.3 point better this year.

GOVERNMENT INTERVENTION IN THE ECONOMY
Score: 3.5–Worse (high level)

The World Bank reports that the government consumed 23.8 percent of GDP in 2003, up from the 19.3 percent reported in the 2005 *Index*. In the 2003–2004 fiscal year, based on data from the central bank, Ethiopia received 13.53 percent of its total revenues from state-owned enterprises and government ownership of property. On net, Ethiopia's government intervention score is 0.5 point worse this year.

MONETARY POLICY
Score: **3**–Stable (moderate level of inflation)

From 1995 to 2004, based on data from the International Monetary Fund's *2005 World Economic Outlook*, Ethiopia's weighted average annual rate of inflation was 8.52 percent.

CAPITAL FLOWS AND FOREIGN INVESTMENT
Score: **3**–Stable (moderate barriers)

Ethiopia is taking steps to liberalize its foreign investment sector, but official and unofficial barriers still deter foreign investment. According to the Economist Intelligence Unit, "foreign investors may now freely undertake certain activities that were previously the preserve of state bodies, including air freight and the import of propane and butane gas. The travel agency and tour operator businesses have also been opened to foreigners." However, "Certain areas, notably banking, remain off limits…. Fewer than 35 foreign firms are active." The government has lowered the minimum capital investment for wholly and partially owned foreign investments. The U.S. Department of Commerce reports that the Ethiopian government "has eliminated most of the discriminatory tax, credit and foreign trade treatment of the private sector, simplified administrative procedures, and established a clear and consistent set of rules regulating business activities. Though bureaucratic hurdles continue to affect implementation of projects, the Ethiopian Investment Commission, the main contact point for foreign investors, has improved its services and is now providing a highly expedited 'one-stop shop' service that significantly cuts the time and cost of acquiring investment and business licenses." The International Monetary Fund reports that foreign exchange accounts, payments, and current transfers are subject to controls and restrictions. There are significant controls on capital transactions. Purchase of real estate by nonresidents is prohibited. All investments must be approved and certified by the government.

BANKING AND FINANCE
Score: **4**–Stable (high level of restrictions)

It is only since 1994 that the government has permitted private banks and insurance companies. These services are limited to domestic concerns; foreign firms are prohibited from investing in the banking and insurance sectors. The presence of private banks and insurance firms in the financial sector has grown, and the Economist Intelligence Unit reports that by 2003, there were nine private banks operating alongside the Commercial Bank of Ethiopia and two smaller state-owned banks. According to the U.S. Department of Commerce, "The state-owned Commercial Bank of Ethiopia has approximately 70 percent

of the assets of the entire banking system and an official non-performing loans ratio of about 45 percent." The government affects the allocation of credit. According to the EIU, the government continues to resist International Monetary Fund recommendations to open "the banking system to foreign capital and [end] government control over the National Bank of Ethiopia (the central bank). The government believes that the banking system is not yet strong enough to cope with foreign competition and that full central bank independence is not warranted at this stage."

WAGES AND PRICES
Score: **3**–Stable (moderate level of intervention)

The U.S. Department of Commerce reports, "All retail prices except petroleum, fertilizers and pharmaceuticals have been decontrolled." The government influences prices through state-owned utilities and the large number of state-owned enterprises. The government mandates a minimum wage for both private and public employees, and individual industries and services have established their own minimum wages.

PROPERTY RIGHTS
Score: **4**–Stable (low level of protection)

The judicial system does not offer a high level of property protection. The U.S. Department of Commerce reports that "Ethiopia's judicial system remains underdeveloped, poorly staffed and inexperienced, although efforts are underway to strengthen its capacity. While property and contractual rights are recognized and there are written commercial and bankruptcy laws, judges lack understanding of commercial matters. There is no guarantee that the decision of an international arbitration body will be fully accepted and implemented by Ethiopian authorities."

REGULATION
Score: **4**–Stable (high level)

Ethiopia's cumbersome bureaucracy deters investment. According to the Economist Intelligence Unit, "Corruption in Ethiopia poses various problems for [the] business environment, as patronage networks are firmly entrenched and political clout is often used to gain economic prowess." The U.S. Department of Commerce reports that "Ethiopia's regulatory system is generally considered fair and honest, but not always transparent. There are instances in which burdensome regulatory or licensing requirements have prevented the local sale of…exports, particularly personal hygiene and health care products." The EIU reports that corruption imposes a serious burden on economic activity.

INFORMAL MARKET
Score: **4**–Stable (high level of activity)

Transparency International's 2004 score for Ethiopia is 2.3. Therefore, Ethiopia's informal market score is 4 this year.

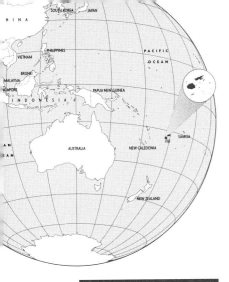

FIJI

Rank: 90

Score: 3.15

Category: Mostly Unfree

Present & Past Scores

(Best) 1
2
3
4
(Worst) 5

3.49 3.24 3.23 3.23 3.29 3.29 3.50 3.49 3.48 3.06 3.28 3.15

'95 '96 '97 '98 '99 '00 '01 '02 '03 '04 '05 '06

QUICK STUDY

SCORES

Trade Policy	4
Fiscal Burden	3.5
Government Intervention	2
Monetary Policy	1
Foreign Investment	4
Banking and Finance	3
Wages and Prices	3
Property Rights	4
Regulation	3
Informal Market	4

Population: 835,000

Total area: 18,270 sq. km

GDP: $1.9 billion

GDP growth rate: 4.8%

GDP per capita: $2,328

Major exports: garments, sugar, fish, gold, timber

Exports of goods (fob): $671 million

Major export trading partners: US 23.3%, Australia 19.3%, UK 13.4%, Japan 4.8%

Major imports: machinery and transport equipment, manufactured goods, food, mineral fuels

Imports of goods (cif): $1.2 billion

Major import trading partners: Australia 35.0%, Singapore 19.1%, New Zealand 17.1%, Japan 4.8%

Foreign direct investment (net): –$5.1 million

2003 Data (in constant 2000 US dollars)

Fiji is the most advanced parliamentary democracy among the Pacific island economies. Its large subsistence agriculture sector accounts for around 16 percent of GDP. Driven mainly by tourism and construction, the Fiji economy has performed well during the past several years. According to the most recently available figures, tourism reached a record 506,000 in 2004—an 18 percent increase over 2003. Relatively strong local private-sector investor confidence continues to underpin economic expansion. However, despite government efforts to make the economy more business-friendly, the protection of property rights still remains uncertain. The government has drafted legislation for the transfer of beach ownership from the state to the coastal indigenous Fijian clans that claim historical ownership. According to the Economist Intelligence Unit, this "legislation has been viewed with alarm by hoteliers and developers, owing to concerns over potential demands for payment for access." The next parliamentary election is scheduled for 2006. Fiji's fiscal burden of government score is 0.2 point worse this year; however, its government intervention score is 0.5 point better, and its monetary policy score is 1 point better. As a result, Fiji's overall score is 0.13 point better this year.

TRADE POLICY
Score: **4–Stable** (high level of protectionism)

According to the World Bank, Fiji's average tariff rate in 2002 (the most recent year for which World Bank data are available) was 12.4 percent. The U.S. Department of Commerce reports that "some goods are absolutely restricted and some subject to quotas." In addition, some products are subject to specific import licensing. Based on the revised trade factor methodology, Fiji's trade policy score is unchanged.

FISCAL BURDEN OF GOVERNMENT
Score—Income Taxation: **3–Stable** (moderate tax rates)
Score—Corporate Taxation: **4–Stable** (high tax rates)
Score—Change in Government Expenditures: **3–Worse** (very low decrease)
Final Score: **3.5–Worse** (high cost of government)

Fiji's top individual income tax rate is 30 percent. The top corporate tax rate is 31 percent. In 2003, according to the Asian Development Bank, government expenditures as a share of GDP decreased by 0.2 percentage point to 30.6 percent, compared to a 2.1 percentage point decrease in 2002. On net, Fiji's fiscal burden of government score is 0.2 point worse this year.

GOVERNMENT INTERVENTION IN THE ECONOMY
Score: **2–Better** (low level)

The International Monetary Fund reports that the government consumed 16.1 percent of GDP in 2003, down from the 31.6 percent reported in the 2005 *Index*. As a result, Fiji's government intervention score is 0.5 point better this year. In the same year, according to the Reserve Bank, Fiji received 1.6 percent of its total revenues from state-owned enterprises and government ownership of property.

MONETARY POLICY
Score: **1**–Better (very low level of inflation)

From 1995 to 2004, Fiji's weighted average annual rate of inflation was 2.72 percent, down from the 3.27 percent from 1994 to 2003 reported in the 2005 *Index*. As a result, Fiji's monetary policy score is 1 point better this year.

CAPITAL FLOWS AND FOREIGN INVESTMENT
Score: **4**–Stable (high barriers)

Fiji places a number of restrictions on foreign investment but also offers a number of tax incentives to would-be investors in preferred activities. The government must approve all potential foreign investments and requires potential investors to undergo a series of bureaucratic registration and regulatory processes. According to the International Monetary Fund, "The foreign investment approvals process contains unnecessary discretion and unclear criteria." Fiji discourages foreign acquisition of a controlling interest in established Fijian businesses unless such acquisition is in the "national interest." The IMF reports that residents may hold foreign exchange accounts subject to approval by the government. Non-residents may hold foreign exchange accounts subject to certain regulations. Most payments and transfers are subject to government approval and limitations on amounts. Capital transfers in excess of specified amounts require approval by the central bank, the South Pacific Stock Exchange, or commercial banks.

BANKING AND FINANCE
Score: **3**–Stable (moderate level of restrictions)

Fiji's banking system includes two merchant banks and five foreign-owned commercial banks. The commercial banks are permitted to offer a wide range of services. The government remains active in the banking sector. According to the Economist Intelligence Unit, "The government effectively withdrew from the commercial banking sector after bailing out the state-owned National Bank of Fiji in 1998. An Australian financial services group, Colonial Ltd, acquired 51% of the bank in 1999. It is now known as Colonial National Bank and is the largest network in the country, with a majority holding in one of the two merchant banks in Fiji." The government also owns the Fiji Development Bank, which provides business development loans, especially for agriculture and tourism.

WAGES AND PRICES
Score: **3**–Stable (moderate level of intervention)

According to the U.S. Department of Commerce, "There are a number of basic food items under price control. The Minister responsible is empowered under the Counter-Inflation Act to alter, remove or add any item from price control." The International Monetary Fund reports that approximately one-third of the goods and services that make up the consumer price index are subject to price controls. The government also affects prices through state-owned enterprises in the utilities and sugar sectors. There is no national minimum wage, but the Ministry for Labor sets and enforces minimum wages for certain sectors of the economy.

PROPERTY RIGHTS
Score: **4**–Stable (low level of protection)

Protection of property is highly uncertain in Fiji. According to the U.S. Department of State, "The courts had a significant backlog of cases, and processing was slowed by, among other things, a shortage of prosecutors." In addition, "Prior to the May [2000] takeover of Parliament, the judiciary was independent; however, with the purported abrogation of the Constitution and other events, including abolition of the Supreme Court, the status of the Judiciary is uncertain." The Economist Intelligence Unit reports that "the difficulties [involved] in obtaining secure titles to land are serious obstacles to investment and growth."

REGULATION
Score: **3**–Stable (moderate level)

The U.S. Department of Commerce reports that "enactment of the Foreign Investment Act of 1999 establishes transparent and simple procedures for the registration of foreign investors and is expected to streamline and reduce the time required for foreign investment approvals…. [T]he transparency of implementation is yet to be seen." There also "is room for greater transparency, both in the government procurement and in the investigative processes." Continuing political instability makes regulatory reform difficult.

INFORMAL MARKET
Score: **4**–Stable (high level of activity)

Fiji has an active informal market. Piracy of such intellectual property as sound recordings and motion pictures is rampant. According to the U.S. Department of Commerce, "many of Fiji's people are underemployed, engaged in subsistence agriculture, or are part of the large casual labor force."

FINLAND

Rank: 12

Score: 1.85

Category: Free

Present & Past Scores

(Best) 1
2
3
4
(Worst) 5

2.39 2.23 2.09 2.19 2.11 2.09 1.94 1.85 2.00 1.90 1.85

'95 '96 '97 '98 '99 '00 '01 '02 '03 '04 '05 '06
n/a

QUICK STUDY

SCORES

Trade Policy	2
Fiscal Burden	3
Government Intervention	2.5
Monetary Policy	1
Foreign Investment	2
Banking and Finance	2
Wages and Prices	2
Property Rights	1
Regulation	2
Informal Market	1

Population: 5,200,000

Total area: 337,030 sq. km

GDP: $131.5 billion

GDP growth rate: 3.7%

GDP per capita: $25,288

Major exports: metal, machinery and transport equipment, electrical and optical equipment, chemicals, travel services, insurance

Exports of goods and services: $54.4 billion

Major export trading partners: Sweden 11.0%, Germany 10.7%, Russia 8.9%, UK 7.1%, US 6.4%

Major imports: raw materials, consumer goods, foodstuffs, chemicals, petroleum products, insurance, travel services

Imports of goods and services: $41.7 billion

Major import trading partners: Germany 14.7%, Russia 13.2%, Sweden 10.9%

Foreign direct investment (net): $5.2 billion

2004 Data (in constant 2000 US dollars)

D riven by abundant forest resources, capital investments, and high-technology industry, Finland's economy is one of the best in the European Union, ranking among the top in terms of competitiveness and transparency. As a committed member of the EU, Finland has started to plan for its EU presidency during the second half of 2006, and continued EU integration and relations with Russia are among the country's major foreign policy issues. In 2004, the economy continued to expand at a sound 3.7 percent. Although reforms have been implemented, the current government's main domestic issue is the improvement of labor market conditions. Finland's unemployment rate of around 9 percent remains above the EU average, and its relatively inflexible labor market and high employer-paid social security taxes hamper employment growth. The government is headed by Matti Vanhanen, whose popularity has remained stable. Vanhanen introduced a modest cut in the corporate tax rate, from 29 percent to 26 percent, which became effective in January 2005. The next presidential election is scheduled for January 2006. Finland's fiscal burden of government score is 0.5 point better this year. As a result, its overall score is 0.05 point better this year.

TRADE POLICY
Score: **2**–Stable (low level of protectionism)

As a member of the European Union, Finland was subject to a common EU weighted average external tariff of 1.3 percent in 2003, down from the 2.4 percent for 2002 reported in the 2005 *Index*, based on World Bank data. According to the World Trade Organization and the U.S. Trade Representative, the EU imposes non-tariff trade barriers through a complex regulatory system and export subsidies. According to the U.S. Department of Commerce, "Some agricultural goods are subject to the standard import-licensing system, EU-wide quotas, import taxes or other provisions." Based on the revised trade factor methodology, Finland's trade policy score is unchanged.

FISCAL BURDEN OF GOVERNMENT
Score—Income Taxation: **3**–Better (moderate tax rates)
Score—Corporate Taxation: **3**–Better (moderate tax rates)
Score—Change in Government Expenditures: **3**–Better (very low decrease)
Final Score: **3**–Better (moderate cost of government)

According to Deloitte, Finland's top income tax rate is 33.5 percent, down from the 35.5 percent reported in the 2005 *Index*. Effective January 2005, the top corporate tax rate was cut to 26 percent, down from the 29 percent reported in the 2005 *Index*. In 2004, government expenditures as a share of GDP fell 0.2 percentage point to 50.7 percent, compared to a 0.9 percentage point increase in 2003. On net, Finland's fiscal burden of government score is 0.5 point better this year.

GOVERNMENT INTERVENTION IN THE ECONOMY
Score: **2.5**–Stable (moderate level)

According to Finland's Statistics Bureau, the government consumed 22.4 percent of GDP in 2004. In 2003, based on data from the same source, Finland received 2.73 percent of its total revenues from state-owned enterprises and government ownership of property.

MONETARY POLICY
Score: **1**–Stable (very low level of inflation)

Finland is a member of the euro zone. From 1995 to 2004, Finland's weighted average annual rate of inflation was 0.58 percent.

CAPITAL FLOWS AND FOREIGN INVESTMENT
Score: **2**–Stable (low barriers)

Finland welcomes foreign investment, and few restrictions remain in effect. Foreign investments do not require prior approval, but the U.S. Department of Commerce reports that some "acquisitions of large Finnish companies may require follow-up clearance from the Ministry of Trade and Industry in accordance with the Act on the Control of Foreign Acquisitions of Finnish Companies. The purpose of the clearance is to protect 'essential national interests'." According to the International Monetary Fund, "Acquisition of shares giving at least one-third of the voting rights in a Finnish defense enterprise to a single foreign owner requires prior confirmation by the Ministry of Defense...." Non–European Economic Area investors must apply for a license to invest in a number of monitored industries, including national security–related sectors, banking and insurance, mining, travel agencies, and restaurants. Restrictions on the purchase of land apply only to non-residents purchasing land in the Aaland Islands for recreational purposes or secondary residences. The International Monetary Fund reports no exchange controls and no restrictions on current transfers or repatriation of profits, and both residents and non-residents may hold foreign exchange accounts.

BANKING AND FINANCE
Score: **2**–Stable (low level of restrictions)

Finland's banking system is generally in line with the rest of the European Union. The market determines interest rates, and foreigners have access to the system in a nondiscriminatory manner. The Organisation for Economic Co-operation and Development reports that Sampo-Leonia Plc is "A partially (40.3 %) state-owned financial conglomerate providing banking, asset management, insurance and investment banking services to private persons, companies and corporations." However, even though the government has an ownership stake in a bank that competes with private banks, the industry is open to foreign competition. The Economist Intelligence Unit reports that in 2003, 343 domestic banks and 10 foreign banks with branches were operating in Finland. The foreign banks together accounted for a small portion of total banking assets. Banking assets are concentrated with the three largest banking groups—Nordea, the Okobank group, and the Sampo financial group—which, according to the EIU, account for 91 percent of euro deposits. Banks may engage in some related financial services, such as the buying and selling of securities.

WAGES AND PRICES
Score: **2**–Stable (low level of intervention)

The market determines most wages and prices. The government controls the price of health care services and taxis. It also affects agricultural prices through Finland's participation in the Common Agricultural Policy, a program that heavily subsidizes agricultural goods. Finland does not have a legislated minimum wage, but it does require all employers to meet minimum wages that are established through collective bargaining agreements in each industrial sector.

PROPERTY RIGHTS
Score: **1**–Stable (very high level of protection)

Property rights are well protected. The Economist Intelligence Unit reports that "contractual obligations, for both government and business, are strictly honored in Finland. The quality of the judiciary and the civil service is generally high." According to the U.S. Department of Commerce, "There is no record of any significant investment dispute in the last four decades." Expropriation is unlikely.

REGULATION
Score: **2**–Stable (low level)

Finland maintains an open and transparent regulatory structure. The conduct of business, especially for non–European Economic Area residents or companies, is subject to some legal requirements. The U.S. Department of Commerce reports that "Finnish tax, labor, health and safety, and related laws and policies are largely neutral towards the efficient mobilization and allocation of investment." According to the World Bank, starting a business is easy and simple. Construction and environmental permits are required to protect the environment, and many activities that are deemed to have a detrimental effect on the environment are prohibited. The labor market has been made more flexible in recent years but still remains fairly rigid relative to other countries in the region. Bureaucratic corruption is almost nonexistent.

INFORMAL MARKET
Score: **1**–Stable (very low level of activity)

Transparency International's 2004 score for Finland is 9.7. Therefore, Finland's informal market score is 1 this year.

Finland qualifies for the Global Free Trade Alliance.

FRANCE

Rank: 44

Score: 2.51

Category: Mostly Free

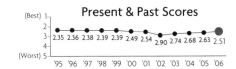

Present & Past Scores

(Best) 1
2
3
4
(Worst) 5

2.35 2.36 2.38 2.39 2.39 2.49 2.54 2.90 2.74 2.68 2.63 2.51

'95 '96 '97 '98 '99 '00 '01 '02 '03 '04 '05 '06

QUICK STUDY

SCORES

Trade Policy	2
Fiscal Burden	4.1
Government Intervention	3
Monetary Policy	1
Foreign Investment	3
Banking and Finance	3
Wages and Prices	2
Property Rights	2
Regulation	3
Informal Market	2

Population: 62,230,800

Total area: 547,030 sq. km

GDP: $1.39 trillion

GDP growth rate: 2.1%

GDP per capita: $22,723

Major exports: intermediate goods, capital goods, motor vehicles and transport equipment, processed foods and drinks

Exports of goods and services: $377 billion

Major export trading partners: Germany 15.0 %, Spain 10.4%, UK 9.4%, Italy 9.3%

Major imports: intermediate goods, motor vehicles and transport equipment, energy

Imports of goods and services: $372.2 billion

Major import trading partners: Germany 17.4%, Italy 9.0%, US 8.0%, Spain 7.4%, UK 7.4%

Foreign direct investment (net): –$17.4 billion

2004 Data (in constant 2000 US dollars)

An over-regulated labor market and overly intrusive state remain the biggest drags on France's economy. France has striven to preserve its statist political economy culture by adopting protectionist trading stances. As a result, growth has remained sluggish (2.1 percent in 2004), the unemployment rate is persistently high, and France has violated the European Union Stability and Growth Pact's deficit limit for the third year in a row. Some progress, however, has been made. The government has reduced the long-term unemployment benefit cut-off period for workers under age 50 from three years to two and has weakened the 35-hour workweek mandate by allowing employers to offer workers a higher rate of pay for additional hours. In May 2005, the French people voted against the EU constitution. This, plus the anti-capitalist rhetoric of the campaign, makes it appear unlikely that further economic reform will occur in the medium term. France's capital flows and foreign investment score is 1 point worse this year; however, its fiscal burden of government score is 0.2 point better, and its government intervention score is 2 points better. As a result, France's overall score is 0.12 point better this year.

TRADE POLICY
Score: **2–Stable** (low level of protectionism)

As a member of the European Union, France was subject to a common EU weighted average external tariff of 1.3 percent in 2003, down from the 2.4 percent for 2002 reported in the 2005 *Index*, based on World Bank data. According to the World Trade Organization and the U.S. Trade Representative, the EU imposes non-tariff trade barriers through a complex regulatory system and export subsidies. The U.S. Trade Representative reports that France applies standards, quotas, or regulations beyond EU standards on selected items. Based on the revised trade factor methodology, France's trade policy score is unchanged.

FISCAL BURDEN OF GOVERNMENT
Score—Income Taxation: **4.5–Stable** (very high tax rates)
Score—Corporate Taxation: **4.5–Stable** (very high tax rates)
Score—Change in Government Expenditures: **3–Better** (very low decrease)
Final Score: **4.1–Better** (high cost of government)

According to Deloitte, France's top income tax rate is 48.1 percent, down from the 49.64 percent reported in the 2005 *Index*. The top corporate tax rate has been reduced to 33.83 percent from 34.3 percent (a 33.33 percent corporate tax rate plus a surcharge of 1.5 percent, down from 3 percent). In 2004, government expenditures as a percent of GDP decreased 0.1 percentage point to 54.4 percent, compared to the 1.1 percentage point increase in 2003. On net, France's fiscal burden of government score is 0.2 point better this year.

GOVERNMENT INTERVENTION IN THE ECONOMY
Score: **3–Better** (moderate level)

Data from the Ministry of Finance indicate that the government consumed 23.7 percent of GDP in 2004. In 2003, based on data from France's Cours des Comptes, France received 5.5 percent of its total revenues from state-owned enterprises and government ownership of property. Based on newly available data for revenues from state-owned enterprises, France's government intervention score is 2 points better this year.

MONETARY POLICY
Score: **1**–Stable (very low level of inflation)

France is a member of the euro zone. From 1995 to 2004, France's weighted average annual rate of inflation was 2.09 percent.

CAPITAL FLOWS AND FOREIGN INVESTMENT
Score: **3**–Worse (moderate barriers)

According to the U.S. Department of Commerce, "certain sector-based foreign investment restrictions…tend to favor investors from other EU countries." The Economist Intelligence Unit reports that there are "persistent obstacles to foreign takeovers of domestic companies." The *Financial Times* reports that a legislative amendment adopted in November 2004 "increase[s] the government's discretionary powers to block the take over of strategically important French companies by foreign investors." There are restrictions on foreign investment in agriculture, aircraft production, air transport, audiovisual, banking and financial and accounting services, insurance, maritime transport, publishing, radio and television media, road transportation, telecommunications, and tourism. The International Monetary Fund reports that both residents and non-residents may hold foreign exchange accounts. There are no restrictions or controls on payments, transfers, or repatriation of profits, and non-residents may purchase real estate. Based on evidence of constraints on foreign investment, France's capital flows and foreign investment score is 1 point worse this year.

BANKING AND FINANCE
Score: **3**–Stable (moderate level of restrictions)

There are no distinctions in France between commercial and investment banking, and holders of banking licenses may engage in any banking activity. France had 925 banks and financial institutions at the end of 2003, including 304 commercial banks, 167 of which were foreign-owned subsidiaries and branches. The Economist Intelligence Unit reports that the French banking system is very concentrated: "The government's Credit Establishments and Investments Enterprises Committee…found that the six top banks accounted for 80% of lending and 90% of deposits." According to the U.S. Department of Commerce, "The French government has sold its majority stakes in major banks and insurance companies. However, it retains ownership of the Caisse des Depots et Consignations and minority stakes in several major financial institutions. The French postal service, La Poste, an independent public entity, holds 10 percent of the French financial services market." According to the EIU, "There is no sign that the French government has any intention of withdrawing altogether from banking."

WAGES AND PRICES
Score: **2**–Stable (low level of intervention)

The market freely determines the prices of most goods and services. The government, reports the Economist Intelligence Unit, controls the prices of pharmaceuticals and books. The government also controls prices in state monopolies, such as utilities and telephone services, and affects agricultural prices through France's participation in the Common Agricultural Policy, a program that heavily subsidizes agricultural goods. France has a minimum wage that is revised whenever the cost of living index increases by 2 percent.

PROPERTY RIGHTS
Score: **2**–Stable (high level of protection)

According to the Economist Intelligence Unit, "Contractual agreements are secure in France, and both the judiciary and the civil service are highly professional. The bureaucracy is competent, though entanglements in the apparatus are common and can be time consuming." The constitution states that any company defined as a national public service or natural monopoly must pass into state ownership.

REGULATION
Score: **3**–Stable (moderate level)

The World Bank reports that registering property in France is highly bureaucratic. According to *The Wall Street Journal*, the government introduced a measure to "sidestep" the mandatory 35-hour workweek "by allowing employers to offer staff extra working hours at a higher rate of pay. It also enables workers to sell part of their vacation entitlement back to employers or put it toward training or early retirement." Despite this increase in labor flexibility, reports the Economist Intelligence Unit, labor laws remain "comprehensive, establishing minimum working conditions and covering all aspects of employer-employee relations." Companies are concerned with local standards, including rigorous testing and approval procedures that must be undertaken before goods—particularly those that entail risk—can be sold in France. The U.S. Department of Commerce reports that "deregulation is far from complete and the state remains very involved in economic life."

INFORMAL MARKET
Score: **2**–Stable (low level of activity)

Transparency International's 2004 score for France is 7.1. Therefore, France's informal market score is 2 this year.

GABON

Rank: 102

Score: 3.28

Category: Mostly Unfree

Present & Past Scores

(Best) 1
2
3
4
(Worst) 5

3.19 3.63 3.31 3.18 3.09 3.26 3.38 3.33 3.18 3.43 3.40 3.28

'95 '96 '97 '98 '99 '00 '01 '02 '03 '04 '05 '06

P resident Omar Bongo Ondimba has ruled Gabon since 1967 and was re-elected to a seven-year term in 1998 amid charges of voting irregularities. With his Gabonese Democratic Party and allied parties controlling 107 of the 120 seats in the National Assembly and a majority of seats in the Senate, Ondimba was also expected to win re-election in December 2005. Gabon's economy depends heavily on trade in the government-owned oil and timber industries. Oil accounted for nearly 47 percent of GDP and over 80 percent of exports in 2004, in addition to being the primary source of government revenues, but production has declined in recent years, and the economy must diversify if growth is to continue. Mismanagement and a lack of transparency in government finances, particularly oil revenues, remain problems, and corruption is common. Together, servicing the debt and financing the public sector accounted for approximately 54 percent of government spending in 2004. In an effort to meet the requirements of the International Monetary Fund agreement and open the door to debt rescheduling with the Paris Club, the government has reluctantly agreed to long-delayed reforms to curtail spending and privatize inefficient, state-owned enterprises. Gabon's fiscal burden of government score is 0.2 point better this year, and its trade policy and informal market scores are both 0.5 point better. As a result, Gabon's overall score is 0.12 point better this year.

TRADE POLICY
Score: **4.5**–Better (very high level of protectionism)

Gabon is a member of the Central African Economic and Monetary Community (CEMAC). According to the World Bank, Gabon's weighted average tariff rate in 2002 (the most recent year for which World Bank data are available) was 14.9 percent. (The World Bank has revised the figure for 2002 downward from the 15.8 percent reported in the 2005 *Index*.) The International Monetary Fund reports that Gabon continues to have "significant non-tariff barriers." Based on the lower tariff rate, as well as a revision of the trade factor methodology, Gabon's trade policy score is 0.5 point better this year.

FISCAL BURDEN OF GOVERNMENT
Score—Income Taxation: **5**–Stable (very high tax rates)
Score—Corporate Taxation: **4.5**–Stable (very high tax rates)
Score—Change in Government Expenditures: **1**–Better (very high decrease)
Final Score: **3.8**–Better (high cost of government)

According to the International Monetary Fund, Gabon's top income tax rate is 50 percent. The corporate tax rate is 35 percent. In 2003, according to the African Development Bank, government expenditures as a share of GDP decreased 5.8 percentage points to 22.4 percent, compared to a 2.6 percentage point decrease in 2002. On net, Gabon's fiscal burden of government score is 0.2 point better this year.

GOVERNMENT INTERVENTION IN THE ECONOMY
Score: **3**–Stable (moderate level)

The Economist Intelligence Unit reports that the government consumed 10.3 percent of GDP in 2003. In 2002 (the most recent year for which data are available), based on data from the International Monetary Fund, Gabon received 10.36 percent of its total revenues just from the state-owned oil company.

QUICK STUDY

SCORES

Trade Policy	4.5
Fiscal Burden	3.8
Government Intervention	3
Monetary Policy	1
Foreign Investment	3
Banking and Finance	4
Wages and Prices	3
Property Rights	3
Regulation	4
Informal Market	3.5

Population: 1,344,433

Total area: 267,667 sq. km

GDP: $5.2 billion

GDP growth rate: 2.8%

GDP per capita: $3,865

Major exports: petroleum, timber, manganese

Exports of goods and services: $2.0 billion

Major export trading partners: US 51.2%, France 8.7%, China 7.4%

Major imports: machinery and mechanical appliances, prepared foodstuffs

Imports of goods and services: $1.9 billion

Major import trading partners: France 51.0%, US 5.1%, UK 4.4%

Foreign direct investment (net): $50 million

2003 Data (in constant 2000 US dollars)

MONETARY POLICY
Score: 1–Stable (very low level of inflation)

As a member of the Central African Economic and Monetary Community, Gabon uses the CFA franc, pegged to the euro. From 1995 to 2004, based on data from the International Monetary Fund's *2005 World Economic Outlook*, Gabon's weighted average annual rate of inflation was 1.21 percent.

 CAPITAL FLOWS AND FOREIGN INVESTMENT
Score: 3–Stable (moderate barriers)

"The Gabonese Investment Code follows the general model used in French-speaking Africa, but provides more liberal terms than other Francophone African countries," reports the U.S. Department of Commerce. "However, Gabon does not formally recognize the principle of equal national treatment because it reserves the right to favor Gabonese firms." According to the International Monetary Fund, "On the basis of [Foreign Investment Advisory Service] recommendations, the government in the coming months intends to implement a package of measures aimed at minimizing regulatory and administrative requirements as the basis for an effective investment promotion policy." The International Monetary Fund reports that residents may hold foreign exchange accounts subject to some restrictions. Non-residents may hold foreign exchange accounts but must report them to the government. The government must approve most transfers and payments to countries other than France, Monaco, members of the West African Economic and Monetary Union, members of the CEMAC, and Comoros. Capital transactions are subject to various reporting requirements, controls, and official authorization. According to the IMF, "All [real estate] transactions must be supported by appropriate documents and reported to the [Ministry of Economy, Finance, Budget, and Privatization]."

 BANKING AND FINANCE
Score: 4–Stable (high level of restrictions)

The Economist Intelligence Unit notes that Gabon's banking sector is small and "dominated by five commercial banks (mainly with French parent companies)." The banking system is open to both foreign and domestic competition, but the state maintains a significant role; all banks but one are partially or fully owned by the state, according to the World Bank. "Banks—which dominate the financial sector—find their activities and growth potential limited by the size of the non-oil economy, given that financing of the oil sector is largely undertaken outside the country," reports the World Bank. "The government retains a strong role in the financial sector, both as owner and as client, either directly or through public enterprises. In total, banks accounting for more than 85 percent of assets are subject to some government ownership." The EIU notes that only 15 percent of the population has bank accounts.

 WAGES AND PRICES
Score: 3–Stable (moderate level of intervention)

According to the International Monetary Fund, "Price setting is in principle free. Restrictions do exist, however, for the following items: petroleum, school books, water and electricity, certain kinds of bread, cement, certain kinds of cooking oil, drinking water, medical glasses, surgical equipment, local beer, sugar and public transportation." The government also affects prices through subsidies to its many state-owned enterprises. Gabon has a minimum wage.

 PROPERTY RIGHTS
Score: 3–Stable (moderate level of protection)

Private property is moderately well protected in Gabon. According to the Economist Intelligence Unit, "The president…effectively controls the judiciary (including the Constitutional Court) [and] both chambers of parliament (where the [Gabonese Democratic Party] has large majorities)…." The U.S. Department of Commerce reports that "Gabon and other countries doing business in Gabon do not always treat giving or accepting a bribe as a criminal act." Expropriation is unlikely.

 REGULATION
Score: 4–Stable (high level)

Both the U.S. Department of Commerce and the Economist Intelligence Unit report that corruption is pervasive and that complex regulations impede business. According to the Department of Commerce, "Corruption is prevalent and is an obstacle for…business in Gabon." Parastatals employ 20 percent of formal-sector workers, and although the government has made efforts to reduce bureaucracy and regulation, success has been limited, largely because of entrenched political interests.

 INFORMAL MARKET
Score: 3.5–Better (high level of activity)

Transparency International's 2004 score for Gabon is 3.3. Therefore, Gabon's informal market score is 3.5 this year—0.5 point better than last year.

THE GAMBIA

Rank: 123

Score: 3.51

Category: Mostly Unfree

Present & Past Scores

(Best) 1-
2-
3-
4-
(Worst) 5-

3.60 3.71 3.55 3.69 3.64 3.29 3.44 3.49 3.45 3.51

'95   '96   '97   '98   '99   '00   '01   '02   '03   '04   '05   '06
n/a   n/a

QUICK STUDY

SCORES

Trade Policy	4.5
Fiscal Burden	3.6
Government Intervention	2
Monetary Policy	4
Foreign Investment	3
Banking and Finance	3
Wages and Prices	3
Property Rights	4
Regulation	4
Informal Market	4

Population: 1,420,895

Total area: 11,300 sq. km

GDP: $459.9 million

GDP growth rate: 6.7%

GDP per capita: $324

Major exports: groundnut products, fish

Exports of goods and services: $192.1 million

Major export trading partners: US 22.3%, India 19.7%, China 7.7%, Germany 7.0%, Belgium 4.9%

Major imports: food and beverages, machinery and transport equipment, minerals and fuels

Imports of goods and services: $213.7 million

Major import trading partners: China 25.4%, Senegal 9.1%, UK 6.8%, Brazil 6.0%, US 5.8%

Foreign direct investment (net): $50.2 million

2003 Data (in constant 2000 US dollars)

P resident Alhaji Yahya Jammeh was re-elected in 2001 in a process that international observers judged to be free and fair, and his party won a majority in the National Assembly in the 2002 elections. However, corruption remains a problem at all levels of government and in the judiciary. In response to donor demands, Jammeh has taken steps to curb corruption through his "Operation No Compromise" campaign. This effort has resulted in a number of firings, arrests, and convictions for corruption, including many involving high-profile politicians and government officials in Jammeh's own party. Most of the population is engaged in subsistence agriculture, and the agricultural sector accounted for about 33 percent of GDP in 2003. Many parts of the government are poorly managed, lacking in transparency, and rife with inefficiency. The government has announced its commitment to improving the country's poor infrastructure, privatizing government-owned businesses, and removing regulatory impediments to business, but progress has been slow, and this is likely to curtail multilateral and bilateral donor funding as well as foreign investment. The Gambia's fiscal burden of government score is 0.4 point better this year, but its trade policy score is 1 point worse. As a result, The Gambia's overall score is 0.06 point worse this year.

TRADE POLICY
Score: **4.5**–Worse (high level of protectionism)

According to the World Trade Organization, The Gambia's average tariff rate in 2003 was 12.7 percent. The Economist Intelligence Unit reports problems with fraud and delays in customs. The World Bank reports that the government imposes licensing arrangements and sanitary and phytosanitary prohibitions on a few products. Based on increasing evidence of non-tariff barriers, as well as a revision of the trade factor methodology, The Gambia's trade policy score is 1 point worse this year.

FISCAL BURDEN OF GOVERNMENT
Score—Income Taxation: **3.5**–Stable (high tax rates)
Score—Corporate Taxation: **4.5**–Stable (very high tax rates)
Score—Change in Government Expenditures: **2**–Better (moderate decrease)
Final Score: **3.6**–Better (high cost of government)

According to the International Monetary Fund, The Gambia's top income tax rate is 35 percent. Deloitte reports that the top corporate tax rate is also 35 percent. In 2003, according to the African Development Bank, government expenditures as a share of GDP decreased 2.5 percentage points to 22.9 percent, compared to 0.6 percentage point decrease in 2002. On net, The Gambia's fiscal burden of government score is 0.4 point better this year.

GOVERNMENT INTERVENTION IN THE ECONOMY
Score: **2**–Stable (low level)

The World Bank reports that the government consumed 11.1 percent of GDP in 2003. In the same year, based on data from the International Monetary Fund, The Gambia received 2.91 percent of its total revenues from state-owned enterprises and government ownership of property.

MONETARY POLICY
Score: **4**–Stable (high level of inflation)

From 1995 to 2004, The Gambia's weighted average annual rate of inflation was 13.88 percent.

CAPITAL FLOWS AND FOREIGN INVESTMENT
Score: **3**–Stable (moderate barriers)

The government welcomes foreign investment and grants equal treatment to domestic and foreign investors. The only sectors officially closed to foreign investment are those that are reserved for the state. According to the U.S. Department of State, "There are no economic or industrial strategies that have discriminatory effects on foreign investors. There are no limits on foreign ownership or control of businesses in all sectors except television broadcasting and defense matters which are closed to private sector participation." There is repatriation of profits, and foreign investors are allowed to invest without a local partner, although the government does state its intent to encourage joint ventures. According to the International Monetary Fund, "regulatory barriers—including the absence of a transparent competition law—would need to be urgently addressed, in order to attract the necessary foreign capital to jump-start a sustainable growth...." The IMF reports that residents and non-residents may hold foreign exchange accounts. There are no restrictions on payments and transfers. Some capital transactions are controlled.

BANKING AND FINANCE
Score: **3**–Stable (moderate level of restrictions)

Although the government has privatized some of its holdings in the banking sector—it sold a majority of its share in the Trust Bank to private investors between 1997 and 1999, for example—it continues to affect the allocation of credit. According to the Economist Intelligence Unit, "Gambia Commercial and Development Bank was wholly owned by the government but has now been sold to private interests, and the other commercial bank, the International Bank for Commerce and Industry, is also privately owned. A new development bank, the Arab Gambian Islamic Bank, opened in Banjul in January 1998." The EIU reports that the banking sector as a whole is healthy, with non-performing loans as a percent of total loans falling to 5.5 percent in 2003, but notes that "weak institutional capacity and corruption still pose problems on a more practical level." According to the International Monetary Fund, the government provides credit to the agricultural sector.

WAGES AND PRICES
Score: **3**–Stable (moderate level of intervention)

The market sets some prices, but the government influences prices through the many state-owned companies in the agriculture, maritime, water and electricity, aviation, public transport, and telecommunications sectors. The government sets gas prices. Minimum wages are set through six industrial councils (with participation from the government, labor, and employers on each council) that govern commerce, artisans, transport, port operations, agriculture, and fisheries.

PROPERTY RIGHTS
Score: **4**–Stable (low level of protection)

"The Constitution provides for an independent judiciary," reports the U.S. Department of State; "however, the judiciary reportedly at times was subject to executive branch pressure, especially at lower levels." According to the Economist Intelligence Unit, "The independence and objectivity of the judiciary has been called into question in recent years.... [There are complaints about] intimidation of lawyers, a lack of independence and a lack of technical support for the legal profession.... The absence of an independent and transparent judicial system has deterred investors." The Supreme Court is in disarray and has not been operating for a year.

REGULATION
Score: **4**–Stable (high level)

Establishing a business in The Gambia can be difficult because of bureaucratic inefficiency, lack of transparency, and what the Economist Intelligence Unit characterizes as "institutional corruption." The U.S. Department of Commerce reports that the agricultural sector—one of the largest sectors in the economy—cannot increase production because "structural problems remain a hindrance, particularly within the groundnut sector." In addition, corruption "is becoming increasingly institutionalized. Business people occasionally encounter extortion, bribery, or fraud." Political uncertainty adds to the problem.

INFORMAL MARKET
Score: **4**–Stable (high level of activity)

Transparency International's 2004 score for The Gambia is 2.8. Therefore, The Gambia's informal market score is 4 this year.

GEORGIA

Rank: 68

Score: 2.98

Category: Mostly Free

Present & Past Scores

(Best) 1
2
3
4
(Worst) 5

3.99 3.93 3.83 3.90 3.85 3.63 3.53 3.40 3.14 3.29 2.98

'95 '96 '97 '98 '99 '00 '01 '02 '03 '04 '05 '06
n/a

QUICK STUDY

SCORES

Trade Policy	3.5
Fiscal Burden	2.3
Government Intervention	1.5
Monetary Policy	2
Foreign Investment	3
Banking and Finance	2
Wages and Prices	3
Property Rights	4
Regulation	4
Informal Market	4.5

Population: 4,800,000

Total area: 69,700 sq. km

GDP: $3.73 billion

GDP growth rate: 11.1%

GDP per capita: $777

Major exports: ferro alloys, scrap metals and aluminum, machinery, chemicals

Exports of goods and services: $770 million

Major export trading partners: Russia 17.7%, Turkey 17.3%, Turkmenistan 12.3%, Armenia 8.6%, UK 5.9%

Major imports: oil products, machinery and machines, medicine

Imports of goods and services: $1.4 billion

Major import trading partners: Russia 14.0%, UK 12.8%, Turkey 9.9%, Azerbaijan 8.3%, US 8.0%, Germany 7.3%

Foreign direct investment (net): $315 million

2003 Data (in constant 2000 US dollars)

Mikheil Saakashvili's victory in the 2004 presidential elections and the removal of Adjara separatist leader Aslan Abashidze have highlighted Georgia's pioneering role as home of the "Rose Revolution." A recent Organization for Security and Co-operation in Europe report suggests that Georgia is making genuine electoral progress as the volatility that had threatened the government has begun to subside. However, Georgia continues to struggle against the Russian-supported separatist enclaves of South Ossetia and Abkhazia. It also suffered a severe blow as a result of the February 2005 death of Prime Minister Zurab Zhvania. The anticipated completion of the Baku–Tbilisi–Ceyhan oil pipeline in late 2005 and construction of the South Caucasus gas pipeline could have a positive effect on a number of domestic industries, including transportation, communications, hotels, and catering. The agricultural sector is also improving. Saakashvili's party remains six seats shy of a two-thirds constitutional majority, but the mandate given to his National Movement–Democrats will enable them to proceed with important economic and governance reforms. The main challenge will continue to be fighting corruption and creating a workable state. Georgia's fiscal burden of government score is 0.1 point better this year, and its monetary policy, foreign investment, and banking and finance scores are all 1 point better. As a result, its overall score is 0.31 point better this year, causing Georgia to be classified as a "mostly free" country.

TRADE POLICY
Score: **3.5**–Stable (high level of protectionism)

According to the World Bank, Georgia's weighted average tariff rate in 2004 was 8.7 percent, down from the 9.9 percent in 1999 reported in the 2005 *Index*, based on World Bank data. Some goods require an import license. The Economist Intelligence Unit reports that customs corruption is widespread. Based on the revised trade factor methodology, Georgia's trade policy score is unchanged.

FISCAL BURDEN OF GOVERNMENT
Score—Income Taxation: **1.5**–Better (low tax rates)
Score—Corporate Taxation: **2**–Stable (low tax rates)
Score—Change in Government Expenditures: **3.5**–Stable (low increase)
Final Score: **2.3**–Better (low cost of government)

Georgia implemented a flat income tax rate of 12 percent in January 2005, down from the top 20 percent progressive rate reported in the 2005 *Index*. The top corporate tax rate is 20 percent. In 2003, according to the central bank, government expenditures as a share of GDP increased 0.9 percentage point to 18.3 percent, compared to a 0.6 percentage point increase in 2002. On net, Georgia's fiscal burden of government score is 0.1 point better this year.

GOVERNMENT INTERVENTION IN THE ECONOMY
Score: **1.5**–Stable (low level)

The World Bank reports that the government consumed 8.9 percent of GDP in 2003. In the same year, according to the International Monetary Fund's Government Financial Statistics CD–ROM, Georgia received 0.47 percent of its total revenues from state-owned enterprises and government ownership of property.

MONETARY POLICY
Score: **2**–Better (low level of inflation)

From 1995 to 2004 Georgia's weighted average annual rate of inflation was 5.47 percent, down from the 6.39 percent from 1994 to 2003 reported in the 2005 *Index*. As a result, Georgia's monetary policy score is 1 point better this year.

CAPITAL FLOWS AND FOREIGN INVESTMENT
Score: **3**–Better (moderate barriers)

Foreign investment receives equal treatment under the law. There are no restrictions on purchases of or investment in domestic companies, stocks, bonds, or any other property, and local participation in businesses or investments is not required. Most sectors of the economy are open to foreign investment, although exceptions exist for some infrastructure projects and agricultural land. According to the Economist Intelligence Unit, the economy should benefit "from the new government's commitment to improve the business environment and to attract foreign investors. Predatory tax enforcement, a lack of adequate legal protection, pervasive corruption and arbitrary application of rules and regulations were the major reasons why foreign investors previously stayed away." The International Monetary Fund reports that tax reforms that entered into force on January 1, 2005, are designed "to improve the business climate [and] establish favorable conditions for both local and foreign investors." In addition, "measures aimed at promotion of industry and investments, eradication of barriers to business…[reducing the] number of controlling agencies, and ensuring transparency in the process of granting licenses and rights are parts of the initiative." Residents and non-residents may hold foreign exchange accounts. There are limits and *bona fide* tests for payments and current transfers. Capital transactions are not restricted but must be registered. Based on increasing evidence of liberalization, Georgia's capital flows and foreign investment score is 1 point better this year.

BANKING AND FINANCE
Score: **2**–Better (low level of restrictions)

"Reform of the banking sector began in mid-1995," reports the Economist Intelligence Unit, "with the National Bank of Georgia (NBG, the central bank) assuming a supervisory role. The NBG instituted bank consolidation and reform, imposing increasingly stringent reporting requirements.… Minimum capital requirements have been raised progressively." The Georgian embassy reports that there were 21 banks operating as of March 2005, including 19 Georgian commercial banks and two foreign bank branches. Foreign investors are majority owners of seven banks, which jointly account for over 65 percent of banking assets. Over 10 percent of the population possessed banking accounts in 2005 versus only 3 percent several years before. The government does not have a stake in any bank. Based on evidence of minimal government influence, Georgia's banking and finance score is 1 point better this year.

WAGES AND PRICES
Score: **3**–Stable (moderate level of intervention)

Most prices have been liberalized, although the Georgian embassy reports that the government regulates the prices of city transport services, communication services, electricity, gas, water, and communal services. The government also subsidizes the health care and agricultural sectors. Georgia has a minimum wage for state workers but not for the private sector.

PROPERTY RIGHTS
Score: **4**–Stable (low level of protection)

Judicial corruption is still a problem despite the government's substantial improvement in trying to raise the level of efficiency and fairness in the courts. *The Economist* reports that "corruption and crime have raged through government, the judiciary, business and the lives of ordinary citizens for most of the past decade. The authorities lost control not only of bureaucratic details, but of chunks of the country…." According to *The Washington Times*, "In adjudicating [business] disputes, the performance of the Georgian court system has been mixed. Both foreign and Georgian investors have expressed a lack of confidence in the competence, independence, and impartiality of lower court decisions, in addition to the ever present concerns about their ability to be corrupted."

REGULATION
Score: **4**–Stable (high level)

Despite government efforts to foster a market economy, establishing a business can be difficult. "Streamlining procedures within a bureaucracy…is a major challenge for Georgia's reformers," reports the U.S. Department of Commerce. "Investors face innumerable petty obstacles and near constant frustration at the day-to-day difficulties of doing business in Georgia." The Economist Intelligence Unit reports that "small and medium-sized enterprises (SMEs)…have been prevented from developing by unfavourable legislation and widespread corruption."

INFORMAL MARKET
Score: **4.5**–Stable (very high level of activity)

Transparency International's 2004 score for Georgia is 2. Therefore, Georgia's informal market score is 4.5 this year.

GERMANY

Rank: 19

Score: 1.96

Category: Free

Present & Past Scores

(Best) 1–
2–
3– 2.20 2.31 2.20 2.41 2.31 2.29 2.09 2.05 2.03 2.08 2.00 1.96
4–
(Worst) 5–
'95 '96 '97 '98 '99 '00 '01 '02 '03 '04 '05 '06

QUICK STUDY

SCORES

Trade Policy	2
Fiscal Burden	3.1
Government Intervention	2
Monetary Policy	1
Foreign Investment	1
Banking and Finance	3
Wages and Prices	2
Property Rights	1
Regulation	3
Informal Market	1.5

Population: 82,600,000

Total area: 357,021 sq. km

GDP: $1.9 trillion

GDP growth rate: 1.6%

GDP per capita: $23,002

Major exports: motor vehicles, machinery, textiles, chemical products, telecommunications technology, financial services, insurance

Exports of goods and services: $702.7 billion

Major export trading partners: France 10.3%, US 8.9%, UK 8.3%, Italy 7.2%, Netherlands 6.2%

Major imports: chemical products, motor vehicles, machinery, mineral oil and gas, financial services, insurance

Imports of goods and services: $641 billion

Major import trading partners: France 9.1%, Netherlands 7.8%, US 7.4%, Italy 6.1%, UK 6.1%

Foreign direct investment (net): –$28.9 billion

2004 Data (in constant 2000 US dollars)

Germany has the European Union's largest economy—and one of its weakest. In terms of individual companies and export strategy, the economy remains world-class but has underperformed its potential in recent years. In May 2005, over 5 million Germans were unemployed. Growth in 2004 was 1.6 percent, continuing a trend of little if any growth in the past four years. Germany's 2004 deficit once again violated the EU Stability and Growth Pact, which Berlin originally advocated. For the first time, national per capita income is below the EU average. Germany's non-wage labor costs are among the world's highest, making fundamental economic reform of the welfare and labor market systems imperative. In spring 2003, following his re-election, Chancellor Gerhard Schroeder proposed a series of reforms limiting unemployment benefits, initiating cuts in health care spending, and allowing employers hiring and firing flexibility. Even these limited reforms were repudiated. Following a May 2005 defeat in the North Rhine–Westphalia elections, Schroeder moved up national elections to the fall of 2005. The result was a clear demonstration of the German public's rejection of desperately needed economic reforms and produced a split result between conservatives and Social Democrats that has led to a political stalemate. Germany's fiscal burden of government score is 0.4 point better this year. As a result, its overall score is 0.04 point better this year, causing Germany to be classified as a "free" country.

 TRADE POLICY
Score: **2**–Stable (low level of protectionism)

As a member of the European Union, Germany was subject to a common EU weighted average external tariff of 1.3 percent in 2003, down from the 2.4 percent for 2002 reported in the 2005 *Index*, based on World Bank data. According to the World Trade Organization and the U.S. Trade Representative, the EU imposes non-tariff trade barriers through a complex regulatory system and export subsidies. The U.S. Department of Commerce reports that "Germany's regulations and bureaucratic procedures can be a difficult hurdle…. Complex safety standards, not normally discriminatory but sometimes zealously applied, complicate access to the market." Based on the revised trade factor methodology, Germany's trade policy score is unchanged.

 FISCAL BURDEN OF GOVERNMENT
Score—Income Taxation: **4**–Better (high tax rates)
Score—Corporate Taxation: **3**–Stable (moderate tax rates)
Score—Change in Government Expenditures: **2.5**–Better (low decrease)
Final Score: **3.1**–Better (moderate cost of government)

According to Deloitte, Germany's top income tax rate is 44.3 percent (a reduced top income tax rate of 42 percent plus a 5.5 percent surcharge), down from the 47 percent reported in the 2005 *Index*. The top corporate tax rate is 25 percent, but an additional 5.5 percent solidarity tax raises this rate to 26.4 percent. In 2004, government expenditures as a share of GDP decreased 1.1 percentage points to 47.7 percent, compared to a 0.1 percentage point increase in 2003. On net, Germany's fiscal burden of government score is 0.4 point better this year.

 GOVERNMENT INTERVENTION IN THE ECONOMY
Score: **2**–Stable (low level)

Based on data from Germany's Federal Statistical Office, the government consumed 18.7 percent

193

of GDP in 2004. In the same year, according to the same source, Germany received 1.21 percent of its total revenues from state-owned enterprises and government ownership of property.

MONETARY POLICY
Score: 1–Stable (very low level of inflation)

Germany is a member of the euro zone. From 1995 to 2004, Germany's weighted average annual rate of inflation was 1.50 percent.

CAPITAL FLOWS AND FOREIGN INVESTMENT
Score: 1–Stable (very low barriers)

Foreign and domestic investors receive equal treatment and face the same regulatory hurdles in establishing a business. The International Monetary Fund reports no restrictions or barriers with respect to capital transactions or current transfers, real estate purchases, repatriation of profits, or access to foreign exchange. "The German government officially, and the population in general, welcomes foreign investment that provides new jobs," reports the Economist Intelligence Unit. "There are no serious limitations on new projects, except for a law passed in July 2004 requiring prior government permission for the sale of defence companies to foreign investors. No permanent currency or administrative controls on foreign investments apply." According to Deloitte, "Foreign investment that provides new jobs is welcomed, but the government opposes hostile takeovers." The EIU likewise notes that the government "will remain sceptical of takeovers of key German companies by foreign groups." Some businesses, including certain financial institutions, passenger transport businesses, and real estate agencies, require licenses.

BANKING AND FINANCE
Score: 3–Stable (moderate level of restrictions)

Germany's banking system is well regulated and dominated by public-sector financial institutions. According to the Economist Intelligence Unit, "Germany has a basically non-discriminatory, well-developed financial services infrastructure. Germany's universal banking systems allows the country's more than 39,000 bank offices not only to take deposits and make loans to customers, but also to trade in securities…. Private banks control roughly 30 percent of the market…. A state-owned bank, KfW, provides special credit services, including financing homeowner mortgages, providing guarantees to small and medium-sized businesses, financing projects in disadvantaged regions in Germany and providing export financing for projects in developing countries." The government owns a majority of the post office, which also offers banking services. The German embassy reports that there are 2,147 credit institutions, including 477 savings banks that account for 15 percent of bank market share, or 34 percent when combined with the 12 *Landesbanken* (wholesale banks owned by savings-banks associations and state governments). The government has removed its guarantees on *Landesbanken* loans.

Commercial banks account for 28 percent of bank market share. The U.S. Department of Commerce reports that credit is available on market terms.

WAGES AND PRICES
Score: 2–Stable (low level of intervention)

The market sets most prices. According to the Economist Intelligence Unit, "Price controls are limited to maximum prices (for example, rent increases), minimum prices (mainly for agricultural products, under EU regulations [i.e., Common Agricultural Policy]) and price-calculation ordinances (such as for public utilities and insurance premiums). The Federal Cartel Office (Bundeskartellamt) moves against companies that abuse their dominant market position through 'excessive' price increases." Germany does not impose a minimum wage; the minimum wage is set by collective bargaining.

PROPERTY RIGHTS
Score: 1–Stable (very high level of protection)

Property is well protected in Germany. The judiciary is both independent and efficient. The Economist Intelligence Unit reports that "contractual agreements are secure…and both the judiciary and the civil service are highly professional. The courts are decentralized, reflecting the country's federal system; there are separate supreme courts to deal with cases on commercial, tax, labour and constitutional issues."

REGULATION
Score: 3–Stable (moderate level)

The government is streamlining regulations by increasingly using the Internet to reduce bureaucratic steps; however, businesses still must contend with a vast and confusing web of regulations. Labor reforms implemented during the past three years ("Hartz" reforms) focus mostly on reducing welfare benefits for the unemployed. However, Germany's wages and fringe benefits remain among the world's highest, and the ability of businesses to fire workers is subject to rigid conditions, all of which serves a strong disincentive to invest and create jobs. Corruption is minimal, although Transparency International reports that "the construction sector, the privatization of former East German enterprises, and the awarding of public contracts represent areas of some continued concern."

INFORMAL MARKET
Score: 1.5–Stable (low level of activity)

Transparency International's 2004 score for Germany is 8.2. Therefore, Germany's informal market score is 1.5 this year.

If Germany were to improve its regulation score, it would qualify for the Global Free Trade Alliance.

GHANA

Rank: 105

Score: 3.29

Category: Mostly Unfree

Present & Past Scores

(Best) 1
2
3
4
(Worst) 5

'95	'96	'97	'98	'99	'00	'01	'02	'03	'04	'05	'06
3.54	3.54	3.43	3.29	3.29	3.24	3.24	3.54	3.54	3.35	3.25	3.29

P resident John Agyekum Kufuor was re-elected in 2004 in a process that was generally deemed free and fair, but there have been allegations of corruption among government officials and in the judiciary. Agriculture accounts for over half of employment, almost 40 percent of GDP, and about one-third of total exports. Reliance on agriculture as the chief component of the economy, and on commodities (primarily gold and cocoa) as a source of foreign exchange, makes Ghana's economy vulnerable to global price fluctuations. Donors, especially the International Monetary Fund, play a central role in economic policy. Under President Kufuor, Ghana has generally followed through on economic reforms. Over 200 state-owned enterprises have been privatized, but some proposed privatizations and hikes in subsidized prices have been delayed because of political concerns. The price of fuel was increased by 50 percent (but not fully liberalized) in early 2005. The increase was very unpopular, and discontent could threaten other reforms. Ghana is eligible for assistance from the U.S. Millennium Challenge Account. Ghana's monetary policy score and banking and finance score are both 1 point better this year; however, its trade policy score is 1 point worse, its fiscal burden of government score is 0.9 point worse, and its government intervention score is 0.5 point worse. As a result, Ghana's overall score is 0.04 point worse this year.

TRADE POLICY
Score: **4.5**–Worse (very high level of protectionism)

According to the World Bank, Ghana's weighted average tariff rate in 2004 was 14.8 percent, up from the 9.5 percent in 2000 reported in the 2005 *Index*, based on World Bank data. The U.S. Trade Representative reports that "some imports, such as pharmaceuticals, mercury, gambling machines, handcuffs, condensed or evaporated milk, arms and ammunition, and live plants and animals require special permits." The same source reports various fees and taxes levied on imports. Based on the higher tariff rate, as well as a revision of the trade policy methodology, Ghana's trade policy score is 1 point worse this year.

FISCAL BURDEN OF GOVERNMENT
Score—Income Taxation: **3**–Stable (moderate tax rates)
Score—Corporate Taxation: **4**–Stable (high tax rates)
Score—Change in Government Expenditures: **4.5**–Worse (high increase)
Final Score: **3.9**–Worse (high cost of government)

Ghana's top income tax rate is 30 percent. The top corporate tax rate is also 30 percent, down from the 32.5 percent reported in the 2005 *Index*. In 2003, according to the African Development Bank, government expenditures as a share of GDP increased 2.9 percentage points to 29 percent, compared to a 6.6 percentage point decrease in 2002. On net, Ghana's fiscal burden of government score is 0.9 point worse this year.

GOVERNMENT INTERVENTION IN THE ECONOMY
Score: **2**–Worse (low level)

The World Bank reports that the government consumed 11.5 percent of GDP in 2003, up from the 9.9 percent reported in the 2005 *Index*. As a result, Ghana's government intervention score is 0.5 point worse this year. In the same year, based on data from the International Monetary Fund,

---

QUICK STUDY

SCORES

Trade Policy	4.5
Fiscal Burden	3.9
Government Intervention	2
Monetary Policy	4
Foreign Investment	3
Banking and Finance	3
Wages and Prices	3
Property Rights	3
Regulation	3
Informal Market	3.5

Population: 20,669,260

Total area: 238,540 sq. km

GDP: $5.7 billion

GDP growth rate: 5.2%

GDP per capita: $276

Major exports: gold, cocoa, timber, diamonds, aluminum

Exports of goods and services: $2.5 billion

Major export trading partners: Netherlands 11.3%, UK 10.7%, France 7.6%, Germany 6.2%, US 4.3%

Major imports: petroleum, foodstuffs

Imports of goods and services: $3.7 billion

Major import trading partners: Nigeria 12.9%, China 9.1%, UK 7.1%, US 5.9%

Foreign direct investment (net): $76.7 million

2003 Data (in constant 2000 US dollars)

Ghana received 2.89 percent of its total revenues from state-owned enterprises and government ownership of property.

MONETARY POLICY
Score: **4**–Better (high level of inflation)

From 1995 to 2004, Ghana's weighted average annual rate of inflation was 16.89 percent, down from the 24.03 percent from 1994 to 2003 reported in the 2005 *Index*. As a result, Ghana's monetary policy score is 1 point better this year.

CAPITAL FLOWS AND FOREIGN INVESTMENT
Score: **3**–Stable (moderate barriers)

The foreign investment code eliminates screening of foreign investment, guarantees capital repatriation, and does not discriminate against foreign investors. The U.S. Department of Commerce reports that the government "has passed laws that encourage foreign investment and replaced some that previously stifled it." According to the International Monetary Fund, however, "Foreign investments…require the prior approval of the Ghana Investment Promotion Center (GIPC) if they are to benefit from…the right to transfer income from investments and, in the event of sale or liquidation, capital proceeds." The GIPC law restricts petty trading, taxi services, gambling and lotteries, beauty salons, and barbershops to Ghanaians. "Although registration is relatively easy," reports the U.S. Department of Commerce, "the entire process of establishing a business…is lengthy, complex, and requires compliance with regulations and procedures of at least 5 government agencies." The IMF reports that residents may hold foreign exchange accounts and non-residents may hold them subject to restrictions. Payments and current transfers are subject to restrictions. The Bank of Ghana must approve most capital transactions, and foreign direct investment faces a minimum capital requirement.

BANKING AND FINANCE
Score: **3**–Better (moderate level of restrictions)

The government has taken steps to increase the independence of the central bank by limiting government borrowing from the central bank and prohibiting central bank loan guarantees to private organizations. According to the Economist Intelligence Unit, "There are 18 banks—ten commercial banks, five merchant banks, and three development banks. There are five foreign banks…[which] play a leading role in the sector and are slowly stimulating competition, mainly by offering more and better services." Three banks held over 55 percent of total banking assets at the end of 2003. The Ghana Stock Exchange's performance has been strong in recent years. As of April 2005, reports the U.S. Department of Commerce, "all banks [were to] be authorized to provide services in the commercial, development and merchant sectors. Until recently banking was dominated by state-owned institutions and showed few signs of competition. Within the last six years, however, two state-owned banks have been privatized." Based on evidence of less government intervention, Ghana's banking and finance score is 1 point better this year.

WAGES AND PRICES
Score: **3**–Stable (moderate level of intervention)

The government influences the prices of utilities through the state-owned companies. It also maintains some food subsidies, manipulates prices through its remaining government enterprises, and influences the prices of cocoa (Ghana's major export) by forcing farmers to sell their crops to the parastatal Ghana Cocoa Board. The government has created an independent body to fix the price of fuel. According to the Economist Intelligence Unit, "The pricing mechanism is likely to link the fuel price to international oil prices and the performance of the currency…." A tripartite commission composed of representatives of government, labor, and employers sets the minimum wage.

PROPERTY RIGHTS
Score: **3**–Stable (moderate level of protection)

According to the U.S. Department of Commerce, "in some cases, land records are incomplete or non-existent and therefore clear title may be impossible to establish." Ghana's judicial system suffers from corruption, although the problem is less acute than it is in some other African countries. "There is a history of government intervention in the court system," reports the U.S. Department of Commerce, "although somewhat less so in commercial matters.… [T]he courts have been slow in disposing of cases and at times face challenges in enforcing decisions, largely due to resource constraints and institutional inefficiencies. There is a growing interest in alternative dispute resolution, especially as it applies to commercial cases."

REGULATION
Score: **3**–Stable (moderate level)

Regulations are moderately burdensome. According to the U.S. Department of Commerce, "The [Ghana Investment Promotion Center] was established [in] 1994 as a one-stop shop for economic, commercial and investment information for entrepreneurs interested in starting a business or investing in Ghana." According to the U.S. Trade Representative, however, "Bureaucratic inertia is sometimes a problem…and administrative approvals often take longer than they should." The U.S. Department of Commerce notes that corruption exists but to a lesser extent than in many other countries in the region.

INFORMAL MARKET
Score: **3.5**–Stable (high level of activity)

Transparency International's 2004 score for Ghana is 3.6. Therefore, Ghana's informal market score is 3.5 this year.

GREECE

Rank: 57

Score: 2.80

Category: Mostly Free

Present & Past Scores

(Best) 1-
2-
3-
4-
(Worst) 5-

3.20 3.00 2.86 2.94 2.93 2.74 2.74 2.89 2.79 2.85 2.80 2.80

'95 '96 '97 '98 '99 '00 '01 '02 '03 '04 '05 '06

F ollowing his center–right party's unexpected sweep in the March 2004 parliamentary elections, new Prime Minister Costas Karamanlis was faced with the task of rescuing Greece's flailing efforts to host the 2004 summer Olympic Games. The games came off as a great success but contributed to a very large budget deficit of 6.1 percent of GDP in 2004—double the limit of 3 percent specified under the European Union's Stability and Growth Pact. Tourism and construction associated with the Olympic Games helped the economy to grow at a rate of 4.2 percent in 2004 following 4.7 percent growth in 2003. However, unemployment and inflation have remained high relative to other countries in the euro zone. Greece's share of handouts from the European Union will fall sharply in 2007. Corruption is still rife within state enterprises, and a corrupt, dysfunctional bureaucracy continues to deter foreign investors. Greece's overall score is unchanged this year.

TRADE POLICY
Score: 2–Stable (low level of protectionism)

As a member of the European Union, Greece was subject to a common EU weighted average external tariff of 1.3 percent in 2003, down from the 2.4 percent for 2002 reported in the 2005 *Index*, based on World Bank data. According to the World Trade Organization and the U.S. Trade Representative, the EU imposes non-tariff trade barriers through a complex regulatory system and export subsidies. According to the U.S. Department of Commerce, "Agricultural products from non-EU countries are subject to a complicated protection system…. Greece occasionally bans imports of some types of agricultural products that compete with similar domestically produced ones." Based on the revised trade factor methodology, Greece's trade policy score is unchanged.

FISCAL BURDEN OF GOVERNMENT
Score—Income Taxation: **4**–Stable (high tax rates)
Score—Corporate Taxation: **4**–Better (high tax rates)
Score—Change in Government Expenditures: **4**–Worse (moderate increase)
Final Score: **4**–Stable (high cost of government)

According to Deloitte, Greece's top income tax rate is 40 percent. The top corporate tax rate, formerly 35 percent, was cut to 32 percent on income earned in 2005. In 2004, government expenditures as a share of GDP increased 1.9 percentage points to 52 percent, compared to the 0.1 percentage point increase in 2003.

GOVERNMENT INTERVENTION IN THE ECONOMY
Score: **2**–Stable (low level)

The World Bank reports that the government consumed 15.5 percent of GDP in 2003. In the same year, based on data from the central bank, Greece received 0.34 percent of its total revenues from state-owned enterprises and government ownership of property.

QUICK STUDY

SCORES

Trade Policy	2
Fiscal Burden	4
Government Intervention	2
Monetary Policy	2
Foreign Investment	3
Banking and Finance	3
Wages and Prices	3
Property Rights	3
Regulation	3
Informal Market	3

Population: 11,040,650

Total area: 131,940 sq. km

GDP: $133.9 billion

GDP growth rate: 4.2%

GDP per capita: $12,128

Major exports: food and beverages, chemicals, textiles, manufactured goods, petroleum products

Exports of goods and services: $26.1 billion

Major export trading partners: Germany 12.6%, Italy 10.5%, UK 7.0%, France 4.2%

Major imports: manufactured goods, foodstuffs, chemicals

Imports of goods and services: $38 billion

Major import trading partners: Germany 12.3%, Italy 12.0%, France 6.5%, Netherlands 5.1%

Foreign direct investment (net): $688 million

2004 Data (in constant 2000 US dollars)

MONETARY POLICY
Score: **2**–Stable (low level of inflation)

Greece is a member of the euro zone. From 1995 to 2004, Greece's weighted average annual rate of inflation was 3.13 percent.

CAPITAL FLOWS AND FOREIGN INVESTMENT
Score: **3**–Stable (moderate barriers)

Although Greece officially welcomes foreign investment, it also maintains a number of restrictions. The government restricts both foreign and domestic investment in utilities but has begun to liberalize the telecommunications and energy sectors. The U.S. Department of Commerce reports that "non-EU investors receive less advantageous treatment than domestic or EU investors in the banking, mining, broadcasting, maritime, and air transport sectors (these sectors were opened to EU citizens due to EU single market rules)." According to the June 21, 2005, *Financial Times*, "Obstacles for investors include an inefficient bureaucracy, high tax rates, ill-defined land use and popular resistance to the notion of foreigners benefiting from the development of Greek assets…. Processing of applications has been slow and the issuing of licenses and permits even slower." The International Monetary Fund reports that both residents and non-residents may hold foreign exchange accounts. There are no restrictions or controls on payments, real estate transactions, transfers, or repatriation of profits. The IMF reports that investments in border regions are restricted to EU residents.

BANKING AND FINANCE
Score: **3**–Stable (moderate level of restrictions)

The Economist Intelligence Unit reports that in 2003, there were 60 banks, 21 of which were foreign. As a condition of membership in the European Union, the government has liberalized the banking system in ways that facilitate foreign competition and have led to the sale of some public-sector banks. The government has been withdrawing from the banking sector. According to the U.S. Department of Commerce, "A few state-controlled banks dominate the Greek banking industry. Private Greek and foreign banks do, however, comprise an increasingly competitive and generally profitable private sector, holding about 59 percent of the banking system's assets." The same source notes that the state banks have large exposure to state-owned enterprises and are in questionable financial health. The government indirectly controls two large commercial banks: National Bank and Emporiki. According to the Economist Intelligence Unit, the government has sold 11 percent of its stake in the National Bank of Greece, reducing its direct holding to 7.5 percent.

WAGES AND PRICES
Score: **3**–Stable (moderate level of intervention)

The market determines most prices. According to the Economist Intelligence Unit, "the state can control prices [in the petroleum-product market] through mandatory storage requirements and adjustments to excise duties…. Fares for urban transport, inter-urban railways, domestic air travel and domestic ferry transport continue to be set administratively for reasons of social policy." The government also controls the prices of pharmaceuticals and affects agricultural prices through Greece's participation in the Common Agricultural Policy, a program that heavily subsidizes agricultural goods. The minimum wage is set through collective bargaining and legally enforced.

PROPERTY RIGHTS
Score: **3**–Stable (moderate level of protection)

The U.S. Department of Commerce reports that enforcing property and contractual rights through the court system is highly time-consuming. According to the Economist Intelligence Unit, "Contractual agreements can be problematic…. The judiciary is supposed to be non-partisan but tends to reflect the political sensibilities of the government of the day…. In Greece it is wise to seek legal assistance from the outset [instead of when encountering legal difficulties] to avoid pitfalls." Expropriation of property is unlikely.

REGULATION
Score: **3**–Stable (moderate level)

The government is very bureaucratic, and regulations are not fully transparent. According to the U.S. Department of Commerce, "the complexity of government regulations and procedures—and the perceived inconsistent implementation by the Greek civil administration—[are considered] to be the greatest impediment to investing and operating in Greece." The government has created the Hellenic Centre for Investments to answer investors' concerns, but investors still find the bureaucracy burdensome. Labor laws are somewhat rigid; they limit working hours and restrict part-time employment and the dismissal of personnel.

INFORMAL MARKET
Score: **3**–Stable (moderate level of activity)

Transparency International's 2004 score for Greece is 4.3. Therefore, Greece's informal market score is 3 this year.

GUATEMALA

Rank: 74

Score: 3.01

Category: Mostly Unfree

Present & Past Scores

(Best) 1
2
3
4
(Worst) 5

3.36 3.10 2.94 2.96 2.94 2.91 2.88 3.00 3.01 3.16 3.18 3.01

'95 '96 '97 '98 '99 '00 '01 '02 '03 '04 '05 '06

QUICK STUDY

SCORES

Trade Policy	2.5
Fiscal Burden	3.6
Government Intervention	1
Monetary Policy	3
Foreign Investment	3
Banking and Finance	3
Wages and Prices	2
Property Rights	4
Regulation	4
Informal Market	4

Population: 12,307,091

Total area: 108,890 sq. km

GDP: $20.6 billion

GDP growth rate: 2.1%

GDP per capita: $1,675

Major exports: coffee, sugar, bananas, apparel, petroleum

Exports of goods and services: $3.8 billion

Major export trading partners: US 58.6%, El Salvador 8.6%, Mexico 3.1%

Major imports: fuels, construction materials, machinery and transport equipment

Imports of goods and services: $6.4 billion

Major import trading partners: US 34.3%, Mexico 8.9%, South Korea 7.9%, El Salvador 5.4%, China 4.6%

Foreign direct investment (net): $91.3 million

2003 Data (in constant 2000 US dollars)

Guatemala is Central America's most populous country. Traditionally, coffee, sugar, and fruit have been the primary exports, with more than 50 percent of the workforce engaged in agriculture, but tourism and apparel assembly now earn more, and remittances ($2.5 billion in 2004) make up the bulk of foreign exchange. President Oscar Berger has managed to get a series of fiscal measures through Congress even though his coalition lacks a majority. In June 2004, his administration reduced the armed forces by more than one-third and cut their budget to 0.33 percent of GDP. The government has steadily withdrawn from owning services and energy utilities. The DR–CAFTA trade pact, ratified by both Guatemala and the U.S. in 2005, could boost trade and employment prospects for those working in the large informal sector. High crime rates and rising youth gang membership challenge Guatemala's more numerous and better-trained police, and a weak judiciary still faces a backlog of cases and remains plagued by intimidation and corruption. Guatemala's banking and finance score is 1 point worse this year; however, its trade policy score is 0.5 point better, its fiscal burden of government score is 0.2 point better, and its government intervention score and capital flows and foreign investment score are both 1 point better. As a result, Guatemala's overall score is 0.17 point better this year.

TRADE POLICY
Score: **2.5**–Better (moderate level of protectionism)

According to the World Bank, Guatemala's weighted average tariff rate in 2004 was 4.9 percent, down from the 5.8 percent in 2001 reported in the 2005 *Index*, based on World Bank data. Red tape and customs corruption hinder trade. "Imports are generally not subject to non-tariff trade barriers," reports the U.S. Department of Commerce, "though there are occasional cases of arbitrary customs valuation and excessive bureaucratic obstacles." Based on the lower tariff rate, as well as a revision of the trade factor methodology, Guatemala's trade policy score is 0.5 point better this year.

FISCAL BURDEN OF GOVERNMENT
Score—Income Taxation: **3**–Stable (moderate tax rates)
Score—Corporate Taxation: **4**–Better (high tax rates)
Score—Change in Government Expenditures: **3.5**–Worse (low increase)
Final Score: **3.6**–Better (high cost of government)

According to Deloitte, Guatemala's top income tax rate is 31 percent. The top corporate tax rate is also 31 percent, down from the 35 percent reported in the 2005 *Index*. In 2003, based on data from the central bank, government expenditures as a share of GDP increased 1 percentage point to 13.4 percent, compared to a 0.5 percentage point decrease in 2002. On net, Guatemala's fiscal burden of government score is 0.2 point better this year.

GOVERNMENT INTERVENTION IN THE ECONOMY
Score: **1**–Better (very low level)

The World Bank reports that the government consumed 4.9 percent of GDP in 2003, down from the 7.6 percent reported in the 2005 *Index*. In the same year, based on data from the Ministry of Public Finance, Guatemala received 2.28 percent of its total revenues from state-owned enterprises and government ownership of property, down from the 5.04 percent reported in the

2005 *Index*. As a result, Guatemala's government intervention score is 1 point better this year.

MONETARY POLICY
Score: **3**–Stable (moderate level of inflation)

From 1995 to 2004, Guatemala's weighted average annual rate of inflation was 6.98 percent.

CAPITAL FLOWS AND FOREIGN INVESTMENT
Score: **3**–Better (moderate barriers)

Guatemala grants foreign investors national treatment and allows the full repatriation of profits. The Economist Intelligence Unit reports that restrictions on foreign investment include prohibition of "rendering of licensed professional services" by foreign firms and limits on foreign ownership of domestic airlines, newspapers and commercial radio stations, mining and forestry operations, petroleum operations, and real estate. According to the U.S. Department of Commerce, "Though Guatemala passed a foreign investment law in 1998 to streamline and facilitate foreign investment, time-consuming administrative procedures, arbitrary bureaucratic impediments and judicial decisions, a high crime rate and corruption" impede investment. Minerals, petroleum, and natural resources are considered the property of the state. The International Monetary Fund reports that residents and non-residents may hold foreign exchange accounts. There are no restrictions or controls on payments, transactions, and transfers. Based on evidence that foreign investment is welcomed in most sectors, Guatemala's capital flows and foreign investment score is 1 point better this year.

BANKING AND FINANCE
Score: **3**–Worse (moderate level of restrictions)

According to the International Monetary Fund, "Prudential norms have been tightened under the new legal and regulatory framework adopted in 2002; bank supervision has been strengthened; and offshore banks have been brought into the regulatory framework." The Economist Intelligence Unit reports that 25 banks, one of which was foreign, were operating in Guatemala as of October 2004. The government owns or partially owns two of the nation's largest banks, which account for slightly less than 10 percent of total banking assets. The U.S. Department of Commerce reports that "recent progress in money laundering and bank regulatory reform led to Guatemala's removal from the Financial Action Task Force's list of non-cooperating countries in the fight against money laundering in July 2004." According to the EIU, "Foreign corporations are legally prohibited from writing most kinds of insurance, though they may offer a full product line through local subsidiaries." Based on evidence of government involvement in the banking sector and restrictions on financial activities, Guatemala's banking and finance score is 1 point worse this year.

WAGES AND PRICES
Score: **2**–Stable (low level of intervention)

According to the Economist Intelligence Unit, "Guatemala has no price controls and is gradually eliminating subsidies on various economic activities and products (such as fuel).... [T]he government maintains some 24,000 direct subsidies, among them a Q[uetzal]12,000-per-house subsidy on construction costs." Guatemala has a minimum wage law, but the U.S. Department of State reports that noncompliance is common in the rural and informal sectors.

PROPERTY RIGHTS
Score: **4**–Stable (low level of protection)

The Economist Intelligence Unit characterizes the judicial system as "backlogged and often influenced by political machinations." According to the U.S. Department of Commerce, "Resolution of business disputes through Guatemala's judicial system is time-consuming and often unreliable. Civil cases can take as long as a decade to resolve.... Corruption in the judiciary is not uncommon." In addition, "Land invasions by squatters are increasingly common in rural areas. It can be difficult to obtain and enforce eviction notices, as land title is often clouded and the police tend to avoid actions against squatters that could provoke violence."

REGULATION
Score: **4**–Stable (high level)

Vague regulations cause significant bureaucratic obstacles to establishing a business. According to the U.S. Department of Commerce, problems include "time-consuming administrative procedures, arbitrary bureaucratic impediments, corruption, and a sometimes anti-business attitude of the current administration." In addition, "regulations often contain few explicit criteria for government administrators, resulting in ambiguous requirements that are applied inconsistently or retroactively by different government agencies." The Economist Intelligence Unit reports that labor laws are somewhat rigid.

INFORMAL MARKET
Score: **4**–Stable (high level of activity)

Transparency International's 2004 score for Guatemala is 2.2. Therefore, Guatemala's informal market score is 4 this year.

GUINEA

Rank: 127

Score: 3.55

Category: Mostly Unfree

Present & Past Scores

(Best) 1
2
3 3.29 3.13 3.39 3.16 3.19 3.34 3.21 3.45 3.26 3.24 3.33 3.55
4
(Worst) 5
'95 '96 '97 '98 '99 '00 '01 '02 '03 '04 '05 '06

QUICK STUDY

SCORES

Trade Policy	5
Fiscal Burden	4
Government Intervention	1.5
Monetary Policy	4
Foreign Investment	4
Banking and Finance	3
Wages and Prices	2
Property Rights	4
Regulation	4
Informal Market	4

Population: 7,908,905

Total area: 245,857 sq. km

GDP: $3.4 billion

GDP growth rate: 1.2%

GDP per capita: $431

Major exports: bauxite, gold, aluminum, diamonds, coffee, agricultural products

Exports of goods and services: $760.7 million

Major export trading partners: South Korea 14.6%, Spain 10.5%, US 9.9%, Russia 8.9%, France 8.7%

Major imports: petroleum products, metals, transport equipment, machinery

Imports of goods and services: $947.5 million

Major import trading partners: France 16.2%, China 9.0%, Belgium 6.9%, Italy 6.4%

Foreign direct investment (net): $5.7 million

2003 Data (in constant 2000 US dollars)

P resident Lansana Conte has ruled Guinea since seizing power in a 1984 military coup and, despite health concerns, won a 2003 election that was boycotted by all major opposition parties because of questions about the electoral system's fairness. The president's party won 91 of 114 seats in the 2002 legislative election, also boycotted by major opposition parties. Should Conte become incapacitated or die, whether through violence or because of poor health, there could be substantial disruption because there is no clear successor. The government is marked by corruption, lack of transparency, and extra-budgetary expenditures. Opposition to economic reform among many high-level officials raises doubts about Guinea's ability to meet multilateral donors' reform expectations, upon which debt relief hinges. Electricity and water shortages are common. Economic growth will depend on performance in traditional economic activities, particularly mining and agriculture. More than three-quarters of the population is engaged in subsistence agriculture. Mining is also important: Bauxite, aluminum, gold, and diamonds accounted for more than 85 percent of export earnings in 2002. The government controls prices on key goods, such as rice and fuel, although it has been forced to raise prices on fuel. Guinea's fiscal burden of government score is 0.3 point better this year; however, its trade policy score is 0.5 point worse, and its monetary policy score and banking and finance score are both 1 point worse. As a result, Guinea's overall score is 0.22 point worse this year.

 ### TRADE POLICY
Score: 5–Worse (very high level of protectionism)

According to the World Bank, Guinea's weighted average tariff rate in 2002 (the most recent year for which World Bank data are available) was 18.6 percent, up from the 13.9 percent in 2002 reported in the 2005 *Index*, based on World Bank data. (The revised figure for 2002 was based on correspondence with the Bank.) According to the U.S. Department of Commerce, importers need a formal import authorization from the central bank to import quantities that exceed US$5,000 in value, and corruption "remains a significant factor in clearing products through customs." Based on the higher tariff rate, as well as a revision of the trade factor methodology, Guinea's trade policy score is 0.5 point worse this year.

 ### FISCAL BURDEN OF GOVERNMENT
Score—Income Taxation: 4–Stable (high tax rates)
Score—Corporate Taxation: 4.5–Stable (very high tax rates)
Score—Change in Government Expenditures: 3–Better (very low decrease)
Final Score: 4–Better (high cost of government)

The International Monetary Fund reports that Guinea's top income tax rate is 40 percent. The top corporate tax rate is 35 percent. In 2003, according to the African Development Bank, government expenditures as a share of GDP remained unchanged at 18.3 percent, compared to a 1.1 percentage point increase in 2002. On net, Guinea's fiscal burden of government score is 0.3 point better this year.

 ### GOVERNMENT INTERVENTION IN THE ECONOMY
Score: 1.5–Stable (low level)

The World Bank reports that the government consumed 7.5 percent of GDP in 2003. In the same year, based on data from the International Monetary Fund, Guinea received 1.46 percent

201

of its total revenues from state-owned enterprises and government ownership of property.

MONETARY POLICY
Score: **4**–Worse (high level of inflation)

From 1995 to 2004, based on data from the International Monetary Fund's *2005 World Economic Outlook*, Guinea's weighted average annual rate of inflation was 14.60 percent, up from the 9.61 percent from 1994 to 2003 reported in the 2005 *Index*. As a result, Guinea's monetary policy score is 1 point worse this year.

CAPITAL FLOWS AND FOREIGN INVESTMENT
Score: **4**–Stable (high barriers)

Guinea's investment code welcomes foreign investment and provides national treatment to foreign investors, but investment is still hampered by corruption and bureaucratic inefficiency. The lack of basic services also poses a disincentive. The Economist Intelligence Unit reports that "provision of the most basic services (water, sanitation and electricity) remains virtually non-existant in most parts of the country…. The non-delivery of basic services deters all but the most adventurous of those willing to invest." According to the U.S. Department of Commerce, "Businesspersons assert that application procedures are sufficiently opaque to allow for significant corruption, and regulatory activity is often applied based on personal interest…. The business and political cultures encourage corruption. Business is routinely conducted through the payment of bribes rather than by the rule of law." Foreign investors are restricted from majority ownership in radio, television, and newspapers. The International Monetary Fund reports that both residents and non-residents may hold foreign exchange accounts, but residents may hold such accounts abroad only with central bank approval. Payments and transfers are subject to government approval in some cases, and repatriation is controlled. All capital transfers through the official exchange market and many capital transactions, including all real estate transactions and all outward direct investment, must be authorized by the central bank.

BANKING AND FINANCE
Score: **3**–Worse (moderate level of restrictions)

There are few restrictions on banks, and foreign banks are welcome. Most banks are in private hands pursuant to a massive privatization in the late 1980s and early 1990s. According to the Economist Intelligence Unit, "The financial sector consists of the [central bank], six deposit-taking banks, four insurance companies, a social security institution, two small co-operative banks and some 50 or so bureaux de change. The financial sector is largely controlled by foreign-owned banks…. The banking system is progressively gaining public confidence, as demonstrated by the steady rise in demand deposits." Overall, however, Guinea's banking system remains fragile and unable to meet the private sector's development needs. The

EIU reports that recent attempts by the governor of the central bank to seek reimbursement from two individuals may have been politically motivated and that, "given the regional instability," Guinea's banks "are risk averse, and therefore prefer to finance trade, lending at high real interest rates." On net, Guinea's banking and finance score is 1 point worse this year.

WAGES AND PRICES
Score: **2**–Stable (low level of intervention)

The market determines most prices. The government has made some significant progress in privatization but still influences prices through the state-owned utilities. Under the labor code, the government can set a minimum wage by decree, but it has not yet done so.

PROPERTY RIGHTS
Score: **4**–Stable (low level of protection)

Property is weakly protected in Guinea. According to the U.S. Department of Commerce, "Although the Guinean constitution creates an independent judiciary, businesspersons frequently claim that poorly trained magistrates, high levels of corruption, and nepotism plague the administration of justice." The government intends to reform the judiciary with the help of international donor agencies. To that end, it established an arbitration court in 1999, but much remains to be done.

REGULATION
Score: **4**–Stable (high level)

Red tape and a large bureaucracy deter investment. The U.S. Department of Commerce reports that "Guinea's laws are designed to promote free enterprise and competition. According to local and expatriate businesspersons, the government lacks transparency in the application of the law. Businesspersons assert that application procedures are sufficiently opaque to allow for significant corruption, and regulatory activity is often applied based on personal interest." In addition, "rampant corruption negatively impacts even the most basic business transactions. Virtually every U.S. company and U.S. businessperson with ties to Guinea has reported one or more of the following experiences: an arbitrary tax assessment… requests from government officials for specific gifts, pressure to participate in government infrastructure projects that were not in the company's best interest, pressure to hire certain individuals, threats of or actual imprisonment, impounding of vehicles, and closure of the business's office."

INFORMAL MARKET
Score: **4**–Stable (high level of activity)

Guinea has an active informal market. According to the Economist Intelligence Unit, "Also thriving is the informal sector (by definition unrecorded), which satisfies the needs of much of the population. Formal sector manufacturing represents less than 4% of GDP."

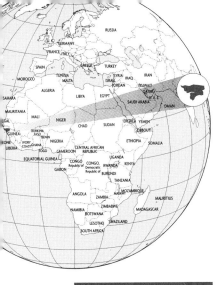

GUINEA–BISSAU

Rank: 131

Score: 3.65

Category: Mostly Unfree

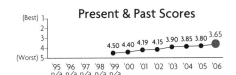

Present & Past Scores

(Best) 1
2
3
4
(Worst) 5

4.50 4.40 4.19 4.15 3.90 3.85 3.80 3.65

'95 '96 '97 '98 '99 '00 '01 '02 '03 '04 '05 '06
n/a n/a n/a n/a n/a

QUICK STUDY

SCORES

Trade Policy	4.5
Fiscal Burden	4
Government Intervention	2
Monetary Policy	1
Foreign Investment	3
Banking and Finance	4
Wages and Prices	3
Property Rights	5
Regulation	5
Informal Market	5

Population: 1,489,209

Total area: 36,120 sq. km

GDP: $201.5 million

GDP growth rate: 0.6%

GDP per capita: $135

Major exports: cashew nuts, fish and shrimp

Exports of goods and services: $76.3 million

Major export trading partners: India 66.9%, Nigeria 16.8%, Italy 7.7%

Major imports: foodstuffs, petroleum products

Imports of goods and services: $84 million

Major import trading partners: Senegal 20.6%, Portugal 16.7%, China 10.7%, Italy 10.1%

Foreign direct investment (net): $1.9 million

2003 Data (in constant 2000 US dollars)

Guinea-Bissau is one of the world's poorest countries and has a history of instability. A September 2003 military coup forced President Kumba Yala to resign after he postponed the legislative elections, dismissed the prime minister, and dissolved the National Assembly. The military appointed a civilian transitional government, and legislative elections were held in March 2004. An October 2004 mutiny by soldiers demanding back pay resulted in the death of the army chief of staff. The June 2005 presidential election had a high turnout and was judged to be free and fair by international observers. Two former rulers, Yala and João Bernardo Vieira, were among the contenders in spite of being banned from politics under the transitional charter. The initial vote did not result in a clear majority. Significantly, Yala accepted his loss and announced that he will abide by the run-off election between Vieira and Malam Bacai Sanha of the ruling party. Agriculture and forestry comprise the bulk of GDP, and cashew nuts are the primary export. Instability has greatly hindered economic growth, and parts of the economy have reverted to barter during the worst disruptions. Guinea-Bissau's fiscal burden of government score is 1 point worse this year; however, its government intervention score is 0.5 point better, and its monetary policy score and banking and finance score are both 1 point better. As a result, Guinea-Bissau's overall score is 0.15 point better this year.

TRADE POLICY
Score: **4.5**–Stable (very high level of protectionism)

Guinea–Bissau is a member of the West African Economic and Monetary Union (WAEMU.) According to the World Bank, Guinea–Bissau's weighted average tariff rate in 2004 was 13.6 percent, down from the 14.3 percent in 2001 reported in the 2005 *Index*, based on World Bank data. The International Monetary Fund reports abuses in customs, including irregularities in the valuation of imports and difficulty tracking and monitoring goods. Based on the revised trade factor methodology, Guinea–Bissau's trade policy score is unchanged.

FISCAL BURDEN OF GOVERNMENT
Score—Income Taxation: **2**–Stable (low tax rates)
Score—Corporate Taxation: **4.5**–Stable (very high tax rates)
Score—Change in Government Expenditures: **5**–Worse (very high increase)
Final Score: **4**–Worse (high cost of government)

The International Monetary Fund reports that Guinea–Bissau's top income tax rate is 20 percent. According to Deloitte, the top corporate tax rate is 35 percent. In 2003, according to the African Development Bank, government expenditures as a share of GDP increased 3.7 percentage points to 37.1 percent, compared to a 9.6 percentage point decrease in 2002. On net, Guinea–Bissau's fiscal burden of government score is 1 point worse this year.

GOVERNMENT INTERVENTION IN THE ECONOMY
Score: **2**–Better (low level)

The World Bank reports that the government consumed 13 percent of GDP in 2003. In the same year, based on data from the International Monetary Fund, Guinea–Bissau received 3.93 percent of its total revenues from state-owned enterprises and government ownership of property, down from the 6.83 percent reported in the 2005 *Index*. As a result, Guinea–Bissau's government intervention score is 0.5 point better this year.

MONETARY POLICY
Score: **1–Better** (very low level of inflation)

As a member of the West African Economic and Monetary Union, Guinea–Bissau uses the CFA franc, pegged to the euro. From 1995 to 2004, Guinea–Bissau's weighted average annual rate of inflation was 0.26 percent, down from the 3.34 percent from 1994 to 2003 reported in the 2005 *Index*. As a result, Guinea–Bissau's monetary policy score is 1 point better this year.

 CAPITAL FLOWS AND FOREIGN INVESTMENT
Score: **3–Stable** (moderate barriers)

Political and economic instability, a weak infrastructure, an unskilled workforce, and a small local market have discouraged foreign investment in Guinea–Bissau. However, there is some foreign investment in the fishing industry and oil exploration, and there is potential for foreign investment in the mining sector. The government has entered into agreements with foreign oil companies, allowing them to fund all exploration costs, and the state-owned PetroGuin oil company will bear 30 percent of the costs if commercial operations are approved. The investment code provides for investment incentives and guarantees against nationalization and expropriation. The International Monetary Fund reports that non-residents may hold foreign exchange accounts with permission of the Central Bank of West African States, or BCEAO, and residents may hold them with permission of the Ministry of Finance and the BCEAO. Capital transfers to members of the WAEMU are unrestricted, aside from direct investments, which require government authorization. The government must approve most personal capital movements between residents and non-residents, such as personal loans, gifts or inheritances, or transfer of assets.

 BANKING AND FINANCE
Score: **4–Better** (high level of restrictions)

The BCEAO, a central bank common to the eight members of the WAEMU, governs Guinea–Bissau's banking system. According to the Economist Intelligence Unit, "There is one commercial bank, Banco Africano Ocidental, which was established in 2001 with local and Portuguese capital.... All banks were closed during the civil war and only reopened in July 1999. Banking has been severely weakened, as local businesses were decapitalised during the war and many loans are now unrecoverable." Of the other two banks that were active briefly after the conflict, the Banco Totta & Acores withdrew from the country in March 2002, and the Banco Internationales da Guiné–Bissau has been liquidated. Although armed violence has subsided and the economy is recovering, Guinea–Bissau's banking system remains in transition. On net, Guinea–Bissau's banking and finance score is 1 point better this year.

 WAGES AND PRICES
Score: **3–Stable** (moderate level of intervention)

Although the government has liberalized some prices, it still continues to influence the prices of many goods and services. The government influences prices through state-owned enterprises in the electricity, water, and transport sectors. According to the *Financial Times*, it also directly controls the price of cashew nuts, which account for 95 percent of exports. The Council of Ministers sets a minimum wage annually for various categories of work.

 PROPERTY RIGHTS
Score: **5–Stable** (very low level of protection)

Protection of property in Guinea–Bissau is extremely weak. According to the U.S. Department of State, "The Constitution provides for an independent judiciary; however, in the past, the judiciary was subject to executive influence and control, and members of the Supreme Court were appointed and often replaced by the former President. During the year, the judiciary made major strides in establishing its constitutional independence...and in conjunction with regional courts, began hearing case backlogs.... [J]udges continued to be poorly trained and paid and sometimes were subject to corruption." In addition, "Traditional practices still prevailed in most rural areas, and persons who lived in urban areas often brought judicial disputes to traditional counselors to avoid the costs and bureaucratic impediments of the official system. The police often resolved disputes."

 REGULATION
Score: **5–Stable** (very high level)

According to the Economist Intelligence Unit, "the greatest risk [for investors] arises from the country's political instability, depressed business environment, periodic inability of the government to honour its financial and commercial obligations, and slow, weakly functioning local institutions on which investors or other foreign parties may depend. Enforcement of contracts cannot be assured through the local justice system." The same source reports that corruption is a substantial problem in the public sector.

 INFORMAL MARKET
Score: **5–Stable** (very high level of activity)

Guinea–Bissau's informal market is so large that it eclipses the legal market. The U.S. Department of State reports that "Guinea–Bissau has an unofficial money transfer system...." According to the Economist Intelligence Unit, "there is an active trade in smuggled diamonds from Guinea–Conakry and Liberia" as well as "a thriving regional trade in food products, which is unrecorded. Large amounts of exports of fishing products also appear to be unrecorded."

GUYANA

Rank: 85

Score: 3.11

Category: Mostly Unfree

Present & Past Scores

(Best) 1
2
3 3.70 3.38 3.40 3.55 3.30 3.35 3.35 3.23 3.15 3.08 3.08 3.11
4
(Worst) 5
'95 '96 '97 '98 '99 '00 '01 '02 '03 '04 '05 '06

QUICK STUDY

SCORES

Trade Policy	4
Fiscal Burden	4.1
Government Intervention	3
Monetary Policy	2
Foreign Investment	3
Banking and Finance	2
Wages and Prices	2
Property Rights	3
Regulation	4
Informal Market	4

Population: 768,888

Total area: 214,970 sq. km

GDP: $724.4 million

GDP growth rate: −0.6%

GDP per capita: $942

Major exports: sugar, gold, aluminum, bauxite, rice, rum, timber

Exports of goods (fob): $512.8 million

Major export trading partners: Canada 24.5%, US 20.9%, UK 13.1%, Jamaica 5.9%

Major imports: machinery, food, manufactures, petroleum

Imports of goods (fob): $571.7 million

Major import trading partners: US 22.5%, Trinidad and Tobago 19.2%, Italy 11.2%, UK 7.2%, Cuba 5.3%

Foreign direct investment (net): $24.1 million

2003 Data (in constant 2000 US dollars)

According to the Economist Intelligence Unit, Guyana's ruling party (People's Progressive Party–Civic) and opposition party (People's National Congress–Reform) remain suspicious of each other and have been unable to reach compromise even on minor issues. The country still depends heavily on foreign aid. The government has implemented some structural reforms in the fiscal and procurement process under an agreement with the World Bank and the International Monetary Fund and plans to use more aid funds on infrastructure and social spending aimed at alleviating poverty. Severe flooding of coastal areas in 2005 led to extensive crop losses and major infrastructure damage and is also bound to have a profound impact on fiscal restraint. The government is looking to secure private investment in the two most important sectors of the economy—sugar and bauxite—and is still negotiating the liberalization of the telecommunications sector, which could help to develop subsectors such as call centers and Internet connections. Guyana's fiscal burden of government score is 0.3 point worse this year. As a result, its overall score is 0.03 point worse this year.

TRADE POLICY
Score: **4–Stable** (high level of protectionism)

As a member of the Caribbean Community and Common Market (CARICOM), Guyana has a common external tariff rate that ranges from 5 percent to 20 percent. According to the World Bank, Guyana's weighted average tariff rate in 2001 (the most recent year for which World Bank data are available) was 10.6 percent. The World Trade Organization reports that "Guyana applies import licensing requirements on a relatively large number of products…[including] some important products of national industries, such as rice and cane sugar, and some of the most significant imports." The U.S. Department of Commerce reports delays and accusations of corruption in customs. Based on the revised trade factor methodology, Guyana's trade policy score is unchanged.

FISCAL BURDEN OF GOVERNMENT
Score—Income Taxation: **3–Stable** (moderate tax rates)
Score—Corporate Taxation: **5–Stable** (very high tax rates)
Score—Change in Government Expenditures: **3.5–Worse** (low increase)
Final Score: **4.1–Worse** (high cost of government)

Guyana's top income tax rate is 33.3 percent. The top corporate tax rate is 45 percent. In 2003, based on data from the Bank of Guyana, government expenditures as a share of GDP increased 0.5 percentage point to 44.1 percent, compared to a 1.2 percentage point decrease in 2002. On net, Guyana's fiscal burden of government score is 0.3 point worse this year.

GOVERNMENT INTERVENTION IN THE ECONOMY
Score: **3–Stable** (moderate level)

The World Bank reports that the government consumed 27.7 percent of GDP in 2003. In the same year, based on data from the central bank, Guyana received 9.44 percent of its total revenues from state-owned enterprises and government ownership of property.

MONETARY POLICY
Score: **2**–Stable (low level of inflation)

From 1995 to 2004, Guyana's weighted average annual rate of inflation was 5.02 percent.

CAPITAL FLOWS AND FOREIGN INVESTMENT
Score: **3**–Stable (moderate barriers)

Although Guyana's investment regime can be bureaucratic, non-transparent, and slow, it is becoming more attractive to foreign investors. According to the U.S. Department of Commerce, although Guyana has been moving toward a more welcoming environment for foreign investors, the government remains cautious about approving new foreign investment and encourages joint ventures with the government. The International Monetary Fund reports that both residents involved in exporting activities (subject to approval) and non-residents may hold foreign exchange accounts. Payments and transfers are not restricted. The IMF reports that, while most capital transactions are unrestricted, all credit operations are controlled. Guyana's constitution guarantees the right of foreigners to own property or land.

BANKING AND FINANCE
Score: **2**–Stable (low level of restrictions)

Guyana's banking system is becoming more competitive but remains underdeveloped and hindered by few sound lending opportunities. According to the Economist Intelligence Unit, non-performing loans have fallen sharply as a percent of total lending, from 37 percent in 2002 to 18 percent in 2004. However, the improvement is largely due to debt write-offs, and some banks remain burdened by bad debt. There are six commercial banks, the two largest of which—the Bank of Nova Scotia and National Bank of Industry and Commerce (NBIC)—are foreign-owned. In March 2003, the last state-owned bank, the Guyana National Co-Operative Bank (GNCB), was sold to the NBIC. The International Monetary Fund reports that banks must obtain approval from the Ministry of Finance before lending to non-resident enterprises. In June 2003, Guyana opened a stock exchange, with 11 local companies listed. The government has announced its intention to finance a loan scheme for poor farmers in the interior of the country.

WAGES AND PRICES
Score: **2**–Stable (low level of intervention)

The market determines most prices, but the government affects prices through some state-owned enterprises and the sugar industry, which the Economist Intelligence Unit reports accounted for 12 percent of GDP in 2003. The Labor Act and the Wages Council Act give the Labor Minister the authority to set minimum wages, but Guyana does not have a legislated private-sector minimum wage.

PROPERTY RIGHTS
Score: **3**–Stable (moderate level of protection)

Guyana's judicial system is often slow, inefficient, and subject to corruption. According to the U.S. Department of State, "The Constitution provides for an independent judiciary, but law enforcement officials and prominent lawyers questioned the independence of the judiciary and accused the Government of intervening in certain cases." In addition, "Delays in judicial proceedings are caused by shortages of trained court personnel and magistrates, inadequate resources…occasional alleged acts of bribery, poor tracking of cases, and slowness of police preparing cases for trial."

REGULATION
Score: **4**–Stable (high level)

Some sectors of the economy, such as utilities and other state-owned industries, are highly regulated, and the bureaucracy is extensive. "Bureaucratic procedures are cumbersome and time-consuming," reports the U.S. Department of Commerce. "Decision-making is centralized and businesspersons, both Guyanese and foreign, say it is often difficult to know who the decision-makers are on a given issue or what the rationale was for decisions made. One of the biggest obstacles in establishing a business is navigating land deeds and title registries. Getting clear title to land is one of the most frequent administrative difficulties for prospective businesses." In addition, businessmen complain that "government officials have solicited bribes as a prerequisite for the granting of licenses and permits needed to operate their businesses."

INFORMAL MARKET
Score: **4**–Stable (high level of activity)

Guyana has a large informal market. The U.S. Department of State's *International Narcotics Control Strategy* report indicates that the informal economy, driven largely by drug proceeds, could be equivalent to from 50 percent to 60 percent of formal sector economic activity.

2006 Index of Economic Freedom

HAITI

Rank: 147

Score: 4.03

Category: Repressed

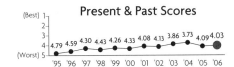

E stablishing order, mending government institutions, holding free elections, energizing a weak economy, and paying down its $1.4 billion external debt have been priorities for Haiti's interim government since the 2004 resignation of President Jean-Bertrand Aristide. Violence continues to afflict the capital and major provincial towns as Haiti's 4,000-member police force, assisted by security forces from the U.N. Stabilization Mission, attempts to dismantle armed gangs and criminals. The U.S. Department of State reports that poorly functioning judicial and penal systems hamper the processing of those charged with crimes, and many of the prisons destroyed during the uprising that led to Aristide's departure have not been rehabilitated. More than 100 parties signed up to take part in local and national elections scheduled for late 2005. However, in March 2005, only $220 million of $1.3 billion in reconstruction aid had been disbursed. Following the property destruction and business closures associated with the collapse of the Aristide regime, coupled with subsequent flood damage, economic growth came to a halt. In January 2005, Haiti repaid $52 million in over-due World Bank interest payments, permitting the disbursement of $73 million in new credit. Haiti's fiscal burden of government score is 0.4 point worse this year, but its trade policy score is 1 point better. As a result, Haiti's overall score is 0.06 point better this year.

QUICK STUDY

SCORES

Trade Policy	2.5
Fiscal Burden	4.3
Government Intervention	3
Monetary Policy	5
Foreign Investment	4
Banking and Finance	4
Wages and Prices	3
Property Rights	5
Regulation	5
Informal Market	4.5

Population: 8,439,799

Total area: 27,750 sq. km

GDP: $3.9 billion

GDP growth rate: 0.4%

GDP per capita: $467

Major exports: coffee, cocoa, mangoes, oil

Exports of goods and services: $646.9 million

Major export trading partners: US 83.6%, Dominican Republic 6.4%, Canada 3.6%

Major imports: raw material, machinery and equipment, fuels, foodstuffs

Imports of goods and services: $1.9 billion

Major import trading partners: US 54.8%, Dominican Republic 6.0%, Colombia 2.9%

Foreign direct investment (net): $6.9 million

2003 Data (in constant 2000 US dollars)

TRADE POLICY
Score: **2.5**–Better (moderate level of protectionism)

The World Trade Organization reports that Haiti's average tariff rate in 2003 (the most recent year for which WTO data are available) was 2.9 percent, down from the 9 percent in 2003 reported in the 2005 *Index*, based on World Bank data. According to the U.S. Department of Commerce, the inefficiency of the state-owned international seaport remains a significant barrier, and "corruption among customs officers is a serious problem: bribes are sometimes demanded to clear shipments." Imports of agricultural products require a license. Based on the lower tariff rate, as well as a revision of the trade factor methodology, Haiti's trade policy score is 1 point better this year.

FISCAL BURDEN OF GOVERNMENT
Score—Income Taxation: **3**–Stable (moderate tax rates)
Score—Corporate Taxation: **4.5**–Stable (very high tax rates)
Score—Change in Government Expenditures: **5**–Worse (very high increase)
Final Score: **4.3**–Worse (high cost of government)

According to the International Monetary Fund, Haiti's top income tax rate is 30 percent. Deloitte reports that the top corporate income tax rate is 35 percent. In 2003, according to the central bank, government expenditures as a share of GDP increased 4 percentage points to 15.1 percent, compared to a 1 percentage point increase in 2002. On net, Haiti's fiscal burden of government score is 0.4 point worse this year.

GOVERNMENT INTERVENTION IN THE ECONOMY
Score: **3**–Stable (moderate level)

Based on United Nations data, the government consumed 10 percent of GDP in 2002. According to the U.S. Department of Commerce, the government still owns several major enterprises: "None of the major infrastructure-related enterprises (the airport, seaport, telephone company, or electric company) have been privatized. The privatization of two state-held banks as well as an essential oil plant is also unlikely in the near future."

MONETARY POLICY
Score: **5**–Stable (very high level of inflation)

From 1995 to 2004, Haiti's weighted average annual rate of inflation was 25.08 percent.

CAPITAL FLOWS AND FOREIGN INVESTMENT
Score: **4**–Stable (high barriers)

Haiti has made efforts to attract foreign investment. "Some investments, however, still require special government authorization," according to the U.S. Department of Commerce. "Investments in electricity, water, and telecommunications require both government concession and approval. Additionally, investments in the public health sector must first receive authorization." There are restrictions on foreign ownership of land. The U.S. Department of Commerce reports numerous unofficial barriers to investment, including judicial inadequacies, lack of transparency, corruption, inefficient bureaucracy, poor financial services, and a paucity of clear and enforceable laws and regulations. Political instability also hinders foreign investment. The government intends to remove discrimination against foreign investors, but the U.S. Department of Commerce reports that its "commitment to modernize commercial laws, investment, banking, and tax codes has not produced results." The International Monetary Fund reports that residents may hold foreign exchange accounts only for specified purposes and that non-residents may hold them without restriction. There are no restrictions on payments, transfers, or capital transactions.

BANKING AND FINANCE
Score: **4**–Stable (high level of restrictions)

Haiti's banking sector remains undeveloped. The U.S. Department of Commerce reports that there are seven locally incorporated banks, two foreign banks, a private development financial institution, two mortgage banks, and two state-owned banks. According to the Economist Intelligence Unit, the two state-owned banks accounted for approximately 10 percent of total bank deposits in 2004. The International Monetary Fund notes that non-performing loans rose to 8.3 percent as of December 2004. According to the U.S. Department of State, "banks are not required to comply with internationally recognized accounting standards, or to be audited by internationally recognized accounting firms.... Nonetheless, most private banks follow international accounting norms and use consolidated reporting." Credit is available on market terms, and banks may offer a full range of banking services, but poor records and lack of proper titles hinder access to credit. The EIU notes that instability makes banks reluctant to extend new loans.

WAGES AND PRICES
Score: **3**–Stable (moderate level of intervention)

The government influences prices. "There is no set pricing structure in Haiti," reports the U.S. Department of Commerce, "but the government does impose restrictions on the mark-up of some products. For example, retailers are prohibited from marking up pharmaceutical products by more than 40 percent." In addition, "Primary export products benefit from a price insurance fund called Stabex, part of a system created to compensate for losses due to world price fluctuations." The government also influences prices through the extensive state-owned sector, which includes (but is not limited to) enterprises in the telecommunications, energy, port, airport, agriculture, and banking sectors. A tripartite commission composed of six members appointed by the president sets Haiti's minimum daily wage.

PROPERTY RIGHTS
Score: **5**–Stable (very low level of protection)

Property is not secure in Haiti. According to the U.S. Department of Commerce, "The protection and guarantees that Haitian law extends to investors are severely compromised by weak enforcement mechanisms, a lack of updated laws to handle modern commercial practices and a dysfunctional, resource-poor legal system. Business litigants are often frustrated with the legal process and most commercial disputes are settled out of court." In addition, "widespread corruption has allowed disputing parties to purchase favorable outcomes."

REGULATION
Score: **5**–Stable (very high level)

It is virtually impossible to open a business legally under Haitian law. According to *The Economist*, "it takes 203 days to register a new company...." The U.S. Department of Commerce characterizes Haitian law as "deficient in a number of areas, including...publication of laws, regulations and official notices; establishment of companies; land tenure and real property law and procedures; bank and credit operations; insurance and pension regulation; accounting standards; civil status documentation; customs law and administration; international trade and investment promotion; foreign investment regime; and regulation of market concentration and competition." The same source reports that businesses cite corruption as an impediment to investing in Haiti.

INFORMAL MARKET
Score: **4.5**–Stable (very high level of activity)

Transparency International's 2003 score for Haiti is 1.5. Therefore, Haiti's informal market score is 4.5 this year.

HONDURAS

Rank: 102

Score: 3.28

Category: Mostly Unfree

Present & Past Scores

(Best) 1
2
3 — 3.58 3.58 3.58 3.51 3.71 3.51 3.50 3.38 3.24 3.53 3.43 3.28
4
(Worst) 5
'95 '96 '97 '98 '99 '00 '01 '02 '03 '04 '05 '06

QUICK STUDY

SCORES

Trade Policy	3.5
Fiscal Burden	3.3
Government Intervention	3
Monetary Policy	3
Foreign Investment	3
Banking and Finance	2
Wages and Prices	3
Property Rights	4
Regulation	4
Informal Market	4

Population: 6,968,512

Total area: 112,090 sq. km

GDP: $6.45 billion

GDP growth rate: 3.0%

GDP per capita: $927

Major exports: coffee, bananas, shrimp, lobster, tobacco, fruit, timber

Exports of goods and services: $2.6 billion

Major export trading partners: US 66.1%, El Salvador 2.6%, Guatemala 2.4%

Major imports: manufactures and industrial raw materials, machinery and transport equipment, food and animal products

Imports of goods and services: $3.6 billion

Major import trading partners: US 54.0%, El Salvador 3.5%, Mexico 3.0%

Foreign direct investment (net): $186.9 million

2003 Data (in constant 2000 US dollars)

Democratic governance and a market economy continue to survive in Honduras despite pervasive poverty, violent crime, and a weak justice system. Coffee and bananas are the principal exports, and the Honduran clothing-assembly industry is the largest Central American exporter of textile products to the United States. Tourism is another rising sector, employing some 85,000 workers according to the Economist Intelligence Unit. Yet 45 percent of the population lives in extreme poverty. Unemployment has remained at about 28 percent from 2001–2004, according to the CIA *World Factbook*. The country may benefit, however, from DR–CAFTA. The U.S. Department of Commerce reports that it can take up to two months to register a new business in Honduras. Although no current data are available, INTERPOL has reported that Honduras had a murder rate of 154 per 100,000 in 1998, while the U.S. Department of State reports a 2003 murder rate of 53 per 100,000. Many homicides are attributable to gangs affiliated with groups in the United States, Mexico, and other Central American countries. Although Honduras has adopted stronger anti-crime laws, its justice system is undermanned and poorly paid, and its prisons are 200 percent over capacity. Honduras has signed a Millennium Challenge Account compact with the United States. Honduras's trade policy score is 0.5 point worse this year; however, its government intervention and foreign investment scores are both 1 point better. As a result, Honduras's overall score is 0.15 point better this year.

TRADE POLICY
Score: **3.5**–Worse (high level of protectionism)

According to the World Bank, Honduras's weighted average tariff rate in 2004 was 7.8 percent, up from the 7.3 percent in 2001 reported in the 2005 *Index*, based on World Bank data. The U.S. Department of Commerce reports limits on imports of corn, rice, and poultry. The World Trade Organization reports limited use of non-tariff barriers and lack of transparency in customs regulations. Based on the higher tariff rate, as well as a revision of the trade factor methodology, Honduras's trade policy score is 0.5 point worse this year.

FISCAL BURDEN OF GOVERNMENT
Score—Income Taxation: **2.5**–Stable (moderate tax rates)
Score—Corporate Taxation: **4**–Stable (high tax rates)
Score—Change in Government Expenditures: **2.5**–Stable (low decrease)
Final Score: **3.3**–Stable (moderate cost of government)

According to Deloitte, Honduras's top income tax rate is 25 percent. The top corporate tax rate is 30 percent (a 25 percent corporate tax rate plus a 5 percent temporary social contribution tax). In 2003, based on data from Honduras's central bank and the World Bank, government expenditures as a share of GDP decreased 1.8 percentage points to 26.8 percent, compared to the 0.6 percentage point decrease in 2002.

GOVERNMENT INTERVENTION IN THE ECONOMY
Score: **3**–Better (moderate level)

The World Bank reports that the government consumed 13.7 percent of GDP in 2003. In 2004, based on data from the Secretary of Finance, Honduras received 11.48 percent of its total revenues from state-owned enterprises and government ownership of property. Based on newly available data for revenues from state-owned enterprises, Honduras's government intervention score is 1 point better this year.

MONETARY POLICY
Score: **3**–Stable (moderate level of inflation)

From 1995 to 2004, Honduras's weighted average annual rate of inflation was 8.10 percent.

CAPITAL FLOWS AND FOREIGN INVESTMENT
Score: **3**–Better (moderate barriers)

Honduras welcomes foreign investment, which is generally accorded the same rights as domestic investment. According to the U.S. Department of Commerce, "Restrictions and performance requirements are fairly limited.... Honduras' investment climate is hampered by high levels of crime, a weak judicial system, high levels of corruption, low educational levels among the population, a troubled financial sector, and limited infrastructure." In addition, the constitution "requires that all foreign investment complement, but not substitute for, national investment." Government authorization is required for foreign investment in basic health services, telecommunications, electricity, air transport, fishing and hunting, exploration and exploitation of minerals, forestry, agriculture, insurance and financial services, and private education. Foreign ownership of land near the coast or along borders is generally prohibited but may be allowed in some cases with government permission. The International Monetary Fund reports that both residents and non-residents may hold foreign exchange accounts. Payments and transfers are not restricted, and few capital transactions require approval. Although Honduras restricts some investment, most barriers are informal. On net, Honduras's capital flows and foreign investment score is 1 point better this year.

BANKING AND FINANCE
Score: **2**–Stable (low level of restrictions)

Honduras's banking sector, according to the U.S. Department of Commerce, "is considered weak and in need of further consolidation." The Economist Intelligence Unit reports that the collapse of several banks in 1999, 2001, and 2002 has led to greater capital-adequacy rules, clarification of the role of the central bank, and greater oversight of banks' financial standing and offshore operations. "As of October 2004," reports the EIU, "there were 16 private commercial banks, two state-owned banks, two second-tier banks and three foreign bank representative offices operating in Honduras.... Most domestic banks are family-run and are tight-fisted in their lending practices. Often, only affiliated businesses and individuals are granted credit." State-owned bank operations have been sharply reduced in recent years. The U.S. Department of Commerce reports that seven of the 16 commercial banks have majority foreign ownership.

WAGES AND PRICES
Score: **3**–Stable (moderate level of intervention)

According to the U.S. Department of Commerce, "The Honduran government controls the prices for coffee and medicines, and regulates the prices of gasoline, diesel, and liquid propane gas. In addition, it keeps an informal control over prices of certain staple products such as milk and sugar, by pressuring producers and retailers to keep prices as low as possible." The government also influences prices through state-owned enterprises, which include (but are not limited to) enterprises in the telecommunications, port, electricity, highways, and postal sectors. A minimum wage system established in 2000 applies to all sectors of the economy but varies according to work and geographic area.

PROPERTY RIGHTS
Score: **4**–Stable (low level of protection)

Protection of property is weak. According to the U.S. Department of Commerce, "The most important political issues affecting the business climate in Honduras are the administration of justice and rule of law. The lack of judicial security, a deteriorating security environment, and endemic corruption pose real risks, making business disputes difficult to resolve." Expropriation of property is possible. "The Honduran government generally expropriates property for purposes of land reform," reports the U.S. Department of Commerce. "Compensation for land expropriated under the Agrarian Reform Law, when awarded, is paid in 20-year government bonds."

REGULATION
Score: **4**–Stable (high level)

Businesses are subject to significant red tape, lack of transparency, and the absence of an established rule of law. According to the U.S. Department of Commerce, "Honduran labor laws and the civil procedures code are outdated. The Honduran government often lacks the resources or political will to implement or enforce existing laws." The government also "does not publish regulations before they enter into force and there is no formal mechanism for providing proposed regulations to the public for comment. Procedural red tape to obtain government approval for investment activities is very common." Property registration often is not up to date, nor can the results of title searches be relied upon. The U.S. Trade Representative reports that corruption remains endemic.

INFORMAL MARKET
Score: **4**–Stable (high level of activity)

Transparency International's 2004 score for Honduras is 2.3. Therefore, Honduras's informal market score is 4 this year.

HONG KONG

Rank: 1

Score: 1.28

Category: Free

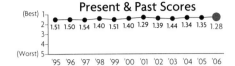

Present & Past Scores

(Best) 1
2 1.51 1.50 1.54 1.40 1.51 1.40 1.29 1.39 1.44 1.34 1.35 1.28
3
4
(Worst) 5
'95 '96 '97 '98 '99 '00 '01 '02 '03 '04 '05 '06

QUICK STUDY

SCORES

Trade Policy	1
Fiscal Burden	1.8
Government Intervention	1.5
Monetary Policy	1
Foreign Investment	1
Banking and Finance	1
Wages and Prices	2
Property Rights	1
Regulation	1
Informal Market	1.5

Population: 6,882,600

Total area: 1,092 sq. km

GDP: $186.6 billion

GDP growth rate: 8.1%

GDP per capita: $27,114

Major exports: insurance services, financial services, transportation, travel services, electrical machinery and apparatus, textiles, jewelry

Exports of goods and services: $311.1 billion

Major export trading partners: China 44.0%, US 16.9%, Japan 5.3%, UK 3.3%

Major imports: electrical machinery and appliances, telecommunications and sound equipment, travel services, transportation (a large share of which is re-exported)

Imports of goods and services: $299.5 billion

Major import trading partners: China 43.5%, Japan 12.1%, Taiwan 7.3%, US 5.3%

Foreign direct investment (net): –$5.7 billion

2004 Data (in constant 2000 US dollars)

The Special Administrative Region (SAR) of Hong Kong remains a model of economic freedom. It is a free port with no barriers to trade; has simple procedures for starting enterprises, free entry of foreign capital and repatriation of earnings, and transparency; and operates under the rule of law. The government has outlined a plan to balance the budget by fiscal year 2006–2007, primarily by reducing the size of the civil service to 160,000 by 2006–2007 from 2004 levels of 172,000. It also has raised the standard salary tax rate to 16 percent from 15 percent and has reduced personal tax deductions. Hong Kong weathered political storms during 2004 and 2005. After suffering a loss of confidence following massive pro-democracy demonstrations in 2003 and 2004, Chief Executive C. H. Tung finally announced his resignation in March 2005. Tung's departure raised hopes of early democratic reforms. Instead, China bent Hong Kong's constitutional strictures, announcing that Tung's successor would complete the term and run for re-election by the 800-person election committee in 2007. Because there is no provision in the Basic Law for election reforms prior to the 2007 selection process, this announcement forecloses reforms until at least 2012. Nonetheless, China's new leadership seemed comfortable with the prospect of Tung's deputy, Chief Secretary Donald Tsang, a practicing Roman Catholic and Knight of the British Empire, becoming his successor. Tsang was formally installed in June 2005, and polls showed that 74 percent of Hong Kong citizens would have voted for him—if they could vote. Hong Kong's fiscal burden of government score is 0.2 point better this year, and its government intervention score is 0.5 point better. As a result, Hong Kong's overall score is 0.07 point better this year.

TRADE POLICY
Score: **1**–Stable (very low level of protectionism)

Hong Kong is basically duty-free. The World Trade Organization reports that Hong Kong's weighted average tariff rate in 2003 (the most recent year for which WTO data are available) was 0 percent. According to the U.S. Department of Commerce, "Non-tariff barriers such as labeling requirements, standards, etc. are minimal." Based on the revised trade factor methodology, Hong Kong's trade policy score is unchanged.

FISCAL BURDEN OF GOVERNMENT
Score—Income Taxation: **1.5**–Stable (low tax rates)
Score—Corporate Taxation: **1.5**–Stable (low tax rates)
Score—Change in Government Expenditures: **2.5**–Better (low decrease)
Final Score: **1.8**–Better (low cost of government)

According to the Financial Services and the Treasury Bureau, Hong Kong maintains a dual income tax system under which individuals are taxed either progressively, between 2 percent and 20 percent, on income adjusted for deductions and allowances or at a flat rate of 16 percent on their gross income, depending on which liability is lower. For purposes of grading the *Index*, the top income tax rate is based on the flat rate of 16 percent. The top corporate tax rate is 17.5 percent. In 2004, according to the government of the Hong Kong Special Administrative Region, government expenditures as a share of GDP decreased 1.9 percentage points to 20.7 percent, compared to the 1.1 percentage point increase in 2003. On net, Hong Kong's fiscal burden of government score is 0.2 point better this year.

GOVERNMENT INTERVENTION IN THE ECONOMY
Score: **1.5**–Better (low level)

According to the Hong Kong Census and Statistics Bureau, the government consumed 9.9 percent of GDP in 2004, down from the 10.53 percent reported in the *2005 Index*. As a result, Hong Kong's government intervention score is 0.5 point better this year. In the April 2004–March 2005 fiscal year, according to the Economic and Trade Office, Hong Kong received 1.7 percent of its total revenues from state-owned enterprises and government ownership of property.

MONETARY POLICY
Score: **1**–Stable (very low level of inflation)

Hong Kong has a currency board system pegging the Hong Kong dollar to the U.S. dollar. From 1995 to 2004, Hong Kong's weighted average annual rate of inflation was –1.23 percent.

CAPITAL FLOWS AND FOREIGN INVESTMENT
Score: **1**–Stable (very low barriers)

Hong Kong is receptive to investment and does not discriminate between foreign and domestic investors. According to the Economist Intelligence Unit, "Attracting foreign investment is a priority, and the government has a worldwide network of economic and trade offices to promote overseas investment in Hong Kong. Foreign investment is widely considered beneficial, even crucial, for economic stability…. [T]here are no restrictions on foreign ownership of property or companies and no foreign-exchange controls." The U.S. Department of Commerce reports that foreign entities may own no more than 49 percent of local broadcast stations. The Hong Kong dollar is freely convertible, and the International Monetary Fund reports that there are no controls or requirements on current transfers, purchase of real estate, access to foreign exchange, or repatriation of profits.

BANKING AND FINANCE
Score: **1**–Stable (very low level of restrictions)

Hong Kong is a global banking center. According to the Economist Intelligence Unit, 71 of the world's largest 100 banks operate in the territory. The government does not own any banks. Banking regulations under the Banking Ordinance are not onerous and are intended to ensure adequate liquidity and capital adequacy ratios and to guard against improper lending activity. Hong Kong has passed legislation making it easier for foreign banks to enter the market by removing restrictions on the number of branches foreign banks can operate in Hong Kong (November 2001) and by lowering asset and deposit criteria for new foreign bank branches (May 2002). In April 1998, Hong Kong intervened in the stock market by purchasing $15.2 billion in private stocks. The government has largely divested itself of its holdings but, according to the U.S. Department of Commerce, also "decided to retain a portion of the stocks (worth about $410 million) as a long-term investment." The Hong Kong Economic

and Trade Office reports that the retained portion of the investment is managed by external managers to avoid any conflict of interest. According to the U.S. Department of Commerce, "Credit … is allocated strictly on market terms and is available to foreign investors on a non-discriminatory basis." The government reports that, of the 206 authorized banks operating as of April 2005, 123 were incorporated outside of Hong Kong.

WAGES AND PRICES
Score: **2**–Stable (low level of intervention)

Hong Kong's market largely sets wages and prices, although price controls are imposed on rent for some residential properties and on public transport and electricity. There is no minimum wage for local employees.

PROPERTY RIGHTS
Score: **1**–Stable (very high level of protection)

According to the Economist Intelligence Unit, "Contractual arrangements are generally secure in Hong Kong, aided by its transparent common-law legal system inherited from the UK. Protection of private property and freedom of exchange are enshrined in Hong Kong's mini-constitution; they are in no danger of being weakened in the foreseeable future." The same source reports that "the government controls all land in Hong Kong, and renewable land leases are granted or sold via public auction, tender or (in special circumstances) private treaty…. [L]eases [are] valid up to 2047 for land in all areas of the Special Administrative Region…." The EIU cautions, however, that "there is considerable uncertainty about the future of these leases after 2047 vis-à-vis China's land policy."

REGULATION
Score: **1**–Stable (very low level)

Business regulations are streamlined and applied uniformly. According to the Economist Intelligence Unit, "The simplicity of procedures for investing, expanding and establishing a local company is a major attraction for foreign investment in Hong Kong. It is relatively easy to start a company: ready-made firms (known as shelf companies) are widely available and enable a businessperson to walk off a plane in the morning and start operating a firm in the afternoon." Hong Kong's labor code is strictly enforced, but the regulations are not significantly burdensome. The EIU also reports that "new building construction requires permits, and polluting industries face increasingly strict controls. Pharmaceutical operations face strict rules on importation, manufacture, sale and distribution…."

INFORMAL MARKET
Score: **1.5**–Stable (low level of activity)

Transparency International's 2004 score for Hong Kong is 8. Therefore, Hong Kong's informal market score is 1.5 this year.

> Hong Kong qualifies for the Global Free Trade Alliance.

HUNGARY

Rank: 40

Score: 2.44

Category: Mostly Free

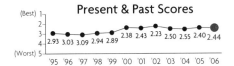

Present & Past Scores

(Best) 1
2
3
4
(Worst) 5

2.93 3.03 3.09 2.94 2.89 2.38 2.43 2.23 2.50 2.55 2.40 2.44

'95 '96 '97 '98 '99 '00 '01 '02 '03 '04 '05 '06

A new entrant into the European Union, Hungary has been a success story of post-communist transformation, but the August 2004 selection of a new prime minister, Ferenc Gyurcsany, followed by the failed December referendum on hospital privatization and dual citizenship, reinforced the ruling Socialists' political position in the coalition. Economic liberalization and privatization implemented by prior governments have led to majority foreign ownership in major industries, including a technologically advanced export sector. High interest rates have attracted foreign capital, but Hungary has increasingly come under competitive pressure from neighboring countries. Compared to the low flat-tax rates in Romania, Hungary's high labor taxes cause the country to lose investment opportunities. However, tax reform is unlikely until the parliamentary elections in May 2006. Hungary's economy, about 40 percent of which is export-driven and closely linked to the major markets in the EU, has suffered as a result of the economic stagnation that has plagued the EU core. A number of industries, including electricity, gas, and telecommunications, remain uncompetitive and subsidized by the government. Hungary's trade policy score is 1 point better this year; however, its fiscal burden of government score is 0.4 point worse, and its monetary policy score is 1 point worse. As a result, Hungary's overall score is 0.04 point worse this year.

TRADE POLICY
Score: **2**–Better (low level of protectionism)

Hungary adopted the trade policies of the European Union when it joined the EU in May 2004. As a member of the EU, Hungary is subject to a common EU weighted average external tariff, which was 1.3 percent in 2003, down from the 7.5 percent for 2002 reported in the 2005 *Index*, based on World Bank data. According to the World Trade Organization and the U.S. Trade Representative, the EU imposes non-tariff trade barriers through a complex regulatory system and export subsidies. The U.S. Department of Commerce reports that EU phytosanitary regulations operate as non-tariff barriers. Based on the lower tariff rate, as well as a revision of the trade factor methodology, Hungary's trade policy score is 1 point better this year.

FISCAL BURDEN OF GOVERNMENT
Score—Income Taxation: **3.5**–Stable (high tax rates)
Score—Corporate Taxation: **1.5**–Stable (low tax rates)
Score—Change in Government Expenditures: **3**–Worse (very low decrease)
Final Score: **2.4**–Worse (low cost of government)

According to Deloitte, Hungary's top income tax rate is 38 percent. The top corporate income tax rate is 16 percent. In 2004, government expenditures as a share of GDP fell 0.5 percentage point to 49.3 percent, compared to the 2.8 percentage point decrease in 2003. On net, Hungary's fiscal burden of government score is 0.4 point worse this year.

GOVERNMENT INTERVENTION IN THE ECONOMY
Score: **2**–Stable (low level)

Based on data from the Economist Intelligence Unit, the government consumed 10.8 percent of GDP in 2003. In the same year, based on data from the Ministry of Finance, Hungary received 2.22 percent of its total revenues from state-owned enterprises and government ownership of property.

QUICK STUDY

SCORES

Trade Policy	2
Fiscal Burden	2.4
Government Intervention	2
Monetary Policy	3
Foreign Investment	2
Banking and Finance	2
Wages and Prices	3
Property Rights	2
Regulation	3
Informal Market	3

Population: 10,088,000

Total area: 93,030 sq. km

GDP: $53.8 billion

GDP growth rate: 4.0%

GDP per capita: $5,333

Major exports: food, machinery and equipment, beverages and tobacco, raw materials, fuels and electricity

Exports of goods and services: $41.5 billion

Major export trading partners: Germany 30.4%, Austria 11.2%, US 5.8%, Italy 4.5%

Major imports: manufactures, machinery and equipment, food products

Imports of goods and services: $44.7 billion

Major import trading partners: Germany 28.6%, Austria 8.7%, Italy 7.5%, Russia 6.7%

Foreign direct investment (net): $3.4 billion

2004 Data (in constant 2000 US dollars)

213

MONETARY POLICY
Score: **3**–Worse (moderate level of inflation)

From 1995 to 2004, Hungary's weighted average annual rate of inflation was 6.30 percent, up from the 5.48 percent from 1994 to 2003 reported in the 2005 *Index*. As a result, Hungary's monetary policy score is 1 point worse this year.

CAPITAL FLOWS AND FOREIGN INVESTMENT
Score: **2**–Stable (low barriers)

Hungary is very open to foreign investment. The U.S. Department of Commerce reports that foreign companies account for two-thirds of the manufacturing sector, 90 percent of the telecommunications sector, and 60 percent of the energy sector. The government allows 100 percent foreign ownership in almost all firms, with the exception of some defense-related industries, airlines, and broadcasting. The law does not discriminate against foreign investors, and Law XXIV of 1988 provides for national treatment. Government approval is not required for foreign investment in most cases. Foreigners may not purchase agricultural land or protected natural areas. The International Monetary Fund reports that both residents and non-residents may hold foreign exchange accounts. Hungary places no restrictions or controls on payments for or proceeds from invisible transactions, current transfers, or repatriation of profits. The IMF reports no restrictions on issues or sales of capital market securities, bonds, debt securities, derivatives, credits, and direct investments, although there are some reporting requirements.

BANKING AND FINANCE
Score: **2**–Stable (low level of restrictions)

The banking industry is increasingly competitive. Banks are relatively free from burdensome government oversight, and foreign banks face no barriers to entry into the Hungarian market. According to the U.S. Department of Commerce, "Foreigners do not need government of Hungary approval to establish bank subsidiaries or to establish more than a 10 percent stake in existing banks." The Economist Intelligence Unit reports that there are 30 commercial banks, 27 of which were foreign-owned, operating in Hungary at the end of 2004. The top 10 banks controlled over 78 percent of all banking assets. Foreign investors accounted for 81 percent of combined registered capital in the banking sector as of September 2004. Only the Hungarian Development Bank and the Hungarian Export–Import Bank remain 100 percent state-owned, and the Land Credit and Mortgage Bank remains majority state-owned.

WAGES AND PRICES
Score: **3**–Stable (moderate level of intervention)

The Hungarian government controls some prices. According to the Economist Intelligence Unit, "the state's role as a regulator is still strong, as demonstrated by the government's price limitations on privately owned firms...." The Hungarian embassy reports that the government controls the prices of "electricity, gas, railways, buses, water, sewerage disposal, postal service, telephone services, motorway charge and rents (for social flats)." The same source notes that the government subsidizes agriculture through the European Union's Common Agricultural Policy. Hungary has a minimum wage.

PROPERTY RIGHTS
Score: **2**–Stable (high level of protection)

The constitution provides for an independent judiciary, and the government respects this provision in practice. The threat of expropriation is low. According to the Economist Intelligence Unit, the court system is slow and severely overburdened, and it may take more than a year to obtain a final ruling on a contract dispute.

REGULATION
Score: **3**–Stable (moderate level)

Much of Hungary's regulatory regime corresponds with European Union standards. A business license is required for some activities, and the government has streamlined the process for obtaining a license. However, regulations are not always transparent or evenly applied. Retail businesses still encounter a web of regulations that make it difficult to open a store. According to the Economist Intelligence Unit, "The efficiency, reliability and integrity of public-sector employees vary, and corruption is not unknown. Personal connections can considerably accelerate and improve the chances of success in bureaucratic and many other processes."

INFORMAL MARKET
Score: **3**–Stable (moderate level of activity)

Transparency International's 2004 score for Hungary is 4.8. Therefore, Hungary's informal market score is 3 this year.

If Hungary were to improve its regulation score, it would qualify for the Global Free Trade Alliance.

ICELAND

Rank: 5

Score: 1.74

Category: Free

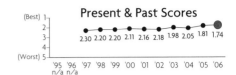

Present & Past Scores

(Best) 1
2
3
4
(Worst) 5

2.30 2.20 2.20 2.11 2.16 2.18 1.98 2.05 1.81 1.74

'95 '96 '97 '98 '99 '00 '01 '02 '03 '04 '05 '06
n/a n/a

QUICK STUDY

SCORES

Trade Policy	2.5
Fiscal Burden	2.4
Government Intervention	2.5
Monetary Policy	1
Foreign Investment	3
Banking and Finance	1
Wages and Prices	1
Property Rights	1
Regulation	2
Informal Market	1

Population: 290,000

Total area: 103,000 sq. km

GDP: $9.5 billion

GDP growth rate: 5.9%

GDP per capita: $32,758

Major exports: marine products, aluminum, ferrosilicon, agricultural products

Exports of goods and services: $3.3 billion

Major export trading partners: UK 19.0%, Germany 17.7%, Netherlands 10.7%, US 9.3%, Spain 6.9%

Major imports: industrial supplies and capital goods, transport equipment, fuel and lubricants, consumer goods

Imports of goods and services: $3.4 billion

Major import trading partners: Germany 12.6%, US 10.1%, Norway 9.6%, Denmark 7.6%, UK 6.8%

Foreign direct investment (net): −$1.9 billion

2004 Data (in constant 2000 US dollars)

Iceland, a parliamentary democracy with a market economy, has a relatively young labor force compared to EU members. It also boasts an 18 percent corporate tax rate, one of the lowest to be found in any of the Organisation for Economic Co-operation and Development's member countries. Structural reforms and market liberalization have enabled Iceland to enjoy strong economic performance, with a 2004 GDP growth rate of 5.9 percent. Although the marine sector remains important, the economy has become increasingly diverse. The service sector employs two-thirds of the working population. The European Union is Iceland's largest trading partner, although differences over fishing policies have been a major issue in considering EU membership. In addition, public opinion has not favored joining the EU, partly because of unsympathetic signals from Brussels. According to the Economist Intelligence Unit, no significant policy shift regarding EU membership is likely, despite the 2004 appointment of pro-EU Prime Minister Halldor Asgrimsson. In November 2004, the government announced its plan for tax reform, including cuts in the personal income tax rate and removal of net wealth taxes on individuals and companies. Iceland's capital flows and foreign investment score is 1 point worse this year; however, its fiscal burden of government score is 0.2 point better, its government intervention score is 0.5 point better, and its monetary policy score is 1 point better. As a result, Iceland's overall score is 0.07 point better this year.

TRADE POLICY
Score: **2.5** Stable (moderate level of protectionism)

According to the World Bank, Iceland's weighted average tariff rate in 2001 (the most recent year for which World Bank data are available) was 3.4 percent. "Since joining the European Economic Area in 1994, Iceland has been forced to adopt European product standards and regulations in many areas. Implementation of these new standards…has created problems for importers," reports the U.S. Department of Commerce, "Iceland maintains strict phytosanitary regulations, since many animal diseases common elsewhere are not present in the country." Based on the revised trade factor methodology, Iceland's trade policy score is unchanged.

FISCAL BURDEN OF GOVERNMENT
Score—Income Taxation: **2.5**–Better (moderate tax rates)
Score—Corporate Taxation: **2**–Stable (low tax rates)
Score—Change in Government Expenditures: **3**–Better (very low decrease)
Final Score: **2.4**–Better (low cost of government)

Iceland's top income tax rate is 26.75 percent (a general rate of 24.75 percent plus a 2 percent high income tax rate), down from the 30.75 percent reported in the 2005 *Index*, The top corporate tax rate is 18 percent. In 2004, government expenditures as a share of GDP decreased 0.4 percentage point to 47.6 percent, compared to the 2.2 percentage point increase in 2003. On net, Iceland's fiscal burden of government score is 0.2 point better this year.

GOVERNMENT INTERVENTION IN THE ECONOMY
Score: **2.5**–Better (moderate level)

According to the Economist Intelligence Unit, the government consumed 26.6 percent of GDP in 2004. In 2003, based on data from Statistics Iceland, Iceland received 4.89 percent of its total revenues from state-owned enterprises and government ownership of property, down from the 7.14 percent reported in the 2005 *Index*. As a result, Iceland's government intervention score is 0.5 point better this year.

MONETARY POLICY
Score: **1**–Better (very low level of inflation)

From 1995 to 2004, Iceland's weighted average annual rate of inflation was 2.97 percent, down from the 3.26 percent from 1994 to 2003 reported in the 2005 *Index*. As a result, Iceland's monetary policy score is 1 point better this year.

CAPITAL FLOWS AND FOREIGN INVESTMENT
Score: **3**–Worse (moderate barriers)

Iceland generally welcomes foreign investment, and foreign investors receive domestic treatment, although the government still maintains some restrictions in such key areas as fishing, aviation, and energy. The International Monetary Fund reports that residents and non-residents may own foreign exchange accounts, subject to reporting requirements. There are no controls or requirements on payments or current transfers, access to foreign exchange, or repatriation of profits. Foreign governments or other authorities may not issue debt instruments without permission of the central bank, and foreign governments or public authorities may not invest in Iceland. There are substantial restrictions on foreign ownership of real estate and in the fishing and fish processing industry, which is a major portion of the economy. Foreign ownership in the fishing industry is limited to 25 percent. The IMF reports that individuals must live in Iceland to purchase real estate, unlimited companies must be 100 percent Icelandic-owned, and joint stock companies must be 80 percent Icelandic-owned. Based on the evidence of restrictions, Iceland's capital flows and foreign investment score is 1 point worse this year.

BANKING AND FINANCE
Score: **1**–Stable (very low level of restrictions)

Since joining the European Economic Area, Iceland has complied with European Union directives by liberalizing and deregulating financial markets, allowing Icelandic financial institutions to operate on a cross-border basis in the EEA, and allowing EEA financial institutions to operate similarly in Iceland. The Icelandic Investment Bank has been completely privatized. "Since the late 1990s a large number of state-owned enterprises have been sold off, most notably the Icelandic Investment Bank in 1998–99 and, more recently, the government's remaining stakes in the Agricultural Bank (Bunadarbanki) and the National Bank of Iceland (Landsbanki), at the time the country's second- and third-largest retail banks respectively," reports the Economist Intelligence Unit. "The state has now withdrawn completely from the commercial banking sector."

WAGES AND PRICES
Score: **1**–Stable (very low level of intervention)

The market sets most prices in Iceland, although agriculture remains subsidized. According to the Economist Intelligence Unit, "The agricultural sector is one of the most heavily subsidized and protected in the world." However, the very low portion of economic output resulting from the agricultural sector (1.4 percent of GDP in 2003) minimizes the impact of agricultural subsidies. Collective bargaining agreements set workers' pay, hours, and working conditions; government plays a minor role, primarily as a mediator, in this process. Iceland does not have a minimum wage.

PROPERTY RIGHTS
Score: **1**–Stable (very high level of protection)

Private property is well protected in Iceland. The U.S. Department of State reports that "the Constitution and law provide for an independent judiciary, and the Government generally respected this provision in practice.... With limited exceptions, trials were public and conducted fairly, with no official intimidation."

REGULATION
Score: **2**–Stable (low level)

Over the past several years, significant deregulation and some privatization have opened the economy to greater competition and efficiency. According to PricewaterhouseCoopers, "Operating licenses are required for businesses in certain sectors, for example manufacturing industries, and are granted on fulfillment of clearly defined rules.... As a member of the European Economic Area, Iceland operates its regulatory environment on the same principles as the European Union." The fishing industry uses a transferable quota system to distribute fishing rights. Opponents of membership in the EU find the EU's common fisheries policy unacceptable for an economy that relies so heavily on fishing.

INFORMAL MARKET
Score: **1**–Stable (very low level of activity)

Transparency International's 2004 score for Iceland is 9.5. Therefore, Iceland's informal market score is 1 this year.

INDIA

Rank: 121

Score: 3.49

Category: Mostly Unfree

Present & Past Scores

(Best) 1
2
3 3.93 3.93 3.88 3.83 3.93 3.93 3.91 3.61 3.58 3.53 3.53 3.49
4
(Worst) 5

'95 '96 '97 '98 '99 '00 '01 '02 '03 '04 '05 '06

QUICK STUDY

SCORES

Trade Policy	5
Fiscal Burden	3.9
Government Intervention	3
Monetary Policy	2
Foreign Investment	3
Banking and Finance	4
Wages and Prices	3
Property Rights	3
Regulation	4
Informal Market	4

Population: 1,064,398,592

Total area: 3,287,590 sq. km

GDP: $543.7 billion

GDP growth rate: 8.6%

GDP per capita: $511

Major exports: textile goods, gems and jewelry, iron and steel, chemicals, leather goods

Exports of goods and services: $88.6 billion

Major export trading partners: US 18.6%, United Arab Emirates 7.6%, UK 4.8%, China 4.5%

Major imports: petroleum and petroleum products, machinery, fertilizer

Imports of goods and services: $83.7 billion

Major import trading partners: US 5.4%, China 5.3%, UK 4.4%

Foreign direct investment (net): $3.2 billion

2003 Data (in constant 2000 US dollars)

Despite concerns that the Congress Party–led United Progressive Alliance might hinder economic reforms to appease its leftist partners, progress continues, albeit slowly. Peace dialogues with Pakistan, including discussions about forging closer economic ties, are ongoing. In 2005, foreign investors hailed the scrapping of Press Note 18, which required foreign companies to secure permission from local joint venture partners before setting up an intra-industry rival. While tax rates are still too high, some are being reduced. The Congress Party remains committed to selective privatization. To meet India's growing energy needs, plans are underway to restructure state-owned oil and gas firms, including allowing private-sector competition. Recent discussions with Wal-Mart and other global chains indicate that India might soon relax its ban on foreign investment in the retail sector. India's labor laws, which require companies employing more than 100 employees to seek government permission to fire employees, remain an obstacle to exploiting India's full economic potential in both the manufacturing and service sectors. Nevertheless, the continued commitment to economic reform displayed by Indian leaders of all stripes indicates that there are grounds for cautious optimism about the long-term prospects for successful economic reform. India's fiscal burden of government score is 0.4 point better this year. As a result, its overall score is 0.04 point better this year.

TRADE POLICY
Score: **5–Stable** (very high level of protectionism)

According to the World Bank, India's weighted average tariff rate in 2004 was 28 percent, up from the 21 percent in 2001 reported in the 2005 *Index*, based on World Bank data. The U.S. Trade Representative reports that non-tariff barriers remain extensive, including a high level of confusing bureaucracy, onerous standards and certifications on many goods, discriminatory sanitary and phytosanitary measures, and a negative import list that bans or restricts imports. Based on the revised trade factor methodology, India's trade policy score is unchanged.

FISCAL BURDEN OF GOVERNMENT
Score—Income Taxation: **3–Stable** (moderate tax rates)
Score—Corporate Taxation: **4.5–Better** (very high tax rates)
Score—Change in Government Expenditures: **3.5–Better** (low increase)
Final Score: **3.9–Better** (high cost of government)

According to Deloitte, India's top income tax rate is 33 percent (a top rate of 30 percent plus a 10 percent surcharge), up from the 30 percent reported in the 2005 *Index*. The top corporate tax rate has been cut to 33 percent (a reduced top rate of 30 percent plus an increased surcharge of 10 percent) from the 36.8 percent reported in the 2005 *Index*. In 2003, according to the Asian Development Bank, government expenditures as a share of GDP increased 1 percentage point to 29.1 percent, compared to the 0.4 percentage point increase in 2002. On net, India's fiscal burden of government score is 0.4 point better this year.

GOVERNMENT INTERVENTION IN THE ECONOMY
Score: **3–Stable** (moderate level)

The World Bank reports that the government consumed 12.8 percent of GDP in 2003. In the same year, according to the International Monetary Fund's Government Financial Statistics

CD–ROM, India received 17.9 percent of its total revenues from state-owned enterprises and government ownership of property.

 MONETARY POLICY
Score: **2**–Stable (low level of inflation)

From 1995 to 2004, India's weighted average annual rate of inflation was 3.85 percent.

 CAPITAL FLOWS AND FOREIGN INVESTMENT
Score: **3**–Stable (moderate barriers)

According to the U.S. Department of Commerce, "India controls foreign investment with limits on equity and voting rights, mandatory government approvals, and capital controls." The Economist Intelligence Unit characterizes India as "a difficult market for foreign companies. Most economic activities are bound by restrictions, public services and infrastructure are poor, and the government continues to impede the free flow of capital across its borders." However, India is taking gradual steps to attract more foreign investment, and foreign ownership is permitted in most sectors. The U.S. Department of Commerce reports that in January 2005, "the GOI [Government of India] relaxed restrictions on new [foreign direct investment] in India by foreign partners of joint ventures. The previous rules, issued in Press Note 18 in 1998, had required a release by the Indian partner and GOI approval for any new investment, a provision often subject to abuse. The new rules maintain restrictions on the majority of existing joint ventures, but leave new ones to negotiate their own terms on a commercial basis." Sectors off-limits to foreign investment include agriculture, legal services, railways, real estate, retailing, and security services. The International Monetary Fund reports that central bank approval is required for residents to open foreign currency accounts, either domestically or abroad, and that such accounts are subject to significant restrictions. Non-residents may hold foreign exchange and domestic currency accounts, subject to approval and conditions. Some payments and transfers face quantitative limits. The IMF reports that capital transactions and some credit operations are subject to certain restrictions and requirements.

 BANKING AND FINANCE
Score: **4**–Stable (high level of restrictions)

The government has adopted a more tolerant policy toward foreign banks in recent years, but it still dominates the banking sector. According to the U.S. Department of Commerce, "There are approximately 80 scheduled commercial banks, Indian and foreign; almost 200 regional rural banks; more than 350 central cooperative banks, 20 land development banks; and a number of primary agricultural credit societies.... In terms of business, the state-owned banks account for more than 70 percent of deposits and loans. Private banks handle 17 percent of the market, and foreign banks located in metropolitan areas account for approximately 13 percent of the market."

The foreign equity ceiling for private banks has been raised from 49 percent to 74 percent but is capped at 20 percent in the state-owned banks. However, the government is reluctant to liberalize the sector. "The 20 public sector banks, representing three quarters of all banking assets, are still at least 51% owned by the state and will stay that way. The [central bank] will also keep a tight rein on any investment by foreign banks in local private banks above a 10% limit," reports the May 19, 2005, edition of *The Economist*. "The central bank puts moral pressure on banks to charge low interest on loans to 'priority' sectors such as small companies and agriculture."

 WAGES AND PRICES
Score: **3**–Stable (moderate level of intervention)

The government continues to influence prices on several goods and services. The Economist Intelligence Unit reports that the Essential Commodities Act of 1955 applies price controls at the factory, wholesale, and retail levels on "essential" commodities. Electricity, some petroleum products, and certain types of coal are the only items with fully administered prices. The government also controls the prices of pharmaceuticals. The government mandates minimum wages that vary by state and industry.

 PROPERTY RIGHTS
Score: **3**–Stable (moderate level of protection)

Protection of property rights is applied unevenly in India. The Economist Intelligence Unit reports that "large backlogs create delays—sometimes years long—in reaching decisions. Consequently, foreign corporations often include clauses for international arbitration in their contracts." According to the U.S. Department of Commerce, "Critics say that liquidating a bankrupt company may take as long as 20 years." Protection of property for local investors, particularly the smallest ones, is weak.

 REGULATION
Score: **4**–Stable (high level)

Businesses must contend with extensive federal and state regulation. According to the U.S. Department of Commerce, "firms have identified corruption as one obstacle to...investment. Indian businessmen agree that red tape and wide-ranging administrative discretion serve as a pretext to extort money." In addition, labor laws are rigid. *The Economist* reports that "any company employing more than 100 people requires the permission of the state authorities to sack workers...."

 INFORMAL MARKET
Score: **4**–Stable (high level of activity)

Transparency International's 2004 score for India is 2.8. Therefore, India's informal market score is 4 this year.

INDONESIA

Rank: 134

Score: 3.71

Category: Mostly Unfree

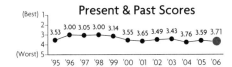

Present & Past Scores

(Best) 1
2
3
4
(Worst) 5

3.53 3.00 3.05 3.00 3.14 3.55 3.65 3.49 3.43 3.76 3.59 3.71

'95 '96 '97 '98 '99 '00 '01 '02 '03 '04 '05 '06

In 2004, with the direct election of President Susilo Bambang Yudhoyono and the seating of a fully elected legislature, Indonesia completed its 12-year transition to democracy and became the world's youngest and third-largest democracy. Now the new president and the legislature must contend with the legacy of 30 years of authoritarian dictatorship and the lackluster performance of the government during the democratic transition. Among the challenges to be faced are rampant corruption, weak rule of law, and the management of both state-owned enterprises and military-owned businesses. The president acknowledged that Indonesians had elected him because they believed he was best suited to curb corruption and revitalize the economy. He launched an aggressive anti-corruption campaign that has resulted in some arrests and is working to deregulate Indonesia's economy. His politically courageous initiatives include substantially reducing Indonesia's burdensome fuel subsidies and starting to implement tax reform. As a result of these activities and others, Indonesia is experiencing solid economic growth and is attracting foreign investment inflows at twice the rate it did during the transition period. Indonesia's trade policy score is 0.5 point worse this year, and its fiscal burden of government score is 0.7 point worse. As a result, Indonesia's overall score is 0.12 point worse this year.

QUICK STUDY

SCORES

Trade Policy	3
Fiscal Burden	4.1
Government Intervention	3.5
Monetary Policy	3
Foreign Investment	4
Banking and Finance	4
Wages and Prices	3
Property Rights	4
Regulation	4
Informal Market	4.5

Population: 214,674,160

Total area: 1,919,440 sq. km

GDP: $167.7 billion

GDP growth rate: 4.1%

GDP per capita: $781

Major exports: textiles and garments, crude petroleum and products, liquefied natural gas

Exports of goods and services: $68.7 billion

Major export trading partners: Japan 22.3%, US 12.1%, Singapore 8.9%, South Korea 7.1%, China 6.2%

Major imports: raw materials and intermediates, capital goods, chemicals and fuels

Imports of goods and services: $52.7 billion

Major import trading partners: Japan 13.0%, Singapore 12.8%, China 9.1%, US 8.3%, South Korea 4.7%

Foreign direct investment (net): –$686.1 million

2003 Data (in constant 2000 US dollars)

TRADE POLICY
Score: **3–Worse** (moderate level of protectionism)

According to the World Bank, Indonesia's weighted average tariff rate in 2003 (the most recent year for which World Bank data are available) was 5.2 percent, up from the 3.9 percent in 2001 reported in the 2005 *Index*, based on World Bank data. The World Trade Organization reports restrictions on the import and export of certain goods. The U.S. Department of Commerce notes that corruption among customs officials is pervasive and that several goods are subject to import bans and other restrictions. Based on the higher tariff rate, as well as a revision of the trade factor methodology, Indonesia's trade policy score is 0.5 point worse this year.

FISCAL BURDEN OF GOVERNMENT
Score—Income Taxation: **3.5–Stable** (high tax rates)
Score—Corporate Taxation: **4–Stable** (high tax rates)
Score—Change in Government Expenditures: **5–Worse** (high increase)
Final Score: **4.1–Worse** (high cost of government)

According to Deloitte, Indonesia's top income tax rate is 35 percent. The top corporate income tax rate is 30 percent. In 2004, according to the Asian Development Bank, government expenditures as a share of GDP increased 3.3 percentage points to 21.6 percent, compared to a 1.1 percentage point increase in 2003. On net, Indonesia's fiscal burden of government score is 0.7 point worse this year.

GOVERNMENT INTERVENTION IN THE ECONOMY
Score: **3.5–Stable** (high level)

The World Bank reports that the government consumed 9.2 percent of GDP in 2003. In 2004, according to the central bank, Indonesia received 3.28 percent of its total revenues from state-owned enterprises and government ownership of property. Indonesia's Statistics Office, however, reports that the government employs over 20 percent of the labor force. According to

219

the U.S. Department of Commerce, "State-owned Enterprises (SOEs) play a dominant role in many sectors, including oil & gas, retail distribution, electric power generation & transmission, civil aviation, banking, fertilizer production and wholesale distribution." Based on the apparent unreliability of reported figures for government consumption and total revenue, 2 points have been added to Indonesia's government intervention score: 1 point for government consumption and 1 point for total revenue.

MONETARY POLICY
Score: 3–Stable (moderate level of inflation)

From 1995 to 2004, Indonesia's weighted average annual rate of inflation was 7.09 percent.

CAPITAL FLOWS AND FOREIGN INVESTMENT
Score: 4–Stable (high barriers)

Foreign investment is restricted by both official and unofficial barriers. According to the U.S. Department of Commerce, "official appeals for investment have not been matched by action on serious issues facing investors such as judicial reform, rampant corruption, security, and taxation and labor issues…. [F]oreign investors are increasingly troubled by judicial corruption and abuses of the legal process that result in a lack of legal certainty, difficulties negotiating and enforcing contracts, unequal treatment and a disregard for arbitration and award judgments." The Economist Intelligence Unit notes that Indonesia's "negative list" was updated in 2000 to close 11 business sectors to both foreign and domestic investment and close eight others to foreign investment (although restrictions on one of the eight—broadcast media—were loosened in 2003). Subject to restrictions, residents and non-residents may hold foreign exchange accounts. Most capital transactions are restricted. Non-residents are not allowed to purchase real estate, although they can purchase the right to use real estate, according to the IMF. A number of investments require domestic partners.

BANKING AND FINANCE
Score: 4–Stable (high level of restrictions)

"Indonesia's banking industry is recovering after having been devastated in the Asian financial crisis of 1997–98," reports the Economist Intelligence Unit. "Officials have taken steps to return nationalised banks to the private sector and winnow the number of ailing financial institutions that remain in government hands." The government has privatized and sold stakes in many nationalized banks to private investors during the past few years. However, the EIU reports that the top five domestic banks in terms of assets remain state-owned. According to the May 7, 2005, *Asia Times*, "The country's largest bank, Bank Mandiri, majority owned by the government, plans to acquire several banks…and fulfill its ambition to be the dominant player in the banking sector…. However, the bank is being investigated by the attorney general following irregularities uncovered by a BPK probe of the bank's financial reports." The March 29, 2005, *Jakarta Post* reports that money

laundering by high-ranking Indonesian officials remains "vigorous" despite Indonesia's removal from the Financial Action Task Force list of non-cooperative countries.

WAGES AND PRICES
Score: 3–Stable (moderate level of intervention)

According to the Economist Intelligence Unit, "A handful of commodities and services remained classified as under 'administered prices.' These include petrol, electricity, liquefied petroleum gas, rice, cigarettes, cement, hospital services, potable/piped water, city transport, air transport, telephone charges, trains, salt, toll-road tariffs and postage." The government also influences prices through the extensive state-owned sector; subsidizes some services, such as telecommunications; and reviews most prices of fuel, petrol, diesel, and kerosene every month.

PROPERTY RIGHTS
Score: 4–Stable (low level of protection)

Court rulings can be arbitrary and inconsistent, and the judicial system suffers from corruption. According to the U.S. Department of Commerce, "The unpredictable nature of the judicial process and the arbitrary actions of local officials are two problems cited by many businesses as particularly difficult to overcome. In some cases, judges rule against foreigners in commercial disputes, ignoring the facts of the case and the contracts between the parties. It is also difficult to get international arbitration awards enforced by Indonesian courts, often leaving no recourse for international investors." *The Economist* reports that "judges regularly have to be bribed."

REGULATION
Score: 4–Stable (high level)

Indonesia's regulatory environment is plagued by corruption and red tape. The U.S. Department of Commerce reports that "Indonesia has a tangled regulatory and legal environment where most firms, both foreign and domestic, attempt to avoid the justice system. Laws and regulations are often vague and require substantial interpretation by implementing offices, leading to business uncertainty and rent seeking opportunities. Deregulation has been somewhat successful in removing barriers, creating more transparent trade and investment regimes, and has alleviated, but not eliminated, red tape. U.S. businesses routinely cite transparency problems and red tape as factors hindering operations." A survey from the International Business Chamber in August 2004 reported that 88 percent of businesses in Indonesia reported negative experiences with corruption.

INFORMAL MARKET
Score: 4.5–Stable (very high level of activity)

Transparency International's 2004 score for Indonesia is 2. Therefore, Indonesia's informal market score is 4.5 this year.

IRAN

Rank: 156

Score: 4.51

Category: Repressed

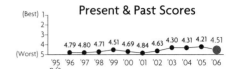

Present & Past Scores

(Best) 1
2
3
4
(Worst) 5

4.79 4.80 4.71 4.51 4.69 4.84 4.63 4.30 4.31 4.21 4.51

'95 '96 '97 '98 '99 '00 '01 '02 '03 '04 '05 '06
n/a

QUICK STUDY

SCORES

Trade Policy	4.5
Fiscal Burden	3.6
Government Intervention	5
Monetary Policy	4
Foreign Investment	5
Banking and Finance	5
Wages and Prices	4
Property Rights	5
Regulation	5
Informal Market	4

Population: 66,392,020

Total area: 1,648,000 sq. km

GDP: $113.9 billion

GDP growth rate: 6.6%

GDP per capita: $1,715

Major exports: petroleum, iron and steel, carpets

Exports of goods and services: $22.1 billion

Major export trading partners: Japan 22.2%, China 9.9%, Italy 6.4%, South Korea 5.5%

Major imports: intermediate goods and industrial raw materials, foodstuffs and other consumer goods

Imports of goods and services: $31 billion

Major import trading partners: Germany 10.8%, France 8.5%, China 8.3%, Italy 8.0%, United Arab Emirates 7.8%

Foreign direct investment (net): −$1.3 billion

2003 Data (in constant 2000 US dollars)

I ran's economy was crippled by the 1979 Islamic revolution, the Iran–Iraq war, and widespread economic mismanagement. Hopes for reform were raised under former President Mohammed Khatami, but he was hamstrung by opposition from entrenched bureaucrats in state agencies and by Islamic hard-liners in the judiciary and other state institutions. Khatami and his allies suffered a major political defeat in the February 2004 legislative elections. Iran's new parliament has adopted more populist and nationalist economic policies while reversing President Khatami's tentative economic reforms. Reformers also were defeated in the June 2005 presidential election, which elevated Tehran Mayor Mahmoud Ahmadinejad to the presidency. During the campaign, Ahmadinejad promised to give poor Iranians a greater share of the country's oil wealth and called for greater state control of the economy. Although high world oil prices have raised export revenues and helped to service Iran's large foreign debt, the country's state-dominated economy remains troubled by high unemployment, inflation, corruption, expensive subsidies, and a bloated and inefficient public sector. Iran's trade policy score is 2 points worse this year, and its capital flows and foreign investment score is 1 point worse. As a result, Iran's overall score is 0.3 point worse this year.

TRADE POLICY
Score: **4.5**–Worse (very high level of protectionism)

According to the World Bank, Iran's weighted average tariff rate in 2004 was 14.8 percent, up from the 3.1 percent in 2000 reported in the 2005 *Index*, based on World Bank data. The European Commission Market Access Sectoral and Trade Barriers Database reports that sanitary and phytosanitary regulations are a non-tariff barrier and that the government bans imports of specified products. Based on the higher tariff rate, as well as a revision of the trade factor methodology, Iran's trade policy score is 2 points worse this year.

FISCAL BURDEN OF GOVERNMENT
Score—Income Taxation: **3.5**–Stable (high tax rates)
Score—Corporate Taxation: **3**–Stable (moderate tax rates)
Score—Change in Government Expenditures: **5**–Stable (very high increase)
Final Score: **3.6**–Stable (high cost of government)

Iran's top income tax rate is 35 percent. The top corporate tax rate is 25 percent. In 2003, according to the Economist Intelligence Unit, government expenditures as a share of GDP increased 11 percentage points to 31 percent, compared to the 0.9 percentage point increase in 2002.

GOVERNMENT INTERVENTION IN THE ECONOMY
Score: **5**–Stable (very high level)

The World Bank reports that the government consumed 14 percent of GDP in 2003. In the same year, according to the International Monetary Fund's Government Financial Statistics CD–ROM, Iran received 53.83 percent of its total revenues from state-owned enterprises and government ownership of property. However, the Economist Intelligence Unit reports that "major sectors (such as oil and gas, transport, telecommunications, industry, and banking and finance) remain overwhelmingly under the purview of the state and its entities. The state directly owns well over 500 companies, and there are another 1,000 or so semi-public companies." Based on the apparent unreliability of the reported figure for government consumption, 1 point has been added to Iran's government intervention score.

MONETARY POLICY
Score: **4**–Stable (high level of inflation)

From 1995 to 2004, Iran's weighted average annual rate of inflation was 15.04 percent.

CAPITAL FLOWS AND FOREIGN INVESTMENT
Score: **5**–Worse (very high barriers)

In May 2002, the government updated its foreign investment code for the first time in over 50 years by enacting the Law on the Attraction and Protection of Foreign Investment. According to the Economist Intelligence Unit, however, "The conservative-dominated Majlis (parliament)...have objected to giving banking, telecommunications, transport, and border control responsibilities to foreign firms." Article 44 of Iran's constitution mandates state ownership of power generation, postal services, telecommunications, and other large-scale industries. According to the EIU, "The Expediency Council moved in October 2004 to resolve these constitutional issues by interpreting Article 44 to allow for the sale of 65% of the shares of state-owned enterprises, except for defence and security-related industries and the National Iranian Oil Company." *The Economist* reports that Iran's constitution forbids foreigners to own any concessions, operate projects, or participate in production-sharing agreements in the oil and gas sector. The government instead uses a buy-back system where foreign companies that finance and develop a project are reimbursed in dollars. The Majlis has given itself the power to veto projects in which foreign investors have a majority stake and has blocked two proposed investments. The International Monetary Fund reports that most payments, transfers, credit operations, and capital transactions are subject to limitations, quantitative limits, or approval requirements. Based on the evidence of the government's anti–foreign investment policies, Iran's foreign investment and capital flows score is 1 point worse this year.

BANKING AND FINANCE
Score: **5**–Stable (very high level of restrictions)

All banks were nationalized following the 1979 revolution. Iran's constitution requires that the banking sector be fully state-owned. According to the Economist Intelligence Unit, "The central bank issued a licence in August 2001 to Bank-e-Eqtesadi Novine (Modern Economic Bank), making it Iran's first private bank since the sector was nationalised in the aftermath of the 1979 revolution…. Other private banks established in Iran include the Karafarin Bank, which received a full-service banking licence in December 2001, and Saman Bank, in August 2002." Private banks are extremely small, however, and the state dominates banking activity. The ability of banks to charge interest is restricted under Iran's interpretation of

Islamic law. "The bulk of commercial banks' loan portfolio," reports the EIU, "is taken up with low-return loans to state agencies and parastatals…."

WAGES AND PRICES
Score: **4**–Stable (high level of intervention)

According to the Economist Intelligence Unit, "Iran does not regulate pricing for most commercial products with the exception of fuel (such as petrol, natural gas or diesel) and wheat for the production of bread." The U.S. Energy Information Administration reports that Iran provides about $3 billion in subsidies to lower the price of oil. The government also affects prices through its extensive state-owned enterprises and sets minimum wages for each sector and region.

PROPERTY RIGHTS
Score: **5**–Stable (very low level of protection)

"The rule of law in Iran is inconsistent and unsatisfactory," reports the Economist Intelligence Unit. "Recourse to the courts is unwieldy and often counter-productive and rarely leads to the swift resolution of outstanding disputes…. Few foreign firms have had satisfactory experiences when seeking to bring a contract dispute before a court." In addition, "written agreements offer very little protection for the contracting party. Foreign companies often find that engaging an influential, and experienced, local business partner who also enjoys substantial political patronage is the most effective form of protection."

REGULATION
Score: **5**–Stable (very high level)

The government effectively discourages the establishment of new businesses. According to the Economist Intelligence Unit, "The most common form of company in Iran is the joint-stock company, or sherkat-e sahami, in which the liability of a shareholder is limited to the capital invested in the company." In addition, "Contract negotiations are often lengthy, prolonged by the exhaustive details demanded by state agencies, and the slow functioning bureaucracy, which often requires approval from an extensive number of higher officials before legal agreement can be concluded." The EIU reports that corruption is a continuing problem.

INFORMAL MARKET
Score: **4**–Stable (high level of activity)

Transparency International's 2004 score for Iran is 2.9. Therefore, Iran's informal market score is 4 this year.

IRAQ

Rank: Suspended

Score: n/a

Category: n/a

Present & Past Scores

(Best) 1
2
3
4.85 4.85 4.85 4.85 4.90 4.90 5.00
4
(Worst) 5

'95 '96 '97 '98 '99 '00 '01 '02 '03 '04 '05 '06
n/a   n/a n/a n/a n/a

QUICK STUDY

SCORES

Trade Policy	n/a
Fiscal Burden	n/a
Government Intervention	n/a
Monetary Policy	n/a
Foreign Investment	n/a
Banking and Finance	n/a
Wages and Prices	n/a
Property Rights	n/a
Regulation	n/a
Informal Market	n/a

Population: 24, 699, 000

Total area: 437,072 sq. km

GDP: n/a

GDP growth rate: n/a

GDP per capita: n/a

Major exports: crude oil

Exports of goods and services: n/a

Major export trading partners: n/a

Major import: food, medicine, manufactures

Imports of goods and services: n/a

Major import trading partners: n/a

Foreign direct investment (net): n/a

2003 Data

Iraq gained its independence from Britain in 1932 and was a constitutional monarchy until a 1958 military coup led to a series of dictatorships. Both the recent war to overthrow Saddam Hussein and its chaotic aftermath, characterized by looting, terrorism, and sabotage, severely undermined the economy. The Economist Intelligence Unit reports that real GDP fell an estimated 20 percent in 2003, followed by a rise of 35 percent in 2004. Iraq's oil industry, which provides more than 90 percent of hard-currency earnings, has been hurt by pipeline sabotage, electricity outages, and years of neglect and postponed maintenance during Saddam's reign. According to the U.S. Department of State, oil production rose to about 2 million barrels per day by the end of 2004 and generated about $17 billion in annual revenue. Postwar economic recovery will be aided by high oil prices, as well as generous economic aid from the United States and other foreign donors, but will be hampered by continued insurgency and political uncertainty. In January 2005, the Iraqi people elected a Transitional National Assembly that was charged with writing a new constitution and holding another round of elections at the end of 2005 to form a permanent government.

 TRADE POLICY
Score: Not graded

Iraq is in the process of rebuilding its economy. According to the U.S. Department of Commerce, Iraq applied a flat tariff rate of 5 percent in 2004. Trade sanctions were lifted after the war. The U.S. Department of Commerce reports that "trade in arms, trade in certain cultural artifacts illegally removed from Iraq and trade with previously designated persons and certain Baath party officials continue to be banned."

 FISCAL BURDEN OF GOVERNMENT
Score—Income Taxation: Not graded
Score—Corporate Taxation: Not graded
Score—Change in Government Expenditures: Not graded
Final Score: Not graded

According to the Economist Intelligence Unit, "the CPA [Coalition Provisional Authority] took the decision to introduce a taxation system in order to send a message to international donors that Iraqis are bearing part of the cost of their own reconstruction and to avoid any potential moral hazard related to economic profligacy…. Under inherited plans individual taxes are to be assessed on a modestly progressive basis, with the top individual rate of 15% on incomes of about US$700 a year or more. Corporate income is to be taxed at a flat rate of 15%." Data on government expenditures are not available.

 GOVERNMENT INTERVENTION IN THE ECONOMY
Score: Not graded

The World Bank estimates that the government consumed 50.5 percent of GDP in 2004. In the same year, based on data from the Coalition Provisional Authority, Iraq received 93.47 percent of its total revenues from state-owned enterprises and government ownership of property. Data on revenues from state-owned enterprises are not available.

223

MONETARY POLICY
Score: Not graded

From 1995 to 2004, based on data from the Economist Intelligence Unit, Iraq's weighted average annual rate of inflation was 46.30 percent.

 CAPITAL FLOWS AND FOREIGN INVESTMENT
Score: Not graded

The Economist Intelligence Unit reports that the Foreign Investment Law of 2003 "allows foreign companies to own up to 100% of Iraqi companies, but specifically excludes the energy sector." Under this legislation, foreign companies are treated the same as Iraqi companies, and foreign investors may acquire 40-year leases on—but not ownership of—real estate. Nonetheless, reports the EIU, "Iraq continues to face substantial difficulties in attracting investment, largely as a result of the security situation and the lack of a binding legal framework or 'permanent' decision makers (with the government in transition)."

 BANKING AND FINANCE
Score: Not graded

Iraq's banking sector is weak and undeveloped, consisting of six state-owned banks and 17 private banks as of September 2004, according to the International Monetary Fund, which also reports that the two largest state-owned banks—Rafidain and Rasheed—accounted for 90 percent of banking sector assets. "In September 2003," reports the Economist Intelligence Unit, "the CPA issued the Iraqi Banking Law, which, together with the Central Bank Law, laid out regulations covering virtually all aspects of banking operations in the country. The former required the country's private banks to have paid-in capital of around NID10bn (around US$5m at that point), although the country's 17 existing private banks were given 18 months to reach that amount. The law also allows six foreign banks to have majority-owned subsidiaries in Iraq during the next five years and permits an unlimited number of foreign banks to buy up to 50% of an existing Iraqi bank." The EIU reports that three foreign banks (from Kuwait, Jordan, and Lebanon) have acquired stakes in one of Iraq's banks but that "none of the foreign banks licensed by the Central Bank to operate in Iraq have opened branches or operations through subsidiaries." The Central Bank of Iraq Law, passed by the Coalition Provisional Authority in March 2004, gave the central bank independence and established procedures from managing foreign reserves to supervising banks. Interest rates on loans, deposits, and securities were fully liberalized in March 2004.

 WAGES AND PRICES
Score: Not graded

According to the Economist Intelligence Unit, the "backdrop of high inflation has led to calls from many Iraqis for more stringent price controls and subsidies. Concerns over social stability in the current environment of high insecurity are therefore likely to slow price liberalisation and subsidy elimination."

 PROPERTY RIGHTS
Score: Not graded

There is no protection of property in Iraq. The aftermath of the war resulted in high insecurity, rioting, and looting, discouraging any kind of investment. The Economist Intelligence Unit reports that "the absence of an enforceable legal system means that foreigners are further disadvantaged in terms of dispute resolution, although this affects local investors to a large degree as well." U.S. forces are trying to help Iraqis feel safer, but that remains a daunting task.

 REGULATION
Score: Not graded

According to the U.S. Department of Commerce, "While most United Nations and U.S. economic sanctions against Iraq were lifted in May 2003, the Iraqi legal and regulatory system as well as an inadequate infrastructure and an unstable security situation pose numerous obstacles to doing business in Iraq."

 INFORMAL MARKET
Score: Not graded

Transparency International's 2004 score for Iraq is 2.1. Therefore, Iraq would have an informal market score of 4 this year if grading were not suspended.

IRELAND

Rank: 3
Score: 1.58
Category: Free

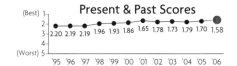
QUICK STUDY

SCORES

Trade Policy	2
Fiscal Burden	2.3
Government Intervention	2
Monetary Policy	1
Foreign Investment	1
Banking and Finance	1
Wages and Prices	2
Property Rights	1
Regulation	2
Informal Market	1.5

Population: 4,040,600

Total area: 70,280 sq. km

GDP: $116.2 billion

GDP growth rate: 4.9%

GDP per capita: $28,762

Major exports: machinery and transport equipment, manufactured materials, computer services and information, travel services, financial services

Exports of goods and services: $134.8 billion

Major export trading partners: UK 28.5%, US 13.9%, Germany 7.5%, China 5.7%

Major imports: chemicals, manufactured materials, food and live animals, insurance services, financial services

Imports of goods and services: $108.1 billion

Major import trading partners: US 19.7%, UK 16.0%, Belgium 14.7%, Germany 7.7%

Foreign direct investment (net): $2.5 billion

2004 Data (in constant 2000 US dollars)

Ireland's modern, highly industrialized economy grew by 80 percent during the 1990s. The country has one of the world's most pro-business environments, especially for foreign businesses and investments, and Prime Minister Bertie Ahern, whose Fianna Fail party governs in coalition with the Progressive Democrats, has maintained this impressive inheritance. In January 2003, the Ahern government lowered the corporate tax rate to 12.5 percent—far below the European Union's average of 30 percent—from 16 percent. Ireland has become a major center for U.S. investment in Europe. Although accounting for only 1 percent of the euro zone market, it receives nearly one-third of U.S. investment in the EU. Due largely to close trading ties with the U.S., Ireland is the world's largest exporter per capita. Compared to the rest of Western Europe, Irish growth can be measured in leaps and bounds: GDP grew by 4.9 percent in 2004. However, there are some clouds on the horizon. Ireland is saddled with an underperforming health service, whose costs have tripled in seven years with only limited gains in output, and government expenditures amounted to 34.3 percent of GDP in 2004. Ireland's fiscal burden of government score is 0.2 point better this year, and its monetary policy score is 1 point better. As a result, Ireland's overall score is 0.12 point better this year.

TRADE POLICY
Score: **2**–Stable (low level of protectionism)

As a member of the European Union, Ireland was subject to a common EU weighted average external tariff of 1.3 percent in 2003, down from the 2.4 percent for 2002 reported in the 2005 *Index*, based on World Bank data. According to the World Trade Organization and the U.S. Trade Representative, the EU imposes non-tariff trade barriers through a complex regulatory system and export subsidies. Based on the revised trade factor methodology, Ireland's trade policy score is unchanged.

FISCAL BURDEN OF GOVERNMENT
Score—Income Taxation: **4**–Stable (high tax rates)
Score—Corporate Taxation: **1**–Stable (very low tax rates)
Score—Change in Government Expenditures: **3**–Better (very low decrease)
Final Score: **2.3**–Better (low cost of government)

Ireland's top income tax rate is 42 percent. The top corporate tax rate is 12.5 percent. In 2004, government expenditures as a percent of GDP decreased 0.1 percentage point to 34.3 percent, compared to the 0.5 percentage point increase in 2003. On net, Ireland's fiscal burden of government score is 0.2 point better this year.

GOVERNMENT INTERVENTION IN THE ECONOMY
Score: **2**–Stable (low level)

According to the Ministry of Finance, the government consumed 14.4 percent of GDP in 2004. In the same year, based on data from the Ministry of Finance, Ireland received 1.9 percent of its total revenues from state-owned enterprises and government ownership of property.

MONETARY POLICY
Score: **1**–Better (very low level of inflation)

Ireland is a member of the euro zone. From 1995 to 2004, Ireland's weighted average annual rate of inflation was 2.83 percent, down from the 3.91 percent from 1994 to 2003 reported in the 2005 *Index*. As a result, Ireland's monetary policy score is 1 point better this year.

CAPITAL FLOWS AND FOREIGN INVESTMENT
Score: **1**–Stable (very low barriers)

Ireland welcomes foreign investment, and barriers are minimal. The government does not distinguish between domestic and foreign investment, and all firms incorporated in Ireland receive equal treatment. The only constraints on foreign investment involve ownership of Irish airlines by non-EU residents and restrictions on the purchase of agricultural lands. Foreign investors can participate in the sale of Irish state-owned companies. According to the U.S. Department of Commerce, "Ireland, with one percent of the EU's population, attracted twenty-five percent of all new U.S. investment in the EU over the last decade. In 2003, U.S. investment flow into Ireland was roughly USD 9.1 billion, two-and-a-half times the amount of U.S. investment flow into China." There is no approval process for foreign investment or capital inflows unless the company is applying for incentives. There are no restrictions or barriers with respect to current transfers, repatriation of profits, or access to foreign exchange.

BANKING AND FINANCE
Score: **1**–Stable (very low level of restrictions)

Ireland's banking and financial system is advanced and competitive. In 2004, total assets of licensed credit institutions represented over 400 percent of GDP—the second largest ratio in the EU after Luxembourg. According to the Economist Intelligence Unit, "The banking industry is diverse with around 90 banks and other credit institutions authorised to conduct business in 2002, most of which are foreign." The EIU reports that two large banks (Allied Irish Banks and Bank of Ireland) control 70 percent of the market. According to the U.S. Department of Commerce, "ACC Bank is the sole state-owned financial institution providing a broad range of retail and business banking services, with a particular emphasis on the agricultural sector." Dublin has attracted a number of foreign banks through its International Financial Services Center, which offers banks a corporate tax rate of 12.5 percent (up from the 10 percent originally offered). The European Commission views this corporate tax rate as an aid to industry, but the U.S. Department of Commerce reports that "the Irish Government has resolutely resisted efforts to harmonize taxes at a single EU rate."

WAGES AND PRICES
Score: **2**–Stable (low level of intervention)

The market determines most prices. According to the Economist Intelligence Unit, "There are no government-imposed price controls, and price-fixing arrangements are specifically prohibited under the 1991 Competition Act." The government affects agricultural prices through Ireland's participation in the Common Agricultural Policy, a program that heavily subsidizes agricultural goods. It also intervenes in public and private wage setting through the National Wage Partnership Program. Ireland implemented a new national minimum wage in 2001.

PROPERTY RIGHTS
Score: **1**–Stable (very high level of protection)

Expropriation of property is highly unlikely. Property receives good protection from the court system. The Economist Intelligence Unit reports that "contractual agreements are secure in Ireland, and both the judiciary and the civil service are of high quality."

REGULATION
Score: **2**–Stable (low level)

Overall, Ireland's policy framework promotes an open and competitive business environment. According to the U.S. Department of Commerce, "The Irish Government generally employs a transparent and effective policy framework that fosters competition between private businesses in a non-discriminatory fashion…. Most tax, labor, environment, health and safety, and other laws are compatible with European Union regulations, and they do not adversely affect investment. Bureaucratic procedures generally are transparent and reasonably efficient." The Economist Intelligence Unit reports that "the government has put increasing emphasis on 'precautionary' and 'polluter pays' principles." Mining investments need authorization from the Department of Public Enterprise. The U.S. Department of Commerce reports that "Irish labor force regulation is less restrictive compared with most continental EU countries." Corruption is not a serious problem for investors.

INFORMAL MARKET
Score: **1.5**–Stable (low level of activity)

Transparency International's 2004 score for Ireland is 7.5. As a result, Ireland's informal market score is 1.5 this year.

Ireland qualifies for the Global Free Trade Alliance.

ISRAEL

Rank: 36

Score: 2.36

Category: Mostly Free

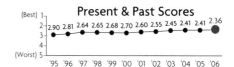
Present & Past Scores

(Best) 1
2 — 2.90 2.81 2.64 2.65 2.68 2.70 2.60 2.55 2.45 2.41 2.41 **2.36**
3
4
(Worst) 5

'95 '96 '97 '98 '99 '00 '01 '02 '03 '04 '05 '06

QUICK STUDY

SCORES

Trade Policy	2
Fiscal Burden	4.1
Government Intervention	2.5
Monetary Policy	1
Foreign Investment	2
Banking and Finance	3
Wages and Prices	2
Property Rights	2
Regulation	3
Informal Market	2

Population: 6,800,000

Total area: 20,770 sq. km

GDP: $115.7 billion

GDP growth rate: 4.3%

GDP per capita: $17,014

Major exports: electronic communication, medical and scientific equipment, chemicals, chemical products and cut diamonds

Exports of goods and services: $42.1 billion

Major export trading partners: US 42.4%, Belgium 6.1%, UK 4.7%, Germany 4.4%, Netherlands 3.7%

Major imports: machinery and equipment, fuel, chemicals

Imports of goods and services: $47.8 billion

Major import trading partners: US 22.4%, Germany 8.9%, Belgium 8.4%, UK 7.3%

Foreign direct investment (net): $1.7 billion (2003)

2004 Data (in constant 2000 US dollars)

Israel won its independence from Britain in 1948 and fought a series of wars against its Arab neighbors that imposed a high defense burden on the state-dominated economy. Despite few natural resources, Israel has developed a modern economy with a thriving technology sector. The collapse of the 1993 Oslo peace agreement with the Palestinians and the onset of the *intifada* in September 2000 depressed tourism, discouraged foreign investment, and contributed to economic recession. Since his landslide re-election in January 2003, Prime Minister Ariel Sharon has focused on reducing the continued threat of Palestinian terrorism. His plan for unilateral withdrawal from Gaza has divided his Likud Party and led him into a fragile governing coalition with the Labor Party. While Sharon has made security his top priority, former Finance Minister Benjamin Netanyahu spearheaded efforts to rein in public-sector growth and reinvigorate the privatization program. Further sales of government stakes in companies such as Bank Leumi and Bezeq are expected. Economic growth could improve if the January 2005 election of Palestinian President Mahmoud Abbas leads to progress in peace negotiations. Israel's trade policy score is 0.5 point better this year. As a result, its overall score is 0.05 point better this year.

TRADE POLICY
Score: **2**–Better (low level of protectionism)

Based on information from the Economist Intelligence Unit and the International Monetary Fund, Israel's average tariff rate in 2003 (the most recent year for which data are available) was 2 percent, down from the 4 percent in 1993 reported in the 2005 *Index*, based on World Bank data. Because Israel's weighted average tariff data for 1993 from the World Bank were extremely dated, it was deemed that the 2003 average tariff rate data reflected Israel's trade policy more accurately. According to the U.S. Trade Representative, "The cost of labeling has acted as a deterrent…. Technical standards are increasingly becoming a prominent non-tariff barrier." Based on the lower tariff rate, as well as a revision of the trade factor methodology, Israel's trade policy score is 0.5 point better this year.

FISCAL BURDEN OF GOVERNMENT
Score—Income Taxation: **5**–Stable (very high tax rates)
Score—Corporate Taxation: **4.5**–Stable (very high tax rates)
Score—Change in Government Expenditures: **2.5**–Stable (low decrease)
Final Score: **4.1**–Stable (high cost of government)

According to Deloitte, Israel's top income tax rate is 50 percent. The top corporate tax rate has been cut to 34 percent from 35 percent, effective January 2005. In 2004, based on data from the International Monetary Fund, government expenditures as a share of GDP decreased 1.6 percentage points to 51.6 percent, compared to a 1 percentage point decrease in 2003.

GOVERNMENT INTERVENTION IN THE ECONOMY
Score: **2.5**–Stable (moderate level)

Based on Central Bureau of Statistics data, the government consumed 29.2 percent of GDP in 2004. In the same year, based on data from the Ministry of Finance, Israel received 1.49 percent of its total revenues from state-owned enterprises and government ownership of property.

MONETARY POLICY
Score: **1**–Stable (very low level of inflation)

From 1995 to 2004, Israel's weighted average annual rate of inflation was 0.47 percent.

CAPITAL FLOWS AND FOREIGN INVESTMENT
Score: **2**–Stable (low barriers)

There are few significant barriers to foreign investment. "There are few restrictions on foreign investors," reports the U.S. Department of Commerce, "except for parts of the defense industry that are closed to outside investors on national security grounds. There is no screening of foreign investment and no regulations regarding acquisitions, mergers, and takeovers that differ from those that Israelis must follow.... Investments in regulated industries (e.g. banking, insurance), however, require prior government approval." According to the International Monetary Fund, both residents and non-residents may hold foreign exchange accounts, and there are no controls or restrictions on current transfers, repatriation of profits, or other transactions. Israel's bureaucracy can be difficult to navigate. The U.S. Department of Commerce reports that on January 1, 2003, Israel removed the "last restrictions placed on the ability of institutional investors to invest abroad...." Political instability is a disincentive to investment. The IMF reports that the government has equalized the tax applied to foreign securities and domestically traded securities.

BANKING AND FINANCE
Score: **3**–Stable (moderate level of restrictions)

Although the government is divesting itself from the banking sector, it retains significant shares of some of Israel's largest banks. According to the Economist Intelligence Unit, "The five largest banks—two of them majority government-owned—dominate the sector, although a number of more nimble private and foreign banks have enjoyed some success. Virtually all Israeli banks are universal banks, offering both traditional corporate and retail services, while also pursuing capital-market activities." The top five banks control over 95 percent of total banking assets, and the top two (Bank Hapoalim and Bank Leumi) control 60 percent. The government is pursuing plans to sell its stake in Bank Leumi and Israel Discount Bank. The Economist Intelligence Unit reports that the government owns the Industrial Development Bank but is selling it off and winding down its loan portfolio. The U.S. Department of Commerce reports that investments in the banking and insurance sector require prior government approval. The government is in the process of forcing banks to divest their asset management operations and insurance companies.

WAGES AND PRICES
Score: **2**–Stable (low level of intervention)

Most price controls have been lifted. According to the Economist Intelligence Unit, however, "The Ministry of Industry and Trade [can] impose price controls on goods and services supplied by a monopoly, or in the framework of restricted trade. Controls may also be imposed if there is a large concentration in the supply of a good, or if the goods and services are subsidised, or their producers receive support from the state budget. The government is entitled to impose price controls on goods and services deemed vital." Israel has a minimum wage.

PROPERTY RIGHTS
Score: **2**–Stable (high level of protection)

"In spite of the fractious political environment," reports the Economist Intelligence Unit, "contractual arrangements in Israel are generally secure. The country's legal system is largely based on the UK's but is increasingly influenced by US attitudes and trends. It is widely perceived to be independent, fair and honest." According to the U.S. Department of Commerce, "Israel has a written and consistently applied commercial law based on the British Companies Act of 1948 as amended." Expropriation is possible, particularly for Palestinians, but reportedly occurs only if the property is linked to a terrorist threat and expropriation is deemed to be in the interest of national security.

REGULATION
Score: **3**–Stable (moderate level)

According to the Economist Intelligence Unit, "After complying with the formal requirements and paying capitalisation and registration fees, a firm must file with the Registrar of Companies to be recognised as a legal entity. Registration documents are usually filed in Hebrew, with financial data expressed in shekels, though corporate documents in English are accepted." The U.S. Department of Commerce reports that "tax, labor, health, and safety laws can be impediments to...investors. Although the current trend is towards deregulation, Israel's bureaucracy can still be difficult to navigate.... It is important that potential investors get approvals or other commitments made by regulatory officials in writing before proceeding, rather than relying on unofficial oral promises." Bribery and corruption are not regarded as serious impediments.

INFORMAL MARKET
Score: **2**–Stable (low level of activity)

Transparency International's 2003 score for Israel is 6.4. Therefore, Israel's informal market score is 2 this year.

> If Israel were to improve its regulation score, it would qualify for the Global Free Trade Alliance.

ITALY

Rank: 42

Score: 2.50

Category: Mostly Free

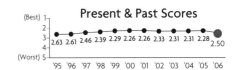

Present & Past Scores

(Best) 1
2
3
4
(Worst) 5

2.63 2.61 2.46 2.39 2.29 2.26 2.26 2.33 2.31 2.31 2.28 2.50

'95 '96 '97 '98 '99 '00 '01 '02 '03 '04 '05 '06

QUICK STUDY

SCORES

Trade Policy	2
Fiscal Burden	4
Government Intervention	2
Monetary Policy	1
Foreign Investment	2
Banking and Finance	3
Wages and Prices	2
Property Rights	3
Regulation	3
Informal Market	3

Population: 58,100,000

Total area: 301,230 sq. km

GDP: $1.1 trillion

GDP growth rate: 1.2%

GDP per capita: $18,932

Major exports: engineering products, textiles, clothing and leather, transport equipment, chemicals, food and beverages

Exports of goods and services: $286.8 billion

Major export trading partners: Germany 14.1%, France 12.5%, US 8.3%, UK 7.1%

Major imports: transport equipment, energy products, textiles and clothing

Imports of goods and services: $292.3 billion

Major import trading partners: Germany 18.1%, France 11.4%, Netherlands 5.8%, UK 4.8%

Foreign direct investment (net): −$2.2 billion

2004 Data (in constant 2004 US dollars)

The May 2001 election of Prime Minister Silvio Berlusconi seemed to give Italy a chance to advance economic reforms, but little has been done. The state's huge pension liabilities, labor market rigidities, and bureaucratic burdens remain unaddressed, and cuts in individual income taxes have been minuscule. Italian law forces large firms in effect to take on workers for life, since dismissing employees remains difficult. The European Commission has repeatedly warned Italy to open up its credit market, yet in 2005, the central bank opposed bids by two foreign institutions to buy Italian banks. A subsequent scandal erupted over allegations of collusion between the central bank governor and the Italian banks. Italian competitiveness has declined on international markets. The economy has underperformed the rest of the euro zone throughout the past half-decade. In 2004, GDP grew by only 1.2 percent, public debt remained at 106 percent of GDP, and unemployment was a relatively high 8.1 percent. Population is stagnant. In April 2005, Berlusconi's center–right coalition was trounced in regional elections, losing 12 of 14 contests, and Berlusconi was forced to form a new government more committed to helping the country's poorer southern region and to decreasing corporate taxes than to implementing Berlusconi's previously promised cuts in the income tax. It therefore seems unlikely that this new government will fare much better than the last one did. Italy's fiscal burden of government score is 0.3 point better this year; however, its banking and finance score and property rights score are both 1 point worse, and its informal market score is 0.5 point worse. As a result, Italy's overall score is 0.22 point worse this year.

TRADE POLICY
Score: **2**–Stable (low level of protectionism)

As a member of the European Union, Italy was subject to a common EU weighted average external tariff of 1.3 percent in 2003, down from the 2.4 percent for 2002 reported in the 2005 *Index*, based on World Bank data. According to the World Trade Organization and the U.S. Trade Representative, the EU imposes non-tariff trade barriers through a complex regulatory system and export subsidies. The U.S. Department of Commerce reports prohibitions on certain foodstuffs, animal products, plants, and similar items. Based on the revised trade factor methodology, Italy's trade policy score is unchanged.

FISCAL BURDEN OF GOVERNMENT
Score—Income Taxation: **4**–Better (high tax rates)
Score—Corporate Taxation: **4.5**–Stable (very high tax rates)
Score—Change in Government Expenditures: **3**–Better (very low decrease)
Final Score: **4**–Better (high cost of government)

Italy's top income tax rate has been cut to 43 percent from 45.6 percent. The top corporate income tax rate has been reduced to 33 percent from 34 percent. In 2004, government expenditures as a percent of GDP decreased 0.6 percentage point to 48.6 percent, compared to a 0.8 percentage point increase in 2003. On net, Italy's fiscal burden of government score is 0.3 point better this year.

GOVERNMENT INTERVENTION IN THE ECONOMY
Score: **2**–Stable (low level)

Based on data from the Economist Intelligence Unit, the government consumed 18.3 percent of GDP in 2004. In the same year, based on data from the Ministry of Economy and Finance, Italy received 1.34 percent of its total revenues from state-owned enterprises and government ownership of property.

MONETARY POLICY
Score: 1–Stable (very low level of inflation)

Italy is a member of the euro zone. From 1995 to 2004, Italy's weighted average annual rate of inflation was 2.36 percent.

CAPITAL FLOWS AND FOREIGN INVESTMENT
Score: 2–Stable (low barriers)

Italy welcomes foreign investment, although the government can veto mergers and acquisitions involving foreign investors for "reasons essential to the national economy" or if the foreign investor's home country applies restrictions against Italian investors. The government does not screen foreign investment, and the tax code does not discriminate against foreign investments. Foreign investment is prohibited or closely regulated in the defense, aircraft manufacturing, domestic airlines, and shipping sectors. According to the U.S. Department of Commerce, "Foreign investors generally find no major impediments to investing…. Analyses and surveys," however, "routinely cite excessive bureaucracy, inadequate infrastructure and a rigid labor market as disincentives for foreign investment in Italy." Foreign citizens may not buy land along the Italian border. Residents and non-residents may hold foreign exchange accounts, and there are no barriers to repatriation of profits, transfers, payments, or current transfers.

BANKING AND FINANCE
Score: 3–Worse (moderate level of restrictions)

Italy's banking sector was dominated by the state until a recent spate of privatizations. According to the Economist Intelligence Unit, "Now, only two major state-owned financial institutions [Cassa Depositi e Prestiti and Banco Posta] continue to survive and will remain in state hands." At the end of 2003, Italy had 788 banks, including 244 commercial banks, 38 popular banks, 445 cooperative banks, and 61 subsidiaries of foreign banks. There has been increasing consolidation as private banks have merged with or bought stakes in former state banks; in 2003, the five largest bank groups had a market share of 51 percent. Approval from the Bank of Italy is required for a foreign investor to own more than 5 percent of an Italian bank. A number of foreign banks have a small stake in Italian banks. In early 2005, the government announced that foreign banks would not be allowed to gain a controlling stake in Italian banks. Based on this policy, Italy's banking and finance score is 1 point worse this year.

WAGES AND PRICES
Score: 2–Stable (low level of intervention)

The market determines most wages and prices, but the gov-

ernment can introduce price controls through the Interministerial Committee on Economic Programming. According to the Economist Intelligence Unit, "Goods and services now subject to rate setting at the national level include drinking water, electricity, gas, highway tolls, prescription drugs reimbursed by the national health service, postal tariffs, radio and television licenses, telephone rates and certain fares for domestic travel (air, lake ferry, bus and railway)." In addition, "the Italian Competition Authority can control a dominant firm's pricing." The government affects agricultural prices through Italy's participation in the Common Agricultural Policy, a program that heavily subsidizes agricultural goods.

PROPERTY RIGHTS
Score: 3–Worse (moderate level of protection)

The Economist Intelligence Unit reports that "contractual agreements in Italy are generally secure" but that "the prospect of long delays in the overburdened judicial system often leads companies to settle disputes out of court…. [C]orruption and improper business practices are more common than in Northern Europe." According to the U.S. Department of Commerce, "Given the slowness of the Italian judicial system (normally at least five years for trial in a civil matter plus many more years for two automatic appeals), investors are advised to choose arbitration, which can be Italian or international." Also, "Italian judges are very politically oriented…." Based on this new evidence, Italy's property rights score is 1 point worse this year.

REGULATION
Score: 3–Stable (moderate level)

Red tape and regulations that vary from region to region and are inefficiently implemented contribute to a non-transparent system. According to the Economist Intelligence Unit, "The local one-stop shop (sportello unico), where activated, has significantly reduced the time needed to set up a business. It now takes an average of three months, a notable improvement on the previous 2–5 years." Still, many procedures are complicated. The EIU reports that "more than 40,000 laws…make up Italian environmental legislation; they are highly fragmented, and regional authorities interpret them inconsistently." Labor laws are rigid. The U.S. Department of Commerce reports that "surveys of the business community in Italy routinely identify…domestic corruption as a disincentive to investing or doing business in the south and some other less-developed areas of Italy."

INFORMAL MARKET
Score: 3–Worse (moderate level of activity)

Transparency International's 2004 score for Italy is 4.8. Therefore, Italy's informal market score is 3 this year—0.5 point worse than last year.

IVORY COAST

Rank: 88

Score: 3.14

Category: Mostly Unfree

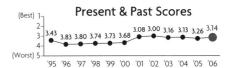

Present & Past Scores

(Best) 1
2
3 3.43 3.83 3.80 3.74 3.73 3.68 3.08 3.00 3.16 3.13 3.26 3.14
4
5 (Worst)

'95 '96 '97 '98 '99 '00 '01 '02 '03 '04 '05 '06

QUICK STUDY

SCORES

Trade Policy	4
Fiscal Burden	4.4
Government Intervention	1.5
Monetary Policy	1
Foreign Investment	3
Banking and Finance	2
Wages and Prices	3
Property Rights	4
Regulation	4
Informal Market	4.5

Population: 16,835,416

Total area: 322,460 sq. km

GDP: $10.0 billion

GDP growth rate: −3.8%

GDP per capita: $597

Major exports: cocoa, coffee, petroleum, timber

Exports of goods and services: $4.3 billion

Major export trading partners: France 19.0%, Netherlands 17.7%, US 7.1%, Spain 5.6%

Major imports: petroleum, food, transport equipment

Imports of goods and services: $3.5 billion

Major import trading partners: France 32.7%, Nigeria 14.4%, UK 7.0%

Foreign direct investment (net): $365.7 million

2003 Data (in constant 2000 US dollars)

Ivory Coast (Côte d'Ivoire) has seen significant unrest since an attempted coup by exiled members of the military in September 2002 sparked a full-scale rebellion that split the country. Hope for lasting peace and transition to an elected government acceptable to all parties resides in the Pretoria Accord brokered in April 2005 by South African President Thabo Mbeki. If the Pretoria Accord fails, the country will remain divided, the economy stalled, and peace threatened by the prospect of renewed fighting. Elections were scheduled for October 2005, but their credibility depended on significant progress in dealing with such political and logistical challenges as voter registration and disarmament. President Laurent Gbagbo had agreed to let Alassane Ouattara, former prime minister and opposition leader, run for president in the scheduled elections. Political unrest, corruption, and a lack of accountability in the executive and judicial branches of government all impede growth. The economy relies on cash crops that are generally raised on small farms, but the government's policy of squeezing the cocoa sector for revenue has created disincentives to produce. Ivory Coast's informal market score is 0.5 point worse this year; however, its fiscal burden of government score is 0.2 point better, its government intervention score is 0.5 point better, and its monetary policy score is 1 point better. As a result, Ivory Coast's overall score is 0.12 point better this year.

TRADE POLICY
Score: **4–Stable** (high level of protectionism)

Ivory Coast is a member of the West African Economic and Monetary Union (WAEMU). According to the World Bank, Ivory Coast's weighted average tariff rate in 2004 was 10.7 percent, down from the 12 percent in 2002 reported in the 2005 *Index*, based on World Bank data. According to the U.S. Trade Representative, import prohibitions, restrictions, or prior authorization apply to "petroleum products, animal products, live plants, seeds, arms and munitions, plastic bags, distilling equipment, pornography, saccharin, narcotics, explosives, illicit drugs, and toxic waste." The USTR also reports corruption in customs. Based on the revised trade factor methodology, Ivory Coast's trade policy score is unchanged.

FISCAL BURDEN OF GOVERNMENT
Score—Income Taxation: **5–Stable** (very high tax rates)
Score—Corporate Taxation: **4.5–Stable** (very high tax rates)
Score—Change in Government Expenditures: **3.5–Better** (low increase)
Final Score: **4.4–Better** (high cost of government)

Ivory Coast's top income tax rate is 60 percent. The top corporate income tax rate is 35 percent. According to the African Development Bank, government expenditures as a share of GDP increased less in 2003 (0.2 percentage point to 19.7 percent) than they did in 2002 (2.9 percentage points). On net, Ivory Coast's fiscal burden of government score is 0.2 point better this year.

GOVERNMENT INTERVENTION IN THE ECONOMY
Score: **1.5–Better** (low level)

The World Bank reports that the government consumed 8.2 percent of GDP in 2003, down from the 11.4 percent reported in the 2005 *Index*. As a result, Ivory Coast's government intervention score is 0.5 point better this year. In 2002, based on data from the International Monetary

Fund, Ivory Coast received 3.36 percent of its total revenues from state-owned enterprises and government ownership of property.

MONETARY POLICY
Score: 1–Better (very low level of inflation)

As a member of the West African Economic and Monetary Union, Ivory Coast uses the CFA franc, pegged to the euro. From 1995 to 2004, based on data from the International Monetary Fund's *2005 World Economic Outlook*, Ivory Coast's weighted average annual rate of inflation was 2.16 percent, down from the 3.33 percent from 1994 to 2003 reported in the 2005 *Index*. As a result, Ivory Coast's monetary policy score is 1 point better this year.

CAPITAL FLOWS AND FOREIGN INVESTMENT
Score: 3–Stable (moderate barriers)

The government welcomes foreign investment, but political instability poses a significant disincentive. "There are no significant limits on foreign investment," reports the U.S. Department of Commerce, "nor are there generally differences in treatment of foreign and national investors…. The [government] does not screen investments and has no overall economic and industrial strategy that discriminates against foreign-owned firms." According to the U.S. Trade Representative, "corruption [is] an obstacle to investment in Cote d'Ivoire." The International Monetary Fund reports that foreign exchange accounts by residents are permitted but must be approved by the government and the Central Bank of West African States, or BCEAO, and that non-residents can hold them with approval of the BCEAO. Transfers to countries other than France, Monaco, members of the WAEMU, members of the Central African Economic and Monetary Community (CEMAC), and Comoros must also be approved by the government. Other transfers are subject to numerous requirements, controls, and authorization depending on the transaction. Capital transactions are subject to government authorization in many cases.

BANKING AND FINANCE
Score: 2–Stable (low level of restrictions)

The BCEAO, a central bank common to the eight members of the WAEMU, governs Ivory Coast's banking system. The Economist Intelligence Unit reports that commercial banks have been closed since the start of the civil war in areas controlled by the rebels. According to the U.S. Department of Commerce, "Cote d'Ivoire's financial system remains functional. Banks generally make lending and investment decisions on business criteria. The banking and financial system, however, offers only certain kinds of instruments and financial markets are thin. [Government] policies generally encourage the free flow of capital…. The [government] relinquished its interest in smaller banks and retains only a small minority share in several large banks." At the end of 2003, there were 22 banks and financial institutions. The largest banks have a foreign ownership stake.

WAGES AND PRICES
Score: 3–Stable (moderate level of intervention)

The government has approved a Bourse du Café et Cacao to monitor and set minimum producer prices every three months, the Autorité de Regulation du Café et Cacao to manage a system of purchasing quotas, and the Fond de Régulation et de Contrôle to finance price stabilization through taxation on cocoa exports and forward selling. The government sets a minimum wage.

PROPERTY RIGHTS
Score: 4–Stable (low level of protection)

According to the U.S. Department of State, "The Constitution provides for an independent judiciary; however, in practice the judiciary was subject to executive branch, military, and other outside influences…. Judges served at the discretion of the executive, and there were credible reports that they submitted to political pressure and financial influence. The judiciary was slow and inefficient."

REGULATION
Score: 4–Stable (high level)

Ivory Coast's bureaucracy obstructs business activity. The Economist Intelligence Unit reports that "heavy red tape pervades public administration, making it sometimes slow and inefficient." The government has made some efforts to increase regulatory transparency. According to the U.S. Department of Commerce, Ivory Coast is a member of "OHADA (Organization pour l'Harmonization en Afrique du Droit des Affaires): an organization that harmonizes a broad range of legal systems which previously were widely disparate in their approach to business law, codes, rules, regulations and local conventions affecting business. The agreement creates a number of uniform acts and sets up organizations when necessary to implement the acts." The same source reports that companies see corruption as an impediment to doing business.

INFORMAL MARKET
Score: 4.5–Worse (very high level of activity)

Transparency International's 2004 score for Ivory Coast is 2. Therefore, Ivory Coast's informal market score is 4.5 this year—0.5 point worse than last year.

JAMAICA

Rank: 54

Score: 2.76

Category: Mostly Free

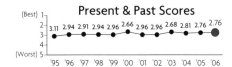

Present & Past Scores

(Best) 1
2
3
4
(Worst) 5

3.11 2.94 2.91 2.94 2.96 2.66 2.96 2.96 2.68 2.81 2.76 2.76

'95 '96 '97 '98 '99 '00 '01 '02 '03 '04 '05 '06

QUICK STUDY

SCORES

Trade Policy	3.5
Fiscal Burden	4.1
Government Intervention	2.5
Monetary Policy	3
Foreign Investment	1
Banking and Finance	2
Wages and Prices	2
Property Rights	3
Regulation	3
Informal Market	3.5

Population: 2,642,628

Total area: 10,990 sq. km

GDP: $8.34 billion

GDP growth rate: 2.3%

GDP per capita: $3,156

Major exports: alumina, bauxite, sugar, bananas, coffee, rum

Exports of goods and services: $3.4 billion

Major export trading partners: US 29.2%, Canada 11.7%, UK 10.8%, France 7.8%, Norway 6.8%

Major imports: raw materials, machinery and transport equipment, fuels

Imports of goods and services: $4.9 billion

Major import trading partners: US 39.8%, Trinidad and Tobago 9.7%, Germany 5.6%, Venezuela 4.5%

Foreign direct investment (net): $416 million

2003 Data (in constant 2000 US dollars)

Jamaica is the Caribbean's fourth most popular tourist destination. For two decades, expanding tourism has been the top foreign exchange earner, although receipts have declined slightly in the past two years following a rise in violent crime. Twenty percent of the labor force works in agriculture, which generates only 7 percent of GDP, incurs high production costs, and is susceptible to drought and floods. Other industries include mining for bauxite and alumina. Jamaica's market economy contracted in 1999 but has slowly returned to expansion, growing by 1 percent in 2002 and 2.3 percent in 2003, according to the Economist Intelligence Unit. Such lackluster growth has contributed to sustained unemployment rates of about 15 percent in the past three years. Joblessness and Jamaica's geographic location in the middle of drug smuggling routes from South America to the United States contribute to high crime rates. Current challenges to the economy include rising energy prices and inadequate infrastructure. Jamaica remains highly dependent on oil imports from Mexico and Venezuela, and its highway infrastructure is in poor condition. Jamaica is a member of the British Commonwealth, and both of its principal political parties favor policies attractive to foreign investors. Jamaica's overall score is unchanged this year.

 TRADE POLICY
Score: **3.5**–Stable (high level of protectionism)

As a member of the Caribbean Community and Common Market (CARICOM), Jamaica has a common external tariff rate that ranges from 5 percent to 20 percent. According to the World Bank, Jamaica's weighted average tariff rate in 2003 (the most recent year for which World Bank data are available) was 9.8 percent, up from the 7.8 percent in 2001 reported in the 2005 *Index,* based on World Bank data. The U.S. Department of Commerce reports that some items require import licenses and others are banned. The World Trade Organization reports that non-tariff barriers are low, but certain charges are applied exclusively to imports, and the government imposes selective import licensing. Based on the revised trade factor methodology, Jamaica's trade policy score is unchanged.

 FISCAL BURDEN OF GOVERNMENT
Score—Income Taxation: **2.5**–Stable (moderate tax rates)
Score—Corporate Taxation: **4.5**–Stable (very high tax rates)
Score—Change in Government Expenditures: **5**–Stable (very high increase)
Final Score: **4.1**–Stable (high cost of government)

Jamaica's top income tax rate is 25 percent. The top corporate tax rate is 33.3 percent. In 2003, based on data from Jamaica's central bank, government expenditures as a share of GDP increased 3.6 percentage points to 39 percent, compared to the 2.6 percentage point increase in 2002.

 GOVERNMENT INTERVENTION IN THE ECONOMY
Score: **2.5**–Stable (moderate level)

The World Bank reports that the government consumed 15.1 percent of GDP in 2003. In the April 2003–March 2004 fiscal year, based on data from the International Monetary Fund, Jamaica received 8.07 percent of its total revenues from state-owned enterprises and government ownership of property.

MONETARY POLICY
Score: **3**–Stable (moderate level of inflation)

From 1995 to 2004, Jamaica's weighted average annual rate of inflation was 11.99 percent.

 CAPITAL FLOWS AND FOREIGN INVESTMENT
Score: **1**–Stable (very low barriers)

Jamaica encourages foreign investment in all sectors. Foreign investors and domestic interests receive equal treatment, and foreign investors are not excluded from acquiring privatized state-owned enterprises. According to the U.S. Department of Commerce, "The [government] encourages foreign investment as a source of development and has no policies or regulations that reserve areas exclusively for Jamaicans." There is no screening of foreign investments, but the U.S. Department of Commerce notes that, even though no sector is officially closed to foreign investment, "projects that affect national security, have a negative impact on the environment, or involve sectors such as life insurance, media or mining are subjected to some restrictions." The International Monetary Fund reports that there are no restrictions on foreign exchange accounts, which may be held by both residents and non-residents. There are no restrictions on transactions, transfers, or repatriation of funds, and non-residents may purchase real estate. Capital or money market instruments are subject to government approval in some cases.

 BANKING AND FINANCE
Score: **2**–Stable (low level of restrictions)

A mid-1990s financial crisis prompted by non-performing loans led to a government bailout of the banking and insurance sectors, as well as strengthened supervision and regulation. The Financial Sector Adjustment Company (FINSAC) was created to provide funding, to reorganize illiquid and close insolvent financial institutions, and then to divest their assets. By 1998, the government owned controlling stakes in Jamaica's seven largest domestic banks. The Economist Intelligence Unit reports that FINSAC ultimately assumed control of more than 100 financial institutions and related companies. "Now that the sale of its major assets has taken place," however, its "mandate is considered to be largely complete." There were 15 deposit-taking institutions at the beginning of 2005, including six commercial banks, five merchant banks, and four building societies. According to the U.S. Department of Commerce, "The non-performing loans portfolio as a percentage of the total asset base has moved from seven percent in 2000 to 1 percent at the end of September 2004. Since the financial sector crisis, significant strides have also been made in terms of the regulatory framework, which are now in line with international standards." The Jamaican embassy reports that the government no longer has any stake in a commercial bank. The government continues to be involved in the sector by providing concessionary financing through development banks.

 WAGES AND PRICES
Score: **2**–Stable (low level of intervention)

According to the U.S. Department of Commerce, "Most prices are freely determined by the market. Notable exceptions are utility services, such as electricity, water and bus fares. The Office of Utilities Regulation has been set up to monitor pricing and other activities for utility companies.... While there are no official or government policies on price regulation or control, the Fair Trading Commission (FTC) and the Consumer Affairs Commission (CAC) do monitor pricing of consumer items." Jamaica has a minimum wage law, but most workers are paid more than the minimum.

 PROPERTY RIGHTS
Score: **3**–Stable (moderate level of protection)

The U.S. Department of Commerce reports that "Jamaica's legal system is based on English common law principles and the rules in relation to the enforceability of contracts are therefore based on the English common law. The Jamaican judicial system therefore recognizes and upholds the sanctity of contracts." However, the judiciary lacks adequate resources; in some cases, according to the U.S. Department of State, "trials... are delayed for years, and other cases are dismissed because files cannot be located." An inadequate police force further weakens the security of property rights; the U.S. Department of Commerce reports that "crime poses a greater threat to foreign investment than do politically motivated activities." Expropriation is unlikely.

 REGULATION
Score: **3**–Stable (moderate level)

Most regulations are moderately burdensome, and red tape can be a problem. According to the U.S. Department of Commerce, "A cumbersome bureaucracy has been identified as a major disincentive to investment in Jamaica." In addition, "Although there has been improvement in the approval process for most investment projects, the time can take anywhere from three months for Free Zone projects to over a year for large mining and greenfield projects." Approval of new developments requires environmental impact assessments. The U.S. Department of Commerce and other sources identify corruption as a problem and the country's high crime rate as a deterrent to investment.

 INFORMAL MARKET
Score: **3.5**–Stable (high level of activity)

Transparency International's 2004 score for Jamaica is 3.3. Therefore, Jamaica's informal market score is 3.5 this year.

JAPAN

Rank: 27

Score: 2.26

Category: Mostly Free

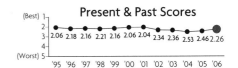

Present & Past Scores

(Best) 1
2
3 — 2.06 2.18 2.16 2.21 2.16 2.06 2.04 2.34 2.36 2.53 2.46 2.26
4
(Worst) 5
'95 '96 '97 '98 '99 '00 '01 '02 '03 '04 '05 '06

Japan's growth was robust early in 2004 but slowed to an annual 2.7 percent by year's end. Prime Minister Junichiro Koizumi was expected to step down when his term as leader of the ruling Liberal Democratic Party was scheduled to end in September 2006, but that plan was put in jeopardy when Koizumi was handed a defeat on the privatization of postal savings and insurance businesses in August 2005, forcing him to call a September "snap" election of the lower house of the Diet. In March 2005, in an effort to address a large budget deficit (6.5 percent of GDP in 2004), the Diet passed a fiscal budget with projected revenue growth of 5.4 percent but also with spending of $547 billion, which is unchanged from the previous year. Overseas markets and conditions abroad have an important impact on economic recovery, since consumer spending, which accounts for 60 percent of GDP, has been flat or falling amid steadily declining incomes. Complicating Japan's increasing economic interdependence with China, which is now Japan's largest trading partner, are tensions regarding China's increasingly aggressive military programs. Such tensions are particularly unsettling, given continued North Korean provocations, and contribute to economic uncertainties in the region. Japan's capital flows and foreign investment score and banking and finance score are both 1 point better this year. As a result, Japan's overall score is 0.2 point better this year.

QUICK STUDY

SCORES

Trade Policy	2
Fiscal Burden	3.6
Government Intervention	2
Monetary Policy	1
Foreign Investment	2
Banking and Finance	3
Wages and Prices	2
Property Rights	2
Regulation	3
Informal Market	2

Population: 127,687,000

Total area: 377, 835 sq. km

GDP: $5.1 trillion

GDP growth rate: 2.7%

GDP per capita: $39,941

Major exports: financial services, computer and information services, travel services, transport equipment, electrical machinery

Exports of goods and services: $572.1 billion

Major export trading partners: US 22.4%, China 13.1%, South Korea 7.8%, Taiwan 7.4%

Major imports: machinery and equipment, mineral fuels, food, chemicals, raw materials

Imports of goods and services: $476.1 billion

Major import trading partners: China 20.7%, US 13.7%, South Korea 4.8%, Australia 4.3%

Foreign direct investment (net): −$21.4 billion

2004 Data (in constant 2000 US dollars)

TRADE POLICY
Score: **2–Stable** (low level of protectionism)

According to the World Bank, Japan's weighted average tariff rate in 2004 was 2.4 percent, up from the 2.2 percent in 2002 reported in the 2005 *Index*, based on World Bank data. The World Trade Organization reports that "Japan has few non-tariff border measures. Those currently applied involve some import prohibitions and quantitative import restrictions (for example, on certain fish and silk). In addition, imports of certain goods are subject to licensing requirements…. Certain aspects of the import quota system can be intricate." According to the U.S. Department of Commerce, "While tariffs are generally low, Japan does have barriers that impede or delay the importation of foreign products…." These barriers include standards unique to Japan, requirements for prior experience in Japan's shutting out new entrants to the market, discriminatory regulation, licensing, and cartels. Based on the revised trade factor methodology, Japan's trade policy score is unchanged.

FISCAL BURDEN OF GOVERNMENT
Score—Income Taxation: **3.5–Stable** (high tax rates)
Score—Corporate Taxation: **4–Stable** (high tax rates)
Score—Change in Government Expenditures: **3–Stable** (very low decrease)
Final Score: **3.6–Stable** (high cost of government)

According to Deloitte, Japan's top income tax rate is 37 percent. The top corporate tax rate is 30 percent. In 2004, government expenditures as a share of GDP decreased 0.3 percentage point to 37.3 percent, compared to a 0.7 percentage point decrease in 2003.

GOVERNMENT INTERVENTION IN THE ECONOMY
Score: **2–Stable** (low level)

Based on Economist Intelligence Unit data, the government consumed 17.6 percent of GDP in 2004. In the same year, based on data from the Ministry of Finance, Japan received 1.13 percent of its total revenues from state-owned enterprises and government ownership of property.

MONETARY POLICY
Score: 1–Stable (very low level of inflation)

From 1995 to 2004, Japan's weighted average annual rate of inflation was –0.17 percent.

CAPITAL FLOWS AND FOREIGN INVESTMENT
Score: 2–Better (low barriers)

Most direct legal restrictions on foreign investment have been removed, but many bureaucratic and informal barriers remain in effect, as evidenced by Japan's last-place standing among the Organisation for Economic Co-operation and Development nations in foreign investment as a percentage of output. According to the U.S. Department of Commerce, "Corporate practices and market rules…inhibit foreign acquisition of Japanese firms, such as insufficient financial disclosure practices, cross-holding of shares among companies belonging to the same business grouping (keiretsu), the low proportion of publicly traded common stock relative to total capital in many companies, and public attitudes about foreign takeovers; Exclusive buyer-supplier networks and alliances are still maintained by some keiretsu, which limit competition from foreign firms and domestic newcomers; [and] Laws and regulations…directly or indirectly restrict the establishment of business facilities and hinder market access for foreign products, services, and FDI." Foreign investors must notify and obtain approval from the government for investments in the following restricted areas: agriculture, forestry, petroleum, electricity, gas, water, aerospace, telecommunications, and leather manufacturing. There are no restrictions or controls on the holding of foreign exchange accounts or on transactions, current transfers, repatriation of profits, or real estate transactions by residents or non-residents. Barriers are largely unofficial, and nearly all sectors of the economy are open to foreign investment. As a result, Japan's capital flows and foreign investment score is 1 point better this year. If implemented, proposed revisions in Japan's commercial code and tax laws that would penalize foreign investors and discourage mergers and acquisitions could affect Japan's capital flows and foreign investment score in future editions of the *Index*.

BANKING AND FINANCE
Score: 3–Better (moderate level of restrictions)

Japan's banking system is competitive but continues to suffer from non-performing loans resulting from the collapse of the asset-price bubble in the late 1980s and early 1990s. Banks have forged a number of mergers and alliances to bolster their balance sheets; the five largest domestic banking groups are the result of mergers in the past few years. "At the end of 2004," reports the Economist Intelligence Unit, "the Japanese banking

system included seven city banks, one long-term credit bank, five trust banks, 64 first-tier regional banks, 48 second-tier regional banks (which are all collectively known as commercial banks); 69 foreign banks; 301 credit associations; and 181 credit co-operatives." The government has announced plans to privatize the Postal Savings system—the country's largest financial institution and the world's largest depository institution—beginning in 2007, but that effort stalled in August 2005. Other government-affiliated financial institutions include the Development Bank of Japan, Japan Bank for International Co-operation, Government Housing Loan Corporation, Japan Finance Corporation for Small Business, National Life Finance Corporation, Shoko Chukin Bank, and Okinawa Development Finance Corporation. Japan has passed several laws liberalizing financial services, strengthening capital requirements, making regulations more transparent, allowing banks and insurance companies to engage in securities businesses, and permitting foreign exchange trading on the margin. According to the U.S. Department of Commerce, "Banks are often large shareholders in publicly traded corporations, have close relationships with both local governments and national regulatory agencies, and often play a coordinating role among their clients." The government does not hinder the formation of foreign banks, but it does affect the supply of credit through its state-run financial institutions. Although the government remains significantly involved in the financial sector, most institutions are privately held. On net, Japan's banking and finance score is 1 point better this year.

WAGES AND PRICES
Score: 2–Stable (low level of intervention)

According to the Economist Intelligence Unit, "Japan has no formal price controls except on rice (for which there are also import quotas). But indirect regulation continues to influence prices on a wide range of products…. The present government policy is to encourage lower prices by eliminating regulations, rationalising the distribution system and increasing anti-monopoly efforts." The government also maintains a price support program for agricultural goods, although the EIU reports that the "new food law…put into effect in April 2004, calls for a gradual shift away from government control over rice production and distribution." The U.S. Department of State reports that minimum wages are set with input advisory councils composed of representatives of business, workers, and "public interest" organizations.

PROPERTY RIGHTS
Score: 2–Stable (high level of protection)

In general, property rights are secure in Japan. According to the Economist Intelligence Unit, "Japan has civil courts for enforcing property and contractual rights. The courts do not discriminate against foreign investors, but these courts are ill suited for litigation of investment and business disputes." In addition, "the Japanese tend to write their contractual agreements in general terms, entrusting the details to the presumably fair judgment of the parties involved. Contracts are highly respected despite this lack of precision, and it is unusual for a business dispute to be settled through litigation." The same source reports that the courts can be very slow in settling disputes.

REGULATION
Score: **3**–Stable (moderate level)

Regulations impose a substantial burden on businesses. According to the U.S. Department of Commerce, "Japan's reputation for protectionism and red tape…is well deserved…. [T]he Japanese economy remains over-regulated and those regulations can be used to hinder foreign firms' attempts to gain access to the market." Bureaucrats and regulators are much more powerful in Japan than in other countries. According to the *Financial Times*, a typical goal of the bureaucracy is to "create national champions [as opposed to promoting competition] by skewing regulations in favour of selected incumbents." The U.S. Department of Commerce reports that the "Prime Minister launched an initiative, called the Special Zones for Structural Reform, that empowers local governments in Japan to take the lead on deregulation by establishing zones where businesses can be unfettered by onerous regulations."

INFORMAL MARKET
Score: **2**–Stable (low level of activity)

Transparency International's 2004 score for Japan is 6.9. Therefore, Japan's informal market score is 2 this year.

> If Japan were to improve its regulation score, it would qualify for the Global Free Trade Alliance.

JORDAN

Rank: 57

Score: 2.80

Category: Mostly Free

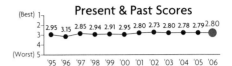

Present & Past Scores

(Best) 1
2 2.95 3.15 2.85 2.94 2.91 2.95 2.80 2.73 2.80 2.78 2.79 2.80
3
4
(Worst) 5
'95 '96 '97 '98 '99 '00 '01 '02 '03 '04 '05 '06

Jordan, which gained its independence from Britain in 1946, is a constitutional monarchy with relatively few natural resources and an economy that historically has been supported by foreign loans, aid, and remittances from expatriate workers, many of whom work in the Persian Gulf oil kingdoms. King Abdullah II has undertaken a bold program of economic reform since coming to power in 1999. Jordan joined the World Trade Organization in 2000 after implementing extensive legislative and regulatory reforms and improving security measures for foreign-owned intellectual property. It also signed a free trade agreement with the United States in 2000 and an association agreement with the European Union in 2001. Jordan suffers from high unemployment, a heavy debt burden, and the high cost of oil imports. Although tourism has been hurt by terrorism in Israel and the disputed Palestinian territories, the economy has benefited from the "Iraq effect," which has allowed Jordan to share the increased trade and postwar reconstruction efforts in neighboring Iraq. Real economic growth in 2004 was 6.1 percent. The private sector received a boost when the Jordanian Telecommunications Company lost its monopoly control over fixed-line and international services in January 2005 and the entire telecommunications sector was opened to private companies. Jordan's wages and prices score is 1 point better this year, and its informal market score is 0.5 point better; however, its fiscal burden of government score is 0.1 point worse, its government intervention score is 0.5 point worse, and its capital flows and foreign investment score is 1 point worse. As a result, Jordan's overall score is 0.01 point worse this year.

QUICK STUDY

SCORES

Trade Policy	4
Fiscal Burden	4
Government Intervention	3.5
Monetary Policy	1
Foreign Investment	3
Banking and Finance	2
Wages and Prices	2
Property Rights	3
Regulation	3
Informal Market	2.5

Population: 5,307,895

Total area: 92,300 sq. km

GDP: $9.56 billion

GDP growth rate: 3.2%

GDP per capita: $1,801

Major exports: manufactured goods, pharmaceuticals, machinery and transport equipment

Exports of goods and services: $4.3 billion

Major export trading partners: US 21.5%, India 6.5%, Switzerland 6.5%, Saudi Arabia 5.2%

Major imports: machinery and transport equipment, manufactured goods, food and live animals

Imports of goods and services: $6.4 billion

Major import trading partners: Saudi Arabia 11.3%, China 7.9%, Germany 7.9%, US 6.8%

Foreign direct investment (net): $354.8 million

2003 Data (in constant 2000 US dollars)

 ### TRADE POLICY
Score: **4**–Stable (high level of protectionism)

According to the World Bank, Jordan's weighted average tariff rate in 2003 (the most recent year for which World Bank data are available) was 11.4 percent, up from the 11.3 percent in 2002 reported in the 2005 *Index*, based on World Bank data. The U.S. Department of Commerce reports numerous restrictions on imports through prohibition, licensing, and restricting the right to import some goods to specific companies. Based on the revised trade factor methodology, Jordan's trade policy score is unchanged.

 ### FISCAL BURDEN OF GOVERNMENT
Score—Income Taxation: **2.5**–Stable (moderate tax rates)
Score—Corporate Taxation: **4.5**–Stable (very high tax rates)
Score—Change in Government Expenditures: **4.5**–Worse (high increase)
Final Score: **4**–Worse (high cost of government)

The International Monetary Fund reports that Jordan's top income tax rate is 25 percent. The top corporate tax rate is 35 percent. In 2003, according to the Ministry of Finance, government expenditures as a share of GDP increased 2.4 percentage points to 37.3 percent, compared to the 1.6 percentage point decrease in 2002. On net, Jordan's fiscal burden of government score is 0.1 point worse this year.

 ### GOVERNMENT INTERVENTION IN THE ECONOMY
Score: **3.5**–Worse (high level)

The World Bank reports that the government consumed 23.2 percent of GDP in 2003. In the same year, based on data from the central bank, Jordan received 13.96 percent of its total revenues from state-owned enterprises and government ownership of property, up from the 7.6 percent reported in the 2005 *Index*. As a result, Jordan's government intervention score is 0.5 point worse this year.

MONETARY POLICY
Score: **1**–Stable (very low level of inflation)

From 1995 to 2004, Jordan's weighted average annual rate of inflation was 2.74 percent.

CAPITAL FLOWS AND FOREIGN INVESTMENT
Score: **3**–Worse (moderate barriers)

The government promotes foreign investment. There is no formal screening process, but foreign investors face a minimum capital requirement of JD 50,000 on any one investment, according to the International Monetary Fund. The IMF reports that residents and non-residents may hold foreign exchange accounts. There are no restrictions or controls on payments, transactions, transfers, purchase of real estate (provided Jordan and the country of residence for the individual or business have a reciprocal relationship and Cabinet approval is obtained), or repatriation of profits. According to the U.S. Department of Commerce, foreign investments may not exceed 50 percent in construction, wholesale and retail trade, transport, wastewater treatment, food services, travel agent services, import and export services, and advertising. The same source notes that foreigners are prohibited from investing in investigation and security services, sports clubs, stone quarrying, custom clearance services, and land transportation. Based on increasing evidence of restrictions on foreign investment, Jordan's capital flows and foreign investment score is 1 point worse this year.

BANKING AND FINANCE
Score: **2**–Stable (low level of restrictions)

Jordan's banking system is open to foreign investment. According to the Economist Intelligence Unit, "In Middle Eastern terms, Jordan's financial services sector is relatively well developed. Until 2004 it was served by nine local commercial banks, two Islamic banks, five investment banks, and five foreign banks. In 2004 two Lebanese banks—Banque Audi and Banque du Liban et d'Outre Mer—and National Bank of Kuwait all entered the market." The central bank administers two banks—the Philadelphia Investment Bank and the Jordan Gulf Bank. Supervision has been strengthened, and regulations have been clarified and updated, through banking reform. The U.S. Department of Commerce reports that the banking law passed in 2000 "protects depositors' interests, diminishes money market risk, guards against the concentration of lending, and includes articles on new banking practices (e-commerce and e-banking) and money laundering." The Economist Intelligence Unit reports that the Arab Bank dominates the sector, accounting for about 60 percent of total banking assets. The banking system remains burdened by non-performing loans. According to the U.S. Department of Commerce, "While [central bank] officials

estimate the rate of non-performing loans at 15%, unofficial estimates put the figure closer to 20% or more."

WAGES AND PRICES
Score: **2**–Better (low level of intervention)

The government has removed most price controls but determines the price of fuel through subsidies and sets the price of electricity, public transportation, and flour. According to the Economist Intelligence Unit, the government froze public-sector salaries and cut subsidies for water and basic commodities as part of an agreement with the International Monetary Fund. The government subsidizes oil. There is a minimum wage for all workers except domestic servants, those working in small family businesses, and agricultural workers. Based on newly available data on prices, Jordan's wages and prices score is 1 point better this year.

PROPERTY RIGHTS
Score: **3**–Stable (moderate level of protection)

The judiciary is generally independent, although the Economist Intelligence Unit reports that the king is the country's ultimate authority. According to the U.S. Department of State, "The Ministry of Justice has great influence over a judge's career and subverts the judicial system in favor of the executive branch." The U.S. Department of State reports that the purpose of a law passed in June 2001 was "to limit the Ministry of Justice's influence over a judge's career and prevent it from subverting the judicial system in favor of the executive branch…. [However], judges complain of telephone surveillance by the government." Expropriation is unlikely.

REGULATION
Score: **3**–Stable (moderate level)

Jordan's regulatory environment is moderately bureaucratic and burdensome, but the government is attempting to reform the system and reduce red tape. According to the Economist Intelligence Unit, in order to improve the investment climate, "Changes have been made to customs, taxation, company law and the financial market…. Yet bureaucratic resistance and infighting has often weakened the impact of reforms…. Despite Jordan's new lure, foreign investors still complain about some aspects of the kingdom's investment climate. Western businessmen often find that after an initially enthusiastic response from Jordanian officials their investment bids become bogged down in red tape, with few officials willing to make a decision. Business start-up costs are high, while there is still plenty of scope to make employment regulations more flexible."

INFORMAL MARKET
Score: **2.5**–Better (moderate level of activity)

Transparency International's 2004 score for Jordan is 5.3. Therefore, Jordan's informal market score is 2.5 this year—0.5 point better than last year.

KAZAKHSTAN

Rank: 113

Score: 3.35

Category: Mostly Unfree

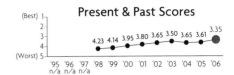

Present & Past Scores

(Best) 1
2
3
4
(Worst) 5

4.23 4.14 3.95 3.80 3.65 3.50 3.65 3.61 3.35
'95 '96 '97 '98 '99 '00 '01 '02 '03 '04 '05 '06
n/a n/a n/a

QUICK STUDY

SCORES

Trade Policy	3.5
Fiscal Burden	3.5
Government Intervention	2.5
Monetary Policy	3
Foreign Investment	4
Banking and Finance	2
Wages and Prices	3
Property Rights	4
Regulation	4
Informal Market	4

Population: 14,878,100

Total area: 2,717,300 sq. km

GDP: $24.9 billion

GDP growth rate: 9.2%

GDP per capita: $1,673

Major exports: mineral products, ferrous metals, food products, chemicals, oil

Exports of goods and services: $13.3 billion

Major export trading partners: Russia 15.2%, Switzerland 13.0%, China 12.8%

Major imports: machinery and equipment, mineral products, ferrous metals, chemicals

Imports of goods and services: $8.7 billion

Major import trading partners: Russia 39.0%, Germany 8.7%, China 6.2%, US 5.6%

Foreign direct investment (net): $2.1 billion

2003 Data (in constant 2000 US dollars)

Kazakhstan enjoys large oil and gas reserves and high per capita foreign investment due to its resource-rich energy sector, but energy exports are constrained by the insufficient capacity of the export pipelines that run primarily through Russia. Kazakhstan is building an oil pipeline to China, may supply the Baku–Tbilisi–Ceyhan pipeline by tanker, and is interested in a pipeline to Iran. During the past five years, non-energy sectors have also demonstrated robust growth. The country is politically stable, and tolerance between ethnic and religious groups prevails despite the strife in neighboring Kyrgyzstan and Uzbekistan. In September 2004, President Nursultan Nazarbayev's Otan party won 60 percent of the seats in parliament. In February 2005, the Nazarbayev government, which has been criticized in the past for violating civil rights and restricting the media, introduced a comprehensive program of state modernization. Western investors may face increasing state intervention in the management of hydrocarbon projects. The scale of projects and the presence of large oil reserves make Kazakhstan an important country for major international oil activity. Development of the giant Karachaganak field in the country's western region and a rapidly increasing oil export market should spur growth in 2006. Kazakhstan's fiscal burden of government score is 0.4 point worse this year; however, its capital flows and foreign investment score is 1 point better, and its banking and finance score is 2 points better. As a result, Kazakhstan's overall score is 0.26 point better this year.

TRADE POLICY
Score: 3.5–Stable (high level of protectionism)

According to the U.S. Trade Representative, Kazakhstan's average tariff rate in 2004 was 7.9 percent, down from the 10 percent in 2002 reported in the 2005 *Index*, based on USTR data. Customs corruption acts as a non-tariff barrier. The U.S. Department of Commerce reports problems with corruption and with the "[i]nconsistent and arbitrary implementation or interpretation of customs regulations." Based on the revised trade factor methodology, Kazakhstan's trade policy score is unchanged.

FISCAL BURDEN OF GOVERNMENT
Score—Income Taxation: 2–Stable (low tax rates)
Score—Corporate Taxation: 4–Stable (high tax rates)
Score—Change in Government Expenditures: 4–Worse (moderate increase)
Final Score: 3.5–Worse (high cost of government)

Kazakhstan's top income tax rate is 20 percent. The top corporate tax rate is 30 percent. According to the Asian Development Bank, government expenditures as a share of GDP increased by 1.5 percentage points to 23.2 percent in 2003, compared to a 1.3 percentage point decrease in 2002. On net, Kazakhstan's fiscal burden of government score is 0.4 point worse this year.

GOVERNMENT INTERVENTION IN THE ECONOMY
Score: 2.5–Stable (moderate level)

The World Bank reports that the government consumed 11.5 percent of GDP in 2003. In the same year, according to the International Monetary Fund's Government Financial Statistics CD–ROM, Kazakhstan received 5.06 percent of its total revenues from state-owned enterprises and government ownership of property.

MONETARY POLICY
Score: **3**–Stable (moderate level of inflation)

From 1995 to 2004, Kazakhstan's weighted average annual rate of inflation was 6.84 percent.

CAPITAL FLOWS AND FOREIGN INVESTMENT
Score: **4**–Better (high barriers)

A new Investment Law passed in January 2003 did not substantially improve the foreign investment regime. The U.S. Department of Commerce reports that "market-oriented reform and successful attraction of investment has been progressively undermined over the last four years by a growing tendency on the part of the government to challenge contractual rights, to legislate preferences for domestic companies, and to create mechanisms for government intervention in foreign companies' operations, particularly procurement decisions." The same source notes that legal provisions are vague and often arbitrarily and inconsistently enforced. No sector of the economy is closed to investment, but the government imposes a 25 percent cap on foreign capital in the banking system and a 20 percent ceiling on foreign ownership in media companies. It also screens foreign investment proposals in a process that is often non-transparent, arbitrary, and slow. Foreign individuals and companies may only lease land. The International Monetary Fund reports that, subject to restrictions, foreign exchange accounts may be held by residents and non-residents. Most capital transactions, payments, and transfers are subject to government approval, quantitative limits, and strict documentary requirements. Although Kazakhstan is a very restricted investment environment, its laws do provide for nonexpropriation, currency convertibility, and guaranteed contracts. On net, Kazakhstan's capital flows and foreign investment score is 1 point better this year.

BANKING AND FINANCE
Score: **2**–Better (low level of restrictions)

Kazakhstan's banking system, according to the U.S. Department of Commerce, "is the most developed in Central Asia, and rapidly moving towards adoption of international banking standards." According to the Economist Intelligence Unit, "All banks have to adopt international banking standards, including the risk-weighted 8% capital-adequacy ratio set by the Bank for International Settlements (BIS). The scheme has cut the number of banks in Kazakhstan from 130 at the end of 1995 to 35 by July 2004." The December 15, 2004, *Financial Times* reports that "Kazakhstan has privatized all its banks and the private sector is enjoying healthy competition.... Kazakhstan's banks are really in the business of taking deposits and lending money to individuals and corporations." There are 15 banks with at least partial foreign ownership. Foreign insurance companies may not operate in Kazakhstan except through joint ventures with domestic firms. Foreign capital in the banking sector is capped at 25 percent. Based on evidence of limited government involvement in the banking sec-

tor, Kazakhstan's banking and finance score is 2 points better this year.

WAGES AND PRICES
Score: **3**–Stable (moderate level of intervention)

The market sets most prices, but the government still controls prices when considered necessary. The U.S. Department of Commerce reports that "the government subsidized two programs on development of leasing of food processing machinery and a program for decreasing interest rates at Commercial banks for food processing companies." According to the Economist Intelligence Unit, "Monopoly prices, administrative prices and imperfect market competition more generally create significant distortions...." The government also sets a monthly minimum wage.

PROPERTY RIGHTS
Score: **4**–Stable (low level of protection)

Kazakhstan's legal system does not provide sufficient protection for private property. The U.S. Department of Commerce reports that most business disputes arise from "breaches of contract or non-payment on the part of Kazakhstani state entities." According to the Economist Intelligence Unit, "Observance of contracts in Kazakhstan is poor and getting worse.... Little progress has been made...on developing an independent and competent Judiciary.... [C]orruption remains widespread, and the judiciary views itself more as an arm of the executive than as an enforcer of contracts or guardian of fundamental rights." The EIU also reports that "legislation severely curtails private land ownership."

REGULATION
Score: **4**–Stable (high level)

According to the U.S. Department of Commerce, "Transparency in the application of laws remains...an obstacle to expanded trade and investment.... [I]nvestors complain of moving goalposts and corruption.... Often, contradictory norms hinder the functioning of the legal system. While Kazakhstan has recently defined more clearly which laws take precedence in the event of a contradiction, it has become clear that stability clauses granted investors under previous versions of the Foreign Investment Law or other legislation may not necessarily protect investors from changes in the legal and tax regulatory regime." The Economist Intelligence Unit reports that "the bureaucracy is inefficient, and by the government's own admission corruption is widespread."

INFORMAL MARKET
Score: **4**–Stable (high level of activity)

Transparency International's 2004 score for Kazakhstan is 2.2. Therefore, Kazakhstan's informal market score is 4 this year.

KENYA

Rank: 94

Score: 3.20

Category: Mostly Unfree

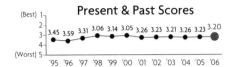

Present & Past Scores

(Best) 1
2
3.45 3.59 3.31 3.06 3.14 3.05 3.26 3.23 3.21 3.26 3.23 3.20
3
4
(Worst) 5

'95 '96 '97 '98 '99 '00 '01 '02 '03 '04 '05 '06

QUICK STUDY

SCORES

Trade Policy	4
Fiscal Burden	3.5
Government Intervention	2.5
Monetary Policy	3
Foreign Investment	3
Banking and Finance	3
Wages and Prices	2
Property Rights	3
Regulation	4
Informal Market	4

Population: 31,915,850

Total area: 582,650 sq. km

GDP: $10.8 billion

GDP growth rate: 1.8%

GDP per capita: $341

Major exports: tea, coffee, fish products, petroleum products

Exports of goods and services: $3.2 billion

Major export trading partners: Uganda 12.6%, UK 12.5%, US 9.4%, Egypt 4.6%, Tanzania 4.2%

Major imports: petroleum products, iron and steel, motor vehicles

Imports of goods and services: $3.7 billion

Major import trading partners: United Arab Emirates 13.4%, Saudi Arabia 9.8%, South Africa 8.7%, UK 7.5%, China 6.4%

Foreign direct investment (net): $75.2 million

2003 Data (in constant 2000 US dollars)

President Mwai Kibaki and his National Rainbow Coalition government came to power in December 2002 on promises to reform Kenya after 24 years of corruption and economic mismanagement under former President Daniel arap Moi. Despite initial progress, such as enactment of laws on corruption and a code of ethics that requires executive and judicial officials and parliamentarians to declare their assets when entering and leaving office, the coalition has fractured over the new constitution and has failed to follow through on many reforms. Most large parastatals are scheduled for at least partial privatization, but political opposition to privatization remains strong and key economic sectors remain dominated by state-owned enterprises, monopolies, and marketing boards. Bureaucracy is extensive, and the government wage bill accounts for 9 percent of GDP. Despite pledges to foreign donors, the new government has not aggressively pursued high-level corruption. Agriculture, forestry, and fishing account for 24 percent of GDP and employ over 70 percent of the population. The generally poor condition of the infrastructure, including unreliable provision of electricity and non-mobile telephony and decaying roads, inhibits investment and the production and transport of goods. Kenya is eligible for assistance as a threshold country for the U.S. Millennium Challenge Account. Kenya's fiscal burden of government score is 0.2 point worse this year, and its government intervention score is 0.5 point worse; however, its trade policy and informal market scores are both 0.5 point better. As a result, Kenya's overall score is 0.03 point better this year.

TRADE POLICY
Score: 4–Better (high level of protectionism)

According to the World Bank, Kenya's weighted average tariff rate in 2004 was 10.3 percent, down from the 14.4 percent in 2002 reported in the 2005 *Index*, based on World Bank data. According to the U.S. Department of Commerce, "Non tariff barriers include the requirement to use a [government of Kenya] appointed inspection firm for imports. Some U.S. firms may find packaging and labeling requirements difficult to meet." Based on the lower tariff rate, as well as a revision of the trade factor methodology, Kenya's trade policy score is 0.5 point better this year.

FISCAL BURDEN OF GOVERNMENT
Score—Income Taxation: 3–Stable (moderate tax rates)
Score—Corporate Taxation: 4–Stable (high tax rates)
Score—Change in Government Expenditures: 3–Worse (very low decrease)
Final Score: 3.5–Worse (high cost of government)

Deloitte reports that Kenya's top income tax rate is 30 percent. The top corporate income tax rate is also 30 percent. In 2003, according to the African Development Bank, government expenditures as a share of GDP remained unchanged at 24.1 percent, compared to the 1.6 percentage point decrease in 2002. On net, Kenya's fiscal burden of government score is 0.2 point worse this year.

GOVERNMENT INTERVENTION IN THE ECONOMY
Score: 2.5–Worse (moderate level)

The World Bank reports that the government consumed 17.9 percent of GDP in 2003. In fiscal year July 2003–June 2004, based on data from the World Bank, Kenya received 7.53

243

percent of its total revenues from state-owned enterprises and government ownership of property, up from the 0.008 percent reported in the 2005 *Index*. As a result, Kenya's government intervention score is 0.5 point worse this year.

MONETARY POLICY
Score: **3**–Stable (moderate level of inflation)

From 1995 to 2004, Kenya's weighted average annual rate of inflation was 10.14 percent.

CAPITAL FLOWS AND FOREIGN INVESTMENT
Score: **3**–Stable (moderate barriers)

Kenya's government has relaxed its screening standards and has established the Investment Promotion Center for investment approval. According to Deloitte, "Foreign investment is welcome if it spurs job creation and has no negative impact on security or the environment. Foreigners face ownership restrictions in only a few industries, including infrastructure, insurance and the media." Branches of non-resident companies are assessed at a higher tax rate (37.5 percent) than are resident companies (30 percent). Work permits, which even expatriates find increasingly hard to obtain, are required for all foreign nationals who wish to work in the country. Foreign ownership of companies listed on the Nairobi Stock Exchange is limited to 75 percent, and foreign brokerage and fund management firms must have minimum Kenyan ownership of 30 percent and 51 percent, respectively. The International Monetary Fund reports that both residents and non-residents may hold foreign exchange accounts. There are no controls or requirements on payments and transfers. Most capital transactions are permitted, but government approval is required for the sale or issue of most capital and money market instruments and for the purchase of real estate by non-residents. "If Kenya is to attract meaningful foreign investment," notes the U.S. Trade Representative, "it will need to address rampant corruption; degraded road, rail, and telecommunications infrastructure; relatively high energy costs; and inefficient government expenditures."

BANKING AND FINANCE
Score: **3**–Stable (moderate level of restrictions)

Kenya's banking system is fragile. The Economist Intelligence Unit reports that "Kenya began 2005 with 44 commercial banks, one non-bank financial institution, two building societies and two mortgage-finance companies. There are five dominant banks in the sector: Standard Chartered (UK), Barclays (UK), Kenya Commercial Bank, National Bank of Kenya and Co-operative Bank of Kenya." The government influences the sector through state-owned banks, including the large, state-controlled Kenya Commercial Bank and National Bank of Kenya. The banking sector remains hindered by non-performing loans, particularly from state-owned banks to state-owned enterprises, although the ratio has improved from over 30 percent of total loans in December 2002 to 23.4 percent in June 2004. According to the Economist Intelligence Unit, proposed

legislation limiting the amount of interest and charges that can be applied to non-performing loans is being held up by a dispute between the president and parliament over whether the law should apply retroactively.

WAGES AND PRICES
Score: **2**–Stable (low level of intervention)

According to the Economist Intelligence Unit, "Part IV (Section 35) of the Restrictive Trade Practices, Monopolies and Price Controls Act reserves to the minister of finance the right to set maximum prices in certain instances. Officially, however, price controls were dismantled in 1994." The government controls the prices of some of the most important agricultural goods through marketing boards and regulates the price of some utilities. Kenya has a minimum wage for blue-collar workers.

PROPERTY RIGHTS
Score: **3**–Stable (moderate level of protection)

The U.S. Department of Commerce reports that "Kenya's judicial system is modeled after the British.... In addition, there is a separate industrial court that hears disputes over wages and labor terms. Its decisions cannot be appealed. Kenya established commercial courts to deal with commercial cases in 2000. Property and contractual rights are enforceable, but long delays in resolving commercial cases are common." The government has taken some steps to address corruption in the judiciary, but the Economist Intelligence Unit reports that "Kenya still has a long way to go before real change can be seen.... [T]he court [lacks] independence from executive pressure over sensitive matters.... [J]udicial officers are reluctant to prosecute their colleagues; terms of service for officers are poor, making them vulnerable to bribes; and resources, such as training, are lacking."

REGULATION
Score: **4**–Stable (high level)

Kenya's bureaucracy remains significantly burdensome. According to the U.S. Department of Commerce, "Investment in Kenya has historically been constrained by a time-consuming and highly discretionary approval and licensing system that have been [*sic*] vulnerable to corrupt practices. The amended investment law is to address the concerns through its 'one-stop-office', to process applications for foreign investors within one month." In addition, "Government approval for ventures in agriculture, distributive trade, and small-scale enterprises has become more difficult to secure as the government seeks to indigenize."

INFORMAL MARKET
Score: **4**–Better (high level of activity)

Transparency International's 2003 score for Kenya is 2.1. Therefore, Kenya's informal market score is 4 this year—0.5 point better than last year.

KOREA, DEMOCRATIC PEOPLE'S REPUBLIC OF (NORTH KOREA)

Rank: 157

Score: 5.00

Category: Repressed

Present & Past Scores

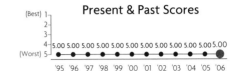

(Best) 1—
2—
3—
4— 5.00 5.00 5.00 5.00 5.00 5.00 5.00 5.00 5.00 5.00 5.00 5.00
(Worst) 5—
'95 '96 '97 '98 '99 '00 '01 '02 '03 '04 '05 '06

QUICK STUDY

SCORES

Trade Policy	5
Fiscal Burden	5
Government Intervention	5
Monetary Policy	5
Foreign Investment	5
Banking and Finance	5
Wages and Prices	5
Property Rights	5
Regulation	5
Informal Market	5

Population: 22,500,000

Total area: 120,540 sq. km

GDP: n/a

GDP growth rate: 1.8%

GDP per capita: n/a

Major exports: minerals, metallurgical products, machinery, textiles, fishery products

Exports of goods and services: n/a

Major export trading partners: China 37.1%, South Korea 27.1%, Japan 16.3%

Major imports: petroleum, coking coal, machinery and equipment, textiles, grain

Imports of goods and services: n/a

Major import trading partners: China 30.6%, South Korea 21.2%, Thailand 9.9%

Foreign direct investment (net): n/a

2003 Data

The Democratic People's Republic of Korea is undergoing some economic changes. In 2002, the government initiated tentative steps toward markets and entrepreneurship by creating semi-private markets, shops, and small business across the country. Part of these reforms included the phasing out of a decades-old food rationing and public distribution system and allowing prices and exchange rates to float. Nevertheless, the country remains firmly rooted in its communist and authoritarian system with its central command economy, and deeper institutional reform is constrained by the degeneration of North Korea's industrial, transportation, and energy infrastructure, which continues to be neglected for the sake of the government's military policy. Although reports indicate that there is greater economic activity in Pyongyang and other cities, economic deprivation seems to be worsening for most of the population. The country remains heavily dependent on external assistance for its food supplies, and there are indications that the economy is opening up to more trade with its two neighbors, China and South Korea. North Korea's trade volume in 2004 is estimated to have reached its highest level since 1991—$2.85 billion. However, the possibility that North Korea might open wide-scale trade remains low because of lingering tensions about its nuclear weapons program. The Democratic People's Republic of Korea's overall score is unchanged this year.

TRADE POLICY
Score: 5–Stable (very high level of protectionism)

The government controls all imports and exports, and trade is minimal. The Economist Intelligence Unit reports that "North Korean trade data are compiled from trading partners' statistics and published by the South's Korea Trade-Investment Promotion Agency.... [M]uch trade is de facto aid, mainly with North Korea's two main partners, China and South Korea." According to the Korea Trade-Investment Promotion Agency, North Korea imported slightly over $2 billion in goods in 2003 while exporting slightly more than $1 billion.

FISCAL BURDEN OF GOVERNMENT
Score—Income Taxation: n/a
Score—Corporate Taxation: n/a
Score—Change in Government Expenditures: n/a
Final Score: 5–Stable (very high cost of government)

No data on income or corporate tax rates are available. Given the absence of published official macroeconomic data, such figures as are available with respect to North Korea's government expenditures are highly suspect and outdated.

GOVERNMENT INTERVENTION IN THE ECONOMY
Score: 5–Stable (very high level)

The government owns all property and sets production levels for most products, and state-owned industries account for nearly all GDP. "The State directs all significant economic activity," reports the U.S. Department of Commerce, "and only government-controlled labor unions are permitted." According to the Economist Intelligence Unit, "Until 2002 hopes of long-overdue economic reform, raised by Kim Jong-Il's business-oriented trip to Shanghai in January 2001, went unfulfilled. In September 1998 the revised constitution gave only slightly more space to private enterprise and the use of price and profit."

MONETARY POLICY
Score: **5**–Stable (very high level of inflation)

In July 2002, North Korea introduced price and wage reforms that consisted of reducing government subsidies and telling producers to charge prices that more closely reflect costs. According to the Economist Intelligence Unit, "with no matching supply-side measures to boost output, the result of these measures has been rampant inflation for many staple goods."

CAPITAL FLOWS AND FOREIGN INVESTMENT
Score: **5**–Stable (very high barriers)

"North Korea has the dubious distinction of being first in and last out of the developing world's debt crisis, initially defaulting in the 1970s and remaining mired in debt today," reports the Economist Intelligence Unit. "This dire debt record has not stopped North Korea from seeking new foreign investment. Its first special economic zone, at Rajin-Sonbong in the northeast, was gazetted in 1991. A raft of detailed foreign business laws in the 1990s suggested serious intent, but found few takers. Rajin-Sonbong is remote and still lacks basic infrastructure. Wage rates were unrealistically high, as the state controls labour supply and insists on taking its share. More recent special zones, at Mt Kumgang and Kaesong, are more enticing…. Continued nuclear defiance will inevitably deter investors from what remains largely a leap into the unknown." Aside from these few economic zones where investment is approved on a case-by-case basis, foreign investment is prohibited.

BANKING AND FINANCE
Score: **5**–Stable (very high level of restrictions)

"As a communist command economy," reports the Economist Intelligence Unit, "North Korea largely lacked a financial sector in the capitalist sense. Most funding for industry came from the state, which also earned revenue by taking a percentage on transactions among enterprises…. At least two foreign aid agencies have recently set up microcredit schemes…. Reports in early 2005 suggested that a radical overhaul of the financial system is under way. As a next step in market reforms, investment funds will no longer be allocated by the state under a plan. Instead, as normal elsewhere, firms will have to borrow from banks, whose role and importance are therefore set to grow and change markedly." Because of debts dating back to the 1970s, most foreign banks will not consider entering North Korea. The central bank also serves as a commercial bank with a network of 227 local branches. A South Korean bank has opened a branch in the Kaesong zone, and a Hong Kong hotel and casino in Rajin-Sonbong includes a bank. The state holds a monopoly on insurance through the State Insurance Bureau and the Korea Foreign Insurance Company. The state continues to dominate the financial sector.

WAGE AND PRICES
Score: **5**–Stable (very high level of intervention)

The government controls and determines all wages and prices. According to the Economist Intelligence Unit, "Only in 2002 did real change begin. In July wages and (more so) prices were raised drastically for producers and consumers typically tenfold or more. Enterprises were told to charge prices that reflected their costs, and no longer expect subsidies." In addition, "the government had adopted a law that acknowledged the existence of farmers' markets for the first time [in 2003]. However, with no matching supply-side measures to boost output, the result of these tentative reforms has been rampant inflation for many staple goods." According to the U.S. Department of State, "Government ministries set wages."

PROPERTY RIGHTS
Score: **5**–Stable (very low level of protection)

Property rights are not guaranteed in North Korea. Almost all property belongs to the state, and the U.S. Department of State reports that "the judiciary is not independent."

REGULATION
Score: **5**–Stable (very high level)

The government regulates the economy heavily. According to the *Financial Times*, Kim Jong-Il refuses to follow China's example of opening to foreign investment and relaxing borders, and this refusal has serious implications because "the country's economy, stripped of its industries and starved of energy, is unsustainable." *The Economist* reports that the government has implemented some modest reforms: "Farmers are [now] allowed their own small gardens, and farmers' markets are now referred to simply as 'markets', because, as well as food, they sell consumer goods."

INFORMAL MARKET
Score: **5**–Stable (very high level of activity)

North Korea's informal market is immense even though the government imprisons many who engage in such activity. Informal market activity in agricultural goods flourishes as a result of famines and oppressive government policies. There is also an active informal market in currency and in trade with China.

KOREA, REPUBLIC OF (SOUTH KOREA)

Rank: 45
Score: 2.63
Category: Mostly Free

Present & Past Scores

(Best) 1
2
3 2.46 2.54 2.36 2.35 2.43 2.55 2.40 2.54 2.75 2.64 2.64 2.63
4
(Worst) 5
'95 '96 '97 '98 '99 '00 '01 '02 '03 '04 '05 '06

QUICK STUDY

SCORES

Trade Policy   3.5
Fiscal Burden   3.3
Government Intervention 2.5
Monetary Policy   2
Foreign Investment   2
Banking and Finance   3
Wages and Prices   2
Property Rights   2
Regulation   3
Informal Market   3

Population: 48,100,000

Total area: 98,730 sq. km

GDP: $614.9 billion

GDP growth rate: 4.6%

GDP per capita: $12,783

Major exports: electronic products, passenger cars, machinery, chemical products, steel, ships, textiles

Exports of goods and services: $299.1 billion

Major export trading partners: China 19.6%, US 16.9%, Japan 8.5%

Major imports: crude petroleum, machinery and equipment, chemicals and chemical products

Imports of goods and services: $269.8 billion

Major import trading partners: Japan 20.6%, China 13.2%, US 12.8%, Saudi Arabia 5.3%

Foreign direct investment (net): $3.1 billion

2004 Data (in constant 2000 US dollars)

In 2004, following a brief recession, South Korea achieved solid growth of 4.6 percent, driven largely by strong export performance in key industries such as automobiles and electronics. Several positive steps toward economic reform have been implemented in recent years. The bankruptcy law, which has long been viewed as a serious hurdle to corporate restructuring, was integrated and simplified by the National Assembly. The corporate tax rate was reduced to 25 percent from 27 percent, effective January 2005. Yet the outlook going forward may be less bright because of political and economic volatility and the diminishing authority of President Roh Moo Hyun and his Uri Party. The Uri Party's inability to regain its parliamentary majority in April 2005 impedes the government's ability to enact much-needed economic reforms in the labor market because of dependence on the minority Democratic Labor Party, which is closely linked to the militant unions. Creating further uncertainty are South Korea's ambiguous foreign policies. Flare-ups with Japan over historical issues, a seemingly passive stance toward North Korean provocations, and rising tensions with the United States all raise concerns at a time when regional cooperation has never been more critical. South Korea's trade policy score is 0.5 point worse this year, but its fiscal burden of government score is 0.6 point better. As a result, South Korea's overall score is 0.01 point better this year.

TRADE POLICY
Score: **3.5**–Worse (high level of protectionism)

According to the World Bank, South Korea's weighted average tariff rate in 2002 (the most recent year for which World Bank data are available) was 10 percent. (The World Bank has revised the figure for 2002 upward from the 5.7 percent reported in the 2005 *Index*.) According to the World Trade Organization, "The Korean tariff remains a relatively complex instrument and as such constitutes a potential distortion to competition." Korea also restricts imports through a negative list of over 1,000 items and utilizes export subsidies. Based on the higher tariff rate, as well as a revision of the trade factor methodology, South Korea's trade policy score is 0.5 point worse this year.

FISCAL BURDEN OF GOVERNMENT
Score—Income Taxation: **3.5**–Stable (high tax rates)
Score—Corporate Taxation: **3**–Better (moderate tax rates)
Score—Change in Government Expenditures: **3.5**–Better (low increase)
Final Score: **3.3**–Better (moderate cost of government)

According to the Ministry of Finance and Economy, South Korea's top income tax rate is 38.5 percent (a 35 percent income tax rate plus a 10 percent surcharge), down from the 39.6 percent reported in the 2005 *Index*. Effective January 2005, the top corporate tax rate was cut to 25 percent from 27 percent. In 2004, government expenditures as a share of GDP increased 0.1 percentage point to 27.3 percent, compared to the 2.4 percentage point increase in 2003. On net, South Korea's fiscal burden of government score is 0.6 point better this year.

GOVERNMENT INTERVENTION IN THE ECONOMY
Score: **2.5**–Stable (moderate level)

Based on data from the Economist Intelligence Unit, the government consumed 13.4 percent of

GDP in 2004. In the same year, based on data from the Ministry of Planning and Budget, South Korea received 5.33 percent of its total revenues from state-owned enterprises and government ownership of property.

MONETARY POLICY
Score: 2–Stable (low level of inflation)

From 1995 to 2004, South Korea's weighted average annual rate of inflation was 3.50 percent.

CAPITAL FLOWS AND FOREIGN INVESTMENT
Score: 2–Stable (low barriers)

The Foreign Investment Promotion Act of November 1998 and other reforms substantially opened South Korea's economy to foreign investment. According to the U.S. Trade Representative, 27 sectors (primarily media and communications, electric power–related sectors, and certain agricultural sectors) are partially closed to foreign investment, and two sectors (radio and television broadcasting) are completely closed. The same source notes that labor market inflexibility, labor–management disputes, and insufficient regulatory transparency hinder investment. The government has removed restrictions on foreign investors that acquire companies through mergers and acquisitions. The Korean embassy reports that 16,181 foreign companies were operating in Korea at the end of 2004, up from 5,130 in 1997. According to the International Monetary Fund, both residents and non-residents may hold foreign exchange accounts. Payments, transactions, transfers, or repatriation of profits are subject to reporting requirements or restrictions on amounts permitted for specified periods.

BANKING AND FINANCE
Score: 3–Stable (moderate level of restrictions)

In the period following the 1997–1998 financial crisis, the government closed many insolvent banks, nationalized others, and forced weak banks to merge with other banks to improve their financial standing. The government has been selling its stake in private banks—the World Bank reports that the government holds stakes in only two banks following the privatization of Korea First Bank—but continues to have influence over the sector. According to the Economist Intelligence Unit, "At end-2004, South Korea's financial system included 14 commercial banks, 39 foreign banks operating branches, five specialised banks, two merchant banking corporations, 42 securities firms, 50 insurers, 47 asset-management companies, 18 leasing companies and eight credit-card issuers. The numerous non-bank financial institutions included many mutual savings banks, credit unions, community credit co-operatives, a postal savings and insurance network, and instalment-credit companies." An amendment to the Banking Act raised the ceiling on foreign ownership of a national commercial bank, but official approval is required when foreign ownership exceeds 10 percent, 25 percent, and 33 percent, and the 15 percent limit on foreign ownership of a regional bank

remains in place. Non-performing loans have been reduced substantially since the crisis.

WAGES AND PRICES
Score: 2–Stable (low level of intervention)

The market sets most prices. "Official price controls still exist in certain areas, including farm products and telecommunications services," reports the Economist Intelligence Unit; the government sets prices for "(1)...rail and subway fares, electricity rates, telecoms tariffs, postal rates, school textbooks, health-insurance premiums, cigarettes, television services, entrance fees to national museums and monuments, motorway tolls and other public-facility fees; (2)...taxi and bus fares, school tuition, water and sewage rates, and sanitation services; (3)...diesel fuel, liquefied petroleum gas and other petrochemical products; (4) coal products specifically packaged for home heating...(5) government-surplus rice." South Korea maintains a minimum wage that is reviewed annually.

PROPERTY RIGHTS
Score: 2–Stable (high level of protection)

Private property is secure, and expropriation is highly unlikely. However, the justice system can be inefficient and slow. The Economist Intelligence Unit reports that "a contract is often considered a broadly defined consensus statement that allows for flexibility and adjustment.... Strict adherence to contractual terms is often frowned upon, and emphasis on informal unwritten consent can work to the disadvantage of both parties to a contract. To avoid possible litigation, both parties should ensure that the obligations spelled out in a negotiated contract are fully understood.... [L]egal procedures in South Korea can be cumbersome and expensive."

REGULATION
Score: 3–Stable (moderate level)

Labor regulations are highly burdensome. According to the U.S. Department of Commerce, "Laws and regulations are framed in general terms and are subject to differing interpretations by government officials, who rotate frequently. The regulatory process is not transparent and frequent informal discussions with the bureaucracy are necessary. Mid-level bureaucrats rely on unpublished ministerial guidelines and unwritten administrative advice for direction.... [T]he rule-making process continues to be opaque and non-transparent." The same source reports that there is corruption in the bureaucracy. The government increasingly uses the Internet both to improve access to regulations and to eliminate bureaucratic steps to businesses.

INFORMAL MARKET
Score: 3–Stable (moderate level of activity)

Transparency International's 2004 score for South Korea is 4.5. Therefore, South Korea's informal market score is 3 this year.

KUWAIT

Rank: 50

Score: 2.74

Category: Mostly Free

Present & Past Scores

(Best) 1
2
3
4
(Worst) 5

2.55 2.44 2.55 2.45 2.50 2.53 2.66 2.58 2.75 2.81 2.74

'95 '96 '97 '98 '99 '00 '01 '02 '03 '04 '05 '06
n/a

QUICK STUDY

SCORES

Trade Policy	2.5
Fiscal Burden	1.4
Government Intervention	4.5
Monetary Policy	1
Foreign Investment	3
Banking and Finance	3
Wages and Prices	3
Property Rights	3
Regulation	3
Informal Market	3

Population: 2,396,417

Total area: 17,820 sq. km

GDP: $40.11 billion

GDP growth rate: 9.9%

GDP per capita: $16,738

Major exports: oil, fertilizers and refined products

Exports of goods and services: $16.1 billion

Major export trading partners: Japan 22.0%, South Korea 15.4%, US 11.9%, Singapore 10.2%

Major imports: food, construction materials, clothing, vehicles and parts

Imports of goods and services: $11 billion

Major import trading partners: US 14.5%, Japan 10.1%, Germany 9.4%, UK 6.0%

Foreign direct investment (net): –$4.6 billion

2003 Data (in constant 2000 US dollars)

K uwait, a small constitutional monarchy that gained its independence from Britain in 1961, is endowed with 96 billion barrels of oil reserves—roughly 10 percent of the world's oil supply. The oil sector accounts for nearly 50 percent of GDP and 95 percent of export revenues. The ruling Al-Sabah dynasty has used state-owned oil revenues to build a modern infrastructure and a cradle-to-grave welfare system for Kuwait's small population. Prime Minister Sabah al-Ahmad al-Jabr Al-Sabah leads a government that is committed to cautious economic reforms but faces opposition from Islamist and populist members of parliament and foot dragging from entrenched bureaucrats. Yet the government remains committed to incremental liberalization and to Project Kuwait, a $7 billion plan to encourage foreign investment and development of oilfields in northern Kuwait. The parliament approved legislation to allow foreign banks to operate in Kuwait, and the first foreign bank, BNP Paribas, began operations in August 2004. The government also has established a free trade zone to boost both Kuwaiti participation in the postwar reconstruction of Iraq and trade with Iran. Kuwait has signed a Trade and Investment Framework agreement with the United States as a first step toward a free trade agreement. Kuwait's informal market score is 0.5 point worse this year; however, its fiscal burden of government score is 0.2 point better, and its capital flows and foreign investment score is 1 point better. As a result, Kuwait's overall score is 0.07 point better this year.

TRADE POLICY
Score: **2.5**–Stable (moderate level of protectionism)

According to the World Bank, Kuwait's weighted average tariff rate in 2002 (the most recent year for which World Bank data are available) was 3.9 percent, up from the 3.6 percent average tariff for 2003 reported in the 2005 Index, based on World Bank data. According to the U.S. Trade Representative, "the import clearing process is time-consuming, requiring numerous transfers, large quantities of paperwork, and numerous redundancies. The process is prone to errors and fraud…. Kuwait maintains restrictive standards that impede the marketing of some exports." The U.S. Department of Commerce reports that foreign companies need a local agent or sponsor to do any work with the government. Based on the revised trade factor methodology, Kuwait's trade policy score is unchanged.

FISCAL BURDEN OF GOVERNMENT
Score—Income Taxation: **1**–Stable (very low tax rates)
Score—Corporate Taxation: **1**–Stable (very low tax rates)
Score—Change in Government Expenditures: **2.5**–Better (low decrease)
Final Score: **1.4**–Better (very low cost of government)

Kuwait's top income tax rate is 0 percent. The top corporate tax rate is also 0 percent. In 2003, according to the Economist Intelligence Unit, government expenditures as a share of GDP decreased 1.7 percentage points to 44.4 percent, compared to a 0.7 percentage point increase in 2002. On net, Kuwait's fiscal burden of government score is 0.2 point better this year.

GOVERNMENT INTERVENTION IN THE ECONOMY
Score: **4.5**–Stable (very high level)

The World Bank reports that the government consumed 25.9 percent of GDP in 2003. In fiscal year April 2003–March 2004, based on data from the Central Bank of Kuwait, Kuwait received

88.65 percent of its total revenues from state-owned enterprises and government ownership of property in the oil sector.

 MONETARY POLICY
Score: **1**–Stable (very low level of inflation)

From 1995 to 2004, Kuwait's weighted average annual rate of inflation was 1.16 percent.

 CAPITAL FLOWS AND FOREIGN INVESTMENT
Score: **3**–Better (moderate barriers)

Kuwait is open to some types of foreign investment, but there are significant restrictions. A 2001 law permitted foreign investors to open companies without a local partner. According to the Economist Intelligence Unit, "Despite the [2001] Foreign Investment Law and its associated bylaws, which allow foreigners to own up to 100% of Kuwaiti companies in certain sectors, significant restrictions on foreign direct investment remain." The U.S. Trade Representative reports that foreign investors are now permitted majority ownership in new investments and 100 percent ownership in "infrastructure projects such as water, power, waste water treatment or communications; investment and exchange companies; insurance companies; information technology and software development; hospitals and pharmaceuticals; air, land and sea freight; tourism, hotels, and entertainment; housing projects and urban development." According to the U.S. Department of Commerce, "Foreign-owned firms and the foreign-owned portions of joint ventures are the only businesses subject to corporate income tax, which applies to domestic and offshore income…. The licensing authority of the Ministry of Commerce and Industry screens all proposals for direct foreign investment." Except for Gulf Cooperation Council citizens, foreigners may not own real estate. Kuwait still restricts foreign investment in the upstream petroleum sector. The International Monetary Fund reports that residents and non-residents may hold foreign exchange accounts, and there are no restrictions or controls on payments, transactions, transfers, or repatriation of profits. Although some restrictions remain in place, the evidence indicates that Kuwait has liberalized its foreign investment laws. As a result, Kuwait's capital flows and foreign investment score is 1 point better this year.

 BANKING AND FINANCE
Score: **3**–Stable (moderate level of restrictions)

Banking in Kuwait is competitive and meets international standards. Foreign investors are permitted to own 100 percent (although central bank approval is required to own more than 5 percent) of Kuwaiti banks. The government has permitted three foreign banks to open branches under the January 2004 banking legislation, but strict restrictions still apply, including mandatory approval by the cabinet to enter the market, having a maximum of one branch, and a requirement that, within three years, half of their employees be Kuwaiti. "Kuwait has seven, largely privately owned commercial banks," reports the Economist Intelligence Unit, "including one operating on

Islamic banking principles, which together have around 140 branches. The Kuwait Investment Authority (KIA) acquired stakes in a number of banks after the 1982 stockmarket crash. Divestment of these assets remains an aim of government economic policy." According to the U.S. Department of Commerce, "There are three specialized government banks in Kuwait that provide medium and long term financing."

 WAGES AND PRICES
Score: **3**–Stable (moderate level of intervention)

The government sets some prices. According to the U.S. Department of Commerce, "Kuwait's surging population and subsidized prices…have created rapidly rising demand for electricity and water." The Economist Intelligence Unit reports that the government heavily subsidizes oil prices, housing, and some export commodities. The government does not mandate a minimum wage in the private sector, but it does set wages in the public sector, which employs over 93 percent of Kuwaitis.

 PROPERTY RIGHTS
Score: **3**–Stable (moderate level of protection)

The Economist Intelligence Unit reports that the constitution and law provide for an independent judiciary; in practice, however, the Amir appoints all judges. In addition, the majority of the judges are non-citizens, and renewal of their appointments is subject to government approval. According to the U.S. Department of State, "Noncitizen judges hold 1- to 3-year renewable contracts, which undermines their independence. The Ministry of Justice may remove judges for cause, but rarely does so. Foreign residents involved in legal disputes with citizens frequently claimed that the courts showed a bias in favor of citizens." The U.S. Department of Commerce reports that trials are lengthy.

 REGULATION
Score: **3**–Stable (moderate level)

According to the U.S. Department of Commerce, "Kuwait has a developed legal system and a strong trading history. It has a civil code system influenced by Islamic law. As a traditional trading nation, the judiciary is familiar with international commercial laws." State involvement in the economy is considerable, and competition with state-owned or private Kuwaiti concerns is difficult. The Economist Intelligence Unit reports that "much of the country's limited private-sector activity is driven by public-sector spending. There is also a considerable suspicion of economic reform proposals in the National Assembly (parliament)." Bureaucratic corruption exists, but it does not represent a heavy burden on businesses.

 INFORMAL MARKET
Score: **3**–Worse (moderate level of activity)

Transparency International's 2004 score for Kuwait is 4.6. Therefore, Kuwait's informal market score is 3 this year—0.5 point worse than last year.

KYRGYZ REPUBLIC

Rank: 71

Score: 2.99

Category: Mostly Free

Present & Past Scores

(Best) 1
2
3   3.95 3.68 3.73 3.75 3.60 3.46 3.41 3.34   2.99
4
(Worst) 5

'95 '96 '97 '98 '99 '00 '01 '02 '03 '04 '05 '06
n/a n/a n/a

Widespread protests after the February 2005 parliamentary elections forced President Askar Akayev to flee to Russia and resign. The Kyrgyz Republic's autocratic neighbors, such as Uzbekistan and Kazakhstan, support the new government; in addition, political parties are underdeveloped. The Kyrgyz Republic receives multilateral health, education, and agriculture aid from the International Monetary Fund until at least 2007. In return, the government agreed to prioritize foreign direct investment, tax, and banking sector reforms; reduce foreign debt; and maintain fiscal prudence. To convince foreign investors that it is serious about structural reform, the government must overcome its reluctance to privatize state assets and address corruption. With Kurmanbek Bakiev winning the July 2005 presidential elections, and with parliamentary elections scheduled for late 2005, it was unlikely that all of the government's planned reforms would be implemented quickly, although agriculture, which has suffered in recent years, might undergo a second round of reform. Despite another poor harvest, growth in wages and real GDP will continue, in part because of an increase in production by the Kumtor gold mine and the return of global gold prices to over $400 per troy ounce. Gold accounts for over 40 percent of foreign currency earnings. The Kyrgyz Republic's government intervention score is 0.5 point better this year, and its trade policy, fiscal burden of government, and capital flows and foreign investment scores are all 1 point better. As a result, its overall score is 0.35 point better this year, causing the Kyrgyz Republic to be classified as a "mostly free" country.

TRADE POLICY
Score: **2.5**–Better (moderate level of protectionism)

According to the World Bank, the Kyrgyz Republic's weighted average tariff rate in 2003 (the most recent year for which World Bank data are available) was 4.3 percent, down from the 7.8 percent in 2002 reported in the 2005 *Index*, based on World Bank data. The U.S. Department of Commerce reports that significant non-tariff barriers include import taxes, extensive certification requirements, and licensing. According to the same source, "Corruption is found in every aspect of a company's interaction with the government, including licensing, dispute settlement, government procurement, regulatory activity and taxation." Based on the lower tariff rate, as well as a revision of the trade factor methodology, the Kyrgyz Republic's trade policy is 1 point better this year.

FISCAL BURDEN OF GOVERNMENT
Score—Income Taxation: **2**–Stable (low tax rates)
Score—Corporate Taxation: **2**–Better (low tax rates)
Score—Change in Government Expenditures: **3.5**–Stable (low increase)
Final Score: **2.4**–Better (low cost of government)

The International Monetary Fund reports that the Kyrgyz Republic's top income tax rate is 20 percent. According to Deloitte, the top corporate tax rate is also 20 percent, down from the 30 percent reported in the 2005 *Index*. In 2003, according to the Asian Development Bank, government expenditures as a share of GDP increased 0.2 percentage point to 25 percent, compared to the 2.0 percentage point increase in 2002. On net, the Kyrgyz Republic's fiscal burden of government score is 1 point better this year.

QUICK STUDY

SCORES

Trade Policy	2.5
Fiscal Burden	2.4
Government Intervention	2
Monetary Policy	2
Foreign Investment	3
Banking and Finance	3
Wages and Prices	3
Property Rights	4
Regulation	4
Informal Market	4

Population: 5,052,000

Total area: 198,500 sq. km

GDP: $1.53 billion

GDP growth rate: 6.7%

GDP per capita: $305

Major exports: electricity, machinery, foodstuffs

Exports of goods and services: $614 million

Major export trading partners: United Arab Emirates 24.8%, Switzerland 20.3%, Russia 16.7%, Kazakhstan 9.8%, China 4.0%

Major imports: machinery, oil and gas, chemicals, foodstuffs

Imports of goods and services: $646.2 million

Major import trading partners: Russia 24.7%, Kazakhstan 24.0%, China 10.2%, US 6.7%

Foreign direct investment (net): $18.5 million

2003 Data (in constant 2000 US dollars)

251

GOVERNMENT INTERVENTION IN THE ECONOMY
Score: 2–Better (low level)

The World Bank reports that the government consumed 17.2 percent of GDP in 2003. In 2004, based on data from the National Statistics Committee, the Kyrgyz Republic received 4.65 percent of its total revenues from state-owned enterprises and government ownership of property, down from the 9.14 percent reported in the *2005 Index*. On net, the Kyrgyz Republic's government intervention score is 0.5 point better this year.

MONETARY POLICY
Score: 2–Stable (low level of inflation)

From 1995 to 2004, based on data from the International Monetary Fund's *2005 World Economic Outlook*, the Kyrgyz Republic's weighted average annual rate of inflation was 4.07 percent.

CAPITAL FLOWS AND FOREIGN INVESTMENT
Score: 3–Better (moderate barriers)

The Kyrgyz Republic has opened most of its economy to foreign investment, has adopted guarantees against expropriation or nationalization, and permits investors to bid on privatized firms. "The legal concept of the sanctity of a contract is not consistently observed," reports the U.S. Department of Commerce. "Individual investors have become involved in disputes over licensing, registration, and enforcement of contracts. Corruption is a serious problem…. There is no evidence of discrimination against foreign investors. However, procedures for licensing and approvals are not transparent, which can make the process seem discriminatory." According to the Economist Intelligence Unit, "Reforms are needed to improve the tax system, strengthen corporate governance, fight corruption and ease the level of regulation. Without these reforms, the Kyrgyz Republic will continue to be unable to mobilise the domestic and foreign investment required." The EIU also reports that legal entities and foreign corporations may not purchase land. The International Monetary Fund reports that residents and non-residents may hold foreign exchange accounts. There are no restrictions on payments and transfers, but most capital transactions must be registered with the relevant government authority or are subject to controls. Although there are substantial unofficial barriers to investment, the official investment code is open and consistent with international standards. On net, the Kyrgyz Republic's capital flows and foreign investment score is 1 point better this year.

BANKING AND FINANCE
Score: 3–Stable (moderate level of restrictions)

The Kyrgyz Republic's banking system is improving, but it remains underdeveloped. As of July 2004, there were 21 commercial banks, all but two of them private. Three banks are entirely foreign-owned, and several others are partially foreign-owned. The central bank, which is nominally independent and subject to political pressure, has improved super-

vision and established minimum capital requirements for banks. According to the Economist Intelligence Unit, "Even after the closure of several insolvent banks in 2001, the banking sector is far from being able to play any sort of central role in investment financing. Substantial improvements are required to increase the capitalisation of the sector, mobilise savings, improve bank supervision and strengthen the legislative framework governing the sector." The small stock exchange listed 18 companies as of July 2004.

WAGES AND PRICES
Score: 3–Stable (moderate level of intervention)

The government lifted most price controls and removed most subsidies in 1994 but continues to influence prices through its state-owned enterprises, which include enterprises in agriculture, mining, telecommunications, energy, aviation, and printing. The Kyrgyz Republic maintains a minimum wage.

PROPERTY RIGHTS
Score: 4–Stable (low level of protection)

The legal system does not protect private property sufficiently. "The judiciary is nominally independent," reports the Economist Intelligence Unit, "but suffers from a lack of reform, low salaries and corruption. The president recommends appointments to the constitutional court, the supreme court and the supreme court of arbitration…." According to the U.S. Department of Commerce, "The legal concept of the sanctity of a contract is not consistently observed. Individual investors have become involved in disputes over licensing, registration, and enforcement of contracts. Corruption is a serious problem."

REGULATION
Score: 4–Stable (high level)

According to the U.S. Department of Commerce, "the transition to a market economy is only partially complete. Property rights and the legal system remain weak. Lack of transparency and corruption plague the country's economic development." In addition, "Although the body of new commercial law promises to be an effective basis for commerce, implementing regulations and court procedures, in many cases, remain to be worked out and the law is not always implemented fully. In an effort to assist foreign investors on a variety of issues, the state committee for foreign investments and economic development established an agency based on the 'one-stop-shop' model. However, businesses report that registration with this new agency does not prevent bureaucratic holdups in other parts of the Kyrgyz government." The European Bank for Reconstruction and Development reports that "corruption is widespread."

INFORMAL MARKET
Score: 4–Stable (high level of activity)

Transparency International's 2004 score for the Kyrgyz Republic is 2.2. Therefore, the Kyrgyz Republic's informal market score is 4.

LAOS

Rank: 149

Score: 4.08

Category: Repressed

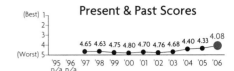

Present & Past Scores

(Best) 1
2
3
4
(Worst) 5

4.65 4.63 4.75 4.80 4.70 4.76 4.68 4.40 4.33 **4.08**

'95 '96 '97 '98 '99 '00 '01 '02 '03 '04 '05 '06
n/a n/a

QUICK STUDY

SCORES

Trade Policy	4.5
Fiscal Burden	3.8
Government Intervention	1.5
Monetary Policy	4
Foreign Investment	4
Banking and Finance	4
Wages and Prices	4
Property Rights	5
Regulation	5
Informal Market	5

Population: 5,659,834

Total area: 236,800 sq. km

GDP: $1.99 billion

GDP growth rate: 5.0%

GDP per capita: $352

Major exports: electricity, garments, timber and wood products, coffee

Exports of goods and services: $378 million

Major export trading partners: Thailand 20.8%, Vietnam 15.8%, France 7.4%, Germany 5.2%, Belgium 4.0%

Major imports: machinery and equipment, textiles, gold and silver

Imports of goods and services: $524 million

Major import trading partners: Thailand 59.8%, China 12.9%, Vietnam 10.3%

Foreign direct investment (net): −$53.3 million

2003 Data (in constant 2000 US dollars)

The ruling Laos People's Revolutionary Party remains firmly in power in the absence of a coherent political opposition. Laos has undertaken several reform initiatives, such as implementation of anti-corruption legislation and privatization of state-owned enterprises, but any significant change in the near future is unlikely. Laos continues to improve relations with its neighbors, particularly Thailand and Vietnam, through growing trade and investment relations and the exchange of high-level official visits. The Laotian government began official negotiations for accession to the World Trade Organization in October 2004, and the next round of talks were expected to take place in late 2005. Additionally, the U.S. granted normal trade relations with Laos in 2004. In April 2005, the World Bank and the Asian Development Bank elected to provide $50 million and $120 million, respectively, in risk guarantees for Laos's Nam Theun II hydroelectric power project despite lack of revenue-management oversight. The government remains cautious of avian flu and has established a number of joint ministerial-level task forces to prevent the spread of the disease. Laos's trade policy score is 0.5 point worse this year; however, its fiscal burden of government score is 0.5 point better, its government intervention score is 1.5 points better, and its banking and finance score is 1 point better. As a result, Laos's overall score is 0.25 point better this year.

 TRADE POLICY
Score: **4.5**–Worse (very high level of protectionism)

The World Bank reports that Laos's weighted average tariff rate in 2001 (the most recent year for which World Bank data are available) was 13.5 percent. (The World Bank has revised the figure for 2001 upward from the 12.2 percent reported in the 2005 *Index*.) According to the U.S. Department of Commerce, "non-tariff barriers, such as a quota on the import of automobiles, still exist…. Importing from and exporting to Laos still requires authorization from several national and local authorities, which can be a time-consuming and less-than-transparent process." Based on the higher tariff rate, as well as a revision of the trade factor methodology, Laos's trade policy score is 0.5 point worse this year.

 FISCAL BURDEN OF GOVERNMENT
Score—Income Taxation: **4**–Stable (high tax rates)
Score—Corporate Taxation: **4.5**–Stable (very high tax rates)
Score—Change in Government Expenditures: **2**–Better (moderate decrease)
Final Score: **3.8**–Better (high cost of government)

According to the International Monetary Fund, Laos's top income tax rate is 40 percent. Deloitte reports that the top corporate tax rate is 35 percent. In 2003, according to the Asian Development Bank, government expenditures as a share of GDP decreased 2.9 percentage points to 18.8 percent, compared to a 1.5 percentage point increase in 2002. On net, Laos's fiscal burden of government score is 0.5 point better this year.

 GOVERNMENT INTERVENTION IN THE ECONOMY
Score: **1.5**–Better (low level)

According to the World Bank, the government consumed 4.8 percent of GDP in 2003, down from the 15.5 percent reported in the 2005 *Index*. As a result, Laos's government intervention score is 1 point better this year. In fiscal year October 2003–September 2004, based on data from the International Monetary Fund, Laos received 9.3 percent of its total revenues from state-owned enterprises and government ownership of property, down from the 11.22 percent reported in the 2005 *Index*. As a result, Laos's government intervention score is an additional 0.5 point better this year for a total improvement of 1.5 points.

 ## MONETARY POLICY
Score: **4**–Stable (high level of inflation)

From 1995 to 2004, Laos's weighted average annual rate of inflation was 12.37 percent.

 ## CAPITAL FLOWS AND FOREIGN INVESTMENT
Score: **4**–Stable (high barriers)

In 2000, the U.S. Department of Commerce reported that Laos's "foreign investment law guarantees foreign investors protection on their investments and property from government confiscation, seizure or nationalization without compensation; operations free from government interference; the right to lease [but not own] land, transfer leasehold interests, and make improvements on land or buildings; and repatriate earnings. Foreign investors may invest in either joint ventures with Lao partners or in wholly foreign-owned entities." According to the Economist Intelligence Unit, "Foreign direct investment (FDI) is picking up, despite the government's failure to improve the investment environment…. FDI is threatened by the country's macroeconomic instability, particularly the tendency for the currency to weaken, and the potential for a deterioration in security." The International Monetary Fund reports that both residents and non-residents may hold foreign exchange accounts, subject to certain restrictions and government approval. Some payments and transfers face quantitative restrictions. All capital transactions require central bank approval.

 ## BANKING AND FINANCE
Score: **4**–Better (high level of restrictions)

According to the Economist Intelligence Unit, "State banks continue to dominate the banking sector—nearly 50% of total assets are owned by the state-owned Banque pour le Commerce Extérieur Lao (BCEL), which handles foreign trade and other overseas transactions." In addition, "The Bank of the Lao People's Democratic Republic (the central bank) has announced a series of reforms designed to make commercial banks more competitive, but politically directed lending remains the norm. The central bank is largely ineffective, with monetary policy subordinate to fiscal policy." There are two state-owned commercial banks in addition to the BCEL, an official Lao–Viet export–import bank, and a government-owned rural credit bank. Foreign banks may open full branches but are limited to operating in the Vientiene municipality. The insurance sector is dominated by Assurance Générales du Laos, in which the government has a 49 percent stake. Although the government dominates the financial sector, private and foreign banks are permitted to operate, and the banking system is stable. On net, Laos's banking and finance score is 1 point better this year.

 ## WAGES AND PRICES
Score: **4**–Stable (high level of intervention)

The government is the largest force in the economy, according to the Economist Intelligence Unit, and impedes the ability of the market to freely set prices in most sectors. In 2000, the U.S. Department of Commerce reported that the "government still sets production targets for the agricultural sector, as well as for some industries, and controls the price on a few essential goods, such as cement and gasoline." Since agriculture is the principal sector, constituting 49.9 percent of total output in 2002, these controls are a major constraint. The government also controls the price of electricity and influences prices through its extensive state-owned sector. Laos maintains a daily minimum wage.

 ## PROPERTY RIGHTS
Score: **5**–Stable (very low level of protection)

The Economist Intelligence Unit reports that the judiciary "is in no sense independent…." According to the U.S. Department of Commerce, "foreign investors are generally advised to seek arbitration outside of Laos, since Laos' domestic arbitration authority lacks the ability to enforce its decisions." The same source reports that "impunity is a problem as is corruption. Many observers believe that judges can be bribed." Foreigners are not allowed to own land.

 ## REGULATION
Score: **5**–Stable (very high level)

"The environment for both domestic firms and foreign investors is still far from easy, owing to persistent red tape and corruption," reports the Economist Intelligence Unit. According to the U.S. Department of Commerce, "Foreign investors most frequently cite inconsistencies in the interpretation and application of existing laws as among the greatest impediments to investment. The lack of transparency in an increasingly centralized decision-making process, as well as the difficulty encountered in obtaining general information, augments the perception of the regulatory framework as arbitrary and inscrutable."

 ## INFORMAL MARKET
Score: **5**–Stable (very high level of activity)

The informal market in Laos is larger than the formal economy. There are no copyright or patent laws, piracy is rampant, and the informal market in currency is thriving. The Economist Intelligence Unit reports that there is extensive informal market activity in the logging industry and slash-and-burn cultivation.

LATVIA

Rank: 39

Score: 2.43

Category: Mostly Free

Present & Past Scores

(Best) 1
2
3
4
(Worst) 5

3.19 2.86 2.84 2.74 2.69 2.49 2.49 2.35 2.41 2.31 2.43

'95 '96 '97 '98 '99 '00 '01 '02 '03 '04 '05 '06
n/a

QUICK STUDY

SCORES

Trade Policy	2
Fiscal Burden	2.3
Government Intervention	2.5
Monetary Policy	2
Foreign Investment	2
Banking and Finance	2
Wages and Prices	2
Property Rights	3
Regulation	3
Informal Market	3.5

Population: 2,321,000

Total area: 64,589 sq. km

GDP: $9.6 billion

GDP growth rate: 7.5%

GDP per capita: $4,116

Major exports: wood and wood products, textiles, metals, machinery and equipment

Exports of goods and services: $3.9 billion

Major export trading partners: UK 15.6%, Germany 14.8%, Sweden 10.6%, Lithuania 8.2%

Major imports: machinery and equipment, chemicals, fuels

Imports of goods and services: $5.2 billion

Major import trading partners: Germany 16.1%, Lithuania 9.7%, Russia 8.7%, Finland 7.4%

Foreign direct investment (net): $309.5 million

2003 Data (in constant 2000 US dollars)

Latvia marked the beginning of 2005 with strong economic growth, an inflation spike nearing 10 percent, and a budget surplus due to higher tax inflows. The republic's rapidly expanding banking sector has propelled its main industries: construction, wholesale trade, retail, transport, and telecommunications. Exports of machinery, wood, and chemicals to Estonia, Lithuania, and Russia have also grown. However, economists are wary of the increased government spending, credit expansion, and consumer imports that contribute to the widening account deficit. Latvia's plans to adopt the euro in 2008 can proceed only if the country adopts a number of important reforms—specifically, administrative and legal reforms, as well as a revival of the privatization agenda, which has been sluggish in recent years. Latvian–Russian diplomatic relations have become tense due to the absence of a post–World War II peace treaty, lack of recognition and demarcation of the Latvian–Russian border, and differences in perceptions of the postwar Soviet occupation. Acrimonious debates with Moscow about the education of Russian-speaking schoolchildren in the Latvian language and Russia's embargo of the oil pipeline to the oil terminal in Ventspils have further strained relations. Latvia's fiscal burden of government score is 0.2 point worse this year, and its monetary policy score is 1 point worse. As a result Latvia's overall score is 0.12 point worse this year.

TRADE POLICY
Score: **2**–Stable (low level of protectionism)

Latvia adopted the trade policies of the European Union when it joined the EU in May 2004. The common EU weighted average external tariff was 1.3 percent in 2003, based on World Bank data. According to the World Trade Organization and the U.S. Trade Representative, the EU imposes non-tariff trade barriers through a complex regulatory system and export subsidies. Based on its adoption of EU trade policies, and on the revised trade factor methodology, Latvia's trade policy score is unchanged.

FISCAL BURDEN OF GOVERNMENT
Score—Income Taxation: **2.5**–Stable (moderate tax rates)
Score—Corporate Taxation: **1.5**–Stable (low tax rates)
Score—Government Expenditures: **3.5**–Worse (low increase)
Final Score: **2.3**–Worse (low cost of government)

Latvia has a flat income tax rate of 25 percent. The corporate tax rate is 15 percent. In 2004, according to the Ministry of Finance, government expenditures as a share of GDP increased 0.7 percentage point to 40.4 percent, compared to the 1.1 percentage point increase in 2003. On net, Latvia's fiscal burden of government score is 0.2 point worse this year.

GOVERNMENT INTERVENTION IN THE ECONOMY
Score: **2.5**–Stable (moderate level)

The Central Statistics Bureau reports that the government consumed 20.9 percent of GDP in 2004. In 2003, according to the International Monetary Fund's Government Financial Statistics CD–ROM, Latvia received 1.9 percent of its total revenues from state-owned enterprises and government ownership of property.

MONETARY POLICY
Score: **2**–Worse (low level of inflation)

From 1995 to 2004, Latvia's weighted average annual rate of inflation was 4.90 percent, up from the 2.64 percent from 1994 to 2003 reported in the 2005 *Index*. As a result, Latvia's monetary policy score is 1 point worse this year.

CAPITAL FLOWS AND FOREIGN INVESTMENT
Score: **2**–Stable (low barriers)

Latvia welcomes foreign investment, and foreigners receive national treatment. The government has no screening process, but all investments must be registered in the commercial register, the only exceptions being for partnerships and individual entrepreneurs. According to the Economist Intelligence Unit, "Since 1996 virtually all restrictions on foreign investment have been removed; foreign investors enjoy equal treatment and protection under the law…. Latvia offers one of the lowest corporate income taxes in Europe…. Bureaucratic obstacles include poor availability of information on government procedures and insufficient professionalism of many civil servants." Foreign investors may invest in most industries but are not allowed to hold controlling shares in companies involved in security services, air transport, or raffles and gambling interests. Foreign investors may own land for agricultural or forestry purposes if there is an existing investment protection agreement between Latvia and the country in which the investor is based, or if more than 50 percent of the fixed capital is owned by a Latvian citizen or the government. The International Monetary Fund reports that both residents and non-residents may hold foreign exchange accounts; there are no restrictions or controls on payments, transactions, transfers, or repatriation of profits; and non-residents may purchase buildings and land unless the land is near the border or in an environmentally sensitive area.

BANKING AND FINANCE
Score: **2**–Stable (low level of restrictions)

Banking crises in 1995 and 1998 led to the liquidation and consolidation of a number of Latvia's banks. The banking system has largely recovered, and regulations now require minimum accounting and financial standards, minimum capital requirements, restrictions on exposure, and open foreign exchange positions. A foreign non–European Economic Area bank may open a branch in Latvia if its capital is equal to at least the minimum capital required by law (EUR 5 million) and, if the bank is not licensed in a country that is a member of the World Trade Organization, it has been operating for at least three years. In 2004, 22 banks and one branch of a foreign bank were operating in Latvia. Banking standards and requirements apply equally to foreign and domestic banks, and foreign banks are welcome; according to the Economist Intelligence Unit, only one large bank is not owned by a West European bank. The Latvian government reports that it is sole owner of the JSC Hipoteku banka (the Mortgage Bank), which accounted for

4 percent of total banking assets at the end of 2004. All other commercial banking institutions are privately held.

WAGES AND PRICES
Score: **2**–Stable (low level of intervention)

The market determines most wages and prices. According to the Latvian embassy, the government controls the price of home rentals, utilities, some health services, and public transport services. Accession to the European Union has made Latvia eligible to subsidize agricultural prices through the Common Agricultural Policy. The government mandates a minimum wage.

PROPERTY RIGHTS
Score: **3**–Stable (moderate level of protection)

Latvia's constitution provides for an independent judiciary, which in practice is inefficient. The Economist Intelligence Unit reports that "judicial institutions enjoy independence from political influence, but are regarded as inefficient, with long delays in court hearings and enforcement of decisions…. Judges are under-qualified and overworked…." According to the U.S. Department of Commerce, "improvements in the judicial system are needed to accelerate the adjudication of cases, to strengthen the enforcement of court decisions, and to upgrade professional standards."

REGULATION
Score: **3**–Stable (moderate level)

Establishing a business is relatively easy, but some regulations are confusing and contradictory, leading to a lack of transparency. According to the U.S. Department of Commerce, "Government bureaucracy, corruption and organized crime, typical of the old Soviet Bloc countries, have been the main impediments to…trade and investment…in Latvia." In addition, "it is often alleged that bribe-taking—ranging from low-level bureaucrats in a position to delay or speed up bureaucratic procedures, to high-level officials involved in awarding government contracts—is not uncommon." Labor laws are somewhat rigid.

INFORMAL MARKET
Score: **3.5**–Stable (high level of activity)

Transparency International's 2004 score for Latvia is 4. Therefore, Latvia's informal market score is 3.5 this year.

LEBANON

Rank: 73
Score: 3.00
Category: Mostly Unfree

Present & Past Scores

(Best) 1
2
3
4
(Worst) 5

2.91 2.73 3.06 3.03 3.06 2.70 3.01 3.04 3.13 3.10 3.00

'95 '96 '97 '98 '99 '00 '01 '02 '03 '04 '05 '06
n/a

QUICK STUDY

SCORES

Trade Policy	3
Fiscal Burden	2
Government Intervention	3
Monetary Policy	1
Foreign Investment	4
Banking and Finance	2
Wages and Prices	3
Property Rights	4
Regulation	4
Informal Market	4

Population: 4,497,669

Total area: 10,400 sq. km

GDP: $17.65 billion

GDP growth rate: 2.7%

GDP per capita: $3,925

Major exports: food products, jewelry, chemical products, metal products

Exports of goods and services: $2.9 billion

Major export trading partners: Switzerland 11.0%, United Arab Emirates 10.1%, Saudi Arabia 7.6%, US 7.4%

Major imports: food products, vehicles, mineral products, chemical products

Imports of goods and services: $7.6 billion

Major import trading partners: France 13.5%, Germany 11.8%, Italy 10.8%, US 4.5%

Foreign direct investment (net): $246.5 million

2003 Data (in constant 2000 US dollars)

L ebanon gained its independence from France in 1943 and developed one of the Middle East's most advanced economies as a trading center and financial hub. With a thriving international banking sector, it was known as "the Switzerland of the Middle East" until its disastrous 1975–1990 civil war. Syria intervened, ostensibly to tamp down the fighting, and established a stranglehold on Lebanese politics. The cost of rebuilding the country's war-torn infrastructure and chronic fiscal deficits pushed public debt to 190 percent of GDP by the end of 2004. In response, the government adopted a fiscal adjustment program focusing on tax reforms, privatization, and improved debt management. However, Prime Minister Rafiq Hariri's plans for economic reform were frustrated by opposition from pro-Syrian President Emile Lahoud. Hariri resigned as prime minister in 2004, and his February 2005 assassination, which many Lebanese suspect was orchestrated by Syria, ignited a popular revolt against the presence of Syrian troops. Lebanese demonstrations and the threat of U.N. sanctions led Syria to withdraw its troops in April 2005. Political uncertainty has shaken confidence in the economy. Lebanon's trade policy and fiscal burden of government scores are both 0.5 point better this year. As a result, Lebanon's overall score is 0.1 point better this year.

TRADE POLICY
Score: **3**–Better (moderate level of protectionism)

The World Bank reports that Lebanon's weighted average tariff rate in 2002 (the most recent year for which World Bank data are available) was 6.3 percent. (The World Bank has revised the figure for 2002 downward from the 8 percent reported in the 2005 *Index*.) According to the U.S. Department of Commerce, "The import and export of goods is subject to a number of trade barriers imposed by ten Lebanese government state bodies. Measures include prohibitions, licenses, quotas, visas, veterinary certificates, and phytosanitary certificates." Corruption is also a problem. Based on the lower tariff rate, as well as a revision of the trade factor methodology, Lebanon's trade policy score is 0.5 point better this year.

FISCAL BURDEN OF GOVERNMENT
Score—Income Taxation: **2**–Stable (low tax rates)
Score—Corporate Taxation: **1.5**–Stable (low tax rates)
Score—Change in Government Expenditures: **3**–Better (very low decrease)
Final Score: **2**–Better (low cost of government)

Lebanon's top income tax rate is 20 percent. The top corporate tax rate is 15 percent. In 2003, according to the Ministry of Finance, government expenditures as a share of GDP decreased 0.1 percentage point to 38.9 percent, compared to the 0 percentage point change in 2002. On net, Lebanon's fiscal burden of government score is 0.5 point better this year.

GOVERNMENT INTERVENTION IN THE ECONOMY
Score: **3**–Stable (moderate level)

The World Bank reports that the government consumed 12.8 percent of GDP in 2003. In 2004, based on data from the Ministry of Finance, Lebanon received 19.27 percent of its total revenues from state-owned enterprises and government ownership of property.

MONETARY POLICY
Score: **1**–Stable (very low level of inflation)

From 1995 to 2004, based on data from the International Monetary Fund's *2005 World Economic Outlook*, Lebanon's weighted average annual rate of inflation was 2.35 percent.

CAPITAL FLOWS AND FOREIGN INVESTMENT
Score: **4**–Stable (high barriers)

Although Lebanon does not discriminate between national and foreign investments in most sectors and has taken a number of steps to make its foreign investment climate more attractive in recent years, the government reports that foreign investment in real estate, insurance, media companies, and banks is restricted, and foreign companies require a license to operate in other sectors. According to the U.S. Department of Commerce, "Lebanon's free market economy, the absence of controls on the movement of capital and foreign exchange, a highly educated labor force, and the quality of life have encouraged a number of foreign companies to set up offices or regional offices in Lebanon in recent years.... However, some foreign companies have left, or decided to move their regional offices to neighboring countries, or refrained from investing in Lebanon because of frustration resulting from red tape and corruption, arbitrary licensing decisions, archaic legislation, an ineffectual judicial system, high taxes and fees, and a lack of adequate protection of intellectual property." The International Monetary Fund reports that both residents and non-residents may hold foreign exchange accounts, but central bank approval is required to purchase treasury securities, money market instruments, and derivatives, and some credit operations are prohibited. All foreigners must obtain a license from the government to acquire real estate. There are no restrictions on payments and transfers. According to the IMF, "Foreign investments in some sectors are subject to specific ceilings and, in some cases, to prior authorization."

BANKING AND FINANCE
Score: **2**–Stable (low level of restrictions)

Lebanon's banking regime is the region's most liberal, with few restrictions on domestic bank formation and few barriers to foreign banks. "At the end of 2003," reports the Economist Intelligence Unit, "there were 53 commercial banks operating in Lebanon under the license of Banque du Liban (the central bank), in addition to ten investment banks and 16 representative offices of foreign banks." According to the U.S. Department of Commerce, "Strict bank regulation has helped Lebanon avoid the emerging markets crisis.... The [Banking Control Commission (BCC)] complies with most of the core principles of the Basel Committee on banking control and ensures that all banks comply with Basel regulations on capital adequacy ratio.... All credit transactions are subject to timely and accurate disclosure. Bank financial statements are in compliance with international accounting standards. Annual accounts are audited by independent auditors and

several banks utilize internationally recognized accounting firms." The EIU reports that many private-sector borrowers are crowded out of the market because more than 60 percent of bank credit goes to the government. In June 2002, Lebanon was removed from the list of countries judged not to be cooperating with international efforts to fight money laundering.

WAGES AND PRICES
Score: **3**–Stable (moderate level of intervention)

According to the U.S. Department of Commerce, the government controls the price of bread and petroleum derivatives and surveys supermarket prices of consumer goods every two months. The government also controls the prices of pharmaceuticals. The Economist Intelligence Unit reports that the government subsidizes the production of certain crops, such as tobacco, and indirectly affects the prices of some utilities, such as electricity, through its state-owned enterprises. It also mandates a monthly minimum wage.

PROPERTY RIGHTS
Score: **4**–Stable (low level of protection)

"The judiciary is nominally independent," reports the Economist Intelligence Unit, "but in reality often acquiesces to the demands of the security services and the police. Courts deal with civil and criminal cases, which are brought by a government-appointed prosecuting magistrate, who exerts considerable influence over judges, for example recommending verdict and sentence. Trials, particularly commercial cases, have nevertheless been known to drag on for many years."

REGULATION
Score: **4**–Stable (high level)

According to the U.S. Department of Commerce, "Transparency has never been strong in Lebanon. The government does not always establish clear rules of the game." In addition, many companies have "refrained from investing here due to frustrations resulting from red tape and corruption, arbitrary licensing decisions, archaic legislation, an ineffectual judicial system, high taxes and fees, and a lack of adequate protection of intellectual property.... Transparency, clear regulations and fair consideration of bids have never been the rule in Lebanon." Bureaucratic corruption is common.

INFORMAL MARKET
Score: **4**–Stable (high level of activity)

Transparency International's 2004 score for Lebanon is 2.7. Therefore, Lebanon's informal market score is 4 this year.

LESOTHO

Rank: 99

Score: 3.24

Category: Mostly Unfree

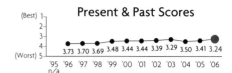

Present & Past Scores

(Best) 1 –
2 –
3 –
4 –
(Worst) 5 –

3.73 3.70 3.69 3.48 3.44 3.44 3.39 3.29 3.50 3.41 3.24

'95 '96 '97 '98 '99 '00 '01 '02 '03 '04 '05 '06
n/a

Lesotho's constitutional monarch, King Letsie III, is head of state but has no executive authority. Prime Minister Pakalitha Mosisili was re-elected in 2002 in free and fair elections, and his party controls a large majority in parliament. Lesotho is completely surrounded by South Africa, with which it is closely linked both politically and economically. About 26 percent of the adult male work force is employed in South Africa. Lesotho's agricultural sector is small as a percentage of GDP, but over 20 percent of the population is engaged in subsistence agriculture. Corruption is problematic. The government has made strides in privatizing agro-industrial business and agribusiness. Private businesses are the rule in manufacturing and construction. The U.S. African Growth and Opportunity Act has had a positive economic impact. The United States is now Lesotho's main export market, primarily because of increased textile exports, but the January 2005 expiration of textile quotas under the Multi-Fiber Arrangement has forced Lesotho to compete with low-cost Asian producers, and this could undermine the textile sector. Lesotho will continue to seek assistance for its HIV/AIDS epidemic, which the government recognizes as a threat to stability. Lesotho is eligible for U.S. Millennium Challenge Account assistance. Lesotho's fiscal burden of government score is 0.7 point better this year, and its government intervention score is 1 point better. As a result, Lesotho's overall score is 0.17 point better this year.

QUICK STUDY

SCORES

Trade Policy	2.5
Fiscal Burden	3.4
Government Intervention	2.5
Monetary Policy	3
Foreign Investment	4
Banking and Finance	3
Wages and Prices	3
Property Rights	3
Regulation	4
Informal Market	4

Population: 1,792,000

Total area: 30,355 sq. km

GDP: $950 million

GDP growth rate: 2.7%

GDP per capita: $530

Major exports: food and live animals, clothing, footwear, wool

Exports of goods and services: $414 million

Major export trading partners: US 76.4%, SACU 22.9%, EU 0.2% (2002)

Major imports: food, vehicles, machinery, medicine, petroleum products

Imports of goods and services: $925 billion

Major import trading partners: SACU 73.5%, Asia 23.7%, EU 1.1% (2002)

Foreign direct investment (net): $39.5 million

2003 Data (in constant 2000 US dollars)

TRADE POLICY

Score: **2.5**–Stable (moderate level of protectionism)

Lesotho belongs to the Southern African Customs Union (SACU), a regional trade arrangement with South Africa, Botswana, Namibia, and Swaziland. The World Bank reports that in 2001 (the most recent year for which World Bank data are available), SACU had a weighted average tariff rate of 3.6 percent. According to the U.S. Trade Representative, "Lesotho applies a permit system for all imports from non-SACU members…. The [government] monitors the level of [egg, sugar, and legume] production…and issues import licenses in the event of short supply…. [N]o licenses for [imports of] used clothing are issued, with the effect of a de facto ban on this product. Liquor imports are prohibited." Based on the revised trade factor methodology, Lesotho's trade policy score is unchanged.

FISCAL BURDEN OF GOVERNMENT

Score—Income Taxation: **3.5**–Stable (high tax rates)
Score—Corporate Taxation: **4.5**–Stable (very high tax rates)
Score—Change in Government Expenditures: **1**–Better (very high decrease)
Final Score: **3.4**–Better (moderate cost of government)

The Ministry of Finance and Development Planning reports that Lesotho's top income tax rate is 35 percent. The top corporate tax rate is also 35 percent. In 2003, according to the African Development Bank, government expenditures as a share of GDP decreased 5.6 percentage points to 41.7 percent, compared to the 3.9 percentage point increase in 2002. On net, Lesotho's fiscal burden of government score is 0.7 point better this year.

GOVERNMENT INTERVENTION IN THE ECONOMY

Score: **2.5**–Better (moderate level)

The African Development Bank reports that the government consumed 31.8 percent of GDP in 2003. In fiscal year April 2003–March 2004, based on data from the Ministry of Finance and Development Planning, Lesotho received 3.69 percent of its total revenues from state-owned enterprises and government ownership of property, down from the 11.37 percent reported in the 2005 *Index*. As a result, Lesotho's government intervention score is 1 point better this year.

MONETARY POLICY
Score: **3**–Stable (moderate level of inflation)

From 1995 to 2004, based on data from the International Monetary Fund's *2005 World Economic Outlook*, Lesotho's weighted average annual rate of inflation was 6.55 percent.

CAPITAL FLOWS AND FOREIGN INVESTMENT
Score: **4**–Stable (high barriers)

The U.S. Trade Representative reports that "Lesotho welcomes foreign investment. Foreign investors have participated in the country's privatization program without discrimination." However, political instability and a lack of transparency discourage foreign investment. According to the Economist Intelligence Unit, "Serious incidents in both 1991 and 1998 have shown how general discontent can quickly turn into aggression directed specifically at foreigners. Foreign-owned businesses…have been major victims of destruction of property…. [T]he underlying potential for unrest should be taken seriously." The International Monetary Fund reports that residents and non-residents no longer require government permission to hold foreign exchange accounts, but quantitative restrictions apply. Some payments and transfers are subject to prior government approval and limitations. Many capital transactions face restrictions or quantitative limits, and real estate purchases abroad require government approval.

BANKING AND FINANCE
Score: **3**–Stable (moderate level of restrictions)

The banking system remains small, underdeveloped, and hindered by non-performing loans. According to the Economist Intelligence Unit, "This is owing to a culture of non-repayment, which stems from historical reasons—politicians exploited Lesotho Bank and parastatals crowded out the private sector." However, "Inefficient financial institutions have been dealt with through a combination of privatisation, recapitalisation and closures, and a programme of measures is under way to improve the efficiency of banking supervision…. The [central bank] is trying to encourage more competition in the banking sector, particularly from South African banks. In October 2004, First National Bank Lesotho (the subsidiary of a South African Bank) became the fourth commercial bank operating in Lesotho." The government privatized the Lesotho Bank in 1999 and liquidated the Lesotho Agricultural Development Bank in 2000. The state owns two development banks that provide industrial credits and other services. The central bank established a Rural Credit Guarantee Fund in 2003 to encour-

age rural lending and in 2004 announced the establishment of the Lesotho PostBank to provide banking services to the poor and in rural areas through the post office network.

WAGES AND PRICES
Score: **3**–Stable (moderate level of intervention)

Many prices have been liberalized, but the government still influences prices through large state-owned utilities and direct intervention in the agricultural sector, which employs approximately 57 percent of the labor force. According to the Economist Intelligence Unit, "A history of direct government involvement has limited private-sector involvement in the commercial development of the [agriculture] sector…. The programme for privatising agricultural parastatals has not made much headway either, with little interest being shown by the private sector." The Wage Advisory Board (a tripartite group of unions, government, and employers) sets a national minimum wage annually.

PROPERTY RIGHTS
Score: **3**–Stable (moderate level of protection)

Private property is guaranteed, and expropriation is unlikely. According to the Economist Intelligence Unit, "Lesotho's legal system is based on Roman–Dutch law and is close to that practised in South Africa. The judiciary is independent and has generally been allowed to carry out its role effectively, even during the years of military rule. However, draconian internal security legislation gives considerable power to the police and restricts the right of assembly and some forms of industrial action."

REGULATION
Score: **4**–Stable (high level)

The Economist Intelligence Unit reports that some sectors of the economy "have been growing rapidly owing to a favourable tax regime and trading arrangements, although the framework for attracting investment has been criticised for being ad hoc and lacking transparency." Corruption is present, "especially at the petty level where civil servants, who have been without significant pay increases for several years supplement their incomes." The government has pledged to address labor market inflexibility and the inefficient public sector as part of its International Monetary Fund agreement, but specific results have yet to be seen.

INFORMAL MARKET
Score: **4**–Stable (high level of activity)

Lesotho has a substantial informal market, primarily in consumer goods. Smuggling is common. According to the Institute for Security Studies, "One of the distinctive features of Lesotho's economy is its huge informal sector that exists alongside a small, but predominantly commercial, modern sector."

LIBYA

Rank: 152

Score: 4.16

Category: Repressed

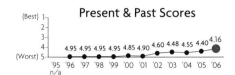

Present & Past Scores

(Best) 1
2
3
4
(Worst) 5

4.95 4.95 4.95 4.95 4.85 4.90 4.60 4.48 4.55 4.40 4.16

'95 '96 '97 '98 '99 '00 '01 '02 '03 '04 '05 '06
n/a

QUICK STUDY

SCORES

Trade Policy	5
Fiscal Burden	4.6
Government Intervention	4
Monetary Policy	1
Foreign Investment	4
Banking and Finance	4
Wages and Prices	5
Property Rights	5
Regulation	5
Informal Market	4

Population: 5,559,289

Total area: 1,759,540 sq. km

GDP: $22.7 billion

GDP growth rate: 9.1%

GDP per capita: $4,083

Major exports: refined petroleum products, crude oil

Exports of goods (fob): $14.7 billion

Major export trading partners: Italy 39.1%, Germany 13.5%, Spain 13.5%, Turkey 7.1%

Major imports: manufactured goods, food, machinery and transport equipment

Imports of goods (fob): $7.2 billion

Major import trading partners: Italy 27.8%, Germany 10.5%, UK 7.0%, Tunisia 6.3%, France 5.8%

Foreign direct investment (net): $566.1 million

2003 Data (in constant 2000 US dollars)

Libya's state-dominated economy depends heavily on oil revenues, which generate almost all export earnings and about one-quarter of GDP. Despite one of Africa's highest per capita GDPs, the economy has been hurt by more than 30 years of socialist economic policies and international sanctions. Libya accepted civil liability for its role in the 1989 Lockerbie bombing and agreed to pay compensation to the victims' families, and the U.N. lifted sanctions in September 2003. After Libyan leader Muammar Qadhafi's December 2003 announcement of his willingness to abandon efforts to build weapons of mass destruction, the U.S. lifted its travel ban in March 2004 and removed most of its unilateral sanctions in April 2004. However, Libya is still prohibited from buying U.S. arms or dual-use items because it remains on the U.S. Department of State's list of state sponsors of terrorism. In 2003, Qadhafi appointed American-educated Prime Minister Shokri Ghanem to preside over economic reforms, particularly in the oil industry, which is seeking substantial foreign investment, but bureaucratic resistance and policy reversals by Qadhafi have frustrated Ghanem's efforts. Libya has applied to join the World Trade Organization but still needs to institute significant market reforms to meet the WTO's stringent accession criteria. Libya's fiscal burden of government score is 0.4 point better this year, and its capital flows and foreign investment score and banking and finance score are both 1 point better. As a result, Libya's overall score is 0.24 point better this year.

TRADE POLICY
Score: **5**–Stable (very high level of protectionism)

According to the World Bank, Libya's weighted average tariff rate in 2002 (the most recent year for which World Bank data are available) was 25.2 percent. (The World Bank has revised the figure for 2002 upward from the 15.9 percent reported in the 2005 *Index*.) The European Commission's Market Access Sectoral and Trade Barriers Database reports that sanitary and phytosanitary regulations serve as a non-tariff barrier. According to the Economist Intelligence Unit, "Import controls, despite being eased since the lifting of UN sanctions, remain tight even by regional standards." The customs system lacks transparency and is subject to corruption. Based on the revised trade factor methodology, Libya's trade policy score is unchanged.

FISCAL BURDEN OF GOVERNMENT
Score—Income Taxation: **3.5**–Better (high tax rates)
Score—Corporate Taxation: **5**–Stable (very high tax rates)
Score—Change in Government Expenditures: **5**–Stable (very high increase)
Final Score: **4.6**–Better (very high cost of government)

According to the International Monetary Fund, Libya's top income tax rate is 38 percent (35 percent plus a 3 percent jihad tax), down from the 90 percent reported in the 2005 *Index*. Deloitte reports that the top corporate tax rate is 64 percent (60 percent plus a 4 percent jihad tax), up from the 44 percent reported in the 2005 *Index*. In 2003, according to the International Monetary Fund, government expenditures as a share of GDP increased by 3.3 percentage points, compared to the 3.4 percentage point decrease in 2002. On net, Libya's fiscal burden of government score is 0.4 point better this year.

GOVERNMENT INTERVENTION IN THE ECONOMY
Score: **4**–Stable (high level)

The African Development Bank reports that the government consumed 17.7 percent of GDP in 2003. In 2004, based on data from the International Monetary Fund, Libya received 86.41 percent of its total revenues from state-owned enterprises and government ownership of property in the oil sector.

 MONETARY POLICY
Score: **1**–Stable (very low level of inflation)

From 1995 to 2004, Libya's weighted average annual rate of inflation was –2.25 percent.

 CAPITAL FLOWS AND FOREIGN INVESTMENT
Score: **4**–Better (high barriers)

According to the Economist Intelligence Unit, "Foreign direct investment (FDI) in Libya has been almost exclusively in the hydrocarbons sector. The past sanctions regime, combined with the country's erratic economic policy, have, in the past, provided little incentive for investors in other sectors." The September 23, 2004, issue of *The Economist* notes that Libya's "bumbling, grasping, and erratic bureaucracy" is an impediment to investment. The International Monetary Fund reports that both residents and non-residents may hold foreign currency accounts with prior approval. Payments for authorized imports are not restricted; other payments require government approval or are subject to quantitative limits. Repatriation and most capital transactions, including transactions involving capital and money market instruments, credit operations, direct investment, and real estate, are subject to controls, including approval requirements. The government has partially liberalized rules on foreign investment, permitting it in some sectors and creating a one-stop-shop for foreign investors, but the IMF reports that the regulatory and bureaucratic environment suffers from "major deficiencies." Lifting of United Nations sanctions and the U.S. embargo should open up new opportunities for investment. Based on evidence of partial liberalization of foreign investment rules, Libya's capital flows and foreign investment score is 1 point better this year.

 BANKING AND FINANCE
Score: **4**–Better (high level of restrictions)

Libya's banking system has been under state control since the 1970s and remains highly centralized. "In 2002," reports the Economist Intelligence Unit, "Libyan finance and banking officials indicated that they are considering privatising some of the country's banks. However, no clear privatisation plan or prospectus has been published and foreign investor interest remains low…. Indeed, foreign banks have only cautiously welcomed new legislation, approved by the General People's Congress in March 2005, to permit foreign banks to open branches in Libya for the first time…. Investors are deterred

by bureaucratic regulation and antiquated administrative procedures, as well as poor transparency and the heavy debt burdens of some state banks…. [T]here is no capital market to speak of." A 1993 law permits both foreign and private banking. The first private bank since 1969 opened in December 1996. The only foreign banks with representative offices in Libya include the Arab Banking Corporation, Malta's Bank of Valletta, and Egypt's Suez Bank. The International Monetary Fund reports that Libya is modernizing and enhancing banking supervision. Based on evidence of foreign and private banks represented or operating in Libya and legislation permitting foreign branches, Libya's banking and finance score is 1 point better this year.

 WAGES AND PRICES
Score: **5**–Stable (very high level of intervention)

The government controls most prices. According to the Economist Intelligence Unit, the government uses its extensive subsidy system "to negate the need for a salary increase, or, in the times when prices dropped, as a substitute for salary increases." The government sets most wages because it employs 70 percent of the labor force.

 PROPERTY RIGHTS
Score: **5**–Stable (very low level of protection)

The U.S. Department of State reports that Libya's judiciary "is not independent…[and] the private practice of law is illegal; all lawyers must be members of the Secretariat of Justice." According to the Economist Intelligence Unit, there is little land ownership, and the government may re-nationalize the little private property that is granted, especially to foreign companies.

 REGULATION
Score: **5**–Stable (very high level)

According to the Economist Intelligence Unit, Libya is gradually integrating into the international economy and easing restrictions on private enterprise. In addition, "Since 1999, private-sector growth has resumed and been given extra impetus by changes in laws on trading and import activities and on the formation of private companies or partnerships." The government allows private small farming, some private banking, private-sector retail, and foreign investment in the oil sector, although it heavily regulates business activities. The EIU reports that corruption is widespread.

 INFORMAL MARKET
Score: **4**–Stable (high level of activity)

Transparency International's 2004 score for Libya is 2.5. Therefore, Libya's informal market score is 4 this year.

LITHUANIA

Rank: 23

Score: 2.14

Category: Mostly Free

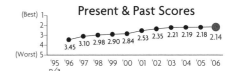

Present & Past Scores

(Best) 1
2
3
4
(Worst) 5

3.45 3.10 2.98 2.90 2.84 2.53 2.35 2.21 2.19 2.18 2.14

'95 '96 '97 '98 '99 '00 '01 '02 '03 '04 '05 '06
n/a

QUICK STUDY

SCORES

Trade Policy	2
Fiscal Burden	2.4
Government Intervention	2
Monetary Policy	1
Foreign Investment	2
Banking and Finance	1
Wages and Prices	2
Property Rights	3
Regulation	3
Informal Market	3

Population: 3,454,000

Total area: 65,200 sq. km

GDP: $14.0 billion

GDP growth rate: 9.0%

GDP per capita: $4,078

Major exports: mineral products, transport equipment, textiles, machinery and equipment, chemicals

Exports of goods and services: $7.8 billion

Major export trading partners: Switzerland 11.6%, Russia 10.1%, Germany 9.9%, Latvia 9.7%, UK 6.4%

Major imports: machinery and equipment, mineral products, transport equipment, chemicals, clothing

Imports of goods and services: $8.8 billion

Major import trading partners: Russia 22.0%, Germany 16.2%, Poland 5.2%, Italy 4.3%, France 4.2%

Foreign direct investment (net): $134 million

2003 Data (in constant 2000 US dollars)

Despite rising political uncertainty, Lithuania continues to enjoy impressive economic successes. Two rounds of parliamentary elections in October 2004 brought a left-wing, four-party coalition to power. The new government is already experiencing tensions because of certain policies that have engendered opposition. The two populist coalition members favor higher social spending, but the Social Democrats and New Union–Social Liberals, which retain the Prime Minister, Minister of Finance, and Parliament Speaker positions, are committed to a tight fiscal policy, and right-wing parties in parliament pose a well-organized opposition to the governing coalition, creating a system of checks and balances. Already a member of the European Union, Lithuania is focusing on joining the euro zone in 2007. It has met most of the Maastricht criteria, including fiscal reforms, income tax reduction, increased revenue from the value-added tax, and the introduction of a real estate tax. According to the Economist Intelligence Unit, economic growth was an impressive 6.7 percent in 2004. Growth in real wages, diminishing unemployment, and the availability of markets for exports in the Baltic countries and Russia signal an optimistic short-term economic outlook. Lithuania's fiscal burden of government score is 0.4 point better this year. As a result, its overall score is 0.04 point better this year.

TRADE POLICY
Score: **2**–Stable (low level of protectionism)

Lithuania adopted the trade policies of the European Union when it joined the EU in May 2004. The common EU weighted average external tariff was 1.3 percent in 2003, based on World Bank data. According to the World Trade Organization and the U.S. Trade Representative, the EU imposes non-tariff trade barriers through a complex regulatory system and export subsidies. The U.S. Department of Commerce reports licensing requirements on some goods beyond EU requirements. Based on its adoption of EU trade policies, and on the revised trade factor methodology, Lithuania's trade policy score is unchanged.

FISCAL BURDEN OF GOVERNMENT
Score—Income Taxation: **3**–Stable (moderate tax rates)
Score—Corporate Taxation: **1.5**–Stable (low tax rates)
Score—Change in Government Expenditures: **3.5**–Better (low increase)
Final Score: **2.4**–Better (low cost of government)

The Embassy of Lithuania reports that Lithuania has a flat income tax rate of 33 percent. The top corporate tax rate is 15 percent. In 2004, according to the Embassy of Lithuania, government expenditures as a share of GDP increased 0.6 percentage point to 34.7 percent, compared to the 0.2 percentage point decrease in 2003. On net, Lithuania's fiscal burden of government score is 0.4 point better this year.

GOVERNMENT INTERVENTION IN THE ECONOMY
Score: **2**–Stable (low level)

Based on data from the Bank of Lithuania, the government consumed 17.5 percent of GDP in 2004. In 2003, according to the International Monetary Fund's Government Financial Statistics CD–ROM, Lithuania received 2.71 percent of its total revenues from state-owned enterprises and government ownership of property.

MONETARY POLICY
Score: **1**–Stable (very low level of inflation)

Lithuania has a currency board pegging its litas to the euro. From 1995 to 2004, Lithuania's weighted average annual rate of inflation was 0.58 percent.

CAPITAL FLOWS AND FOREIGN INVESTMENT
Score: **2**–Stable (low barriers)

Lithuania maintains few barriers to foreign investment. Foreign companies are accorded the same treatment as domestic firms. The International Monetary Fund reports that all sectors of the economy are open to foreign investment, with the exception of the security and defense sectors and the organization of lotteries. According to the U.S. Department of Commerce, "The law provides for equal protection to foreign and domestic investors. No special permit is required from government authorities to invest foreign capital in Lithuania and there are no prohibitions or limitations on investment, provided the investor complies with Lithuanian laws. Foreign investors have free access to all sectors of the economy, with some limited exceptions." Activities involving increased danger to human life, health, environment, manufacturing, or trade in weapons require prior permission or a license. The Economist Intelligence Unit reports that "Lithuania is a potentially attractive investment proposition…. However, complex regulations and procedures continue to be obstacles for investors." The IMF reports that since January 23, 2003, foreigners have been allowed to purchase agricultural and non-agricultural land. Residents may hold foreign exchange accounts; non-residents must obtain approval to hold foreign exchange accounts if the country from which they have come requires approval. There are no controls or restrictions on repatriation of profits, current transfers, or payments. Some capital transactions must be registered with the central bank, and there are limits on open foreign exchange positions by banks.

BANKING AND FINANCE
Score: **1**–Stable (very low level of restrictions)

Lithuania's banking system has recovered from its collapse in 1995 and emerged relatively unscathed from the Russian financial crisis in 1998. The crisis led to consolidation as the number of commercial banks fell from 28 in 1995 to 10 as of January 2004. "The sector is already highly concentrated," reports the Economist Intelligence Unit. "The share of total assets held by the three largest banks—Vilniaus Bankas, Hansabankas and Nord/LB Lietuva—was 75% as of the beginning of December 2004." Scandinavian banks dominate the banking sector, in which foreign banks accounted for just under 90 percent of banking capital as of October 2004. Privatization of Zemes Ukio Bankas (LZUB), Lithuania's last remaining state-owned bank, was completed on March 19, 2002. According to the U.S. Department of Commerce, "Government policies do not interfere in the free flow of financial resources or the allocation of credit."

WAGES AND PRICES
Score: **2**–Stable (low level of intervention)

According to the Economist Intelligence Unit, "Most prices had been liberalised by 1993, and steep increases in administratively controlled prices, such as rents, heating and transport, were introduced subsequently to bring them up to cost-recovery level." Information provided by the Lithuanian embassy reflects that price controls remain in effect on electricity, water, and natural gas. Accession to the European Union has made Lithuania eligible to subsidize agricultural prices through the Common Agricultural Policy. The government maintains a minimum wage.

PROPERTY RIGHTS
Score: **3**–Stable (moderate level of protection)

According to the U.S. Department of State, "The Constitution provides for an independent judiciary, and the government generally respected this provision in practice." The European Bank for Reconstruction and Development reports that "weakness of the judicial system is viewed as a deterrent for foreign investors to enforce their rights in local courts." However, reports the Economist Intelligence Unit, "EU accession has played a major role in reforming the judicial system, including strengthening its independence and streamlining proceedings to clear up the backlog of criminal cases."

REGULATION
Score: **3**–Stable (moderate level)

According to the U.S. Department of Commerce, "Business in Lithuania is still fairly heavily regulated…. Investors and lawyers complain that many laws and regulations are vague, confusing, and often contradictory. The government gives the business community little advance notice of new legislation, and still less opportunity for comment." The same source reports that small and medium entrepreneurs "describe lower level bureaucrats as rigid, unhelpful, corrupt, and often abusive…. The Lithuanian press is replete with stories of tax inspectors, economic police, and customs officials who make unreasonable demands on small businesses. Many companies agree that the government appears to be biased in favor of big business…." Environmental and labor laws are established along the lines of EU regulation.

INFORMAL MARKET
Score: **3**–Stable (moderate level of activity)

Transparency International's 2004 score for Lithuania is 4.6. Therefore, Lithuania's informal market score is 3 this year.

LUXEMBOURG

Rank: 4
Score: 1.60
Category: Free

Present & Past Scores

(Best) 1-
2- 2.04 2.01 2.01 2.00 1.89 1.84 1.93 1.68 1.76 1.63 1.60
3-
4-
(Worst) 5-
'95 '96 '97 '98 '99 '00 '01 '02 '03 '04 '05 '06
n/a

2004 Data (in constant 2000 US dollars)

QUICK STUDY

SCORES

Trade Policy	2
Fiscal Burden	3
Government Intervention	2
Monetary Policy	1
Foreign Investment	1
Banking and Finance	1
Wages and Prices	2
Property Rights	1
Regulation	2
Informal Market	1

Population: 461,000

Total area: 2,586 sq. km

GDP: $21.9 billion

GDP growth rate: 4.5%

GDP per capita: $47,505

Major exports: machinery and transport equipment, manufactured metal products, financial services, travel services, insurance services

Exports of goods and services: $30.9 billion

Major export trading partners: Germany 26.1%, France 19.9%, Belgium 12.0%

Major imports: machinery and equipment, chemicals, computer and information services, financial services

Imports of goods and services: $26.8 billion

Major import trading partners: Belgium 35.8%, Germany 27.0%, France 13.9%

Foreign direct investment (net): –$1.8 billion

Luxembourg, a founding member of the European Union, is also its smallest member. During the first half of 2005, it held the rotating EU presidency. Despite a deceleration in per capita GDP in recent years, Luxembourg maintains one of the world's highest GDP income levels. During the 20th century, it evolved from an agrarian society into a manufacturing and services economy. With a financial services industry that accounts for about one-third of GDP, Luxembourg is one of the world's richest countries. In addition to being Europe's principal center for mutual funds and a major force in the banking and insurance industries, it is an ideal location for information technology companies, with a skilled workforce and well-developed infrastructure. There are no restrictions that apply specifically to foreign investors, the liberal regulatory structure is fair and transparent, and labor strife is minimal. After the June 2004 election, a center–left government was formed. Like the previous center–right government, it is headed by the leader of the Christian Social Party, Jean-Claude Junker, who is both prime minister and finance minister. Luxembourg's GDP grew an impressive 4.5 percent in 2004. Luxembourg's fiscal burden of government score is 0.3 point better this year. As a result, its overall score is 0.03 point better this year.

TRADE POLICY
Score: **2**–Stable (low level of protectionism)

As a member of the European Union, Luxembourg was subject to a common EU weighted average external tariff of 1.3 percent in 2003, down from the 2.4 percent for 2002 reported in the 2005 *Index,* based on World Bank data. According to the World Trade Organization and the U.S. Trade representative, the EU imposes non-tariff trade barriers through a complex regulatory system and export subsidies. Based on the revised trade factor methodology, Luxembourg's trade policy score is unchanged.

FISCAL BURDEN OF GOVERNMENT
Score—Income Taxation: **3.5**–Stable (high tax rates)
Score—Corporate Taxation: **2.5**–Stable (moderate tax rates)
Score—Change in Government Expenditures: **3.5**–Better (low increase)
Final Score: **3**–Better (moderate cost of government)

Luxembourg's top income tax rate is 38.95 percent (38 percent plus a 2.5 percent surcharge). The top corporate tax rate is 22.9 percent. In 2004, government expenditures as a share of GDP increased 0.8 percentage point to 45.9 percent, compared to the 1.4 percentage point increase in 2003. On net, Luxembourg's fiscal burden of government score is 0.3 point better this year.

GOVERNMENT INTERVENTION IN THE ECONOMY
Score: **2**–Stable (low level)

The Ministry of Economy reports that the government consumed 18.3 percent of GDP in 2004. In the same year, according to the national statistical agency, Luxembourg received 1.88 percent of its revenues from state-owned enterprises and government ownership of property.

MONETARY POLICY
Score: **1–Stable** (very low level of inflation)

Luxembourg is a member of the euro zone. From 1995 to 2004, Luxembourg's weighted average annual rate of inflation was 2.19 percent.

 CAPITAL FLOWS AND FOREIGN INVESTMENT
Score: **1–Stable** (very low barriers)

Luxembourg has a very open foreign investment regime and actively promotes foreign investment. Foreign and domestic businesses receive equal treatment, and there are no local content requirements. The Economist Intelligence Unit reports that non–European Economic Area banks need a license from the Commission de Surveillance du Secteur Financier to set up a branch or subsidiary. Luxembourg's investment regulatory structure is fair and transparent. The government restricts investments that directly affect national security. The International Monetary Fund reports that both residents and non-residents may hold foreign exchange accounts. There are no restrictions or barriers with respect to capital transactions or current transfers, repatriation of profits, purchase of real estate, or access to foreign exchange.

 BANKING AND FINANCE
Score: **1–Stable** (very low level of restrictions)

Banking is one of Luxembourg's largest industries, and the banking system is highly competitive and subject to little government regulation, although banks are restricted in their ability to engage in some financial services, such as real estate. According to the Economist Intelligence Unit, "At end-January 2005 Luxembourg boasted 161 banks from more than 20 different countries; of the world's 50 leading institutions, 30 have subsidiaries in the Grand Duchy." With its bank secrecy laws and no withholding tax on interest, Luxembourg is an attractive environment in which to do business. The EIU reports, however, that "Luxembourg, Austria and Belgium have promised to impose a 15% withholding tax on accounts held by non-residents from July 2005; this rate is due to rise to 20% in 2008 and finally to 35% in 2011. The other member states will establish a system that will exchange information between banks and tax offices to keep track of savings held elsewhere in the EU." Luxembourg has one state-owned bank, Société Nationale de Crédit et d'Investissement (SNCI), which makes medium- to long-term loans, primarily for exports and foreign investment.

 WAGES AND PRICES
Score: **2–Stable** (low level of intervention)

The market sets most prices, but the Ministry of Economy reports that fuel, drugs, and taxi fares remain subject to price controls. Luxembourg affects agricultural prices through its participation in the Common Agricultural Policy, a program that heavily subsidizes agricultural goods. There is a minimum wage.

 PROPERTY RIGHTS
Score: **1–Stable** (very high level of protection)

Private property is well-protected in Luxembourg. The Economist Intelligence Unit reports that "contractual agreements… are secure, and the country's judiciary and civil service are highly regarded."

 REGULATION
Score: **2–Stable** (low level)

The process for establishing a business in Luxembourg is relatively simple. The government's one-stop-shopping system for business registration applies to foreign and domestic enterprises alike, and regulations are fair, transparent, and applied evenly in most cases. Despite some rigidities in the labor legislation, labor costs relative to wages are considerably lower than in the rest of the European Union. According to the U.S. Department of Commerce, "Luxembourg's government is pro-business" and "provides a variety of incentives to…investors, including subsidies, tax relief, legislation protecting investors' rights, and a transparent regulatory structure. Its multilingual labor force is efficient, educated, and highly productive; labor strife is minimal." Corruption is virtually nonexistent.

 INFORMAL MARKET
Score: **1–Stable** (very low level of activity)

Transparency International's 2004 score for Luxembourg is 8.4. Therefore, Luxembourg's informal market score is 1 this year.

Luxembourg qualifies for the Global Free Trade Alliance.

MACEDONIA

Rank: 57

Score: 2.80

Category: Mostly Free

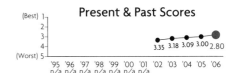

Present & Past Scores

(Best) 1–
2–
3–
4–
(Worst) 5–

3.35 3.18 3.09 3.00 2.80

'95 '96 '97 '98 '99 '00 '01 '02 '03 '04 '05 '06
n/a n/a n/a n/a n/a n/a n/a

QUICK STUDY

SCORES

Trade Policy	3.5
Fiscal Burden	1.5
Government Intervention	3
Monetary Policy	1
Foreign Investment	3
Banking and Finance	2
Wages and Prices	2
Property Rights	4
Regulation	4
Informal Market	4

Population: 2,049,000

Total area: 25,333 sq. km

GDP: $3.56 billion

GDP growth rate: 3.2%

GDP per capita: $1,740

Major exports: iron and steel, manufactures, food and beverages, tobacco

Exports of goods and services: $1.5 billion

Major export trading partners: Serbia and Montenegro 30.8%, Germany 22.0%, Greece 8.2%, US 4.9%

Major imports: foodstuffs, fuels, machinery and equipment, chemicals

Imports of goods and services: $2.2 billion

Major import trading partners: Greece 18.8%, Germany 13.4%, Serbia and Montenegro 9.7%, Slovenia 8.4%

Foreign direct investment (net): $88.9 million

2003 Data (in constant 2000 US dollars)

In 2001, Macedonia dissolved in ethnic conflict. An August 2001 truce averted full-blown civil war, but the coalition government, in which the country's ethnic Albanians and majority Macedonian Slavs share power, remains fragile. Despite recent local election setbacks, pro-Western President Branko Crvenkovski remains the leader most likely to maintain the delicate political stability that followed the 2001 crisis, although he faces a political challenge in turning more power over to local governments. Corruption still pervades the economy, and the criminal underworld thrives on traffic in weapons, drugs, and people. A 2005 European Commission report made it plain that organized crime poses an increasing challenge to state authority and Macedonian society. This, coupled with political instability, has discouraged foreign investment, which has totaled less than $1 billion since 1991. However, there has been some progress. Price and trade liberalization and banking sector supervision are well-established, even if the general regulatory structure—particularly as it relates to judicial reform and a swollen and corrupt bureaucracy—remains weak. Real GDP increased by 2.9 percent in 2004, and the reported 30 percent unemployment rate remains one of the highest in the Balkans. Macedonia's trade policy score is 1 point better this year, and its fiscal burden of government score and government intervention score are 0.5 point better. As a result, Macedonia's overall score is 0.2 point better this year, causing Macedonia to be classified as a "mostly free" country.

TRADE POLICY
Score: **3.5**–Better (high level of protectionism)

The World Bank reports that Macedonia's weighted average tariff rate in 2004 was 8.1 percent, down from the 13.8 percent in 2001 reported in the 2005 *Index*, based on World Bank data. Customs corruption acts as a non-tariff barrier. According to the International Monetary Fund, major trade reform eliminated many non-tariff barriers, such as licensing requirements, but "despite reforms in customs administration, that administration remained notoriously corrupt as late as 2002, constituting an informal trade tax." Based on the lower tariff rate, as well as a revision of the trade factor methodology, Macedonia's trade policy score is 1 point better this year.

FISCAL BURDEN OF GOVERNMENT
Score—Income Taxation: **2**–Worse (low tax rates)
Score—Corporate Taxation: **1.5**–Stable (low tax rates)
Score—Change in Government Expenditures: **1**–Better (very high decrease)
Final Score: **1.5**–Better (low cost of government)

Macedonia's top income tax rate is 24 percent, up from the 18 percent reported in the 2005 *Index*. The top corporate income tax rate is 15 percent. In 2003, according to the European Bank for Reconstruction and Development, government expenditures as a share of GDP decreased 6.9 percentage points to 34.1 percent, compared to the 0.6 percentage point decrease in 2002. On net, Macedonia's fiscal burden of government score is 0.5 point better this year.

GOVERNMENT INTERVENTION IN THE ECONOMY
Score: **3**–Better (moderate level)

According to the World Bank, the government consumed 12 percent of GDP in 2003, down from the 22.4 percent reported in the *2005 Index*. In 2004, based on data from the Ministry of Finance, Macedonia received 4.49 percent of its total revenues from state-owned enterprises and government ownership of property. This figure should be viewed with caution, however. According to the Economist Intelligence Unit, the quality of the data produced by Macedonia's statistical office is poor, and its figures are not reliable. Because of the apparent unreliability of official figures on revenues from state-owned enterprises, 1 point has been added to Macedonia's government intervention score. Based on the decline in government consumption, Macedonia's government intervention score is 0.5 point better this year.

MONETARY POLICY
Score: **1**–Stable (very low level of inflation)

From 1995 to 2004, Macedonia's weighted average annual rate of inflation was 0.46 percent.

CAPITAL FLOWS AND FOREIGN INVESTMENT
Score: **3**–Stable (moderate barriers)

Macedonia grants foreign and domestic investors equal treatment and—with the exception of a few sectors, such as arms manufacturing—permits non-residents to invest in domestic firms, establish new firms, or launch joint ventures without restrictions. Foreign investors can also acquire state-owned firms that are slated for privatization. The European Bank for Reconstruction and Development reports that foreign direct investment "is at a low level as many foreign investors continue to be deterred by a difficult investment climate and perceived political and security risks." According to the Economist Intelligence Unit, Macedonia has received $1 billion in foreign investment since gaining its independence, but "FDI has dried up since then because of the sharply increased political risk and continued weaknesses in the business environment." The International Monetary Fund reports that residents may hold foreign exchange accounts with approval from the central bank and that non-residents may hold foreign exchange accounts subject to some restrictions. Payments and transfers face few controls and restrictions. Most capital and money market activities require the approval of or must be registered with the government. Residents are generally not permitted to buy real estate abroad.

BANKING AND FINANCE
Score: **2**–Stable (low level of restrictions)

Overall, the banking system is weak and suffers from a legacy of bad loans. "[B]anking sector supervision standards are well advanced, but the regulatory framework for non-bank financial institutions is still weak," reports the European Bank for Reconstruction and Development. "Despite the steady progress in the banking sector reform especially in the area of privatisation (direct and indirect state ownership of banks' capital has fallen to 13 percent), the banking sector...remains highly concentrated and is still not competitive enough. The three largest banks hold about three-quarters of total deposits in the banking sector..... Foreign ownership amounted to almost 48.6 per cent of total bank capital at the end of 2003." Of the 21 banks in Macedonia as of March 2005, seven are majority foreign-owned, including two of the three largest. The government operates one state-owned bank.

WAGES AND PRICES
Score: **2**–Stable (low level of intervention)

The market determines most wages and prices. The government influences prices through the remaining state-owned sectors, but many state-owned enterprises have been privatized, and this influence is declining. The Economist Intelligence Unit reports that the government controls the price of electricity. Macedonia has a minimum wage that is set by law at two-thirds of the average wage.

PROPERTY RIGHTS
Score: **4**–Stable (low level of protection)

Protection of property in Macedonia still needs to be strengthened. According to the Economist Intelligence Unit, "the judiciary is politicised, especially in cases involving minorities.... Macedonia is making only slow progress in harmonising its laws and judicial standards with those of the EU and the Council of Europe." The U.S. Agency for International Development identifies "an inefficient judiciary and a lack of rule of law [as] key impediments to the economic and democratic development of the country."

REGULATION
Score: **4**–Stable (high level)

Organized crime is a serious threat and a barrier to doing business. "There is some danger of organised crime against businesses, both foreign and domestic," reports the Economist Intelligence Unit, "although violence tends to be between criminal gangs." The government has made some effort to establish a regulatory system to promote competitiveness. In some areas, according to the European Bank for Reconstruction and Development, legislation supporting free markets "fall[s] short of what is generally acceptable internationally." In addition, poor enforcement of legislation "undermines the utility of specific laws in issue and [diminishes] the confidence that both local and foreign investors and traders have in the legal system as a whole."

INFORMAL MARKET
Score: **4**–Stable (high level of activity)

Transparency International's 2004 score for Macedonia is 2.7. Therefore, Macedonia's informal market score is 4 this year.

MADAGASCAR

Rank: 52

Score: 2.75

Category: Mostly Free

Present & Past Scores

(Best) 1
2
3
4
(Worst) 5

3.74 3.55 3.49 3.51 3.45 3.39 3.29 3.29 2.85 3.14 2.73 2.75

'95 '96 '97 '98 '99 '00 '01 '02 '03 '04 '05 '06

QUICK STUDY

SCORES

Trade Policy	2.5
Fiscal Burden	4
Government Intervention	1.5
Monetary Policy	3
Foreign Investment	2
Banking and Finance	3
Wages and Prices	2
Property Rights	3
Regulation	3
Informal Market	3.5

Population: 16,893,000

Total area: 587,040 sq. km

GDP: $3.9 billion

GDP growth rate: 9.8%

GDP per capita: $233

Major exports: petroleum products, fish, vanilla, sugar

Exports of goods and services: $1.6 billion

Major export trading partners: France 37.4%, US 29.2%, Germany 5.5%, Mauritius 5.2%

Major imports: capital goods, raw materials, consumer goods

Imports of goods and services: $2.5 billion

Major import trading partners: China 15.5%, France 14.4%, South Africa 6.9%, Iran 6.8%, India 4.1%

Foreign direct investment (net): $46.9 million

2003 Data (in constant 2000 US dollars)

Madagascar has largely recovered from the violence and chaos that followed its fraudulent 2001 presidential election, in which former President Didier Ratsiraka inspired protests after claiming victory. President Marc Ravalomanana's party enjoyed success in the 2002 legislative elections and 2003 municipal elections, which were judged to be free and fair. Madagascar is a poor nation, recovering from the anti-market economic policies adopted under Ratsiraka. The economy remains vulnerable to the impact of poor weather on harvests, which threatens the livelihood of the three-quarters of the population that are engaged in agriculture. Corruption remains a problem. Government-owned utilities and enterprises are inefficient, and service failures are common. However, economic growth has been strong since 2002 when the government began implementing economic reforms. At the behest of the International Monetary Fund, the government is considering privatization, particularly of the electricity and water utilities and the airline industries. The January 2005 expiration of textile quotas under the Multi-Fiber Arrangement has forced Madagascar's textile industry to compete with low-cost Asian producers. Madagascar signed a $110 million compact in 2005 for development grants from the U.S. Millennium Challenge Account. Madagascar's capital flows and foreign investment score is 1 point better this year, and its informal market score is 0.5 point better; however, its fiscal burden of government score is 0.7 point worse, and its monetary policy score is 1 point worse. As a result, Madagascar's overall score is 0.02 point worse this year.

TRADE POLICY
Score: **2.5**–Stable (moderate level of protectionism)

The World Bank reports that Madagascar's weighted average tariff rate in 2001 (the most recent year for which World Bank data are available) was 3.6 percent. (The World Bank has revised the figure for 2001 upward from the 2.9 percent reported in the 2005 *Index*.) According to the European Commission's Market Access Sectoral and Trade Barriers Database, "Madagascar maintains a limited number of import restrictions. Restrictions currently in force are retained for reasons of health, security or morals, and concern products such as arms, explosives, and radioactive products. Import restrictions also apply to products considered by the Government to be strategic (e.g. vanillin and precious stones). Importation of all these products is either prohibited or requires prior authorization by the relevant Ministry…. [P]rior authorization is also required for imports of telecommunication items and equipment in order to ensure compatibility with established standards." Based on the revised trade factor methodology, Madagascar's trade policy score is unchanged.

FISCAL BURDEN OF GOVERNMENT
Score—Income Taxation: **3**–Stable (moderate tax rates)
Score—Corporate Taxation: **4**–Stable (high tax rates)
Score—Change in Government Expenditures: **5**–Worse (very high increase)
Final Score: **4**–Worse (high cost of government)

According to the International Monetary Fund, Madagascar's top income tax rate is 30 percent. Deloitte reports that the top corporate income tax rate is also 30 percent. In 2003, according to the African Development Bank, government expenditures as a share of GDP increased 3.8 percentage points to 19.5 percent, compared to a 2.7 percentage point decrease in 2002. On net, Madagascar's fiscal burden of government score is 0.7 point worse this year.

GOVERNMENT INTERVENTION IN THE ECONOMY
Score: **1.5**–Stable (low level)

The World Bank reports that the government consumed 9.2 percent of GDP in 2003. In 2004, based on data from the International Monetary Fund, Madagascar received 3.83 percent of its total revenues from state-owned enterprises and government ownership of property.

MONETARY POLICY
Score: **3**–Worse (moderate level of inflation)

From 1995 to 2004, Madagascar's weighted average annual rate of inflation was 10.23 percent, up from the 4.08 percent from 1994 to 2003 reported in the 2005 *Index*. As a result, Madagascar's monetary policy score is 1 point worse this year.

CAPITAL FLOWS AND FOREIGN INVESTMENT
Score: **2**–Better (low barriers)

In 2001, the U.S. Department of Commerce reported that "foreign investors are compelled to deal with a thicket of bureaucratic obstacles as they seek the necessary permits and approvals." According to the World Bank and the International Monetary Fund, "In the past year, the Government has taken measures to improve the investment climate. This includes a one-stop shop for facilitating enterprise creation which became operational in October 2003 in the capital and Toamasina. The one-stop shop has reduced considerably to less than a week the time needed to set up a firm. Legislation allowing foreigners to own land was also passed." Most sectors of the economy are open to 100 percent foreign ownership, and the government has established Export Processing Zones to facilitate investment. The International Monetary Fund reports that both residents and non-residents may open foreign exchange accounts, subject to certain restrictions and government approval. There are no restrictions on payments or transfers, though profits must be repatriated within 30 days. Most capital movements with other nations require government authorization, including outward direct investment by residents, but inward direct investment "may be freely conducted within Madagascar without authorization or investment approval." Based on evidence of few formal barriers to investment and progress in addressing informal barriers, Madagascar's capital flows and foreign investment score is 1 point better this year.

BANKING AND FINANCE
Score: **3**–Stable (moderate level of restrictions)

The political crisis threw the financial system into disarray during the first half of 2002. According to the Economist Intelligence Unit, non-performing loans increased to 19 percent in 2002, up from 10 percent in 2001, and the central bank continues to hold about a third of financial sector assets even though the government has withdrawn from commercial banking. "All major banks have been transferred to private ownership," reports the EIU, and "all the major commercial institutions are now at least partly privatised, with a strong involvement by major French names; this has provided an underpinning of international support at this difficult time." Two new banks are entering the sector; the locally based Compagnie Malgache de Banque was recently licensed, and an existing savings institution (Caisse d'Epargne de Madagascar or CEM) is converting to a commercial bank.

WAGES AND PRICES
Score: **2**–Stable (low level of intervention)

In its last *Trade Policy Review* of Madagascar, in 2001, the World Trade Organization reported that "most marketing boards have been liquidated and price controls abolished on virtually all [agricultural] products. Monopolies held or exclusive rights exercised by state-owned companies, which are still operating in the agriculture sector, have virtually been abolished." The government still manages a parastatal that markets cotton production. The Ministry of Civil Service, Labor, and Social Laws enforces wages set by the labor code and supporting legislation.

PROPERTY RIGHTS
Score: **3**–Stable (moderate level of protection)

"The Constitution provides for an autonomous judiciary," reports the U.S. Department of State; "however, at all levels, the judiciary was susceptible to the influence of the executive and at times susceptible to corruption." According to the U.S. Department of Commerce, "Investors in Madagascar face a legal environment in which security of private property and the enforcement of contracts are inadequately protected by the judicial system." Land titling, reports *The Wall Street Journal*, is a very bureaucratic process that is subject to corruption.

REGULATION
Score: **3**–Stable (moderate level)

Despite efforts to streamline the regulatory process, lack of transparency and red tape remain problems. "The bureaucratic process for establishing a new enterprise is time consuming and requires considerable maneuvering," reports the U.S. Department of Commerce. "Ministerial overlap and bureaucratic struggles for dominance are serious problems. Often, investors have no idea which ministries to approach, or where to start. While there has been a recent move to simplify, the process is still lacking in transparency and corruption is a persistent problem." According to the Economist Intelligence Unit, "Reform of the civil service, to be piloted in a small number of ministries, has been under discussion for some time but has yet to make substantial progress."

INFORMAL MARKET
Score: **3.5**–Better (high level of activity)

Transparency International's 2004 score for Madagascar is 3.1. Therefore, Madagascar's informal market score is 3.5 this year—0.5 point better than last year.

MALAWI

Rank: 130

Score: 3.63

Category: Mostly Unfree

Present & Past Scores

(Best) 1 —
2 —
3 — 3.74 3.64 3.86 3.96 3.89 3.84 3.76 3.59 3.63 3.51 3.65 3.63
4 —
(Worst) 5 —
'95 '96 '97 '98 '99 '00 '01 '02 '03 '04 '05 '06

The period after Bingu wa Mutharika was declared the winner of Malawi's 2004 presidential elections was marred by violence and allegations of fraud by opposition parties. Less than one year later, Mutharika resigned from the ruling United Democratic Front and formed his own Democratic Progressive Party. Although Mutharika is supported by a bloc of parliamentarians, his reform agenda is threatened by political instability. The International Monetary Fund has been pressing the government to loosen state-run agricultural marketing arrangements, privatize state-owned enterprises, adopt fiscal discipline and accountability, and diversify the economy. Despite some privatization, the economy remains hindered by numerous state-owned enterprises and utilities. Malawi is very poor, and more than 80 percent of the population is engaged in the agricultural sector, which accounts for 40 percent of GDP. Extreme weather can create food shortages, resulting in famine. Tobacco is the primary export. Industrial activity is a small part of the overall economy, and the country possesses few natural resources. Corruption remains a problem. An estimated 14 percent of the population is infected with HIV/AIDS. Malawi is eligible for assistance as a threshold country for the U.S. Millennium Challenge Account. Malawi's fiscal burden of government score is 0.3 point worse this year, and its government intervention score is 0.5 point worse; however, its banking and finance score is 1 point better. As a result, Malawi's overall score is 0.02 point better this year.

QUICK STUDY

SCORES

Trade Policy 4
Fiscal Burden 4.3
Government Intervention 4
Monetary Policy 4
Foreign Investment 3
Banking and Finance 3
Wages and Prices 3
Property Rights 3
Regulation 4
Informal Market 4

Population: 10,962,000

Total area: 118,480 sq. km

GDP: $1.7 billion

GDP growth rate: 4.4%

GDP per capita: $157

Major exports: tea, tobacco, sugar, cotton, wood products, coffee

Exports of goods and services: $474 million

Major export trading partners: South Africa 23.2%, US 13.4%, Germany 11.2%, Egypt 5.6%

Major imports: food, petroleum products, consumer goods, transportation equipment

Imports of goods and services: $679 million

Major import trading partners: South Africa 53.1%, India 6.3%, Tanzania 3.8%

Foreign direct investment (net): $18.4 million

2003 Data (in constant 2000 US dollars)

TRADE POLICY
Score: **4**–Stable (high level of protectionism)

The World Bank reports that Malawi's weighted average tariff rate in 2001 (the most recent year for which World Bank data are available) was 10.2 percent. (The World Bank has revised the figure for 2001 downward from the 12.5 percent reported in the 2005 *Index*.) "Trade licensing covers thirteen import and six export commodities," reports the U.S. Department of Commerce. "There are serious incidences/allegations of corruption, particularly in the area of customs...." Based on the revised trade factor methodology, Malawi's trade policy score is unchanged.

FISCAL BURDEN OF GOVERNMENT
Score—Income Taxation: **4**–Stable (high tax rates)
Score—Corporate Taxation: **4**–Better (high tax rates)
Score—Change in Government Expenditure: **5**–Worse (very high increase)
Final Score: **4.3**–Worse (high cost of government)

The International Monetary Fund reports that Malawi's top income tax rate is 40 percent. The top corporate tax rate is 30 percent, down from the 35 percent reported in the 2005 *Index*. In 2003, according to the African Development Bank, government expenditures as a share of GDP increased 4.1 percentage points to 36.5 percent, compared to the 0.7 percentage point decrease in 2002. On net, Malawi's fiscal burden of government score is 0.3 point worse this year.

GOVERNMENT INTERVENTION IN THE ECONOMY
Score: **4**–Worse (high level)

The World Bank reports that the government consumed 20.1 percent of GDP in 2003, up from the 18.2 percent reported in the 2005 *Index*. As a result, Malawi's government intervention score is 0.5 point worse this year. In fiscal year July 2003–June 2004, based on data from the World Bank, Malawi received 5.45 percent of its total revenues from state-owned enterprises and government ownership of property. However, this figure may underestimate the real level of government intervention in the economy. The Economist Intelligence Unit notes that government parastatals employ 500,000 people and account for around 20 percent of GDP. Based on this evidence of significant government intervention in the economy, 1 point has been added to Malawi's government intervention score.

MONETARY POLICY
Score: **4**–Stable (high level of inflation)

From 1995 to 2004, Malawi's weighted average annual rate of inflation was 12.14 percent.

CAPITAL FLOWS AND FOREIGN INVESTMENT
Score: **3**–Stable (moderate barriers)

According to the U.S. Department of Commerce, "the Government's overall economic and industrial policy does not have discriminatory effects on foreign investors. Since industrial licensing in Malawi applies to both domestic and foreign investment, and is only restricted to a short list of products, it does not impede investment, limit competition, protect domestic interests, or discriminate against foreign investors at any stage of investment." Restrictions based on environmental, health, and national security concerns affect investment in weapons, explosives, and manufacturing that involves the treatment or disposal of hazardous waste or radioactive material. The International Monetary Fund reports that residents may not hold foreign exchange accounts abroad. Non-residents may hold foreign exchange accounts, subject to restrictions and government approval in some cases. Some payments and transfers face quantitative limits. Most capital transactions by residents—including outward direct investment—require approval.

BANKING AND FINANCE
Score: **3**–Better (moderate level of restrictions)

"Malawi's financial services, although developing, are basic and unsophisticated," reports the Economist Intelligence Unit. "The lack of competition in the banking sector has allowed banks to maintain wide spreads between lending and borrowing rates, harming private sector borrowing." Malawi had five commercial lending operations in 2005. The National Bank of Malawi and Commercial Bank of Malawi dominate the sector and together accounted for 80 percent of the market as of December 2003. According to the U.S. Department of Commerce, "The conglomerate Press Corporation Limited (PCL), in which the government holds a 49% stake, sold [its shares of Commercial Bank of Malawi (CBM)] but increased its holding in rival National Bank of Malawi (NBM)." The state also owns the Malawi Development Corporation. Fincom is partly owned by the South African Nedbank, and Standard Bank of South Africa purchased 60 percent of CBM in 2001. Although the government is involved in the sector, private and foreign banks operate freely and control a majority of the banking assets. As a result, Malawi's banking and finance score is 1 point better this year.

WAGES AND PRICES
Score: **3**–Stable (moderate level of intervention)

According to the U.S. Department of Commerce, "Prices for most goods are generally market-determined. Petroleum and sugar are still subject to some degree of price controls. The Agricultural Development and Marketing Corporation (ADMARC) has intervened in the maize market in the recent past, [controlling the prices before the domestic harvest was in full swing in an effort] to stabilize prices. State-provided utilities and services (telephones, water, electricity, etc.) are also subject to varying degrees of government price administration." As most Malawians are active in the agricultural sector, these price restrictions affect a substantial portion of the economy. The Ministry of Labor and Vocational Training sets different urban and rural minimum wages.

PROPERTY RIGHTS
Score: **3**–Stable (moderate level of protection)

Malawi's laws protect all rights to property, including real property and intellectual property. According to the U.S. Department of Commerce, however, "there have on occasion been allegations of government involvement—largely through public comments made by politicians on certain cases. There are also frequent allegations of bribery in civil and criminal cases. Administration of the courts is weak, and due process can be very slow. Serious shortcomings in the judicial system include poor record keeping, a lack of attorneys and trained personnel, heavy caseloads, and insufficient financial resources." *The Economist* reports that "the cost of recovering a $100 debt through the courts is close to $900, so Malawian businessfolk tend to deal only with people they know."

REGULATION
Score: **4**–Stable (high level)

Malawi's regulatory environment is significantly burdensome. The government's "industrial and trade reform program...has produced written guidelines intended to increase government use of transparent and effective policies to foster competition. No tax, labor, environment, health and safety or other laws distort or impede investment," reports the U.S. Department of Commerce. "However, procedural delays, red tape, and corrupt practices continue to impede the business and investment approval process. These include decision making, which is often neither transparent nor based purely on merit, and required land-access approvals."

INFORMAL MARKET
Score: **4**–Stable (high level of activity)

Transparency International's 2004 score for Malawi is 2.8. Therefore, Malawi's informal market score is 4 this year.

MALAYSIA

Rank: 68

Score: 2.98

Category: Mostly Free

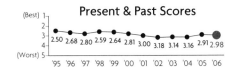

Present & Past Scores

(Best) 1
2
3
4
(Worst) 5

2.50 2.68 2.80 2.59 2.64 2.81 3.00 3.18 3.14 3.16 2.91 2.98

'95 '96 '97 '98 '99 '00 '01 '02 '03 '04 '05 '06

QUICK STUDY

SCORES

Trade Policy	2.5
Fiscal Burden	3.3
Government Intervention	3
Monetary Policy	1
Foreign Investment	4
Banking and Finance	4
Wages and Prices	3
Property Rights	3
Regulation	3
Informal Market	3

Population: 24,774,252

Total area: 329,750 sq. km

GDP: $99.4 billion

GDP growth rate: 5.3%

GDP per capita: $4,011

Major exports: electronics, petroleum, natural gas, textiles, clothing, travel services, transportation, financial services, construction

Exports of goods and services: $115.5 billion

Major export trading partners: US 19.6%, Singapore 15.7%, Japan 10.7%, China 6.5%, Hong Kong 6.5%

Major imports: capital goods, transport equipment, manufactured goods, insurance services, financial services

Imports of goods and services: $96.3 billion

Major import trading partners: Japan 17.3%, US 15.5%, Singapore 11.9%, China 8.8%, Thailand 4.6%

Foreign direct investment (net): $1.04 billion

2003 Data (in constant 2000 US dollars)

Despite some initial optimism about a change of government after 22 years of authoritarian rule, not much is different in Malaysia since Abdullah Badawi succeeded Mahathir Mohamad as prime minister. For example, the ASEAN Free Trade Area is still stymied by Malaysia's protection of its national automobile, the Proton. Badawi did reduce tariffs on the import of foreign-made, or at least ASEAN-made, automobiles but then raised the excise taxes on the same vehicles. There was some hope that Malaysia might permit foreign ownership of banks when Bank Negara allowed a Singapore company to purchase some equity in a local bank, but that one incident has not expanded into opening the banking industry to foreign ownership. Malaysia has pegged the ringgit to the U.S. dollar since 1998. The economy remains strong, growing at 7.2 percent in 2004. The United States and Malaysia signed a Trade and Investment Framework Agreement in May 2004. Malaysia's fiscal burden of government score is 0.2 point worse this year, and its informal market score is 0.5 point worse. As a result, Malaysia's overall score is 0.07 point worse this year.

TRADE POLICY
Score: **2.5**–Stable (moderate level of protectionism)

According to the World Bank, Malaysia's weighted average tariff rate in 2003 (the most recent year for which World Bank data are available) was 4.2 percent, down from the 4.6 percent in 2001 reported in the 2005 *Index*, based on World Bank data. The U.S. Trade Representative reports that 17 percent of Malaysia's tariff lines are subject to non-automatic import licensing. According to the Economist Intelligence Unit, "The country uses import licences (and export controls) to ensure adherence to safety, environmental-protection and copyright requirements, but it also often uses them to protect domestic producers. This policy seeks to ensure adequate supply of essential raw materials and yet provide temporary protection to infant and strategic industries.... Moreover, the persistent denial of sanitary certificates for products such as chicken, pork, liquid milk and eggs effectively acts to prohibit imports." Based on the revised trade factor methodology, Malaysia's trade policy score is unchanged.

FISCAL BURDEN OF GOVERNMENT
Score—Income Taxation: **2.5**–Stable (moderate tax rates)
Score—Corporate Taxation: **3.5**–Stable (high tax rates)
Score—Change in Government Expenditures: **3.5**–Worse (low increase)
Final Score: **3.3**–Worse (moderate cost of government)

According to Deloitte, Malaysia's top income tax rate is 28 percent. The top corporate tax rate is also 28 percent. In 2003, according to the Asian Development Bank, government expenditures as a share of GDP increased 0.1 percentage point to 28.8 percent, compared to a 0.6 percentage point decrease in 2002. On net, Malaysia's fiscal burden of government score is 0.2 point worse this year.

GOVERNMENT INTERVENTION IN THE ECONOMY
Score: **3**–Stable (moderate level)

The World Bank reports that the government consumed 13.9 percent of GDP in 2003. In the same year, based on data from the Ministry of Finance, Malaysia received 16.41 percent of its total revenues from state-owned enterprises and government ownership of property.

MONETARY POLICY
Score: **1**–Stable (very low level of inflation)

From 1995 to 2004, Malaysia's weighted average annual rate of inflation was 1.40 percent.

CAPITAL FLOWS AND FOREIGN INVESTMENT
Score: **4**–Stable (high barriers)

The International Monetary Fund reports substantial restrictions on foreign investment in Malaysia, including general rules requiring government approval for any direct investment over a specified amount, any investment giving a single foreign investor over 15 percent of the voting share in a Malaysian company, or investments giving foreign investors over 30 percent jointly. The U.S. Department of Commerce notes that the government "increased the level of foreign ownership allowed in telecommunications firms from 30% to 61% in 1998.... Foreigners are permitted to hold a 70% stake in shipping companies, 49% in forwarding agencies, and 51% in insurance companies." In 2003, the government announced that the temporary policy allowing 100 percent ownership in manufacturing would continue indefinitely. According to the U.S. Department of Commerce, "The government often requires foreign and domestic non-manufacturing firms to take on bumiputra partners (usually 30% of share capital) and to maintain a workforce that proportionately reflects Malaysia's ethnic composition." Malaysia restricts investments in the automotive industry because the government views it as a strategic industry. The International Monetary Fund reports that residents and non-residents may hold foreign exchange accounts, but government approval is required in many cases. Nearly all capital transactions are prohibited, are subject to restrictions, or require government approval.

BANKING AND FINANCE
Score: **4**–Stable (high level of restrictions)

Malaysia had 25 commercial banks (10 domestically owned, 13 locally incorporated but foreign-owned, and two Islamic) as of November 2004. "Islamic banking and insurance services represented nearly 10% of banking system assets at the end of 2003," according to First Initiative, which also reports that "there were 53 offshore banks, 50 insurance firms, and numerous other financial companies in the Labuan Offshore Financial Center" in 2003. The U.S. Trade Representative reports that the government "limits foreign participation in financial services in an effort to encourage the development of domestic financial services providers.... Foreign banks currently operate in Malaysia under a grandfathering provision.... [F]oreign banks must operate as locally controlled subsidiaries." Overall, foreign participation in commercial banking is limited to 30 percent of equity in any single institution. According to the Economist Intelligence Unit, "The government also has a majority share in two of Malaysia's largest local commercial banks: Malayan Banking (Maybank) and Bumiputra-Commerce Bank. The government has traditionally used them to

help fund political programmes and to grant loans to cronies in exchange for political favours." Foreign insurance companies are not allowed more than 49 percent ownership without approval from the government.

WAGES AND PRICES
Score: **3**–Stable (moderate level of intervention)

The market determines most wages and prices. According to the Ministry of International Trade and Industry, the government controls the prices of fuel, steel, cement, wheat flour, sugar, condensed milk, bread, chicken, and cooking oil and subsidizes fuel and paddy (rice). The EIU notes that CDs, VCDs, DVDs, and computer software were placed under the Price Control Act in June 2003. Malaysia does not have a national minimum wage.

PROPERTY RIGHTS
Score: **3**–Stable (moderate level of protection)

Private property is protected in Malaysia, but the judiciary is subject to political influence. According to the Economist Intelligence Unit, "The government acknowledges that the rule of law is important to economic success. Recent independent rulings...have inspired further confidence that the law will continue to provide adequate protection of private property and contractual agreements and a healthy business environment.... Most corporate lawsuits come to trial within 12–18 months of filing."

REGULATION
Score: **3**–Stable (moderate level)

The U.S. Department of Commerce reports that the "government encourages foreign direct investment, particularly in export-oriented manufacturing and high-tech industries, but retains considerable discretionary authority in approving individual investment projects...." According to the Economist Intelligence Unit, "Affirmative-action policies oblige firms to employ bumiputras (Malays and other indigenous peoples) at all levels in proportions reflecting the local ethnic composition." The U.S. Department of Commerce notes that "corruption remains a serious concern."

INFORMAL MARKET
Score: **3**–Worse (moderate level of activity)

Transparency International's 2004 score for Malaysia is 5. Therefore, Malaysia's informal market score is 3 this year—0.5 point worse than last year.

MALI

Rank: 88

Score: 3.14

Category: Mostly Unfree

Present & Past Scores

(Best) 1
2
3
4
(Worst) 5

3.48 3.39 3.45 3.28 3.19 3.08 3.15 3.10 3.20 3.29 3.18 3.14

'95 '96 '97 '98 '99 '00 '01 '02 '03 '04 '05 '06

Mali had its first successful democratic transfer of power in 2002 when General Amadou Toumani Touré won the presidency as an independent candidate in an election that observers judged to be free and fair. Since 2002, Touré and his agenda have enjoyed broad support from parliament. Instability in Ivory Coast is a security and humanitarian concern—an estimated 2 million Malian citizens live or work in Ivory Coast—and also hurts Mali's economy. Mali faces numerous challenges, including desertification, deforestation, illiteracy, inadequate infrastructure, and corruption. Most of the labor force works in agriculture and animal husbandry, which are vulnerable to adverse weather conditions. Drought and locusts have caused food shortages, and the risk of famine is significant. The government has expressed commitment to its International Monetary Fund program of economic liberalization, anti-corruption efforts, and stronger public-sector accountability, but the pace of privatization and deregulation has been slow. Unemployment contributes to unrest. The judiciary is inefficient and impaired by corruption. Mali has benefited from the African Growth and Opportunity Act, which has increased the competitiveness of its clothing and textile exports, and is eligible for assistance from the U.S. Millennium Challenge Account. Mali's trade policy score is 1 point worse this year; however, its fiscal burden of government score is 0.4 point better, and its government intervention and informal market scores are 0.5 point better. As a result, Mali's overall score is 0.04 point better this year.

QUICK STUDY

SCORES

Trade Policy	4
Fiscal Burden	3.9
Government Intervention	2
Monetary Policy	1
Foreign Investment	3
Banking and Finance	4
Wages and Prices	3
Property Rights	4
Regulation	3
Informal Market	3.5

Population: 11,651,000

Total area: 1,240,000 sq. km

GDP: $3.0 billion

GDP growth rate: 6.0%

GDP per capita: $258

Major exports: gold, cotton, livestock

Exports of goods and services: $956 million

Major export trading partners: Thailand 13.9%, China 12.0%, India 11.9%, Italy 7.5%

Major imports: capital goods, petroleum, foodstuffs, textiles

Imports of goods and services: $1.15 billion

Major import trading partners: France 15.2%, Senegal 7.6%, Ivory Coast 7.0%

Foreign direct investment (net): $109.2 million

2003 Data (in constant 2000 US dollars)

TRADE POLICY
Score: **4–Worse** (high level of protectionism)

Mali is a member of the West African Economic and Monetary Union (WAEMU), which imposes a common external tariff with four rates: 0 percent, 5 percent, 10 percent, and 20 percent. According to the World Bank, Mali's weighted average tariff rate in 2004 was 10.6 percent, down from the 11.4 percent in 2002 reported in the 2005 *Index*, based on World Bank data. The World Trade Organization reports that Mali employs "measures of a restrictive nature (reference values, supplementary taxes, high domestic taxes)…under policies implemented in favour of certain domestic products (for example sugar, meat, tobacco, cigarettes)." Some imports are banned, and others can enter only with a license. Based on new evidence of non-tariff barriers, as well as a revision of the trade factor methodology, Mali's trade policy score is 1 point worse this year.

FISCAL BURDEN OF GOVERNMENT
Score—Income Taxation: **4–Stable** (high tax rates)
Score—Corporate Taxation: **4.5–Stable** (very high tax rates)
Score—Change in Government Expenditures: **2.5–Better** (low decrease)
Final Score: **3.9–Better** (high cost of government)

According to the International Monetary Fund, Mali's top income tax rate is 40 percent. Deloitte reports that the top corporate tax rate is 35 percent. In 2003, according to the African Development Bank, government expenditures as a share of GDP decreased 1.3 percentage points to 22.5 percent, compared to the 0.6 percentage point increase in 2002. On net, Mali's fiscal burden of government score is 0.4 point better this year.

GOVERNMENT INTERVENTION IN THE ECONOMY
Score: **2–Better** (low level)

The World Bank reports that the government consumed 9.9 percent of GDP in 2003, down from the 10.7 percent reported in the 2005 *Index*. In the same year, based on data from the International Monetary Fund, Mali received 8.35 percent of its total revenues from state-owned enterprises and government ownership of property. As a result, Mali's government intervention score is 0.5 point better this year.

MONETARY POLICY
Score: **1–Stable** (very low level of inflation)

As a member of the West African Economic and Monetary Union, Mali uses the CFA franc, pegged to the euro. From 1995 to 2004, Mali's weighted average annual rate of inflation was –1.68 percent.

CAPITAL FLOWS AND FOREIGN INVESTMENT
Score: **3–Stable** (moderate barriers)

The government has an established investment code and permits 100 percent foreign ownership of any new business. Foreign investors may purchase privatized state-owned enterprises and invest in most areas of the economy; they must go through the same screening process as domestic investors. According to the U.S. Department of Commerce, "Foreign investors sometimes report that tax collectors interpret tax laws to discriminate against foreign companies or companies with foreign capital." The Economist Intelligence Unit reports that corruption "is most pervasive in government procurement, where lower and middle-ranking civil servants may request bribes to expedite paperwork, but is not a serious impediment to foreign investment." The International Monetary Fund reports that residents may hold foreign exchange accounts with permission of the government and the Central Bank of West African States, or BCEAO, and non-residents may hold them with permission of the BCEAO. Some payments and transfers to countries other than France, Monaco, members of the WAEMU, members of the Central African Economic and Monetary Community, and Comoros require government approval. Credit and loan operations, and issues and purchases of securities, derivatives, and other instruments, are subject to various requirements, controls, and authorization depending on the transaction. The purchase of real estate requires prior authorization from the Ministry of Finance. All investments outside of the WAEMU by residents require government approval.

BANKING AND FINANCE
Score: **4–Stable** (high level of restrictions)

The BCEAO, a central bank common to the eight members of the WAEMU, governs Mali's banking system. Member countries use the CFA franc, which is issued by the BCEAO and pegged to the euro. Mali's bank-dominated financial sector is small, underdeveloped, and concentrated in urban areas, leaving rural services to the rapidly increasing number of microfinance lenders. In mid-2004, according to First Initiative, Mali had nine commercial banks, including a development bank, an agricultural bank, and a housing bank. Over 300 microfinance institutions were operating in 2004. In addition to the banking sector, Mali has five insurance firms and two pension funds (one for private-sector employees and one for public-sector employees). "The sector is characterised by heavy government ownership," reports the Economist Intelligence Unit; "only three of the nine banks are 100% privately owned. This has led to the availability of only a limited range of financial products and weak intermediation." The International Monetary Fund notes that privatization of Banque Internationale du Mali and Banque du Développement du Mali has been delayed and that the ratio of non-performing loans to total credit rose from 8.4 percent to 10.5 percent from the end of 2003 to August 2004.

WAGES AND PRICES
Score: **3–Stable** (moderate level of intervention)

The market determines most wages and prices, but the government directly controls the price of cotton, one of the most important sectors of the economy. The International Monetary Fund reports that the government subsidizes the water and energy sectors. The government also sets a national minimum wage.

PROPERTY RIGHTS
Score: **4–Stable** (low level of protection)

The constitution provides for an independent judiciary, which in practice is corrupt and subject to political influence. The U.S. Department of Commerce reports that corruption in dispute settlement is pervasive, and the Economist Intelligence Unit reports that "the World Bank describes Mali's judicial system as notoriously inefficient and corrupt, with numerous examples of bribery and influence peddling in the courts."

REGULATION
Score: **3–Stable** (moderate level)

Despite government efforts to improve the regulatory structure and reform the civil service, businesses still must contend with corruption, inconsistent application of regulations, and inefficient bureaucracy. The Economist Intelligence Unit reports that "corruption is most pervasive in government procurement, where lower and middle-ranking civil servants may request bribes to expedite paperwork, but is not a serious impediment to foreign investment."

INFORMAL MARKET
Score: **3.5–Better** (high level of activity)

Transparency International's 2003 score for Mali is 3.2. Therefore, Mali's informal market score is 3.5 this year—0.5 point better than last year.

MALTA

Rank: 24
Score: 2.16
Category: Mostly Free

Present & Past Scores

(Best) 1
2
3
4
(Worst) 5

3.44 3.24 3.25 3.15 3.14 3.09 2.84 2.73 2.71 2.46 2.28 2.16

'95 '96 '97 '98 '99 '00 '01 '02 '03 '04 '05 '06

QUICK STUDY

SCORES

Trade Policy   2
Fiscal Burden   4.1
Government Intervention 2.5
Monetary Policy   1
Foreign Investment   3
Banking and Finance   2
Wages and Prices   2
Property Rights   1
Regulation   2
Informal Market   2

Population: 399,000

Total area: 316 sq. km

GDP: $3.8 billion

GDP growth rate: −1.7%

GDP per capita: $9,568

Major exports: machinery and transport equipment, manufactures

Exports of goods and services: $3.7 billion

Major export trading partners: Singapore 17.4%, US 11.7%, UK 9.4%, Germany 8.8%, France 7.5%, China 7.0%

Major imports: machinery and transport equipment, manufactured goods, food, beverages, tobacco

Imports of goods and services: $4.0 billion

Major import trading partners: Italy 19.1%, France 13.5%, UK 8.4%, Germany 6.5%, US 4.0%

Foreign direct investment (net): $336 million

2003 Data (in constant 2000 US dollars)

Malta, which gained its independence from Great Britain in 1964, depends on tourism, foreign trade, and manufacturing. Its well-trained workers, cheap labor costs, and proximity to the European Union market have long attracted foreign companies. Like its neighbor Cyprus, now that it has joined the EU, Malta hopes to adopt the euro as soon as possible, and this means introducing more politically painful reforms. Fiscal consolidation and job creation remain the major economic policy challenges. Malta also maintains a sprawling socialist market economy, with the majority of government spending allocated to housing, education, and health care. As a result, debt is over 60 percent of GDP, which is above the Maastricht target criteria for members of the euro zone. Although the budget deficit was reduced to 5.2 percent of GDP in 2004 from its 2003 rate of 10 percent, it remains well above the accepted level of 3 percent that euro membership demands. In addition, growth remains anemic, with GDP increasing only 0.7 percent in 2004. In response to Malta's dash to economic modernization, unions have become restive, and the government's goal of forging a social pact among unions, employers, and the public sector has proved elusive. Malta's banking and finance score is 1 point worse this year; however, its fiscal burden of government score is 0.2 point better, its informal market score is 1 point better, and its trade policy and government intervention scores are 0.5 point better. As a result, Malta's overall score is 0.12 point better this year.

TRADE POLICY
Score: **2**–Better (low level of protectionism)

Malta adopted the trade policies of the European Union when it joined the EU in May 2004. The common EU weighted average external tariff was 1.3 percent in 2003, based on World Bank data. In the 2005 *Index*, based on World Bank data, Malta had a tariff of 4.64 percent. According to the World Trade Organization and the U.S. Trade Representative, the EU imposes non-tariff trade barriers through a complex regulatory system and export subsidies. Based on the revised trade factor methodology, Malta's trade policy score is 0.5 point better this year.

FISCAL BURDEN OF GOVERNMENT
Score—Income Taxation: **3.5**–Stable (high tax rates)
Score—Corporate Taxation: **4.5**–Stable (very high tax rates)
Score—Government Expenditures: **4**–Better (moderate increase)
Final Score: **4.1**–Better (high cost of government)

Malta's top income tax rate is 35 percent. The top corporate tax rate is also 35 percent. In 2003, according to the International Monetary Fund, government expenditures as a share of GDP increased 1.8 percentage points to 46.4 percent, compared to a 2.4 percentage point increase in 2002. On net, Malta's fiscal burden of government score is 0.2 point better this year.

GOVERNMENT INTERVENTION IN THE ECONOMY
Score: **2.5**–Better (moderate level)

The World Bank reports that the government consumed 21.4 percent of GDP in 2003. In the same year, based on data from Malta's Treasury Department, Malta received 3.71 percent of its total revenues from state-owned enterprises and government ownership of property,

277

down from the 6.41 percent reported in the 2005 *Index*. As a result, Malta's government intervention score is 0.5 point better this year.

MONETARY POLICY
Score: 1–Stable (very low level of inflation)

From 1995 to 2004, Malta's weighted average annual rate of inflation was 2.21 percent.

CAPITAL FLOWS AND FOREIGN INVESTMENT
Score: 3–Stable (moderate barriers)

Malta seeks to attract foreign investment, at least in selected sectors. "Direct investment by nonresidents is usually permitted in all sectors except real estate, wholesale retail trade, and public utilities," reports the International Monetary Fund. "Nonresident participation may not exceed 50% of equity in businesses involved in information technology services." According to the U.S. Department of Commerce, "Proposals for investment are considered on a case-by-case basis by [the Malta Development Corporation]. Virtually, all manufacturing sectors are open to export-oriented investors. While there are no overt legal prohibitions against such activity, the government carefully screens foreign proposals [that are] oriented principally toward the domestic market or are in direct competition with local business. Certain economic activities, such as energy, are…effectively closed to new private investment [both foreign and domestic]…. There are no reported incidents of discrimination against foreign investors…." However, foreign investors may purchase privatized state-owned enterprises. The IMF reports that both residents and non-residents may hold foreign exchange accounts, subject to maximum amounts for residents and restricted to income earned in Malta for non-residents, and that some capital transactions, including selected capital and money market transactions and real estate purchases by non-residents, require government approval. The Economist Intelligence Unit reports that the remaining exchange controls—primarily controls on short-term flows—were removed in May 2004 when Malta became a member of the European Union.

BANKING AND FINANCE
Score: 2–Worse (low level of restrictions)

Malta's financial sector is small but competitive. Formerly state-owned banks are now largely privatized, and foreign banks have a significant presence. According to the U.S. Department of Commerce, "The government has in recent years privatized a number of state controlled firms, including the country's largest bank…. The government has announced its intention to sell its controlling interest (40%) in Malta's second largest bank, the Bank of Valletta." However, the Economist Intelligence Unit reports continuing delays in plans to divest the state's controlling interest in the Bank of Valletta. HSBC (Malta) Ltd., which purchased the government's stake in Malta's largest bank in 1999, and the Bank of Valletta con-

trol about 80 percent of the banking market. Malta's stock exchange is small but active. Commercial banks may offer all forms of commercial banking services. Based on evidence of government involvement in the banking sector, Malta's banking and finance score is 1 point worse this year.

WAGES AND PRICES
Score: 2–Stable (low level of intervention)

The market determines most wages and prices. According to the Ministry of Finance and Economic Affairs, the government amended the Supplies and Services Act in 2003 to repeal the price orders that had been issued under the previous act, although temporary price orders may still be issued. The government mandates a minimum wage.

PROPERTY RIGHTS
Score: 1–Stable (very high level of protection)

Malta's judiciary is independent, both under the constitution and in practice. "Acquisition and disposition of property rights is adequately protected and facilitated in the Maltese legal system," reports the U.S. Department of Commerce. "Private property is only expropriated for public purposes, in a non-discriminatory manner, and in accordance with established principles of international law. Investors and lenders of expropriated property receive adequate and effective compensation. There have not been any expropriations in the last decade."

REGULATION
Score: 2–Stable (low level)

Companies are requested to submit a business proposal to the Malta Development Corporation before establishing operations. The U.S. Department of Commerce reports that the government "has adopted transparent and effective policies and regulations to foster competition. It is striving to eliminate unnecessary bureaucratic procedure and has taken steps to revise labor, safety, health and other laws in general to conform to EU standards." Corruption is rare.

INFORMAL MARKET
Score: 2–Better (low level of activity)

Transparency International's 2004 score for Malta is 6.8. Therefore, Malta's informal market score is 2 this year—1 point better than last year.

> If Malta were to improve its capital flows and foreign investment score, it would qualify for the Global Free Trade Alliance.

MAURITANIA

Rank: 81

Score: 3.08

Category: Mostly Unfree

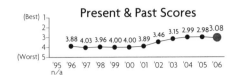

Present & Past Scores

(Best) 1
2
3   3.88 4.03 3.96 4.00 4.00 3.89 3.46 3.15 2.99 2.98 3.08
4
(Worst) 5
'95 '96 '97 '98 '99 '00 '01 '02 '03 '04 '05 '06
n/a

QUICK STUDY

SCORES

Trade Policy	4
Fiscal Burden	2.8
Government Intervention	2
Monetary Policy	3
Foreign Investment	2
Banking and Finance	3
Wages and Prices	2
Property Rights	4
Regulation	4
Informal Market	4

Population: 2,847,000

Total area: 1,030,700 sq. km

GDP: $1.0 billion

GDP growth rate: 4.9%

GDP per capita: $372

Major exports: iron ore, fish, gold

Exports of goods and services: $306 million

Major export trading partners: France 14.5%, Japan 12.2%, Spain 11.1%, Italy 10.1%, Germany 7.3%

Major imports: machinery and equipment, petroleum products, foodstuffs

Imports of goods and services: $757.6 million

Major import trading partners: France 16.8%, Spain 7.7%, China 6.3%, Belgium 5.1%, Germany 4.8%

Foreign direct investment (net): $202 million

2003 Data (in constant 2000 US dollars)

Mauritania is a nominally Islamic republic dominated by a strong executive branch. The fragility of its political situation is demonstrated by three failed coup attempts in 2003 and 2004 and the successful bloodless coup in August 2005. Deposed President Maaouiya Ould Sid'Ahmed Taya seized power in 1984 through a military coup and ruled as elected president from 1992 until the August 2005 coup, though international observers routinely condemned the elections as neither free nor fair. The coup was condemned by other nations and by the United Nations. The African Union suspended Mauritania's membership and demanded that "constitutional order" be restored. The military leaders of the junta dissolved the legislature, established a military council to rule the country, and announced their intention to hold elections within two years. Mauritania is beset by frequent drought, poor harvests, desertification, and extensive unemployment. The largest locust invasions in 15 years struck in 2004 and 2005 and greatly harmed agriculture, creating food shortages deemed "critical" by the Food and Agriculture Organization. The government lacks transparency and accountability, and the U.S. Department of State reports that wealth is concentrated in the hands of the political elite and the president's tribe. In 2002, close to 99 percent of Mauritania's exports consisted of iron ore and fish. Efforts to diversify the economy have met with little success, although oil production is expected to boost GDP growth. Mauritania's fiscal burden of government score is 0.5 point better this year, and its wages and prices score is 1 point better; however, its trade policy score is 0.5 point worse, and its monetary policy and banking and finance scores are 1 point worse. As a result, its overall score is 0.1 point worse, causing Mauritania to be classified as a "mostly unfree" country.

TRADE POLICY
Score: **4–Worse** (high level of protectionism)

The World Bank reports that Mauritania's weighted average tariff rate in 2001 (the most recent year for which World Bank data are available) was 11.2 percent. (The World Bank has revised the figure for 2001 upward from the 9 percent reported in the 2005 *Index*.) According to the U.S. Department of Commerce, "Foreign investors frequently complain of corruption and complexity in customs procedures.... Customs procedures are extremely complicated and discouraging for importers who are not familiar with the Mauritanian system." Based on the higher tariff rate, as well as a revision of the trade factor methodology, Mauritania's trade policy score is 0.5 point worse this year.

FISCAL BURDEN OF GOVERNMENT
Score—Income Taxation: **3.5–Better** (high tax rates)
Score—Corporate Taxation: **2–Stable** (low tax rates)
Score—Change in Government Expenditures: **3.5–Better** (low increase)
Final Score: **2.8–Better** (moderate cost of government)

The Ministry of Economy and Development reports that Mauritania's top income tax rate is 35 percent, down from the 40 percent reported in the 2005 *Index*. According to Deloitte, the top corporate tax rate is 20 percent. In 2003, according to the African Development Bank, government expenditures as a share of GDP increased 0.2 percentage point to 31.6 percent, compared to a 5.3 percentage point increase in 2002. On net, Mauritania's fiscal burden of government score is 0.5 point better this year.

GOVERNMENT INTERVENTION IN THE ECONOMY
Score: 2–Stable (low level)

According to the World Bank, the government consumed 18.9 percent of GDP in 2003. In 2002, based on data from the International Monetary Fund, Mauritania received 4.9 percent of its total revenues from state-owned enterprises and government ownership of property.

MONETARY POLICY
Score: 3–Worse (moderate level of inflation)

From 1995 to 2004, Mauritania's weighted average annual rate of inflation was 8.33 percent, up from the 4.86 percent from 1994 to 2003 reported in the 2005 *Index*. As a result, Mauritania's monetary policy score is 1 point worse this year.

CAPITAL FLOWS AND FOREIGN INVESTMENT
Score: 2–Stable (low barriers)

"No sectors are closed to investment. The mining, fishing, banking, energy and tourism sectors actively seek foreign direct investment," reports the U.S. Department of Commerce. "With the exception of fishing boats, where foreign investment is limited to a 49 percent share, Mauritania has no discriminatory policies against foreign investment." The Economist Intelligence Unit reports that in 2002, "the government adopted a new investment code to encourage local and foreign investors and give them greater security. In particular, foreign investors will be exempted from all customs duties on equipment and goods imported for a start-up, export-oriented project. Also guaranteed is the free transfer of convertible currencies earned from new investments, the right to national or international arbitration in the event of a dispute, and the simplification of administrative formalities with the opening of a 'one-stop shop' to provide advice and to mediate in dealings with the various ministries." The code, however, does not cover the country's two most important sectors: mining and fisheries. Foreign participation is encouraged in the privatization process. The International Monetary Fund reports that both residents and non-residents may hold foreign exchange accounts, but non-resident accounts are subject to some restrictions. Capital movements are subject to exchange controls, and payments and transfers are subject to quantitative limits, *bona fide* tests, and prior approval in some cases. According to the U.S. Department of Commerce, "no U.S. firm represented here has identified corruption as a major obstacle to foreign direct investment. Corruption is most pervasive in government procurement, bank loans, fishing license attribution, land distribution, and tax payments."

BANKING AND FINANCE
Score: 3–Worse (moderate level of restrictions)

Mauritania's banking sector has been liberalized and is becoming more competitive, but it remains underdeveloped, with only seven commercial banks and one government-owned development bank. The government has a 50 percent stake in Chinguetti Bank. According to the Economist Intelligence Unit, "The IMF's latest review of the economy and policies, of January 2003, noted that steady progress was being made in strengthening banking supervision. However, it was concerned that as of mid-August 2002, some 36% of the commercial banking sector's deposit base was made up of government-owned funds." First Initiative reports that six private insurers compete with the state-owned insurance firm. The EIU also reports that the government owns a non-commercial bank, the Banque Al Amana pour le développement et l'habitat. Based on evidence of greater government involvement in the banking sector, Mauritania's banking and finance score is 1 point worse this year.

WAGES AND PRICES
Score: 2–Better (low level of intervention)

The Economist Intelligence Unit reports that the government has removed most price controls. The government maintains a monthly minimum wage. Prices are also distorted by subsidies to businesses and state-owned utilities like electricity and water. Based on a reassessment of available data, Mauritania's wages and prices score is 1 point better this year.

PROPERTY RIGHTS
Score: 4–Stable (low level of protection)

Mauritania's judicial system is chaotic and corrupt. The U.S. Department of Commerce reports that "impartial application of the law by the Mauritanian judiciary has been a problem for some local companies." According to the Economist Intelligence Unit, "the judiciary is prone to executive influence." The U.S. Department of State notes that "poorly educated and poorly trained judges who are susceptible to social, financial, tribal, and personal pressures limit the judicial system's fairness."

REGULATION
Score: 4–Stable (high level)

The Economist Intelligence Unit reports that the government introduced a new investment code in 2002 to facilitate economic activity for local and foreign investors, including a one-stop shop to simplify bureaucratic formalities and advise on dealings with various ministries. According to the U.S. Department of Commerce, however, "Corruption exists at all levels of government and society. While Mauritania has laws, regulations, and penalties against corruption, enforcement is very limited. As a result, some wealthy business groups and [government] officials receive favors from authorities. The meager salaries of [government] employees at all levels foster corruption."

INFORMAL MARKET
Score: 4–Stable (high level of activity)

Mauritania's informal market includes consumer goods, agricultural products, and entertainment products. According to the Ministry of Economy and Development, the informal sector represents about 30 percent of the economy.

MAURITIUS

Rank: 77

Score: 3.03

Category: Mostly Unfree

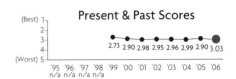

Present & Past Scores

(Best) 1-
2-
3-
4-
(Worst) 5-

2.73 2.90 2.98 2.95 2.96 2.99 2.90 3.03

'95 '96 '97 '98 '99 '00 '01 '02 '03 '04 '05 '06
n/a n/a n/a n/a

QUICK STUDY

SCORES

Trade Policy	4.5
Fiscal Burden	3.3
Government Intervention	3
Monetary Policy	2
Foreign Investment	2
Banking and Finance	3
Wages and Prices	4
Property Rights	2
Regulation	3
Informal Market	3.5

Population: 1,222,000

Total area: 1,860 sq. km

GDP: $5.0 billion

GDP growth rate: 3.2%

GDP per capita: $4,167

Major exports: clothing, food, beverages and tobacco, textiles, sugar

Exports of goods and services: $3.2 billion

Major export trading partners: UK 31.0%, France 21.4%, US 17.5%, Madagascar 6.3%

Major imports: textile fiber, machinery and transport equipment, food, beverages, mineral fuels, chemicals

Imports of goods and services: $3.0 billion

Major import trading partners: South Africa 12.1%, France 12.0%, China 8.4%, India 8.2%

Foreign direct investment (net): $27.1 million

2003 Data (in constant 2000 US dollars)

Mauritius has one of Africa's strongest economies and is a natural bridge to Asia. It has a well-established democratic tradition, and the judiciary is independent. Key sectors include offshore banking and financial services, textile manufacturing, tourism, and sugar. Traditional economic mainstays such as sugar and textiles, however, face increasing international competition, and unemployment is rising. The government has been trying to address unemployment through business-friendly policies, government-provided training, and improvements in the information technology environment, including an ambitious effort to make the island nation a high-tech communications hub with countrywide broadband wireless Internet access. However, the regulatory environment can be difficult because the government has an interest in discouraging competition with parastatals like Mauritius Telecom. The growing financial and business services sector represented over 19 percent of GDP in 2004. The legal and commercial infrastructure is well developed. In its 2005–2006 budget, the government announced favorable tax rules for investors, simplified land-acquisition procedures, and creation of an extended Duty Free Zone that reduces or eliminates many duties and customs levies with the eventual goal of having 80 percent of all tariff lines duty-free. Mauritius's trade policy score is 0.5 point better this year, and its capital flows and foreign investment score is 1 point better; however, its fiscal burden of government score is 0.3 point worse, its government intervention and banking and finance scores are both 1 point worse, and its informal market score is 0.5 point worse. As a result, its overall score is 0.13 point worse this year, causing Mauritius to be classified as a "mostly unfree" country.

TRADE POLICY

Score: **4.5**–Better (very high level of protectionism)

The World Bank reports that Mauritius's weighted average tariff rate in 2002 (the most recent year for which World Bank data are available) was 13 percent. (The World Bank has revised the figure for 2002 downward from the 15.8 percent reported in the 2005 *Index*.) According to the European Commission's Market Access Sectoral and Trade Barriers Database, "The liberalization reforms have fallen short of further dismantling non-tariff measures maintained on various grounds. The number of products subject to import ban, or import control by means of permit, has increased. Import quotas still apply to table-potatoes and salt. Several parastatal bodies, including the State Trading Corporation and the Agricultural Marketing Board, purchase, import, and store 'strategic' products (including flour, ration rice, petroleum products, cement, table potatoes, onions, and garlic).… A permit is required for the exportation of products of 'strategic importance' and of goods eligible for preferential-quota treatment in importing countries." Based on the lower tariff rate, as well as a revision of the trade factor methodology, Mauritius's trade policy score is 0.5 point better this year.

FISCAL BURDEN OF GOVERNMENT

Score—Income Taxation: **3**–Worse (moderate tax rates)
Score—Corporate Taxation: **3**–Stable (moderate tax rates)
Score—Change in Government Expenditures: **4**–Worse (moderate increase)

Final Score: **3.3**–Worse (moderate cost of government)

Mauritius's top income tax rate is 30 percent, up from the 25 percent reported in the 2005 *Index*. The top corporate income tax rate is 25 percent. In 2003, according to the African Development Bank, government expenditures as a share of GDP increased 1.9 percentage points to

26.4 percent, compared to a 0.6 percentage point increase in 2002. On net, Mauritius's fiscal burden of government score is 0.3 point worse this year.

 GOVERNMENT INTERVENTION IN THE ECONOMY
Score: 3–Worse (moderate level)

The World Bank reports that the government consumed 13 percent of GDP in 2003, up from the 8.5 percent reported in the 2005 *Index*. In the same year, according to the International Monetary Fund's Government Financial Statistics CD–ROM, Mauritius received 11.94 percent of its total revenues from state-owned enterprises and government ownership of property, up from the 9.84 percent reported in the 2005 *Index*. As a result, Mauritius's government intervention score is 1 point worse this year.

 MONETARY POLICY
Score: 2–Stable (low level of inflation)

From 1995 to 2004, Mauritius's weighted average annual rate of inflation was 4.70 percent.

 CAPITAL FLOWS AND FOREIGN INVESTMENT
Score: 2–Better (low barriers)

Mauritius generally welcomes foreign investment and has a transparent and well-defined foreign investment code. According to the International Monetary Fund, foreigners may not own land without prior permission from the Prime Minister and the Minister of Internal Affairs. The Embassy of Mauritius reports that the only restrictions on foreign ownership of businesses apply to casinos, where the state is required to own 51 percent, and public utilities. The IMF reports that both residents and non-residents may hold foreign exchange accounts. There are no controls on payments or transfers, and few controls on capital transactions. Based on evidence of a low level of restrictions, Mauritius' capital flows and foreign investment score is 1 point better this year.

 BANKING AND FINANCE
Score: 3–Worse (moderate level of restrictions)

Mauritius has an open, efficient, and competitive banking system. First Initiative reports that there were 10 onshore and 12 offshore commercial banks in 2004, with some licensed to operate both on and offshore. The two largest domestic banks—Mauritius Commercial Bank and State Bank of Mauritius—account for 70 percent of the banking market, and the two largest foreign banks—HSBC and Barclays—account for 22 percent. There are 22 insurance firms, including three foreign-owned companies, but three firms account for approximately 75 percent of the market, according to First Initiative. The Embassy of Mauritius reports that banks totally or partially owned by the government (the Development Bank of Mauritius Ltd and Mauritius Post and Cooperative Bank Ltd)

controlled 29 percent of assets and 28 percent of deposits as of March 2005. Mauritius has come under Organisation for Economic Co-operation and Development scrutiny because of suspected money laundering. The stock market is professional and modern, if small, listing 39 stocks. Based on evidence that wholly or partially state-owned banks control a substantial portion of assets and deposits, Mauritius's banking and finance score is 1 point worse this year.

 WAGES AND PRICES
Score: 4–Stable (high level of intervention)

The Embassy of Mauritius reports that the government directly controls the prices of bread, cement, cooking gas, fertilizers, flour, iron/steel bars, onions, petroleum products, rice, salted snock, and sugar, in addition to subsidizing a few commodities, including rice, flour, fertilizers, and bus transportation. The government also controls key utility services and administratively sets a minimum wage that varies according to sector and is indexed to inflation.

 PROPERTY RIGHTS
Score: 2–Stable (high level of protection)

Expropriation of property is unlikely. The judiciary is independent and provides citizens with a fair trial. According to the U.S. Department of Commerce, "The domestic legal system is generally non-discriminatory and transparent. Members of the judiciary are independent of the legislature and the government. The highest court of appeal is the judicial committee of the Privy Council of England." In addition, "corruption exists but is much less than what is encountered elsewhere in Africa."

 REGULATION
Score: 3–Stable (moderate level)

"To streamline the bureaucratic procedures," reports the U.S. Department of Commerce, "the government has…set up a Board of Investment, which acts as a one-stop-shop for investors." However, regulations are burdensome, and the bureaucracy can cause significant delays. The same source reports that corruption falls below levels seen in the rest of Africa and that the government has made anti-corruption efforts a priority. The government has revised some regulations—for example, in financial services—in an effort to improve the business environment.

 INFORMAL MARKET
Score: 3.5–Worse (high level of activity)

Transparency International's 2004 score for Mauritius is 4.1. Therefore, Mauritius's informal market score is 3.5 this year—0.5 point worse than last year.

MEXICO

Rank: 60

Score: 2.83

Category: Mostly Free

Present & Past Scores

(Best) 1 — 2 — 3 — 4 — (Worst) 5

3.05 3.31 3.35 3.41 3.30 3.09 3.05 2.96 2.81 2.90 2.84 2.83

'95 '96 '97 '98 '99 '00 '01 '02 '03 '04 '05 '06

Although Mexico's Congress has yet to approve most of his proposed political or economic reforms, President Vicente Fox has streamlined procedures for licensing small businesses; Mexico has signed a total of 11 free trade agreements with 43 countries; a new federal investigative force comparable to the U.S. Federal Bureau of Investigation has been established; and civil service reform now enables the government to employ workers based on merit, not just party affiliation. However, the judiciary and local police still have problems of unprofessionalism, inefficiency, and corruption; state enterprises like Petroleos de México (Pemex) still need to be privatized; and the Mexican economy must create enough jobs to meet the number of new workers entering the labor force each year (approximately 1 million). About one-quarter of Mexico's 105 million people live in rural areas and depend on subsistence agriculture, which is still common, although the Economist Intelligence Unit reports that agriculture contributes only about 4 percent of GDP. The North American Free Trade Agreement continues to benefit Mexico. In 2004, exports to the United States increased 12.9 percent, rising to $155.8 billion. Mexico is second only to Brazil in receipts of foreign direct investment inflows in Latin America, estimated at $14 billion for 2004. Mexico's fiscal burden of government score is 0.1 point better this year. As a result, its overall score is 0.01 point better this year.

TRADE POLICY
Score: **2.5**–Stable (moderate level of protectionism)

According to the Ministry of Finance, Mexico's weighted average tariff rate in 2004 was 4.2 percent, down from the 4.9 percent for 2002 reported in the 2005 *Index*, based on World Bank data. The U.S. Department of Commerce reports complaints about "Mexican customs administration procedures, including insufficient prior notification of procedural changes, inconsistent interpretation of regulatory requirements at different border posts, and uneven enforcement of Mexican standards and labeling rules…. Mexican inspection and clearance procedures for some agricultural goods are long, burdensome, non-transparent and unreliable." Many imports are subjected to license requirements, standards, and restriction or prohibition. Corruption is another problem. Based on the revised trade factor methodology, Mexico's trade policy score is unchanged.

FISCAL BURDEN OF GOVERNMENT
Score—Income Taxation: **3**–Stable (moderate tax rates)
Score—Corporate Taxation: **4**–Better (high tax rates)
Score—Change in Government Expenditures: **4**–Worse (moderate increase)
Final Score: **3.8**–Better (high cost of government)

Deloitte reports that Mexico's top income tax rate was cut to 30 percent, effective January 2005, down from the 33 percent reported in the 2005 *Index*. The top corporate tax rate was also reduced to 30 percent from 33 percent. In 2003, according to the International Monetary Fund, government expenditures increased 1.1 percentage points to 24.4 percent, compared to a 0.8 percentage point increase in 2002. On net, Mexico's fiscal burden of government score is 0.1 point better this year.

QUICK STUDY

SCORES

Trade Policy	2.5
Fiscal Burden	3.8
Government Intervention	3.5
Monetary Policy	2
Foreign Investment	3
Banking and Finance	2
Wages and Prices	2
Property Rights	3
Regulation	3
Informal Market	3.5

Population: 105,000,000

Total area: 1,972,550 sq. km

GDP: $617.1 billion

GDP growth rate: 4.2%

GDP per capita: $5,877

Major exports: agricultural products, oil, mining products, manufactures

Exports of goods and services: $177.9 billion

Major export trading partners: US 87.7%, Canada 1.8%, Germany 1.2%, Spain 0.9%

Major imports: electrical equipment, car parts for assembly, repair parts for motor vehicles, aircraft and aircraft parts, capital goods

Imports of goods and services: $189.2 billion

Major import trading partners: US 68.0%, China 6.1%, Japan 4.9%, Germany 4.0%

Foreign direct investment (net): $12.1 billion

2004 Data (in constant 2000 US dollars)

GOVERNMENT INTERVENTION IN THE ECONOMY
Score: **3.5**–Stable (high level)

The World Bank reports that the government consumed 12.7 percent of GDP in 2003. In the same year, based on data from the Ministry of Finance, the government received 29.11 percent of its total revenues from state-owned enterprises and government ownership of property.

MONETARY POLICY
Score: **2**–Stable (low level of inflation)

From 1995 to 2004, Mexico's weighted average annual rate of inflation was 4.88 percent.

CAPITAL FLOWS AND FOREIGN INVESTMENT
Score: **3**–Stable (moderate barriers)

Mexico maintains a number of formal restrictions that impede foreign investment. "Although the country has no restrictions on capital flows," reports the Economist Intelligence Unit, "foreign investors remain barred from important sectors of the economy like petroleum and electricity. Infrastructure remains outdated and unreliable in many parts of the country." According to the U.S. Department of Commerce, "The Mexican Foreign Investment Law identifies 704 activities, 656 of which are open for 100 percent FDI stakes. There are 18 activities in which foreigners may only invest 49 percent; 13 of which require Foreign Investment National Commission approval for a 100 percent stake; 5 reserved for Mexican nationals; and 10 reserved for the Mexican state." Foreigners may invest in real estate subject to certain restrictions. According to the EIU, "A number of improvements have simplified foreign investment in recent years: less legal and administrative red tape, higher ceilings on foreign equity, fewer local content requirements, better intellectual property legislation and the elimination of most import-license requirements." The International Monetary Fund reports that residents and non-residents may hold foreign exchange accounts. Most payments, transactions, and transfers are permissible. Some capital transactions, including capital and money market instruments and derivatives, are subject to government permission and controls.

BANKING AND FINANCE
Score: **2**–Stable (low level of restrictions)

Mexico's banking sector is becoming more competitive and is among the most developed in Latin America. The government has significantly reduced its holdings in commercial banking. According to First Initiative, "Foreign banks have established a significant presence in the Mexican banking sector since limitations were lifted in the late 1990s. In 2003, all of the major banks in Mexico were controlled by foreign firms, save one. Since the 1995 financial crisis, the banking sector has seen much consolidation and restructuring, leaving the five largest banks holding 88% of the banking sector's assets (2003)…. The insurance sector is well developed and highly concentrated, with 65% of policies

underwritten by the five largest companies (2003)." The government also has increased its transparency and efficiency by adopting U.S. Generally Accepted Accounting Principles-based accounting standards and has updated its bankruptcy law to allow a wider range of property to be used as collateral and speed foreclosure. The government owns eight development banks that provide financing to specific areas in the economy, such as small and medium-size enterprises, public works and infrastructure, agriculture, and foreign trade, but these banks play only a small role in the banking sector. The International Monetary Fund reports numerous restrictions on foreign insurance practitioners.

WAGES AND PRICES
Score: **2**–Stable (low level of intervention)

According to the Economist Intelligence Unit, "Mexico maintains suggested retail prices for medicines and limits increases to a percentage of the amount that producers invest in research and development." The U.S. Department of Commerce reports that "Mexican authorities have set minimum prices for a wide range of imported products, including textiles, clothing, leather products, shoes, some metals, stationary products, tools, some glass products, bicycles, children's accessories, and others." The government also controls prices through some state-owned utilities and the energy sector. A government-set minimum wage varies by region.

PROPERTY RIGHTS
Score: **3**–Stable (moderate level of protection)

The threat of expropriation is low. According to the U.S. Department of Commerce, "There have been numerous cases in which foreign investors…have spent years dealing with Mexican courts trying to resolve their disputes. Many cases include allegations of judicial corruption…." The Economist Intelligence Unit reports that Mexico's "judiciary branch…is independent to the point that it can uphold many government decisions…. Contractual agreements are generally upheld in Mexico."

REGULATION
Score: **3**–Stable (moderate level)

According to Mexico's Ministry of Economy, people can open a business or request a license in one business day. The primary beneficiaries are businesses carrying out any of the 685 activities most frequently carried out by small and medium-size enterprises. However, according to the U.S. Department of Commerce, "Foreign firms continue to list bureaucracy, slow government decision-making, lack of transparency, a heavy tax burden, and a rigid labor code among the principal negative factors inhibiting investment in Mexico."

INFORMAL MARKET
Score: **3.5**–Stable (high level of activity)

Transparency International's 2004 score for Mexico is 3.6. Therefore, Mexico's informal market score is 3.5 this year.

MOLDOVA

Rank: 83

Score: 3.10

Category: Mostly Unfree

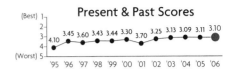

QUICK STUDY

SCORES

Trade Policy	2.5
Fiscal Burden	2.5
Government Intervention	2
Monetary Policy	3
Foreign Investment	4
Banking and Finance	3
Wages and Prices	3
Property Rights	3
Regulation	4
Informal Market	4

Population: 4,237,600

Total area: 33,843 sq. km

GDP: $1.6 billion

GDP growth rate: 6.3%

GDP per capita: $370

Major exports: foodstuffs, textiles, vegetable products, machinery and equipment

Exports of goods and services: $1.0 billion

Major export trading partners: Russia 39.0%, Romania 11.4%, Italy 10.4%, Germany 7.1%, Ukraine 7.1%

Major imports: mineral products, machinery and equipment, textiles, chemicals

Imports of goods and services: $1.7 billion

Major import trading partners: Ukraine 22.0%, Russia 13.0%, Romania 11.8%, Germany 9.7%, Italy 8.3%

Foreign direct investment (net): −$100 million

2003 Data (in constant 2000 US dollars)

One of Europe's poorest nations, the Republic of Moldova has resisted pursuing the types of reforms that have vastly improved the economies of some of its Eastern European neighbors. The Communist Party retained political control after winning the March 2005 parliamentary elections and re-elected its leader, Vladimir Voronin, as president in collaboration with the opposition. Although the government maintains a pro-Western stance, it has had trouble pursuing structural reforms and has made little progress on the International Monetary Fund's program to attract external financial resources. The parliament approved the government's economic growth and strategy paper in December 2004, but international financial institutions and Western investors will not be satisfied until the government begins to address fiscal adjustment, wage restraint, and payment of debt arrears. Despite the fact that the pace of privatization and industrial output has slowed, GDP growth was 7.3 percent in 2004, consumption continues to grow, and the currency continues to appreciate. The impasse in the pro-Russian and communist-dominated Transnistria enclave, plagued by corruption and the smuggling of arms and contraband, continues despite international attempts at mediation. Moldova's fiscal burden of government score is 0.1 point better this year. As a result, its overall score is 0.01 point better this year.

TRADE POLICY
Score: **2.5**–Stable (moderate level of protectionism)

According to the World Bank, Moldova's weighted average tariff rate in 2001 (the most recent year for which World Bank data are available) was 2.8 percent. (The World Bank has revised the figure for 2001 downward from the 3.9 percent reported in the 2005 *Index*.) A 2004 World Bank report notes a "range of informal barriers to both imports and exports in Moldova, such as cumbersome and restrictive trade procedures, corruption, burdensome and inappropriate regulations and high transport costs." Based on the revised trade factor methodology, Moldova's trade policy score is unchanged.

FISCAL BURDEN OF GOVERNMENT
Score—Income Taxation: **2**–Stable (low tax rates)
Score—Corporate Taxation: **2**–Stable (low tax rates)
Score—Change in Government Expenditures: **4**–Better (moderate increase)
Final Score: **2.5**–Better (moderate cost of government)

Moldova's top income tax rate is 22 percent. The top corporate tax rate has been cut to 18 percent from 20 percent, effective January 2005. In 2003, government expenditures as a share of GDP increased 1.2 percentage points to 33.6 percent, compared to the 3.0 percentage point increase in 2002. On net, Moldova's fiscal burden of government score is 0.1 point better this year.

GOVERNMENT INTERVENTION IN THE ECONOMY
Score: **2**–Stable (low level)

The World Bank reports that the government consumed 17.7 percent of GDP in 2003. In the same year, based on data from the International Monetary Fund, Moldova received 4.93 percent of its revenues from state-owned enterprises and government ownership of property.

MONETARY POLICY
Score: **3**–Stable (moderate level of inflation)

Between 1995 and 2004, Moldova's weighted average annual rate of inflation was 11.99 percent.

CAPITAL FLOWS AND FOREIGN INVESTMENT
Score: **4**–Stable (high barriers)

The Moldovan government does not maintain many formal barriers to foreign investment, and the Moldovan embassy reports that foreign investors are free to "place their investments throughout the Republic of Moldova, in any area of business activity, as long as it does not go against the interests of the national security, anti-monopoly legislation, environment protection norms, public health and public order." However, there are significant informal barriers and indications that the formal reasons to block investment are liberally applied. According to the International Monetary Fund, "despite efforts to simplify licensing and business registration, there has been no significant improvement in the business climate. Moreover, the privatization program has stalled, while corruption remains widespread and governance weak. Government interference in the private sector…casts doubt over the authorities' commitment to market-oriented reforms." The Economist Intelligence Unit reports that the "poor investment climate, including annulments of some earlier sales, continues to deter many Western investors. Between 2001 and 2004 the government privatized less than 60 of the 480-odd enterprises scheduled for sale." Foreign investors may not purchase agricultural or forest land. The IMF reports that both residents and non-residents may hold foreign exchange accounts, but approval is required in some cases. Payments and transfers require supporting documentation and approval of the National Bank of Moldova if they exceed specified amounts. Nearly all capital transactions require approval by or registration with the National Bank of Moldova.

BANKING AND FINANCE
Score: **3**–Stable (moderate level of restrictions)

There are no official barriers to founding foreign banks or branches in Moldova. The central bank has increased the minimum capital requirement, which is expected to contribute to consolidation in the banking sector. First Initiative reports that the banking sector "consists of 16 commercial banks (2003). There are 14 locally-owned banks, while the two remaining ones are from Russia and Romania. The banking sector is highly concentrated with the five largest banks accounting for over 70% of lending in 2002. Unlike the banking sector, the insurance sector has high levels of foreign-participation. The largest insurance firm in Moldova, the former state insurance company, is owned by an Australian company." Moldova's stock exchange is very small, listing fewer than 25 companies in 2002. The Moldovan embassy reports that the government holds shares in two banks—JSCB "Banca de Economii" SA and JSCB "EuroCreditBank"—including a controlling share of

Banca de Economii. The Economist Intelligence Unit reports that foreign investment accounts for approximately 50 percent of total banking capital.

WAGES AND PRICES
Score: **3**–Stable (moderate level of intervention)

The government influences prices through the large state-owned sector. According to the Ministry of Economy, the state regulates the prices of goods and services provided by monopolies and the prices of electric or thermal energy, land, medical services, and services offered by local tax regions. Moldova has two legal monthly minimum wages: one wage for state employees and another, higher wage for the private sector.

PROPERTY RIGHTS
Score: **3**–Stable (moderate level of protection)

The U.S. Department of Commerce reports that the "legal system has improved in recent years. Moldova has a documented and consistently applied commercial law." Nevertheless, much more needs to be done. According to the U.S. Department of State, "The Constitution provides for an independent judiciary; however, the executive branch has exerted undue influence on the judiciary. Many observers believe that arrears in salary payments also make it difficult for judges to remain independent from outside influences and free from corruption."

REGULATION
Score: **4**–Stable (high level)

"Bureaucratic procedures are not always transparent and red tape often makes processing unnecessarily long," reports the U.S. Department of Commerce. "[C]ommercial law is a confusing patchwork of narrow statutes and an outdated civil code. With USAID experts, a draft civil code has been developed which follows the current European practice of incorporating commercial law provisions." The same source reports that anti-corruption laws "are not effectively enforced and corruption exists at an advanced level." A report provided by the World Bank indicates that labor laws are somewhat rigid.

INFORMAL MARKET
Score: **4**–Stable (high level of activity)

Transparency International's 2004 score for Moldova is 2.3. Therefore, Moldova's informal market score is 4 this year.

MONGOLIA

Rank: 60

Score: 2.83

Category: Mostly Free

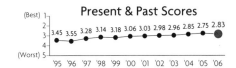

Present & Past Scores

(Best) 1—
2—
3— 3.45 3.55 3.28 3.14 3.18 3.06 3.03 2.98 2.96 2.85 2.75 2.83
4—
(Worst) 5—
'95 '96 '97 '98 '99 '00 '01 '02 '03 '04 '05 '06

QUICK STUDY

SCORES

Trade Policy	2.5
Fiscal Burden	3.3
Government Intervention	2.5
Monetary Policy	2
Foreign Investment	2
Banking and Finance	2
Wages and Prices	2
Property Rights	4
Regulation	4
Informal Market	4

Population: 2,480,000

Total area: 1,565,000 sq. km

GDP: $1.05 billion

GDP growth rate: 5.6%

GDP per capita: $424

Major exports: livestock, copper, animal products, cashmere, apparel

Exports of goods and services: $681 million

Major export trading partners: China 46.2%, US 23.2%, Russia 6.7%, Singapore 5.7%

Major imports: machinery and equipment, fuels, food products, chemicals, sugar, tea

Imports of goods and services: $874 million

Major import trading partners: Russia 33.1%, China 21.5%, South Korea 8.4%, Japan 7.9%

Foreign direct investment (net): $124.1 million

2003 Data (in constant 2000 US dollars)

Despite serious economic challenges, Mongolia has shown signs of economic development since its political democratization in 1990, but more needs to be done. The Great Hural (parliament), split almost evenly between the socialist-leaning Mongolian People's Revolutionary Party and free-market Democrats, functions constructively under a multi-party coalition. Livestock herding employs a majority of the population, but Mongolia has one of the world's most productive copper mines. In 2004, GDP grew by 10.6 percent, driven largely by high prices in international metals exchanges. Mongolia's once-profitable cashmere industry is now depressed with the expiration of the international Multi-Fiber Arrangement. Official jobless statistics are pegged at 6 percent to 7 percent. Some trade barriers exist, including a uniform 5 percent tariff (or excise tax) on certain imports. Mongolia is eligible for assistance as a threshold country for the U.S. Millennium Challenge Account. Mongolia's fiscal burden of government score is 0.2 point better this year, and its capital flows and foreign investment score and banking and finance score are both 1 point better; however, its trade policy, property rights, and informal market scores are all 1 point worse. As a result, Mongolia's overall score is 0.08 point worse this year.

TRADE POLICY
Score: **2.5**–Worse (moderate level of protectionism)

The Mongolian embassy reports that Mongolia's average tariff rate in 2004 was 4 percent, the same rate as that reported for 2003 in the 2005 *Index*, based on World Bank data. According to the World Trade Organization, "Mongolia has a few non-tariff border measures, such as import prohibitions and import licensing requirements." The U.S. Department of Commerce reports that "customs is widely considered the most corrupt government institution." Based on increasing evidence of non-tariff barriers, as well as a revision of the trade factor methodology, Mongolia's trade policy score is 1 point worse this year.

FISCAL BURDEN OF GOVERNMENT
Score—Income Taxation: **3**–Stable (moderate tax rates)
Score—Corporate Taxation: **4**–Stable (high tax rates)
Score—Change in Government Expenditures: **2**–Better (moderate decrease)
Final Score: **3.3**–Better (moderate cost of government)

The Embassy of Mongolia reports that Mongolia's top income tax rate is 30 percent. The top corporate tax rate is also 30 percent. In 2003, according to the Asian Development Bank, government expenditures as a share of GDP decreased 2.5 percentage points to 42.2 percent, compared to the 2.6 percentage point increase in 2002. On net, Mongolia's fiscal burden of government score is 0.2 point better this year.

GOVERNMENT INTERVENTION IN THE ECONOMY
Score: **2.5**–Stable (moderate level)

The World Bank reports that the government consumed 18.9 percent of GDP in 2003. In 2004, based on data from the Embassy of Mongolia, Mongolia received 7.43 percent of its total revenues from state-owned enterprises and government ownership of property.

MONETARY POLICY
Score: **2**–Stable (low level of inflation)

From 1994 to 2003, Mongolia's weighted average annual rate of inflation was 4.85 percent.

CAPITAL FLOWS AND FOREIGN INVESTMENT
Score: **2**–Better (low barriers)

The U.S. Department of Commerce reports that "Mongolia supports foreign direct investment in all sectors and businesses—at whatever levels investors want. Its industrial and economic strategies do not discriminate…against foreign investors. Mongolia screens neither investments nor investors…." However, "individual agencies and elements of the judiciary often use their respective powers to hinder investments into such sectors as meat production or pharmaceuticals. Both domestic and foreign investors report similar abuses of inspections, permits, and licenses by Mongolian regulatory agencies." According to the International Monetary Fund, "The Law on Foreign Investment guarantees that foreign firms will not be nationalized and that foreign investors will have the right to dispose of their assets." Foreigners may own land but must register it with the State Real Estate Registry. The IMF reports that residents may hold foreign exchange accounts in authorized banks and that non-residents may hold foreign exchange accounts but must register them with the government. There are no restrictions on payments and transfers. The issuing of capital market securities and similar financial instruments is prohibited. Most credit and loan operations must be registered with the central bank. Based on evidence of an open foreign investment regime, Mongolia's capital flows and foreign investment score is 1 point better this year.

BANKING AND FINANCE
Score: **2**–Better (low level of restrictions)

According to the Mongolian embassy, there were 17 banks operating as of the end of 2004, of which one was wholly state-owned and another was partly state-owned. The Economist Intelligence Unit reports that the Trade and Development Bank was sold to an international consortium in 2002 and that the Agricultural Bank was sold to a Japanese company in 2003. The central bank raised the minimum capital requirement for banks in 2004 and again for 2006. According to the U.S. Department of Commerce, "Mongolia has three generally well-regarded banks owned by American/Swiss, Japanese, and Mongolian interests respectively…. However, concerns remain among these bankers about the effectiveness of the legal and regulatory environment…. [T]he problem is…the will of the regulator, Mongol Bank, to execute mandated functions, particularly in regard to capital reserve requirements and non-performing loans…." There were 72 non-bank financial institutions (not subject to the same regulations as commercial banks) in 2003. The Mongolia Stock Exchange lists some 400 stocks. The government privatized the largest insurer, Mongol Daatgal, in 2002. Based on limited government influence in the financial sector, Mongolia's banking and finance score is 1 point better this year.

WAGES AND PRICES
Score: **2**–Stable (low level of intervention)

Mongolia liberalized most wages and prices in the early 1990s. The U.S. Department of Commerce reports that the government controls the price of airline tickets for domestic routes and that it intervenes in the market to adjust prices for grain and other commodities. The government liberalized energy prices in 1996 but still controls the price of fuel. A minimum wage that is applied to both public-sector and private-sector employees is enforced by the Ministry of Social Welfare and Labor.

PROPERTY RIGHTS
Score: **4**–Worse (low level of protection)

The enforcement of laws protecting private property is weak. According to the U.S. Department of Commerce, "too many judges remain willfully ignorant of commercial principles. They dismiss such concepts as the sanctity of the contract…. In several cases courts have willfully misinterpreted provisions regarding leases and loan contracts. Judges regularly ignore terms of a contract in their decisions. If someone defaults on a loan, the courts often order assets returned without requiring the debtor to compensate the creditor for any loss of value." In addition, "corruption…is increasingly an obstacle to honest business and efficiency." Based on new evidence of the weakness of the rule of law, Mongolia's property rights score is 1 point worse this year.

REGULATION
Score: **4**–Stable (high level)

The vast number of regulations implemented over the past several years, combined with the continuing restructuring of the government, imposes a sizeable burden on business. Labor laws limit employers' ability to hire people. The U.S. Department of Commerce identifies "corruption in the bureaucracy; lack of transparency in regulatory and legislative processes; some abuse of phyto-sanitary and licensing regimes in both the pharmaceutical and food production industries to protect existing state and private interests" as the main market challenges for investors.

INFORMAL MARKET
Score: **4**–Worse (high level of activity)

Transparency International's 2004 score for Mongolia is 3. Therefore Mongolia's informal market score is a 4 this year—1 point worse than last year.

MOROCCO

Rank: 97

Score: 3.21

Category: Mostly Unfree

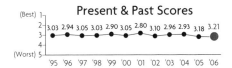

Present & Past Scores

(Best) 1 —
2 — 3.03 2.94 3.05 3.03 2.90 3.05 2.80 3.10 2.96 2.93 3.18 3.21
3 —
4 —
(Worst) 5 —
'95 '96 '97 '98 '99 '00 '01 '02 '03 '04 '05 '06

QUICK STUDY

SCORES

Trade Policy   5
Fiscal Burden   4.1
Government Intervention   2.5
Monetary Policy   1
Foreign Investment   2
Banking and Finance   4
Wages and Prices   3
Property Rights   4
Regulation   3
Informal Market   3.5

Population: 30,113,000

Total area: 446,550 sq. km

GDP: $38.5 billion

GDP growth rate: 5.2%

GDP per capita: $1,278

Major exports: consumer goods, food, drink, tobacco, minerals, petroleum products

Exports of goods and services: $11.7 billion

Major export trading partners: France 26.9%, Spain 17.1%, UK 7.2%, Italy 5.0%

Major imports: machinery and equipment, consumer goods, semifinished goods

Imports of goods and services: $15.4 billion

Major import trading partners: France 20.6%, Spain 12.4%, Italy 7.1%, Germany 5.2%

Foreign direct investment (net): $2.1 billion

2003 Data (in constant 2000 US dollars)

Morocco gained its independence from France in 1956 and evolved into a stable constitutional monarchy and close U.S. ally, both in the Cold War and more recently in the struggle against radical Islam. King Mohammed VI has encouraged political and economic reform, the expansion of civil rights, and the elimination of corruption. The 2002 appointment of Prime Minister Driss Jettou bolstered prospects for free-market reforms, privatization, enhancement of the private sector, and liberalization of social laws. During 2004, the government also sold some of its shares in the state telecommunications company and the largest state-owned bank. Morocco has rich resources, including the world's largest phosphate reserves, and a large tourist industry and growing manufacturing sector. However, agriculture remains the backbone of the economy, accounting for 20 percent of GDP and employing 40 percent of the population. Tourism revenues, depressed by post-9/11 fears of terrorism and the May 2003 Casablanca bombings, recovered by early 2004. A free trade agreement with the United States, signed in June 2004, eliminated tariffs on 95 percent of bilateral trade, with all remaining tariffs to be eliminated in nine years. As of June 30, 2005, Morocco was negotiating with the U.S. for Millennium Challenge Account assistance. Morocco's fiscal burden of government score is 0.3 point worse this year. As a result, its overall score is 0.03 point worse this year.

 TRADE POLICY
Score: 5–Stable (very high level of protectionism)

The World Bank reports that Morocco's weighted average tariff rate in 2003 (the most recent year for which World Bank data are available) was 24.9 percent, down from the 28.2 percent in 2002 reported in the 2005 *Index*, based on World Bank data. According to the U.S. Department of Commerce, "The greatest barriers to trade in Morocco are irregularities in the government procurement procedures, lack of transparent governmental and judicial bureaucracies and contraband." Based on the revised trade factor methodology, Morocco's trade policy score is unchanged.

 FISCAL BURDEN OF GOVERNMENT
Score—Income Taxation: **4–Stable** (high tax rates)
Score—Corporate Taxation: **4.5–Stable** (very high tax rates)
Score—Change in Government Expenditures: **3.5–Worse** (low increase)
Final Score: 4.1–Worse (high cost of government)

The International Monetary Fund reports that Morocco's top income tax rate is 44 percent. The top corporate tax rate is 35 percent. In 2003, according to the IMF, government expenditures increased 0.2 percentage point, compared to the 1.2 percentage point decrease in 2002. On net, Morocco's fiscal burden of government score is 0.3 point worse this year.

 GOVERNMENT INTERVENTION IN THE ECONOMY
Score: 2.5–Stable (moderate level)

The World Bank reports that the government consumed 21 percent of GDP in 2003. In the same year, based on data from the Economist Intelligence Unit, Morocco received 4.82 percent of its total revenues from state-owned enterprises and government ownership of property.

MONETARY POLICY
Score: 1–Stable (very low level of inflation)

Between 1995 and 2004, Morocco's weighted average annual rate of inflation was 1.83 percent.

CAPITAL FLOWS AND FOREIGN INVESTMENT
Score: 2–Stable (low barriers)

Morocco treats foreign and locally owned investments equally and permits 100 percent foreign ownership in most sectors. There is no screening requirement, but foreign investment in some sectors—notably phosphate mining—is restricted. Moroccan governments have tried to attract investment by "reforming investment laws, lowering import barriers, freeing up prices, reforming the judiciary and the labour market, reducing red tape and corruption, improving the financial sector, privatizing state firms and offering concessions," reports the Economist Intelligence Unit, but "Morocco's unwieldy bureaucracy remains a major constraint on the competitiveness of the economy and deters investors." The U.S. Department of Commerce notes, however, that "the government is streamlining paperwork associated with investment and has established a series of Regional Investment Centers to decentralize and accelerate investment-related bureaucratic procedures." The International Monetary Fund reports that residents and non-residents may hold foreign exchange accounts, subject to restrictions and requirements. Personal payments, transfer of interest, and travel payments are subject to limits, documentation requirements, and approval in some cases. Some capital transactions, including many capital and money market transactions and credit operations, require government approval.

BANKING AND FINANCE
Score: 4–Stable (high level of restrictions)

Despite gradual liberalization of the financial sector, including greater autonomy for the central bank, First Initiative reports that "the government retains significant influence over many financial institutions.... As of mid-2004, there were 14 commercial banks. In addition, there are five government-owned specialized financial institutions, 30 credit agencies and 12 leasing companies (2003).... Commercial banks, by law, must be at least 51% Moroccan-owned. The specialized banks are all state-owned and control approximately 43% of the banking sector's assets."Credit is allocated on market terms, and foreign investors have access to domestic credit. The U.S. Department of Commerce reports that Morocco's "banking system is still used by the government to channel domestic savings to finance government debt, and the banks are required to hold a part of their assets in bonds paying below market interest rates."

WAGES AND PRICES
Score: 3–Stable (moderate level of intervention)

"Social pressures and a legacy of government subsidies on staple goods have resulted in price controls being phased out only gradually," reports the Economist Intelligence Unit. "A range of basic consumer goods, including food staples, health products, and some educational materials, are still subsidised, although the subsidy on edible oils was removed at end-2000." According to the U.S. Department of Commerce, "The market freely determines commodity prices without government involvement with the exception of staple commodities such as gasoline, vegetable oil, sugar and subsidized flour. In June 2003, Morocco implemented a new tariff system for grains (barley, wheat, and corn) that resulted in a significant increase in tariffs for bread wheat." The government also influences prices through the country's many state-owned enterprises. Morocco has one minimum wage for the industrial sector and another for the agricultural sector.

PROPERTY RIGHTS
Score: 4–Stable (low level of protection)

The king "presides over the judiciary," reports the Economist Intelligence Unit, and exercises ultimate authority. The EIU cites a World Bank report as saying that "the inefficiency of the judicial system is holding back economic development.... [T]he courts move too slowly in dealing with cases, bankruptcy protection and liquidation procedures are inefficient and the courts often fail to enforce legal rulings.... [M]any of those working in the judiciary had inadequate expertise.... [T]he courts have [an estimated] backlog of 600,000 cases." A survey among businesses by the American Chamber of Commerce in Morocco revealed that corruption in the legal system is regarded as one of the main impediments to doing business.

REGULATION
Score: 3–Stable (moderate level)

Regulations and bureaucracy remain significantly burdensome despite the government's attempts at reform. The Economist Intelligence Unit reports that corruption is widespread throughout the bureaucracy. The EIU also reports that the government has made labor regulations more flexible, although the regulatory cost of labor is still significantly high. According to the U.S. Department of Commerce, "Even in areas where the regulations are favorable on paper, there are often problems in practice. Government procedures are not always transparent, efficient or quick. Routine permits, especially those required by local governments, can be difficult to obtain." The government has set up a network of Regional Investment Centres to speed up the investment process and has introduced measures to promote small and medium enterprises.

INFORMAL MARKET
Score: 3.5–Stable (high level of activity)

Transparency International's 2004 score for Morocco is 3.2. Therefore, Morocco's informal market score is 3.5 this year.

MOZAMBIQUE

Rank: 113

Score: 3.35

Category: Mostly Unfree

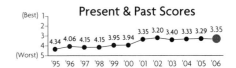

Present & Past Scores

(Best) 1—
2—
3— 4.34 4.06 4.15 4.15 3.95 3.94   3.35 3.20 3.40 3.33 3.29 3.35
4—
(Worst) 5—
'95 '96 '97 '98 '99 '00 '01 '02 '03 '04 '05 '06

QUICK STUDY

SCORES

Trade Policy	3.5
Fiscal Burden	3
Government Intervention	2
Monetary Policy	4
Foreign Investment	3
Banking and Finance	3
Wages and Prices	3
Property Rights	4
Regulation	4
Informal Market	4

Population: 18,791,000

Total area: 801,590 sq. km

GDP: $4.8 billion

GDP growth rate: 7.1%

GDP per capita: $255

Major exports: aluminum, prawns, electricity, cotton, sugar

Exports of goods and services: $996 million

Major export trading partners: Belgium 25.7%, South Africa 14.3%, Italy 9.6%, Spain 9.3%, Zimbabwe 4.7%

Major imports: machinery, vehicles, transport equipment, fuel, textiles

Imports of goods and services: $1.5 billion

Major import trading partners: South Africa 20.6%, Australia 9.0%, US 3.8%

Foreign direct investment (net): $317.7 million

2003 Data (in constant 2000 US dollars)

Mozambique's controversial 2004 elections, which were marred by allegations of fraud, produced the transition from former President Joaquim Chissano of the Frente de Libertação de Moçambique (FRELIMO) to FRELIMO candidate Armando Guebuza. Although the irregularities may not have affected the outcome of the presidential contest, they probably did affect some legislative elections, and tensions between FRELIMO and the opposition Resistência Nacional de Moçambique (RENAMO) remain high. Liberalization, privatization, and relative peace and stability have led to strong economic growth during the past decade, making Mozambique a model for economic development and post-war recovery, but further reform is needed in simplifying regulations, reducing bureaucracy, loosening labor rigidities, and strengthening judicial and public-sector accountability. Guebuza has announced plans to address inadequacies in the judicial system and the rampant corruption that affects all levels of government, the judiciary, and business. More than three-quarters of the population is engaged in agriculture, many in subsistence agriculture. Both unemployment and underemployment are high, and much of the workforce is employed in the informal sector. HIV/AIDS is a growing problem. Mozambique is eligible for assistance from the U.S. Millennium Challenge Account. Mozambique's fiscal burden of government score is 0.4 point better this year, but its capital flows and foreign investment score is 1 point worse. As a result, Mozambique's overall score is 0.06 point worse this year.

TRADE POLICY
Score: **3.5**–Stable (high level of protectionism)

The World Bank reports that Mozambique's weighted average tariff rate in 2003 (the most recent year for which World Bank data are available) was 9.9 percent, up from the 9.4 percent in 2002 reported in the 2005 *Index*, based on World Bank data. According to the U.S. Department of Commerce, "The time-consuming and bureaucratic customs clearance procedures are considered by many to be a significant non-tariff barrier." Corruption is a problem. Based on the revised trade factor methodology, Mozambique's trade policy score is unchanged.

FISCAL BURDEN OF GOVERNMENT
Score—Income Taxation: **3**–Worse (moderate tax rates)
Score—Corporate Taxation: **4**–Stable (high tax rates)
Score—Change in Government Expenditures: **1**–Better (very high decrease)
Final Score: **3**–Better (moderate cost of government)

Mozambique's top income tax rate is 32 percent, up from the 27.6 percent reported in the 2005 *Index*. The top corporate income tax rate is also 32 percent. In 2003, according to the African Development Bank, government expenditures as a share of GDP decreased by 4 percentage points to 29.8 percent, compared to a 0.8 percentage point decrease in 2002. On net, Mozambique's fiscal burden of government score is 0.4 point better this year.

GOVERNMENT INTERVENTION IN THE ECONOMY
Score: **2**–Stable (low level)

The World Bank reports that the government consumed 11.5 percent of GDP in 2003. In the same year, based on data from the Ministry of Financial Planning, Mozambique received 1.71 percent of its total revenues from state-owned enterprises and government ownership of property.

MONETARY POLICY
Score: **4**–Stable (high level of inflation)

From 1995 to 2004, Mozambique's weighted average annual rate of inflation was 12.04 percent.

CAPITAL FLOWS AND FOREIGN INVESTMENT
Score: **3**–Worse (moderate barriers)

Most sectors of Mozambique's economy are open to 100 percent foreign investment, and foreign investors generally receive the same treatment as domestic investors. Some restrictions remain in effect; outright private ownership of land, for example, is prohibited, and mining and management contracts are subject to specific performance requirements. "In the past," reports the U.S. Department of Commerce, "political risk, corruption, bureaucratic red tape, dilapidated infrastructure, and the relatively small size of the market served as strong deterrents to foreign investment. While these issues have not been entirely resolved, they have improved markedly…. [The government] generally does not limit foreign ownership or control of companies. Lengthy registration procedures can be problematic for any investor, national or foreign…. Foreign investors have participated in Mozambique's privatization program with some impediments…. All foreign and domestic investment must be approved." Mozambique allows 100 percent repatriation of profits and retention of earned foreign exchange in domestic accounts. According to the Economist Intelligence Unit, the Investment Promotion Center, which processes foreign investment, "has yet to live up to its billing as a 'one-stop shop' for investors, as the services it offers remain limited." The International Monetary Fund reports that both residents and non-residents may hold foreign exchange accounts. Payments and transfers are subject to maximum amounts, above which they must be approved by the central bank. Capital transactions, money market instruments, and derivatives are subject to controls. Based on the evidence of capital controls, Mozambique's capital flows and foreign investment score is 1 point worse this year.

BANKING AND FINANCE
Score: **3**–Stable (moderate level of restrictions)

The banking system is recovering from the 2000–2001 banking crisis, during which two large banks were declared insolvent. Although Mozambique has adopted a number of reforms in the banking and financial sector, including establishing an independent central bank, the financial system remains small and dominated by banking. There are eight commercial banks, all of which are majority foreign-owned. The Economist Intelligence Unit reports that the government owns 33 percent of the country's largest bank, Banco Internacional de Mocambique, which controls 45 percent of the banking market. The government has sold its minority stake in Banco Austral, the country's fourth largest bank in terms of assets. According to the EIU, "Credit risk…is determined by the poor domestic lending environment, involving what the World Bank terms 'legal and institutional' barriers to credit selection and recovery. This is an apparent reference to weak assurances of contract enforcement through the legal system and the absence of property markets as a form of loan collateral." First Initiative reports that capital markets "are very small and centered around the Bolsa de Valores de Mozambique (BVM), which opened in 1999. Trading, however, is limited to secondary trading in government bonds and a few corporate bonds. The insurance and pension sectors are also small. Despite recent privatization efforts, the insurance market remains dominated by the state-owned insurer."

WAGES AND PRICES
Score: **3**–Stable (moderate level of intervention)

According to the Embassy of Mozambique, the government maintains price controls on fuel, urban transport, electricity, water, and bread. The Economist Intelligence Unit reports that the government controls the price of fuel. A minimum wage for industry and agriculture is set by ministerial decree, based on the advice of annual tripartite (labor unions, government, and employers) meetings.

PROPERTY RIGHTS
Score: **4**–Stable (low level of protection)

Property rights are weakly protected, and the judiciary is corrupt. According to the Economist Intelligence Unit, "The judicial system in Mozambique is close to paralysis. There is a severe shortage of qualified legal personnel and a substantial backlog of cases. Enforcement of contracts and legal redress cannot be assured through the court system." The EIU also reports corruption in the justice system, and the U.S. Department of Commerce reports that most commercial disputes are settled privately because of the judicial system's inefficiency.

REGULATION
Score: **4**–Stable (high level)

Corruption reportedly continues to characterize Mozambique's regulatory environment. The Economist Intelligence Unit reports that "labyrinthine procedures [are] required for relatively simple activities such as registering a company. The commercial code has now been updated to meet the needs of a modern commercial economy…. However, implementation of reforms…is significantly behind schedule owing to the complexity of the process and the multiplicity of government ministries and departments involved…. The private sector still complains that it faces extensive and opaque regulation, with a lack of predictability in determining how long it will take to complete procedures."

INFORMAL MARKET
Score: **4**–Stable (high level of activity)

Transparency International's 2004 score for Mozambique is 2.8. Therefore, Mozambique's informal market score is 4 this year.

NAMIBIA

Rank: 85

Score: 3.11

Category: Mostly Unfree

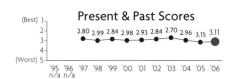

Present & Past Scores

(Best) 1 —
2 —
2.80 2.99 2.84 2.98 2.93 2.84 2.70 2.96 3.15 3.11
3 —
4 —
(Worst) 5 —

'95   '96   '97   '98   '99   '00   '01   '02   '03   '04   '05   '06
n/a n/a

In 2005, political power in Namibia was transferred through democratic elections that, despite irregularities, were judged to be free and fair. Former President Sam Nujoma was replaced by Hifikepunye Pohamba, former Minister of Lands, Resettlement, and Rehabilitation. Pohamba's party, the South West Africa People's Organization, also won a majority in the National Assembly. Namibia is rich in uranium, gem-quality diamonds, lead, silver, tin, tungsten, and zinc. The economy is dependent on mining, fishing, and tourism, but a majority of Namibians are employed in subsistence agriculture. The new president is committed to redistribution of land—through expropriation, if necessary—and commercial farmers are under increasing pressure to cooperate with the government's compulsory purchase of farms. Pohamba has pledged to clamp down on corruption and rein in excessive public spending. The government opposes privatization of state-owned enterprises, despite pressure from the International Monetary Fund, but has announced its commitment to improving management. Several tax increases have been adopted, including luxury taxes, excise taxes, an environmental tax, and amendments to income taxes that eliminate some offsets. Poverty, HIV/AIDS, and high unemployment remain problems. Namibia's fiscal burden of government score is 0.1 point worse this year, and its informal market score is 0.5 point worse; however, its monetary policy score is 1 point better. As a result, Namibia's overall score is 0.04 point better this year.

QUICK STUDY

SCORES

Trade Policy	2.5
Fiscal Burden	4.1
Government Intervention	3
Monetary Policy	2
Foreign Investment	3
Banking and Finance	3
Wages and Prices	3
Property Rights	4
Regulation	3
Informal Market	3.5

Population: 2,015,000

Total area: 825,418 sq. km

GDP: $3.7 billion

GDP growth rate: 3.7%

GDP per capita: $1,845

Major exports: diamonds, preserved fish, metal ores, food products, gold, zinc

Exports of goods and services: $1.75 billion

Major export trading partners: South Africa 31.5%, Angola 24.9%, Spain 12.8%

Major imports: transport equipment, chemical products, plastic products, refined petroleum products, machinery and equipment

Imports of goods and services: $1.7 billion

Major import trading partners: South Africa 80.5%, Germany 2.3%, Switzerland 2.3%

Foreign direct investment (net): $84.6 million

2003 Data (in constant 2000 US dollars)

TRADE POLICY
Score: **2.5**–Stable (moderate level of protectionism)

Namibia belongs to the Southern African Customs Union (SACU), a regional trade arrangement with South Africa, Botswana, Lesotho, and Swaziland. The World Bank reports that SACU's weighted average tariff rate in 2001 (the most recent year for which World Bank data are available) was 3.6 percent. According to the U.S. Trade Representative, "A limited number of products are subject to non-automatic import licensing: medicines; chemicals; frozen, chilled, fish and meat; live animals and genetic materials; controlled petroleum products; firearms and explosives; diamonds, gold and other minerals; and seemingly all second-hand goods such as clothing and motor vehicles." Based on the revised trade factor methodology, Namibia's trade policy score is unchanged.

FISCAL BURDEN OF GOVERNMENT
Score—Income Taxation: **3.5**–Stable (high tax rates)
Score—Corporate Taxation: **4.5**–Stable (very high tax rates)
Score—Change in Government Expenditures: **4**–Worse (moderate increase)
Final Score: **4.1**–Worse (high cost of government)

Namibia's top income tax rate is 35 percent. The top corporate tax rate is also 35 percent. In 2003, according to the African Development Bank, government expenditures as a share of GDP increased 1.8 percentage points to 36.8 percent, compared to the 0.9 percentage point decrease in 2002. On net, Namibia's fiscal burden of government score is 0.1 point worse this year.

GOVERNMENT INTERVENTION IN THE ECONOMY
Score: **3**–Stable (moderate level)

The World Bank reports that the government consumed 28.8 percent of GDP in 2003. In 2004, according to the Bank of Namibia, Namibia received 5.75 percent of its total revenues from state-owned enterprises and government ownership of property.

 MONETARY POLICY
Score: **2**–Better (low level of inflation)

From 1995 to 2004, Namibia's weighted average annual rate of inflation was 5.57 percent, down from the 8.43 percent from 1994 to 2003 reported in the 2005 *Index*. As a result, Namibia's monetary policy score is 1 point better this year.

 CAPITAL FLOWS AND FOREIGN INVESTMENT
Score: **3**–Stable (moderate barriers)

Namibia guarantees foreign investors national treatment for most sectors. An increasing concern is the effect that Namibia's land redistribution program will have on foreign investment. "The Namibian Constitution provides for the expropriation of property in the public interest subject to the payment of 'just' compensation," notes the U.S. Trade Representative. "The government considers foreign-owned and non-productive farmland primary targets for expropriation" and "is poised to implement a new land tax (originally scheduled to take effect in April 2002) in an effort to raise money for land acquisition. Absentee landowners will be subject to higher tax rates per hectare than resident farmers." Promoting black economic empowerment (BEE) is a key government priority; according to the Economist Intelligence Unit, "It will become increasingly necessary (although not legally required) for every new foreign investor to form a partnership with a local BEE firm or trust." Companies that are 75 percent or more foreign-owned are subject to exchange controls. Residents may hold foreign exchange accounts, subject to prior approval and some restrictions. Non-residents may hold foreign currency accounts only if they operate in an export-processing zone. Capital transactions, transfers, and payments are subject to various restrictions, approvals, and quantitative limits. Investments abroad by residents are capped at N$750,000. Examples of expropriation of land or making partnerships with local BEE firms mandatory for foreign investors could affect Namibia's score in future editions of the *Index*.

 BANKING AND FINANCE
Score: **3**–Stable (moderate level of restrictions)

Namibia's small but sound financial sector is closely tied to South Africa's financial system. There were four commercial banks in 2004, all at least partially foreign-owned. According to First Initiative, "The largest two banks are owned by South African banks, while the remaining banks include a Swiss owned bank and one that is jointly owned by Namibian and South African firms…. The Namibian insurance sector consists of 22 insurance companies and two re-insurers (2004)…. The Namibian Stock Exchange (NSX), which opened in 1992, listed 35 shares in early 2004, the majority of which are South African companies that are cross-listed on the Johannesburg Stock Exchange." The government owns the Agricultural Bank of Namibia, NamPost, and the Namibia Development Corporation and the Namibia

National Reinsurance Corporation (NamibRe). It also affects the allocation of credit through subsidized credits for subsistence farmers. Since 1995, the government has required domestic insurance companies to invest a minimum of 35 percent of assets in specified areas of the local market instead of in South Africa, where they traditionally had been invested.

 WAGES AND PRICES
Score: **3**–Stable (moderate level of intervention)

The government continues to influence prices through its many state-owned industries and through large subsidies to its parastatals. According to the Economist Intelligence Unit, "The Namibia Agronomic Board (NAB) determines guideline prices for maize and controls exports and imports of white-maize and wheat, with the aim of encouraging processors to purchase all home-produced supplies before resorting to imports." The Ministry of Labor established a minimum wage for farmers in 2002.

 PROPERTY RIGHTS
Score: **4**–Stable (low level of protection)

The threat of expropriation has escalated significantly. The government claims to follow a policy of "willing buyer–willing seller" to purchase land from white farmers and sell it to black ones, but the president is increasingly vocal about the alleged unwillingness of white farmers to sell their land. In May 2004, the *Financial Times* reported that "at least six farmers…received letters…ordering [them] to sell the property [to the government] within two weeks." According to the U.S. Department of State, "The lack of qualified magistrates, other court officials, and private attorneys has resulted in a serious backlog of criminal cases, which often translates in delays of up to a year or more between arrest and trial."

 REGULATION
Score: **3**–Stable (moderate level)

The Economist Intelligence Unit reports that "Namibia is burdened by an oversized civil service, which accounts for an unsustainably high proportion of government spending." The same source also reports that investors are increasingly under pressure to hire black Namibians in senior positions. The U.S. Department of Commerce and other sources continue to cite concerns about corruption. Burdensome regulations include health and safety standards and a requirement that businesses submit an environmental impact statement for proposed new investments and construction. According to the EIU, "the government enacted separate investment incentive packages for manufacturing and export-oriented activities…."

 INFORMAL MARKET
Score: **3.5**–Worse (high level of activity)

Transparency International's 2004 score for Namibia is 4.1. Therefore, Namibia's informal market score is 3.5 this year— 0.5 point worse than last year.

NEPAL

Rank: 125

Score: 3.53

Category: Mostly Unfree

Present & Past Scores

(Best) 1—
2—
3— 3.86 3.89 3.71 3.49 3.79 3.65 3.51 3.63 3.53 3.55 3.53
4—
(Worst) 5—

'95 '96 '97 '98 '99 '00 '01 '02 '03 '04 '05 '06
n/a

QUICK STUDY

SCORES

Trade Policy	5
Fiscal Burden	2.8
Government Intervention	2.5
Monetary Policy	2
Foreign Investment	4
Banking and Finance	4
Wages and Prices	3
Property Rights	4
Regulation	4
Informal Market	4

Population: 24,660,000

Total area: 140,800 sq. km

GDP: $5.9 billion

GDP growth rate: 3.1%

GDP per capita: $241

Major exports: garments, woolen carpets, jute goods, vegetables, carpet, leather goods

Exports of goods and services: $974 million

Major export trading partners: India 43.7%, US 29.6%, Germany 7.5%

Major imports: petroleum products, textiles, gold and silver, vehicles

Imports of goods and services: $1.7 billion

Major import trading partners: India 44.9%, China 9.6%, United Arab Emirates 8.9%, Singapore 5.1%

Foreign direct investment (net): $28.3 million

2003 Data (in constant 2000 US dollars)

On February 1, 2005, King Gyanendra dismissed his government and assumed executive power. Suspending fundamental freedoms and plunging his extremely poor and underdeveloped country into a humanitarian crisis, the king proclaimed the ineptitude of the current government in dealing with the Maoist threat as the reason for his actions. Nevertheless, the Maoist insurgency remains strong, civil unrest is growing, and the people endure unexplained disappearances, abductions, and other human rights violations. As the security situation continues to deteriorate, Nepal's economically vital tourist industry is likewise declining. In addition, the garment industry, which currently accounts for about 40 percent of foreign-exchange earnings, is trying to cope with increased competition from China; pervasive corruption makes direct investment unacceptably risky; protection of property rights is not well-enforced; and the legal system lacks transparency. In November 2004, the government banned the employment of children under 14 years of age. It also continues to discuss further deregulation of certain industries and reform of its financial sector. The government finally allowed petroleum prices to rise in January 2005 and promises to allow them eventually to reach world prices. Nepal's trade policy and government intervention scores are 0.5 point worse this year; however, its fiscal burden of government score is 0.2 point better, and its informal market score is 1 point better. As a result, Nepal's overall score is 0.02 point better this year.

TRADE POLICY
Score: **5**–Worse (very high level of protectionism)

The World Bank reports that Nepal's weighted average tariff rate in 2004 was 15.6 percent, up from the 14.3 percent in 2002 reported in the 2005 *Index*, based on World Bank data. According to the U.S. Department of Commerce, the government bans or employs quantitative restrictions on imports of "(a) products injurious to health… (b) arms and ammunition, explosive materials… (c) communications equipment, including computers and home entertainment products such as television sets and VCRs; (d) valuable metals and jewelry; and (e) beef and beef products." Corruption is a problem. Based on the higher tariff rate, as well as a revision of the trade factor methodology, Nepal's trade policy score is 0.5 point worse this year.

FISCAL BURDEN OF GOVERNMENT
Score—Income Taxation: **2.5**–Stable (moderate tax rates)
Score—Corporate Taxation: **3**–Stable (moderate tax rates)
Score—Change in Government Expenditures: **2.5**–Better (low decrease)
Final Score: **2.8**–Better (moderate cost of government)

Nepal's top income tax rate is 25 percent. The top corporate tax rate is also 25 percent. In 2003, according to the Asian Development Bank, government expenditures as a share of GDP decreased 1 percentage point to 16 percent, compared to the 0.6 percentage point decrease in 2002. On net, Nepal's fiscal burden of government score is 0.2 point better this year.

GOVERNMENT INTERVENTION IN THE ECONOMY
Score: **2.5**–Worse (moderate level)

The World Bank reports that the government consumed 10.3 percent of GDP in 2003, up from the 10 percent reported in the 2005 *Index*. As a result, Nepal's government intervention score is 0.5 point worse this year. In 2003, according to the International Monetary Fund's Government

Financial Statistics CD–ROM, Nepal received 8.53 percent of total revenues from state-owned enterprises and government ownership of property.

MONETARY POLICY
Score: 2–Stable (low level of inflation)

From 1995 to 2004, Nepal's weighted average annual rate of inflation was 3.52 percent.

CAPITAL FLOWS AND FOREIGN INVESTMENT
Score: 4–Stable (high barriers)

Nepal permits 100 percent foreign ownership in some sectors, simplified licensing and regulations, and opened up the telecommunications and civil aviation sectors. But many sectors, such as business and management consulting, accounting, engineering, legal services, defense, alcohol and cigarette production, travel and trekking agencies, and retail sales, remain closed. According to the U.S. Department of Commerce, implementation of pro-investment policies is "often distorted by bureaucratic delays and inefficiency…. [T]here is often a wide discrepancy between the letter of the law and the law's implementation. Foreign investors constantly complain about complex and opaque government procedures and a working-level attitude that is more hostile than accommodating." Instability and corruption also impede investment. The International Monetary Fund reports that residents may hold foreign exchange accounts only in specific instances. Most non-residents may hold foreign exchange accounts. Most payments and transfers are subject to prior approval by the government. There are restrictions on most capital transactions, and all real estate transactions are subject to controls.

BANKING AND FINANCE
Score: 4–Stable (high level of restrictions)

The government dominates Nepal's banking system, which consisted of 17 commercial banks, 11 development banks, five rural development banks, 57 finance institutions, and six microfinance institutions as of 2004. "While the financial sector was officially deregulated in the 1990s," reports First Initiative, "the state retains a tight grip on financial activities…. The government wholly owns one commercial bank and controls 40% of another, allowing the state to account for approximately 60% of total banking sector lending…. The largest insurance firm is the National Insurance Company, which is majority-owned by the government." According to the U.S. Department of Commerce, "Legal, regulatory, and accounting systems are neither fully transparent nor consistent with international norms." The same source notes that the state-owned banks "have a large number of non-performing loans and are technically insolvent." Foreign banks have been permitted to establish joint ventures since 1984. Majority ownership was not permitted until 2001 when foreign banks were permitted to own up to two-thirds of a joint venture.

WAGES AND PRICES
Score: 3–Stable (moderate level of intervention)

The government has eliminated most price controls. The U.S. Department of Commerce reports that "there are special subsidies and preferred credit arrangements for individual public and private companies in select sectors, such as rural electrification, fertilizer importation, and the provision of agricultural credit." According to the Economist Intelligence Unit, "The government lowered the prices of kerosene and liquefied petroleum gas (LPG), with effect from February 12th [2005]." The government sets a minimum wage for children from 14 to 16 years old, as well as for unskilled workers, skilled workers, and highly skilled workers.

PROPERTY RIGHTS
Score: 4–Stable (low level of protection)

Nepal's judicial system suffers from corruption and inefficiency. According to the U.S. Department of State, the Supreme Court has demonstrated independence, but "lower level courts remain vulnerable to political pressure and bribery of judges and court staff is endemic." The U.S. Department of Commerce reports that "property disputes account for half of the current backlog in Nepal's overburdened court system and such cases can take years to be settled…. [L]aws and regulations are unclear, and interpretation can vary from case to case." The Economist Intelligence Unit reports that "Nepal's 1990 constitution was effectively suspended in October 2002.… The constitutional abeyance became more pronounced when, on February 1st 2005, King Gyanendra sacked the prime minister and decided to rule as chairman of the council of ministers."

REGULATION
Score: 4–Stable (high level)

Nepal's regulatory regime is not transparent. The U.S. Department of Commerce reports that obstacles to investment include "inadequate and obscure commercial legislation and unclear rules regarding labor relations. Policies intended to…simplify necessary interactions between investor and host government have produced few results…. [I]nvestors constantly complain about complex and opaque government procedures and a working-level attitude that is more hostile than accommodating." In addition, "Facilities granted under certain Acts or policies are often either contradicted or negated by another set of rules or policies…. Some companies report that the process of terminating unsatisfactory employees is cumbersome…. [I]nvestors have identified pervasive corruption as an obstacle to maintaining and expanding their…investments in Nepal."

INFORMAL MARKET
Score: 4–Better (high level of activity)

Transparency International's 2004 score for Nepal is 2.8. Therefore, Nepal's informal market score is 4 this year—1 point better than last year.

THE NETHERLANDS

Rank: 16

Score: 1.90

Category: Free

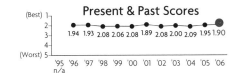

Present & Past Scores

(Best) 1
2
3
4
(Worst) 5

1.94 1.93 2.08 2.06 2.08 1.89 2.08 2.00 2.09 1.95 1.90

'95 '96 '97 '98 '99 '00 '01 '02 '03 '04 '05 '06
n/a

QUICK STUDY

SCORES

Trade Policy	2
Fiscal Burden	4
Government Intervention	3
Monetary Policy	1
Foreign Investment	1
Banking and Finance	1
Wages and Prices	2
Property Rights	1
Regulation	3
Informal Market	1

Population: 16,300,000

Total area: 41,526 sq. km

GDP: $380.1 billion

GDP growth rate: 1.4%

GDP per capita: $23,319

Major exports: chemicals, machinery, foodstuffs, transportation, travel services, financial services

Exports of goods and services: $366.3 billion

Major export trading partners: Germany 24.3%, Belgium 11.7%, UK 10.2%, France 10.0%

Major imports: transport equipment, machinery, fuels, clothing, computer and information services, financial services

Imports of goods and services: $334.7 billion

Major import trading partners: Germany 19.9%, Belgium 11.4%, US 7.8%, UK 7.3%

Foreign direct investment (net): –$5.6 billion

2004 Data (in constant 2000 US dollars)

The Netherlands, despite developing a large, European-style safety net over the years, maintains its openness to the rest of the world. Rotterdam remains the world's largest port as measured by tonnage of goods, and there are few restrictions on foreign direct investment. Since 1997, Dutch labor costs have increased faster than those of European competitors. Rapidly declining competitiveness—the result of wage increases and an overly generous pension system, as well as a decline in the number of workers—has brought the Dutch to an economic crossroads. Recently, GDP has grown at a snail's pace, increasing by only 1.4 percent in 2004. Following the close January 2003 parliamentary election, outgoing Christian Democrat Prime Minister Jan Peter Balkenende was narrowly returned to power, managing a three-party coalition government. Balkenende has been forced to try to alter the cherished "polder model," whereby business, unions, and the government have traditionally negotiated economic matters. In 2004, the government rejected a deal on pension reform negotiated between the unions and Dutch employers. The coalition's reform program has trimmed welfare benefits and has tried to liberalize the labor market while scrapping tax breaks for early retirees. The Netherlands' fiscal burden of government score is 0.5 point better this year. As a result, its overall score is 0.05 point better this year.

TRADE POLICY
Score: **2–Stable** (low level of protectionism)

As a member of the European Union, the Netherlands was subject to a common EU weighted average external tariff of 1.3 percent in 2003, down from the 2.4 percent for 2002 reported in the 2005 *Index*, based on World Bank data. According to the World Trade Organization and the U.S. Trade Representative, the EU imposes non-tariff trade barriers through a complex regulatory system and export subsidies. Based on the revised trade factor methodology, the Netherlands' trade policy score is unchanged.

FISCAL BURDEN OF GOVERNMENT
Score—Income Taxation: **5–Stable** (very high tax rates)
Score—Corporate Taxation: **4–Better** (high tax rates)
Score—Change in Government Expenditures: **3–Better** (very low decrease)
Final Score: **4–Better** (high cost of government)

According to Deloitte, the Netherlands' top income tax rate is 52 percent. Effective January 2005, the top corporate tax rate was cut to 31.5 percent from 34.5 percent. In 2004, government expenditures as a share of GDP decreased 0.4 percentage point to 48.6 percent, compared to the 1.2 percentage point increase in 2003. On net, the Netherlands' fiscal burden of government score is 0.5 point better this year.

GOVERNMENT INTERVENTION IN THE ECONOMY
Score: **3–Stable** (moderate level)

Based on data from the Economist Intelligence Unit, the government consumed 25.3 percent of GDP in 2004. In 2003, based on data from the central bank, the Netherlands received 5.29 percent of its total revenues from state-owned enterprises and government ownership of property.

MONETARY POLICY
Score: **1–Stable** (very low level of inflation)

The Netherlands is a member of the euro zone. From 1995 to 2004, the Netherlands' weighted average annual rate of inflation was 1.76 percent.

 CAPITAL FLOWS AND FOREIGN INVESTMENT
Score: **1–Stable** (very low barriers)

The Netherlands actively promotes foreign investment. According to the U.S. Department of Commerce, "The Netherlands' trade and investment policy is among the most open in the world…. With the exception of a few public and private monopolies from which foreign and domestic private investment is banned (the Netherlands Central Bank, Netherlands railways, national airport Amsterdam Schiphol, and public broadcasting), foreign firms are able to invest in any sector and are entitled under the law to equal treatment with domestic firms." The government requires no screening for investments, 100 percent foreign ownership is allowed in the areas where foreign investment is permitted, and foreign investors receive national treatment. There are no restrictions or barriers on current transfers, repatriation of profits, purchase of real estate, or access to foreign exchange. Capital transactions are not restricted but are subject to reporting requirements under the External Financial Relations Act.

 BANKING AND FINANCE
Score: **1–Stable** (very low level of restrictions)

The Netherlands has been one of Europe's financial and banking centers for centuries, and its banking system operates freely with little government regulation. Banks established in the Netherlands may engage in a variety of financial services, such as buying, selling, and holding securities, insurance policies, and real estate. Three Dutch bank conglomerates—ABN Amro, Rabobank, and ING bank—dominate the sector, accounting for approximately 75 percent of total lending. "Foreign financial service providers face no special conditions or restrictions, and receive full national treatment," reports the U.S. Department of Commerce. "However, one provision of the Dutch 1992 Banking Act does reflect the EU Banking Directive's 'reciprocity' provision. The Finance Ministry says this section has never been used, and that all applications from non-EU parent banks are handled on a national treatment basis." The government is minimally involved in the banking sector. According to the Economist Intelligence Unit, "The government sold its remaining 14.7% stake in NIB Capital, a formerly stateowned financing bank, for €14.7m in June 2004." The EIU also reports that banks and insurance firms must have at least one board member with Dutch banking or insurance experience.

 WAGES AND PRICES
Score: **2–Stable** (low level of intervention)

Wages and prices in the Netherlands are set primarily by the market. According to the Economist Intelligence Unit, "The Price Control Act gives the government substantial powers to control prices, especially in times of high inflation." However, "hardly any sectors have had price controls since 1983. Legislation was passed in January 1996 to introduce price controls for medicines." The government also affects agricultural prices through the country's participation in the Common Agricultural Policy, a program that heavily subsidizes agricultural goods. The Netherlands maintains a minimum wage.

 PROPERTY RIGHTS
Score: **1–Stable** (very high level of protection)

Private property is secure. The Economist Intelligence Unit reports that "contractual agreements remain very secure in the Netherlands. The judiciary and the civil service are of high quality."

 REGULATION
Score: **3–Stable** (moderate level)

According to the U.S. Department of Commerce, laws and regulations affecting investment are non-discriminatory and applied evenly. In general, it is relatively easy to start a business. In 2004, a new corporate governance code of conduct came into effect, seeking to increase accountability for managers and transparency for shareholders. Environmental laws are somewhat stringent. Most available building land is owned by local governments, which limit the number of building permits issued. Combined with the scarcity of land and high property prices, this makes establishing a business more challenging. The government has expanded laws allowing for increased part-time work. *The Economist* reports that "labour laws in the Netherlands, unlike those in France and Germany, are sufficiently flexible to permit job cuts."

 INFORMAL MARKET
Score: **1–Stable** (very low level of activity)

Transparency International's 2004 score for the Netherlands is 8.7. Therefore, the Netherlands' informal market score is 1 this year.

> If the Netherlands were to improve its regulation score, it would qualify for the Global Free Trade Alliance.

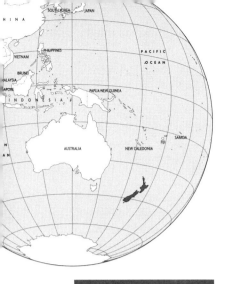

NEW ZEALAND

Rank: 9

Score: 1.84

Category: Free

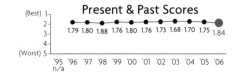

Present & Past Scores

(Best) 1
2   1.79 1.80 1.88 1.76 1.80 1.76 1.73 1.68 1.70 1.75 1.84
3
4
(Worst) 5
'95 '96 '97 '98 '99 '00 '01 '02 '03 '04 '05 '06
n/a

A s one of the world's least-regulated economies, New Zealand has enjoyed high GDP growth (4 percent on average) since 1999. The restructuring and sale of state-owned enterprises in the 1990s significantly reduced the government's role in the economy. New Zealand has the lowest unemployment rate of any country in the Organisation for Economic Co-operation and Development following two decades of sustained implementation of sound economic policies and structural reforms. Economic growth was 4.8 percent in 2004. Amendments to the Employment Relations Act became effective in 2005, along with other measures affecting the labor market. In light of this development, the International Monetary Fund has concluded that "maintaining New Zealand's labor market flexibility is a critical element in sustaining high medium-term growth." New Zealand is still heavily dependent on agricultural commodities for export earnings. The agricultural sector accounts for 9.7 percent of GDP but receives the lowest farm subsidies in the world. The number of international visitors has been rising in recent years, and tourism is becoming an important and growing sector of the economy. New Zealand's fiscal burden of government score is 0.1 point better this year, but its capital flows and foreign investment score is 1 point worse. As a result, New Zealand's overall score is 0.09 point worse this year.

QUICK STUDY

SCORES

Trade Policy	2.5
Fiscal Burden	3.9
Government Intervention	2
Monetary Policy	1
Foreign Investment	2
Banking and Finance	1
Wages and Prices	2
Property Rights	1
Regulation	2
Informal Market	1

Population: 4,009,000

Total area: 268,680 sq. km

GDP: $77.1 billion

GDP growth rate: 4.8%

GDP per capita: $19,243

Major exports: dairy products, forest products, fruit and vegetables, aluminum, wool, fish, machinery

Exports of goods and services: $28.4 billion

Major export trading partners: Australia 20.8%, US 14.4%, Japan 11.2%, China 5.7%

Major imports: machinery and mechanical appliances, vehicles, electrical machinery and equipment, mineral fuels and oils

Imports of goods and services: $28.8 billion

Major import trading partners: Australia 22.4%, Japan 11.2%, US 11.2%, China 9.7%

Foreign direct investment (net): $1.6 billion

2004 Data (in constant 2000 US dollars)

TRADE POLICY
Score: **2.5**–Stable (moderate level of protectionism)

The World Bank reports that New Zealand's weighted average tariff rate in 2004 was 2.9 percent, up from the 2.8 percent in 2002 reported in the 2005 *Index*, based on World Bank data. According to the World Trade Organization, "New Zealand maintains some restrictions on imports and exports mainly for health, safety and sanitary and phytosanitary reasons." The Economist Intelligence Unit reports that New Zealand has "strict health, content, safety and origin-labelling rules for imported and domestically produced goods, and there are stringent animal and plant health requirements." Based on the revised trade factor methodology, New Zealand's trade policy score is unchanged.

FISCAL BURDEN OF GOVERNMENT
Score—Income Taxation: **3.5**–Stable (high tax rates)
Score—Corporate Taxation: **4.5**–Stable (very high tax rates)
Score—Change in Government Expenditures: **3**–Better (very low decrease)
Final Score: **3.9**–Better (high cost of government)

According to Deloitte, New Zealand's top income tax rate is 39 percent. The top corporate tax rate is 33 percent. In 2004, government expenditures as a share of GDP decreased 0.1 percentage point to 34.1 percent, compared to the 0.9 percentage point decrease in 2003. On net, New Zealand's fiscal burden of government score is 0.1 point better this year.

GOVERNMENT INTERVENTION IN THE ECONOMY
Score: **2**–Stable (low level)

Based on data from Statistics New Zealand, the government consumed 17.6 percent of GDP in 2004. In fiscal year July 2003–June 2004, based on data from the International Monetary Fund, New Zealand received 3.2 percent of its total revenues from state-owned enterprises and government ownership of property.

MONETARY POLICY
Score: 1–Stable (very low level of inflation)

From 1995 to 2004, New Zealand's weighted average annual rate of inflation was 2.20 percent.

CAPITAL FLOWS AND FOREIGN INVESTMENT
Score: 2–Worse (low barriers)

New Zealand encourages foreign investment, and barriers to investment are minimal. Foreign ownership is restricted in Telecom New Zealand, Air New Zealand, fishing, and real estate (although approval for ownership of real estate is sometimes possible). "For foreign investment in certain types of land," reports the International Monetary Fund, "the investor must undergo a bona fide test, and the investment must be in the national interest. Authorization is required for acquisitions of the following: land exceeding 5 hectares in area or where the consideration exceeds $NZ 10 million; islands or land containing or adjoining reserves, historic, or heritage areas; foreshore or lakes in excess of 0.4 hectares; and land containing or adjoining foreshore in excess of 0.2 hectares." Foreign investments involving acquisition of an existing New Zealand business where foreign ownership would be 25 percent or greater or the investment exceeds NZ$50 million require approval from the Overseas Investment Commission (OIC). Foreign ownership of Telecom Corporation of New Zealand is limited to 49.5 percent. Permission is required for a non-resident to acquire or hold a fishing quota. The Embassy of New Zealand reports that the OIC received 272 applications and approved 262 investments (96 percent) in 2004. According to the U.S. Department of Commerce, "Amid a growing public outcry about the purchases of coastal properties by foreign buyers, the New Zealand government in November 2003 launched a review of OIC's powers. That review led to proposed legislation in November 2004 that would raise the minimum threshold at which scrutiny of proposed business purchases is required, but toughen the screening and monitoring of land purchases." There are no restrictions on current transfers, repatriation of profits, or access to foreign exchange. Based on evidence of rules and restrictions governing foreign investment, New Zealand's capital flows and foreign investment score is 1 point worse this year.

BANKING AND FINANCE
Score: 1–Stable (very low level of restrictions)

New Zealand's banking system is deregulated, and foreign banks are welcome; foreigners own or control all but two of the 16 registered banks, accounting for approximately 90 percent of banking assets. The government owns one small bank, Kiwibank Limited, which began operations in February 2002. The Reserve Bank of New Zealand is limited to prudential supervision. The government does not provide deposit insurance for financial institutions; instead, banks provide full disclosure of their financial condition to the public on a quarterly basis. Banking services may be offered by non-bank financial institutions, provided they meet banking regulations

and public disclosure requirements. The Labour government has returned control of workplace accident insurance to the state monopoly.

WAGES AND PRICES
Score: 2–Stable (low level of intervention)

The market determines almost all prices and wages. The Embassy of New Zealand reports that no goods are subject to price controls. According to the Economist Intelligence Unit, however, "The Ministry of Economic Development (MED) and Commerce Commission have the power…to control prices in markets where effective competition is absent…." New Zealand has a minimum wage.

PROPERTY RIGHTS
Score: 1–Stable (very high level of protection)

Private property is well protected in New Zealand. According to the Economist Intelligence Unit, "Strict rules governing appointments and protecting tenure in office maintain the judiciary's constitutional independence and protect against the influence of other branches of government…. Contracts and court decisions are generally very well respected."

REGULATION
Score: 2–Stable (low level)

According to the Ministry of Foreign Affairs and Trade, business registrations are "conducted via a simple online service that is completed in a matter of hours…. Incorporation fees are minimal, and once a company is incorporated, online filing of annual returns, and maintenance of company and director details are free of charge." Non–limited liability businesses are not required to register under the Companies Act. The Resource Management Act of 1991 created a three-layer regulatory system involving national, regional, and local authorities that requires businesses to acquire a resource consent, or permit, for most types of business activity. The result is an inconsistent system in which each of the country's 83 different local authorities interprets the law in its own way and accusations of environmental violations can be filed on a broad-ranging basis. This process can take as much as two years, and the system is overloaded with cases. Efforts to fine-tune this act to make it less burdensome have met with only marginal results. Labor laws, while somewhat rigid, are much less so than in other developed countries. In general, New Zealand's business environment is open and competitive.

INFORMAL MARKET
Score: 1–Stable (very low level of activity)

Transparency International's 2004 score for New Zealand is 9.6. Therefore, New Zealand's informal market score is 1 this year.

> If New Zealand were to improve its trade policy score, it would qualify for the Global Free Trade Alliance.

NICARAGUA

Rank: 80

Score: 3.05

Category: Mostly Unfree

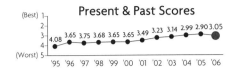

Present & Past Scores

(Best) 1
2
3
4
(Worst) 5

4.08 3.65 3.75 3.68 3.65 3.65 3.49 3.23 3.14 2.99 2.90 3.05

'95 '96 '97 '98 '99 '00 '01 '02 '03 '04 '05 '06

QUICK STUDY

SCORES

Trade Policy	2.5
Fiscal Burden	4
Government Intervention	2
Monetary Policy	3
Foreign Investment	2
Banking and Finance	2
Wages and Prices	3
Property Rights	4
Regulation	4
Informal Market	4

Population: 5,480,000

Total area: 129,494 sq. km

GDP: $4.2 billion

GDP growth rate: 2.3%

GDP per capita: $767

Major exports: coffee, shrimp and lobster, beef, sugar

Exports of goods and services: $1.1 billion

Major export trading partners: US 35.9%, El Salvador 17.3%, Costa Rica 8.1%, Honduras 7.2%, Mexico 4.6%

Major imports: raw materials, petroleum products, consumer goods

Imports of goods and services: $2.1 billion

Major import trading partners: US 24.8%, Venezuela 9.7%, Costa Rica 9.0%, Mexico 8.4%, Guatemala 7.3%, El Salvador 4.9%

Foreign direct investment (net): $185.8 million

2003 Data (in constant 2000 US dollars)

Nicaragua is Central America's poorest country, with an average per capita GDP of $767 and unemployment close to 41 percent. During 2004 and 2005, the country fell victim to a spiraling power play between President Enrique Bolaños Geyer and two of the dominant party leaders who control 80 of the National Assembly's 92 seats. At issue was a 2000 "pact" formed by President Arnoldo Alemán of the Liberal Party and Daniel Ortega of the opposition Sandinista Party that is aimed at stacking the supreme court, the electoral council, and the comptroller's office with cronies to avoid prosecution for their official misdeeds. In October 2004, the two leaders attempted to charge Bolaños with election finance violations in order to remove him from office. When that failed, they pressed loyal Assembly members to pass laws transferring presidential appointment powers to the legislature. The Central American Court of Justice, to which Nicaragua is a signatory, ruled these measures unconstitutional. On June 7, 2005, the Organization of American States General Assembly resolved to invoke its Inter-American Democratic Charter and send Secretary General José Miguel Insulza to investigate. In the midst of this power play, Nicaragua was unable to approve the DR–CAFTA trade agreement before ratification by the United States. Nicaragua's capital flows and foreign investment score is 1 point better this year; however its trade policy score is 0.5 point worse, and its fiscal burden of government and monetary policy scores are 1 point worse. As a result, its overall score is 0.15 point worse this year, causing Nicaragua to be classified as a "mostly unfree" country.

TRADE POLICY
Score: **2.5**–Worse (moderate level of protectionism)

According to the World Bank, Nicaragua's weighted average tariff rate in 2004 was 3.7 percent, up from the 2.3 percent in 2002 reported in the 2005 *Index*, based on World Bank data. The U.S. Department of Commerce reports that importers complain about "secondary customs costs, including customs declarations form charges, consular fees, and fees for mandatory employment of licensed customs agents." A license is required to import sugar. Based on the higher tariff rate, as well as a revision of the trade factor methodology, Nicaragua's trade policy score is 0.5 point worse this year.

FISCAL BURDEN OF GOVERNMENT
Score—Income Taxation: **3**–Worse (moderate tax rates)
Score—Corporate Taxation: **4**–Stable (high tax rates)
Score—Change in Government Expenditures: **5**–Worse (very high increase)
Final Score: **4**–Worse (high cost of government)

According to the Economist Intelligence Unit, Nicaragua's top income tax rate is 30 percent, up from the 25 percent reported in the 2005 *Index*. The top corporate tax rate is also 30 percent. In 2003, based on data from the central bank, government expenditures as a share of GDP increased 3.4 percentage points to 23.8 percent, compared to the 0.1 percentage point decrease in 2002. On net, Nicaragua's fiscal burden of government score is 1 point worse this year.

GOVERNMENT INTERVENTION IN THE ECONOMY
Score: **2**–Stable (low level)

The World Bank reports that the government consumed 15.8 percent of GDP in 2003. In the same year, according to the International Monetary Fund, Nicaragua received 3.07 percent of its

total revenues from state-owned enterprises and government ownership of property.

MONETARY POLICY
Score: 3–Worse (moderate level of inflation)

From 1995 to 2004, Nicaragua's weighted average annual rate of inflation was 7.32 percent, up from the 5.39 percent from 1994 to 2003 reported in the 2005 *Index*. As a result, Nicaragua's monetary policy score is 1 point worse this year.

CAPITAL FLOWS AND FOREIGN INVESTMENT
Score: 2–Better (low barriers)

Nicaragua has liberalized its foreign investment sector. Investment is guaranteed equal treatment, is not screened, and faces no performance requirements. Investors are permitted to own and use property. The U.S. Trade Representative notes other positive reforms, including creation of the Pro-Nicaragua investment promotion agency and efforts toward a "one-stop shop" for foreign investors. However, informal barriers continue to discourage investment. The U.S. Trade Representative identifies poor protection of property rights as a disincentive, and the U.S. Department of Commerce reports that "Nicaragua's legal and regulatory framework remains cumbersome. The rules are not fully transparent, and much business is still conducted on a 'who you know' basis. Some regulatory authorities can be arbitrary, negligent, or slow in their application of existing laws, at times in an apparent effort to favor one competitor over another." The International Monetary Fund reports that residents may hold foreign exchange accounts, but the only non-residents who may hold such accounts are those with approved immigration status (such as diplomats). There are no controls or restrictions on payments and transfers. There are very few restrictions on capital transactions. Based on evidence that the government permits foreign investment in nearly all sectors and has liberalized capital flows, Nicaragua's capital flows and foreign investment score is 1 point better this year.

BANKING AND FINANCE
Score: 2–Stable (low level of restrictions)

Nicaragua's banking system is improving but remains weak and underdeveloped. "As of early 2004," reports First Initiative, "the Nicaraguan banking system consisted of six commercial banks and three finance companies; only one bank is state owned…. The insurance market is small but growing with the entry of private firms into a previously state-run market. The sector has four private insurance companies competing with the state-owned INISER, the country's largest insurance company. Capital markets…are centered on the Bolsa de Valores, a small stock exchange which opened in 1993." According to the U.S. Department of Commerce, "Between November 2000 and March 2002, banking regulators intervened to liquidate four banks…amid findings of fraud, mismanagement, and failure to comply with regulatory norms for solvency. The remain-

ing six banks have not exhibited the extreme weaknesses of the four liquidated banks." Banking reforms increased capital adequacy ratio requirements to 10 percent, created a maximum cap on bank shares held by any one private shareholder, placed limits on loans to any one borrower, and curbed the ability of banks to lend to related companies. In 2000 and 2001, mismanagement and fraud in a number of banks led to a banking crisis. Microfinance credit unions are increasingly important in rural Nicaragua.

WAGES AND PRICES
Score: 3–Stable (moderate level of intervention)

The market determines some wages and prices. According to the U.S. Department of Commerce, "The only price controls in effect are on pharmaceutical sales margins, sugar, domestically produced soft drinks and cigarettes, liquefied natural gas, and public utilities. Other prices are established by market supply and demand." The minimum wage system applies different rates to different economic sectors. The various rates are set through tripartite negotiations involving business, government, and labor and confirmed by the National Assembly.

PROPERTY RIGHTS
Score: 4–Stable (low level of protection)

Protection of property rights is weak. The U.S. Trade Representative reports that "poorly enforced property rights and the resulting proliferation of property disputes are among the most serious barriers to investment in Nicaragua." According to the Economist Intelligence Unit, "The judiciary remains politicised, corrupt and ineffective in resolving property and other disputes."

REGULATION
Score: 4–Stable (high level)

The government has established a "single-window for investment" in an attempt to streamline the bureaucracy, but the U.S. Department of Commerce reports that the "legal and regulatory framework remains cumbersome. The rules are not fully transparent, and much business is still conducted on a 'who you know' basis…. Although the 1997 tax law eliminated many special tax exonerations, investors still express frustration at a high level of discretion and overcentralized decision making in taxation and customs procedures." According to the Economist Intelligence Unit, employees are entitled to generous fringe benefits. Both the Economist Intelligence Unit and the U.S. Department of Commerce have characterized corruption as pervasive.

INFORMAL MARKET
Score: 4–Stable (high level of activity)

Transparency International's 2004 score for Nicaragua is 2.7. Therefore, Nicaragua's informal market score is 4 this year

NIGER

Rank: 115

Score: 3.38

Category: Mostly Unfree

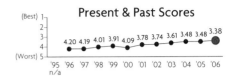

Present & Past Scores

(Best) 1
2
3 4.20 4.19 4.01 3.91 4.09 3.78 3.74 3.61 3.48 3.48 3.38
4
(Worst) 5
'95 '96 '97 '98 '99 '00 '01 '02 '03 '04 '05 '06
n/a

Niger has recovered from the instability created by coups in 1996 and 1999. Mamadou Tandja, first elected president in 1999, was re-elected in 2004 in free and fair elections. More than 80 percent of the population is engaged in subsistence farming and herding. Per capita income is very low, and informal markets are common. Ongoing concerns, such as deforestation, desertification, and poverty, were exacerbated by drought and locusts in 2004 and have led to severe food shortages. The Tandja government negotiated a new International Monetary Fund arrangement committing it to deficit reduction through increased taxation, privatization, and public-sector reform. An effort to increase revenues by extending the value-added tax (VAT) to basic foodstuffs and utilities resulted in protests. After efforts to suppress the protests, the government agreed to lift the VAT on flour and milk but raised it for electricity and water consumption. Uranium, livestock, onions, and cowpeas are the principal exports. Landlocked Niger has strong economic ties with its neighbors, particularly Nigeria, which serves as a key trading partner and conduit to international markets. Niger's informal market score is 1 point better this year. As a result, its overall score is 0.1 point better this year.

QUICK STUDY

SCORES

Trade Policy	4.5
Fiscal Burden	4.3
Government Intervention	3
Monetary Policy	1
Foreign Investment	3
Banking and Finance	3
Wages and Prices	3
Property Rights	4
Regulation	4
Informal Market	4

Population: 11,762,000

Total area: 1,267,000 sq. km

GDP: $2.1 billion

GDP growth rate: 5.3%

GDP per capita: $178

Major exports: uranium ore, livestock

Exports of goods and services: $437 million

Major export trading partners: France 42.3%, Nigeria 28.7%, Japan 17.2%, Spain 4.6%

Major imports: consumer goods, machinery, petroleum

Imports of goods and services: $688 million

Major import trading partners: France 16.4%, Ivory Coast 13.9%, China 10.5%, Nigeria 7.7%, US 5.5%

Foreign direct investment (net): $30.9 million

2003 Data (in constant 2000 US dollars)

TRADE POLICY
Score: **4.5**–Stable (very high level of protectionism)

Niger is a member of the West African Economic and Monetary Union (WAEMU). The World Bank reports that Niger's weighted average tariff rate in 2004 was 13.7 percent, down from the 14.1 percent in 2002 reported in the 2005 *Index*, based on World Bank data. According to the U.S. Department of Commerce, "Importing companies must have a business certificate issued by the Ministry of Commerce and a certificate of payment of dues from both the Chamber of Commerce and the Nigerien Counsel of Public Transportation.... All companies must be listed in the trade and employers registries and possess business and import licenses." In addition, "To import the following goods requires further special authorization from the Ministry of Commerce: petroleum products, metal containers, sheet metal, bottled carbonated drinks and lemonade, bottled beer, wax print cotton cloth, paint primer (lime), soap, and non-alcohol based perfume." Corruption is common, and the bureaucratic process is inefficient. Based on the revised trade factor methodology, Niger's trade policy score is unchanged.

FISCAL BURDEN OF GOVERNMENT
Score—Income Taxation: **4.5**–Stable (very high tax rates)
Score—Corporate Taxation: **5**–Worse (very high tax rates)
Score—Change in Government Expenditures: **2.5**–Better (low decrease)
Final Score: **4.3**–Stable (high cost of government)

The International Monetary Fund reports that Niger's top income tax rate is 45 percent. According to Deloitte, the top corporate tax rate is 40 percent, up from the 35 percent reported in the 2005 *Index*. In 2003, according to the African Development Bank, government expenditures as a share of GDP decreased by 1 percentage point to 17.4 percent, compared to the 1.7 percentage point increase in 2002.

GOVERNMENT INTERVENTION IN THE ECONOMY
Score: **3**–Stable (moderate level)

The World Bank reports that the government consumed 11.3 percent of GDP in 2003. In the

303

same year, based on data from the International Monetary Fund, Niger received 1.86 percent of its total revenues from state-owned enterprises and government ownership of property. According to the U.S. Department of Commerce, however, "Several industrial enterprises are para-statals wholly or partially owned by the government." The Economist Intelligence Unit reports that "the public sector...is the only significant formal employer...." The government still owns the electricity utility, the company importing petroleum products, and a hotel, as well as three financial institutions and the postal service. Based on the apparent unreliability of official figures on revenues from state-owned enterprises, 1 point has been added to Niger's government intervention score.

MONETARY POLICY
Score: **1**–Stable (very low level of inflation)

As a member of the West African Economic and Monetary Union, Niger uses the CFA franc, pegged to the euro. From 1995 to 2004, Niger's weighted average annual rate of inflation was 0.18 percent.

CAPITAL FLOWS AND FOREIGN INVESTMENT
Score: **3**–Stable (moderate barriers)

Niger does not screen foreign investment and grants national treatment to foreign investors. "Total foreign ownership is permitted in all sectors except those few restricted for national security purposes," reports the U.S. Department of Commerce. "[O]wnership of land is permitted, but requires authorization.... Barriers to investment include the small scale of the economy, limited buying power, and low rates of capital accumulation. In addition, transportation costs are high and the government bureaucracy can be cumbersome and slow." The International Monetary Fund reports that residents may hold foreign exchange accounts, subject to some restrictions, with the approval of the government and the Central Bank of West African States, or BCEAO, and that non-residents may hold them with BCEAO approval. Payments and transfers to countries other than France, Monaco, members of the Central African Economic and Monetary Community, members of the WAEMU, and Comoros are subject to quantitative limits and approval in some cases. Some capital transactions to countries other than members of the WAEMU are subject to authorization. Real estate purchases by non-residents must be declared to the government prior to purchase.

BANKING AND FINANCE
Score: **3**–Stable (moderate level of restrictions)

The BCEAO, a central bank common to the eight members of the WAEMU, governs Niger's banking system. The banking system remains underdeveloped, and credit is difficult to obtain. "As of September 2004," reports First Initiative, "four commercial banks were in operation, however banks have a high percentage of non-performing loans and banking services are limited in their reach. There are over 160 micro-finance institutions, however there is little organization and co-operation,

limiting their potential reach to rural areas." According to the Economist Intelligence Unit, "To mobilise savings for domestic investment, there are plans for reforms in the financial sector, including the privatisation of a number of state-owned banks.... Financial sector reforms include completing the restructuring and possible privatisation of three institutions in which the government is the majority shareholder: Crédit du Niger, Caisse de prêts aux collectivités territoriales and Office national de la poste et de l'épargne." Although the government is involved in the financial system, private banks and foreign banks operate freely and account for most bank resources and deposits.

WAGES AND PRICES
Score: **3**–Stable (moderate level of intervention)

"With the exception of petroleum products," reports the U.S. Department of Commerce, "prices are set by market forces, not by the government. For petroleum products, prices are set by the Ministry of Commerce and are [a] function of world market prices and the US dollar exchange rate." The government also sets rates for the state-owned utilities. Minimum wages for salaried workers differ by sector, and Niger's large public sector affects wages and prices.

PROPERTY RIGHTS
Score: **4**–Stable (low level of protection)

The Economist Intelligence Unit reports that "Niger's judicial system is under resourced and, as a result, is subject to pressure from the executive and other influences. Delays in bringing people to trial often result in long periods of pre-trial confinement. Political interference in judicial affairs is rife. Corruption is pervasive, partly fuelled by low salaries and inadequate training programmes." According to the U.S. Department of State, "Judges sometimes feared reassignment or having their financial benefits reduced if they rendered a decision unfavorable to the government...."

REGULATION
Score: **4**–Stable (high level)

According to the Economist Intelligence Unit, "Public administration in Niger is under resourced, largely inefficient and a drain on state resources. Cutting the bloated bureaucracy is an enormous challenge, as it involves politically sensitive changes including civil-service reform and privatisation. There is a lack of transparency and financial malpractice is deeply rooted at all levels of public administration." The U.S. Department of Commerce reports that "investors should be prepared for delays caused by the process of acquiring inter-ministerial approvals." Corruption is an admitted problem.

INFORMAL MARKET
Score: **4**–Better (high level of activity)

Transparency International's 2004 score for Niger is 2.2. Therefore, Niger's informal market score is 4 this year—1 point better than last year.

NIGERIA

Rank: 146

Score: 4.00

Category: Repressed

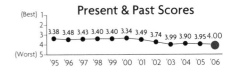

Present & Past Scores

(Best) 1
2
3 3.38 3.48 3.43 3.40 3.40 3.34 3.49 3.74 3.99 3.90 3.95 4.00
4
(Worst) 5
'95 '96 '97 '98 '99 '00 '01 '02 '03 '04 '05 '06

QUICK STUDY

SCORES

Trade Policy	5
Fiscal Burden	3
Government Intervention	4.5
Monetary Policy	4
Foreign Investment	4
Banking and Finance	4
Wages and Prices	3
Property Rights	4
Regulation	4
Informal Market	4.5

Population: 136,460,000

Total area: 923,768 sq. km

GDP: $48.8 billion

GDP growth rate: 10.7%

GDP per capita: $357

Major exports: petroleum, cocoa, rubber

Exports of goods and services: $25.3 billion

Major export trading partners: US 38.3%, India 9.9%, Brazil 6.8%, Spain 6.2%, France 5.6%

Major imports: machinery and transport, chemicals, food and live animals

Imports of goods and services: $21.6 billion

Major import trading partners: US 15.5%, UK 9.5%, Germany 7.3%, China 7.1%

Foreign direct investment (net): $1.04 billion

2003 Data (in constant 2000 US dollars)

President Olusegun Obasanjo won re-election in April 2003, and his People's Democratic Party won 70 percent of the legislative seats and 75 percent of the governorships, in elections that were marred by political violence, fraud, and other irregularities. Nigeria has Africa's largest population, estimated at over 130 million, including 250 ethnic groups and the continent's second-largest Muslim population. Ethnic and religious violence is increasingly common. Obasanjo has assembled a reform-minded team to implement an economic plan focused on reducing government involvement in the economy through privatization and deregulation. The pace of reform has been slow, however, because vested interests continue to block significant change. Per capita income remains low, and corruption, poor infrastructure, and periodic labor strikes undermine economic growth and investment. Most of the population is engaged in small-scale farming, which accounts for over one-third of formal-sector GDP. The oil sector also accounts for about one-third of annual GDP but provides over 70 percent of federal government revenues and 90 percent of exports. Despite stronger efforts to hold government officials accountable for illicit activities, corruption remains common at all levels of government and in the judiciary. Much economic activity is carried on in the informal sector. Nigeria's government intervention score is 0.5 point worse this year. As a result, its overall score is 0.05 point worse this year, causing Nigeria to be classified as a "repressed" country.

TRADE POLICY
Score: **5**–Stable (very high level of protectionism)

The World Bank reports that Nigeria's weighted average tariff rate in 2002 (the most recent year for which World Bank data are available) was 16.9 percent. (The World Bank has revised the figure for 2002 upward from the 15.8 percent reported in the 2005 *Index*). According to the U.S. Trade Representative, "Importers face long clearance procedures, high berthing and unloading costs, erratic application of customs regulations, and corruption…. High tariffs and uneven application of import and labeling regulations make importing high-value perishable products into Nigeria difficult." Nigeria also bans imports of numerous items, including "sorghum, millet, wheat flour, cassava, frozen meat and poultry products, vegetable oil (in bulk), biscuits, pasta, bottled water, fruit juice in retail packs, cookies, confectionery and chocolate products, beer, kaolin, gypsum, mosquito repellent coils, printed fabrics, used clothing, cars more than eight years old, and bagged cement…men's footwear, leather bags and plastic bags (excluding ladies purses), all textiles and yarn, furniture, toothpaste, household plastic ware, soap and detergents, fresh and plastic flowers, and fresh fruits." Based on the revised trade factor methodology, Nigeria's trade policy score is unchanged.

FISCAL BURDEN OF GOVERNMENT
Score—Income Taxation: **2.5**–Stable (moderate tax rates)
Score—Corporate Taxation: **4**–Stable (high tax rates)
Score—Change in Government Expenditures: **1.5**–Stable (high decrease)
Final Score: **3**–Stable (moderate cost of government)

The International Monetary Fund reports that Nigeria's top income tax rate is 25 percent. The corporate tax rate is 30 percent. In 2003, according to the African Development Bank, government expenditures as a share of GDP decreased 3.5 percentage points to 37.9 percent, compared to the 9.2 percentage point increase in 2002.

GOVERNMENT INTERVENTION IN THE ECONOMY
Score: **4.5**–Worse (very high level)

The World Bank reports that the government consumed 23.3 percent of GDP in 2003. In the same year, based on data from the International Monetary Fund, Nigeria received 51.51 percent of its total revenues from state-owned enterprises and government ownership of property in the oil sector, up from the 36.15 percent reported in the 2005 *Index*. As a result, Nigeria's government intervention score is 0.5 point worse this year.

MONETARY POLICY
Score: **4**–Stable (high level of inflation)

From 1995 to 2004, Nigeria's weighted average annual rate of inflation was 14.48 percent.

CAPITAL FLOWS AND FOREIGN INVESTMENT
Score: **4**–Stable (high barriers)

Nigeria's government updated its investment code in 1995 to allow 100 percent foreign ownership in every industry with the exception of petroleum and national security industries. According to the U.S. Trade Representative, "Despite efforts to improve the country's investment climate, disincentives to investing in Nigeria continue to plague foreign entrepreneurs. Potential investors must contend with poor infrastructure, complex tax administration procedures, confusing land ownership laws, arbitrary application of regulations, corruption, and extensive crime. The sanctity of contracts is often violated, and Nigeria's court system for settling commercial disputes is weak and sometimes biased." The International Monetary Fund reports that residents and non-residents may hold foreign exchange accounts. Some capital transactions are subject to documentation requirements and restrictions. Most payments and transfers must be conducted through banks.

BANKING AND FINANCE
Score: **4**–Stable (high level of restrictions)

"The banking sector, which includes 90 commercial and merchant banks as of 2004, is the largest part of Nigeria's financial system," reports First Initiative. "A large number of Nigeria's banks are subsidiaries of foreign banks, particularly European banks, and the ten largest banks account for over 50 percent of banking assets…. The insurance sector…is comprised of 118 insurance firms, including the state owned NICON Insurance Corporation and Nigerian Reinsurance Corporation." Nigeria also has over 700 community banks focusing on microfinance lending and six development banks. According to the U.S. Department of Commerce, "The Central Bank of Nigeria's end-March 2004 assessment of the banking industry revealed that of the 89 banks, 62 were classified sound and satisfactory, 14 as marginal, 11 as unsound and two could not be assessed because they did not render returns for the period." Foreign banks must acquire licenses from the central bank in order to operate. According to the Economist Intelligence Unit, "A

few intrepid foreign banks operate subsidiaries, and a number of others hold important minority stakes in domestic institutions." The government maintains ownership of the Bank of Industry and the Nigerian Agricultural and Rural Development Bank. It also affects the allocation of credit. Under the Small Medium Industries Equity Investment Scheme (SMIEIS), banks must deposit 10 percent of their profit after tax to fund SMIEIS loan programs. In 2000, Nigeria introduced universal banking, which allows banks to engage in money market activities, capital market activities, and insurance services.

WAGES AND PRICES
Score: **3**–Stable (moderate level of intervention)

According to the Economist Intelligence Unit, "There are no price-control laws for manufactured goods and products, but the government still regulates domestic fuel prices…[and] regulates the price of domestic air travel." The government also influences prices through several state-owned enterprises. Nigeria has a minimum wage.

PROPERTY RIGHTS
Score: **4**–Stable (low level of protection)

The Economist Intelligence Unit reports that Nigeria's "judicial system is still deeply undermined by corruption and hugely underfunded, resulting in poor administration and long delays in the hearing of cases. Contractual agreements are recognised, but trials can last more than two years, and the appeals process can drag on for more than four years." According to the U.S. Department of Commerce, "Several factors undermine effective enforcement [of judgements]: the severe lack of available court facilities; hand-written judgements and the lack of computerized systems to facilitate document processing; the arbitrary adjournment of court sessions due to power outages; and easily corrupted court officials and judges. In some instances, decrees have been promulgated and backdated to circumvent court rulings."

REGULATION
Score: **4**–Stable (high level)

The Economist Intelligence Unit describes Nigeria's civil service as "bloated, corrupt and inefficient." According to the U.S. Department of Commerce, "The primary problem regarding Nigeria's regulatory system is lax and uneven enforcement." In addition, "Multiple taxes are a problem for businesses at state and local levels…. [C]orruption is an endemic problem… and permeates all aspects of society, despite laws and penalties on the books. Foreign investors are convenient targets for extortion, bribery, and other corruptive acts since they are viewed as both relatively easy to coerce and profitable."

INFORMAL MARKET
Score: **4.5**–Stable (very high level of activity)

Transparency International's 2004 score for Nigeria is 1.6. Therefore, Nigeria's informal market score is 4.5 this year.

NORWAY

Rank: 30

Score: 2.29

Category: Mostly Free

Present & Past Scores

(Best) 1
2
3 2.44 2.44 2.28 2.28 2.25 2.44 2.40 2.28 2.35 2.33 2.29
4
(Worst) 5

'95 '96 '97 '98 '99 '00 '01 '02 '03 '04 '05 '06
n/a

QUICK STUDY

SCORES

Trade Policy 2
Fiscal Burden 3.4
Government Intervention 3.5
Monetary Policy 1
Foreign Investment 3
Banking and Finance 3
Wages and Prices 2
Property Rights 1
Regulation 3
Informal Market 1

Population: 4,562,000

Total area: 324,220 sq. km

GDP: $179.1 billion

GDP growth rate: 2.9%

GDP per capita: $39,259

Major exports: crude oil, natural gas and refined petroleum products, machinery, food, beverages and tobacco

Exports of goods and services: $76.4 billion

Major export trading partners: Sweden 12.6%, Germany 11.4%, UK 10.5%, US 8.4%, Denmark 6.1%

Major imports: machinery and transport equipment, chemicals, food, beverages and tobacco

Imports of goods and services: $66.3 billion

Major import trading partners: Sweden 16.0%, Germany 13.8%, Denmark 7.5%, UK 6.6%, US 4.9%

Foreign direct investment (net): $271 million

2004 Data (in constant 2000 US dollars)

Norway is an advanced, oil-rich country with a mixed economy that combines public and private ownership. Abundant oil and natural gas resources give it one of the world's most financially healthy economies and account for a large foreign trade surplus. Although Norway is not a member of the European Union, it has a close trade relationship with EU members through the European Economic Area (EEA) agreement. With the exception of a highly protected agricultural sector, Norway implements most of the obligations of EU members as an EEA signatory. Norwegians enjoy high living standards because of the wealth derived from the oil industry. The country's large welfare state provides many welfare programs that are subsidized by high taxes and oil revenues. The private sector, especially traditional manufacturing, has faced increasingly tough international competition that has led to calls for private-sector wage restraint. According to the Economist Intelligence Unit, Norway's business environment is still shackled by "an excessively regulated labor market, high labor costs and limited market opportunity." Pension reform is one of the foremost issues facing the government. Norway's fiscal burden of government score is 0.4 point better this year. As a result, its overall score is 0.04 point better this year.

TRADE POLICY
Score: **2–Stable** (low level of protectionism)

The World Bank reports that Norway's weighted average tariff rate in 2004 was 0.4 percent, down from the 0.7 percent for 2002 reported in the 2005 *Index*, based on World Bank data. According to the World Trade Organization, "Norway requires import licences for surveillance and quota management purposes. Non-automatic licences are maintained to administer 60 tariff quotas on agricultural products, including minimum access quotas, other global quotas, and bilateral quotas.... Norway requires export licences for arms and other strategic goods and minke whale products." Based on the revised trade factor methodology, Norway's trade policy score is unchanged.

FISCAL BURDEN OF GOVERNMENT
Score—Income Taxation: **4.5–Stable** (high tax rates)
Score—Corporate Taxation: **3.5–Stable** (high tax rates)
Score—Change in Government Expenditures: **2–Better** (moderate decrease)
Final Score: **3.4–Better** (moderate cost of government)

Norway's top income tax rate is 47.5 percent (a 28 percent standard tax rate plus a 19.5 percentage point surtax on incomes above NOK 872,000). The top corporate tax rate is 28 percent. In 2004, government expenditures as a share of GDP decreased 2.3 percentage points to 46.6 percent, compared to the 1.4 percentage point increase in 2003. On net, Norway's fiscal burden of government score is 0.4 point better this year.

GOVERNMENT INTERVENTION IN THE ECONOMY
Score: **3.5–Stable** (high level)

Based on data from Norway's National Statistics, the government consumed 22 percent of GDP in 2004. In the same year, based on data from the same source, Norway received 15.4 percent of its total revenues from state-owned enterprises and government ownership of property.

MONETARY POLICY
Score: **1**–Stable (very low level of inflation)

From 1995 to 2004, Norway's weighted average annual rate of inflation was 1.13 percent.

CAPITAL FLOWS AND FOREIGN INVESTMENT
Score: **3**–Stable (moderate barriers)

In 1995, Norway adopted European Economic Area rules guaranteeing national treatment for foreign investors and liberalizing regulations that constrain foreign investment in industrial companies. The U.S. Trade Representative reports that the government still restricts investment in certain sectors, including sectors in which the government has a monopoly, "financial services, mining, hydropower, property acquisition, and areas considered politically sensitive." The World Trade Organization reports nationality restrictions on activities and ownership in the fishing and maritime transport sectors. According to the U.S. Department of Commerce, "While the Norwegian government officially endorses a level playing field for foreign investors, existing regulations, standards and practices often marginally favor Norwegian, Scandinavian and EEA investors, in that order." The International Monetary Fund reports that both residents and non-residents may hold foreign exchange accounts. There are no restrictions on payments, transfers, or repatriation of profits.

BANKING AND FINANCE
Score: **3**–Stable (moderate level of restrictions)

Norway's banking system is composed of 15 commercial banks, 129 savings banks, and some specialized state-owned banks. "In 2003, Norway repealed a requirement that an investor—foreign or domestic—obtain permission from the Ministry of Finance before purchasing more than 10 percent of the equity of a Norwegian financial institution," reports the U.S. Department of Commerce. "Current regulations require that the Norwegian Financial Supervisory Authority grant permission for ownership levels that exceed certain thresholds.... The Authority applies national treatment to non-bank foreign financial groups and institutions, but applies nationality restrictions to bank ownership. At least half the members of the board and half the members of the corporate assembly of a financial institution must be nationals and permanent residents of Norway or another EEA nation. Effective January 1, 2005, there will be no ceiling on foreign equity in a Norwegian financial institution, provided the Authority has granted a concession." The government has reduced its holdings in Norway's two largest banks and has sold its stake in the third largest to private investors. The Economist Intelligence Unit reports that after the merger of Den norske Bank and Gjensidige NOR in November 2003, the government's stake fell from 47.8 percent in DNB to 34 percent in the merged bank. According to the U.S. Department of Commerce, "There are special banks for fisheries, agriculture, shipping, industry, house building, and export finance. The State, to varying degrees, participates in all of these."

WAGES AND PRICES
Score: **2**–Stable (low level of intervention)

The government exercises indirect control over some wages and prices. "Indirect price controls and price fixing exist in several industries," reports the Economist Intelligence Unit. "Besides the oil-sector cases...the government has defended the right of utilities to practice price discrimination and to refuse to sell power outside of their distribution areas." In addition, "There is also a central purchasing agency for whale meat, in Lofoten, which sets non-negotiable prices for suppliers and has exclusive rights to sell the meat." The Embassy of Norway reports that the government regulates the price of prescription drugs and subsidizes agricultural goods. There is no legislated minimum wage.

PROPERTY RIGHTS
Score: **1**–Stable (very high level of protection)

Private property is safe from expropriation. The Economist Intelligence Unit reports that "contractual agreements are secure, with solid legal basis, and Norwegians generally place a high value on meeting these obligations. The civil service and the Judiciary are both of high quality...."

REGULATION
Score: **3**–Stable (moderate level)

The U.S. Department of Commerce reports that "Norway's market, with the notable exception of agricultural products and ancillary processed foods, is transparent and quite open...although there are stringent regulations for chemicals and foodstuffs." The pharmaceutical industry is probably the most heavily regulated. According to the U.S. Department of Commerce, pharmacies have been highly regulated, and despite a 2001 law to increase competition, 78 percent of the market is dominated by monopolies that are protected by outdated laws and regulations. Building permits are subject to considerable government oversight and can take some time to approve. Environmental laws are set in line with European Union standards. When key sectors like the oil and gas industry and transportation are threatened by strikes, the government imposes mandatory wage mediation.

INFORMAL MARKET
Score: **1**–Stable (very low level of activity)

Transparency International's 2004 score for Norway is 8.9. Therefore, Norway's informal market score is 1 this year.

OMAN

Rank: 74

Score: 3.01

Category: Mostly Unfree

Present & Past Scores

(Best) 1 — 2 — 3 — 4 — (Worst) 5

2.70 2.85 2.79 2.74 2.85 2.93 2.65 2.63 2.70 2.75 2.81 3.01

'95 '96 '97 '98 '99 '00 '01 '02 '03 '04 '05 '06

2003 Data (in constant 2000 US dollars)

QUICK STUDY

SCORES

Trade Policy	4.5
Fiscal Burden	1.6
Government Intervention	4.5
Monetary Policy	1
Foreign Investment	3
Banking and Finance	3
Wages and Prices	4
Property Rights	3
Regulation	3
Informal Market	2.5

Population: 2,599,000

Total area: 212,460 sq. km

GDP: $20.5 billion

GDP growth rate: 1.9%

GDP per capita: $7,876

Major exports: oil, metals, fish, textiles

Exports of goods (fob): $10.9 billion

Major export trading partners: South Korea 18.7%, China 18.5%, Japan 16.2%, Thailand 12.2%

Major imports: machinery and electrical equipment, food, beverages and tobacco

Imports of goods (fob): $5.8 billion

Major import trading partners: United Arab Emirates 21.6%, Japan 17.1%, US 6.2%, UK 5.7%

Foreign direct investment (net): $131 million

The Sultanate of Oman, an absolute monarchy ruled by the Al Said family since the middle of the 18th century, has sought in recent years to modernize its oil-dominated economy without diluting the ruling family's power. The country has escaped the political violence that has recently troubled some of its neighbors, although in January 2005 nearly 100 Islamists suspected of trying to overthrow the state were arrested. Additionally, the heirless Sultan's refusal to designate a successor has created political uncertainty. Oman is a relatively small oil producer, and production has declined steadily since 2001. The strength of international oil prices has offset the decline in oil production, which was expected to continue falling in 2005 before rising again in 2006. The government has made economic diversification a priority and seeks to expand natural gas exports and develop gas-based industries. It has encouraged foreign investment in the petrochemical, electrical power, telecommunications, and other industries and is preparing for the privatization of Omantel, the state-owned telecommunications monopoly. Unemployment remains dangerously high, leading the government to place a high priority on "Omanization," or the replacement of foreign workers with local staff. Oman's trade policy score is 1.5 points worse this year, and its informal market score is 0.5 point worse. As a result, its overall score is 0.2 point worse this year, causing Oman to be classified as a "mostly unfree" country.

TRADE POLICY
Score: **4.5**–Worse (very high level of protectionism)

The World Bank reports that Oman's weighted average tariff rate in 2002 (the most recent year for which World Bank data are available) was 13.6 percent. (The World Bank has revised the figure for 2002 upward from the 6.7 percent reported in the 2005 *Index*.) According to the U.S. Trade Representative, "Importation of certain classes of goods, such as alcohol, livestock, poultry and their respective products, firearms, narcotics and explosives, requires a special license, and media imports are subject to censorship…. Oman provides a 10 percent price preference to tenders that contain a high content of local goods or services." Based on the higher tariff rate, as well as a revision of the trade factor methodology, Oman's trade policy score is 1.5 points worse this year.

FISCAL BURDEN OF GOVERNMENT
Score—Income Taxation: **1**–Stable (very low tax rates)
Score—Corporate Taxation: **1**–Stable (very low tax rates)
Score—Change in Government Expenditures: **3.5**–Stable (low increase)
Final Score: **1.6**–Stable (low cost of government)

Oman imposes no income taxes on individuals. The top corporate tax rate is 12 percent. In 2003, according to the central bank, government expenditures as a share of GDP increased 0.7 percentage point to 38.3 percent, compared to a 0.3 percentage point increase in 2002.

GOVERNMENT INTERVENTION IN THE ECONOMY
Score: **4.5**–Stable (very high level)

Based on data from the International Monetary Fund, the government consumed 22.2 percent of GDP in 2003. In the same year, based on data from the central bank, Oman received 70.13

309

percent of its total revenues from state-owned enterprises and government ownership of property in the oil sector.

MONETARY POLICY
Score: **1**–Stable (very low level of inflation)

From 1995 to 2004, Oman's weighted average annual rate of inflation was 0.03 percent.

CAPITAL FLOWS AND FOREIGN INVESTMENT
Score: **3**–Stable (moderate barriers)

When Oman became a member of the World Trade Organization, it adopted a policy of automatic approval of majority foreign ownership up to 70 percent; foreign ownership above 70 percent is allowed with Minister of Commerce and Industry approval. "In September 2003," reports the U.S. Trade Representative, "Oman amended its tax law and extended the national tax treatment (i.e., a corporate tax rate of 12 percent) to all Omani and [Gulf Cooperation Council] companies regardless of the percentage of foreign ownership. Taxes on branches of foreign-owned companies remained at 30 percent…. Oman now permits 100 percent foreign-ownership on a case-by-case basis with the approval of the Minister of Commerce and Industry, although only a handful of companies have taken advantage of this opportunity." The official "Omanization" requirement that only Omanis may work in specified occupational categories is an impediment to foreign investment. According to the U.S. Department of Commerce, "the approval process for establishing a business can be tedious, particularly with respect to land acquisition and labor requirements." Both residents and non-residents may hold foreign exchange accounts. Restrictions on payments, transactions, and transfers generally apply only to Israel. Non-residents are generally not permitted to own land, but exceptions apply to citizens of Gulf Cooperation Council countries.

BANKING AND FINANCE
Score: **3**–Stable (moderate level of restrictions)

Oman's banking sector consists of 14 domestic and foreign commercial banks and three specialized banks, which provide housing and industrial loans to Omani citizens at favorable terms. The Economist Intelligence Unit reports that five of these 14 banks are domestic and that nine are foreign branches. According to the U.S. Department of Commerce, "The [Central Bank of Oman] recently raised its minimum capital requirements, forcing several bank mergers…. Foreign banks find onerous CBO requirements to maintain a 12 percent level of capital adequacy and restrict consumer lending to 42.5% percent of the loan portfolio." The central bank also imposes a maximum interest rate that can be paid to depositors. The EIU reports that a 2000 banking law limited investments in foreign securities, raised capital requirements, and granted the central bank the authority to reject candidates for senior positions in commercial banks. Unlike many other equity markets in the region, the Muscat Securities Market is open to foreign investors.

WAGES AND PRICES
Score: **4**–Stable (high level of intervention)

The government controls the price of many goods and services through subsidies and free services. The Economist Intelligence Unit reports that "continuing price controls on electricity and water contribute to the low inflationary environment." The government also controls the prices of some commodities and affects prices through state-owned monopolies. "In all other areas [of the consumer price index]," reports the EIU, "prices either fell or were unchanged, in many cases (such as electricity) because government-set prices remained fixed." Oman has a minimum wage.

PROPERTY RIGHTS
Score: **3**–Stable (moderate level of protection)

The threat of expropriation is low, although the judiciary is subject to political influence. "The ultimate adjudicator of business disputes within Oman," reports the U.S. Department of Commerce, "is the Commercial Court, which was reorganized in mid-1997 from the former Authority for Settlement of Commercial Disputes (ASCD)…. There have been complaints that powerful businessmen utilized their connections to secure an unfair advantage in ASCD rulings."

REGULATION
Score: **3**–Stable (moderate level)

The U.S. Department of Commerce describes Oman's regulatory system as "not always transparent and sometimes contradictory…. [T]here is no complete body of regulations codifying Omani labor and tax laws and many government decisions are made on an ad hoc basis." The system can be characterized by red tape, confusion, and considerable delay, as the private sector must run a gantlet of government ministries to win approval for business plans. The labor laws, which enforce the "Omanization" requirement that private-sector firms meet quotas for hiring native Omani workers, are similarly burdensome.

INFORMAL MARKET
Score: **2.5**–Worse (moderate level of activity)

Transparency International's 2004 score for Oman is 6.1. Therefore, Oman's informal market score is 2.5 this year—0.5 point worse than last year.

PAKISTAN

Rank: 110

Score: 3.33

Category: Mostly Unfree

Present & Past Scores

(Best) 1
2
3 — 3.34 3.26 3.29 3.31 3.50 3.50 3.50 3.49 3.44 3.35 3.73 3.33
4
(Worst) 5
'95 '96 '97 '98 '99 '00 '01 '02 '03 '04 '05 '06

QUICK STUDY

SCORES

Trade Policy	4.5
Fiscal Burden	4.3
Government Intervention	2.5
Monetary Policy	2
Foreign Investment	3
Banking and Finance	3
Wages and Prices	3
Property Rights	4
Regulation	3
Informal Market	4

Population: 148,438,000

Total area: 803,940 sq. km

GDP: $81.1 billion

GDP growth rate: 5.1%

GDP per capita: $546

Major exports: textiles, cotton (fabrics and yarn), rice, chemicals, manufactures

Exports of goods and services: $15.7 billion

Major export trading partners: US 23.1%, United Arab Emirates 9.4%, UK 7.1%, Germany 5.1%, Hong Kong 4.6%

Major imports: machinery, chemicals, minerals, fuels

Imports of goods and services: $12.7 billion

Major import trading partners: United Arab Emirates 11.2%, Saudi Arabia 10.9%, China 7.3%, Japan 6.6%, US 6.0%

Foreign direct investment (net): $1.3 billion

2003 Data (in constant 2000 US dollars)

Pakistan gained its independence from Great Britain in 1947 and has fought three major wars against India, including the 1971 war in which Bangladesh seceded. The Pakistani economy has been hampered by heavy state involvement, widespread corruption, political instability, and chronic tensions with India. President Pervez Musharraf has committed his government to cautious political and economic reform. After 2001, Musharraf's swift abandonment of Pakistan's Taliban allies and cooperation in the war against al-Qaeda paid large economic dividends in the form of a major U.S. aid package, the dropping of U.S. economic sanctions imposed because of Pakistan's nuclear program, the rescheduling of Pakistan's large foreign debt, and increased economic aid from international organizations. The Musharraf government's substantial economic reforms have helped to spur growth, particularly in industrial production, and have left the economy less dependent on agriculture. The privatization program, announced in 2003, picked up momentum in 2005 with the privatization of some of the country's most prominent public-sector companies, including Pak Arab Fertilizer and portions of Pakistan Telecom, the state communications monopoly. Pakistan's trade policy and government intervention scores are 0.5 point better this year, and its capital flows and foreign investment score, banking and finance score, and wages and prices score are 1 point better. As a result, Pakistan's overall score is 0.4 point better this year.

TRADE POLICY
Score: **4.5**–Better (very high level of protectionism)

The World Bank reports that Pakistan's weighted average tariff rate in 2004 was 13 percent, down from the 15.2 percent for 2002 reported in the 2005 *Index*, based on World Bank data. According to the U.S. Trade Representative, Pakistan "continued to ban the import of 30 items, mostly on religious, environmental, security, and health grounds." The USTR also reports local content requirements. Based on the lower tariff rate, as well as a revision of the trade factor methodology, Pakistan's trade policy score is 0.5 point better this year.

FISCAL BURDEN OF GOVERNMENT
Score—Income Taxation: **3.5**–Stable (high tax rates)
Score—Corporate Taxation: **5**–Stable (very high tax rates)
Score—Change in Government Expenditures: **3.5**–Stable (low increase)
Final Score: **4.3**–Stable (high cost of government)

According to Deloitte, Pakistan's top income tax rate is 35 percent. The top corporate tax rate is 39 percent, down from 41 percent. In 2003, according to the Asian Development Bank, government expenditures as a share of GDP increased 0.2 percentage point to 18.7 percent, compared to the 0.9 percentage point increase in 2002.

GOVERNMENT INTERVENTION IN THE ECONOMY
Score: **2.5**–Better (moderate level)

The World Bank reports that the government consumed 11.7 percent of GDP in 2003. In fiscal year July 2003–June 2004, according to the Ministry of Finance, Pakistan received 9.4 percent of its total revenues from state-owned enterprises and government ownership of property, down from the 11.78 percent reported in the 2005 *Index*. As a result, Pakistan's government intervention score is 0.5 point better this year.

311

MONETARY POLICY
Score: **2**–Stable (low level of inflation)

From 1995 to 2004, Pakistan's weighted average annual rate of inflation was 5.85 percent.

CAPITAL FLOWS AND FOREIGN INVESTMENT
Score: **3**–Better (moderate barriers)

Foreign investors are permitted to own 100 percent of most businesses. According to the U.S. Trade Representative, the only formal restrictions on foreign investment involve "arms and munitions, high explosives, currency/mint operations, radioactive substances, and new nonindustrial alcohol plants." The USTR also reports that Pakistan requires a minimum initial investment in agriculture, infrastructure, and social services; maintains local content requirements for 16 items in the auto and motorcycle industries; and caps foreign ownership in agricultural investments at 60 percent. In addition, "Corruption and a weak judicial system remain recurrent and substantial disincentives to investment," and the "enforcement [of contracts] is difficult." The International Monetary Fund reports that foreign exchange accounts are subject to restrictions, including government approval in some cases. Payments and transfers are subject to approval, quantitative limits, and other restrictions. Most capital transactions are not permitted or require government approval. Based on evidence of greater openness to foreign investment, Pakistan's capital flows and foreign investment score is 1 point better this year.

BANKING AND FINANCE
Score: **3**–Better (moderate level of restrictions)

"About 75 percent of the banking sector is now privately owned," reports First Initiative. "As of December 2003, the banking system was composed of 40 banks, six development financial institutions and two micro-finance banks. The majority of banking sector assets are held by the five largest banks, all of which were previously publicly owned. At the end of 2003, three of the largest banks had been fully privatized, one was in the process of being privatized, and one had been partially sold…. There are three government-run or owned insurance companies in the country, including the State Life Insurance Company, which controlled approximately 90% of the market in 2001. In addition, there is one state-owned re-insurer." According to the Pakistani embassy, there were seven public-sector banks in 2004—one less than in 2003 following the privatization of Habib Bank. The tax applied to banks has fallen from 47 percent in 2003 to 41 percent in 2005 and is scheduled to be reduced to 35 percent by 2007. The embassy also reports that the state no longer has a policy of directed lending. According to the U.S. Trade Representative, the government recognizes the "right to establish new banks, as well as grandfathering acquired rights of established foreign banks and foreign securities firms…[and] recently clarified that foreign investors are allowed to hold a 51 percent equity share of companies operating in the life and general insur-

ance sectors." Based on evidence of a decreasing state role in the financial sector, Pakistan's banking and finance score is 1 point better this year.

WAGES AND PRICES
Score: **3**–Better (moderate level of intervention)

According to the Economist Intelligence Unit, "Provincial and local authorities occasionally set the price of commodities perceived to be in short supply, and the government effectively fixes prices on locally manufactured goods granted tariff protection. The government fixes prices, mostly at the ex-factory stage, for certain products of state-owned firms, including cars, petroleum and public utilities. The government extends price support to farmers for certain crops (such as rice, cotton, sugarcane and wheat), and it increases imports to keep prices stable." In addition, "The government sets fuel prices, power rates and gas rates, some through government-appointed regulators…. Formal price controls for the private sector are in place only for the pharmaceutical industry." Based on a reassessment of the available data, Pakistan's wages and prices score is 1 point better this year.

PROPERTY RIGHTS
Score: **4**–Stable (low level of protection)

The Economist Intelligence Unit reports that "Pakistan's Judiciary was completely separated from the executive in mid-2001, [but] the legal system still functions poorly, hampered by ineffective implementation of laws, poor security for judges and witnesses, delays in sentencing and a huge backlog of cases." According to the U.S. Department of State, the judiciary suffers from corruption.

REGULATION
Score: **3**–Stable (moderate level)

The government has made some effort to improve Pakistan's business environment in recent years. The president has set up a commission to deregulate the economy and attract investment. The Economist Intelligence Unit reports that investors "often cite the laws on water and power, labour, food, agriculture and social security as particularly obstructive to private and foreign investment." The government is considering reforming the labor laws. According to the U.S. Department of Commerce, "Policy inconsistency, weak implementation and corruption have dampened investor interest and economic growth in Pakistan."

INFORMAL MARKET
Score: **4**–Stable (high level of activity)

Transparency International's 2004 score for Pakistan is 2.1. Therefore, Pakistan's informal market score is 4 this year.

PANAMA

Rank: 49

Score: 2.70

Category: Mostly Free

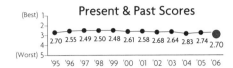

Present & Past Scores

(Best) 1
2
3
4
(Worst) 5

2.70 2.55 2.49 2.50 2.48 2.61 2.58 2.68 2.64 2.83 2.74 2.70

'95 '96 '97 '98 '99 '00 '01 '02 '03 '04 '05 '06

QUICK STUDY

SCORES

Trade Policy	3
Fiscal Burden	3.5
Government Intervention	3
Monetary Policy	1
Foreign Investment	2
Banking and Finance	2
Wages and Prices	2
Property Rights	4
Regulation	3
Informal Market	3.5

Population: 2,984,000

Total area: 78,200 sq. km

GDP: $12.4 billion

GDP growth rate: 4.1%

GDP per capita: $4,167

Major exports: bananas, shrimp, sugar, clothing

Exports of goods and services: $7.3 billion

Major export trading partners: US 13.2%, Nigeria 9.3%, Germany 7.7%, South Korea 7.4%

Major imports: capital goods, food products, oil

Imports of goods and services: $7.2 billion

Major import trading partners: Japan 33.0%, US 11.3%, China 9.0%, South Korea 7.7%, Singapore 7.1%

Foreign direct investment (net): −$173.1 million

2003 Data (in constant 2000 US dollars)

Panama's representative democracy generally respects basic human rights, promotes the rule of law, and maintains policies favorable to foreign and domestic investment, although its institutions are still subject to corruption and political manipulation. Ever since the departure of U.S. military bases and transfer of the Panama Canal, the country has been developing reverted property and investing in infrastructure. Albrook Air Force Base has reopened as a busy regional airport, and a promising City of Knowledge educational center has been established on the former Fort Clayton. Because of Panama's evolution as a transportation and trade crossroads, its service sector (76 percent of GDP in 2003) has overwhelmed manufacturing and production, leaving fewer job opportunities for less-educated citizens. In 2003, the unemployment rate was 12.8 percent, but the economy grew by 4.1 percent and tourism registered an 18 percent revenue increase. Panama's generous social security system is headed for bankruptcy in five years if left unchanged. Demonstrations erupted when President Martin Torrijos, elected in May 2004 on a fiscal reform agenda, backed draconian social security changes that would raise the retirement age and substantially increase contributions even for workers who are not eligible for benefits. Panama's fiscal burden of government score is 0.1 point worse this year; however, its government intervention score is 0.5 point better. As a result, Panama's overall score is 0.04 point better this year.

TRADE POLICY
Score: **3**–Stable (moderate level of protectionism)

The World Bank reports that Panama's weighted average tariff rate in 2001 (the most recent year for which World Bank data are available) was 6.9 percent. (The World Bank has revised the figure for 2001 upward from the 5.7 percent reported in the 2005 *Index*). According to the U.S. Trade Representative, "In addition to tariffs, all imports into Panama are subject to a 5 percent transfer (or ITBM) tax levied on the CIF value, and other handling charges.... Panama's import licensing process is often arbitrary and non-transparent, constituting a major impediment." Based on the revised trade factor methodology, Panama's trade policy score is unchanged.

FISCAL BURDEN OF GOVERNMENT
Score—Income Taxation: **3**–Stable (moderate tax rates)
Score—Corporate Taxation: **4**–Stable (high tax rates)
Score—Change in Government Expenditures: **3**–Worse (very low decrease)
Final Score: **3.5**–Worse (high cost of government)

According to Deloitte, Panama's top income tax rate is 30 percent. The top corporate tax rate is also 30 percent. In 2003, based on data from the Economist Intelligence Unit, government expenditures as a share of GDP decreased 0.5 percentage point to 25.7 percent, compared to the 2.4 percentage point increase in 2002. On net, Panama's fiscal burden of government score is 0.1 point worse this year.

GOVERNMENT INTERVENTION IN THE ECONOMY
Score: **3**–Better (moderate level)

The World Bank reports that the government consumed 10.5 percent of GDP in 2003. In the same year, based on data from the National Statistics Agency, Panama received 15.07 percent of its total revenues from state-owned enterprises and government ownership of property, down from the 22.61 percent reported in the 2005 *Index*. As a result, Panama's government intervention score is 0.5 point better this year.

 MONETARY POLICY
Score: **1**–Stable (very low level of inflation)

Panama has used the U.S. dollar as its legal tender since 1904. From 1995 and 2004, Panama's weighted average annual rate of inflation was 0.58 percent.

 CAPITAL FLOWS AND FOREIGN INVESTMENT
Score: **2**–Stable (low barriers)

Most sectors of the economy are open to foreign investment. The U.S. Trade Representative reports that "Panama maintains an open investment regime and is receptive to foreign investment…. A 1998 investment law aimed to enhance new investment…by guaranteeing that investors will have no restrictions on capital and dividend repatriation, foreign exchange use, and disposal of production inside a limited number of sectors in the economy." According to the U.S. Department of Commerce, "The [government] does impose some limitations on foreign ownership, such as in the retail and media sectors where ownership must be Panamanian. Foreign retailers, however, have been able to work within the confines of Panamanian law primarily through franchise arrangements. Some professions, such as medical practitioners, lawyers, and custom brokers, are reserved for Panamanian citizens." Foreign investors may not purchase land within 10 kilometers of a national border or on an island. Corruption in the judicial, executive, and legislative branches is a barrier to investment. The International Monetary Fund reports that both residents and non-residents may hold foreign exchange accounts; there are no restrictions or controls on payments, transactions, transfers, repatriation of profits, or capital transactions.

 BANKING AND FINANCE
Score: **2**–Stable (low level of restrictions)

Domestic banking competition is relatively high, and major banks from all over the world are represented. "As of February 2005," reports the Economist Intelligence Unit, "there were 72 banks in operation, down from 76 a year earlier. All are private institutions, except for the two state-owned banks: Banco Nacional de Panamá (BNP) and Caja de Ahorros. Of the private banks, 37 had general licences, 27 had international licences and six had representative-office licences." The EIU also reports that the state-owned Banco de Desarollo Agropecuario lends to the agriculture sector. After facing complaints from the anti–money laundering Financial Action Task Group, Panama has strengthened supervision of its banking operations and has been removed from the list of non-cooperating countries. Foreign and domestic banks are treated equally. Domestic banks are permitted to engage in a broad range of services, there are few restrictions on opening banks, and the

government exercises little control over the allocation of credit. A 1998 banking reform law further modernized the system by requiring banks to adopt international standards. The Banking Supervisory Authority (Superintendencia de Bancos) licenses and regulates banks.

 WAGES AND PRICES
Score: **2**–Stable (low level of intervention)

The market sets most wages and prices. According to the Economist Intelligence Unit, "The law limits price regulation to those where monopolistic practices can be demonstrated to do direct or imminent damage to consumers…. Price regulation is applied only to cooking gas and to medicines…. The Ministry of Housing enforces rent control on residential units built before 1984…." The government also imposes a minimum wage.

 PROPERTY RIGHTS
Score: **4**–Stable (low level of protection)

Panama's constitution provides for an independent judiciary, but the Economist Intelligence Unit reports that "Panama continues to have problems with the judiciary and civil service, which still lack independence and have traditionally been plagued with corruption and scandals." According to the U.S. Department of Commerce, "The business community generally lacks confidence in the Panamanian judicial system as an objective, independent arbiter in legal or commercial disputes, especially when the case involves powerful local figures with political influence…. The decision by investors to avoid the court system is moreover understandable, given massive case backlogs and the specter of corruption."

 REGULATION
Score: **3**–Stable (moderate level)

Regulations in Panama are generally transparent, but businesses can be hampered by red tape. According to the Economist Intelligence Unit, "Red tape and the complicated investment-registration process remain the main obstacles for…investors. Changing legal requirements and inflexible labour laws are also serious concerns for prospective investors." The U.S. Department of Commerce reports that businesses complain of the government's "arbitrariness" in assigning import permits and the time it takes the public utility regulating agency to respond to concerns or requests for information. Companies complain that corruption is an obstacle to doing business.

 INFORMAL MARKET
Score: **3.5**–Stable (high level of activity)

Transparency International's 2004 score for Panama is 3.7. Therefore, Panama's informal market score is 3.5 this year.

PARAGUAY

Rank: 109

Score: 3.31

Category: Mostly Unfree

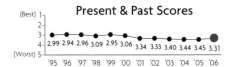

Present & Past Scores

(Best) 1
2
3
4
(Worst) 5

2.99 2.94 2.96 3.09 2.95 3.06 3.34 3.33 3.40 3.44 3.45 3.31

'95 '96 '97 '98 '99 '00 '01 '02 '03 '04 '05 '06

QUICK STUDY

SCORES

Trade Policy	3
Fiscal Burden	2.6
Government Intervention	3
Monetary Policy	3
Foreign Investment	3
Banking and Finance	3
Wages and Prices	3
Property Rights	4
Regulation	4
Informal Market	4.5

Population: 5,643,000

Total area: 406,750 sq. km

GDP: $7.9 billion

GDP growth rate: 2.6%

GDP per capita: $1,407

Major exports: soybeans, cotton, meat, electricity, wood, leather

Exports of goods and services: $2.6 billion

Major export trading partners: Brazil 34.2%, Uruguay 19.6%, Switzerland 7.8%, Argentina 5.3%

Major imports: vehicles, tobacco, petroleum products

Imports of goods and services: $2.9 billion

Major import trading partners: Brazil 32.4%, Argentina 21.6%, China 12.7%

Foreign direct investment (net): $72.1 million

2003 Data (in constant 2000 US dollars)

P araguay needs to boost economic growth, reduce unemployment, and expand infrastructure. Recent economic slowdowns and financial collapse in Brazil and Argentina, its MERCOSUR trading partners, have affected Paraguay's economy. In 2002, GDP contracted 2.3 percent—the worst recession in 20 years—but the economy has since grown by a modest 2 percent to 3 percent per year. Some 45 percent of the workforce is employed in agriculture, which accounts for 90 percent of export earnings. Only half of the population has attended school beyond the 6th grade, and about 40 percent live below the poverty level. Taking office in 2003, President Nicanor Duarte Frutos imposed greater control over public finances and launched reforms to combat corruption and improve the judicial system. He has enjoyed broad support, but peasant farm worker movements have begun to press for land redistribution, and the result has been property invasions and clashes. Smuggling still accounts for an unknown percentage of the economy, and concerns over organized crime and the presence of suspected Middle Eastern terrorist support groups have prompted increased security cooperation with neighboring countries, as well as with the United States. Paraguay's fiscal burden of government score is 0.4 point better this year, and its monetary policy score is 1 point better. As a result, Paraguay's overall score is 0.14 point better this year.

TRADE POLICY
Score: **3**–Stable (moderate level of protectionism)

As a member of the Southern Cone Common Market (MERCOSUR), Paraguay adheres to a common external tariff that ranges from 0 percent to 25 percent. According to the World Bank, Paraguay's weighted average tariff rate in 2004 was 5.2 percent, down from the 12.5 percent for 2001 reported in the 2005 *Index*, based on World Bank data. The World Trade Organization reports that "product-specific registries are still used for imports and, although steps are being taken to address this, export procedures appear cumbersome and time-consuming…. Paraguay increased by up to 50 percent the taxable value of certain imported products subject to excise taxes (beer, cigarettes and lead-free petrol)." Based on the revised trade factor methodology, a lower tariff rate, but new evidence of non-tariff barriers, Paraguay's trade policy score is unchanged.

FISCAL BURDEN OF GOVERNMENT
Score—Income Taxation: **1**–Stable (very low tax rates)
Score—Corporate Taxation: **4**–Stable (high tax rates)
Score—Change in Government Expenditures: **1.5**–Better (high decrease)
Final Score: **2.6**–Better (moderate cost of government)

Paraguay imposes no taxes on income derived from personal work, services provided, or professional services rendered. The top corporate tax rate is 30 percent. In 2003, according to the International Monetary Fund, government expenditures as a share of GDP decreased 3.8 percentage points to 20 percent, compared to the 0.9 percentage point increase in 2002. On net, Paraguay's fiscal burden of government score is 0.4 point better this year.

GOVERNMENT INTERVENTION IN THE ECONOMY
Score: **3**–Stable (moderate level)

The World Bank reports that the government consumed 6.9 percent of GDP in 2003. In the same

315

year, based on data from the International Monetary Fund, Paraguay received 24.38 percent of its total revenues from state-owned enterprises and government ownership of property.

 MONETARY POLICY
Score: **3–Better** (moderate level of inflation)

From 1995 to 2004, Paraguay's weighted average annual rate of inflation was 7.88 percent, down from the 12.46 percent from 1994 to 2003 reported in the 2005 *Index*. As a result, Paraguay's monetary policy score is 1 point better this year.

 CAPITAL FLOWS AND FOREIGN INVESTMENT
Score: **3–Stable** (moderate barriers)

According to the U.S. Department of Commerce, "There are no formal restrictions [on] foreign investment in Paraguay. National treatment of foreign investors is guaranteed, as is full repatriation of capital and profits." The Economist Intelligence Unit reports that a new law prohibits nationals of neighboring countries from purchasing land within 50 kilometers of the border. Other factors, however, such as corruption, a law requiring foreign companies to prove just cause in a Paraguayan court to terminate, modify, or fail to renew contracts or face severe penalties, the lack of property rights protection and the existence of many government-controlled sectors, impede foreign investment. "Government efforts to attract foreign investment through privatization have progressed slowly," reports the U.S. Department of Commerce, "because of residual political opposition and uncertainty about the transparency of the process." According to the EIU, "Foreign investment is deterred by legal insecurity, shortages of skilled labour, deficient infrastructure and the absence of cheap and reliable transport." The International Monetary Fund reports that both residents and non-residents may hold foreign exchange accounts. Most payments and transfers are permitted, although financial enterprises require central bank authorization to transfer earnings. Capital transactions are subject to minimal restrictions.

 BANKING AND FINANCE
Score: **3–Stable** (moderate level of restrictions)

Several financial crises in the 1990s led Paraguay to restructure and consolidate the banking sector and improve oversight, but the economic crisis in neighboring Argentina has affected the financial sector, and the banking system remains weak and poorly supervised. Bank Aleman, the country's third largest bank, collapsed in June 2002, and Multibanco collapsed in May 2003. According to First Initiative, "the banking sector is comprised of 14 commercial banks and the Banco Nacional de Fomento (BNF), the public development bank. The two largest commercial banks...are foreign-owned; as of mid-2004, wholly foreign-owned banks controlled 49% of banking system assets and majority foreign-owned banks controlled 38% of assets.... The BNF retains a high level of non-performing loans and is largely insolvent." In March 2005, reports the Economist Intelligence Unit, "the Senate approved the executive's reform for a public-sector second-tier bank, the Agencia Financiera de Desarrollo (AFD), to replace the Banco Nacional de Fomento, the state development bank. The role of the AFD is to channel long-term external financing through the commercial banking sector to medium and large-scale producers. In early April the Senate also approved a bill for the creation of a first-tier public development bank to be known as the Banco Nacional de Fomento y Desarrollo (BNFD), focusing exclusively on the needs of small producers. However, changes to the bill made in the Senate have awoken fears among multilateral financing institutions that the new body will be exempted from applying some prudent norms under the country's banking law. This could lead to the kind of highly discretionary lending practices that have marred the reputation and performance of the existing Banco Nacional de Fomento."

 WAGES AND PRICES
Score: **3–Stable** (moderate level of intervention)

The market sets most prices, but the Economist Intelligence Unit reports that the government controls the price of fuel. The government also affects prices through state-owned enterprises in the rail, petroleum, cement, electricity, water, and telephone sectors (among others). The Ministry of Justice and Labor sets a private-sector minimum wage.

 PROPERTY RIGHTS
Score: **4–Stable** (low level of protection)

The judiciary is corrupt, and property protection is extremely weak. The U.S. Department of Commerce reports that reforms in the judiciary "are making the legal process more transparent, but will require more training for public prosecutors and judges.... Both the commercial and civil codes cover bankruptcy and give priority for claims first to employees, then to the state, and finally to private creditors." Overall, "Paraguay's judicial system has been characterized by a weak rule of law and corruption.... [I]ncidences of corruption, patronage and bias are part of the current judicial system."

 REGULATION
Score: **4–Stable** (high level)

"Institutionalized corruption is...a significant barrier to investment," reports the U.S. Department of Commerce. "The Civil Code and law 1,034/83 regulate business and industrial activities.... Under the existing framework, the Ministry of Industry and Commerce is charged with overall industrial policy coordination; the Ministry of Finance handles tax and fiscal policy; and the Central Bank is the principal coordinator of monetary policy." According to the World Bank, the cost of starting a business, hiring and firing, and registering property in Paraguay is very high in terms of both time and money.

 INFORMAL MARKET
Score: **4.5–Stable** (very high level of activity)

Transparency International's 2004 score for Paraguay is 1.9. Therefore, Paraguay's informal market score is 4.5 this year.

PERU

Rank: 63

Score: 2.86

Category: Mostly Free

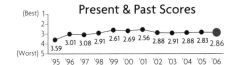

Present & Past Scores

(Best) 1 – 2 – 3 – 4 – (Worst) 5

3.59 3.01 3.08 2.91 2.61 2.69 2.56 2.88 2.91 2.88 2.83 2.86

'95 '96 '97 '98 '99 '00 '01 '02 '03 '04 '05 '06

QUICK STUDY

SCORES

Trade Policy	3.5
Fiscal Burden	3.6
Government Intervention	2
Monetary Policy	1
Foreign Investment	3
Banking and Finance	2
Wages and Prices	2
Property Rights	4
Regulation	4
Informal Market	3.5

Population: 27,148,000

Total area: 1,285,220 sq. km

GDP: $57.8 billion

GDP growth rate: 3.8%

GDP per capita: $2,131

Major exports: gold, copper, fish products, petroleum, coffee

Exports of goods and services: $10.4 billion

Major export trading partners: US 27.1%, UK 12.4%, China 7.7%, Switzerland 7.6%

Major imports: transport equipment, machinery, foodstuffs, chemicals

Imports of goods and services: $10.4 billion

Major import trading partners: US 28.6%, Spain 10.0%, Chile 7.5%, Colombia 4.5%

Foreign direct investment (net): $1.2 billion

2003 Data (in constant 2000 US dollars)

Peru's market-oriented economy has been growing at about 4 percent for the past two years, largely because of construction, mining, and foreign direct investment. In 2004, inflation was 3.5 percent, and the fiscal deficit fell to 1.4 percent of GDP. Notwithstanding general economic success during the past few years, an estimated 54 percent of the people live in poverty, and unemployment and underemployment affect 56 percent of the workforce. The situation has not been aided by the adoption of new taxes, such as the tax on the use of checks, credit cards, and all other financial transactions. Additionally, wealth and commerce are concentrated almost exclusively in Lima and other major cities. Despite public corruption scandals and polls that consistently show him to be Latin America's least popular president, Alejandro Toledo has managed to avoid impeachment. Opposition party members worry about removing him from office and unbalancing the political framework developed since Peru regained its fragile democracy only four years ago. Congress, courts, and the executive seem to balance each other despite corruption and weak rule of law. Toledo's example shows that Latin American governments do not necessarily need centralized, autocratic presidencies to function. Peru's trade policy score is 1 point better this year; however, its fiscal burden of government score is 0.3 point worse, and its capital flows and foreign investment score is 1 point worse. As a result, Peru's overall score is 0.03 point worse this year.

TRADE POLICY
Score: **3.5–Better** (high level of protectionism)

The World Bank reports that Peru's weighted average tariff rate in 2004 was 8.9 percent, down from the 12.6 percent for 2000 reported in the 2005 *Index*. According to the U.S. Trade Representative, "Certain sensitive agricultural products—e.g., corn, rice, sugar and powdered milk—are subject to a Peru-specific 'price band,' or variable levy, which fluctuates to ensure that the import prices of such products equal a predetermined minimum import price.... [T]he following imports are banned: used clothing, used shoes, used tires, remanufactured machine parts, cars over five years old and heavy trucks (weighing three tons or more) over eight years old.... [T]he Peruvian plant and animal health agency, imposes several significant trade barriers (which include bans, import requirements and sanitary permits) on agricultural products." Based on the lower tariff rate, as well as a revision of the trade factor methodology, Peru's trade policy score is 1 point better this year.

FISCAL BURDEN OF GOVERNMENT
Score—Income Taxation: **3**–Stable (moderate tax rates)
Score—Corporate Taxation: **4**–Worse (high tax rates)
Score—Change in Government Expenditures: **3.5**–Worse (low increase)
Final Score: **3.6**–Worse (high cost of government)

Deloitte reports that Peru's top income tax rate is 30 percent. The top corporate tax rate is also 30 percent, up from the 27 percent reported in the 2005 *Index*. In 2003, according to the Economist Intelligence Unit, government expenditures as a share of GDP increased 0.2 percentage point to 28.5 percent, compared to a 0.6 percentage point decrease in 2002. On net, Peru's fiscal burden of government score is 0.3 point worse this year.

GOVERNMENT INTERVENTION IN THE ECONOMY
Score: **2**–Stable (low level)

The World Bank reports that the government consumed 10.1 percent of GDP in 2003. In the same year, according to the International Monetary Fund's Government Financial Statistics CD–ROM, Peru received 4.57 percent of its total revenues from state-owned enterprises and government ownership of property.

MONETARY POLICY
Score: **1**–Stable (very low level of inflation)

From 1995 to 2004, Peru's weighted average annual rate of inflation was 3.00 percent.

CAPITAL FLOWS AND FOREIGN INVESTMENT
Score: **3**–Worse (moderate barriers)

Peru encourages foreign investment. "The 1993 Constitution guarantees national treatment for foreign investors," reports the U.S. Department of Commerce. "The Peruvian government does not screen foreign direct investment nor does it require foreign investors to register their investments. Foreign investment does not require prior approval, except in banking and defense-related industries." According to the U.S. Trade Representative, "Peruvian law restricts majority ownership of broadcast media to Peruvian citizens. Foreigners are also restricted from owning land or investing in natural resources within 50 kilometers of a border, but they can operate within those areas with special authorization. National air and water transportation are restricted to domestic operators." The International Monetary Fund reports that both residents and non-residents may hold foreign exchange accounts. There are no restrictions or controls on payments, transactions, transfers, or repatriation of profits. Capital transactions face minimal restrictions. Peruvian law limits foreign employees to 20 percent of the workforce and no more than 30 percent of the payroll, but there are numerous exemptions. According to the U.S. Department of Commerce, "Several regulatory institutions are notable impediments to business operations…. Business people often complain of excessive red tape." Based on evidence of bureaucratic barriers and constraints on foreign investment, Peru's capital flows and foreign investment score is 1 point worse this year.

BANKING AND FINANCE
Score: **2**–Stable (low level of restrictions)

Peru has a non-discriminatory policy toward foreign banks. The government has opened the country to foreign banks and insurance companies, has established capital requirements, allows banks to set interest rates, and has strengthened prudential standards and disclosure requirements. "As of July 2004," reports the U.S. Department of Commerce, "foreigners were majority owners of nine and had major participation in three commercial banks." According to First Initiative, "The banking sector dominates the Peruvian financial sector, with nearly 80%

of the financial sector's assets in commercial or public-sector banks. As of February 2004, there were 14 commercial banks, with the three largest banks accounting for almost two-thirds of the entire banking sector's assets…. The state participates in the banking sector through the Banco de la Nación, a deposit-taking institution, and the Corporación Financiera de Desarrollo, a development bank." The state-owned financial institutions play a limited role in the financial sector.

WAGES AND PRICES
Score: **2**–Stable (low level of intervention)

The market determines most wages and prices. According to the Economist Intelligence Unit, "Most price controls have been eliminated. Several regulatory committees approve or reject rate hikes proposed by private companies." In addition, "The government [has] created a special fund (Fondo para al Estabilización de Precios de los Combustibles Derivados del Petróleo) to control fuel price increases." Peru maintains a minimum wage.

PROPERTY RIGHTS
Score: **4**–Stable (low level of protection)

The government does not protect private property effectively. "In principle," reports the U.S. Department of Commerce, "secured interests in property, both chattel and real, are recognized. However, the judicial system is often extremely slow to hear cases and to issue decisions. In addition, court rulings and the degree of enforcement have been difficult to predict. The capabilities of individual judges vary substantially, and allegations of corruption and outside interference in the judicial system are common. The Peruvian appeals process also tends to delay final decisions. As a result…investors…have found that contracts are often difficult to enforce in Peru."

REGULATION
Score: **4**–Stable (high level)

Peru remains plagued by an inefficient bureaucracy. According to the U.S. Department of Commerce, "Various procedures—such as obtaining building licenses or certificates of occupancy—require many steps to carry out, and information on necessary procedures is often difficult to obtain. Business people often complain of excessive government red tape…. Peruvian business organizations allege that high government-imposed costs impede investment." In addition, "corruption is a major factor influencing the business climate." According to the World Bank, the cost of starting a business, hiring and firing, and registering property in Peru is moderate in terms of both time and money.

INFORMAL MARKET
Score: **3.5**–Stable (high level of activity)

Transparency International's 2004 score for Peru is 3.5. Therefore, Peru's informal market score is 3.5 this year.

THE PHILIPPINES

Rank: 98

Score: 3.23

Category: Mostly Unfree

Present & Past Scores

(Best) 1
2
3
4
(Worst) 5

3.35 3.14 3.06 2.89 3.03 3.00 3.21 3.05 3.00 3.10 3.30 3.23
'95 '96 '97 '98 '99 '00 '01 '02 '03 '04 '05 '06

QUICK STUDY

SCORES

Trade Policy	2.5
Fiscal Burden	3.8
Government Intervention	2
Monetary Policy	2
Foreign Investment	4
Banking and Finance	3
Wages and Prices	3
Property Rights	4
Regulation	4
Informal Market	4

Population: 81,503,000

Total area: 300,000 sq. km

GDP: $85.3 billion

GDP growth rate: 4.7%

GDP per capita: $1,047

Major exports: electrical and electronic equipment, machinery and transport equipment, garments, chemicals

Exports of goods and services: $43.5 billion

Major export trading partners: US 20.1%, Japan 15.9%, Hong Kong 8.5%, Netherlands 8.1%, Singapore 6.7%

Major imports: semi-processed raw materials, telecommunications equipment, petroleum

Imports of goods and services: $48.6 billion

Major import trading partners: Japan 20.4%, US 19.8%, Singapore 6.8%, South Korea 6.4%, Taiwan 5.0%

Foreign direct investment (net): $151.9 million

2003 Data (in constant 2000 US dollars)

Under President Gloria Macapagal Arroyo, inflation has risen and the economy is both low on capital and high on bureaucratic mismanagement. In 2004, tsunami aid graft was but one sign of rampant corruption, along with human trafficking and a ballooning black market. Amid accusations of fraud in her election, Arroyo began much-needed efforts to reform taxes, clean up corruption, and court overseas investors, but her efforts fell far short of expectations. Foreign direct investment in 2004 leveled off at $1 billion, well below the $3 billion to $4 billion of other ASEAN countries. Arroyo has taken preliminary steps to ease the corporate tax burden, hoping to attract foreign companies. Tax incidence is heavier for corporations than for individuals. The population has increased, exacerbating the problems of an inadequate infrastructure. Arroyo has also increased government spending, which, combined with lagging tax revenues, has led to massive deficits. The government is slow in promoting privatization, as the state still owns a majority of Filipino corporations. The chief obstacles to stable growth remain high tax rates, poor infrastructure, extensive government ownership of business, low foreign investment, and entrenched government corruption. The Philippines' fiscal burden of government score is 0.3 point worse this year, but its banking and finance score is 1 point better. As a result, the Philippines' overall score is 0.07 point better this year.

TRADE POLICY
Score: **2.5**–Stable (moderate level of protectionism)

According to the World Bank, the Philippines' weighted average tariff rate in 2003 (the most recent year for which World Bank data are available) was 2.6 percent, down from the 2.8 percent for 2002 reported in the 2005 *Index*, based on World Bank data. The U.S. Trade Representative reports that "corruption and other irregularities [in customs] remain commonplace." Licensing, quotas, and safeguard measures are widespread. Based on the revised trade factor methodology, the Philippines' trade policy score is unchanged.

FISCAL BURDEN OF GOVERNMENT
Score—Income Taxation: **3**–Stable (moderate tax rates)
Score—Corporate Taxation: **4.5**–Worse (high tax rates)
Score—Change in Government Expenditures: **3**–Stable (very low decrease)
Final Score: **3.8**–Worse (high cost of government)

According to the Embassy of the Philippines, the Philippines' top income tax rate is 32 percent, and the top corporate tax rate was increased in May 2005 to 35 percent from 32 percent. In 2003, according to the Asian Development Bank, government expenditures as a share of GDP decreased 0.4 percentage point to 19.2 percent, compared to a 0 percentage point change in 2002. On net, the Philippines' fiscal burden of government score is 0.3 point worse this year.

GOVERNMENT INTERVENTION IN THE ECONOMY
Score: **2**–Stable (low level)

The World Bank reports that the government consumed 11.4 percent of GDP in 2003. In the same year, based on data from the National Statistics Office, the Philippines received 1.95 percent of its total revenues from state-owned enterprises and government ownership of property.

319

MONETARY POLICY
Score: **2**–Stable (low level of inflation)

From 1995 to 2004, the Philippines' weighted average annual rate of inflation was 5.15 percent.

CAPITAL FLOWS AND FOREIGN INVESTMENT
Score: **4**–Stable (high barriers)

The Philippines maintains barriers to many foreign investments. Two negative lists restrict both foreign investment and the ability of foreigners to practice in numerous sectors, including (but not limited to) engineering, medicine, accounting, law, retail, media, security, marine resources, employee recruitment, advertising, education, public utilities, deep-sea fishing, rice and corn processing, and defense-related industries. Unofficial barriers also impede foreign investment. According to the U.S. Department of Commerce, "High levels of corruption; failure to reform the judicial system; ineffective protection of intellectual property rights; the slow pace of energy sector reform, price liberalization, and privatization; delays in passing key economic and fiscal reform legislation; and political uncertainties...constrain the Government's ability to attract foreign direct investments." The mining sector is now open to 100 percent foreign-owned companies. The International Monetary Fund reports that both residents and non-residents may hold foreign exchange accounts, although non-residents may do so only with foreign currency deposits or proceeds from conversions of property in the Philippines. Payments, capital transactions, and transfers are subject to numerous restrictions, controls, quantitative limits, and authorizations.

BANKING AND FINANCE
Score: **3**–Better (moderate level of restrictions)

The banking sector is recovering from the 50 percent devaluation in the Philippine peso in 1997. Non-performing loans have fallen from a ratio of 17.3 percent in 2001 to 11.3 percent in 2005. "As of 2004," reports First Initiative, "there were 42 commercial banks, 93 thrift banks and approximately 770 rural and co-operative banks.... Recent reforms include the raising of minimum capital requirements for banks in an effort to encourage more consolidation, a trend which is expected to continue.... Foreign companies play a major role in the life insurance market." The commercial banking sector includes 20 foreign-owned or foreign-controlled banks. According to the Philippine embassy, the state owned three commercial banks accounting for 11.1 percent of total banking assets as of December 2004. "Credit is generally granted on market terms. However, there are existing laws that require financial institutions to set aside loans for certain preferred sectors which may translate to increased costs and/or credit risks," reports the U.S. Department of Commerce. "The General Banking Law of 2000...created a seven-year window during which foreign banks may own up to 100 percent of one locally incorporated commercial or thrift bank (up from the previous 60 percent foreign equity ceiling).... Current regulations mandate that majority Filipino-owned domestic banks should, at all times, control at least 70 percent of total banking system assets. Rural banking remains completely closed to foreigners." Although the government is involved in the financial sector, the private sector is the dominant player. As a result, the Philippines' banking and finance score is 1 point better this year.

WAGES AND PRICES
Score: **3**–Stable (moderate level of intervention)

The market sets most wages and prices, but the Economist Intelligence Unit reports that the government controls or influences the price of "electricity distribution, water, telephone charges, public-transport fares, port charges and road tolls." In addition, "Price ceilings are usually imposed only on basic commodities (such as rice, milk, sugar, pork, chicken, cooking oil and flour) in areas that the president declares to be under a state of calamity or emergency, such as those devastated by frequent typhoons." The Philippines maintains a minimum wage.

PROPERTY RIGHTS
Score: **4**–Stable (low level of protection)

The Economist Intelligence Unit reports that the Philippines "has a slow judicial system, hampered by lack of funding and an insufficient number of judges to handle court cases" and that "a series of contract reversals beginning [in] 2002 has undermined the security of contractual arrangements...." According to the U.S. Department of Commerce, "The Philippine judicial system is viewed as a significant disincentive by most foreign investors.... Some observers charge that judges rarely have any background in or thorough understanding of economics, business or a competitive economic system, and that some decisions have strayed from the interpretation of law to policymaking. Also troubling are charges that judges are bribed to issue decisions favorable to a particular interest."

REGULATION
Score: **4**–Stable (high level)

The Philippine government's regulatory agencies lack transparency, and regulations are enforced haphazardly. The U.S. Department of Commerce reports that "investors find business registration, customs, immigration, and visa procedures in the Philippines burdensome and a source of frustration. Some agencies...have established express lanes or 'one-stop shops' to reduce bureaucratic delays, with varying degrees of success...." Labor laws are somewhat rigid. The U.S. Department of Commerce reports that bureaucratic corruption is extensive.

INFORMAL MARKET
Score: **4**–Stable (high level of activity)

Transparency International's 2004 score for the Philippines is 2.6. Therefore, the Philippines' informal market score is 4 this year.

POLAND

Rank: 41

Score: 2.49

Category: Mostly Free

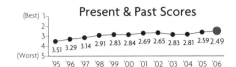

Present & Past Scores

(Best) 1
2
3
4
(Worst) 5

3.51 3.29 3.14 2.91 2.83 2.84 2.69 2.65 2.83 2.81 2.59 2.49

'95 '96 '97 '98 '99 '00 '01 '02 '03 '04 '05 '06

QUICK STUDY

SCORES

Trade Policy	2
Fiscal Burden	2.4
Government Intervention	2
Monetary Policy	1
Foreign Investment	3
Banking and Finance	2
Wages and Prices	3
Property Rights	3
Regulation	3
Informal Market	3.5

Population: 38,196,000

Total area: 312,685 sq. km

GDP: $186.6 billion

GDP growth rate: 5.3%

GDP per capita: $4,885

Major exports: food and live animals, machinery and transport equipment, miscellaneous manufactured goods

Exports of goods and services: $56.7 billion

Major export trading partners: Germany 29.9%, France 6.0%, Italy 6.0%, UK 5.5%

Major imports: mineral fuels and lubricants, machinery and transport equipment, chemicals

Imports of goods and services: $60 billion

Major import trading partners: Germany 24.2%, Italy 7.8%, Russia 7.3%, France 6.7%

Foreign direct investment (net): $4.9 billion

2004 Data (in constant 2000 US dollars)

Poland provides almost half of the economic output of the enlarged European Union's new members, but over 12 million Poles live in poverty, earning less than 2.5 euros per day. Marek Belka, former minister of finance, was appointed prime minister in October 2004. In February 2005, Deputy Prime Minister Jerzy Hausner, Belka's fellow Democratic Left Alliance member, established a centrist Democratic Party that Belka was likely to join before the September 25, 2005, parliamentary elections. Poland's public debt is on track to enter the euro zone in 2009; with each state budget deficit, Poland's debt (43.6 percent of GDP) falls farther below the European Monetary Union's cap for entry (60 percent of GDP). Poland's economic growth (5.3 percent in 2004) continues to outshine major European economies. With one of the EU's lowest wage rates, Poland has received over $65 billion in foreign direct investment since 1990. Privatization has accelerated over the past year, with several major companies going public in 2005. With the development of the Odessa–Brody pipeline and its extension to a refinery in Plotsk and the port of Gdansk, Poland may also diversify its energy sources. Poland's trade policy and fiscal burden of government scores are 0.5 point better this year. As a result, Poland's overall score is 0.1 point better this year.

TRADE POLICY
Score: **2**–Better (low level of protectionism)

Poland adopted the trade policies of the European Union when it joined the EU in May 2004. The common EU weighted average external tariff was 1.3 percent in 2003, based on World Bank data. In the 2005 *Index*, also based on World Bank data, Poland had a tariff of 2.9 percent. According to the World Trade Organization and the U.S. Trade Representative, the EU imposes non-tariff trade barriers through a complex regulatory system and export subsidies. Based on its adoption of EU trade policies, and on the revised trade factor methodology, Poland's trade policy score is 0.5 point better this year.

FISCAL BURDEN OF GOVERNMENT
Score—Income Taxation: **4**–Stable (high tax rates)
Score—Corporate Taxation: **2**–Stable (low tax rates)
Score—Change in Government Expenditures: **1.5**–Better (high decrease)
Final Score: **2.4**–Better (low cost of government)

Poland's top income tax rate is 40 percent. The top corporate tax rate is 19 percent. In 2004, government expenditures as a share of GDP decreased 3.3 percentage points to 44.9 percent, compared to the 0.7 percentage point decrease in 2003. On net, Poland's fiscal burden of government score is 0.5 point better this year.

GOVERNMENT INTERVENTION IN THE ECONOMY
Score: **2**–Stable (low level)

Based on data from the Economist Intelligence Unit, the government consumed 17.3 percent of GDP in 2004. In 2003, according to the International Monetary Fund's Government Financial Statistics CD–ROM, Poland received 4.08 percent of its total revenues from state-owned enterprises and government ownership of property.

MONETARY POLICY
Score: **1**–Stable (very low level of inflation)

From 1995 to 2004, Poland's weighted average annual rate of inflation was 2.91 percent.

CAPITAL FLOWS AND FOREIGN INVESTMENT
Score: **3**–Stable (moderate barriers)

According to Deloitte, "Foreign investors enjoy national treatment if they are permanent residents or nationals of a country where reciprocal treatment is provided to Polish firms." Polish law allows 100 percent foreign ownership of domestic businesses but, according to the U.S. Department of Commerce, also "establishes the following ceilings on the share of foreign ownership: air transport (49 percent); radio and television broadcasting (49 percent); and gambling (0 percent). Furthermore, in some sectors (insurance) it is required that at least two members of management boards know the Polish language. In some fields (e.g., broadcasting) the number of Polish citizens on supervisory and management boards must be higher than the number of foreigners." In addition, "Non-EEA foreigners are allowed to own an apartment, 0.4 hectares (4,000 square meters) of urban land, or up to one hectare of agricultural land without a permit." The International Monetary Fund reports that both residents and non-residents may hold foreign exchange accounts, subject to certain restrictions, including government approval for resident accounts held abroad. Payments, transactions, and transfers over a specified amount must be conducted through a domestic bank. Capital transactions with residents of the European Union, the European Economic Area, and members of the Organisation for Economic Co-operation and Development are free of controls, but many transactions with other nations face restrictions and government approval.

BANKING AND FINANCE
Score: **2**–Stable (low level of restrictions)

The banking sector is now open and competitive. "Of the 75 commercial banks in Poland," reports First Initiative, "45 were controlled by foreign investors (2003). Another aspect of the Polish banking sector is the high degree of consolidation; the 11 largest banks held 75% of all banking sector assets in 2003…. The insurance industry…was composed of 63 companies in 2003, 34 of which are owned by foreign investors." The Economist Intelligence Unit reports that Poland's "banking sector has attracted massive foreign investment, and foreign banks now control around 70% of domestic banking assets. In 2004 the government partially privatised its two last major banks—savings giant PKO Bank Polski (PKO BP) and agriculture lender Bank Gospodarki Zywnosciowej (BGZ)." According to the U.S. Department of Commerce, "The banking sector is dominated by twelve large commercial banks, two of which are controlled by the State Treasury and the remaining ten by foreign institutions." Most credit is allocated on market terms, but the government does provide some low-interest loans to farmers and homeowners.

WAGES AND PRICES
Score: **3**–Stable (moderate level of intervention)

The government has removed a number of price controls but continues to influence the prices of some products. According to the Economist Intelligence Unit, "Official prices apply under the following conditions and products: (1) to goods or services when there are substantial threats to the proper functioning of the economy as specified by the Council of Ministers; (2) to pharmaceutical and medical materials that are covered by health insurance; and (3) to prices for taxi services…. [U]tility prices [are subject to] supervision if the provider dominates the market…." The government also establishes a minimum wage.

PROPERTY RIGHTS
Score: **3**–Stable (moderate level of protection)

Property rights are moderately protected. According to the U.S. Department of Commerce, "Many investors—foreign and domestic—complain about the slowness of the judicial system…. [I]nvestors often voice concern about frequent or unexpected issuance of or changes in laws and regulations." Nevertheless, reports the Economist Intelligence Unit, "firms generally speak well of the local court system…especially compared with the systems of neighbouring countries like Russia." The EIU also reports that corruption is present.

REGULATION
Score: **3**–Stable (moderate level)

According to the U.S. Department of Commerce, "The government acknowledges that its policies are not as transparent as they ought to be and that bureaucratic requirements continue to impose a burden on investors…. Although there are fewer complaints about uneven treatment, regulatory unpredictability and [the] still high level of administrative red tape are recurring complaints of investors, both domestic and foreign." The Embassy of Poland reports that environmental, health, and safety regulations are strict and were strengthened before accession to the European Union.

INFORMAL MARKET
Score: **3.5**–Stable (high level of activity)

Transparency International's 2004 score for Poland is 3.5. Therefore, Poland's informal market score is 3.5 this year.

PORTUGAL

Rank: 30

Score: 2.29

Category: Mostly Free

Present & Past Scores

(Best) 1
2
3
4
(Worst) 5

2.85 2.65 2.46 2.46 2.36 2.39 2.38 2.35 2.40 2.43 2.44 2.29

'95 '96 '97 '98 '99 '00 '01 '02 '03 '04 '05 '06

The Portuguese Socialist Party came to power with a commanding absolute majority in February 2005, and Premier José Socrates has his work cut out for him. Budget tightening to bring the deficit in line with the European Union's Stability and Growth Pact coincided with the beginning of a recession in 2003. The economy grew by only 1 percent in 2004, and the jobless rate has almost doubled in the past three years, reaching 7.1 percent in March 2005. According to *The Economist,* the Portuguese Business Association recently estimated that the notoriously bloated public administration workforce could decrease by 150,000 workers without affecting production. The public sector soaks up the equivalent of 15 percent of GDP in wages alone. In addition, productivity is less than two-thirds of the EU average. Portugal's fiscal burden of government score is 0.5 point better this year, and its monetary policy score is 1 point better. As a result, Portugal's overall score is 0.15 point better this year.

TRADE POLICY
Score: 2–Stable (low level of protectionism)

As a member of the European Union, Portugal was subject to a common EU weighted average external tariff of 1.3 percent in 2003, down from the 2.4 percent for 2002 reported in the 2005 *Index,* based on World Bank data. According to the World Trade Organization and the U.S. Trade Representative, the EU imposes non-tariff trade barriers through a complex regulatory system and export subsidies. Based on the revised trade factor methodology, Portugal's trade policy score is unchanged.

FISCAL BURDEN OF GOVERNMENT
Score—Income Taxation: 4–Stable (high tax rates)
Score—Corporate Taxation: 3–Better (moderate tax rates)
Score—Change in Government Expenditures: 3.5–Stable (low increase)
Final Score: 3.4–Better (moderate cost of government)

Portugal's top income tax rate is 40 percent. The top corporate tax rate is 25 percent, down from the 30 percent reported in the 2005 *Index.* In 2004, government expenditures as a share of GDP increased 0.8 percentage point to 48.4 percent, compared to the 1.6 percentage point increase in 2003. On net, Portugal's fiscal burden of government score is 0.5 point better this year.

GOVERNMENT INTERVENTION IN THE ECONOMY
Score: 2.5–Stable (moderate level)

Based on data from the Economist Intelligence Unit, the government consumed 21.3 percent of GDP in 2004. In the same year, according to the central bank, Portugal received 1.79 percent of its total revenues from state-owned enterprises and government ownership of property.

MONETARY POLICY
Score: 1–Better (very low level of inflation)

Portugal is a member of the euro zone. From 1995 to 2004, Portugal's weighted average annual rate of inflation was 2.74 percent, down from the 3.41 percent reported in the 2005 *Index.* As a result, Portugal's monetary policy score is 1 point better this year.

QUICK STUDY

SCORES

Trade Policy	2
Fiscal Burden	3.4
Government Intervention	2.5
Monetary Policy	1
Foreign Investment	2
Banking and Finance	3
Wages and Prices	2
Property Rights	2
Regulation	3
Informal Market	2

Population: 10,444,000

Total area: 92,391 sq. km

GDP: $108.6 billion

GDP growth rate: 1.0%

GDP per capita: $10,398

Major exports: machinery, clothing and footwear, chemicals

Exports of goods and services: $52.1 billion

Major export trading partners: Spain 24.9%, Germany 13.5%, France 14.0%, UK 9.6%, US 6.1%

Major imports: agricultural products, transport equipment, petroleum, textiles

Imports of goods and services: $65.1 billion

Major import trading partners: Spain 29.3%, Germany 14.3%, France 9.3%, Italy 6.1%, UK 4.6%, US 2.4%

Foreign direct investment (net): –$4.7 billion

2004 Data (in constant 2000 US dollars)

CAPITAL FLOWS AND FOREIGN INVESTMENT
Score: 2–Stable (low barriers)

Portugal has opened most of its industries to foreign investment and has liberalized the bureaucratic process for foreign investors. The government does not discriminate against foreign investments by favoring domestic investors. "Historically," reports the Economist Intelligence Unit, "the majority of FDI projects were export-oriented, which helped to make up for the traditional structural imbalance on the external accounts. However, FDI has dwindled in recent years, and there is now a growing consensus that Portugal needs to improve its business climate and attract higher inflows of FDI. Since 2002, when the former PSD–PP-led coalition came to power, policies have been oriented more towards the creation of a better framework to promote and channel new investment." According to the U.S. Department of Commerce, "Foreigners are permitted to establish themselves in almost all economic sectors open to private enterprise. Currently, however, Portuguese government approval is required for non-EU investment in the following sectors: defense industry, water management, public service telecommunications operators, railways, and maritime transportations. Also, Portugal restricts non-EU investment in regular air transport to 49 percent, and restricts non-EU investment in television operations to 15 percent." The International Monetary Fund reports that residents and non-residents may hold foreign exchange accounts. There are no controls or restrictions on repatriation of profits, current transfers, payments for invisible transactions, or real estate transactions. Foreign employees from non-EU countries may comprise no more than 10 percent of the workforce in businesses with more than five employees.

BANKING AND FINANCE
Score: 3–Stable (moderate level of restrictions)

The U.S. Department of Commerce reports that "Portugal has about 50 banking institutions. The largest five bank groups, however, accounted for a majority of the sector's total assets. Nevertheless, Portugal's bank sector is still undergoing consolidation in order to create banks large enough to compete in the European market. Two banks, including the country's largest, Caixa Geral do Depositos (CGD), are still controlled by the Portuguese government." The Economist Intelligence Unit reports that "[CGD] is still the largest financial group and has on several occasions served as an instrument of government intervention in the economy, usually in defence against unwanted takeover bids from foreign investors. There are currently no immediate plans to privatise CGD." The government influences the allocation of credit through a program designed to assist small and medium-size enterprises. According to the U.S. Department of Commerce, "Portugal's Institute for Supporting Small and Medium-Sized Enterprises and Investment (IAPMEI) has a program of mutual guarantees so that SMEs do not have to use their assets or those of their shareholders to collateralize debt." The Bank of Portugal (for the EU) or the Ministry of Finance (non-EU) must authorize the establishment or acquisition of new credit institutions or finance companies, as well as the establishment of subsidiaries.

WAGES AND PRICES
Score: 2–Stable (low level of intervention)

The market determines most wages and prices. According to the Economist Intelligence Unit, "Price controls remain in special sectors where the government finds price regulation necessary (such as for electricity, water and pharmaceutical products)." The government also affects agricultural prices through Portugal's participation in the Common Agricultural Policy, a program that heavily subsidizes agricultural goods. A mandated minimum wage applies to all full-time workers, rural workers, and domestic employees.

PROPERTY RIGHTS
Score: 2–Stable (high level of protection)

The judiciary is independent, but the court system is painfully slow. According to the U.S. Department of Commerce, "The Portuguese legal system is slow and deliberate, with cases taking years, if not decades, to be resolved. In 2001, there were close to one million pending legal disputes in the national courts, four times the 1992 level.... It takes, for example, an average of 420 days for a bounced check case to wend its way through the court system, double the EU average. In an effort to address this problem, the government introduced reforms in litigation procedures and public administration in 2004."

REGULATION
Score: 3–Stable (moderate level)

Investors complain of onerous red tape. "Decision-making tends to be centralized," reports the U.S. Department of Commerce, "and obtaining government approvals or permits can be time-consuming and costly, for example, in accomplishing such basic tasks as registering companies, filing taxes, receiving value-added tax refunds, and importing vehicles." According to the Financial Times, labor laws "prevent companies from adapting their workforces to production…deter industrial restructuring…and affect Portugal's capacity to attract foreign investors." The government has created a one-stop "Formality Center" to address the bureaucratic problem, but with mixed results. Corruption is present but not overly burdensome to businesses.

INFORMAL MARKET
Score: 2–Stable (low level of activity)

Transparency International's 2004 score for Portugal is 6.3. Therefore, Portugal's informal market score is 2 this year.

> If Portugal were to improve its regulation score, it would qualify for the Global Free Trade Alliance.

QATAR

Rank: 78

Score: 3.04

Category: Mostly Unfree

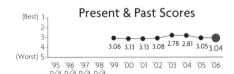

Present & Past Scores

(Best) 1
2
3   3.06 3.13 3.13 3.08 2.78 2.81 3.05 3.04
4
(Worst) 5
'95 '96 '97 '98 '99 '00 '01 '02 '03 '04 '05 '06
n/a n/a n/a n/a

QUICK STUDY

SCORES

Trade Policy	3
Fiscal Burden	1.9
Government Intervention	4
Monetary Policy	2
Foreign Investment	4
Banking and Finance	3
Wages and Prices	3
Property Rights	3
Regulation	4
Informal Market	2.5

Population: 743,000

Total area: 11,437 sq. km

GDP: $22.3 billion

GDP growth rate: 3.3%

GDP per capita: $30,013

Major exports: petroleum products, fertilizers, steel

Exports of goods (fob): $13.4 billion

Major export trading partners: Japan 46.0%, South Korea 18.5%, Singapore 9.5%

Major imports: machinery and transport equipment

Imports of goods (fob): $4.4 billion

Major import trading partners: US 12.2%, Japan 10.5%, Germany 9.6%, UK 8.0%

Foreign direct investment (net): $310.3 million

2003 Data (in constant 2000 US dollars)

The Persian Gulf emirate of Qatar gained its independence from Great Britain in 1971 and has been a leader in Arab political and economic reform during the past decade. Sheikh Hamad bin Khalifa al-Thani, who ousted his father in a bloodless coup in 1995, has encouraged economic growth and foreign investment through accelerated privatization and private-sector development. Qatar's robust economy is dominated by the oil and gas industry, which accounts for more than 55 percent of GDP and roughly 85 percent of export earnings. To better exploit the country's huge natural gas reserves—about 5 percent of the world's total—the government seeks to expand development of offshore natural gas deposits and to become the world's largest producer of liquefied natural gas by 2006. The government announced in January 2005 that $105 billion would be invested over the next five years to diversify the economy, with much of this investment to be financed by foreign banks and investors. A March 19, 2005, suicide bombing by an Egyptian employee of the state-owned Qatar Petroleum Company killed a Briton and wounded 16 others. Although Qatar historically has experienced few terrorist attacks, an upsurge in terrorism could undermine plans for increased foreign investment. Qatar's trade policy score is 0.5 point worse this year; however, its fiscal burden of government score is 0.1 point better, and its government intervention score is 0.5 point better. As a result, Qatar's overall score is 0.01 point better this year.

TRADE POLICY
Score: **3**–Worse (moderate level of protectionism)

According to the World Trade Organization, Qatar's average tariff rate in 2004 was 5.2 percent, up from the 4.2 percent reported in the 2005 *Index*, based on World Bank data. The U.S. Trade Representative reports that "Qatar requires importers to have a license for most products, and only issues import licenses to Qatari nationals. Only authorized local agents are allowed to import specific goods produced by the foreign firms they represent in the local market." Based on the higher tariff rate, as well as a revision of the trade factor methodology, Qatar's trade policy score is 0.5 point worse this year.

FISCAL BURDEN OF GOVERNMENT
Score—Income Taxation: **1**–Stable (very low tax rates)
Score—Corporate Taxation: **1**–Stable (very low tax rates)
Score—Change in Government Expenditures: **4.5**–Better (very high increase)
Final Score: **1.9**–Better (low cost of government)

The government does not impose income taxes on individuals. The top corporate tax rate is 0 percent. In 2003, based on data from the Ministry of Finance, government expenditures as a share of GDP increased by 2.1 percentage points to 30.7 percent, compared to the 4.0 percentage point increase in 2002. On net, Qatar's fiscal burden of government score is 0.1 point better this year.

GOVERNMENT INTERVENTION IN THE ECONOMY
Score: **4**–Better (high level)

The Embassy of Qatar reports that the government consumed 18 percent of GDP in 2003, down from the 20.2 percent reported in the 2005 *Index*. As a result, Qatar's government intervention score is 0.5 point better this year. In fiscal year July 2003–June 2004, based on data from the central bank, Qatar received 63.39 percent of its total revenues just from state-owned oil companies.

MONETARY POLICY
Score: **2**–Stable (low level of inflation)

From 1995 to 2004, Qatar's weighted average annual rate of inflation was 4.93 percent.

CAPITAL FLOWS AND FOREIGN INVESTMENT
Score: **4**–Stable (high barriers)

An October 2000 investment law permits majority and full foreign ownership of businesses in agriculture, industry, health, education, tourism, and projects involved in the development of natural resources. Most sectors, however, are capped at 49 percent foreign ownership. The law still requires foreign businesses to employ a local agent. The Economist Intelligence Unit reports that foreign nationals now own residential properties for renewable 99-year terms that can be passed on to legal heirs and that investors may lease plots for renewable 50-year terms. According to the U.S. Department of Commerce, "the Government is the major buyer and end-user of a wide range of products and services. Government procurement regulations provide a ten percent preference for Qatari bidders and 5 percent for [Gulf Cooperation Council] bidders." The same source notes that foreigners are generally not permitted to invest in privatized public services. The government screens all major foreign investment projects in the oil and gas industry, but 100 percent foreign ownership in the energy sector is permitted with government approval. Foreign companies face a higher tax rate (up to 35 percent) than do domestic companies (0 percent). The International Monetary Fund reports that both residents and non-residents may hold foreign exchange accounts. There are no controls or restrictions on payments and transfers.

BANKING AND FINANCE
Score: **3**–Stable (moderate level of restrictions)

The Economist Intelligence Unit reports that "Qatar has 15 commercial banks, of which seven are locally owned and account for about 80% of the sector's assets…. Loans to the government and to operations related to [liquefied natural gas] developments account for the majority of commercial bank loans." The government influences the banking sector and partially owns the country's largest bank—Qatar National Bank, which accounts for 50 percent of total deposits. Foreign banks are able to operate, and the regulatory system is transparent and up to international standards. According to the U.S. Trade Representative, "In 2004, Law No. 31/2004 amended the Organization of Foreign Capital Investment Law (Law No. 13/2000) to allow foreign investment in the banking sector pending approval by decree from the Cabinet of Ministers. Qatari regulations for local and foreign bank practices are the same…. In 2003, the Qatar Central Bank allowed foreign banks to establish representational offices and the existing foreign banks in Qatar to open new branches." The Doha Securities Market has been opened to foreign investors, but their holdings are restricted to 25 percent of the issued capital of listed companies.

WAGES AND PRICES
Score: **3**–Stable (moderate level of intervention)

The government affects some wages and prices. According to the Economist Intelligence Unit, the government provides extensive subsidies and imposes significant price controls. The government does not mandate a minimum wage, but it does influence wages through its extensive employment of Qatari citizens.

PROPERTY RIGHTS
Score: **3**–Stable (moderate level of protection)

Expropriation of property is not likely, but the judiciary is subject to inefficiencies and influence from the executive. "Contracts are generally secured in Qatar," reports the Economist Intelligence Unit, but "the domestic legal process has a reputation for being long and bureaucratic…. [T]he Qatari system is regarded as adequate in the field of commercial law." According to the U.S. Department of Commerce, the executive influences the judiciary, and the "legal system is biased in favor of citizens and the Government."

REGULATION
Score: **4**–Stable (high level)

According to the U.S. Department of Commerce, "in order to further economic development, the Ministry of Economy and Commerce passed or updated a number of economic and commercial laws in 2003–04, including the Mutual Funds Law, the Auditors and Certified Public Accountants Law, the Foreign Investment Law and the Privatization of Cooperative Societies Law." Government businesses are often exempt from some regulations, leaving private companies to bear a greater regulatory burden. The overall regulatory burden is therefore significant. The U.S. Department of Commerce reports that corruption is most common in procurement.

INFORMAL MARKET
Score: **2.5**–Stable (moderate level of activity)

Transparency International's 2003 score for Qatar is 5.2. Therefore, Qatar's informal market score is 2.5 this year.

ROMANIA

Rank: 92

Score: 3.19

Category: Mostly Unfree

Present & Past Scores

(Best) 1
2
3
4
(Worst) 5

3.65 3.40 3.30 3.21 3.20 3.20 3.59 3.78 3.71 3.71 3.58 3.19

'95 '96 '97 '98 '99 '00 '01 '02 '03 '04 '05 '06

QUICK STUDY

SCORES

Trade Policy   3.5
Fiscal Burden   1.9
Government Intervention   1.5
Monetary Policy   4
Foreign Investment   3
Banking and Finance   3
Wages and Prices   3
Property Rights   4
Regulation   4
Informal Market   4

Population: 21,744,000

Total area: 237,500 sq. km

GDP: $42.7 billion

GDP growth rate: 4.9%

GDP per capita: $1,963

Major exports: textiles and footwear, base metals, machinery and transport equipment, minerals and fuels, agricultural products

Exports of goods and services: $16.9 billion

Major export trading partners: Italy 24.3%, Germany 15.7%, France 7.4%, UK 6.7%

Major imports: machinery and transport equipment, textiles, clothing and footwear, minerals and fuels

Imports of goods and services: $21.3 billion

Major import trading partners: Italy 19.6%, Germany 14.9%, Russia 8.3%

Foreign direct investment (net): $1.4 billion

2003 Data (in constant 2000 US dollars)

Romania remains an important U.S. ally in the strategic Black Sea basin, a transit area for Caspian oil. Together with fellow NATO member Bulgaria, it is changing the strategic balance around the Black Sea. The cabinet formed after the November 2004 legislative elections is headed by the National Liberal Party's Clain Popescu Tariceanu. The governing coalition's four parties—the National Liberal Party, Democratic Party, Hungarian Democratic Union in Romania, and Romanian Humanist Party—are allies only out of necessity. Under a March 2004 agreement with the International Monetary Fund, the government has begun to accelerate reforms in the energy sector, complete its privatization plans, and improve the business environment. In February 2005, Romania reached an agreement with the IMF on macroeconomic targets, focusing primarily on fiscal policy. The IMF has recommended that Romania balance its budget (from a 1.2 percent of GDP deficit in 2004) by raising taxes, but the government has been reluctant to carry out this recommendation. Romania's monetary policy is focused on diminishing double-digit inflation, redenomination of the luel (which occurred in July 2005), and financial liberalization. The rise in foreign direct investment seems to signal an improvement in business. Romania's trade policy score is 0.5 point worse this year; however, its fiscal burden of government score is 1.4 points better, and its government intervention, monetary policy, and capital flows and foreign investment scores are 1 point better. As a result, Romania's overall score is 0.39 point better this year.

 TRADE POLICY
Score: **3.5**–Worse (high level of protectionism)

According to the World Bank, Romania's weighted average tariff rate in 2001 (the most recent year for which World Bank data are available) was 8.3 percent. (The World Bank has revised the figure for 2001 upward from the 7.3 percent reported in the 2005 *Index*). The U.S. Trade Representative reports that corruption is an obstacle to trade, as are sanitary, phytosanitary, and other regulations as Romania harmonizes its standards with those of the European Union. Based on the higher tariff rate, as well as a revision of the trade factor methodology, Romania's trade policy score is 0.5 point worse this year.

 FISCAL BURDEN OF GOVERNMENT
Score—Income Taxation: **1.5**–Better (low tax rates)
Score—Corporate Taxation: **1.5**–Better (low tax rates)
Score—Change in Government Expenditures: **3**–Stable (very low decrease)
Final Score: **1.9**–Better (low cost of government)

Effective January 2005, Romania implemented a flat income tax rate of 16 percent and adopted a flat corporate income tax rate of 16 percent. In 2003, according to the International Monetary Fund, government expenditures as a share of GDP remained unchanged at 32.2 percent, compared to the 1.1 percentage point decrease in 2002. On net, Romania's fiscal burden of government score is 1.4 points better this year.

 GOVERNMENT INTERVENTION IN THE ECONOMY
Score: **1.5**–Better (low level)

The World Bank reports that the government consumed 8.9 percent of GDP in 2003. In 2004, based on data from the International Monetary Fund, Romania received 4.93 percent of its total revenues from state-owned enterprises and government ownership of property. Based on more reliable data and new evidence of lower government consumption and ownership of property, Romania's government intervention score is 1 point better this year.

MONETARY POLICY
Score: 4–Better (high level of inflation)

From 1995 to 2004, Romania's weighted average annual rate of inflation was 14.99 percent, down from the 20.35 percent from 1994 to 2003 reported in the 2005 *Index*. As a result, Romania's monetary policy score is 1 point better this year.

CAPITAL FLOWS AND FOREIGN INVESTMENT
Score: 3–Better (moderate barriers)

Although foreign investment is officially welcome in Romania, the Economist Intelligence Unit reports that "Romania's performance in attracting FDI has lagged far behind potential." According to the U.S. Trade Representative, "A continued impediment to foreign investment is Romania's inconsistent legal and regulatory system. Tax laws change frequently and are unevenly enforced. Tort cases often require lengthy, expensive procedures, and judges' rulings are often not enforced." The government, however, is taking steps to attract more foreign investment. The EIU reports that it has "introduced a new Fiscal Code, which is intended to bring greater certainty to the Romanian tax system…[and] a silent approval procedure for the issuing and renewal of licenses" and has simplified "the procedures for obtaining work permits and long-term visas for expatriates…." The International Monetary Fund reports that residents and non-residents may hold foreign exchange accounts, subject to restrictions and government approval in some cases. All payments and transfers must be documented. Most restrictions on capital transactions have been removed, and the few transactions requiring central bank approval are those involving derivatives. Based on evidence that regulations governing capital flows have been liberalized, Romania's capital flows and foreign investment score is 1 point better this year.

BANKING AND FINANCE
Score: 3–Stable (moderate level of restrictions)

The government has sold a number of state-owned banks but still plays a significant role. "As of mid-2003," reports First Initiative, "there were 38 banks in Romania, 31 of which were majority foreign-owned. The government of Romania and the National Bank of Romania (the Central Bank) made progress in the late 1990s with the liquidation of Bancorex and the privatization of the state-owned Banca Agricola. Banca Comerciala Romana, Romania's largest bank, is now in the process of privatization after extensive delays (2003)." According to the Economist Intelligence Unit, "Out of the 38 banks operating in Romania in December 2003, only three remain in state hands, including the largest commercial bank, BCR. The government sold a 25% share in BCR to the EBRD [European Bank for Recon-

struction and Development] and the International Finance Corporation (IFC) in September 2003, and is seeking a strategic investor to take a majority stake in the bank. The state also holds a majority stake in Eximbank and is the sole owner of the State Savings Bank (CEC), both of which are being restructured in preparation for privatisation…. The share of state-owned banks in total net banking sector assets fell from 75% in 1998 to 26% in 2003, and will fall to 10% when BCR is fully privatised." Majority foreign-owned banks accounted for 59 percent of total bank assets and 55 percent of total deposits in 2004.

WAGES AND PRICES
Score: 3–Stable (moderate level of intervention)

Some prices are set through Romania's state-owned enterprises, which include (but are not limited to) enterprises in the energy, utilities, chemical plants, transportation, movie theaters, and metal sectors. According to the U.S. Department of Commerce, "All prices have been liberalized, with the exception of prices of electricity and gas supplied for domestic consumption, which continue to be controlled by the government." The government establishes a minimum wage.

PROPERTY RIGHTS
Score: 4–Stable (low level of protection)

The U.S. Trade Representative reports that investors' most common complaints include "the frequency with which the government changes its laws…weak enforcement of existing laws, concerns about judicial competence, lack of court impartiality, and corruption." According to the U.S. Department of Commerce, "Judges generally have little experience in the functioning of a market economy, international business methods, or the application of new Romanian commercial laws."

REGULATION
Score: 4–Stable (high level)

The Economist Intelligence Unit reports that among key issues for investors are "the unpredictable legal and regulatory system…[and] excessive red tape…." According to the U.S. Department of Commerce, "investors point to the excessive time it takes to secure necessary zoning permits, property titles, licenses, and utility hook-ups…. [R]egulations change frequently, sometimes literally overnight, often without advance notice. These changes…can significantly add to the costs of doing business [and] make it difficult for investors to develop effective business plans." The Embassy of Romania reports that a "one-stop shop" will streamline the process for registering a business, but the *Financial Times* reports that this reform applies only to "investors with more than [US]$10 m[illion]." Corruption in the bureaucracy is widespread.

INFORMAL MARKET
Score: 4–Stable (high level of activity)

Transparency International's 2004 score for Romania is 2.9. Therefore, Romania's informal market score is 4 this year.

RUSSIA

Rank: 122

Score: 3.50

Category: Mostly Unfree

Present & Past Scores

(Best) 1
2
3 — 3.60 3.70 3.83 3.54 3.65 3.80 3.84 3.74 3.54 3.51 3.61 3.50
4
(Worst) 5
'95 '96 '97 '98 '99 '00 '01 '02 '03 '04 '05 '06

Since his March 2004 re-election, President Vladimir Putin has concentrated on consolidating his power. Russia continues to benefit from high oil prices, and GDP grew by 6.8 percent in 2004, but the crackdown on the Yukos oil company and a $1 billion tax bill against British Petroleum's Russian joint venture partner TNK have hurt the investment climate. Steps by Natural Resources Minister Yurii Trutnev to limit Western investments in raw materials, along with anti-Western investment legislation introduced in May 2005, have led to higher capital outflows. In the energy sector, in addition to the decrepit state-owned pipeline infrastructure, state-owned Rosneft has absorbed Yukos subsidiary Yugansk. Strong inflationary pressures have added to the slowdown. In addition, Russia's population is aging and declining by 0.7 million people per year, and its social indicators are among the worst in the industrial world. Russia earned strong European Union support for its membership in the World Trade Organization by ratifying the Kyoto Protocol on climate change in October 2004. However, the Kremlin's promotion of Viktor Yanukovich (Ukrainian President Viktor Yushchenko's electoral opponent), nuclear cooperation with Iran, intended missile sales to Syria and Brazil, and weapons sales to Venezuela demonstrate that imperial nostalgia continues to drive Russia's policies. Russia's fiscal burden of government score is 0.6 point better this year, and its government intervention score is 0.5 point better. As a result, Russia's overall score is 0.11 point better this year.

QUICK STUDY

SCORES

Trade Policy	3.5
Fiscal Burden	2.5
Government Intervention	2
Monetary Policy	4
Foreign Investment	4
Banking and Finance	4
Wages and Prices	3
Property Rights	4
Regulation	4
Informal Market	4

Population: 143,425,000

Total area: 17,075,200 sq. km

GDP: $306.7 billion

GDP growth rate: 7.3%

GDP per capita: $2,138

Major exports: mineral products, metals, machinery, chemicals, petroleum and natural gas

Exports of goods and services: $148.7 billion

Major export trading partners: Germany 7.8%, Netherlands 6.5%, Italy 6.3%, China 6.2%, Belarus 5.7%, US 4.6%

Major imports: food and agricultural products, machinery and equipment, chemicals, metals

Imports of goods and services: $101.5 billion

Major import trading partners: Germany 14.0%, Belarus 8.6%, Ukraine 7.7%, China 5.8%, US 5.2%

Foreign direct investment (net): −$2.8 billion

2003 Data (in constant 2000 US dollars)

TRADE POLICY
Score: 3.5–Stable (high level of protectionism)

The World Bank reports that Russia's weighted average tariff rate in 2002 (the most recent year for which World Bank data are available) was 8.7 percent. (The World Bank has revised the figure for 2002 upward from the 8.4 percent reported in the 2005 *Index*). According to the U.S. Trade Representative, non-tariff barriers include "tariff-rate quotas, discriminatory and prohibitive charges and fees, and discriminatory licensing, registration, and certification regimes." Based on the revised trade factor methodology, Russia's trade policy score is unchanged.

FISCAL BURDEN OF GOVERNMENT
Score—Income Taxation: **1.5–Stable** (low tax rates)
Score—Corporate Taxation: **3–Stable** (moderate tax rates)
Score—Change in Government Expenditures: **2.5–Better** (low decrease)
Final Score: **2.5–Better** (moderate cost of government)

According to Deloitte, Russia has a flat income tax rate of 13 percent. The top corporate tax rate is 24 percent. In 2003, according to the International Monetary Fund, government expenditures as a share of GDP decreased by 1.5 percentage points to 35.5 percent, compared to a 4.1 percentage point increase in 2002. On net, Russia's fiscal burden of government score is 0.6 point better this year.

GOVERNMENT INTERVENTION IN THE ECONOMY
Score: **2–Better** (low level)

The World Bank reports that the government consumed 15.9 percent of GDP in 2003. In the same year, based on data from the Ministry of Finance, Russia received 4.36 percent of its total revenues from state-owned enterprises and government ownership of property, down from the 8.06 percent reported in the 2005 *Index*. As a result, Russia's government intervention score is 0.5 point better this year.

MONETARY POLICY
Score: **4**–Stable (high level of inflation)

From 1994 to 2003, Russia's weighted average annual rate of inflation was 12.77 percent.

CAPITAL FLOWS AND FOREIGN INVESTMENT
Score: **4**–Stable (high barriers)

Official and unofficial barriers impede foreign investment in Russia. Officially, Russia restricts investments in aerospace, natural gas, insurance, electric power, defense, natural resources, Russian liquor concerns, and large-scale construction projects. "The 1991 investment code guarantees foreign investors rights equal to those of Russian investors. The July 1999 law on foreign investment confirmed the principle of national treatment…. However, in practice, these protections have not been provided," reports the U.S. Department of Commerce. "The uncertainty and lack of clarity of Russian tax law and administration, inconsistent government regulations, the unreliability of the legal system as well as crime and corruption all dissuade investors." In 2005, the government announced a decision barring foreign-controlled companies from bidding on its most lucrative natural resources. According to the U.S. Department of Commerce, "While in previous years the Russian federal leadership was deemed unlikely to nationalize foreign investment or engage in expropriation, the Yukos case may raise some doubts about this assumption. At the sub-federal level, expropriation has been a problem." The International Monetary Fund reports that residents and non-residents may hold foreign exchange accounts, subject to restrictions and government approval in some cases. Payments and transfers are subject to restrictions and surrender requirements. Transactions involving capital and money market instruments, derivatives, and credit operations are subject to central bank authorization in many cases.

BANKING AND FINANCE
Score: **4**–Stable (high level of restrictions)

The banking sector is dominated by two state-owned banks. "As of end-2003," reports First Initiative, "there were approximately 1,300 banks in Russia, the majority of which were small and illiquid. Foreign participation in the banking sector is limited. The largest bank is the state-owned Sberbank, which together with the state-owned Vneshtorgbank held nearly 35% of loans in 2003…. [T]he [insurance] sector is highly concentrated, with the top 100 firms controlling over 90% of the premiums. Foreign participation in the sector is restricted, and foreign-controlled companies may not offer life insurance at all." The Economist Intelligence Unit reports that only 50 of Russia's 1,300 banks "perform any significant banking busi-

ness. The rest are either captive banks of industrial groups or investment funds." An additional concern "is the concentration of the financial industry among the state-owned banks and their links to a handful of major raw-materials exporters." The EIU also reports that a central bank license is required for resident banks to extend foreign currency loans to non-resident companies and individuals for more than 180 days. There is a 49 percent cap on foreign ownership of life insurance firms, and total foreign assets in the sector are capped at 15 percent.

WAGES AND PRICES
Score: **3**–Stable (moderate level of intervention)

The Economist Intelligence Unit reports that the government controls the prices of utilities (gas, electricity, and telecommunications), railways, local transport, communal services and pharmaceuticals. It also controls the prices of companies that have a "dominant" position (that is, +35% of market share). As of this writing, there were 650 such legal entities, of which 400 are medium-sized companies. Russia has a minimum wage.

PROPERTY RIGHTS
Score: **4**–Stable (low level of protection)

Protection of private property in Russia is weak. The Economist Intelligence Unit reports that "Russia's judicial system is still relatively weak and unpredictable. Corruption is rife among law enforcement bodies and judges, and court decisions are often difficult to implement. Many foreign investors have experienced problems in executing court rulings, and in obtaining satisfaction from contractual agreements."

REGULATION
Score: **4**–Stable (high level)

According to the U.S. Department of Commerce, Russia's legal system "is in a state of flux, with various parts of government struggling to create new laws on a broad array of topics…. Russia has implemented only part of its new commercial code (contained within the civil code) and investors must carefully research all aspects of Russian law to ensure that each contract conforms with Russian law and embodies the basic provisions of the new, and where still valid, old codes…. Keeping up with legislative changes, presidential decrees and government resolutions is a challenging task. Uneven implementation of laws creates further complications; various officials, branches of government and jurisdictions interpret and apply regulations with little consistency and the decisions of one may be overruled or contested by another." Bureaucratic corruption is widespread.

INFORMAL MARKET
Score: **4**–Stable (high level of activity)

Transparency International's 2004 score for Russia is 2.8. Therefore, Russia's informal market score is 4 this year.

RWANDA

Rank: 125

Score: 3.53

Category: Mostly Unfree

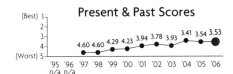

Present & Past Scores

(Best) 1—
2—
3—
4—
(Worst) 5—

4.60 4.60 4.29 4.23 3.94 3.78 3.93 3.41 3.54 3.53

'95 '96 '97 '98 '99 '00 '01 '02 '03 '04 '05 '06
n/a n/a

QUICK STUDY

SCORES

Trade Policy	3
Fiscal Burden	4.3
Government Intervention	2
Monetary Policy	3
Foreign Investment	4
Banking and Finance	3
Wages and Prices	3
Property Rights	4
Regulation	4
Informal Market	5

Population: 8,395,000

Total area: 26,338 sq. km

GDP: $2.2 billion

GDP growth rate: 3.2%

GDP per capita: $260

Major exports: tea, coffee, hides

Exports of goods and services: $206.7 million

Major export trading partners: Indonesia 39.4%, Germany 4.7%, China 4.2%

Major imports: capital goods, machinery and equipment, foodstuffs

Imports of goods and services: $464 million

Major import trading partners: Kenya 23.3%, Germany 7.3%, Belgium 6.4%, Uganda 6.3%

Foreign direct investment (net): $3.8 million

2003 Data (in constant 2000 US dollars)

The largely Tutsi Rwandan Patriotic Front (RFP) took power following the 1994 genocide and ruled through a transition Government of National Unity until the 2003 elections. The RFP's Paul Kagame was elected president in August 2003 in Rwanda's first multi-candidate election since independence. The RFP also won a majority of seats in the legislature in September 2003. The elections, although peaceful, were marred by serious irregularities. Political power remains firmly in the hands of the RFP, and most opposition has been silenced through restrictive regulations. Politicians who speak out on sensitive topics—such as the underrepresentation of Hutus in politics—are treated harshly. The economy has achieved pre-war levels but in many ways is still recovering from the devastating 1994 genocide. Rwanda is very poor, with a majority of the population living in poverty and over 85 percent engaged in subsistence agriculture. Much economic activity occurs in the informal market. Relations between Rwanda and neighboring Uganda remain tense, with each country accusing the other of espionage and threatening its national security. Rwanda will benefit from substantial debt relief now that it has reached its completion point for the International Monetary Fund and World Bank Heavily Indebted Poor Country initiative. Rwanda's monetary policy score is 1 point worse this year; however, its fiscal burden of government score is 0.1 point better, and its banking and finance score is 1 point better. As a result, Rwanda's overall score is 0.01 point better this year.

TRADE POLICY
Score: **3**–Stable (moderate level of protectionism)

According to the World Bank, Rwanda's weighted average tariff rate in 2003 (the most recent year for which World Bank data are available) was 6.6 percent, the same as that reported for 2001 in the 2005 *Index*, also based on World Bank data. According to the World Trade Organization, the only imports expressly prohibited are asbestos and products that contain asbestos. In addition, "For health reasons, the importation of certain products is subject to approval by the Ministry of Health. Imports of products such as explosives or arms require [authorization]." Customs corruption is a problem. Based on the revised trade factor methodology, Rwanda's trade policy score is unchanged.

FISCAL BURDEN OF GOVERNMENT
Score—Income Taxation: **3.5**–Better (high tax rates)
Score—Corporate Taxation: **4.5**–Stable (very high tax rates)
Score—Change in Government Expenditures: **4.5**–Stable (high increase)
Final Score: **4.3**–Better (high cost of government)

Rwanda's top income tax rate is 35 percent, down from the 40 percent reported in the 2005 *Index*. The top corporate tax rate is also 35 percent. In 2003, according to the African Development Bank, government expenditures as a share of GDP increased 2.8 percentage points to 24.1 percent, compared to the 0.3 percentage point increase in 2002. On net, Rwanda's fiscal burden of government score is 0.1 point better this year.

GOVERNMENT INTERVENTION IN THE ECONOMY
Score: **2**–Stable (low level)

The World Bank reports that the government consumed 13.8 percent of GDP in 2003. In 2004, based on data from the International Monetary Fund, Rwanda received 4.55 percent of its total revenues from state-owned enterprises and government ownership of property.

 ## MONETARY POLICY
Score: **3**–Worse (moderate level of inflation)

From 1995 to 2004, based on data from the International Monetary Fund's *2005 World Economic Outlook*, Rwanda's weighted average annual rate of inflation was 9.64 percent, up from the 5.38 percent from 1994 to 2003 reported in the 2005 *Index*. As a result, Rwanda's monetary policy score is 1 point worse this year.

 ## CAPITAL FLOWS AND FOREIGN INVESTMENT
Score: **4**–Stable (high barriers)

Rwanda welcomes foreign investment and has adopted several initiatives, including a one-stop-shop, to facilitate investment. However, it continues to have difficulty attracting foreign investment because of corruption, ongoing concern about latent political instability, and existing political instability in neighboring countries. According to the Economist Intelligence Unit, "the lack of predictability in executing routine matters, owing to slow-moving bureaucratic structures and the lax enforcement of contracts, are among the problems encountered by investors." The government relaxed some restrictions on foreign investment in June 2000 and adopted a floating exchange rate in July 2000, but the International Monetary Fund reports that authorities intervene to influence the rate. The IMF reports that both residents and non-residents may hold foreign exchange accounts, but only if they provide supporting documentation. Payments and transfers are subject to authorizations and maximum allowances and limits. Nearly all capital transactions require the central bank's approval.

 ## BANKING AND FINANCE
Score: **3**–Better (moderate level of restrictions)

"The Rwandan financial sector is very small," reports First Initiative, "and is comprised primarily of a small banking and micro-finance sector. In mid-2004, there were nine commercial banks operating in Rwanda, five of which were established following the war…. In general, the banking sector is plagued by a large percentage of non-performing loans." According to the Economist Intelligence Unit, "The government sold an 80% stake in the Banque commerciale du Rwanda (BCR) in August 2004 to Actis, which manages funds on behalf of the UK's Commonwealth Development Corporation, for US$6m. Also in August 2004, the government sold 80% of the Banque continentale africaine au Rwanda (Bacar) for US$3.8m to a consortium consisting of FINA Bank of Kenya and Enterprise Holdings of Botswana." The state plays a large role in the insurance sector, according to the EIU, which reports that "state-owned Sonarwa is the largest [insurer] and is due to be privatised. Another parastatal, Soras, has 25% of the insurance market and, like Sonarwa, concentrates on vehicle insurance."

Based on evidence that the government is reducing its role in the banking sector, Rwanda's banking and finance score is 1 point better this year.

 ## WAGES AND PRICES
Score: **3**–Stable (moderate level of intervention)

The market sets most prices, but the government reserves its right to control prices in case of market failure. According to the World Trade Organization, "The list of sensitive goods and services for which prices may be fixed is established by ministerial order…. A draft order, once adopted, will confirm price control for goods and services such as: petroleum products, medicines, sugar, rice, cement, medical consultations, water, electricity, public transport and postal services." The government sets minimum wages that vary by type of job.

 ## PROPERTY RIGHTS
Score: **4**–Stable (low level of protection)

Property rights have improved in Rwanda since the genocide in 1994 and 1995, although there is still uncertainty regarding the protection of private property. According to the Economist Intelligence Unit, the judiciary "has never displayed much de facto independence and can usually be relied on to deliver verdicts favourable to the authorities." In addition, "Land ownership is a sensitive issue, and the government is preparing new legislation with extreme caution." The U.S. Department of State reports that Rwanda's judiciary "suffers from inefficiency, a lack of resources, and some corruption. There were occasional reports of bribery of officials, ranging from clerks to judges."

 ## REGULATION
Score: **4**–Stable (high level)

The Economist Intelligence Unit reports that "numerous policy initiatives [are] under way in Rwanda, and in many instances this is leading to confusion and extra layers of bureaucracy." According to the U.S. Department of Commerce, "A private sector regulatory law…passed by the National Assembly in 2001…created a regulatory board to regulate the utility sectors in Rwanda…. A new regulatory agency provides guidance on granting licenses, enforcing regulations, addressing anti-competitive activities, and implementing standards." The EIU also reports that "some local manufacturers and import-exporters insist that graft has worsened and that unofficial payments to state officials are a major impediment to their profitability."

 ## INFORMAL MARKET
Score: **5**–Stable (very high level of activity)

Most economic activity occurs informally. According to the Economist Intelligence Unit, "Officially recorded exports and imports leave a substantial share of Rwanda's total trade unaccounted for and this 'informal' sector is believed to be doing substantially better than the formal sector."

SAUDI ARABIA

Rank: 62

Score: 2.84

Category: Mostly Free

Present & Past Scores

(Best) 1-
2-
3-
4-
(Worst) 5-

3.00 3.00 2.94 3.16 3.20 3.35 3.16 3.09 3.05 2.99 2.84

'95 '96 '97 '98 '99 '00 '01 '02 '03 '04 '05 '06
n/a

QUICK STUDY

SCORES

Trade Policy	3
Fiscal Burden	1.4
Government Intervention	4.5
Monetary Policy	1
Foreign Investment	4
Banking and Finance	3
Wages and Prices	2
Property Rights	3
Regulation	3
Informal Market	3.5

Population: 22,528,000

Total area: 1,960,582 sq. km

GDP: $203.6 billion

GDP growth rate: 7.2%

GDP per capita: $9,038

Major exports: crude oil, oil products

Exports of goods and services: $100.7 billion

Major export trading partners: US 20.7%, Japan 15.4%, South Korea 9.8%, Singapore 4.2%

Major imports: machinery and transport equipment, chemical products

Imports of goods and services: $51.7 billion

Major import trading partners: US 9.3%, Japan 7.6%, Germany 7.3%, UK 6.1%

Foreign direct investment (net): $145.4 million

2003 Data (in constant 2000 US dollars)

Saudi Arabia, the largest Persian Gulf oil kingdom, was founded in 1932 by King Abdul Aziz al-Saud and has been ruled as an absolute monarchy by the Saud dynasty ever since. Crown Prince Abdullah officially became monarch in August 2005 following the death of King Fahd, who had suffered a debilitating stroke 10 years earlier. Saudi Arabia contains the world's largest proven oil reserves, with over 260 billion barrels of oil—about one-quarter of global supplies. As the world's foremost oil producer and exporter, it plays a dominant role in the Organization of Petroleum Exporting Countries (OPEC). Saudi Arabia faces a rapidly growing population, high unemployment rates, and political challenges from Islamic extremists. The traditional alliance between the Saudi dynasty and the Wahhabi religious establishment has been strained by radical young clerics who have denounced the royal family for corruption and close ties to the United States. To stem popular discontent, the government held its first nationwide municipal elections in February 2005, although women were excluded from voting. The government has sought to diversify the economy to reduce its dependence on oil exports and strengthen the private sector. In December 2004, 70 percent of the state-owned National Company for Cooperative Insurance, the largest insurance company in the Arab world, was sold to private investors, and there are plans to privatize other state enterprises. Saudi Arabia's informal market score is 0.5 point worse this year; however, its trade policy score and banking and finance score are 1 point better. As a result, Saudi Arabia's overall score is 0.15 point better this year.

TRADE POLICY
Score: **3–Better** (moderate level of protectionism)

According to the World Bank, Saudi Arabia's weighted average tariff rate in 2004 was 7.3 percent, down from the 11.4 percent for 2000 reported in the 2005 *Index*, based on World Bank data. The U.S. Trade Representative reports that "importation of alcohol, firearms, illegal drugs, pork products, and used clothing is prohibited." Imports of nearly two dozen other products require special approval. Based on the lower tariff rate, as well as a revision of the trade factor methodology, Saudi Arabia's trade policy score is 1 point better this year.

FISCAL BURDEN OF GOVERNMENT
Score—Income Taxation: **1–Stable** (very low tax rates)
Score—Corporate Taxation: **1–Stable** (very low tax rates)
Score—Change in Government Expenditures: **2.5–Stable** (low decrease)
Final Score: **1.4–Stable** (very low cost of government)

According to Deloitte and the Economist Intelligence Unit, Saudi Arabia has no income tax or corporate tax either for Saudi nationals or for citizens of the Gulf Cooperation Council (GCC). However, a fixed 2.5 percent religious tax called *Zakat* is mandated by Islamic law and applied to Saudi and GCC individuals and corporations. In 2003, according to the Economist Intelligence Unit, government expenditures as a share of GDP decreased by 1 percentage point to 32 percent, compared to the 4.2 percentage point decrease in 2002.

GOVERNMENT INTERVENTION IN THE ECONOMY
Score: **4.5–Stable** (very high level)

According to the World Bank, the government consumed 24.6 percent of GDP in 2003. In the same year, based on data from the Saudi Arabian Monetary Agency, Saudi Arabia received 78.84 percent of its total revenues from state-owned oil companies.

 ## MONETARY POLICY
Score: **1**–Stable (very low level of inflation)

From 1995 to 2004, Saudi Arabia's weighted average annual rate of inflation was 0.34 percent.

 ## CAPITAL FLOWS AND FOREIGN INVESTMENT
Score: **4**–Stable (high barriers)

Although Saudi Arabia has taken steps to open its economy to foreign investments, substantial barriers remain. In 2003, the government reduced the "negative list" of sectors that are off-limits to foreign investors from 22 to 19. Foreign investors may own real property, subject to restrictions, and no longer are required to have a local partner. The U.S. Department of Commerce lists "a government requirement that companies hire Saudi nationals, slow payment of some government contracts, an increasingly restrictive visa policy for all workers, [and] enforced segregation of the sexes in most business and social settings" as disincentives to investment. All foreign investment projects must obtain a license from the Saudi government. According to the U.S. Trade Representative, "Only foreign-owned corporations and the foreign-owned portion of joint ventures are subject to the corporate income tax, which ranges from 20 percent to 30 percent of net profits. Domestic corporate partners are subject to a 2.5 percent tax on assets." The International Monetary Fund reports that residents may hold foreign exchange accounts but that approval is required for non-residents. There are no controls or restrictions on payments and transfers. Only Saudi Arabian and Gulf Cooperation Council nationals and corporations may engage in portfolio investment in listed Saudi Arabian companies or buy securities, bonds, or money market instruments, and non-residents must have permission to issue them in Saudi Arabia. Credit operations must be approved.

 ## BANKING AND FINANCE
Score: **3**–Better (moderate level of restrictions)

The U.S. Department of Commerce reports that "there are 11 banks operating in Saudi Arabia, ten majority-owned Saudi banks and one GCC bank, Gulf Investment Bank (Bahrain). Three other GCC-based banks…hold licenses to operate in the Kingdom, but have not yet opened their doors. In 2003, the Saudi Arabian Monetary Agency (SAMA) granted Deutsche Bank the first foreign (non-GCC) banking license in 20 years." According to the Economist Intelligence Unit, "The ten domestic commercial banks are heavily exposed to the government and to contractors dependent on government payments." Most banks are joint ventures with foreign banks. The government owns 50 percent of the National Commercial Bank and five specialized credit institutions. It also recently privatized 70 percent of the largest insurance company—the state-owned National Company for Co-operative Insurance. Foreign investment is now permitted in the insurance sector. Based on evidence that the government is further opening the financial sector to foreign investment, Saudi Arabia's banking and finance score is 1 point better this year.

 ## WAGES AND PRICES
Score: **2**–Stable (low level of intervention)

The market determines most wages and prices. The Economist Intelligence Unit reports that "Islamic law forbids price controls; hence, they are illegal in Saudi Arabia. Although this applies to goods supplied by the private sector, public sector goods are often heavily subsidised and sold at non-market prices…. Medicines are dispensed on a subsidised basis through the health service but not through retail outlets. Price controls on subsidised cement or building materials are administered at both the ex-factory and the wholesale level, depending on whether the item in question is produced locally or imported. A government purchasing agency controls prices for wheat and barley." There is no legal minimum wage.

 ## PROPERTY RIGHTS
Score: **3**–Stable (moderate level of protection)

According to the Economist Intelligence Unit, "Investors and expatriates working in the kingdom continue to question the efficacy and impartiality of Saudi courts.…the workings of the commercial courts are slow and opaque; others suggest that the courts routinely favour Saudi parties, particularly those with connections to the ruling elite, in disputes with foreign firms or individuals. The enforcement and hence the security of contracts are hampered by the complex nature, lengthy process and dubious neutrality of the judiciary."

 ## REGULATION
Score: **3**–Stable (moderate level)

Regulations are not transparent in Saudi Arabia, and bureaucracy poses a substantial hurdle for businesses. Implementation of laws can be inconsistent. According to the U.S. Department of Commerce, "There are few aspects of the Saudi government's regulatory system that are transparent, though Saudi investment policy is less opaque than many other areas. Saudi tax and labor laws and policies tend to favor high-tech transfers and the employment of Saudis rather than fostering competition.… Bureaucratic procedures are cumbersome, but red tape can generally be overcome with persistence." In addition, "Foreign firms have identified corruption as an obstacle to investment.… Bribes, often disguised as 'commissions,' are reputed to be commonplace."

 ## INFORMAL MARKET
Score: **3.5**–Worse (high level of activity)

Transparency International's 2004 score for Saudi Arabia is 3.4. Therefore, Saudi Arabia's informal market score is 3.5 this year—0.5 point worse than last year.

SENEGAL

Rank: 83

Score: 3.10

Category: Mostly Unfree

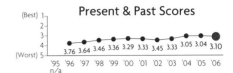

Present & Past Scores

(Best) 1
2
3
4
(Worst) 5

3.76 3.64 3.46 3.36 3.29 3.33 3.45 3.33 3.05 3.04 3.10

'95 '96 '97 '98 '99 '00 '01 '02 '03 '04 '05 '06
n/a

QUICK STUDY

SCORES

Trade Policy	3.5
Fiscal Burden	4.5
Government Intervention	2
Monetary Policy	1
Foreign Investment	3
Banking and Finance	4
Wages and Prices	2
Property Rights	3
Regulation	4
Informal Market	4

Population: 10,240,000

Total area: 196,190 sq. km

GDP: $5 billion

GDP growth rate: 6.5%

GDP per capita: $485

Major exports: fish, groundnuts (peanuts), petroleum products, phosphates, cotton

Exports of goods and services: $1.4 billion

Major export trading partners: India 13.0%, France 12.2%, Italy 8.5%, Spain 5.0%

Major imports: foods and beverages, consumer goods, capital goods, petroleum products

Imports of goods and services: $1.7 billion

Major import trading partners: France 24.9%, Nigeria 12.2%, Thailand 6.7%, Spain 4.3%

Foreign direct investment (net): $63.5 million

2003 Data (in constant 2000 US dollars)

Senegal is one of the few African countries with a long-standing democratic tradition. President Abdoulaye Wade was elected in March 2000 and is permitted by law to stand for re-election in 2007. Wade's governing coalition of allied parties continues to control the legislature, but multiple shuffles have weakened the representation of allied parties in the cabinet, causing support for him to erode. A new peace accord between the government and the rebel Mouvement des Forces Démocratiques de Casamance (MFDC) in southern Senegal's Casamance region was signed in December 2004. MFDC leader Father Augustin Diamacoune Senghor signed the accord, which Wade had initiated, raising hopes that this agreement will be more successful than past efforts. Senegal's superior transportation and telecommunication infrastructure has made it a regional gateway and business center. Services are the largest contributor to GDP, but agriculture and fishing, which involve an estimated three-quarters of the labor force, are also critical to the economy. The government has implemented a series of economic reforms aimed at liberalizing the economy, including breaking up monopolies and privatizing state-owned enterprises. Senegal is eligible for assistance from the U.S. Millennium Challenge Account. Senegal's wages and prices score is 1 point better this year; however, its fiscal burden of government score is 0.1 point worse, its banking and finance score is 1 point worse, and its informal market score is 0.5 point worse. As a result, Senegal's overall score is 0.06 point worse this year.

TRADE POLICY
Score: **3.5**–Stable (high level of protectionism)

Senegal is a member of the West African Economic and Monetary Union (WAEMU), which imposes a common external tariff with four rates: 0 percent, 5 percent, 10 percent, and 20 percent. The World Bank reports that Senegal's weighted average tariff rate in 2004 was 9.2 percent, up from the 8.4 percent for 2002 reported in the 2005 *Index*, based on World Bank data. Customs corruption serves as a trade barrier, but the U.S. Department of Commerce notes that "Customs has initiated an action plan to combat fraud." Based on the revised trade factor methodology, Senegal's trade policy score is unchanged.

FISCAL BURDEN OF GOVERNMENT
Score—Income Taxation: **5**–Stable (very high tax rates)
Score—Corporate Taxation: **4.5**–Stable (very high tax rates)
Score—Change in Government Expenditures: **4**–Better (moderate increase)
Final Score: **4.5**–Worse (very high cost of government)

Senegal's top income tax rate is 50 percent. The top corporate tax rate is 33 percent, down from the 35 percent reported in the 2005 *Index*. In 2003, according to the African Development Bank, government expenditures as a share of GDP increased 1.8 percentage points to 22.8 percent, compared to the 0.7 percentage point decrease in 2002. On net, Senegal's fiscal burden of government score is 0.1 point worse this year.

GOVERNMENT INTERVENTION IN THE ECONOMY
Score: **2**–Stable (low level)

The World Bank reports that the government consumed 14.6 percent of GDP in 2003. In the same year, according to the International Monetary Fund, Senegal received 2.82 percent of its

total revenues from state-owned enterprises and government ownership of property.

MONETARY POLICY
Score: **1**–Stable (very low level of inflation)

As a member of the West African Economic and Monetary Union, Senegal uses the CFA franc, pegged to the euro. From 1995 to 2004, Senegal's weighted average annual rate of inflation was 0.62 percent.

CAPITAL FLOWS AND FOREIGN INVESTMENT
Score: **3**–Stable (moderate barriers)

There is no legal discrimination against foreign investors, and 100 percent foreign ownership of businesses is permitted in most sectors, except in the electricity, telecommunications, mining, and water sectors. Repatriation of profit and capital is guaranteed. However, the unofficial barriers to investment are substantial. "Judicial, tax, customs and other regulatory decisions are frequently inconsistent, tardy and non-transparent," reports the U.S. Department of Commerce. "Few procurement decisions consistently follow [government] guidelines mandating a free and transparent tender process. Labor laws in particular are seen as a disincentive to investment by foreign investors. The firing for cause or malfeasance of employees are [*sic*] sometimes successfully challenged in the court, leading to the reinstatement of the fired employee as well as the payment of damages." According to the International Monetary Fund, the government must approve most capital transfers to countries other than members of the West African Economic and Monetary Union. Other transfers are subject to numerous requirements, controls, and authorization depending on the transaction. Residents must receive approval from the Central Bank of West African States, or BCEAO, and the Senegalese government to hold foreign exchange accounts, and non-residents must receive approval from the BCEAO. Most capital transactions to countries other than members of the WAEMU require approval of or declaration to the government.

BANKING AND FINANCE
Score: **4**–Worse (high level of restrictions)

The BCEAO, a central bank common to the eight members of the WAEMU, governs Senegal's banking system. Member countries use the CFA franc, which is issued by the BCEAO and pegged to the euro. According to First Initiative, "The banking sector dominates the Senegalese financial system, and is comprised of nine commercial banks and two specialized banks that focus on housing and agriculture lending. The banking sector has a high level of foreign ownership, particularly by French financial institutions. In 2003, Senegal had 30 micro-finance institutions. The sector is highly concentrated, with the top four institutions controlling over 80 percent of the market." The Economist Intelligence Unit reports that the government is a shareholder in several major banks, including Banque internationale pour le commerce et l'industrie du Séné-

gal (BICIS) and Compagnie bancaire de l'Afrique occidentale (CBAO), and a majority shareholder in the agricultural bank, Caisse Nationale de Crédit Agricole du Sénégal (CNCAS), and Credit National du Senegal. According to the U.S. Department of Commerce, "A few French-owned banks with conservative lending guidelines and high interest and collateral requirements dominate bank lending.... The system is characterized by the over liquidity of banks and their hesitancy to lend for medium and long-term loans." Based on evidence of heavy government involvement in the banking sector, Senegal's banking and finance score is 1 point worse this year.

WAGES AND PRICES
Score: **2**–Better (low level of intervention)

The market determines most prices, but the government influences many prices through its large state-owned sector. "Since the economic reform programme began in 1994," reports the World Trade Organization, "Senegal has freed certain controlled prices, but others remain in effect (for hydrocarbons, medical services and pharmaceutical products)." Senegal has a monthly minimum wage. Based on new evidence of the government's decreasing role in setting prices, Senegal's wages and prices score is 1 point better this year.

PROPERTY RIGHTS
Score: **3**–Stable (moderate level of protection)

According to the U.S. Department of Commerce, "Senegal lacks commercial courts staffed with trained judges. As a result, decisions are sometimes arbitrary and inconsistent." In addition, "The investment code provides for settlement of disputes via due process of the law prescribed in the cumbersome Senegalese judicial system. In order to overcome the weaknesses of the judicial system in the dispute settlement area and to speed the settlement process, Senegal established, in 1998, an arbitration center administered by the Dakar Chamber of Commerce." Corruption is present in dispute settlement cases.

REGULATION
Score: **4**–Stable (high level)

Regulatory and enforcement agencies are characterized by red tape. According to the U.S. Department of Commerce, "some foreign and domestic investors believe that the investment climate in Senegal is worsening. Judicial, tax, customs and other regulatory decisions are frequently inconsistent, tardy and non-transparent.... Labor laws in particular are seen as a disincentive to investment...." Corruption is a significant obstacle to doing business.

INFORMAL MARKET
Score: **4**–Worse (high level of activity)

Transparency International's 2004 score for Senegal is 3. Therefore, Senegal's informal market score is 4 this year—0.5 point worse than last year.

SERBIA AND MONTENEGRO

Rank: Suspended

Score: n/a

Category: n/a

Present & Past Scores

(Best) 1
2
3   4.21 4.28
4   ●——●
(Worst) 5

'95 '96 '97 '98 '99 '00 '01 '02 '03 '04 '05 '06
n/a n/a n/a n/a n/a n/a n/a   n/a n/a n/a

QUICK STUDY

SCORES

Trade Policy	n/a
Fiscal Burden	n/a
Government Intervention	n/a
Monetary Policy	n/a
Foreign Investment	n/a
Wages and Prices	n/a
Banking and Finance	n/a
Property Rights	n/a
Regulation	n/a
Informal Market	n/a

Population: 8,104,000

Total area: 102,350 sq. km

GDP: $9.7 billion

GDP growth rate: 3.0%

GDP per capita: $1,200

Major exports: manufactured goods, food and live animals, raw materials

Exports of goods and services: $3.2 billion

Major export trading partners: Italy 31.5%, Germany 17.4%, Austria 6.2%

Major imports: machinery and transport equipment, fuels and lubricants, manufactured goods, chemicals, food and live animals, raw materials

Imports of goods and services: $7.0 billion

Major import trading partners: Germany 18.6%, Italy 16.1%, Austria 8.5%

Foreign direct investment (net): $1.3 billion

2003 Data (in constant 2000 US dollars)

Serbia and Montenegro are worse off economically than almost all of Central and Eastern Europe's other transition economies. Under a 2002 agreement, the two countries have run their own economies, currencies (Montenegro uses the euro), and customs unions while remaining part of a decentralized state, and a vote as early as spring 2006 could determine whether they remain tied or go their separate ways. The March 2003 assassination of reformist Prime Minister Zoran Djindjic by members of the Zemun drug cartel demonstrated that, government efforts aside, Belgrade's underground power structure remains in the grip of war criminals, corrupt security chiefs, and ultranationalist politicians. After months of infighting and inconclusive parliamentary elections, nationalist former Yugoslav President Vojislav Kostunica was picked to lead a fragile coalition government. In April 2005, the European Union agreed to begin association talks with Serbia and Montenegro. GDP increased by 6 percent in 2004, and net foreign direct investment more than doubled in 2003, to $1.3 billion, due to foreign investment in the oil and tobacco sectors. While Montenegro has privatized most major industries other than electricity, the pace of privatization in Serbia slowed in 2004 as legislation to improve the business environment stalled. Kostunica, despite heading a minority government, must use his success with the EU to continue desperately needed reforms.

TRADE POLICY
Score: Not graded

The World Bank reports that Serbia and Montenegro's weighted average tariff rate in 2002 (the most recent year for which World Bank data are available) was 7.9 percent, down from the 9.4 percent average tariff for Serbia in 2001 and up from Montenegro's average tariff rate of 3.4 percent in 1999 as reported in the 2005 *Index*, based on World Bank data. According to the U.S. Department of Commerce, "In August 2003, the two republics agreed to an Internal Market and Trade Action Plan on harmonizing tariffs and excise taxes to create a single market. Harmonization has been achieved on 93 percent of products, resulting in an average (outweighed) tariff rate of 7 percent…. The government has phased-out quantitative restrictions although certain goods require a license from the government." Recent efforts have curtailed corruption in customs.

FISCAL BURDEN OF GOVERNMENT
Score—Income Taxation: Not graded
Score—Corporate Taxation: Not graded
Score—Change in Government Expenditures: Not graded
Final Score: Not graded

There are different tax rates in Serbia and Montenegro. Serbia has a flat tax rate of 10 percent for both individual income and corporate income. Montenegro's top income tax rate is 22 percent, while it has a flat corporate tax rate of 9 percent. In 2003, according to the European Bank for Reconstruction and Development, Serbia and Montenegro's government expenditures as a share of GDP decreased 0.5 percentage point to 46.8 percent.

GOVERNMENT INTERVENTION IN THE ECONOMY
Score: Not graded

The World Bank reports that the government of Serbia and Montenegro consumed 18.3 percent of GDP in 2002, the most recent year for which data are available. According to the Economist Intelligence Unit, "by early September 2003 Serbia had sold 843 companies...." In addition, "Privatisation in Montenegro is well advanced, with some 65% of state-owned companies having been sold off and only 25% of banking assets remaining in state or social ownership."

 MONETARY POLICY
Score: Not graded

From 1995 to 2004, based on data from the Economist Intelligence Unit and the International Monetary Fund's *2005 World Economic Outlook*, Serbia and Montenegro's weighted average annual rate of inflation was 14.39 percent. This figure, however, is somewhat misleading because Montenegro has used the more stable euro as its currency since 2002, while Serbia remains wedded to the dinar.

 CAPITAL FLOWS AND FOREIGN INVESTMENT
Score: Not graded

The foreign investment climate in Serbia and Montenegro is improving, and the government is trying to attract more investment. "Although structural barriers still persist at this stage of inchoate transition," reports the U.S. Department of Commerce, "the republic governments recognize the necessity to remove impediments, reform business activity and open the economy to foreign participation." As amended, Serbian law eliminates previous investment restrictions, provides for national treatment, permits transfer and repatriation of profits and dividends, guarantees against expropriation, and provides investment incentives. Montenegro's Foreign Investment Law incorporates these same protections for foreign investors. However, the business environment is still weak. According to the European Bank for Reconstruction and Development, "In both republics, excessive bureaucracy, red tape and corruption are major impediments to existing and potentially new enterprises, and the weak judiciary is ranked both by investors and by the Government as one of the most serious obstacles to doing business." The International Monetary Fund reports that both residents and non-residents may hold foreign exchange accounts, subject to central bank permission or conditions. Payments and transfers are subject to restrictions, and most capital transactions are subject to controls.

 BANKING AND FINANCE
Score: Not graded

Serbia and Montenegro has two separate banking systems. Each republic has its own independent central bank. According to the U.S. Department of Commerce, "There are 45 commercial banks (down from 88 in early 2001) in Serbia, most of which are authorized for international banking operations.... In January 2002, the four largest banks (Beogradska, Jugobanka, Investbanka, Beobanka) were placed in bankruptcy, signaling the government's resolve to reform this sector. These banks accounted for 65 percent of total banking sector assets....

In July 2002, the passage of a new law allowed a debt-for-equity swap between the Serbian government and 18 banks that account for Paris Club debt. The swaps resulted in majority ownership being shifted to the Serbian government." The Economist Intelligence Unit reports that Serbia has made progress in selling the state-owned banks. Foreign investors may establish new banks or make investments in existing banks in Serbia on the condition of reciprocity. The U.S. Department of Commerce reports that "Montenegro's banking system is considerably smaller than Serbia's with only ten licensed banks. Nonetheless, the sector has faced problems although not as severe as in Serbia." Montenegro's last bank with direct government majority ownership is being privatized.

 WAGES AND PRICES
Score: Not graded

"For most goods," reports the U.S. Department of Commerce, "state subsidies and price supports for consumer goods have been eliminated and prices are determined by market forces. Changes in the price of certain basic products (e.g., milk, bread, flour, and cooking oil), however, must be reported to the Ministry of Internal Trade 15 days in advance and the state retains discretionary authority. The state directly controls prices of utilities, public transit, telecom services and petroleum." Serbia and Montenegro has a minimum wage.

 PROPERTY RIGHTS
Score: Not graded

"The union and republic constitutions serve as the foundation of the legal system and create independent judiciaries in Serbia and Montenegro," reports the U.S. Department of Commerce. According to the Economist Intelligence Unit, "Economic or trade matters come under the jurisdiction of economic courts. Judges are elected or removed by the republican assemblies or the federal assembly. The system is overburdened and inefficient; judges need retraining to keep up with recent developments and low levels of pay are an invitation to corruption."

 REGULATION
Score: Not graded

According to the European Bank for Reconstruction and Development, "in both republics, excessive bureaucracy, red tape and corruption are major impediments to existing and potentially new enterprises.... The legal and regulatory environment throughout the Union is difficult and many areas still require improvement."

 INFORMAL MARKET
Score: Not graded

Transparency International's 2004 score for Serbia and Montenegro is 2.7. Therefore, Serbia and Montenegro would have an informal market score of 4 this year if grading were not suspended.

SIERRA LEONE

Rank: 137

Score: 3.76

Category: Mostly Unfree

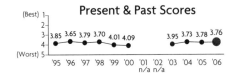

Present & Past Scores

(Best) 1
2
3 — 3.85 3.65 3.79 3.70 4.01 4.09   3.95 3.73 3.78 3.76
4
(Worst) 5
'95 '96 '97 '98 '99 '00 '01 '02 '03 '04 '05 '06
               n/a n/a

QUICK STUDY

SCORES

Trade Policy	4.5
Fiscal Burden	4.1
Government Intervention	2
Monetary Policy	3
Foreign Investment	4
Banking and Finance	4
Wages and Prices	2
Property Rights	5
Regulation	5
Informal Market	4

Population: 5,337,000

Total area: 71,740 sq. km

GDP: $753.7 million

GDP growth rate: 6.6%

GDP per capita: $141

Major exports: diamonds, cocoa, coffee, fish

Exports of goods and services: $161.1 million

Major export trading partners: Belgium 58.6%, Germany 13.3%, UK 4.5%, US 4.4%

Major imports: foodstuffs, fuel, machinery and transport equipment, manufactured goods

Imports of goods and services: $583 million

Major import trading partners: Germany 23.2%, UK 9.8%, US 5.3%, Netherlands 5.2%

Foreign direct investment (net): $7.4 billion

2003 Data (in constant 2000 US dollars)

The civil war that crippled Sierra Leone for over a decade ended in 2002 after a successful British-led military intervention and a subsequent U.N. peacekeeping operation enabled the government to assume control of the entire country. President Ahmed Tejan Kabbah was re-elected in 2002, and his party won a majority of parliamentary seats in elections that, despite some irregularities, were judged to be free and fair. Following the demobilization and disarmament of rebel forces and government-backed militia, the country has returned to relative peace and normality, but stability is fragile, as demonstrated by the U.N. Security Council decision to extend the U.N. peacekeeping operation beyond the original target date. Regional instability poses additional problems; renewed conflict in neighboring Ivory Coast, Liberia, and Guinea, for example, could easily spill over into Sierra Leone. Reforms necessary to revive the economy and combat corruption have been slowed by vested interests. Per capita income is very low, and over two-thirds of the population is engaged in subsistence agriculture. In 2003, agriculture accounted for over 52 percent of GDP and diamonds comprised 69 percent of exports. Economic activity remains hindered by dilapidated infrastructure, rampant corruption, and economic mismanagement. Sierra Leone's monetary policy score is 1 point worse this year; however, its trade policy and government intervention scores are 0.5 point better, and its fiscal burden of government score is 0.2 point better. As a result, Sierra Leone's overall score is 0.02 point better this year.

 TRADE POLICY
Score: **4.5**–Better (very high level of protectionism)

The World Bank reports that Sierra Leone's average tariff rate in 2004 was 13.3 percent, down from the 15.9 percent in 2002 reported in the 2005 *Index*, based on World Bank data. The World Trade Organization reports limited use of local content requirements and requirements for special permits, but that "few import prohibitions and restrictions are maintained for health, safety, security, and environmental reasons." According to the U.S. Department of Commerce, "non-tariff barriers include quotas…and sanitary and phytosanitary rules." Based on the lower tariff rate, as well as a revision of the trade factor methodology, Sierra Leone's trade policy score is 0.5 point better this year.

 FISCAL BURDEN OF GOVERNMENT
Score—Income Taxation: **3.5**–Stable (high tax rates)
Score—Corporate Taxation: **4**–Better (high tax rates)
Score—Change in Government Expenditures: **5**–Worse (very high increase)
Final Score: **4.1**–Better (high cost of government)

The International Monetary Fund reports that the top income tax rate is 35 percent. According to the World Bank, the top corporate tax rate is 30 percent, down from the 35 percent reported in the 2005 *Index*. In 2003, according to the African Development Bank, government expenditures as a share of GDP increased 3.6 percentage points to 32.2 percent, compared to the 1.2 percentage point decrease in 2002. On net, Sierra Leone's fiscal burden of government score is 0.2 point better this year.

GOVERNMENT INTERVENTION IN THE ECONOMY
Score: **2**–Better (low level)

The World Bank reports that the government consumed 19.5 percent of GDP in 2003, down from the 20.8 percent reported in the 2005 *Index*. As a result, Sierra Leone's government intervention score is 0.5 point better this year. In the same year, based on data from the Bank of Sierra Leone, Sierra Leone received 4.86 percent of its total revenues from state-owned enterprises and government ownership of property.

MONETARY POLICY
Score: **3**–Worse (moderate level of inflation)

From 1995 to 2004, Sierra Leone's weighted average annual rate of inflation was 10.73 percent, up from the 4.78 percent from 1994 to 2003 reported in the 2005 *Index*. As a result, Sierra Leone's monetary policy score is 1 point worse this year.

CAPITAL FLOWS AND FOREIGN INVESTMENT
Score: **4**–Stable (high barriers)

Sierra Leone does not discriminate against foreign firms and does not impose any ownership restrictions on foreign firms in any sector. However, unofficial barriers are significant. According to the U.S. Department of Commerce, "the business climate has been hampered by a shortage of foreign exchange, corruption, devastated infrastructure and uncertainty resulting from the now ended 11-year civil war.... Many investors continue to be adversely affected by corruption within Government ranks. Both lower level officials and senior officials, including ministers, are known to harass successful businesses in order to extract bribes or other favors. Arbitrary and inconsistent application of laws and regulations concerning labor, import tariffs and other areas can adversely affect productivity and profitability." Non-citizens and foreign investors are not permitted to participate in certain local industries, including cement block manufacturing, granite and sandstone excavation, and manufacturing of certain consumer durable goods. The International Monetary Fund reports that both residents and non-residents may hold foreign exchange accounts subject to some restrictions. Payments and transfers are generally permitted but face quantitative limits and approval requirements in some instances. Most capital transactions involving capital and money market instruments and credit operations require the Bank of Sierra Leone's approval. Direct investment abroad by residents, including purchase of real estate, is prohibited.

BANKING AND FINANCE
Score: **4**–Stable (high level of restrictions)

According to First Initiative, "Sierra Leone's bloody civil war ravaged the country and the economy. With the return of peace in 2002, a viable financial sector is only now beginning to reemerge.... The financial system is dominated by the banking sector, which consists of six commercial banks (2003). Two commercial banks are state owned, one is privately owned by Sierra Leonean investors, and the three remaining banks are foreign owned." The U.S. Department of Commerce notes that credit is allocated on market terms and that "[l]egal, regulatory and accounting systems are consistent with international norms." According to the Economist Intelligence Unit, "Since the upturn in the security situation, the government majority-owned banks…have been instrumental in generating new business. But the quality of such business is questionable as many loans are believed to have been, and continue to be, offered with little or no security to politically well-connected people."

WAGES AND PRICES
Score: **2**–Stable (low level of intervention)

The government sets few prices and wages, but it does influence the price of utilities through state-owned firms and subsidies. The Economist Intelligence Unit reports that the government made some "weak efforts" to control rising rice prices in September 2003. The government sets a minimum wage.

PROPERTY RIGHTS
Score: **5**–Stable (very low level of protection)

Property is not secure in Sierra Leone. The Economist Intelligence Unit reports that judges "draw salaries but often lack the means to carry out their duties properly—for example, the judiciary is hampered in some of its work that has a political bearing, such as trying corruption cases, as the chief justice is appointed by the president (in accordance with the constitution)." According to the U.S. Department of State, "Traditional justice systems continued to supplement extensively the central government judiciary in cases involving family law, inheritance, and land tenure, especially in rural areas."

REGULATION
Score: **5**–Stable (very high level)

According to the Economist Intelligence Unit, "The government of Ahmad Tejan Kabbah hopes to encourage investment by developing a range of incentives (including tax exemptions) for export- and resource-based industries, as well as for new investors, but weak local demand and foreign-exchange shortages are continuing to inhibit industrial expansion, while foreign companies are reluctant to invest in a country with such high levels of political risk." The government recently established a one-stop shop for business licenses in an effort to streamline the bureaucracy.

INFORMAL MARKET
Score: **4**–Stable (high level of activity)

Transparency International's 2004 score for Sierra Leone is 2.3. Therefore, Sierra Leone's informal market score is 4 this year.

SINGAPORE

Rank: 2

Score: 1.56

Category: Free

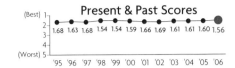

QUICK STUDY

SCORES

Trade Policy	1
Fiscal Burden	2.1
Government Intervention	3.5
Monetary Policy	1
Foreign Investment	1
Banking and Finance	2
Wages and Prices	2
Property Rights	1
Regulation	1
Informal Market	1

Population: 4,240,300

Total area: 647.5 sq. km

GDP: $106.8 billion

GDP growth rate: 8.4%

GDP per capita: $25,186

Major exports: machinery, chemicals, mineral fuels, electronics, consumer goods, travel services, transportation, financial and insurance services

Exports of goods and services: $179.5 billion

Major export trading partners: Malaysia 15.2%, US 12.4%, Hong Kong 9.8%, China 8.6%

Major imports: machinery, mineral fuels, oil, chemicals, foodstuffs, financial and insurance services

Imports of goods and services: $163.8 billion

Major import trading partners: Malaysia 15.2%, US 12.5%, Japan 11.7%, China 9.9%

Foreign direct investment (net): $5.4 billion

2004 Data (in constant 2000 US dollars)

In 2005, the Hong Kong–based Political and Economic Risk Consultancy (PERC) selected Singapore's judicial system as the best in Asia. Opposition politicians rightfully criticize Singapore's judicial system for its record of siding with prominent politicians, but foreign investors are more concerned about commercial law and the efficient way police handle non-political crimes. PERC's ranking could give the economy a much-needed boost. Accustomed to annual growth of 8 percent to 10 percent before the 1997 financial crisis, Singapore experienced only 1.2 percent growth in 2003. Growth rebounded to 8.4 percent in 2004, but Singapore struggles with competition from China and India in some manufactures. In an effort to spur growth, cushion workers, and attract foreign talent, Singapore has cut its corporate income tax rate to 20 percent from 22 percent. It is also party to free trade agreements with the United States, Australia, New Zealand, and Japan. The government is also beginning to divest itself of its non-strategic government-linked companies (GLC) and is introducing more competition into some GLC-dominated services. Although an election is not mandatory before August 2007, there is speculation that Prime Minister Lee Hsien Loong will call early elections in 2006. Singapore's fiscal burden of government score is 0.4 point better this year. As a result, Singapore's overall score is 0.04 point better this year.

TRADE POLICY
Score: 1–Stable (very low level of protectionism)

According to the World Bank, Singapore's weighted average tariff rate in 2003 (the most recent year for which World Bank data are available) was 0 percent. The World Trade Organization reports that "border measures include import and export restrictions, which, with the exception of rice and rubber (the latter for exports only), are maintained mainly for environmental, security and health reasons…. Sanitary and phytosanitary restrictions are strict, with each imported consignment of food products undergoing checks by Singapore Customs." Imports of cars over three years old are banned. Customs corruption is virtually nonexistent.

FISCAL BURDEN OF GOVERNMENT
Score—Income Taxation: **2**–Stable (low tax rates)
Score—Corporate Taxation: **2**–Better (low tax rates)
Score—Change in Government Expenditures: **2.5**–Better (low decrease)
Final Score: **2.1**–Better (low cost of government)

According to Deloitte, Singapore's top income tax rate is 22 percent. Effective from the 2005 year of assessment, the corporate tax rate has been cut to 20 percent from 22 percent. In 2004, based on data from the Singapore Department of Statistics, government expenditures as a share of GDP decreased by 1.2 percentage points to 15.7 percent, compared to a 0.2 percentage point decrease in 2003. On net, Singapore's fiscal burden of government score is 0.4 point better this year.

GOVERNMENT INTERVENTION IN THE ECONOMY
Score: **3.5**–Stable (high level)

Based on data from Singapore's Department of Statistics, the government consumed 10.4 percent of GDP in 2004. In 2003, according to the International Monetary Fund's Government Financial Statistics CD–ROM, Singapore received 22.75 percent of its total revenues from state-

341

owned enterprises and government ownership of property.

MONETARY POLICY
Score: 1–Stable (very low level of inflation)

From 1995 to 2004, Singapore's weighted average annual rate of inflation was 1.18 percent.

CAPITAL FLOWS AND FOREIGN INVESTMENT
Score: 1–Stable (very low barriers)

"Private foreign investment has been the main force behind Singapore's rapid development over the past 30 years," reports the Economist Intelligence Unit. Singapore's investment laws are clear and fair, and they pose few problems for business. Foreign and domestic businesses are treated equally, there are no production or local content requirements, and nearly all sectors are open to 100 percent foreign ownership. According to the World Trade Organization, "Foreign investment in the manufacturing sector remains unrestricted…. In 1999, a 40% foreign shareholding restriction on local banks was lifted. A 70% limit on foreign ownership of Stock Exchange of Singapore (SES) members was also removed. In the telecommunications sector, all FDI restrictions (previously 49% direct and 24.99% indirect) were lifted in 2000. Foreign investment limits continue to be maintained in: broadcasting (up to 49%, unless waived) and newspaper services (raised from 3% to 5% in 2002 and possibly higher if permission is given); foreign law firms and foreign lawyers practicing in Singapore (although liberalized somewhat in 2000); and in some sectors in which government linked companies are dominant (for example, foreign equity in the PSA Corporation, one of two main managers of Singapore's ports, is restricted to 49%). Restrictions are also maintained on foreign ownership of certain landed properties unless permitted by the relevant authority." Residents and non-residents may hold foreign exchange accounts. There are no controls or requirements on current transfers, payments, or repatriation of profits.

BANKING AND FINANCE
Score: 2–Stable (low level of restrictions)

Singapore's financial system is sound and well-regulated, but barriers to foreign banks and bank ownership persist. There were 23 "qualifying full banks" (QFBs), 36 wholesale banks, 111 commercial banks, and 47 offshore banks at the end of 2004. Though the Monetary Authority of Singapore (MAS) has shown greater willingness to grant foreign banks QFB licenses (only six have been granted to foreign banks since 1999) and restricted bank licenses over the past few years, the U.S. Department of Commerce reports that "foreign banks in the domestic retail banking sector still face significant restrictions and are not accorded national treatment. Aside from the limit on the number of foreign QFBs and their customer service locations, foreign QFBs are not allowed to access the local banks' ATM networks, a major competitive disadvantage, although they can share ATMs among themselves and [can] negotiate with the local banks to allow their card holders to obtain cash advances. Customers of foreign banks are also unable to access their accounts for transfers or bill payments at ATMs operated by banks other than their own. Local retail banks do not face similar constraints." The U.S. Trade Representative reports that, "in spite of lifting the formal ceilings on foreign ownership of local banks and finance companies, officials have indicated that they will not allow a foreign takeover of a local bank or finance company. Officials say they want local banks' share of total resident deposits to remain above 50 percent. Foreign penetration of the banking system…is comparatively high, with foreign banks holding about 40 percent of non-bank deposits." According to the Economist Intelligence Unit, "The MAS has discouraged foreign investors from taking control of a local bank by creating local management nominating committees and requiring that the majority of board members be Singapore citizens and permanent residents…. Any foreign institution that wants to accumulate substantial numbers of shares in local banks must get approval from the MAS at the thresholds of 5%, 12% and 20%." The government has significant ownership in financial markets. The EIU reports that the largest bank in Southeast Asia—the Development Bank of Singapore, which accounted for 29 percent of total banking assets in 2004—is publicly listed, but ownership is government-controlled. Temasek (the government's investment arm) reports that it controls 21 first-tier companies (controlling 80 key businesses). Seven of these are listed on the Singapore Exchange, accounting for 21 percent of the Exchange's market capitalization or S$91 billion. Over the past several years the main sources used to evaluate this factor have raised questions about the government's role in Singapore's banking sector. These issues will be scrutinized and verified in the 2007 *Index*.

WAGES AND PRICES
Score: 2–Stable (low level of intervention)

The market sets almost all wages and prices. According to the Economist Intelligence Unit, "The Ministry of Trade and Industry can impose controls as it deems necessary. Rice and live pigs are now the only two price-controlled items under the Price Control Act, administered by the Ministry." Wages are based on annual recommendations made by a tripartite (government, labor, and business) National Wages Council.

PROPERTY RIGHTS
Score: 1–Stable (very high level of protection)

The court system is very efficient and strongly protects private property, and there is no threat of expropriation, although the World Trade Organization reports that "the Government maintains a significant degree of control over the land and labour markets. In the case of land, the Government controls the release and therefore the price of land, particularly industrial land." According to the Economist Intelligence Unit, "Contractual arrangements…are secure, and the professionalism and efficiency of key agencies are widely acknowledged….

Singapore is known for its tough laws, strict enforcement and stiff penalties for offenders, and it exercises expedient and efficient procedures."

REGULATION
Score: 1–Stable (very low level)

According to the U.S. Department of Commerce, "The Singapore Government promotes its regulatory environment as business-friendly, with transparent and clear regulations. Tax, labor, banking and finance, industrial health and safety, arbitration, wage and training rules and regulations are formulated and reviewed with the interests of foreign investors and local enterprises in mind...." In addition, "procedures for obtaining licenses and permits are generally transparent and not burdensome." Most observers and business persons regard Singapore's government as clean and corruption-free.

INFORMAL MARKET
Score: 1–Stable (very low level of activity)

Transparency International's 2004 score for Singapore is 9.3. Therefore, Singapore's informal market score is 1 this year.

Singapore qualifies for the Global Free Trade Alliance.

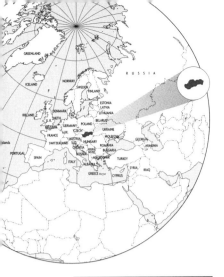

SLOVAK REPUBLIC

Rank: 34

Score: 2.35

Category: Mostly Free

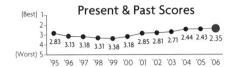

Present & Past Scores

(Best) 1
2
3
4
(Worst) 5

2.83 3.13 3.18 3.31 3.38 3.18 2.85 2.81 2.71 2.44 2.43 2.35

'95 '96 '97 '98 '99 '00 '01 '02 '03 '04 '05 '06

T he Slovak Republic's ruling center–right coalition, headed by Prime Minister Mikulas Dziurinda, has implemented a series of bold reforms to steer the country toward economic prosperity. During the first two years of its rule, the coalition moved forward on pension, tax, health care, social insurance, labor code, and administrative reforms that have begun to produce positive results and attract new investors. Slovakia's economy grew by 4.2 percent in 2003 and 4.9 percent in 2004. The state constrained spending despite a significant increase in tax revenues following implementation of a 19 percent (half the former rate) flat-rate income tax in January 2004. Unemployment dropped from 15.2 percent at the end of 2003 to 14.3 percent at the end of 2004. These significant improvements resulted in increased capital inflows, particularly into heavy industry. Volkswagen, Peugeot–Citroen, and Kia Motors have all invested in Slovakia's automotive sector. However, like other Central European countries, Slovakia is experiencing inflationary pressures. The government is set to adopt the euro in 2009. The Slovak Republic's fiscal burden of government score is 0.2 point worse this year, but its trade policy score is 1 point better. As a result, the Slovak Republic's overall score is 0.08 point better this year.

QUICK STUDY

SCORES

Trade Policy	2
Fiscal Burden	2
Government Intervention	2
Monetary Policy	3
Foreign Investment	2
Banking and Finance	1
Wages and Prices	2
Property Rights	3
Regulation	3
Informal Market	3.5

Population: 5,390,000

Total area: 48,845 sq. km

GDP: $24.2 billion

GDP growth rate: 4.9%

GDP per capita: $4,235

Major exports: machinery and transport equipment, intermediate manufactured goods, chemicals, fuels

Exports of goods and services: $19.7 billion

Major export trading partners: Germany 36.7%, Czech Republic 13.0%, Austria 9.7%, Italy 5.3%

Major imports: machinery, fuels and related products, chemicals, miscellaneous manufactured goods

Imports of goods and services: $19.7 billion

Major import trading partners: Germany 27.4%, Czech Republic 18.3%, Russia 10.8%

Foreign direct investment (net): $518.2 million

2004 Data (in constant 2000 US dollars)

TRADE POLICY
Score: **2**–Better (low level of protectionism)

The Slovak Republic adopted the trade policies of the European Union when it joined the EU in May 2004. The common EU weighted average external tariff was 1.3 percent in 2003, based on World Bank data. In the 2005 *Index*, based on World Trade Organization data, the Slovak Republic had a tariff of 6.1 percent. According to the World Trade Organization and the U.S. Trade Representative, the EU imposes non-tariff trade barriers through a complex regulatory system and export subsidies. Based on its adoption of EU trade policies, and on the revised trade factor methodology, the Slovak Republic's trade policy score is 1 point better this year.

FISCAL BURDEN OF GOVERNMENT
Score—Income Taxation: **1.5**–Stable (low tax rates)
Score—Corporate Taxation: **2**–Stable (low tax rates)
Score—Change in Government Expenditures: **2.5**–Worse (low decrease)
Final Score: **2**–Worse (low cost of government)

The Slovak Republic has a flat income tax rate of 19 percent. The top corporate tax rate is also a flat rate of 19 percent. In 2004, according to the Ministry of Finance, government expenditures as a share of GDP decreased by 1.5 percentage points to 40.6 percent, compared to the 3.2 percentage point decrease in 2003. On net, the Slovak Republic's fiscal burden of government score is 0.2 point worse this year.

GOVERNMENT INTERVENTION IN THE ECONOMY
Score: **2**–Stable (low level)

Based on data from the Slovak Monetary Policy Department, the government consumed 19.4 percent of GDP in 2004. In 2003, according to the International Monetary Fund's Government Financial Statistics CD–ROM, the Slovak Republic received 3.17 percent of its total revenues from state-owned enterprises and government ownership of property.

MONETARY POLICY
Score: **3**–Stable (moderate level of inflation)

From 1995 to 2004, the Slovak Republic's weighted average annual rate of inflation was 7.48 percent.

CAPITAL FLOWS AND FOREIGN INVESTMENT
Score: **2**–Stable (low barriers)

There is no screening process for foreign investment, and both 100 percent foreign ownership and repatriation of profits are permitted. "In its Doing Business in 2005 report, the World Bank named Slovakia as the world's top reformer in improving its investment climate over the last year, allowing it to join the top 20 economies in the world for ease of doing business," reports the U.S. Department of Commerce. "The country's low-cost yet skilled labor force, low taxes, liberal labor code and favorable geographic location have helped it become one of Europe's favorite investment markets." According to the same source, foreign ownership is limited to 49 percent of the natural gas company, the electric power producer, electricity distributors, and an oil pipeline, and the state "must still retain ownership of the railroad rights of way, postal services, water supplies (but not suppliers) and forestry companies." The International Monetary Fund reports that residents may establish foreign exchange accounts when staying abroad or with permission of the National Bank of Slovakia; non-residents may hold foreign exchange accounts. Restrictions on foreign purchase of real estate (except agricultural land) were lifted effective May 1, 2004. There are very few controls on capital transactions, except for rules governing commercial banking and credit institutions, which must abide by existing banking laws.

BANKING AND FINANCE
Score: **1**–Stable (very low level of restrictions)

The Slovak Republic has implemented an aggressive privatization program for its state-owned banks. According to First Initiative, "The banking sector…underwent a series of structural [changes] between 2001 and 2004, including the elimination of financially weak banks and the privatization of the three largest state-owned banks…. Privatizations have left a large number of non-performing loans to be resolved by the Slovak Consolidation Agency. As of June 2004, the banking sector was comprised of 18 Slovak-incorporated commercial banks and numerous branches of three foreign-owned banks." The government has privatized its larger and medium-sized state-owned banks and retains control of two small banks, Postova Banka and Banka Slovakia, both of which are up for privatization and have received bids by foreign banks. According to the Economist Intelligence Unit, "Foreign capital already controls nearly 100% of banking assets." Interest rates have been completely liberalized, and credit limits have been abolished. The capital market is relatively new and still small, with most trading involving government bonds.

WAGES AND PRICES
Score: **2**–Stable (low level)

The government has removed a number of price controls, but the Ministry of Finance reports that one-fifth of the consumer price index is regulated by price controls, particularly for housing and utilities. The government also affects agricultural prices through the Slovak Republic's participation in the Common Agricultural Policy, a program that heavily subsidizes agricultural goods. The government mandates a minimum wage.

PROPERTY RIGHTS
Score: **3**–Stable (moderate level of protection)

According to the U.S. Department of Commerce, "The legal system enforces property and contractual rights, but decisions may take years, thus limiting the utility of the courts for dispute resolution. Slovak courts recognize and enforce foreign judgments, subject to the same delays…. A bankruptcy law exists but has not been as effective as needed and enforcement remains erratic." In addition, "There is a conviction in business circles that corruption still persists [as] a significant factor in the court system."

REGULATION
Score: **3**–Stable (moderate level)

In 2004, according to the World Bank, the Slovak Republic made the greatest improvement in the business environment of any nation by deregulating and cutting taxes. Nevertheless, lack of transparency, the persistence of red tape, and excessive and inefficient bureaucracy continue. The U.S. Department of Commerce reports that "transparency and predictability have been a problem on many issues involving investors" and that the amount of time involved in buying land and obtaining building permits can be significant. The Economist Intelligence Unit reports that the government "enacted a comprehensive overhaul of the Labor Code in 2003. As a result, employers have gained greater flexibility in hiring and firing employees…."

INFORMAL MARKET
Score: **3.5**–Stable (high level of activity)

Transparency International's 2004 score for the Slovak Republic is 4. Therefore, the Slovak Republic's informal market score is 3.5 this year.

SLOVENIA

Rank: 38

Score: 2.41

Category: Mostly Free

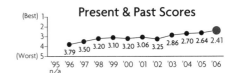

Present & Past Scores

(Best) 1
2
3
4
(Worst) 5

3.79 3.50 3.20 3.10 3.20 3.06 3.25 2.86 2.70 2.64 2.41

'95 '96 '97 '98 '99 '00 '01 '02 '03 '04 '05 '06
n/a

QUICK STUDY

SCORES

Trade Policy	2
Fiscal Burden	3.6
Government Intervention	2
Monetary Policy	2
Foreign Investment	2
Banking and Finance	3
Wages and Prices	2
Property Rights	3
Regulation	2
Informal Market	2.5

Population: 1,995,000

Total area: 20,253 sq. km

GDP: $20.8 billion

GDP growth rate: 2.5%

GDP per capita: $10,411

Major exports: manufactures, machinery and transport equipment, chemicals, food and live animals

Exports of goods and services: $12.5 billion

Major export trading partners: Germany 23.2%, Italy 13.2%, Croatia 9.0%, Austria 7.3%

Major imports: machinery and transport equipment, chemicals, manufactures, mineral fuels and lubricants

Imports of goods and services: $13.1 billion

Major import trading partners: Germany 19.9%, Italy 18.6%, France 10.0%, Austria 8.6%

Foreign direct investment (net): –$116.1 million

2003 Data (in constant 2000 US dollars)

Slovenia is the most advanced of the countries that joined the European Union in 2004. Its per capita GDP makes it almost as rich as Greece, and it was designated in 2003 by the European Commission as the most prepared of the EU's prospective members. Both its strategic location at the crossroads between Eastern and Western Europe and its highly educated and skilled workforce have given it a distinct advantage compared to other developing Central European states. Slovenia has adopted a gradualist approach; the establishment has never accepted the need for radical economic reform, maintaining that a relatively high regional level of economic development renders such drastic change irrelevant. For several years, the sale of key assets to foreigners encountered widespread hostility. Foreign direct investment has been modest because of abundant bureaucratic barriers and the small size of the Slovene market, which is much smaller than those of the Czech Republic and Slovakia. However, GDP grew by a robust 4.6 percent in 2004, while unemployment—a lingering worry—decreased slightly to 10.6 percent. To maintain its economic edge, Slovenia must complete its privatization process and continue to liberalize its monopolistic industrial base. Slovenia's fiscal burden of government score is 0.2 point worse this year; however, its government intervention score is 0.5 point better, and its monetary policy score and capital flows and foreign investment score are 1 point better. As a result, Slovenia's overall score is 0.23 point better this year.

TRADE POLICY
Score: **2**–Stable (low level of protectionism)

Slovenia adopted the trade policies of the European Union when it joined the EU in May 2004. The common EU weighted average external tariff was 1.3 percent in 2003, based on World Bank data. According to the World Trade Organization and the U.S. Trade Representative, the EU imposes non-tariff trade barriers through a complex regulatory system and export subsidies. Based on the adoption of EU trade policies, and on the revised trade factor methodology, Slovenia's trade policy score is unchanged.

FISCAL BURDEN OF GOVERNMENT
Score—Income Taxation: **5**–Stable (very high tax rates)
Score—Corporate Taxation: **3**–Stable (moderate tax rates)
Score—Change in Government Expenditures: **3.5**–Worse (low increase)
Final Score: **3.6**–Worse (high cost of government)

Slovenia's top income tax rate is 50 percent. The top corporate tax rate is 25 percent. In 2004, according to the Embassy of Slovenia, government expenditures as a share of GDP increased 0.4 percentage point to 43.1 percent, compared to the 0.5 percentage point decrease in 2003. On net, Slovenia's fiscal burden of government score is 0.2 point worse this year.

GOVERNMENT INTERVENTION IN THE ECONOMY
Score: **2**–Better (low level)

According to the Embassy of Slovenia, the government consumed 19.8 percent of GDP in 2004, down from the 20.2 percent reported in the 2005 *Index*. As a result, Slovenia's government intervention score is 0.5 point better this year. In 2003, according to the International Monetary Fund's Government Financial Statistics CD–ROM, Slovenia received 2.33 percent of its

347

total revenues from state-owned enterprises and government ownership of property.

MONETARY POLICY
Score: 2–Better (low level of inflation)

From 1995 to 2004, Slovenia's weighted average annual rate of inflation was 4.62 percent, down from the 6.41 percent from 1994 to 2003 reported in the 2005 *Index*. As a result, Slovenia's monetary policy score is 1 point better this year.

CAPITAL FLOWS AND FOREIGN INVESTMENT
Score: 2–Better (low barriers)

Slovenia has opened most sectors to foreign investment. Foreign investors are accorded national treatment, restrictions on portfolio investment have been abolished, and the government has streamlined the investment process. The U.S. Department of Commerce reports that, despite the stated commitment to improving the foreign investment environment, "practical impediments to increased FDI flows" include an incomplete legal framework regulating corporate activities, administrative barriers to business, impediments to securing land and business premises, an "ambivalent attitude toward FDI" that creates uncertainty, and a rigid labor force. The International Monetary Fund reports that residents and non-residents may hold foreign exchange accounts after proving their identity. There are no restrictions on payments and transfers. Nearly all restrictions on capital and money market instruments were removed in 2003. Most direct investment is unrestricted, except a license requirement for investment in trading or producing armaments or military equipment, but non-EU foreigners may face restrictions on investment in real estate. Based on evidence of the liberalization of capital flows and the opening of new sectors to foreign investment, Slovenia's capital flows and foreign investment score is 1 point better this year.

BANKING AND FINANCE
Score: 3–Stable (moderate level of restrictions)

"The banking system is relatively well developed by central European standards," reports the Economist Intelligence Unit. "The system is sound, well capitalised and with a low proportion of nonperforming loans." According to First Initiative, "The banking sector is well developed and concentrated, with the three largest banks controlling approximately 50% of banking sector assets. Approximately 20 commercial banks and two savings institutions are operational as of 2004. Pressure by the European Union and other international organizations prompted the privatization of a number of formerly state-owned banks…. Slovenia's insurance sector consists of 18 firms. The dominant firm in both general and life insurance is the state-owned firm, Zavarovalnica Triglav, which began to be privatized in 2002." The government sold 39 percent of the largest commercial bank, Nova Ljubljanska Banka (NLB), in 2002. The Slovenian embassy reports that the government partially owns two banks—Nova kreditna banka Maribor d.d. (90 percent) and Nova Ljubljanska banka d.d. (35.6 percent).

However, the May 10, 2005, *Financial Times* reports that only one-third of Slovenia's banking assets are private and that the state effectively directs the three largest banks—Nova Ljubljanska, Nova Kreditna Banka Maribor, and Abanka, which control over half of total banking assets.

WAGES AND PRICES
Score: 2–Stable (low level of intervention)

The market determines most wages and prices. According to the Embassy of Slovenia, "The government sets the price of gasoline, electricity, natural gas, railway transport, heating, communal services and school textbooks." The Economist Intelligence Unit reports that administered prices make up 13 percent of the consumer price index. The government also affects agricultural prices through Slovenia's participation in the Common Agricultural Policy, a program that heavily subsidizes agricultural goods. The government mandates a minimum wage.

PROPERTY RIGHTS
Score: 3–Stable (moderate level of protection)

Private property is guaranteed by Slovenia's constitution. According to the Economist Intelligence Unit, "Judges are appointed by the executive branch…but are generally politically neutral." However, "The Slovenian court system is marred by inadequate staffing and slow procedural progress and is in need of further reform." The EIU also reports that investors are usually frustrated about the weak protection afforded by the judiciary.

REGULATION
Score: 2–Stable (low level)

It is becoming easier to establish a business as the government has undertaken regulatory reform, although an entrenched and sometimes inefficient bureaucracy continues to hinder business development. Deregulation of the labor market has not progressed. According to the U.S. Department of Commerce, "the market for workers remains quite rigid and investors will find that termination of workers [is] somewhat more difficult than in the West. In addition, the labor market remains relatively over-protected, and pay scales in public service are very complicated and do not reward performance." The same source reports that corruption exists on a "minor scale." The government has made progress in reforming public administration and identifying and reducing red tape.

INFORMAL MARKET
Score: 2.5–Stable (moderate level of activity)

Transparency International's 2004 score for Slovenia is 6. Therefore, Slovenia's informal market score is 2.5 this year.

> If Slovenia were to improve its regulation score, it would qualify for the Global Free Trade Alliance.

SOUTH AFRICA

Rank: 50

Score: 2.74

Category: Mostly Free

Present & Past Scores

(Best) 1
2
3
4
(Worst) 5

3.23 3.20 2.94 2.88 2.98 3.01 3.00 2.79 2.63 2.79 2.83 2.74

'95 '96 '97 '98 '99 '00 '01 '02 '03 '04 '05 '06

QUICK STUDY

SCORES

Trade Policy	2.5
Fiscal Burden	3.9
Government Intervention	2
Monetary Policy	2
Foreign Investment	3
Banking and Finance	3
Wages and Prices	2
Property Rights	3
Regulation	3
Informal Market	3

Population: 45,829,000

Total area: 1,219,912 sq. km

GDP: $138.7 billion

GDP growth rate: 1.9%

GDP per capita: $3,026

Major exports: metal and metal products, gold, diamonds, machinery and transport equipment

Exports of goods and services: $37.5 billion

Major export trading partners: UK 12.2%, US 12.0%, Japan 8.9%, Germany 7.9%

Major imports: machinery, mineral products, chemicals, transport equipment

Imports of goods and services: $37.6 billion

Major import trading partners: Germany 16.6%, UK 8.5%, US 8.3%, Japan 6.0%

Foreign direct investment (net): $40.4 million

2003 Data (in constant 2000 US dollars)

P resident Thabo Mbeki and his African National Congress have a commanding majority in parliament and control nearly all of South Africa's provincial governments, raising concerns that South Africa may be shifting toward one-party rule. Corruption is a problem; Deputy President Jacob Zuma, for example, was dismissed because of alleged corruption. South Africa has slowly liberalized during the past decade, and economic growth has improved. It remains the economic hub of sub-Saharan Africa, generating 36 percent of regional GDP. Major obstacles to long-term growth and stability include violent crime, an 11 percent HIV/AIDS infection rate, and unemployment officially estimated at over 25 percent (although unofficial estimates place it at nearly 40 percent). Powerful unions oppose the ANC proposal for limited liberalization of labor markets. Plans for privatization are weakened by failure to include major state-owned enterprises such as Transnet, Eskom, and South African Airways. The crisis in Zimbabwe has caused an estimated 3 million Zimbabweans to flee to South Africa, adding to strains on the economy. Mbeki's policy of trying to curb Zimbabwean President Robert Mugabe's excesses and brutality through "quiet diplomacy" has proven ineffective, and his endorsement of Zimbabwe's flawed 2005 parliamentary election has lent Mugabe unwarranted legitimacy. South Africa's fiscal burden of government score is 0.1 point worse this year, but its monetary policy score is 1 point better. As a result, South Africa's overall score is 0.09 point better this year.

TRADE POLICY
Score: **2.5**–Stable (moderate level of protectionism)

South Africa belongs to the Southern African Customs Union (SACU), a regional trade arrangement with Botswana, Lesotho, Namibia, and Swaziland. According to the World Bank, in 2001 (the most recent year for which World Bank data are available), the SACU had a weighted average tariff rate of 3.6 percent. The U.S. Trade Representative reports four "main categories of controlled imports": used goods if those goods or substitutes are produced domestically; waste, scrap, ashes, and residues for health and environmental reasons; harmful substances for environmental, health, and social reasons; and goods subject to quality specifications. Based on the revised trade factor methodology, South Africa's trade policy score is unchanged.

FISCAL BURDEN OF GOVERNMENT
Score—Income Taxation: **4**–Stable (high tax rates)
Score—Corporate Taxation: **4**–Stable (high tax rates)
Score—Change in Government Expenditures: **3.5**–Worse (low increase)
Final Score: **3.9**–Worse (high cost of government)

According to Deloitte, South Africa's top income tax rate is 40 percent. The corporate tax rate is 30 percent. In 2003, according to the African Development Bank, government expenditures as a share of GDP increased by 0.8 percentage point to 26.7 percent, compared to the 0 percentage point change in 2002. On net, South Africa's fiscal burden of government score is 0.1 point worse this year.

GOVERNMENT INTERVENTION IN THE ECONOMY
Score: **2**–Stable (low level)

The World Bank reports that the government consumed 19.1 percent of GDP in 2003. In the

same year, according to the International Monetary Fund's Government Financial Statistics CD–ROM, South Africa received 1.63 percent of its total revenues from state-owned enterprises and government ownership of property.

MONETARY POLICY
Score: 2–Better (low level of inflation)

From 1995 to 2004, South Africa's weighted average annual rate of inflation was 3.30 percent, down from the 6.55 percent from 1994 to 2003 reported in the 2005 *Index*. As a result, South Africa's monetary policy score is 1 point better this year.

CAPITAL FLOWS AND FOREIGN INVESTMENT
Score: 3–Stable (moderate barriers)

South Africa permits foreign investment in most sectors, requires no government approval, and generally does not restrict the form or extent of foreign investment. Foreign ownership of media is capped at 20 percent, and foreign ownership of banks must be approved at two equity levels. The Black Economic Empowerment strategy establishing a scorecard with targets for equity ownership, management, procurement, and equality in employment for "historically disadvantaged individuals" (HDI) became law in January 2004. "A major concern is whether HDI equity ownership will become mandatory and a cost of doing business with the South African government," reports the U.S. Department of Commerce. "Poor or unclear regulations in key sectors, such as telecommunications, are also disincentives to investment." According to the Economist Intelligence Unit, "FDI will continue to be adversely affected by high start-up and input costs, stringent labour regulations, skills shortages, infrastructural limitations and the government's failure to create a single-window, direct investment facility to encourage overseas interest and reduce red tape." The International Monetary Fund reports that residents may establish foreign exchange accounts through authorized dealers, but government approval is required and quantitative limits apply. Non-residents may hold them with authorized dealers. Many payments, capital transactions, and transfers are subject to restrictions, controls, quantitative limits, and prior approval.

BANKING AND FINANCE
Score: 3–Stable (moderate level of restrictions)

According to the U.S. Department of Commerce, "Five large banks dominate the South African banking landscape… accounting for around 90 percent of banking services…. [T]here are approximately 70 foreign banks operating in South Africa, either via representative offices, branches, subsidiaries or joint ventures with local companies." The purchase by Barclays of 60 percent of ABSA for $5.4 billion in 2005 marks the largest single foreign direct investment in South Africa since 1994. "Foreign-equity ownership of banks exceeding 15% require authorisation from the Registrar of Deposit-Taking Institutions," reports the Economist Intelligence Unit, "and stakes exceeding 49% require authorisation from the Ministry of Finance…. Most medium- and long-term domestic loans still come from state institutions,

such as the Industrial Development Corporation." Other state-owned institutions include the Development Bank of Southern Africa, Business Partners, Ntsika Enterprise Promotion, Khula Enterprise Finance, Land Bank, and Postbank.

WAGES AND PRICES
Score: 2–Stable (low level of intervention)

Prices are generally set by the market, the exceptions being the prices of petroleum products, coal, paraffin, and utilities. According to the Economist Intelligence Unit, the Food Pricing Monitoring Committee monitors the prices of a basket of 26 basic food items and investigates sharp or unjust price increases and incidents of predatory and monopolistic tendencies in collaboration with the Competition Commission. "In those sectors in which workers were not organized sufficiently to engage in the collective bargaining process," reports the U.S. Department of State, "the law gives the Minister of Labor the authority to set wages…."

PROPERTY RIGHTS
Score: 3–Stable (moderate level of protection)

The threat of expropriation is low. The judiciary is independent, and contractual arrangements are generally secure. According to the U.S. Department of State, "The Constitution provides for an independent and impartial judiciary, and the Government generally respected this provision in practice; however, the judiciary was understaffed, underfunded, and overburdened." The U.S. Department of Commerce reports that "criminal and judicial entities also lack adequate resources for carrying out anti-corruption policies. U.S. firms have, however, not identified corruption as a serious obstacle to foreign direct investment."

REGULATION
Score: 3–Stable (moderate level)

The government has moved to increase regulatory transparency, but regulation of economic activity can be burdensome. Labor regulations are onerous, especially under the government's black empowerment program. *The Economist* reports that "firing is such a costly headache that many prefer not to hire in the first place. Centralised collective bargaining…strangles the little guys before they have a chance to grow big." According to the Economist Intelligence Unit, "concerns exist over the capacity of the bureaucracy at the various levels of government, and performance is mixed. A further problem has been co-ordination and co-operation between different government departments and different tiers of government…. In provincial and local governments (outside the three main metropolitan areas) these problems tend to be worse."

INFORMAL MARKET
Score: 3–Stable (moderate level of activity)

Transparency International's 2004 score for South Africa is 4.6. Therefore, South Africa's informal market score is 3 this year.

SPAIN

Rank: 33
Score: 2.33
Category: Mostly Free

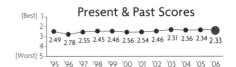
QUICK STUDY

SCORES

Trade Policy	2
Fiscal Burden	4.3
Government Intervention	2
Monetary Policy	2
Foreign Investment	2
Banking and Finance	2
Wages and Prices	2
Property Rights	2
Regulation	3
Informal Market	2

Population: 42,300,000

Total area: 504,782 sq. km

GDP: $622.2 billion

GDP growth rate: 2.7%

GDP per capita: $14,709

Major exports: raw materials, machinery, capital goods, energy products, consumer goods, pharmaceuticals, medicines

Exports of goods and services: $249 billion

Major export trading partners: France 19.6%, Germany 11.7%, Portugal 9.8%, Italy 9.2%, UK 9.2%

Major imports: machinery, fuels, chemicals, consumer goods

Imports of goods and services: $279.8 billion

Major import trading partners: Germany 16.4%, France 15.2%, Italy 9.0%, UK 6.1%

Foreign direct investment (net): –$29.7 billion

2004 Data (in constant 2000 US dollars)

Many years of brisk growth characterized by strong job creation, structural reforms, and sound fiscal policy are a strong part of former Spanish Prime Minister José María Aznar's legacy. Under Aznar, the Spanish economy grew at an average annual rate of 3.6 percent between 1996 and 2003, while unemployment was halved from 22 percent to around 11 percent. However, the March 14, 2004, parliamentary election unexpectedly returned socialists to power. The new premier, Jose Luis Rodríguez Zapatero, won in the wake of the pre-election al-Qaeda bombings in Madrid. As the Economist Intelligence Unit noted in April 2005, the new socialist government has not undone Aznar's achievement. Instead, it has concentrated on dealing with the Basque region, social reform, and reorienting Spain's foreign policy in a more pro-French and pro-German direction. GDP grew 2.7 percent in 2004, and unemployment, long the scourge of modern Spain, declined to 10.8 percent. The key to continued growth lies in improving sluggish labor productivity performance. In March 2005, the Zapatero government announced a package of reforms aimed at bolstering Spain's flagging competitiveness by liberalizing the utilities and financial services markets. Spain's fiscal burden of government score is 0.1 point better this year. As a result, its overall score is 0.01 point better this year.

TRADE POLICY
Score: **2**–Stable (low level of protectionism)

As a member of the European Union, Spain was subject to a common EU weighted average external tariff of 1.3 percent in 2003, down from the 2.4 percent for 2002 reported in the 2005 *Index*, based on World Bank data. According to the World Trade Organization and the U.S. Trade representative, the EU imposes non-tariff trade barriers through a complex regulatory system and export subsidies. Based on the revised trade factor methodology, Spain's trade policy score is unchanged.

FISCAL BURDEN OF GOVERNMENT
Score—Income Taxation: **4.5**–Stable (very high tax rates)
Score—Corporate Taxation: **4.5**–Better (very high tax rates)
Score—Change in Government Expenditures: **3.5**–Worse (low increase)
Final Score: **4.3**–Better (high cost of government)

Spain's top income tax rate is 45 percent. The top corporate rate is 35 percent, rather than the 40 percent reported in the 2005 *Index*. In 2004, government expenditures as a share of GDP increased 1 percentage point to 40.6 percent, compared to a 0.3 percentage point decrease in 2003. On net, Spain's fiscal burden of government score is 0.1 point better this year.

GOVERNMENT INTERVENTION IN THE ECONOMY
Score: **2**–Stable (low level)

Based on data from the central bank, the government consumed 18.3 percent of GDP in 2004. In the same year, based on data from the same source, Spain received 3.97 percent of its total revenues from state-owned enterprises and government ownership of property.

MONETARY POLICY
Score: 2–Stable (low level of inflation)

Spain is a member of the euro zone. From 1995 to 2004, Spain's weighted average annual rate of inflation was 3.05 percent.

CAPITAL FLOWS AND FOREIGN INVESTMENT
Score: 2–Stable (low barriers)

Spain maintains few restrictions on foreign investment. According to the U.S. Department of Commerce, "Spanish law permits foreign investment of up to 100 percent of equity, and capital movements have been completely liberalized. On April 1999, the adoption of royal decree 664/1999 eliminated the need for government authorization of any investments save those in activities 'directly related to national defense,' such as arms production." The government does employ its power to restrict unwanted investment. The Economist Intelligence Unit reports that "both Socialist and conservative Popular Party administrations have acted to protect key domestic companies from foreign domination. They have fostered the formation of a core of Spanish investors in strategic sectors, especially those where privatisation could lead to foreign control. The government's guarantees in this area are generally unwritten, and its actions have most often taken the form of tacit intervention in deals or public expressions of disapproval." There are no restrictions or controls on resident or non-resident foreign exchange accounts, repatriation of profits, and proceeds from invisible transactions. Current transfers are not restricted but must be declared to deposit institutions. The Bank of Spain requires reporting on most credit and lending activities.

BANKING AND FINANCE
Score: 2–Stable (low level of restrictions)

Spain's banking and financial sectors are diverse, modern, and fully integrated into international financial markets. The government has made progress in opening the banking system to foreign competition by removing restrictions on investments from non–European Union investors. The U.S. Department of Commerce reports that there were "77 private banks, 47 savings banks, 85 credit unions, 77 finance houses, [and] 52 branches of foreign banks headquartered in non-EU countries" as of June 22, 2004. Two banks—Banco Santander Central Hispano (BSCH) and Banco Bilbao Vizcaya Argentaria (BBVA)—dominate domestic commercial banking, account for about 40 percent of private banking assets, and rank as the world's 8th and 14th largest banks, respectively. According to the Economist Intelligence Unit, "The Spanish government extends substantial financial aid and tax benefits for industries considered of high priority…. Preferential access to official credit is also granted, together with the subsidies, up to a combined limit for both types of aid." The government provides financing for industrial restructuring and to smaller firms through the Official Credit Institute, subsidizes financing for high-technology projects through the Centre for the Technological Development of Industry, and offers subsidized credit

to Spanish foreign investments through the Spanish Institute for Foreign Trade.

WAGES AND PRICES
Score: 2–Stable (low level of intervention)

The government has removed most price controls but, according to the Economist Intelligence Unit, controls the prices of "farm insurance, stamps, public transport, electricity, natural gas/butane/propane and medicines. Regional governments also control a few prices locally." The government also affects agricultural prices through Spain's participation in the Common Agricultural Policy, a program that heavily subsidizes agricultural goods. The government mandates a minimum wage.

PROPERTY RIGHTS
Score: 2–Stable (high level of protection)

Property is relatively safe from government expropriation. The judiciary is independent in practice, but bureaucratic obstacles at the national and state levels are significant. The Economist Intelligence Unit reports that "contractual agreements are secure although the legal system can be painfully slow, and enforcement becomes a tortuous process when contracts are not honored. Out-of-court settlements are common."

REGULATION
Score: 3–Stable (moderate level)

Although the government has streamlined its regulatory regime, the Economist Intelligence Unit reports that "bureaucratic steps are considerable both at the national and state levels, and many civil servants are un-cooperative, though generational change is helping make dealings with the public sector somewhat more agile." In addition, "The new Socialist government passed a law in December 2004 to limit opening hours for large retailers." Spain has the full array of European Union environmental regulations but does not enforce them effectively. One key area needing reform is the labor market, which the Organisation for Economic Co-operation and Development says is known for strongly segmenting permanent workers, who enjoy enormous benefits, from temporary workers, who have little employment stability.

INFORMAL MARKET
Score: 2–Stable (low level of activity)

Transparency International's 2004 score for Spain is 7.1. Therefore, Spain's informal market score is 2 this year.

> If Spain were to improve its regulation score, it would qualify for the Global Free Trade Alliance.

SRI LANKA

Rank: 92
Score: 3.19
Category: Mostly Unfree

Present & Past Scores

(Best) 1 —
2 —
3 —
4 — 3.06 2.94 2.61 2.76 2.86 2.91 2.84 2.89 3.05 3.06 3.03 3.19
(Worst) 5 —
'95 '96 '97 '98 '99 '00 '01 '02 '03 '04 '05 '06

QUICK STUDY

SCORES

Trade Policy	3
Fiscal Burden	3.4
Government Intervention	2
Monetary Policy	3
Foreign Investment	4
Banking and Finance	4
Wages and Prices	3
Property Rights	3
Regulation	3
Informal Market	3.5

Population: 19,232,000

Total area: 65,610 sq. km

GDP: $17.7 billion

GDP growth rate: 5.9%

GDP per capita: $921

Major exports: textiles and garments, tea, diamonds, petroleum

Exports of goods and services: $6.7 billion

Major export trading partners: US 34.6%, UK 12.5%, India 4.8%, Germany 4.5%

Major imports: textiles, machinery and transport equipment, mineral products, chemicals

Imports of goods and services: $9.0 billion

Major import trading partners: India 16.1%, Hong Kong 8.4%, Singapore 7.8%, Japan 6.7%

Foreign direct investment (net): $211.8 million

2003 Data (in constant 2000 US dollars)

Sri Lanka is still coping with the aftermath of the December 2004 tsunami—the worst natural disaster in the nation's history—and the government's socialist–nationalist policies. Although the international community offered billions of dollars in aid, there are widespread accusations that the money was mishandled by the ruling coalition government, formed between President Chandrika Kumaratunga's party and the Marxist Janatha Vimukhti Peramuna (JVP). The JVP holds 39 seats in the fragile alliance with Kumaratunga's party, and the two factions together hold a majority of 119 seats in the 225-seat parliament. The island nation's energy woes also continue, with the Central Electricity Board (CEB) losing $450,000 per day and shouldering $800 million in total debt. The energy problem is exacerbated by the majority party's unwillingness to adjust to world oil prices. Attempts to restructure the CEB have met with opposition from the powerful JVP, which threatens to withdraw its support from President Kumaratunga should restructuring occur. Sri Lanka remains embroiled in a civil war with the Liberation Tigers of Tamil Eelam. A cease-fire has been in effect since late 2001, but there seems little prospect that either side will offer sufficient compromises to gain a peace agreement. Sri Lanka's trade policy score is 0.5 point worse this year; in addition, its fiscal burden of government score is 0.1 point worse, and its capital flows and foreign investment score is 1 point worse. As a result, Sri Lanka's overall score is 0.16 point worse this year.

TRADE POLICY
Score: 3–Worse (moderate level of protectionism)

According to the World Bank, Sri Lanka's weighted average tariff rate in 2004 was 6.8 percent, up from the 4.2 percent for 2001 reported in the 2005 *Index*, based on World Bank data. The World Trade Organization notes "overlapping jurisdictions in trade and trade-related policies leading to a certain lack of coherence in their formulation and implementation…. Non-tariff barriers, especially licences affect a substantial number of goods." Based on the higher tariff rate, as well as a revision of the trade factor methodology, Sri Lanka's trade policy score is 0.5 point worse this year.

FISCAL BURDEN OF GOVERNMENT
Score—Income Taxation: 3–Stable (moderate tax rates)
Score—Corporate Taxation: 4–Stable (high tax rates)
Score—Change in Government Expenditures: 2.5–Worse (low decrease)
Final Score: 3.4–Worse (moderate cost of government)

Sri Lanka's top income tax rate is 30 percent. The top corporate tax rate is 32.5 percent (a 30 percent corporate tax rate plus a 2.5 percentage point surcharge tax). In 2003, according to the Asian Development Bank, government expenditures as a share of GDP decreased by 1.7 percentage points to 23.7 percent, compared to a 2.1 percentage point decrease in 2002. On net, Sri Lanka's fiscal burden of government score is 0.1 point worse this year.

GOVERNMENT INTERVENTION IN THE ECONOMY
Score: 2–Stable (low level)

The World Bank reports that the government consumed 7.9 percent of GDP in 2003. In the same year, according to the central bank, Sri Lanka received 8.66 percent of its total revenues from state-owned enterprises and government ownership of property.

MONETARY POLICY
Score: **3**–Stable (moderate level of inflation)

From 1995 to 2004, Sri Lanka's weighted average annual rate of inflation was 7.64 percent.

CAPITAL FLOWS AND FOREIGN INVESTMENT
Score: **4**–Worse (high barriers)

Foreign investment up to 100 percent is allowed in many sectors, and foreign firms receive national treatment. However, foreign investment is prohibited in non-bank lending, pawnbroking, and retail trade with a capital investment of less than $1 million (with some exceptions). According to the U.S. Trade Representative, "Investment in additional sectors is restricted and subject to screening and approval on a case-by-case basis, when foreign equity exceeds 40 percent" in a number of important sectors including shipping, mass communications, fishing, timber-based industries, mining, and the growing and primary processing of tea, rubber, coconut, rice, cocoa, sugar, and spices. Foreign investment equity restrictions and regulations apply to other sectors. Outward direct investment must be approved by the government. The World Trade Organization notes that "foreign and domestic investors often complain that the regulatory system allows for too much bureaucratic discretion…. [F]oreign inflows have remained subdued, probably due in part to the civil conflict, but also to other factors including obstacles to clearing products through customs, lack of access to land to build factories, and inadequate infrastructure." The International Monetary Fund reports that residents and non-residents may hold foreign exchange accounts subject to requirements, including government approval in some cases. There are strict reporting requirements and limits on payments and transfers. Capital transactions are subject to many restrictions and government approval in some cases. Based on the level of restrictions, Sri Lanka's capital flows and foreign investment score is 1 point worse this year.

BANKING AND FINANCE
Score: **4**–Stable (high level of restrictions)

Sri Lanka raised foreign-equity limits to 100 percent in commercial banks, insurance services, and stockbroking. Foreign banks must secure central bank approval before opening branches. "As of 2004," reports First Initiative, "there are 26 commercial banks, 14 of which were foreign owned, and two that were state-owned [Bank of Ceylon and People's Bank]. The two state-owned banks hold approximately 50% of all banking sector assets. In addition, there are 14 specialized banks, 10 merchant and investment banks and over 1,400 cooperative rural banks." According to the U.S. Department of Commerce, "The State consumes over 50 percent of the country's domestic financial resources and has a virtual monopoly on the management and use of long term savings…." The same

source reports that the "state banks are weak, with high [non-performing loans], inadequate loan loss provisioning, and low equity/assets ratio. Much of that is due to past government interference." The government privatized Sri Lanka's largest insurance firm in April 2003. The Colombo Stock Exchange listed 242 companies as of early 2004.

WAGES AND PRICES
Score: **3**–Stable (moderate level of intervention)

The government controls some wages and prices. According to the U.S. Department of Commerce, "The state continues to control the price of (basic) bread, flour, petroleum, bus and rail fares, telecom rates, water and electricity." Sri Lanka does not have a national minimum wage, but the law provides for and enforces the decisions of wage boards for specific sectors and industries.

PROPERTY RIGHTS
Score: **3**–Stable (moderate level of protection)

The Economist Intelligence Unit reports that the judiciary's "credibility and independence…has often been called into question in the past, especially since the president appoints judges to the Supreme Court." Delays in litigation are problematic. According to the U.S. Department of Commerce, "Settlement through the…court system is subject to extremely protracted and inexplicable delay. Aggrieved investors (especially those dealing with the Government of Sri Lanka on projects) have frequently pursued out-of-court settlements, which offer the possibility—not frequently realized—of speedier resolution of disputes."

REGULATION
Score: **3**–Stable (moderate level)

Sri Lankan regulations can be difficult to decipher, in addition to which enforcement can be deficient and transparency is sometimes lacking. The U.S. Department of Commerce reports that "some of the laws and regulations are not freely available and are difficult to access. Foreign and domestic investors often complain that the regulatory system allows far too much leeway for bureaucratic discretion…." The bureaucracy often employs cronies and is subject to corruption. The Economist Intelligence Unit reports that "labour laws are archaic and the sacking of employees requires permission of a labour commission."

INFORMAL MARKET
Score: **3.5**–Stable (high level of activity)

Transparency International's 2004 score for Sri Lanka is 3.5. Therefore, Sri Lanka's informal market score is 3.5 this year.

SUDAN

Rank: Suspended

Score: n/a

Category: n/a

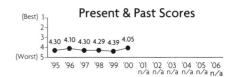

Present & Past Scores

(Best) 1
2
3   4.30 4.10 4.30 4.29 4.39 4.05
4
(Worst) 5
'95 '96 '97 '98 '99 '00 '01 '02 '03 '04 '05 '06
                                      n/a n/a n/a n/a n/a n/a

QUICK STUDY

SCORES

Trade Policy	n/a
Fiscal Burden	n/a
Government Intervention	n/a
Monetary Policy	n/a
Foreign Investment	n/a
Banking and Finance	n/a
Wages and Prices	n/a
Property Rights	n/a
Regulation	n/a
Informal Market	n/a

Population: 33,546,000

Total area: 2,505,810 sq. km

GDP: $14.5 billion

GDP growth rate: 6%

GDP per capita: $433

Major exports: crude oil, cotton, sesame, livestock

Exports of goods and services: $2.2 billion

Major export trading partners: China 40.9%, Saudi Arabia 17.1%, United Arab Emirates 5.4%

Major imports: machinery and equipment, manufactured goods, petroleum, transport equipment

Imports of goods and services: $1.9 billion

Major import trading partners: Saudi Arabia 16.3%, China 14.2%, India 4.2%, France 4.1%

Foreign direct investment (net): $1.3 billion

2003 Data (in constant 2000 US dollars)

The political situation in Sudan, Africa's largest country, is complex. After a 1989 military coup, President Omar Hassan al-Bashir and his inner circle of National Congress Party advisers ruled under a declared state of emergency, with parliament disbanded, parts of the constitution suspended, and civil liberties restricted. On July 9, 2005, pursuant to a January 2005 peace agreement that ended the decades-long civil war between the Arab Islamist government in Khartoum and the Christian African Sudanese People's Liberation Movement/Army that had cost millions of lives, a government of national unity was established under an interim constitution. Under the January agreement, which included compromises on political representation, self-determination, and distribution of oil resources, John Garang, leader of the main southern rebel group, was named vice president. Garang died in a helicopter crash only three weeks after assuming office, but his deputy, Salva Kiir, appears to have no difficulty succeeding him. In the western Darfur region, the government continues to support Arab Muslim militia groups, known as jinjaweed, who are committing genocide against black African Muslims. Estimates indicate that the conflict has resulted in up to 300,000 deaths and has affected 2.5 million persons, including approximately 2 million internally displaced persons in Darfur and refugees in neighboring Chad. Sudan's economy is hindered by instability, conflict-damaged infrastructure, economic mismanagement, and corruption. Oil reserves provide a potential resource for development. Until significant oil production began in 1999, the economy was predominantly agrarian, and most people remain engaged in that sector.

TRADE POLICY
Score: Not graded

According to the World Bank, Sudan's weighted average tariff rate in 2002 (the most recent year for which World Bank data are available) was 19.6 percent, up from the 4.4 percent for 1996 reported in the 2005 *Index*, based on World Bank data. Corruption pervades the customs service.

FISCAL BURDEN OF GOVERNMENT
Score—Income Taxation: Not graded
Score—Corporate Taxation: Not graded
Score—Change in Government Expenditures: Not graded
Final Score: Not graded

Sudan's top income tax rate is 20 percent. The top corporate tax rate is 35 percent. In 2003, according to the International Monetary Fund, government expenditures as a share of GDP increased 2.8 percentage points to 15.8 percent, compared to a 0.7 percentage point increase reported last year.

GOVERNMENT INTERVENTION IN THE ECONOMY
Score: Not graded

According to the African Development Bank, the government consumed 10.6 percent of GDP in 2003. In the same year, based on data from the International Monetary Fund, Sudan received 56.55 percent of its total revenues from state-owned enterprises and government ownership of property in the oil sector.

MONETARY POLICY
Score: Not graded

From 1995 to 2004, based on data from the International Monetary Fund's *2005 World Economic Outlook,* Sudan's weighted average annual rate of inflation was 8.21 percent.

CAPITAL FLOWS AND FOREIGN INVESTMENT
Score: Not graded

Foreign investment in Sudan is restricted by cumbersome regulations, political instability, and corruption. The government is seeking foreign investment, especially in connection with the privatization of state-owned enterprises. According to the Economist Intelligence Unit, however, "The poor state of the SOEs has discouraged potential private operators, who are not only unwilling to take on the companies' debts, but are also aware of the substantial investment many of the firms require after years of neglect. There has been substantial opposition to the privatisation programme among Sudan's influential labour unions…. In addition, accusations of corruption have dogged the privatisation programme, with government officials alleged to have demanded payments, while those linked to the senior ranks of the regime are reported to have bought state assets at prices well below their true value." Most of the interest of foreign investment is directed toward the oil sector. The International Monetary Fund reports that all residents (except the government, public institutions, and public enterprises) may hold foreign exchange accounts. Non-residents may hold foreign exchange accounts only with government approval. Controls apply to all transactions involving capital market securities, money market instruments, credit operations, and outward direct investment.

BANKING AND FINANCE
Score: Not graded

According to First Initiative, "Sudan's financial sector is small and under-developed after over two decades of civil conflict. The majority of financial institutions that do exist… adhere to Islamic financial principles. As of 2004, there were 25 commercial banks in Sudan, 16 of which are completely or mostly privately owned, and seven state-owned commercial banks. The sector also includes four specialized state-owned banks, which provide funds to specific sectors of the economy, and two investment banks. Some state-owned banks are beginning to be privatized." The Economist Intelligence Unit reports that Sudan's banking sector has been one of the few that operate solely according to Islamic principles, which prohibit the charging and payment of interest, and that "the strength of Sudan's monetary policy will be tested, as parallel banking systems—one sharia-compliant, the other not—are to be established as an outcome of the north–south peace deal. Currently an effective banking system only operates in the north, where the financial institutions are all sharia-compliant." The EIU also reports that steps being taken to improve the banking sector include increasing central bank supervision and relaxing firm government control over the allocation of credit.

WAGES AND PRICES
Score: Not graded

Although Sudan has liberalized some prices, price controls on foodstuffs remain in effect, and many goods are subsidized. According to the Economist Intelligence Unit, "Subsidy spending has been high over the post-coup period, while support to ailing state-owned enterprises…has also added to public expenditure, although much has remained off budget." In addition, "The government has continued to subsidise a range of basic goods and services, although the scope and depth of the subsidy programme has eased in line with the economic reform drive." The Ministry of Labor enforces Sudan's minimum wage.

PROPERTY RIGHTS
Score: Not graded

There is little respect for private property in Sudan. "The judiciary is not independent and is largely subservient to the Government," reports the U.S. Department of State. "The authorities do not ensure due process, and the military forces summarily tried and punished citizens. The Government infringed on citizens' privacy rights."

REGULATION
Score: Not graded

Sudan's regulatory burden is heavy and inefficient. Businesses often find it difficult to obtain licenses to operate, and business owners may be harassed by corrupt bureaucrats. One example of the effect of Sudan's burdensome regulations is the agricultural sector, which accounts for more than 80 percent of employment. The Economist Intelligence Unit cites corruption as "endemic."

INFORMAL MARKET
Score: Not graded

Transparency International's 2004 score for Sudan is 2.2. Therefore, Sudan would have an informal market score of 4 this year if grading were not suspended.

SURINAME

Rank: 129

Score: 3.60

Category: Mostly Unfree

Present & Past Scores

(Best) 1
2
3 4.10 4.00 4.10 4.08 3.98 3.98 3.98 4.01 3.96 3.93 3.60
4
(Worst) 5
'95 '96 '97 '98 '99 '00 '01 '02 '03 '04 '05 '06
n/a

Democracy was last restored in Suriname in 1991 but, as in many other Latin American countries, has been built on weak institutions, corruption, a strong government presence, and little economic freedom. As a result, Suriname remains poor and underdeveloped. Suriname is rich in natural resources, especially timber and minerals; there are reserves of bauxite, gold, nickel, and silver. The government is planning to privatize the state-owned banana company this year and to liberalize the telecommunications sector. According to the Economist Intelligence Unit, there is already a short list of cellular communications providers interested in competing with the state-owned company. Agriculture accounts for 8.6 percent of GDP, and mining accounts for over 10 percent. The large public sector is the primary employer, with half of the labor force on its rolls. Fiscal budget deficits remain the most pressing economic problem. Suriname's fiscal burden of government score is 0.3 point better this year, its monetary policy score is 1 point better, and its informal market score is 2 points better. As a result, Suriname's overall score is 0.33 point better this year.

TRADE POLICY
Score: **4**–Stable (high level of protectionism)

As a member of the Caribbean Community and Common Market (CARICOM), Suriname has a common external tariff rate that ranges from 0 percent to 20 percent. According to the World Bank, Suriname's average tariff rate in 2002 (the most recent year for which reliable data are available) was 11.7 percent. The World Trade Organization reports that "Suriname has taken major steps to reduce non-tariff barriers to trade…. Under the new system, imports (and exports) are free from non-tariff barriers except to protect national security, public morality, the environment, and human, animal, and plant life and health." Based on the revised trade factor methodology, Suriname's trade policy score is unchanged.

FISCAL BURDEN OF GOVERNMENT
Score—Income Taxation: **3.5**–Stable (high tax rates)
Score—Corporate Taxation: **5**–Stable (very high tax rates)
Score—Change in Government Expenditures: **2.5**–Better (low decrease)
Final Score: **4**–Better (high cost of government)

Suriname's top income tax rate is 38 percent. The top corporate tax rate is 36 percent. In 2003, according to the International Monetary Fund, government expenditures as a share of GDP decreased 1.3 percentage points to 34.4 percent, compared to the 1.4 percentage point increase in 2002. On net, Suriname's fiscal burden of government score is 0.3 point better this year.

GOVERNMENT INTERVENTION IN THE ECONOMY
Score: **3**–Stable (moderate level)

Based on data from the International Monetary Fund, the government consumed 36.2 percent of GDP in 2003. In the same year, based on data from the same source, Suriname received 7.82 percent of its total revenues from state-owned enterprises and government ownership of property.

QUICK STUDY

SCORES

Trade Policy	4
Fiscal Burden	4
Government Intervention	3
Monetary Policy	4
Foreign Investment	4
Banking and Finance	4
Wages and Prices	3
Property Rights	3
Regulation	4
Informal Market	3

Population: 438,100

Total area: 163,270 sq. km

GDP: 988.8 million

GDP growth rate: 5.1%

GDP per capita: $2,257

Major exports: alumina, shrimp, crude oil, rice

Exports of goods and services: $240.3 million

Major export trading partners: US 24.4%, Norway 19.2%, Belgium 13.1%, France 10.6%

Major imports: foodstuffs, petroleum, cotton

Imports of goods and services: $524 million

Major import trading partners: US 31.6%, Netherlands 18.7%, Trinidad and Tobago 11.1%, China 6.9%, Japan 6.4%

Foreign direct investment (net): −$87.2 million

2003 Data (in constant 2000 US dollars)

MONETARY POLICY
Score: **4**–Better (high level of inflation)

From 1995 to 2004, Suriname's weighted average annual rate of inflation was 14.74 percent, down from the 24.62 percent between 1994 and 2003 reported in the 2005 *Index*. As a result, Suriname's monetary policy score is 1 point better this year.

CAPITAL FLOWS AND FOREIGN INVESTMENT
Score: **4**–Stable (high barriers)

The government has updated its investment code, and slow progress is being made in removing disincentives to foreign investment, but implementation is questionable. "In December 2001," reports the U.S. Department of Commerce, "laws were passed to create a new institute called InvestSur to process applications for investment requests, to settle disputes, and to help investors…. However, new investment laws have been caught up in bureaucratic delays and changes have been slow." Moreover, "While Surinamese companies might escape with bending the rules, foreign companies are generally held to the letter of the law…. Large segments of Surinamese society retain nationalistic suspicion of foreign investors." The International Monetary Fund reports that residents may hold foreign exchange accounts provided that the funds did not come from sales of real estate in Suriname. Non-residents may open foreign exchange accounts in U.S. dollars and with the approval of the Foreign Exchange Commission. Payments and transfers face various quantitative limits and approval requirements. The IMF reports that capital transactions involving outward remittances of foreign exchange require the approval of the Foreign Exchange Commission.

BANKING AND FINANCE
Score: **4**–Stable (high level of restrictions)

Suriname's banking legislation is out of date, and the central bank does not provide adequate oversight. "As of 2004," reports First Initiative, "the Surinamese banking sector is comprised of eight commercial banks, six of which the government is a shareholder of. The three largest banks in Suriname, two of which are partially owned by the state, control over 80% of the financial system's assets. The government fully owns three smaller banks and a development bank, which it plans to merge." According to the Economist Intelligence Unit, the four smaller state-owned banks (Landbouwbank, Surinaamse Postspaarbank, Surinaamse Volkscredietbank, and Nationale Ontwikkelingsbank), which account for 14.7 percent of total bank assets, are in poor financial health and will be merged "with the state taking direct responsibility for non-performing loans of these banks, in preparation for privatisation."

WAGES AND PRICES
Score: **3**–Stable (moderate level of intervention)

According to the World Trade Organization, "Under the Law on Price Setting and Monitoring, the Minister of Trade and Industry is authorized to determine the maximum price or mark-up for any good or service sold in Suriname…." As of April 2004, the government fixed the prices of baby food, bread, cooking gas, fuel, flour, and milk and restricted mark-ups on over 30 food items. The government also regulates the prices of utilities. Although there is no official minimum wage, the government influences wages as employer of approximately 50 percent of the workforce.

PROPERTY RIGHTS
Score: **3**–Stable (moderate level of protection)

Private property is not well protected. The judicial process is inefficient. According to the U.S. Department of Commerce, "the judiciary has a significant shortage of judges…. Surinamese law provides for the right of an individual or company to hold land, buildings and equipment. Settlement of ownership disputes or damage to property, buildings or equipment can be an extremely long process in the undermanned, overworked, legal system."

REGULATION
Score: **4**–Stable (high level)

Suriname's state-owned sector plays a considerable role in the economy and impedes private enterprise. According to the U.S. Department of Commerce, "Surinamese investment legislation, formulated in 1960, is now outdated. As a result, companies negotiate directly with the Surinamese government on concessions, licenses and hiring. Investors are dealt with by the appropriate ministries on an 'ad hoc' basis. The process can be very slow, quixotic, and is not immune from patronage and favoritism." Although a new investment law is designed to ease the burden of doing business, "bureaucratic delays have prohibited it from taking effect. A plethora of government controls in pricing, licensing, and other areas leave considerable space for favoritism and corruption."

INFORMAL MARKET
Score: **3**–Better (moderate level of activity)

Transparency International's 2004 score for Suriname is 4.3. Therefore, Suriname's informal market score is 3 this year—2 points better than last year.

SWAZILAND

Rank: 78

Score: 3.04

Category: Mostly Unfree

Present & Past Scores

(Best) 1—
2—
3—
4— 3.11 3.35 3.26 3.13 3.06 3.16 3.05 3.21 3.05 3.18 3.11 3.04
(Worst) 5—
  '95 '96 '97 '98 '99 '00 '01 '02 '03 '04 '05 '06

QUICK STUDY

SCORES

Trade Policy	2.5
Fiscal Burden	3.9
Government Intervention	3
Monetary Policy	2
Foreign Investment	3
Banking and Finance	3
Wages and Prices	3
Property Rights	3
Regulation	3
Informal Market	4

Population: 1,106,000

Total area: 17,360 sq. km

GDP: $1.5 billion

GDP growth rate: 2.2%

GDP per capita: $1,358

Major exports: sugar, wood pulp, cotton yarn, citrus and canned fruit

Exports of goods and services: $1.3 billion

Major export trading partners: South Africa 59.7%, EU 8.8%, US 8.8%, Mozambique 6.2%

Major imports: motor vehicles, machinery, transport equipment, foodstuffs, petroleum products, chemicals

Imports of goods and services: $1.4 billion

Major import trading partners: South Africa 95.6%, EU 0.9%, Japan 0.9%, Singapore 0.3%

Foreign direct investment (net): $41.9 million

2003 Data (in constant 2000 US dollars)

Swaziland is a monarchy in which King Mswati III and his advisers hold most political power and the judiciary and a partially elected parliament exercise only limited power. Political parties were banned in 1973 when the constitution was suspended by former King Sobhuza. The current political system engenders corruption and mismanagement, and Mswati's spendthrift habits have led to popular discontent. Civil unrest has pushed the government toward political reform, but vested interests resist change and are likely to prevent reform that seriously reduces the powers of the monarchy. Swaziland is landlocked and shares a border with South Africa and Mozambique. The economy is heavily dependent on South Africa, and most trade is conducted with that country. Although most of the population is engaged in subsistence agriculture, industry and services are the largest sources of formal-sector GDP. Up to 40 percent of the working-age population is unemployed or underemployed. Progress toward economic liberalization and privatization has been delayed by opposition among the political elite. Swaziland is believed to have the world's highest HIV/AIDS rate, with nearly 40 percent of people aged 15–49 infected. Swaziland's fiscal burden of government score is 0.3 point worse this year, and its government intervention score is 1 point worse; however, its monetary policy score and capital flows and foreign investment score are 1 point better. As a result, Swaziland's overall score is 0.07 point better this year.

TRADE POLICY
Score: **2.5**–Stable (moderate level of protectionism)

Swaziland belongs to the Southern African Customs Union (SACU), a regional trade arrangement with Botswana, Lesotho, Namibia, and South Africa. According to the World Bank, in 2001 (the most recent year for which World Bank data are available), the SACU had a weighted average tariff rate of 3.6 percent. The U.S. Trade Representative reports that Swaziland has "exercised its right under the SACU Agreement to protect infant industries such as fertilizer, cement, and beer by applying tariff rates [above the common external tariff].… A limited number of products from outside the SACU area require an import permit." Based on the revised trade factor methodology, Swaziland's trade policy score is unchanged.

FISCAL BURDEN OF GOVERNMENT
Score—Income Taxation: **3**–Stable (moderate tax rates)
Score—Corporate Taxation: **4**–Stable (high tax rates)
Score—Change in Government Expenditures: **4.5**–Worse (high increase)
Final Score: **3.9**–Worse (high cost of government)

Swaziland's top income tax rate is 33 percent. The top corporate tax rate is 30 percent. In 2003, according to the African Development Bank, government expenditures as a share of GDP increased 2.8 percentage points to 34 percent, compared to the 1.9 percentage point decrease in 2002. On net, Swaziland's fiscal burden of government is 0.3 point worse this year.

GOVERNMENT INTERVENTION IN THE ECONOMY
Score: **3**–Worse (moderate level)

Based on data from the International Monetary Fund, the government consumed 17.3 percent of GDP in 2003. In fiscal year 2003–2004, based on data from the central bank, the government received 12.8 percent of its total revenues from state-owned enterprises and government ownership of property, up from the 4.44 reported in the 2005 *Index*. As a result, Swaziland's government intervention score is 1 point worse this year.

MONETARY POLICY
Score: **2–Better** (low level of inflation)

From 1995 to 2004, based on data from the International Monetary Fund's *2005 World Economic Outlook*, Swaziland's weighted average annual rate of inflation was 5.30 percent, down from the 8.42 percent from 1994 to 2003 reported in the 2005 *Index*. As a result, Swaziland's monetary policy score is 1 point better this year.

CAPITAL FLOWS AND FOREIGN INVESTMENT
Score: **3–Better** (moderate barriers)

According to the U.S. Department of Commerce, "Swaziland does not have an investment code or securities act. As a result, policies affecting foreign investment are established and influenced more through government statements and decrees than through formal legislative or administrative processes.... There are no formal policies or practices that discriminate against foreign investors. Companies...may be 100 percent foreign-owned and foreign investors are free to invest in most sectors." All foreign workers must have permits—a process that can be time consuming and cumbersome. The International Monetary Fund reports that both residents and non-residents may hold foreign exchange accounts, but residents face restrictions. Payments and transfers, while not usually restricted, are subject to quantitative limits and government approval in some cases. The IMF also reports that the central bank must approve most inward capital transfers. Most other capital transactions require documentation or face restrictions. Real estate transactions by non-residents must be approved. Based on contradictory policies of a relatively open foreign investment regime combined with tight capital restrictions, Swaziland's capital flows and foreign investment score is 1 point better this year.

BANKING AND FINANCE
Score: **3–Stable** (moderate level of restrictions)

First Initiative reports that Swaziland's "financial system is quite small and is characterized by a large degree of state-ownership.... [A]s of 2004 [the banking system] includes four banking institutions, three private banks (all owned by South African banks), the state-owned Swazibank and a housing bank. There are 178 saving and credit unions which provide micro-finance services (2003).... [T]he micro-finance industry continues to be essentially unregulated due to the difficulty of enforcing rules.... The state-owned Swaziland Royal Insurance Corporation monopolizes the insurance sector." The banking system is sound, according to the International Monetary Fund, which notes that "commercial banks are well capitalized, have a relatively low level of nonperforming

loans, and have taken a sound approach to risk management and provisioning."

WAGES AND PRICES
Score: **3–Stable** (moderate level of intervention)

The International Monetary Fund reports that administered prices account for approximately 16 percent of the consumer price index. However, the government affects prices through its many state-owned industries, which include (but are not limited to) state-owned enterprises in the electricity, transportation, and maize sectors. Swaziland has a legally mandated minimum wage that varies according to type of work.

PROPERTY RIGHTS
Score: **3–Stable** (moderate level of protection)

According to the U.S. Department of Commerce, Swaziland's "dual legal system...can be confusing and has, at times, presented problems for foreign-owned business...." The U.S. Department of State reports that "lack of an independent court budget, lack of trained manpower, inadequate levels of salary remuneration and managing case work remain problems" and that "delays in trials are common." According to the Economist Intelligence Unit, "The courts have recently given several important judgements against the government, which has led to growing government interference in the judicial system. In November 2002 the prime minister stated that the rulings of the appeal court would be ignored."

REGULATION
Score: **3–Stable** (moderate level)

"Despite inadequate legislation," reports the U.S. Department of Commerce, "starting a business in Swaziland can be a relatively simple process." The Bank of Swaziland reports that businesses must provide a healthy work environment and must submit an environmental impact assessment. According to the Economist Intelligence Unit, some government regulations (especially those dealing with safety conditions) are applied erratically, and this can lead to uncertainty and confusion. The Bank of Swaziland reports that bureaucratic corruption "is on the high side." The EIU also notes the existence of "some, largely petty, bribery in the civil service. According to a report leaked in 2002, there are over 10,000 ghost employees in the civil service, and regular abuse of overtime and other allowances occurs.... Large government contracts are particularly vulnerable to corrupt practices."

INFORMAL MARKET
Score: **4–Stable** (high level of activity)

Swaziland has an active informal market, primarily in the supply of labor, transportation service, the construction industry, and computer software. The Economist Intelligence Unit reports "high levels of illegal crossborder trade."

SWEDEN

Rank: 19

Score: 1.96

Category: Free

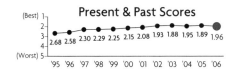

Present & Past Scores

(Best) 1
2
3
4
(Worst) 5

2.68 2.58 2.30 2.29 2.25 2.15 2.08 1.93 1.88 1.95 1.89 1.96

'95 '96 '97 '98 '99 '00 '01 '02 '03 '04 '05 '06

QUICK STUDY

SCORES

Trade Policy	2
Fiscal Burden	3.6
Government Intervention	3
Monetary Policy	1
Foreign Investment	1
Banking and Finance	2
Wages and Prices	2
Property Rights	1
Regulation	3
Informal Market	1

Population: 9,104,000

Total area: 449,964 sq. km

GDP: $259.2 billion

GDP growth rate: 3.5%

GDP per capita: $28,471

Major exports: paper products, pulp and wood, machinery and transport equipment, chemicals, financial and insurance services, travel services

Exports of goods and services: $159.9 billion

Major export trading partners: US 10.7%, Germany 10.2%, Norway 8.5%, UK 7.9%

Major imports: machinery, chemicals, mineral fuels, travel services, financial and insurance services

Imports of goods and services: $131.8 billion

Major import trading partners: Germany 18.9%, Denmark 9.2%, UK 7.7%, Norway 7.6%, Netherlands 6.8%

Foreign direct investment (net): –$12.7 billion

2004 Data (in constant 2000 US dollars)

Sweden is the third-largest country, by area, in Western Europe. Over 66 percent of GDP is derived from the services sector, while the agriculture sector comprises 3 percent. As one of the world's most open and competitive economies, Sweden relies heavily on international trade, with total trade accounting for about 65 percent of GDP in 2004. Although the state owns about 25 percent of the domestic economy, the Economist Intelligence Unit reports that "most operations are run on a strictly commercial basis." Deregulation in major sectors such as telecommunications and banking has put Sweden ahead of the European Union in market openness to new entrants, including foreigners, and has contributed to faster GDP growth than the Organisation for Economic Co-operation and Development's average in recent years. Continuing low inflation and competitive business environments brought the Swedish economy strong economic growth of 3.5 percent in 2004, outpacing the euro area that Swedes voted against joining in 2003. Although high personal tax rates and rigid labor market regulations remain areas of deficiency, Sweden's multi-year tax reform that began in 2000 resulted in tax rate cuts for low- and middle-income earners. The government also abolished inheritance and gift taxes in January 2005. Sweden's fiscal burden of government score is 0.3 point better this year, but its banking and finance score is 1 point worse. As a result, Sweden's overall score is 0.07 point worse this year.

TRADE POLICY
Score: **2**–Stable (low level of protectionism)

As a member of the European Union, Sweden was subject to a common EU weighted average external tariff of 1.3 percent in 2003, down from the 2.4 percent for 2002 reported in the 2005 *Index*, based on World Bank data. According to the World Trade Organization and the U.S. Trade Representative, the EU imposes non-tariff trade barriers through a complex regulatory system and export subsidies. Based on the revised trade factor methodology, Sweden's trade policy score is unchanged.

FISCAL BURDEN OF GOVERNMENT
Score—Income Taxation: **5**–Stable (very high tax rates)
Score—Corporate Taxation: **3.5**–Stable (high tax rates)
Score—Change in Government Expenditures: **2.5**–Better (low decrease)
Final Score: **3.6**–Better (high cost of government)

According to the Economist Intelligence Unit, Sweden's income tax burden is one of the heaviest among the world's industrialized economies: a 60 percent top income tax rate. The top corporate tax rate is 28 percent. In 2004, government expenditures as a share of GDP decreased 1.5 percentage points to 57.1 percent, compared to a 0.3 percentage point increase in 2003. On net, Sweden's fiscal burden of government score is 0.3 point better this year.

GOVERNMENT INTERVENTION IN THE ECONOMY
Score: **3**–Stable (moderate level)

Based on data from the Economist Intelligence Unit, the government consumed 27.8 percent of GDP in 2004. In the same year, based on data from the Ministry of Finance, Sweden received 5.1 percent of its total revenues from state-owned enterprises and government ownership of property.

361

MONETARY POLICY
Score: **1–Stable** (very low level of inflation)

From 1995 to 2004, Sweden's weighted average annual rate of inflation was 0.96 percent.

 CAPITAL FLOWS AND FOREIGN INVESTMENT
Score: **1–Stable** (very low barriers)

Sweden presents few barriers to foreign investment. Foreign companies may purchase Swedish companies without government approval, and domestic companies may not restrict foreign ownership of shares. According to the U.S. Department of Commerce, "Surveys conducted by investors in recent years ranking the investment climate in Sweden show rather uniform results: positives mentioned are competent employees, low corporate tax rates, excellent infrastructure and good access to capital. On the minus side are high cost of labor, rigid labor legislation and the overall high costs in Sweden." Both domestic and foreign investors are prohibited from investing in the retail sale of pharmaceuticals and alcoholic beverages, in which the government maintains a monopoly. The government does not require investors to obtain prior approval of acquisitions. The International Monetary Fund reports that residents and non-residents may hold foreign exchange accounts. There are no controls on payments and transfers or repatriation of profits. A permit may be required for the purchase of real estate by non-residents. The IMF reports that direct investment is controlled in fishing, civil aviation, and transport and communications.

 BANKING AND FINANCE
Score: **2–Worse** (low level of restrictions)

Most commercial banks in Sweden are privately owned and operated. Banks are allowed to offer a full range of services, and foreign banks have access to the banking sector. According to the U.S. Department of Commerce, "Foreign banks, insurance companies, brokerage firms, and cooperative mortgage institutions are permitted to establish branches…on equal terms with domestic firms, although a permit is required." The same source reports that credit is allocated on market terms and that financial regulations and other requirements are transparent and consistent with international norms. "Of the 27 domestic commercial banks in Sweden," reports the Economist Intelligence Unit, "the three most important are Svenska Handelsbanken, SEB (formerly Skandinaviska Enskilda Banken) and ForeningsSparbanken. Another important commercial bank is Nordea Sverige, which is part of the pan-Nordic Nordea group. All four banks are listed on the Stockholm Stock Exchange. Nordea Sverige is listed through the Nordea Group, in which the Swedish government holds a 25.7% stake. Together, the four account for more than 80% of the total Swedish banking market…. At the end of September 2004 there were 21 foreign banks operating in Sweden." The EIU also reports that a "number of agencies…continue to provide concessional finance." Based on evidence of government ownership in a sizeable bank, requirements for foreign financial institutions to get a permit to open a branch in Sweden, and government involvement in the credit market, Sweden's banking and finance score is 1 point worse this year.

 WAGES AND PRICES
Score: **2–Stable** (low level of intervention)

The Economist Intelligence Unit reports that "prices in Sweden are generally set by market forces. Monopolies are the exception. One such is the state-owned chain of liquor stores. Another is the state-owned chemist-chain, Apoteket, which has the only license to sell both prescription and non-prescription medicines." The government affects agricultural prices through Sweden's participation in the Common Agricultural Policy, a program that heavily subsidizes agricultural goods. Wages are set through collective bargaining agreements that traditionally apply to all workers regardless of union affiliation.

 PROPERTY RIGHTS
Score: **1–Stable** (very high level of protection)

Sweden has a well-developed and efficient legal system. The judiciary is independent and provides citizens with a fair judicial process. According to the Economist Intelligence Unit, "Contractual arrangements are generally highly respected in Sweden—morally as well as legally. The quality of the judiciary and civil service is high, and the country's legal code is well developed."

 REGULATION
Score: **3–Stable** (moderate level)

The process for opening a business in Sweden is relatively easy and straightforward. According to the Economist Intelligence Unit, "There is often much less bureaucracy than in continental Europe, and a great deal of information is public under the law. Information is readily available in English. Most agencies have extensive Internet websites and respond reasonably promptly to e-mail enquiries." Many laws have been changed along the lines of European Union standards. The high cost of labor, in terms of payroll taxes and legislation, is one of the biggest deterrents to business. Environmental law continues to become increasingly stringent, surpassing even EU standards.

 INFORMAL MARKET
Score: **1–Stable** (very low level of activity)

Transparency International's 2004 score for Sweden is 9.2. Therefore, Sweden's informal market score is 1 this year.

> If Sweden were to improve its regulation score, it would qualify for the Global Free Trade Alliance.

SWITZERLAND

Rank: 15
Score: 1.89
Category: Free

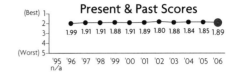

Present & Past Scores

(Best) 1
2
3
4
(Worst) 5

1.99 1.91 1.91 1.88 1.91 1.89 1.80 1.88 1.84 1.85 1.89

'95 '96 '97 '98 '99 '00 '01 '02 '03 '04 '05 '06
n/a

QUICK STUDY

SCORES

Trade Policy	2
Fiscal Burden	2.9
Government Intervention	2
Monetary Policy	1
Foreign Investment	2
Banking and Finance	2
Wages and Prices	2
Property Rights	1
Regulation	3
Informal Market	1

Population: 7,364,000

Total area: 41,290 sq. km

GDP: $253.1 billion

GDP growth rate: 1.9%

GDP per capita: $34,369

Major exports: machinery and electronic devices, chemicals, watches, precision instruments, financial services, travel services, insurance services

Exports of goods and services: $177.1 billion

Major export trading partners: Germany 20.6%, US 10.1%, France 8.6%, Italy 8.5%, UK 4.8%

Major imports: machinery and electronic devices, vehicles, financial services

Imports of goods and services: $149.1 billion

Major import trading partners: Germany 33.9%, Italy 11.7%, France 10.1%, Austria 4.4%, US 4.1%

Foreign direct investment (net): −$19.1 billion

2004 Data (in constant 2000 US dollars)

With its stable currency and politics, relatively low taxes, secure banking system, and federal and cantonal incentives for new investors, Switzerland is an attractive investment location, particularly for small manufacturing. In general, there are no overall restrictions on the percentage of equity that foreign firms may hold, and some cantons waive taxes on new firms for up to 10 years. Larger businesses are highly competitive and international, but smaller businesses, particularly those related to agriculture, are protected, and this has led to higher food prices. Switzerland has two of Europe's five largest banks. As in Germany, however, a consensus-driven business and political system retards further economic liberalization and growth. GDP growth has been weak during the past two decades, reflecting very low productivity growth. Nevertheless, per capita income remains high. The economy was broadly stagnant in 2002 and 2003, and GDP grew only 1.9 percent in 2004. The Swiss are negotiating a bilateral agreement with the European Union, but full accession remains unlikely, so the Swiss have improved their ties with the EU's single market while shunning some of the EU's excessive regulation. Switzerland has announced its intention to pursue a free trade agreement with the United States. Switzerland's fiscal burden of government score is 0.1 point better this year, and its government intervention score is 0.5 point better; however, its banking and finance score is 1 point worse. As a result, Switzerland's overall score is 0.04 point worse this year.

TRADE POLICY
Score: **2–Stable** (low level of protectionism)

The World Bank reports that Switzerland's weighted average tariff rate in 2001 (the most recent year for which World Bank data are available) was 1.5 percent. (This figure has been revised upward from the 0.8 percent for 2001—also based on World Bank data—that was reported in the 2005 *Index*.) According to the World Trade Organization, "Trade controls and restrictions are in place only for security, safety, health and environmental reasons, and to apply UN and certain EU trade sanctions." However, the U.S. Trade Representative notes that "nearly all agricultural products…are subject to import duties and variable import quotas." Based on the revised trade factor methodology, Switzerland's trade policy score is unchanged.

FISCAL BURDEN OF GOVERNMENT
Score—Income Taxation: **3.5–Stable** (high tax rates)
Score—Corporate Taxation: **2.5–Stable** (moderate tax rates)
Score—Change in Government Expenditures: **3–Better** (very low decrease)
Final Score: **2.9–Better** (moderate cost of government)

Switzerland's top cantonal income tax rate is 35.5 percent. (Switzerland taxes its citizens at the federal and cantonal levels. Taxation at the cantonal level is a greater burden on the average citizen than taxation at the federal level; therefore, Switzerland's top income and corporate tax rates are based on the highest cantonal tax rate.) The top cantonal corporate tax rate is 23 percent. In 2004, government expenditures as a share of GDP remained unchanged at 36 percent, compared to the 0.6 percentage point increase in 2003. On net, Switzerland's fiscal burden of government score is 0.1 point better this year.

GOVERNMENT INTERVENTION IN THE ECONOMY
Score: 2–Better (low level)

The Economist Intelligence Unit reports that the government consumed 12 percent of GDP in 2004. In 2003, based on data from the Department of Finance, Switzerland received 4.1 percent of its total revenues from state-owned enterprises and government ownership of property, down from the 7.8 percent reported in the 2005 *Index*. As a result, Switzerland's government intervention score is 0.5 point better this year.

MONETARY POLICY
Score: 1–Stable (very low level of inflation)

From 1995 to 2004, Switzerland's weighted average annual rate of inflation was 0.77 percent.

CAPITAL FLOWS AND FOREIGN INVESTMENT
Score: 2–Stable (low barriers)

Switzerland is generally open to foreign investment. Formal approval is not required, and screening applies only to foreign investment in real estate and national security establishments. According to the U.S. Department of Commerce, "With the exception of areas considered essential to national security, such as hydroelectric and nuclear power, operation of oil pipelines, transportation of explosive materials, and operation of airlines and marine navigation, national treatment is granted to foreign investors." The Economist Intelligence Unit reports that cantonal laws generally require 51 percent Swiss ownership in mining activities and that foreign firms must have less than 51 percent ownership in petroleum exploitation operations. Visas and work permits for non-European foreign workers are strictly controlled. The International Monetary Fund reports that both residents and non-residents may hold foreign exchange accounts. There are no restrictions on repatriation of profits, payments for invisible transactions, or current transfers. Purchases of real estate by non-residents must be approved by the canton in which the property is located.

BANKING AND FINANCE
Score: 2–Worse (low level of restrictions)

Switzerland's banks may offer a wide range of financial services, and credit is allocated on market terms. According to the U.S. Department of Commerce, "There are no private or government efforts to restrict foreign participation in industry standards setting [and] no other practices by private firms to restrict foreign investment, participation, or control in or of domestic enterprises." The Economist Intelligence Unit reports that government permission is required to establish a foreign-owned bank or finance company and that 148 foreign banks accounted for 8.9 percent of total banking assets as of the end of 2003. Switzerland's two biggest banks—UBS and Credit Suisse—control over 60 percent of assets and rank among the world's top 10 financial institutions. According to the U.S. Department of Commerce, "There are 24 cantonal banks (owned by the cantonal govern-

ment) involved mainly in acceptance of savings deposits, granting of mortgages or debentures to satisfy local commercial and private credit needs, and granting loans to public authorities." The EIU reports that the cantonal banks accounted for nearly 14 percent of assets as of the end of 2003. Based on evidence of cantonal ownership of banks, Switzerland's banking and finance score is 1 point worse this year.

WAGES AND PRICES
Score: 2–Stable (low level of intervention)

The market sets most prices. However, according to the Economist Intelligence Unit, "Permanent price and margin controls apply to all agricultural goods and their by-products that are subsidised or protected by the Swiss government. The federal Price Surveillance Office has the right to set maximum prices for these goods." The Embassy of Switzerland reports that the government controls the price of goods and services in the alcohol, medical, mail services, and waste management sectors.

PROPERTY RIGHTS
Score: 1–Stable (very high level of protection)

Switzerland may be one of the world's best protectors of property rights. The judiciary is independent, and the government respects this independence in practice. The Economist Intelligence Unit reports that "contractual arrangements are completely secure in Switzerland, and the judiciary and civil service are of high quality."

REGULATION
Score: 3–Stable (moderate level)

Regulations are extensive, particularly at the local level, but the government applies them evenly and transparently in most cases. It takes about six weeks to register a new business. According to the U.S. Department of Commerce, "Indirect [government] involvement is evident in the extensive number of government regulations.... Building codes, regulated hours of establishment, labor laws, zoning ordinances, environmental regulation (for instance, garbage control), noise codes and administered prices are examples of areas where rules and regulations are...pervasive...." In April 2004, reports the Economist Intelligence Unit, "a new cartel law [gave] the Federal Competition Commission greater powers to fine companies rigging prices and blocking competition, including first-time offenders." In addition, "Companies have relative freedom in hiring and firing. Nevertheless there are usually generous social plans for those who lose their jobs."

INFORMAL MARKET
Score: 1–Stable (very low level of activity)

Transparency International's 2004 score for Switzerland is 9.1. Therefore, Switzerland's informal market score is 1 this year.

> If Switzerland were to improve its regulation score, it would qualify for the Global Free Trade Alliance.

SYRIA

Rank: 145

Score: 3.93

Category: Mostly Unfree

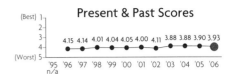

Present & Past Scores

(Best) 1
2
3   4.15 4.14 4.01 4.04 4.05 4.00 4.11 3.88 3.88 3.90 3.93
4
(Worst) 5
'95 '96 '97 '98 '99 '00 '01 '02 '03 '04 '05 '06
n/a

QUICK STUDY

SCORES

Trade Policy	5
Fiscal Burden	3.8
Government Intervention	5
Monetary Policy	2
Foreign Investment	4
Banking and Finance	4
Wages and Prices	4
Property Rights	4
Regulation	4
Informal Market	3.5

Population: 17,384,000

Total area: 185,180 sq. km

GDP: $19.7 billion

GDP growth rate: 2.5%

GDP per capita: $1,135

Major exports: crude oil and petroleum products, food, textiles and textile fibers, raw cotton

Exports of goods and services: $8.2 billion

Major export trading partners: Germany 20.7%, Italy 12.4%, United Arab Emirates 7.5%, Turkey 6.0%, France 5.3%

Major imports: machinery and transport equipment, food, live animals, beverages and tobacco, chemicals, manufactured products

Imports of goods and services: $6.2 billion

Major import trading partners: Germany 7.0%, Italy 6.9%, China 6.2%, Turkey 5.3%

Foreign direct investment (net): $141.5 million

2003 Data (in constant 2000 US dollars)

Syria has been ruled by the Assad regime since Minister of Defense Hafez al-Assad seized power in a 1970 military coup. Under Assad, Syria imposed rigid state controls on the economy. Hafez Assad was succeeded in 2000 by his son Bashar. Bashar Assad first promised cautious economic reforms to energize the stagnant socialist economy; then, to consolidate his power, he reached an accommodation with officials from his father's regime who oppose economic reform. The May 2004 imposition of U.S. economic sanctions and Syria's growing isolation due to its suspected involvement in the February 2005 assassination of former Lebanese Prime Minister Rafiq Hariri have discouraged foreign investment. The Assad regime has allowed the establishment of private banks and seeks to attract investment from Syrian expatriates, but its reluctance to open the markets, which would threaten the power of the ruling Baath Party, is likely to hamper future economic growth. Syria's fiscal burden of government score is 0.2 point better this year, and its banking and finance score is 1 point better; however, its government intervention score is 0.5 point worse, and its monetary policy score is 1 point worse. As a result, Syria's overall score is 0.03 point worse this year.

TRADE POLICY
Score: **5**–Stable (very high level of protectionism)

According to the World Bank, Syria's weighted average tariff rate in 2002 (the most recent year for which World Bank data are available) was 15.5 percent. The *Index* methodology places greater emphasis on weighted average tariff rates; therefore, the weighted tariff rate for 2002 is used instead of the 35 percent average tariff rate for 2003 reported in the 2005 *Index*. The U.S. Department of Commerce reports that Syria prohibits imports of electrical appliances, chocolates, fruit juices, mineral water, cosmetics, and ceramics from non-Arab countries. In addition, "Customs procedures are cumbersome, tedious, and time-consuming because of complex regulations." Corruption is common. Based on the revised trade factor methodology, Syria's trade policy score is unchanged.

FISCAL BURDEN OF GOVERNMENT
Score—Income Taxation: **2**–Stable (low tax rates)
Score—Corporate Taxation: **4.5**–Stable (very high tax rates)
Score—Change in Government Expenditures: **4**–Better (moderate increase)
Final Score: **3.8**–Better (high cost of government)

Syria's top income tax rate is 20 percent. The top corporate tax rate is 35 percent. In 2003, according to the International Monetary Fund, government expenditures as a share of GDP increased by 1.7 percentage points to 33.1 percent, compared to the 1.7 percentage point increase in 2002. On net, Syria's fiscal burden of government score is 0.2 point better this year.

GOVERNMENT INTERVENTION IN THE ECONOMY
Score: **5**–Worse (very high level)

The World Bank reports that the government consumed 10.7 percent of GDP in 2003. In the same year, based on data from the Economist Intelligence Unit, Syria received 43.46 percent of its total revenues from state-owned enterprises and government ownership of property, up from the 39.98 percent reported in the 2005 *Index*. As a result, Syria's government intervention

365

score is 0.5 point worse this year. According to the U.S. Department of Commerce, "The government continues to control all 'strategic' industries such as oil production, oil refining, port operation, telecommunications, air transport, power generation/distribution, and water distribution…." The EIU reports that an "overstaffed and inefficient public sector continues to act as a drain on the economy, soaking up government expenditure…and capital investment." Based on the apparent unreliability of the reported figure for government consumption, 1 point has been added to Syria's government intervention score.

MONETARY POLICY
Score: **2**–Worse (low level of inflation)

From 1995 to 2004, based on data from the International Monetary Fund's *2005 World Economic Outlook*, Syria's weighted average annual rate of inflation was 3.46 percent, up from the 2.96 percent from 1994 to 2003 reported in the 2005 *Index*. As a result, Syria's monetary policy score is 1 point worse this year.

CAPITAL FLOWS AND FOREIGN INVESTMENT
Score: **4**–Stable (high barriers)

Foreigners may own 100 percent of a company and may own land. New laws guarantee against expropriation and permit repatriation. According to the U.S. Department of Commerce, "Almost all sectors of the economy are open to foreign direct investment except for power generation and distribution, air transport, port operation, water bottling, telephony, and oil and gas production and refining." However, the government "has not fully adopted the strong legal and regulatory framework demanded by both foreign and Syrian investors…. [M]ost observers continue to find Syria's business environment a difficult one, plagued by ambiguous regulations and arbitrary government enforcement. Economic reforms in the recent past have been largely symbolic and have done little to improve Syria's overall investment climate." Many capital transactions are subject to controls, and foreign exchange and trade transactions must be approved.

BANKING AND FINANCE
Score: **4**–Better (high level of restrictions)

First Initiative reports that "Syria's banking sector is dominated by the state, led by the Commercial Bank of Syria and other specialized sector banks…. In 2001, the Syrian government began implementing a series of reforms including the legalization of private banks (provided that a 51% stake is Syrian-held), the allowance of foreign stakes in banks, and the creation of the Monetary and Credit Council (MCC) to regulate foreign bank operations and financial markets. In January 2004, three commercial banks began operations and in June 2004, an additional three banks were licensed to operate…. The insurance industry is…entirely government-based." According to the Economist Intelligence Unit, "Credit continues to be predominantly centrally allocated, and the banking sector is still dominated by state-owned institutions. The Central Bank also continues to constrain the workings of the small private banks, setting interest rate caps, for example, and retaining restrictions on foreign-currency operations." While the state continues to dominate the financial sector, the establishment of private banks demonstrates some progress. As a result, Syria's banking and finance score is 1 point better this year.

WAGES AND PRICES
Score: **4**–Stable (high level of intervention)

"Both the Ministry of Industry and the Ministry of Supply control product pricing for many goods," reports the U.S. Department of Commerce. "The pricing regime has relaxed slightly from the rigidity of previous years, but Syrian consumers remain very price conscious and prices are not allowed to fluctuate greatly." According to the Economist Intelligence Unit, the government sets prices, provides subsidies, and controls marketing in the agricultural sector. Syria maintains a minimum wage.

PROPERTY RIGHTS
Score: **4**–Stable (low level of protection)

Protection of property rights is weak. According to the U.S. Department of Commerce, "there is considerable government interference in the court system, and judgments by foreign courts are generally accepted only if the verdict favors the Syrian government. [The bankruptcy law] is not applied fairly and creditors may or may not salvage their investment." The U.S. Department of State reports that "political connections and bribery can influence verdicts."

REGULATION
Score: **4**–Stable (high level)

According to the U.S. Department of Commerce, "Regulations enforced by the Ministry of Supply are aimed at promoting consumer protection…. Fiscal and welfare regulations, such as tax, labor, safety, and health laws, appear to be enforced without systemic discrimination—when they are actually enforced. Bureaucratic procedures for licensing and necessary documentation move slowly and require official approval from many levels within the government. Under-the-table payments are often required, as corruption is endemic at nearly all levels of government…. Labor laws are complex and significantly limit an employer's flexibility to hire and fire employees."

INFORMAL MARKET
Score: **3.5**–Stable (high level of activity)

Transparency International's 2004 score for Syria is 3.4. Therefore, Syria's informal market score is 3.5 this year.

TAIWAN

Rank: 37
Score: 2.38
Category: Mostly Free

Present & Past Scores

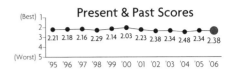

(Best) 1
2
3 - 2.21 2.18 2.16 2.29 2.14 2.03 2.23 2.38 2.34 2.48 2.34 2.38
4
(Worst) 5
'95 '96 '97 '98 '99 '00 '01 '02 '03 '04 '05 '06

QUICK STUDY

SCORES

Trade Policy	2
Fiscal Burden	3.3
Government Intervention	3
Monetary Policy	1
Foreign Investment	2
Banking and Finance	3
Wages and Prices	2
Property Rights	2
Regulation	3
Informal Market	2.5

Population: 22,500,000

Total area: 35,980 sq. km

GDP: $305.3 billion

GDP growth rate: 5.7%

GDP per capita: $13,569

Major exports: electrical equipment and machinery, textiles, metals, plastics, chemicals

Exports of goods and services: $185.5 billion

Major export trading partners: China 19.5%, Hong Kong 17.1%, US 16.2%, Japan 7.6%

Major imports: machinery and electrical equipment, precision instruments, minerals

Imports of goods and services: $174.8 billion

Major import trading partners: Japan 26.0%, US 12.9%, China 9.9%, South Korea 6.9%

Foreign direct investment (net): –$4.8 billion

2004 Data (in constant 2000 US dollars)

Taiwan developed from an agricultural economy in the 1960s to a capital-intensive economy in the 1980s and is now one of the world's leading exporters of high-tech goods. It also continues to lead the way in the innovation of technology-intensive products and has a flourishing service industry. Taiwan is a creditor country and holds the world's third-largest foreign exchange reserves of $239 billion. The economy has been hurt by high oil prices and a general sluggishness in the global economy. In addition, because of less-than-satisfactory economic performance, the government is considering raising business taxes. Even with these problems, however, unemployment reached its lowest point in four years in April 2005 (4 percent), adding 167,000 jobs over the previous year. Significant strides have been made in the enforcement of international property rights, with growing cooperation between Taiwanese law enforcement agencies and corporate victims of intellectual property rights violations. While Taiwan is one of Asia's most dynamic democracies and has been free from Chinese rule for virtually an entire century, it has come under intense pressures from the People's Republic to accept Beijing's suzerainty. Increasingly, Taiwan relies on sister democracies such as the United States and Japan to help maintain a presence co-equal to China's in the World Trade Organization, the Asian Development Bank, the Asia Pacific Economic Cooperation forum and other international trade and financial bodies. Taiwan's trade policy score is 0.5 point better this year, and its fiscal burden of government score is 0.1 point better; however, its banking and finance score is 1 point worse. As a result, Taiwan's overall score is 0.04 point worse this year.

TRADE POLICY
Score: **2–Better** (low level of protectionism)

The Ministry of Finance reports that Taiwan's weighted average tariff rate in 2004 was 1.64 percent, down from the 3.3 percent for 2002 reported in the 2005 *Index*, based on World Bank data. According to the U.S. Trade Representative, Taiwan "maintains Special Safeguards (SSGs) for a number of agricultural products covered by [tariff rate quotas].... Currently, 24 product categories require import permits.... Imports of 65 categories are restricted...and their importation is effectively banned." Based on the lower tariff rate, as well as a revision of the trade factor methodology, Taiwan's trade policy score is 0.5 point better this year.

FISCAL BURDEN OF GOVERNMENT
Score—Income Taxation: **4–Stable** (high tax rates)
Score—Corporate Taxation: **3–Stable** (moderate tax rates)
Score—Change in Government Expenditures: **3–Better** (very low decrease)
Final Score: **3.3–Better** (moderate cost of government)

Taiwan's top income tax rate is 40 percent. The top corporate tax rate is 25 percent. In 2004, according to Taiwan's National Statistics, government expenditures as a share of GDP decreased 0.8 percentage point to 23.1 percent, compared to the 0.4 percentage point increase in 2003. On net, Taiwan's fiscal burden of government score is 0.1 point better this year.

GOVERNMENT INTERVENTION IN THE ECONOMY
Score: **3–Stable** (moderate level)

Based on data from the Economist Intelligence Unit, the government consumed 11.7 percent of GDP in 2004. In the same year, based on data from the Ministry of Finance, Taiwan received

15.53 percent of its total revenues from state-owned enterprises and government ownership of property.

MONETARY POLICY
Score: **1**–Stable (very low level of inflation)

From 1995 to 2004, based on data from the International Monetary Fund's *2005 World Economic Outlook*, Taiwan's weighted average annual rate of inflation was 0.94 percent.

CAPITAL FLOWS AND FOREIGN INVESTMENT
Score: **2**–Stable (low barriers)

Repatriation of profits is unconstrained, and 100 percent ownership is permitted in most sectors. The U.S. Trade Representative reports that "foreign investment remains prohibited in a handful of industries such as agriculture, wireless broadcasting, oil exploration of Taiwan's coastal area, public utilities, and postal services." Foreign investment is limited to 60 percent in the telecommunications sector, and foreign ownership of electricity transmission and distribution and of high-speed railway transportation is limited. "Rules on local licensing of professionals are cited as a barrier to foreign providers of some services," reports the U.S. Department of Commerce. "Some foreign investors complain of lengthy and non-transparent approval processes." The Economist Intelligence Unit reports that foreign investors "complain about inadequate protection of intellectual property rights and difficulty securing government contracts." Legislation approved in February 2002 allows foreigners to purchase land, and the EIU reports that foreign firms may now own 100 percent of domestic financial institutions. According to the U.S. Department of Commerce, "Restrictions on capital flows relating to portfolio investment have been removed. The insurance and securities industries have been liberalized and opened to foreign investment. Access to Taiwan's securities markets by foreign institutional investors has also been broadened."

BANKING AND FINANCE
Score: **3**–Worse (moderate level of restrictions)

As of 2004, Taiwan had 45 domestic banks, five medium-size business banks, 36 foreign banks, 35 credit cooperatives, 253 farmers' credit unions, and 25 fishermen's credit unions. "Since the mid-1980s," reports the U.S. Department of Commerce, "the financial sector as a whole has been steadily opening to private investment. Nevertheless, the market share held by foreign banks remains relatively small (below three percent). The establishment of new securities firms, banks, insurance companies, and holding companies, has underscored this liberalization trend and enhanced competition. Four large state-owned banks were privatized in early 1998, and another four sold to the private sector in 1999. The only reinsurance company was privatized in 2002. Privatization efforts have reduced the number of public banks to five and cut the share of assets controlled by public banks from 61 percent to 21 percent of total assets of all domestic and foreign banks." Based

on evidence that, despite progress in privatization, the government still has a substantial role in the banking sector, Taiwan's banking and finance score is 1 point worse this year.

WAGES AND PRICES
Score: **2**–Stable (low level of intervention)

Most wages and prices are set by the market. According to the Economist Intelligence Unit, "Domestic price controls apply primarily to public utilities or to implement specific government policies." The few price controls in effect apply to electricity, salt, telecommunications, and postage. The state-run Chinese Petroleum Corporation determines the price of oil, natural gas, petrol, and diesel. The government mandates a minimum wage.

PROPERTY RIGHTS
Score: **2**–Stable (high level of protection)

The judiciary may be subject to corruption and political influence, although these problems do not represent a serious impediment to business activity. The U.S. Department of Commerce reports that "Taiwan's court system is generally viewed as independent and free from overt interference by the Executive Branch. Judges are generally over-worked. In response to complaints about the slow pace of the judicial decision-making…simplified courts have been set up to deal with minor cases that can be resolved quickly. Special courts for intellectual property rights (IPR) cases have been established." According to the Economist Intelligence Unit, one of the judiciary's biggest problems, is "corruption associated with 'black gold' (that is, organized crime.)"

REGULATION
Score: **3**–Stable (moderate level)

Taiwan's business regulations can be burdensome. Comprehensive laws and regulations govern taxes, labor, health, and safety. Many investors complain of unrealistic wording in regulations and inconsistent enforcement. According to the U.S. Department of Commerce, " especially for small investors in services the investment approval process can be daunting." In addition, corruption has been "a source of complaints" by investors, even though it is less serious than in other countries.

INFORMAL MARKET
Score: **2.5**–Stable (moderate level of activity)

Transparency International's 2004 score for Taiwan is 5.6. Therefore, Taiwan's informal market score is 2.5 this year.

> If Taiwan were to improve its regulation score, it would qualify for the Global Free Trade Alliance.

TAJIKISTAN

Rank: 137

Score: 3.76

Category: Mostly Unfree

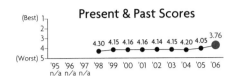

Present & Past Scores

(Best) 1
2
3
4
(Worst) 5

4.30 4.15 4.16 4.16 4.14 4.15 4.20 4.05 3.76

'95 '96 '97 '98 '99 '00 '01 '02 '03 '04 '05 '06
n/a n/a n/a

QUICK STUDY

SCORES

Trade Policy   3
Fiscal Burden   2.6
Government Intervention   4.5
Monetary Policy   3
Foreign Investment   4
Banking and Finance   4
Wages and Prices   4
Property Rights   4
Regulation   4
Informal Market   4.5

Population: 6,305,000

Total area: 143,100 sq. km

GDP: $1.3 billion

GDP growth rate: 10.2%

GDP per capita: $208

Major exports: cotton, vegetables, textiles, electricity, oil

Exports of goods and services: $1 billion

Major export trading partners: Netherlands 25.4%, Turkey 24.4%, Latvia 9.9%, Switzerland 9.7%, Uzbekistan 8.5%, Russia 6.6%

Major imports: foodstuffs, machinery and equipment, petroleum, electricity

Imports of goods and services: $877 million

Major import trading partners: Russia 20.2%, Uzbekistan 15.1%, Azerbaijan 7.1%, Ukraine 7.1%

Foreign direct investment (net): $29.9 million

2003 Data (in constant 2000 US dollars)

ajikistan is one of Central Asia's poorest countries. Millions of Tajiks work in Russia and other post-Soviet states, and income repatriation is an important part of GDP. Tajikistan is rich in minerals, including aluminum ore, and exports hydroelectric energy. Traditional dependence on cotton and aluminum has been augmented by the development of such industries as telecommunications. President Imomali Rahmonov's government has been open to some economic reforms, but external debt and poor implementation of structural reforms continue to hurt economic performance. The Islamic Renaissance Party of Tajikistan, which formerly spearheaded an armed rebellion, is the only Islamic group in Central Asia that has both parliamentary and cabinet-level representation. Tajikistan has agreed to provide Russia with a permanent military base to augment the Russian 201st Motorized Rifle Brigade, which has been responsible for patrolling Tajikistan's borders for 13 years. Tajikistan also granted Russia a 49-year lease on its Nurek space facility, to be used for a ballistic missile early warning system. China recently opened a road from Xinjiang Autonomous Region to Tajikistan to increase trade. Tajikistan's government intervention score is 0.5 point worse this year; however, its trade policy score is 0.5 point better, its fiscal burden of government score is 0.9 point better, and its monetary policy and banking and finance scores are 1 point better. As a result, its overall score is 0.29 point better this year, causing Tajikistan to be classified as a "mostly unfree" country.

TRADE POLICY

Score: **3–Better** (moderate level of protectionism)

According to the World Bank, Tajikistan's weighted average tariff rate in 2002 (the most recent year for which data are available) was 7.1 percent. The *Index* methodology places greater emphasis on weighted average tariff rates. Therefore, the weighted tariff rate for 2002 is used instead of the 8.3 percent average tariff rate for 2003 reported in the 2005 *Index*, based on World Bank data. The International Monetary Fund reports "licensing of trade in alcohol and tobacco, and other goods restricted for health, security, moral, and cultural reasons." Based on the lower tariff rate, as well as a revision of the trade factor methodology, Tajikistan's trade policy score is 0.5 point better this year.

FISCAL BURDEN OF GOVERNMENT

Score—Income Taxation: **1.5–Better** (low tax rates)
Score—Corporate Taxation: **3–Better** (moderate tax rates)
Score—Change in Government Expenditures: **3–Better** (very low decrease)
Final Score: **2.6–Better** (moderate cost of government)

According to the International Monetary Fund, effective January 2005, Tajikistan's top income tax rate was cut to 13 percent from 20 percent. The top corporate tax rate was also reduced to 25 percent from 30 percent. In 2003, according to the IMF, government expenditures as a share of GDP decreased 0.1 percentage point to 19.1 percent, compared to the 0.8 percentage point increase in 2002. On net, Tajikistan's fiscal burden of government score is 0.9 point better this year.

GOVERNMENT INTERVENTION IN THE ECONOMY

Score: **4.5–Worse** (very high level)

The World Bank reports that the government consumed 8.9 percent of GDP in 2003. In the

same year, based on data from the International Monetary Fund, Tajikistan received 13.47 percent of its total revenues from state-owned enterprises and government ownership of property, up from the 9.28 percent reported in the 2005 *Index*. As a result, Tajikistan's government intervention score is 0.5 point worse this year. The Economist Intelligence Unit reports that "many…enterprises in the…construction, transport, communications and agricultural sectors are still largely state-owned" and that "most of the labour force is still employed by the government…." Based on the apparent unreliability of reported figures for government consumption and total revenues, 2 points have been added to Tajikistan's government intervention score.

MONETARY POLICY
Score: **3–Better** (moderate level of inflation)

From 1995 to 2004, based on data from the International Monetary Fund's *2005 World Economic Outlook*, Tajikistan's weighted average annual rate of inflation was 11.31 percent, down from the 18.58 percent from 1994 to 2003 reported in the 2005 *Index*. As a result, Tajikistan's monetary policy score is 1 point better this year.

CAPITAL FLOWS AND FOREIGN INVESTMENT
Score: **4–Stable** (high barriers)

The government has made some efforts to promote increased investment, but substantial barriers to foreign investment remain in effect. The Economist Intelligence Unit reports that "political and economic instability and the country's geographic isolation have discouraged substantial amounts of FDI. Investors are deterred by corruption and the lack of democratic reforms, and the slow pace of the privatisation process." According to the International Monetary Fund, "Investment is restrained by institutional impediments and the restrictive business environment. To achieve higher levels of investment, the authorities will need to create a more supportive business environment by removing ownership restrictions, especially in the banking sector, and enhancing governance and transparency, particularly with regard to tax and business registrations." The IMF reports that both residents and non-residents may hold foreign exchange accounts, although residents face some restrictions. Payments and transfers face documentary requirements. Most capital transactions, including all direct investment transactions, require central bank approval.

BANKING AND FINANCE
Score: **4–Better** (high level of restrictions)

Tajikistan's financial sector is dominated by banking, which was composed of 15 commercial banks and the central bank in 2003. "Many banks have a high rate of non-performing loans," reports First Initiative, "and the government still retains a large degree of influence in the lending process. In early 2004, the [central bank] revoked the licenses of three of the weakest banks." According to the Economist Intelligence Unit, "The four largest banks (of which one, Amonatbank, is still state-owned) dominate the sector, holding roughly 80% of deposits and 70% of non-government loans." The EIU reports that Tajikistan still has barriers to foreign participation in the financial sector, including a ceiling on foreign capital in banks, and that "[y]ears of mistrust of the banking sector, combined with its limited financial instruments, have resulted in most businesses avoiding banks entirely." Overall, despite numerous restrictions, poor supervision, and a substantial government presence in the financial sector, private banks do operate and comprise a majority of the banking sector. As a result, Tajikistan's banking and finance score is 1 point better this year.

WAGES AND PRICES
Score: **4–Stable** (high level of intervention)

Wages and prices are greatly influenced by the large government sector. The government influences prices through extensive state-owned industries, utilities, and state farms, particularly in the production of cotton—the country's main crop. According to the Economist Intelligence Unit, "The level of quasi-fiscal spending that is not captured by the official budget figures remains high. This is mainly attributable to the high level of subsidies to the large number of unrestructured state-owned enterprises, particularly in the energy sector, where the quasi-fiscal deficit has been estimated by the IMF at 7% of GDP." Tajikistan maintains a minimum wage.

PROPERTY RIGHTS
Score: **4–Stable** (low level of protection)

Protection of private property is weak in Tajikistan. The Economist Intelligence Unit reports that corruption and cronyism are "particularly widespread within the judiciary, whose independence is further undermined by political pressure." According to the U.S. Department of State, "In many instances, armed paramilitary groups directly influence judicial officials…. Judges at all levels have extremely poor access to legal reference materials. Bribery of prosecutors and judges appears to be a common practice."

REGULATION
Score: **4–Stable** (high level)

The private sector is not very developed. The procedure for establishing a business can be both tedious and time-consuming. Bureaucratic corruption is the major deterrent to investment. *The Washington Post* reports that "corruption, overregulation, senseless tax policies and inertia have frustrated the development of a private sector beyond retail trade and simple services, according to business people, bankers and diplomats."

INFORMAL MARKET
Score: **4.5–Stable** (very high level of activity)

Transparency International's 2004 score for Tajikistan is 2. Therefore, Tajikistan's informal market score is 4.5 this year.

TANZANIA

Rank: 94

Score: 3.20

Category: Mostly Unfree

Present & Past Scores

(Best) 1
2
3
4
(Worst) 5

3.79 3.73 3.51 3.53 3.41 3.58 3.60 3.51 3.49 3.24 3.41 3.20

'95 '96 '97 '98 '99 '00 '01 '02 '03 '04 '05 '06

QUICK STUDY

SCORES

Trade Policy	3.5
Fiscal Burden	4
Government Intervention	2.5
Monetary Policy	2
Foreign Investment	3
Banking and Finance	2
Wages and Prices	3
Property Rights	4
Regulation	4
Informal Market	4

Population: 35,889,000

Total area: 945,087 sq. km

GDP: $11.1 billion

GDP growth rate: 7.1%

GDP per capita: $309

Major exports: manufactured goods, minerals, tobacco, coffee

Exports of goods and services: $1.8 billion

Major export trading partners: India 9.9%, Japan 9.3%, Germany 5.2%, UK 5.2%

Major imports: machinery and transportation equipment, crude oil

Imports of goods and services: $2.5 billion

Major import trading partners: South Africa 9.9%, China 9.1%, India 7.6%, UK 4.4%

Foreign direct investment (net): $233.5 million

2003 Data (in constant 2000 US dollars)

The United Republic of Tanzania is composed of mainland Tanzania and the Zanzibar archipelago. Although they comprise one country, there are two presidents. Zanzibar also has its own parliament and exercises some autonomy. The 2000 elections were considered to be free and fair in Tanzania but were marred by irregularities and political violence in Zanzibar. Constitutional restrictions prevented Tanzanian President Benjamin Mkapa from running in the October 2005 election. Politically motivated violence has been common in Zanzibar. The historically state-led economy is becoming more market-based but remains hindered by mismanagement, corruption, poor infrastructure, and a high incidence of HIV/AIDS. There has been progress in privatizing state-owned enterprises, and the government generally supports economic reform and has largely followed through on commitments to donors, but vested interests opposed to liberalization have hindered implementation. Agriculture is the dominant sector, employing over 80 percent of the labor force and accounting for more than 44 percent of GDP. Foreign investment in the mining sector in recent years has enabled Tanzania to become a significant producer of gold, the country's leading export. Tanzania is eligible for assistance as a threshold country for the U.S. Millennium Challenge Account. Tanzania's fiscal burden of government score is 0.4 point worse this year; however, its trade policy score is 1.5 points better, and its capital flows and foreign investment score is 1 point better. As a result, Tanzania's overall score is 0.21 point better this year.

TRADE POLICY
Score: **3.5**–Better (high level of protectionism)

The World Bank reports that Tanzania's weighted average tariff rate in 2003 (the most recent year for which World Bank data are available) was 8.2 percent, down from the 15.4 percent for 2000 reported in the 2005 *Index*, based on World Bank data. According to the U.S. Department of Commerce, "the customs department and the port authorities are the greatest hindrance to importers throughout Tanzania. Clearance delays and extra-legal levies are commonplace when dealing with the Tanzanian Customs Department.... Areas in which corruption persists include...customs clearance." Based on the lower tariff rate, as well as a revision of the trade factor methodology, Tanzania's trade policy score is 1.5 points better this year.

FISCAL BURDEN OF GOVERNMENT
Score—Income Taxation: **3**–Stable (moderate tax rates)
Score—Corporate Taxation: **4**–Stable (high tax rates)
Score—Change in Government Expenditures: **5**–Worse (very high increase)
Final Score: **4**–Worse (high cost of government)

Tanzania's top income tax rate is 30 percent. The top corporate tax rate is also 30 percent. In 2003, according to the African Development Bank, government expenditures as a share of GDP increased 3.3 percentage points to 19.9 percent, compared to the 2.4 percentage point decrease in 2002. On net, Tanzania's fiscal burden of government score is 0.4 point worse this year.

GOVERNMENT INTERVENTION IN THE ECONOMY
Score: **2.5**–Stable (moderate level)

The World Bank reports that the government consumed 11.4 percent of GDP in 2003. In fiscal year July 2003–June 2004, based on data from the Ministry of Finance, Tanzania received 8.06 percent of its total revenues from state-owned enterprises and government ownership of property.

MONETARY POLICY
Score: 2–Stable (low level of inflation)

From 1995 to 2004, Tanzania's weighted average annual rate of inflation was 3.81 percent.

CAPITAL FLOWS AND FOREIGN INVESTMENT
Score: 3–Better (moderate barriers)

The 1997 Tanzania Investment Act establishing the Tanzania Investment Center identified investment priorities, overhauled the company registration process, and established investor rights and incentives. "Tanzania is formally open to foreign investment in all sectors, although a successful investor must overcome many procedural barriers," reports the U.S. Department of Commerce. "There is no limit on foreign ownership or control, though land ownership remains restricted…. Remaining obstacles to foreign investment include bureaucratic intransigence, corruption and poor infrastructure." The same source reports that the Capital Markets and Securities Authority "has opened the Dar es Salaam Stock Exchange (DSE) to foreigners. The maximum allowed limit for foreign participation in any single company listed on the DSE is 60 percent. Foreigners are not allowed to participate in Government Securities." The International Monetary Fund reports that residents may hold foreign exchange accounts only for funds acquired outside of Tanzania; otherwise, such accounts are restricted. Non-residents temporarily residing in Tanzania may hold foreign exchange accounts. The IMF reports that all transfers of foreign currency from residents to non-residents must be approved by the central bank. Most capital transactions face reporting requirements, and some are restricted. Foreign purchase of real estate in Tanzania and purchase of real estate abroad by residents must be approved by the government. Overall, there are few official constraints on foreign investment and capital flows. As a result, Tanzania's capital flows and foreign investment score is 1 point better this year.

BANKING AND FINANCE
Score: 2–Stable (low level of restrictions)

The government has made strides since liberalizing banking services in 1995, including removing constraints on interest rates, permitting private financial institutions, and restricting the central bank to regulatory, licensing, and supervisory roles. "In 2004," reports First Initiative, "the banking sector was comprised of 20 commercial banks, with most bank branches concentrated in the capital city, Dar es Salaam…. [T]he majority of micro-finance services are provided by savings and credit cooperatives and foreign NGOs. The [Bank of Tanzania] has slated a number of banks for restructuring and potential privatization…. There were four life insurance and 12 general insurance companies as of the beginning of 2004, however the

sector remains dominated by the state-owned National Insurance Corporation (NIC)." According to the International Monetary Fund, "foreign direct investment in [the banking sector] has also grown very rapidly, and the banking industry is now dominated by foreign banks." The government sold a majority stake in the National Commercial Bank in March 2000 and has privatized the Cooperative and Rural Development Bank. The EIU reports that privatization of the National Microfinance Bank is proceeding and that the government is considering a bid by Rabobank of the Netherlands. The state maintains a role in the banking sector through the Tanzania Investment Bank, the People's Bank of Zanzibar, and the Tanzania Postal Bank. The EIU notes that the government intends to establish new sources of government-supported lending, despite the history of politically motivated lending that led to financial instability in the past.

WAGES AND PRICES
Score: 3–Stable (moderate level of intervention)

According to the U.S. Department of Commerce, "The Tanzanian government has eliminated most price controls; however, the government still regulates the price of gasoline, diesel fuel and kerosene." The government affects agricultural prices through marketing boards for its main export crops. Tanzania has a legal monthly minimum wage.

PROPERTY RIGHTS
Score: 4–Stable (low level of protection)

The U.S. Department of Commerce reports that "the legal system remains slow, and judicial corruption is still a problem…. A commercial court has been established in order to improve the capacity of the legal system to resolve commercial disputes, and this was joined by a land court in late 2002."

REGULATION
Score: 4–Stable (high level)

According to the U.S. Department of Commerce, "The [Tanzania Investment Center] facilitates applications for the variety of permits an investor may need, which greatly decreases the time and effort spent on complying with bureaucratic regulations. The regulatory system can be burdensome…. Government decisions are not always completely transparent, and Ministers and high-level officials have significant authority to make exceptions to the rule. Well-connected companies may obtain allowances or unfair advantages…. Many of the laws and regulations in Tanzania that impact investment (including tax, labor, environment, health and safety) are outdated, but the Government of Tanzania has made an effort to revise and harmonize them."

INFORMAL MARKET
Score: 4–Stable (high level of activity)

Transparency International's 2004 score for Tanzania is 2.8. Therefore, Tanzania's informal market score is 4 this year.

THAILAND

Rank: 71
Score: 2.99
Category: Mostly Free

Present & Past Scores

(Best) 1
2
3
4
(Worst) 5
2.54 2.53 2.53 2.56 2.58 2.76 2.34 2.51 2.71 2.81 3.03 2.99
'95 '96 '97 '98 '99 '00 '01 '02 '03 '04 '05 '06

QUICK STUDY

SCORES

Trade Policy	3.5
Fiscal Burden	3.4
Government Intervention	2.5
Monetary Policy	1
Foreign Investment	4
Banking and Finance	3
Wages and Prices	3
Property Rights	3
Regulation	3
Informal Market	3.5

Population: 61,014,000

Total area: 514,000 sq. km

GDP: $141.1 billion

GDP growth rate: 6.9%

GDP per capita: $2,276

Major exports: machinery and mechanical appliances, electrical apparatus for circuits, computer parts, and electrical appliances

Exports of goods and services: $94.1 billion

Major export trading partners: US 17.0%, Japan 14.2%, Singapore 7.3%, China 7.1%, Hong Kong 5.4%

Major imports: capital goods, raw materials, fuel and lubricants

Imports of goods and services: $82.5 billion

Major import trading partners: Japan 24.1%, US 9.5%, China 8.0%, Singapore 4.3%

Foreign direct investment (net): $1.2 billion

2003 Data (in constant 2000 US dollars)

Prime Minister Thaksin Shinawatra's Thai Rak Thai party easily won re-election in February 2005, but the past year has been a challenging one for his government. The economy contracted in the first quarter in 2005, largely as a result of such problems as the Asian tsunami that devastated Thailand's tourist industry. Drought continues to hamper the agricultural sector, hitting rice producers particularly hard, and rising oil prices and weaker demand for Thai exports are taking a toll on the manufacturing sector. Insurgency and civil unrest persist in Thailand's three Muslim-dominated southern provinces. Thaksin plans to promote growth by spending $40 billion during the next five years on infrastructure projects; he is also committed to keeping the country's current account deficit to 2 percent of GDP. Given that both goals are likely to reduce economic freedom, the prospects for success are poor. Encouragingly, the government has cut diesel subsidies. Thailand remains an active participant in multilateral trade negotiations but a slow implementer of trade liberalization. Tariffs remain high, government ministries own major portions of the economy, and corruption remains a problem. Discussions with the United States on a free trade agreement continue. Thailand's fiscal burden of government score is 0.4 point better this year. As a result, its overall score is 0.04 point better this year, causing Thailand to be classified as a "mostly free" country.

TRADE POLICY

Score: **3.5**–Stable (high level of protectionism)

The World Bank reports that Thailand's weighted average tariff rate in 2003 (the most recent year for which World Bank data are available) was 8.3 percent, down from the 8.7 percent for 2001 reported in the 2005 *Index*, based on World Bank data. According to the World Trade Organization, "Import licensing for various items remains opaque and appears in some cases to be equivalent to quantitative restrictions. Most import licensing requirements are for national security, health, and environment reasons. A number of other non-tariff border measures remain for other reasons, for example to protect infant industries." The U.S. Trade Representative reports that customs corruption is a serious problem. Based on the revised trade factor methodology, Thailand's trade policy score is unchanged.

FISCAL BURDEN OF GOVERNMENT

Score—Income Taxation: **3.5**–Stable (high tax rates)
Score—Corporate Taxation: **4**–Stable (high tax rates)
Score—Change in Government Expenditures: **2**–Better (moderate decrease)
Final Score: **3.4**–Better (moderate cost of government)

Thailand's top income tax rate is 37 percent. The top corporate tax rate is 30 percent. In 2003, according to the Asian Development Bank, government expenditures as a share of GDP decreased by 2 percentage points to 16.2 percent, compared to a 1 percentage point increase in 2002. On net, Thailand's fiscal burden of government score is 0.4 point better this year.

GOVERNMENT INTERVENTION IN THE ECONOMY

Score: **2.5**–Stable (moderate level)

The World Bank reports that the government consumed 10.6 percent of GDP in 2003. In the same year, according to the International Monetary Fund's Government Financial Statistics CD–ROM,

373

Thailand received 7.12 percent of its total revenues from state-owned enterprises and government ownership of property.

 MONETARY POLICY
Score: **1**–Stable (very low level of inflation)

From 1995 to 2004, Thailand's weighted average annual rate of inflation was 2.31 percent.

 CAPITAL FLOWS AND FOREIGN INVESTMENT
Score: **4**–Stable (high barriers)

The law permits 100 percent foreign ownership except in 32 restricted service occupations, which include firms in the cultural and national security sectors and industries deemed by the government to be at a comparative disadvantage relative to those of other countries. Foreign investors face limits on ownership in other sectors. According to the U.S. Department of Commerce, "the Alien Business Act of 1999 governs most investment activity by non-Thai nationals, opens additional business sectors to foreign investment, and increases maximum ownership stakes permitted in some sectors above the standard 49 percent limitation…. In general, non-Thai businesses and citizens are not permitted to own land in Thailand unless the land is on government-approved industrial estates…. [F]oreigners who invest a minimum of 40 million baht (around $964,000) will be permitted to buy up to 1,600 square meters of land for residential use with the permission of the Ministry of Interior." Regulations are not enforced consistently or predictably and remain an obstacle to investment. The International Monetary Fund reports that residents and non-residents may hold foreign exchange accounts, subject to approval in some cases and maximum limits. Foreign exchange transactions, repatriation, some outward direct investments, and transactions involving capital market securities, bonds, debt securities, money market instruments, real estate, and short-term money securities are regulated and require government approval in most cases. Residents may purchase real estate abroad, subject to quantitative limits.

 BANKING AND FINANCE
Score: **3**–Stable (moderate level of restrictions)

"Before the 1997 financial crisis," reports First Initiative, "Thailand had 15 commercial banks, but as of 2004 there were 13 commercial banks, along with a number of state and development banks. Banks in Thailand may apply for an International Banking Facilities (IBF) license from the Bank of Thailand that allows them to engage in both domestic and offshore banking. In 2003, nine commercial banks and 15 foreign banks held IBF licenses…. State-owned commercial and specialized banks are expected to be reduced from the current 13 to three or four. In 2004, the insurance sector was comprised of 27 life insurance companies, 81 general insurance firms, and six health insurance firms. Seven of Thailand's insurance firms were branches of foreign insurers." According to the U.S. Department of Commerce, "The overall health of the banking sector remains affected by the high levels of non-performing loans (NPLs) banks carry on their books. After peaking at 47 percent of total lending in May 1999, NPLs slowly declined to stand at 11.45 percent of total loans in November 2004. The figure actually approaches 24 percent, however, if nonperforming loans transferred to banks' private asset management companies are taken into account." The state still plays a substantial role in the financial sector.

 WAGES AND PRICES
Score: **3**–Stable (moderate level of intervention)

According to the Economist Intelligence Unit, "Manufacturers seeking price hikes for certain goods must first seek approval from the Ministry of Commerce. It monitors a list of 100 products for their retail importance, following the addition in July 2004 of around 30 products—mainly fresh foods and household electrical products." In practice, reports the U.S. Trade Representative, "the Thai government also uses its control of major suppliers of products and services under state monopoly, such as petroleum, aviation, and telecom sectors, to influence prices in the local market." In February 2005, the government decided to cut its 13-month subsidy of diesel fuel. There is a minimum wage.

 PROPERTY RIGHTS
Score: **3**–Stable (moderate level of protection)

Thailand generally protects private property, but there are indications of inefficiency and corruption. According to the Economist Intelligence Unit, "private property rights are generally protected, though vested interests continue to intervene, especially in legal judgments." The U.S. Department of State reports that "the legal system offers inadequate deterrence against corruption…. The legal process is slow in practice…and litigants or third parties sometimes affect judgments through extra-legal means."

 REGULATION
Score: **3**–Stable (moderate level)

Thailand imposes extensive regulation, especially to protect the environment and labor. The U.S. Department of Commerce reports that "consistent and predictable enforcement of government regulations remains an obstacle to investment in Thailand. Gratuity payment to civil servants responsible for regulatory oversight and enforcement unfortunately remains a common practice. Through such payments, regulations can often be by-passed or ignored and approval processes expedited. Firms that refuse to make such payments can be placed at a competitive disadvantage when compared to other firms in the same field."

 INFORMAL MARKET
Score: **3.5**–Stable (high level of activity)

Transparency International's 2004 score for Thailand is 3.6. Therefore, Thailand's informal market score is 3.5 this year.

TOGO

Rank: 134

Score: 3.71

Category: Mostly Unfree

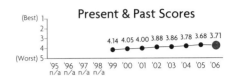

Present & Past Scores

(Best) 1-
2-
3-   4.14 4.05 4.00 3.88 3.86 3.78 3.68 3.71
4-
(Worst) 5-

'95 '96 '97 '98 '99 '00 '01 '02 '03 '04 '05 '06
n/a n/a n/a n/a

QUICK STUDY

SCORES

Trade Policy	3.5
Fiscal Burden	4.6
Government Intervention	3
Monetary Policy	1
Foreign Investment	4
Banking and Finance	4
Wages and Prices	3
Property Rights	4
Regulation	5
Informal Market	5

Population: 4,861,000

Total area: 56,785 sq. km

GDP: $1.4 billion

GDP growth rate: 2.7%

GDP per capita: $292

Major exports: cotton, coffee, cocoa

Exports of goods and services: $507.6 million

Major export trading partners: Burkina Faso 16.6%, Ghana 15.3%, Netherlands 13.0%, Benin 9.5%, Taiwan 4.3%

Major imports: petroleum products, machinery and equipment, foodstuffs

Imports of goods and services: $736.3 million

Major import trading partners: France 21.1%, Netherlands 12.1%, Germany 4.6%, Italy 4.5%, China 4.2%

Foreign direct investment (net): $20.8 million

2003 Data (in constant 2000 US dollars)

Recent events have confirmed that Togo may have the trappings of democracy, but not the reality. Following the death of former President Gnassingbé Eyadéma, who had ruled since coming to power in a 1967 military coup, the military appointed his son Faure Gnassingbé president. A presidential election was held only after violent street protests, condemnation from other nations—including other African states—and imposition of sanctions by the Economic Community of West African States (ECOWAS). Gnassingbé won the April 2005 election, which was marred by massive voter registration fraud, intimidation, stuffing of ballot boxes, and other irregularities. Despite these problems and violent protests following the result, the election was validated by the African Union and ECOWAS. Agriculture employs over 70 percent of Togo's population. In recent years, there has been growth in the service sector based around the port facility at Lomé, which serves as a major re-export location for the landlocked states in the region. Togo's principal exports are cotton and phosphates. Donors had suspended aid to the previous government to protest its anti-democratic policies, violations of human rights, and failure to pay its debt. Togo's fiscal burden of government score is 0.2 point better this year, but its trade policy score is 0.5 point worse. As a result, Togo's overall score is 0.03 point worse this year.

TRADE POLICY
Score: **3.5**–Worse (high level of protectionism)

Togo is a member of the West African Economic and Monetary Union (WAEMU), which imposes a common external tariff with four rates: 0 percent, 5 percent, 10 percent, and 20 percent. According to the World Bank, Togo's weighted average tariff rate in 2004 was 14 percent, up from the 11.5 percent for 2002 reported in the 2005 *Index*, based on World Bank data. There is no evidence of non-tariff barriers. Based on the higher tariff rate, as well as a revision of the trade factor methodology, Togo's trade policy score is 0.5 point worse this year.

FISCAL BURDEN OF GOVERNMENT
Score—Income Taxation: **5**–Stable (very high tax rates)
Score—Corporate Taxation: **5**–Stable (very high tax rates)
Score—Change in Government Expenditures: **3.5**–Better (low increase)
Final Score: **4.6**–Better (very high cost of government)

The International Monetary Fund reports that Togo's top income tax rate is 55 percent. According to Deloitte, the top corporate tax rate is 40 percent. In 2003, according to the African Development Bank, government expenditures as a share of GDP increased 0.6 percentage point to 13.7 percent, compared to the 3.6 percentage point decrease in 2002. On net, Togo's fiscal burden of government score is 0.2 point better this year.

GOVERNMENT INTERVENTION IN THE ECONOMY
Score: **3**–Stable (moderate level)

The World Bank reports that the government consumed 9.8 percent of GDP in 2003. According to the Economist Intelligence Unit, "the privatisation agenda [which includes 15 companies] has been delayed by the freeze in external assistance since 1998 and the poor financial condition of many of the targeted parastatals." The government also owns four banks and the telecommunications company.

MONETARY POLICY
Score: **1**–Stable (very low level of inflation)

As a member of the West African Economic and Monetary Union, Togo uses the CFA franc, pegged to the euro. From 1995 to 2004, Togo's weighted average annual rate of inflation was 0.44 percent.

CAPITAL FLOWS AND FOREIGN INVESTMENT
Score: **4**–Stable (high barriers)

Togo's foreign investment code was liberalized in 1990, but investors still face official and unofficial barriers. The 1990 code includes local content restrictions and requirements on the hiring of Togolese citizens, and there is an overall lack of administrative transparency. Investment is permitted only in certain sectors and is screened on a case-by-case basis. Political instability is also a disincentive. According to the Economist Intelligence Unit, "In particular, private investors have been deterred by the failings of the investment code and of the banking, judicial and land tenure systems." The International Monetary Fund reports that residents may hold foreign exchange accounts after obtaining approval of the government and the Central Bank of West African States, or BCEAO, and that non-residents may hold them with permission from the BCEAO. Payments and transfers to countries other than France, Monaco, members of the Central African Economic and Monetary Community, members of the WAEMU, and Comoros are subject to authorization and quantitative limits in some cases. Purchases of real estate by non-residents for purposes other than business are subject to controls. All investments abroad by residents require government approval. Most capital transactions are subject to controls or require government approval.

BANKING AND FINANCE
Score: **4**–Stable (high level of restrictions)

The BCEAO, a central bank common to the eight members of the WAEMU, governs Togo's banking system. Member countries use the CFA franc, which is issued by the BCEAO and pegged to the euro. Government involvement in banking and lending decisions has caused the banking sector to deteriorate in recent years. According to the Economist Intelligence Unit, "Banking difficulties are most acute within the four state-dominated banks." The country's three private commercial banks—Ecobank-Togo, Banque internationale pour l'Afrique-Togo, and Financial Bank-Togo (co-owned by Swiss-based FBC Genève with 85 percent and France's L'Aiglon with 15 percent)—entered the market in late 2004. The EIU also reports that "Togo initiated privatisation of the four state-run banks—Union togolaise des banques (UTB, 100% government owned), Banque togolaise de crédit et de l'industrie (BTCI, 52% government owned), Banque togolaise de développement (BTD, 43% government owned) and Société nationale d'investissement (SNI, 33% government owned)—in the late 1990s. However, progress has been complicated and, as of mid-2005, only one of the four banks has found a private partner."

WAGES AND PRICES
Score: **3**–Stable (moderate level of intervention)

According to the U.S. Department of Commerce, "Price control and profit margin regulations have been largely eliminated with electricity, water, and telecommunications the only sectors still subject to administrative price controls." The government continues to intervene in agricultural markets, particularly cotton, which accounts for 20 percent–25 percent of export earnings. The Economist Intelligence Unit reports that, responding to a decrease in world prices of cotton in 2002, the government increased farm-gate prices offered by the state-run Société Togolaise de coton (Sotoco). The government sets minimum wages from unskilled workers through professional positions.

PROPERTY RIGHTS
Score: **4**–Stable (low level of protection)

The judicial system does not protect private property sufficiently and is subject to influence from the executive. According to the U.S. Department of Commerce, "Lack of transparency and predictability of the judiciary is a serious obstacle in enforcing property and judgment rights, and similar difficulties apply to administrative procedures." The Economist Intelligence Unit reports that the president's power is "nearly absolute, and both the National Assembly and the judiciary lack independence. Judges that support the government are promoted at the expense of those that do not."

REGULATION
Score: **5**–Stable (very high level)

Togo's regulatory system lacks transparency. The U.S. Department of Commerce reports that "establishing an office in Togo is in theory relatively simple, but administrative obstacles and delays are common." In addition, corruption "has spread as a business practice in recent years…. Bribes, whether to private or government officials, are considered crimes…but [corruption] cases are relatively rare, and appear mostly to [involve] those who have in some way lost official favor."

INFORMAL MARKET
Score: **5**–Stable (very high level of activity)

Togo has a large informal market in computer software, video, and cassette recordings. According to the U.S. Department of State, "Approximately 4 percent of the population was engaged in the private commercial and industrial sector, 2 percent in the public sector, and 22 percent in the informal sector."

TRINIDAD AND TOBAGO

Rank: 42

Score: 2.50

Category: Mostly Free

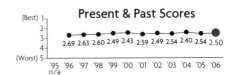

Present & Past Scores

(Best) 1
2
3
4
(Worst) 5

2.69 2.63 2.60 2.49 2.43 2.59 2.49 2.54 2.40 2.54 2.50

'95 '96 '97 '98 '99 '00 '01 '02 '03 '04 '05 '06
n/a

Hydrocarbon-rich Trinidad and Tobago could have a "basket case" economy like many other energy-exporting countries that squander royalties on social programs, but this former British colony manages its public finances responsibly and has pursued orthodox market policies. It has a stabilization fund to guard windfall revenues when oil and gas prices are high so that public expenses can be met when prices are low. It is also the largest supplier of liquefied natural gas in the Americas and has the largest economy in all of the Caribbean Community. Venezuela has larger gas reserves, but its government is unwilling to open development to private investors. In contrast, Trinidad and Tobago has been investor-friendly for more than a decade with its combination of abundant resources, pleasant climate, stable government, and a well-educated workforce. Unemployment on this island of 1.3 million was about 7.7 percent in the third quarter of 2004. Violent crime has increased, with murders and kidnappings higher than they were a year earlier, and both types of crime seem to be linked to drug trafficking. Trinidad and Tobago's fiscal burden of government score is 0.4 point better this year. As a result, its overall score is 0.04 point better this year.

TRADE POLICY
Score: **2.5**–Stable (moderate level of protectionism)

As a member of the Caribbean Community and Common Market (CARICOM) trade bloc, Trinidad and Tobago has a common external tariff rate that ranges from 0 percent to 20 percent. The World Bank reports that Trinidad and Tobago's weighted average tariff rate in 2003 (the most recent year for which World Bank data are available) was 4.9 percent, up from the 2.9 percent for 2002 reported in the 2005 *Index*, based on World Bank data. According to the U.S. Department of Commerce, "Customs clearance can consume much time because of bureaucratic inefficiency and occasional inflexible interpretation of regulations.... Importation of certain goods may require an import license." Based on the revised trade factor methodology, Trinidad and Tobago's trade policy score is unchanged.

FISCAL BURDEN OF GOVERNMENT
Score—Income Taxation: **3**–Stable (moderate tax rates)
Score—Corporate Taxation: **4**–Better (high tax rates)
Score—Change in Government Expenditures: **3**–Better (very low decrease)
Final Score: **3.5**–Better (high cost of government)

Trinidad and Tobago's top income tax rate is 30 percent. The top corporate tax rate is also 30 percent, down from the 35 percent reported in the 2005 *Index*. In 2003, based on data from the Ministry of Finance, government expenditures as a share of GDP decreased 0.6 percentage point to 25.1 percent, compared to a 0.3 percentage point increase in 2002. On net, Trinidad and Tobago's fiscal burden of government score is 0.4 point better this year.

GOVERNMENT INTERVENTION IN THE ECONOMY
Score: **2**–Stable (low level)

The World Bank reports that the government consumed 10.4 percent of GDP in 2003. In the same year, based on data from the central bank, Trinidad and Tobago received 3.98 percent of its total revenues from state-owned enterprises and government ownership of property.

QUICK STUDY

SCORES
Trade Policy 2.5
Fiscal Burden 3.5
Government Intervention 2
Monetary Policy 2
Foreign Investment 2
Banking and Finance 2
Wages and Prices 3
Property Rights 2
Regulation 3
Informal Market 3

Population: 1,313,000

Total area: 5,128 sq. km

GDP: $9.9 billion

GDP growth rate: 13.2%

GDP per capita: $7,520

Major exports: food and live animals, mineral fuels, chemicals, manufactured goods

Exports of goods and services: $5.2 billion

Major export trading partners: US 64.8%, Jamaica 5.6%, France 3.5%

Major imports: transportation equipment, machinery, manufactured goods, food

Imports of goods and services: $4.1 billion

Major import trading partners: US 30.0%, Venezuela 12.9%, UK 4.8%, Japan 4.1%

Foreign direct investment (net): $368.2 million

2003 Data (in constant 2000 US dollars)

MONETARY POLICY
Score: **2**–Stable (low level of inflation)

From 1995 to 2004, Trinidad and Tobago's weighted average annual rate of inflation was 3.84 percent.

CAPITAL FLOWS AND FOREIGN INVESTMENT
Score: **2**–Stable (low barriers)

Trinidad and Tobago is open to foreign investment. The law does not discriminate against foreign firms and prohibits expropriation without just compensation. The government's privatization program is open to foreign investment. According to the U.S. Department of Commerce, "There are no performance requirements for investors written into law, but the [government] strongly encourages, through negotiable incentives, projects that generate employment and foreign exchange; provide training and/or technology transfer; boost exports or reduce imports; have local content; and generally contribute to the welfare of the country. Foreign investment is also screened for its environmental impact." In addition, "Bureaucratic delays in approval of investment packages can be frustrating for investors." Foreign investment in private business is not subject to limitations, but a foreigner must obtain a license to purchase more than 30 percent of a publicly held business. Foreign ownership of land is limited to one acre for residential purposes and five acres for trade purposes. The International Monetary Fund reports that both residents and non-residents may hold foreign exchange accounts. There are no restrictions or controls on payments, transactions, transfers, or repatriation of profits.

BANKING AND FINANCE
Score: **2**–Stable (low level of restrictions)

The banking system is open and well developed. There are no restrictions on foreign banks, and banks are free to engage in a wide range of services. According to First Initiative, "There are six commercial banks in the country, including one state-owned bank (2004). The sector is quite concentrated, with the three largest banks accounting for over half of banking sector assets. Trinidad and Tobago has become the financial center of the English Caribbean, with many of its banks expanding into neighboring islands. Partly as a result of the non-competitive nature of the banking system and partly as a result of banks tightening money-laundering controls, Trinidad and Tobago's over 70 credit unions have become increasingly important." The Economist Intelligence Unit reports that non-performing loans average 20 percent to 25 percent for credit unions, compared to 3 percent for commercial banks.

WAGES AND PRICES
Score: **3**–Stable (moderate level of intervention)

The government affects some wages and prices. According to the U.S. Department of Commerce, "Businesses are generally free to price their products at whatever price meets their marketing objectives. Prices of sugar, schoolbooks and some pharmaceuticals are controlled. Prices may, however, be challenged under Trinidad & Tobago's anti-dumping laws." The International Monetary Fund reports that the government intervenes in the price setting of many utilities. The government subsidizes some agricultural goods and mandates a minimum wage.

PROPERTY RIGHTS
Score: **2**–Stable (high level of protection)

The judiciary is independent and provides a fair judicial process. According to the Economist Intelligence Unit, "The judiciary has defended its independence resolutely in the face of occasional disputes with the executive." However, the judicial process can be time-consuming. "At present," reports the U.S. Department of State, "there is a several year backlog of cases waiting to be heard."

REGULATION
Score: **3**–Stable (moderate level)

Regulations and bureaucratic red tape are burdensome. According to the U.S. Department of Commerce, "investors have…complained about a lack of transparency and delays in the investment approval process. Complaints focus on a perceived lack of delineation of authority for final investment approvals between the various ministries which may be involved in a project, and excessive delays in receiving approvals from the Ministry of Planning and Development's Town and Country Planning Office, which oversees environmental impact assessment approvals. Some projects have been delayed for several years and some potential investors have abandoned [their projects] as a result." There are reports of moderate corruption, but it has not seriously undermined business operations.

INFORMAL MARKET
Score: **3**–Stable (moderate level of activity)

Transparency International's 2004 score for Trinidad and Tobago is 4.2. Therefore, Trinidad and Tobago's informal market score is 3 this year.

TUNISIA

Rank: 99

Score: 3.24

Category: Mostly Unfree

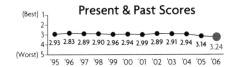

Present & Past Scores

(Best) 1
2
3
4
(Worst) 5

2.93 2.83 2.89 2.90 2.96 2.94 2.99 2.89 2.91 2.94 3.14 **3.24**

'95 '96 '97 '98 '99 '00 '01 '02 '03 '04 '05 '06

QUICK STUDY

SCORES

Trade Policy	5
Fiscal Burden	3.9
Government Intervention	2.5
Monetary Policy	2
Foreign Investment	4
Banking and Finance	4
Wages and Prices	2
Property Rights	3
Regulation	3
Informal Market	3

Population: 9,895,000

Total area: 163,610 sq. km

GDP: $21.9 billion

GDP growth rate: 5.6%

GDP per capita: $2,214

Major exports: textiles, electrical equipment, leather, petroleum

Exports of goods and services: $9.5 billion

Major export trading partners: France 32.6%, Italy 22.1%, Germany 10.7%, Spain 4.7%

Major imports: machinery, textiles, electrical equipment

Imports of goods and services: $10.3 billion

Major import trading partners: France 25.9%, Italy 19.9%, Germany 9.0%, Spain 5.3%

Foreign direct investment (net): $549.6 million

2003 Data (in constant 2000 US dollars)

T unisia gained its independence from France in 1956 and developed a socialist economic system. President Zine al-Abedine Ben Ali, while maintaining a tight grip on political power, has also undertaken gradual free-market economic reforms since the early 1990s, including the privatization of state-owned firms, simplification of the tax code, and more prudent fiscal restraint. The economy includes significant agricultural, mining, energy, tourism, and manufacturing sectors. Tunisia's 1998 association agreement with the European Union, which has helped to create jobs and modernize the economy, was the first such agreement between the EU and an Arab North African country. In recent years, expanding trade and tourism have helped to boost the economy. Real growth slowed to a 15-year low of 1.9 percent in 2002 because of a drought that hurt agriculture and post–September 11 worries about terrorism that hurt tourism, the third-largest employer, but rains and reinvigorated tourism helped to push GDP growth above 5 percent in 2003 and 2004. The government planned to continue its privatization program with the divestment of a 35 percent stake in Tunisie Telecom by early 2006, but bureaucratic red tape and poor access to finance are likely to cause private investment to grow slowly. Tunisia's monetary policy score is 1 point worse this year. As a result, its overall score is 0.1 point worse this year.

 TRADE POLICY
Score: **5**–Stable (very high level of protectionism)

The World Bank reports that Tunisia's weighted average tariff rate in 2002 (the most recent year for which World Bank data are available) was 23.2 percent. (The World Bank has revised the figure for 2002 downward from the 27.4 percent reported in the 2005 *Index*.) According to the U.S. Department of Commerce, "Inconsistent procedures within the…customs administration can be a major obstacle for importers. Government use of non-tariff barriers has sometimes led to delay or rejection of goods shipped to Tunisia but this is not common practice." Based on the revised trade factor methodology, Tunisia's trade policy score is unchanged.

 FISCAL BURDEN OF GOVERNMENT
Score—Income Taxation: **3.5**–Stable (high tax rates)
Score—Corporate Taxation: **4.5**–Stable (very high tax rates)
Score—Change in Government Expenditures: **3**–Stable (very low decrease)
Final Score: **3.9**–Stable (high cost of government)

Tunisia's top income tax rate is 35 percent. The top corporate tax rate is also 35 percent. In 2003, according to the African Development Bank, government expenditures as a share of GDP decreased 0.6 percentage point to 27.2 percent, compared to the 0.8 percentage point decrease in 2002.

 GOVERNMENT INTERVENTION IN THE ECONOMY
Score: **2.5**–Stable (moderate level)

The World Bank reports that the government consumed 16.6 percent of GDP in 2003. In 2004, according to the International Monetary Fund's Government Financial Statistics CD–ROM, Tunisia received 8.11 percent of its total revenues from state-owned enterprises and government ownership of property.

MONETARY POLICY
Score: **2**–Worse (low level of inflation)

From 1995 to 2004, Tunisia's weighted average annual rate of inflation was 3.24 percent, up from the 2.67 percent from 1994 to 2003 reported in the 2005 *Index*. As a result, Tunisia's monetary policy is 1 point worse this year.

CAPITAL FLOWS AND FOREIGN INVESTMENT
Score: **4**–Stable (high barriers)

Tunisia is open to foreign investment generally but does restrict it in some sectors. "The Tunisian government… screens potential FDI to minimize the impact of the investment on domestic competitors and employment," reports the U.S. Department of Commerce. "[T]he Investment Code Law…covers all major sectors of economic activity except mining, energy, the financial sector, and domestic trade. The legislation contains two major hurdles for potential FDI. First, foreign investors are denied national treatment in the agriculture sector as foreign ownership of agricultural land is prohibited, although land can be secured through long-term (up to 40 years) lease…. Second, for onshore companies outside the tourism sector, government authorization is required where foreign capital share exceeds 49 percent. Investment in manufacturing industries, agriculture, agribusiness, public works, and certain services requires only a simple declaration of intent to invest. Other sectors may require a series of [government] authorizations." The International Monetary Fund reports that residents may hold foreign exchange accounts, subject to restrictions and government approval. Non-residents may hold foreign exchange accounts, subject to restrictions. There are some controls, quantitative limits, and other restrictions on payments and transfers. There are many restrictions and controls on capital transactions—including derivatives, capital and money market instruments, purchases abroad by residents, repatriation, and direct investment—and many of these transactions require government approval.

BANKING AND FINANCE
Score: **4**–Stable (high level of restrictions)

Although the government has privatized some of its holdings in the banking sector, it still plays a major role. The government sold its 52 percent stake in the commercial Union Internationale de Banques (UIB) in October 2002 and is attempting to privatize its stake in Banque du Sud (BS). First Initiative reports that "Tunisia's banking sector was comprised of 14 commercial banks and six development banks as of 2004. The state exercises direct control over six commercial banks and all six development banks. The development banks, which lend to specific sectors in the economy, continue to have high percentages of non-performing loans. In recent years, however, the central bank has demanded that banks revise their accounting standards toward international norms." According to the Economist Intelligence Unit, "Banking reform will continue, with the sale of at least one more state-owned bank,

although this process may stall for a while following the government's failure to attract any bids for its sale of a 33.5% stake in Banque du sud." The EIU also reports that the government retains control of most banking assets.

WAGES AND PRICES
Score: **2**–Stable (low level of intervention)

The market determines most wages and prices. According to the Ministry of Development and International Cooperation, market forces determine approximately 87 percent of prices at the production level and 80.6 percent of prices at the distribution level. The U.S. Department of Commerce reports that Tunisia subsidizes food products. The government mandates a minimum wage.

PROPERTY RIGHTS
Score: **3**–Stable (moderate level of protection)

The executive branch is the supreme arbiter of events in the cabinet, government, judiciary, and military. "In general," reports the U.S. Department of Commerce, "complaints about the Tunisian legal system from the commercial sector concern the length and the complexity of unfamiliar legal procedures." According to the Economist Intelligence Unit, "The government appoints, grants tenure to and transfers judges, making them susceptible to government pressure."

REGULATION
Score: **3**–Stable (moderate level)

The bureaucracy can be burdensome. "[D]espite some reform," reports the Economist Intelligence Unit, "labor law is still relatively rigid, with high add-on costs and cumbersome regulations governing the hiring and dismissal of employees." According to the U.S. Department of Commerce, "The Foreign Investment Promotion Agency (FIPA) offers a 'one stop shop' service to investors seeking to establish a business in Tunisia. Generally, it takes approximately two weeks to complete all the necessary work…. [F]irms may need to complete a wide range of regulatory, licensing and logistical procedures before bringing their products or services to the market…. FIPA's simplified registration procedure is not available for all commercial activities. The following activities require prior approval from the relevant government agencies: fisheries, tourism, transportation, communications, education and training, film production, health, real estate development, weapons and ammunition, machine-made carpets, waste treatment and recycling." Corruption is reportedly an obstacle to doing business.

INFORMAL MARKET
Score: **3**–Stable (moderate level of activity)

Transparency International's 2004 score for Tunisia is 5. Therefore, Tunisia's informal market score is 3 this year.

TURKEY

Rank: 85

Score: 3.11

Category: Mostly Unfree

Present & Past Scores

(Best) 1
2
3
4
(Worst) 5

'95 2.95 '96 2.95 '97 2.75 '98 2.66 '99 2.80 '00 2.68 '01 2.93 '02 3.38 '03 3.50 '04 3.39 '05 3.41 '06 3.11

QUICK STUDY

SCORES

Trade Policy	2
Fiscal Burden	3.1
Government Intervention	2.5
Monetary Policy	4
Foreign Investment	3
Banking and Finance	3
Wages and Prices	3
Property Rights	3
Regulation	4
Informal Market	3.5

Population: 72,300,000

Total area: 780,580 sq. km

GDP: $229.3 billion

GDP growth rate: 8.9%

GDP per capita: $3,082

Major exports: food and beverages, textiles and clothing, metals, motor vehicles and parts, agricultural products

Exports of goods and services: $90.9 billion

Major export trading partners: Germany 13.9%, UK 8.8%, US 7.7%, Italy 7.4%, France 5.8%

Major imports: chemicals, crude oil and gas, machinery and equipment, transport equipment

Imports of goods and services: $102 billion

Major import trading partners: Germany 12.8%, Russia 9.3%, Italy 7.0%, France 6.4%, US 4.9%

Foreign direct investment (net): $1.6 billion

2004 Data (in constant 2000 US dollars)

P rime Minister Recep Tayyip Erdogan's government is seeking to reverse decades of corruption, economic incompetence, and authoritarian abuse of power. It has embraced the basic tenets of the Dervis–International Monetary Fund plan, formulated in 2002 after a severe financial crisis threatened Turkey's economic viability. Inflation has fallen sharply to about 9 percent in 2004 from 45 percent in 2002, and lending interest rates have dropped to 35 percent from 70 percent. Further decreases in interest rates remain vital, as the government is forced to roll over a huge internal debt. The government is attempting to pass legislation reforming social security, banking, and tax administration with a view to placing Turkey on a path to sustained growth rather than the boom-and-bust cycles that have characterized much of its modern economic performance. Turkey still faces challenges in decreasing the role of the state; the public sector still dominates energy, telecommunications, transport, and banking. GDP grew by 8.9 percent in 2004 and unemployment fell, although it remained high at 10.3 percent. The European Union agreed to start formal accession talks in October 2005. Turkey's trade policy and fiscal burden of government scores are 0.5 point better this year, and its monetary policy and banking and finance scores are 1 point better. As a result, Turkey's overall score is 0.3 point better this year.

TRADE POLICY
Score: **2**–Better (low level of protectionism)

The World Bank reports that Turkey's weighted average tariff rate in 2003 (the most recent year for which World Bank data are available) was 2 percent, down from the 4.5 percent for 1999 reported in the 2005 *Index*, based on World Bank data. According to the World Trade Organization, "import licences are maintained on health, sanitary, phytosanitary, and environmental grounds." Turkey applies EU policies on non-agricultural imports from third countries. Based on the lower tariff rate, as well as a revision of the trade factor methodology, Turkey's trade policy score is 0.5 point better this year.

FISCAL BURDEN OF GOVERNMENT
Score—Income Taxation: **3.5**–Better (high tax rates)
Score—Corporate Taxation: **4**–Stable (high tax rates)
Score—Change in Government Expenditures: **1**–Better (very high decrease)
Final Score: **3.1**–Better (moderate cost of government)

Effective January 2005, Turkey's top income tax rate was cut to 35 percent from 40 percent. The top corporate tax rate is 30 percent. In 2004, according to the Economist Intelligence Unit, government expenditures as a share of GDP decreased 6.4 percentage points to 32.6 percent, compared to the 1.9 percentage point decrease in 2003. On net, Turkey's fiscal burden of government score is 0.5 point better this year.

GOVERNMENT INTERVENTION IN THE ECONOMY
Score: **2.5**–Stable (moderate level)

According to the central bank, the government consumed 13.2 percent of GDP in 2004. In the same year, based on data from the Ministry of Finance, Turkey received 7.5 percent of its total revenues from state-owned enterprises and government ownership of property.

MONETARY POLICY
Score: **4–Better** (high level of inflation)

From 1995 to 2004, Turkey's weighted average annual rate of inflation was 18 percent, down from the 34.15 percent from 1994 to 2003 reported in the 2005 *Index*. As a result, Turkey's monetary policy score is 1 point better this year.

 CAPITAL FLOWS AND FOREIGN INVESTMENT
Score: **3–Stable** (moderate barriers)

Turkey welcomes foreign investment but maintains a number of formal and informal barriers. The 2003 Foreign Investment Law liberalized rules governing foreign direct investment, guaranteed domestic treatment, and removed minimum capital requirements. Broadcasting, aviation, maritime transportation, and value-added telecommunications services companies and port facilities must be at least 51 percent Turkish-owned. The U.S. Department of Commerce notes "a number of obstacles: excessive bureaucracy, weaknesses in the judicial system, high and inconsistently collected taxes, weaknesses in corporate governance, sometimes unpredictable decisions taken at the municipal level, and frequent, sometimes unclear changes in the legal and regulatory environment." The International Monetary Fund reports that both residents and non-residents may hold foreign exchange accounts. There are few restrictions on payments and transfers. Reporting requirements apply to some capital transactions. Non-residents face restrictions on the purchase of real estate, but foreign companies may acquire real estate through a Turkish legal entity or local partnership.

 BANKING AND FINANCE
Score: **3–Better** (moderate level of restrictions)

Turkey's financial system is recovering from the 2000–2001 financial crisis, and the government has increased transparency and accounting standards. According to First Initiative, "As of end-2003, Turkey had 50 banks, significantly less than it had pre-crisis. The three state-banks control approximately 30% of the banking sector, two of which are planned for privatization.... Foreign participation in banking is very limited (foreign banks accounted for only 3% of banking sector assets as of September 2003), and government holdings continue to make up a significant portion of total bank assets.... The insurance sector...is represented by 60 insurance companies, five of which are foreign-owned and two of which are state-owned firms." Only one insolvent bank remained under Savings Deposit Insurance Fund administration at the end of 2004, the others being liquidated, merged, or sold. Foreign banks face no barriers to entry; the government has sought foreign banks to take over troubled domestic banks. Overall, the government's role in the financial sector is substantial but declining, and the private sector controls most financial assets. As a result, Turkey's banking and finance score is 1 point better this year.

 WAGES AND PRICES
Score: **3–Stable** (moderate level of intervention)

"Despite talk of allowing the enterprises to set their own prices," reports the Economist Intelligence Unit, "the government primarily sets prices of goods produced by state-owned firms.... In general, the government sets annual prices for a range of crops. The municipalities fix ceilings on the price of bread. The Ministry of Health controls drug prices. Permission for price increases depends more on political than on economic criteria." Turkey maintains a minimum wage.

 PROPERTY RIGHTS
Score: **3–Stable** (moderate level of protection)

The U.S. Department of Commerce reports that "Turkey's legal system provides means for enforcing property and contractual rights, and there are written commercial and bankruptcy laws. The court system is overburdened, however, which sometimes results in slow decisions and judges lacking sufficient time to grasp complex issues. The judicial system is also perceived to be susceptible to external influence and to be biased against outsiders."

 REGULATION
Score: **4–Stable** (high level)

Turkish regulations are burdensome. According to the U.S. Department of Commerce, "In general, labor, health and safety laws and policies do not distort or impede investment, although legal restrictions on discharging employees may provide a disincentive to labor-intensive activity in the formal economy. Certain tax policies distort investment decisions.... Bureaucratic 'red tape' remains a significant problem.... Obtaining the approval of both national and local officials for essential permits is a time consuming and often frustrating process." The government has taken steps to simplify the bureaucracy by reducing the number of steps that it takes to open a new business, reports the *Financial Times*, but "petty corruption remains a fact of everyday Turkish life."

 INFORMAL MARKET
Score: **3.5–Stable** (high level of activity)

Transparency International's 2004 score for Turkey is 3.2. Therefore, Turkey's informal market score is 3.5 this year.

TURKMENISTAN

Rank: 148

Score: 4.04

Category: Repressed

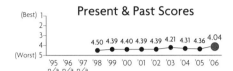

Present & Past Scores

(Best) 1
2
3
4
(Worst) 5

4.50 4.39 4.40 4.39 4.39 4.21 4.31 4.36 4.04

'95 '96 '97 '98 '99 '00 '01 '02 '03 '04 '05 '06
n/a n/a n/a

Turkmenistan possesses the world's fifth-largest reserves of natural gas and is one of the world's top 10 producers of cotton. Its communist-era leader, President Saparmurad Niyazov, was "voted" president for life in December 1999. The educational system has largely been turned into an instrument of political indoctrination. In 2005, Niyazov closed almost all libraries and fired 15,000 state medical personnel, replacing them with military draftees, and ordered all hospitals closed except for those in the capital. The U.S. Department of State reports that human rights abuses are increasing in Turkmenistan. Key industries are still owned by the state, and corruption and over-regulation of the economy limit incentives for foreign investment. In 2003, Niyazov signed the "deal of the century" committing—over the next 25 years—to the export of all Turkmen gas via Russia at less than half of the global market price. Gas and oil remain Turkmenistan's largest sources of export revenue and its principal source of growth. Turkmenistan's capital flows and foreign investment score is 1 point worse this year; however, its trade policy score is 2.5 points better, its fiscal burden of government score is 0.2 point better, its monetary policy score is 1 point better, and its informal market score is 0.5 point better. As a result, Turkmenistan's overall score is 0.32 point better this year.

QUICK STUDY

SCORES

Trade Policy	2.5
Fiscal Burden	2.4
Government Intervention	5
Monetary Policy	3
Foreign Investment	5
Banking and Finance	5
Wages and Prices	4
Property Rights	5
Regulation	4
Informal Market	4.5

Population: 4,863,500

Total area: 488,100 sq. km

GDP: $4.8 billion

GDP growth rate: 16.9%

GDP per capita: $989

Major exports: gas, crude and refined oil, textiles

Exports of goods and services: $3.7 billion

Major export trading partners: Ukraine 39.2%, Italy 18.1%, Iran 14.7%, Turkey 6.5%

Major imports: foodstuffs, machinery and equipment

Imports of goods and services: $3.2 billion

Major import trading partners: Russia 21.5%, Turkey 9.4%, United Arab Emirates 7.6%, China 4.2%

Foreign direct investment (net): $94.3 million

2003 Data (in constant 2000 US dollars)

TRADE POLICY
Score: **2.5**–Better (moderate level of protectionism)

The World Bank reports that Turkmenistan's weighted average tariff rate in 2002 (the most recent year for which World Bank data are available) was 2.9 percent. (The World Bank has revised the figure for 2002 upward from the 1.7 percent reported in the 2005 *Index*.) According to the U.S. Department of State, "Turkmenistan lists about 100 imported goods and materials subject to customs duties and 8 [subject to] to excise taxes. The goods and materials not included in the lists are subject to a five percent customs duty payment…. Export of fertilizers, non-ferrous metals, their alloys, and products made of non-ferrous metals is prohibited." Customs procedures are bureaucratic, slow, and subject to corruption. Based on new, reliable tariff rate data, as well as a revision of the trade factor methodology, Turkmenistan's trade policy score is 2.5 points better this year.

FISCAL BURDEN OF GOVERNMENT
Score—Income Taxation: **1.5**–Stable (low tax rates)
Score—Corporate Taxation: **2**–Better (low tax rates)
Score—Change in Government Expenditures: **4**–Worse (moderate increase)
Final Score: **2.4**–Better (low cost of government)

According to Eurasianet, Turkmenistan's top income tax rate is 10 percent, down from the 12 percent reported in the 2005 *Index*. Deloitte reports that the top corporate tax rate is 20 percent, down from the 25 percent reported in the 2005 *Index*. In 2003, according to the Asian Development Bank, government expenditures as a share of GDP increased 1.9 percentage points to 19.4 percent, compared to the 0.9 percentage point decrease in 2002. On net, Turkmenistan's fiscal burden of government score is 0.2 point better this year.

GOVERNMENT INTERVENTION IN THE ECONOMY
Score: **5**–Stable (very high level)

The World Bank reports that the government consumed 12.8 percent of GDP in 2003. According to the Economist Intelligence Unit, however, "Official fiscal data…hide a large structural deficit in off-budget accounts, debts and arrears." In addition, "Turkmenistan has one of the lowest private sector/GDP ratios in the region…. The majority of employment is still provided by the state…." Based on the apparent unreliability of reported figures for government consumption, 1 point has been added to Turkmenistan's government intervention score. Another point has been added based on the level of state-owned enterprise.

MONETARY POLICY
Score: **3**–Better (moderate level of inflation)

From 1995 to 2004, based on data from the International Monetary Fund's *2005 World Economic Outlook*, Turkmenistan's weighted average annual rate of inflation was 6.71 percent, down from the 12.29 percent from 1994 to 2003 reported in the 2005 *Index*. As a result, Turkmenistan's monetary policy score is 1 point better this year.

CAPITAL FLOWS AND FOREIGN INVESTMENT
Score: **5**–Worse (high barriers)

Turkmenistan's government controls most of the economy and restricts foreign participation. "A host of barriers to investors, both foreign and domestic, have stifled development of the private sector in Turkmenistan," reports the Economist Intelligence Unit. "These include currency and trade restrictions, and the state's reluctance to relinquish management control in those enterprises that it has privatised." According to the U.S. Department of State, "The government…claims it wants to attract foreign investment. However, the government's actions are inconsistent with those statements and the foreign investment climate remains poor. The government selectively chooses its investment partners. In order to function in this peculiar commercial environment a strong relationship with the government is essential…. Finally, the lack of established rule of law, excessive and inconsistent regulation, and unfamiliarity with international business practices are disincentives to foreign investment…. [W]idespread government corruption, usually in the form of bribe requests, [is] an obstacle to investment and business throughout all economic sectors and regions." The International Monetary Fund reports that foreign exchange accounts require government approval. All payments and transfers require government approval. Capital transactions face restrictions and central bank approval in some cases. Based on evidence of discrimination against foreign investors, capital controls, and an opaque and corrupt approval process, Turkmenistan's capital flows and foreign investment score is 1 point worse this year.

BANKING AND FINANCE
Score: **5**–Stable (very high level of restrictions)

"In 2004," reports First Initiative, "a total of 67 banks, both state-owned and commercial, local and foreign, were registered with the State Central Bank of Turkmenistan. Out of this total, two state banks, 52 Daykhanbanks (agricultural banks supervised by the cooperative commercial Daykhan-centerbank) and 13 commercial banks were operational. The state-owned institutions are dominant, with 95% of all loans going to state-owned enterprises…. The government retains significant influence over the Central Bank of Turkmenistan, which supervises the banking sector. Commercial banks function more as administrators of public sector financial transactions than independent lenders." The state-owned insurance company is the sole insurer.

WAGES AND PRICES
Score: **4**–Stable (high level of intervention)

Turkmenistan's government strongly influences prices. According to the Economist Intelligence Unit, "Total domestic subsidies in the oil and gas sector alone were estimated by the World Bank at around…24% of GDP…. Private households are heavily subsidised…and enjoy a substantial quota of free gas." The EIU also reports that the government controls input prices so that it can keep its budget artificially low and continue to claim a sound fiscal position. The government mandates a minimum wage.

PROPERTY RIGHTS
Score: **5**–Stable (very low level of protection)

According to the Economist Intelligence Unit, "The courts and the institutions that implement the law…cannot be trusted to enforce contract rights dispassionately. Turkmenistan's legal system, particularly corporate law, is poorly developed and… poorly enforced…. The judiciary is badly trained and open to bribery. The provision in the constitution for the private ownership of land (Article 9) has yet to be implemented in practice."

REGULATION
Score: **4**–Stable (high level)

According to the U.S. Department of Commerce, "Personal relations with Government officials often play a decisive role in acquiring a contract or running a successful business…. [I]t is difficult for the investor to identify a clear set of rules that apply and that will apply over the term of the investment." Turmenistan's "business environment is extremely difficult, the…regulatory regime is poorly developed [and] corruption is rife," reports the Economist Intelligence Unit. "Laws regulating bankruptcy, financial markets and secured transactions fall well below internationally acceptable standards."

INFORMAL MARKET
Score: **4.5**–Better (very high level of activity)

Transparency International's 2004 score for Turkmenistan is 2. Therefore, Turkmenistan's informal market score is 4.5 this year—0.5 point better than last year.

UGANDA

Rank: 66

Score: 2.95

Category: Mostly Free

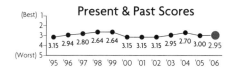

Present & Past Scores

(Best) 1
2
3
4
(Worst) 5

3.15 2.94 2.80 2.64 2.64 3.15 3.15 3.15 2.95 2.70 3.00 2.95

'95 '96 '97 '98 '99 '00 '01 '02 '03 '04 '05 '06

QUICK STUDY

SCORES

Trade Policy	3
Fiscal Burden	3.5
Government Intervention	2
Monetary Policy	2
Foreign Investment	3
Banking and Finance	2
Wages and Prices	2
Property Rights	4
Regulation	4
Informal Market	4

Population: 25,280,000

Total area: 236,040 sq. km

GDP: $7 billion

GDP growth rate: 4.7%

GDP per capita: $277

Major exports: coffee, tea, gold, cotton, fish products

Exports of goods and services: $911.2 million

Major export trading partners: Kenya 14.7%, Switzerland 13.7%, Netherlands 9.2%, UK 6.4%, South Africa 5.6%

Major imports: vehicles, petroleum, medical and pharmaceutical products, cereals

Imports of goods and services: $1.6 billion

Major import trading partners: Kenya 26.1%, India 7.4%, South Africa 7.2%, Japan 6.6%, UK 6.3%

Foreign direct investment (net): $252.7 million

2003 Data (in constant 2000 US dollars)

President Yoweri Museveni, who has ruled Uganda since a 1986 military coup, was elected to a second five-year term in 2001. Although political parties have been officially banned, Museveni has been supported by a state-funded quasi-party. In anticipation of the mid-2006 elections, two amendments to the constitution were voted on by the Ugandan people in July 2005: one to permit political parties and a second to remove the two-term restriction on the presidency and permit Museveni to run in 2006. Both passed. Relations with Rwanda remain tense following the two countries' involvement in the Democratic Republic of Congo, and both Rwanda and Uganda remain concerned about rebel groups in the eastern DRC. Conflict between the Ugandan government and the rebel Lord's Resistance Army continues, and peace is unlikely in the near term. The economy remains heavily dependent on agriculture, which employs the bulk of the workforce and accounted for nearly 40 percent of GDP in 2002. Uganda is behind schedule on privatization and is considering tax increases to reduce its reliance on donor aid, which funds 40 percent of its budget. The government's "abstinence, be faithful, and condoms" (ABC) program has reduced HIV infection. Uganda is eligible for assistance as a threshold country for the U.S. Millennium Challenge Account. Uganda's fiscal burden of government score is 0.5 point better this year. As a result, its overall score is 0.05 point better this year, causing Uganda to be classified as a "mostly free" country.

TRADE POLICY
Score: **3**–Stable (moderate level of protectionism)

The World Bank reports that Uganda's weighted average tariff rate in 2004 was 5.5 percent, down from the 6.8 percent for 2002 reported in the 2005 *Index,* based on World Bank data. According to the U.S. Department of Commerce, "Import certificates, which are non-good-specific, are required and have a validity of 6 months…. In order to export one must first obtain an export certificate from the Ministry of Tourism, Trade and Industry." Based on the revised trade factor methodology, Uganda's trade policy score is unchanged.

FISCAL BURDEN OF GOVERNMENT
Score—Income Taxation: **3**–Stable (moderate tax rates)
Score—Corporate Taxation: **4**–Stable (high tax rates)
Score—Change in Government Expenditures: **3**–Better (very low decrease)
Final Score: **3.5**–Better (high cost of government)

Uganda's top income tax rate is 30 percent. The corporate tax rate is also 30 percent. In 2003, according to the African Development Bank, government expenditures as a share of GDP decreased 0.5 percentage point to 23.3 percent, compared to a 4.1 percentage point increase in 2002. On net, Uganda's fiscal burden of government score is 0.5 point better this year.

GOVERNMENT INTERVENTION IN THE ECONOMY
Score: **2**–Stable (low level)

The World Bank reports that the government consumed 15.2 percent of GDP in 2003. In the July 2003–June 2004 fiscal year, based on data from the International Monetary Fund, Uganda received 1.62 percent of its total revenues from state-owned enterprises and government ownership of property.

MONETARY POLICY
Score: **2**–Stable (low level of inflation)

From 1995 to 2004, Uganda's weighted average annual rate of inflation was 4.03 percent.

 CAPITAL FLOWS AND FOREIGN INVESTMENT
Score: **3**–Stable (moderate barriers)

Uganda is fairly open to foreign investment. The government allows foreign investment in privatized industries, and the U.S. Department of Commerce reports that "Ugandan policies, laws, and regulations generally are investor-friendly. Foreign investors may form 100 percent foreign-owned companies and majority or minority joint ventures with local investors with no restrictions. The [government] permits foreign investors to acquire or takeover domestic enterprises and encourages greenfield investments. Ugandan courts generally uphold the sanctity of contracts." According to the same source, however, "The investment code provides fewer advantages to foreigners as compared with nationals of Uganda. For example, licensing authorities may apply performance obligations on foreign investors, to which nationals are not subject…. [D]ue to byzantine land laws and a slow and non-transparent Land Registry, some foreign companies have encountered difficulty in obtaining land." The International Monetary Fund reports that both residents and non-residents may hold foreign exchange accounts. There are no restrictions or controls on payments, transactions, or transfers.

 BANKING AND FINANCE
Score: **2**–Stable (low level of restrictions)

Uganda's financial system remains dominated by its banking sector. "In 2004," reports First Initiative, "the banking sector was comprised of 16 commercial banks and two development banks and was characterized by a high degree of foreign ownership. The largest bank, the successor to the state-owned Uganda Commercial Bank, was purchased by a South African bank in 2002. Three other foreign banks account for approximately 75% of Uganda's banking sector assets…. In addition to the formal banking institutions, there were seven savings and loan institutions and over 100 micro-finance institutions in 2003. Despite the large number, micro-finance institutions accounted for only 1% of the financial sector, while non-bank institutions accounted for 7% (2003). The insurance sector remains a small part of the financial system. The insurance industry was comprised of fifteen insurance companies in 2003." According to the United Nations *Economic Report on Africa 2003*, "The sale of Uganda Commercial Bank achieved the government's long-standing goal of getting out of the ownership and management of commercial banks." However, the Economist Intelligence Unit notes that the government is still involved in microfinance.

 WAGES AND PRICES
Score: **2**–Stable (low level of intervention)

The government dismantled price controls in January 1994, and the abolition of coffee, cotton, and other government monopolies has allowed the market to set wages and prices in these important sectors. The Economist Intelligence Unit reports that Uganda subsidizes private companies in the electricity sector. The government maintains a minimum wage, but most wages are set through negotiation among individuals, unions, and employers; the government is involved only if it is the employer.

 PROPERTY RIGHTS
Score: **4**–Stable (low level of protection)

The judicial system is not fully independent and lacks resources. According to the U.S. Department of Commerce, "Uganda opened its first commercial court five years ago and now boasts four commercial court judges…. Despite a shortage of judges, lack of funds, and minimal space, the commercial courts normally dispose of disputes within six to seven months…. Commercial court judges estimate that eighty percent of commercial disputes are resolved through Alternative Dispute Resolution. Some foreign businesses have reported that judges may delay ruling on disputes involving politically well-connected parties." The Economist Intelligence Unit reports that "corruption among policemen usually takes the form of small bribes, but…officials in local government and the judiciary are more demanding. A magistrate may demand as much as NUSh100,000 (about US$50) to 'hear a case properly'…."

 REGULATION
Score: **4**–Stable (high level)

Doing business in Uganda is still difficult, particularly for local small businesses. Obstacles include corruption, inefficient government services, and mismanagement. According to the U.S. Department of Commerce, "Uganda has a series of laws, many of which date to the colonial era, that govern commercial activity." In addition, "the regulatory system lacks internal transparency and varies substantially by regulatory body…. [A]gencies at times do not follow standard practices and may not observe all legal provisions. Additionally, the government at times provides ad hoc assistance to well-connected local businessmen…. Many Ugandan agencies maintain substantial red tape…. [S]ome government officials do not have computers or Internet connections…." Bureaucratic corruption is substantial.

 INFORMAL MARKET
Score: **4**–Stable (high level of activity)

Transparency International's 2004 score for Uganda is 2.6. Therefore, Uganda's informal market score is 4 this year.

UKRAINE

Rank: 99

Score: 3.24

Category: Mostly Unfree

Present & Past Scores

(Best) 1
2
3 — 4.00 4.00 3.78 3.83 3.95 3.75 3.88 3.84 3.59 3.49 3.16 3.24
4
(Worst) 5

'95 '96 '97 '98 '99 '00 '01 '02 '03 '04 '05 '06

QUICK STUDY

SCORES

Trade Policy	2.5
Fiscal Burden	2.9
Government Intervention	2
Monetary Policy	3
Foreign Investment	4
Banking and Finance	3
Wages and Prices	3
Property Rights	4
Regulation	4
Informal Market	4

Population: 48,355,700

Total area: 603,700 sq. km

GDP: $39.3 billion

GDP growth rate: 9.4%

GDP per capita: $812

Major exports: metals, minerals, electronics, chemicals, vegetables, fuel and petroleum products

Exports of goods and services: $24.2 billion

Major export trading partners: Russia 17.8%, Germany 5.9%, Italy 5.3%, China 4.1%

Major imports: minerals, electronics, transport equipment, metals

Imports of goods and services: $22.3 billion

Major import trading partners: Russia 35.9%, Germany 9.4%, Turkmenistan 7.2%

Foreign direct investment (net): $1.3 billion

2003 Data (in constant 2000 US dollars)

I n 2004, Ukraine's political system was gripped by the struggle to succeed President Leonid Kuchma, whose nine-year rule expired amid malaise and corruption. The "Orange Revolution" ended with former Prime Minister Viktor Yushchenko claiming victory as president after a December rerun of October's rigged elections, beginning a new chapter of bold political and economic change. The Yushchenko administration has dedicated itself to bringing to justice those responsible for the murder of journalist Georgii Gongadze five years ago. It also has openly expressed its pro-Western stance, pushing for closer relations with the European Union and NATO. Perhaps most important, the government has embarked energetically on policy reforms, although such reforms often do not follow the principles of free markets, privatization, tight monetary policy, low taxes, and property rights. Despite significant dependence on energy imports from Russia, Ukraine continues to seek an equal trading relationship with its neighbor. The economy grew an impressive 12.1 percent in 2004, according to the Economist Intelligence Unit, but high oil prices, increased inflation (now at 13 percent), and political unrest were responsible for an economic slowdown at the beginning of 2005. Ukraine's government intervention score is 0.5 point better this year; however, its fiscal burden of government score is 0.3 point worse, and its monetary policy score is 1 point worse. As a result, Ukraine's overall score is 0.08 point worse this year.

TRADE POLICY
Score: **2.5**–Stable (moderate level of protectionism)

According to the World Bank, Ukraine's weighted average tariff rate in 2002 (the most recent year for which World Bank data are available) was 3.9 percent. (The World Bank has revised the figure for 2002 downward from the 4.4 percent reported in the 2005 *Index*.) The U.S. Department of Commerce reports that Ukraine continues to maintain import barriers, including "discriminatory fees and certification regimes. Non-tariff barriers include non-transparent standards, cumbersome procedures for phytosanitary certification, and import licenses." Based on the revised trade factor methodology, Ukraine's trade policy score is unchanged.

FISCAL BURDEN OF GOVERNMENT
Score—Income Taxation: **1.5**–Stable (low tax rates)
Score—Corporate Taxation: **3**–Stable (moderate tax rates)
Score—Change in Government Expenditures: **4**–Worse (moderate increase)
Final Score: **2.9**–Worse (moderate cost of government)

According to Deloitte, Ukraine has a flat income tax rate of 13 percent. The top corporate tax rate is 25 percent. In 2003, according to the Economist Intelligence Unit, government expenditures as a share of GDP increased by 1.7 percentage points to 28.4 percent, compared to a 0.5 percentage point decrease in 2002. On net, Ukraine's fiscal burden of government score is 0.3 point worse this year.

GOVERNMENT INTERVENTION IN THE ECONOMY
Score: **2**–Better (low level)

The World Bank reports that the government consumed 15.8 percent of GDP in 2003, down from the 20.4 percent reported in the 2005 *Index*. As a result, Ukraine's government intervention score is 0.5 point better this year. In the same year, according to the International

Monetary Fund's Government Financial Statistics CD–ROM, Ukraine received 4.65 percent of its total revenues from state-owned enterprises and government ownership of property.

MONETARY POLICY
Score: **3**–Worse (moderate level of inflation)

From 1995 to 2004, Ukraine's weighted average annual rate of inflation was 7.86 percent, up from the 5.91 percent from 1994 to 2003 reported in the 2005 *Index*. As a result, Ukraine's monetary policy score is 1 point worse this year.

CAPITAL FLOWS AND FOREIGN INVESTMENT
Score: **4**–Stable (high barriers)

Ukraine officially guarantees equal treatment of foreign investment but restricts investment in certain "strategic" enterprises (radio, television, energy, and insurance). According to the U.S. Trade Representative, "An underdeveloped banking system, poor communications networks, a difficult and frequently changing tax and regulatory climate, crime and corruption, and a weak legal system create major obstacles" to investment. In addition, "the privatization process continues to lack transparency…. In the 2004 Presidential election year, the Ukrainian government rushed to privatize large plants including coal mines and steel mills. The privatizations were marked by unclear, non-transparent and changing regulations and by heavy political interference that practically excluded foreign investors from participating in privatization." The new government has said that it will review these privatizations and determine whether they need to be revoked and resold. The International Monetary Fund reports that resident and non-resident foreign exchange accounts are subject to restrictions and government approval in some cases. Payments and transfers are subject to various requirements and quantitative limits. Some capital transactions are subject to controls and licenses. According to the Economist Intelligence Unit, "Ukraine remains a difficult place to conduct business. Businesses are still exposed to pervasive corruption and an unwieldy and unreformed bureaucracy."

BANKING AND FINANCE
Score: **3**–Stable (moderate level of restrictions)

According to the Economist Intelligence Unit, "All parts of the sector—including banks, non-bank financial institutions and the securities market—are still largely underdeveloped and suffer from insufficient capital, an unsatisfactory legal infrastructure and limited investment opportunities." In 2004, reports First Initiative, "the banking sector was comprised of 182 commercial banks, including 20 foreign banks (7 of them with 100% foreign capital) and two state owned banks." The U.S. Department of Commerce notes that the "top ten banks control 55 percent of loans outstanding and own 36 percent of the total capital of the system." A January 2002 law "On Banks and Banking Activity" ended discrimination against foreign banks. According to the U.S. Trade Representative, "Foreign insurance firms and banks are permitted to operate in Ukraine, but they cannot open branches, a prohibition that impedes participation of foreign

businesses in Ukraine. Nevertheless, investors can open 100 percent foreign-owned subsidiaries."

WAGES AND PRICES
Score: **3**–Stable (moderate level of intervention)

The government controls some prices. According to the U.S. Department of Commerce, "The cabinet of Ministers of Ukraine has price-setting authority with products, goods, and services in certain sectors. These lists include basic tariffs (e.g., electricity, telecommunications, transportation, utilities), and some crucial products such as sugar, grain, gas, oil, etc." In April 2005, the government set price caps on electricity in response to a 15 percent sudden price surge, but it removed the caps a few months later. Ukraine has a minimum wage.

PROPERTY RIGHTS
Score: **4**–Stable (low level of protection)

Protection of property is weak. The U.S. Department of State reports that Ukraine's "judiciary is subject to considerable political interference from the executive branch and also suffers from corruption and inefficiency." According to the U.S. Department of Commerce, "Organized crime is alleged to influence court decisions." The Economist Intelligence Unit reports that "the institutional capacity of the state and the judiciary is too weak to combat organised crime effectively. Organised crime and domestic vested interests pose a significant threat to foreign investors who become involved in those areas of the local economy that are considered to be protected." Expropriation is possible. In June 2005, according to the *Financial Times*, the government agreed "to hold a new auction for…the country's largest steel mill, after a court stripped away ownership from businessmen close to…the ousted former president."

REGULATION
Score: **4**–Stable (high level)

The U.S. Department of Commerce reports that "the number of regulations, required certificates, and inspection regimes in Ukraine impose a significant regulatory burden on private enterprise…. The [government] requires enterprises to obtain numerous permits to conduct business. Procedures are complex, unpredictable, burdensome, and duplicative creating confusion, increasing the cost and time to do business in Ukraine, providing opportunities for corruption, and driving business into the shadow economy…. 'One-stop Registration Shops' have been introduced in several cities [for] land use and other permits." According to the Economist Intelligence Unit, "Corruption among public-sector officials stems from the low level of wages and the high level of bureaucracy, which has resulted in pervasive bribery…."

INFORMAL MARKET
Score: **4**–Stable (high level of activity)

Transparency International's 2004 score for Ukraine is 2.2. Therefore, Ukraine's informal market score is 4 this year.

UNITED ARAB EMIRATES

Rank: 65

Score: 2.93

Category: Mostly Free

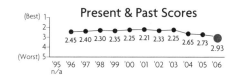

Present & Past Scores

(Best) 1–
2–
3– 2.45 2.40 2.30 2.35 2.25 2.21 2.33 2.25 2.65 2.73
4– 2.93
(Worst) 5–
'95 '96 '97 '98 '99 '00 '01 '02 '03 '04 '05 '06
n/a

QUICK STUDY

SCORES

Trade Policy	2.5
Fiscal Burden	1.3
Government Intervention	4
Monetary Policy	2
Foreign Investment	4
Banking and Finance	4
Wages and Prices	3
Property Rights	3
Regulation	3
Informal Market	2.5

Population: 4,041,000

Total area: 82,880 sq. km

GDP: $74 billion

GDP growth rate: 11.9%

GDP per capita: $19,717

Major exports: natural gas, crude oil

Exports of goods and services: $67.1 billion

Major export trading partners: Japan 26.1%, South Korea 10.5%, Iran 4.4%

Major imports: machinery, manufactured goods, fuel, foodstuffs

Imports of goods and services: $45.8 billion

Major import trading partners: China 9.3%, India 8.5%, US 8.0%, Germany 6.7%, Japan 6.7%, US 6.5%

Foreign direct investment (net): −$483.2 million

2003 Data (in constant 2000 US dollars)

T he United Arab Emirates is a federation of seven small Arab monarchies (Abu Dhabi, Ajman, Dubai, Fujairah, Ras Al-Khaimah, Sharjah, and Umm al-Qaiwain) that gained independence from Great Britain in 1971. Oil and gas production provide about 30 percent of GDP, and energy reserves are expected to last for more than 100 years at current rates of production. Abu Dhabi, which accounts for about 90 percent of oil production, has traditionally taken a leading role in political and economic decision-making at the federal level, although many economic policy decisions are made by the rulers of each emirate. Dubai, whose oil reserves are dwindling, has developed into the UAE's foremost center of finance, commerce, transportation, and tourism. UAE nationals continue to rely heavily on a bloated public sector for employment, subsidized services, and government handouts. The UAE signed a Trade and Investment Framework Agreement with the United States in April 2004 and has begun negotiations for a free trade agreement with Washington. In November 2004, Sheikh Zayed bin Sultan al-Nahyan, ruler of Abu Dhabi and president of the UAE since 1975, died and was succeeded in both offices by his son, Sheikh Khalifa bin Zayed al-Nahyan, who is expected to continue his father's program of economic liberalization. The United Arab Emirates' monetary policy and capital flows and foreign investment scores are 1 point worse this year. As a result, the UAE's overall score is 0.2 point worse this year.

TRADE POLICY
Score: **2.5**–Stable (moderate level of protectionism)

The U.S. Trade Representative reports that the UAE's average tariff rate in 2003 was 5 percent, up from the 4 percent for 2003 reported in the 2005 *Index*, based on World Bank data. According to the same source, "Only firms with an appropriate trade license can engage in importation, and only UAE nationals can obtain such a license (this licensing provision is not applicable to goods imported into free zones)." The U.S. Department of Commerce reports that non-tariff barriers include "restrictive agency/sponsorship/distributorship requirements and restrictive shelf-life requirements for food stuffs." Based on the revised trade factor methodology, the United Arab Emirates' trade policy score is unchanged.

FISCAL BURDEN OF GOVERNMENT
Score—Income Taxation: **1**–Stable (very low tax rates)
Score—Corporate Taxation: **1**–Stable (very low tax rates)
Score—Change in Government Expenditures: **2**–Stable (moderate decrease)
Final Score: **1.3**–Stable (very low cost of government)

The UAE has no income tax or corporate tax. In 2003, based on data from the International Monetary Fund, government expenditures as a share of GDP decreased 2.2 percentage points to 30.7 percent, compared to the 2.8 percentage point decrease in 2002.

GOVERNMENT INTERVENTION IN THE ECONOMY
Score: **4**–Stable (high level)

According to the Economist Intelligence Unit, the government consumed 14.7 percent of GDP in 2003. In the same year, based on data from the central bank, the UAE received 75.06 percent of its total revenues from state-owned enterprises and government ownership of property in the hydrocarbon sector.

389

MONETARY POLICY
Score: **2**–Worse (low level of inflation)

From 1995 to 2004, based on data from the International Monetary Fund's *2005 World Economic Outlook*, the UAE's weighted average annual rate of inflation was 3.44 percent, up from the 2.83 percent from 1994 to 2003 reported in the 2005 *Index*. As a result, the United Arab Emirates' monetary policy score is 1 point worse this year.

 CAPITAL FLOWS AND FOREIGN INVESTMENT
Score: **4**–Worse (high barriers)

Foreign investment in the UAE is restricted. "Except for companies located in one of the free zones," reports the U.S. Trade Representative, "at least 51 percent of a business establishment must be owned by a UAE national. A business engaged in importing and distributing a product must be either a 100 percent UAE owned agency/distributorship or a 51 percent UAE/49 percent foreign limited liability company (LLC).... There is no national treatment for investors in the UAE. Non-GCC [Gulf Cooperation Council] nationals cannot own land.... 22 out of 53 stocks on the UAE stock market are open to foreign investment. Ministry of Economy and Planning rules allow foreign investors to own up to 49 percent of companies on the stock market." Branch offices of foreign companies must have a national agent unless the foreign company has established its office pursuant to an agreement with the government. There are no controls or requirements on current transfers, access to foreign exchange, or repatriation of profits. Foreign ownership of land and stock is restricted. Based on evidence of discrimination against foreign investment, the UAE's capital flows and foreign investment score is 1 point worse this year.

 BANKING AND FINANCE
Score: **4**–Stable (high level of restrictions)

There are 21 domestic banks, some of which have federal or local government ownership, and 26 financial entities. The government remains involved through loan guarantees. The UAE has no corporate income tax, but there is a 20 percent tax on foreign bank profits. Banks also must employ UAE nationals under a quota system. As a condition of membership in the World Trade Organization, the UAE is required to end the current restriction on allowing new foreign banks into the country. According to the U.S. Department of Commerce, "The UAE Central Bank no longer issues licenses for new foreign banks to establish branches in the UAE." Commercial banks are not allowed to engage in non-banking activities. Banks may not lend more than 7 percent of their capital to any single foreign institution.

 WAGES AND PRICES
Score: **3**–Stable (moderate level of intervention)

The government affects prices through extensive subsidies. "Ongoing price controls and subsidies on core goods and services also act as a brake on consumer price growth," reports the Economist Intelligence Unit, "although their partial removal—such as the introduction of healthcare charges for expatriates—has generated some upward pressure on consumer prices." The EIU reports that the government also provides subsidies to various economic sectors. Price setting for the domestic market does not extend to oil exports. There is no minimum wage.

 PROPERTY RIGHTS
Score: **3**–Stable (moderate level of protection)

"Although the UAE has a full complement of institutions for the legislative, executive and judicial branches of government," reports the Economist Intelligence Unit, "in practice all important decisions are made by the ruling families of the emirates, particularly Abu Dhabi.... While tradition dictates that these bodies take decisions in the interest of citizens, the deliberations of these institutions are not transparent or accountable. This leaves considerable scope for inefficiency as instances of incompetence, corruption or excessive red tape are hidden from public view and are rarely open to challenge." All land in Abu Dhabi, the largest of the UAE's seven emirates, is owned by the government.

 REGULATION
Score: **3**–Stable (moderate level)

Establishing a business is easy if the business is not to compete directly with state-owned concerns. The government requires a license only for opening a place of business in the UAE, not for companies exporting to the emirates. According to the U.S. Department of Commerce, "The procedures for obtaining a license vary from emirate to emirate, but are straightforward and publicly available." Trade, industrial, service, professional, and construction licenses are available. Special bylaws apply to business practice in the free zones. The U.S. Department of Commerce reports that "private sector institutions, including banks and foreign oil companies, are not allowed to disseminate statistics to the public." In addition, "corruption is a concern for U.S. firms seeking to do business in the UAE."

 INFORMAL MARKET
Score: **2.5**–Stable (moderate level of activity)

Transparency International's 2004 score for the UAE is 6.1. Therefore, the UAE's informal market score is 2.5 this year.

UNITED KINGDOM

Rank: 5

Score: 1.74

Category: Free

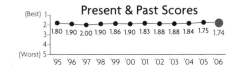

Present & Past Scores

(Best) 1
2 — 1.80 1.90 2.00 1.90 1.86 1.90 1.83 1.88 1.88 1.84 1.75 1.74
3
4
(Worst) 5
'95 '96 '97 '98 '99 '00 '01 '02 '03 '04 '05 '06

QUICK STUDY

SCORES

Trade Policy   2
Fiscal Burden   3.9
Government Intervention   2.5
Monetary Policy   1
Foreign Investment   1
Banking and Finance   1
Wages and Prices   2
Property Rights   1
Regulation   2
Informal Market   1

Population: 59,800,000

Total area: 244,820 sq. km

GDP: $1.6 trillion

GDP growth rate: 3.1%

GDP per capita: $26,391

Major exports: manufactured goods, oil and other fuels, food, travel services, financial and insurance services, transportation, computer services

Exports of goods and services: $525.1 billion

Major export trading partners: US 15.0%, Germany 11.6%, France 9.8%, Ireland 7.0%

Major imports: finished manufactures, semi-manufactures, food, oil, financial services, communications

Imports of goods and services: $595.8 billion

Major import trading partners: Germany 14.0%, US 8.8%, France 8.0%, Netherlands 7.2%

Foreign direct investment (net): $12 billion

2004 Data (in constant 2000 US dollars)

The United Kingdom, with its strong rule of law and political and economic freedom, has become the world's fourth-largest economy, up from sixth largest when Prime Minister Tony Blair assumed power. New Labour's insistence on not undoing the Thatcher revolution continues to pay dividends. GDP grew by 3.1 percent in 2004. However, the government's budget moved from a surplus of 1.6 percent of GDP in 2000–2001 to a 2.9 percent deficit in 2004–2005, chiefly because the Blair team showered money on antiquated public services. Economic storm clouds are looming. The regulatory burden has increased, as companies are expected to do an increasing number of jobs for the government through the use of payrolls. When Labour came to power, 15 such regulations were on the books; the number now stands at 23. In May 2005, the Blair government was returned for an unprecedented third term. Incredibly, given the Labour Party's history, British voters judged Blair a better steward of the economy than the ostensibly pro-business Conservatives. Yet, despite public support following the July 7, 2005, terrorist bombings in London, the prime minister's time is running out. The key question is whether a new Labour leader will maintain similar economic policies and preside over the same type of economic success. The United Kingdom's fiscal burden of government score is 0.1 point better this year. As a result, its overall score is 0.01 point better this year.

TRADE POLICY
Score: **2**–Stable (low level of protectionism)

As a member of the European Union, the United Kingdom was subject to a common EU weighted average external tariff of 1.3 percent in 2003, down from the 2.4 percent for 2002 reported in the 2005 *Index*, based on World Bank data. According to the World Trade Organization and the U.S. Trade Representative, the EU imposes non-tariff trade barriers through a complex regulatory system and export subsidies. Based on the revised trade factor methodology, the United Kingdom's trade policy score is unchanged.

FISCAL BURDEN OF GOVERNMENT
Score—Income Taxation: **4**–Stable (high tax rates)
Score—Corporate Taxation: **4**–Stable (high tax rates)
Score—Change in Government Expenditures: **3.5**–Better (low increase)
Final Score: **3.9**–Better (high cost of government)

The United Kingdom's top income tax rate is 40 percent. The top corporate tax rate is 30 percent. In 2004, government expenditures as a share of GDP increased 0.7 percentage point to 44.1 percent, compared to the 1.6 percentage point increase in 2003. On net, the United Kingdom's fiscal burden of government score is 0.1 point better this year.

GOVERNMENT INTERVENTION IN THE ECONOMY
Score: **2.5**–Stable (moderate level)

Based on data from the Economist Intelligence Unit, the government consumed 21.3 percent of GDP in 2004. In the April 2003–March 2004 fiscal year, based on data from the Government Statistical Service, the United Kingdom received 2.01 percent of its total revenues from state-owned enterprises and government ownership of property.

MONETARY POLICY
Score: 1–Stable (very low level of inflation)

From 1995 to 2004, the United Kingdom's weighted average annual rate of inflation was 2.80 percent.

CAPITAL FLOWS AND FOREIGN INVESTMENT
Score: 1–Stable (very low barriers)

The United Kingdom welcomes foreign investment, and foreign investors receive the same treatment as domestic businesses. "With a few exceptions," reports the U.S. Department of Commerce, "the UK does not discriminate between nationals and foreign individuals in the formation and operation of private companies.... The UK imposes few impediments to foreign ownership.... Government policies are intended to facilitate the free flow of capital and to support the flow of resources in the product and services markets." The UK is one of the most favorable destinations for foreign investment in the European Union, attracting about a quarter of all direct investment in the EU. According to the Economist Intelligence Unit, "The most attractive features of the business environment will be a favourable disposition to foreign investment, deep and sophisticated capital markets, a relaxed attitude to foreign takeovers of domestic companies, and a relatively flexible labour market." The government "has some power to block foreign acquisitions (under the Industry Act 1975) and force divestments" but "generally does not exercise any discriminatory controls over foreign takeovers.... Limits exist in some privatised companies on the amount of voting shares an individual or group may own.... The main regulatory hazards for direct investors, especially those planning acquisitions, stem from Brussels, not London." The International Monetary Fund reports that both residents and non-residents may hold foreign exchange accounts. Payments and proceeds on invisible transactions and current transfers face no restrictions, profits can be repatriated freely, and there are no controls on real estate transactions. The IMF reports that the government can prohibit transfer of control of important domestic manufacturing to a non-resident if the transaction is determined not to be in the national interest. According to the U.S. Department of Commerce, "Foreign investors are able to obtain credit in the local market at normal market terms, and a wide range of credit instruments is available."

BANKING AND FINANCE
Score: 1–Stable (very low level of restrictions)

The London Stock Exchange is one of the world's largest exchanges. The UK has a well-developed, competitive system of universal banking in which banking institutions are permitted to sell securities and insurance products, as well as invest in industrial firms. The U.S. Department of Commerce reports that "London offers all forms of financial services—commercial banking, investment banking, insurance, venture capital, stock and currency brokers, fund managers, commodity dealers, accounting and legal services, as well as electronic clearing and settlement systems and bank payments systems. The UK banking sector is the third largest in the world after the U.S. and Japan, with nearly 700 banks authorized to do business in the UK." According to the Economist Intelligence Unit, "Nearly all major banks around the world have subsidiaries or branches in London authorised to take deposits. Several of these are bigger than the smallest of the top ten British banks.... Foreign banks compete for commercial business in the UK on the same terms as domestic banks." Credit is allocated on market terms.

WAGES AND PRICES
Score: 2–Stable (low level of intervention)

The market sets most prices in the United Kingdom. According to the Economist Intelligence Unit, "The government, either directly or through regulatory agencies, has permanent price-control powers over matches, milk, most public utilities and London taxi fares...." The government also affects agricultural prices through the UK's participation in the Common Agricultural Policy, a program that heavily subsidizes agricultural goods. The United Kingdom has a minimum wage.

PROPERTY RIGHTS
Score: 1–Stable (very high level of protection)

Property rights in the United Kingdom are well secured. The Economist Intelligence Unit reports that "contractual agreements are generally secure in the UK. There is no discrimination against foreign companies in court. The judiciary is of high quality when dealing with commercial cases." In March 2005, Parliament approved a bill to establish a Supreme Court.

REGULATION
Score: 2–Stable (low level)

It is still easier to open a business in the United Kingdom than in other parts of Europe, but the regulatory environment is rapidly worsening. According to *The Economist*, "British business is being buried by a pile of new regulations. Some—such as the working-time directive—come from Brussels.... This supposedly business-friendly government increasingly uses companies as unpaid state employees. Through their payrolls, they now have to do 23 jobs for the government, from doling out maternity pay and tax credits to collecting fines and student loan repayments. When Labour came to power, the number was 15." Some companies spend up to 75 percent of their time dealing with the bureaucracy. Most of the complaints relate to health and safety regulations, environmental rules, and labor laws. These issues will be scrutinized and verified in the 2007 *Index*.

INFORMAL MARKET
Score: 1–Stable (very low level of activity)

Transparency International's 2004 score for the United Kingdom is 8.6. Therefore, the United Kingdom's informal market score is 1 this year.

> The United Kingdom qualifies for the Global Free Trade Alliance.

UNITED STATES

Rank: 9

Score: 1.84

Category: Free

Present & Past Scores

(Best) 1 — 2 — 2.04 1.99 1.93 1.94 1.94 1.89 1.78 1.89 1.86 1.85 1.90 1.84 — 3 — 4 — (Worst) 5

'95 '96 '97 '98 '99 '00 '01 '02 '03 '04 '05 '06

QUICK STUDY

SCORES

Trade Policy	2
Fiscal Burden	3.9
Government Intervention	2
Monetary Policy	1
Foreign Investment	2
Banking and Finance	1
Wages and Prices	2
Property Rights	1
Regulation	2
Informal Market	1.5

Population: 296,667,612

Total area: 9,629,091 sq. km

GDP: $10.7 trillion

GDP growth rate: 4.4%

GDP per capita: $36,067

Major exports: industrial supplies, consumer goods, automotive goods, telecommunication equipment, financial and insurance services, computer and information services

Exports of goods and services: $1.06 trillion

Major export trading partners: Canada 23.2%, Mexico 13.5%, Japan 6.6%, UK 4.4%, China 4.2%, Germany 3.8%

Major imports: crude oil, refined petroleum products, automobiles, consumer goods, financial and insurance services

Imports of goods and services: $1.63 trillion

Major import trading partners: Canada 17.4%, China 13.4%, Mexico 10.6%, Japan 8.8%

Foreign direct investment (net): –$134 billion

2004 Data (in constant 2000 US dollars)

Historically, the U.S. Constitution has provided strong protections for private property and economic liberties. Since World War II, the United States has generally taken a strong leadership position in expanding global trade through lower tariff barriers. Subsequent moves to deregulate, cut tax rates, follow stable monetary policy, and protect intellectual property rights have engendered strong growth. Regrettably, some recent trends have raised questions about such traditions. The U.S. Supreme Court's June 23, 2005, *Kelo v. City of New London* ruling on eminent domain exposes many Americans' property to arbitrary seizure; and while countries in Eastern Europe are adopting flat taxes, deregulating, and privatizing, the U.S. may be drifting toward bigger government. The U.S. has continued a leadership role in free trade with eight ratified free trade agreements, another signed agreement, and ongoing negotiations with other countries. However, continued use of the "anti-dumping" Byrd Amendment, combined with anti-China rhetoric, indicates an ongoing protectionist mindset. Moreover, legislated government spending under such laws as the massive farm subsidies of 2002, the massive Medicare prescription entitlement of 2003, and the massive transportation bill of 2005 has expanded without constraints, and Sarbanes–Oxley and other regulatory laws have raised compliance costs. The United States' trade policy score is 0.5 point better this year, and its fiscal burden of government score is 0.1 point better. As a result, the United States' overall score is 0.06 point better this year.

TRADE POLICY
Score: **2**–Better (low level of protectionism)

The World Bank reports that the United States' weighted average tariff rate in 2004 was 1.8 percent, down from the 2.6 percent for 2002 reported in the 2005 *Index*, based on World Bank data. According to the Economist Intelligence Unit, the government imposes non-tariff barriers, including quotas, tariff rate import quotas, anti-dumping provisions, countervailing duties, and licensing requirements, on a number of goods. Based on the lower tariff rate, as well as a revision of the trade factor methodology, the United States' trade policy score is 0.5 point better this year.

FISCAL BURDEN OF GOVERNMENT
Score—Income Taxation: **3.5**–Stable (high tax rates)
Score—Corporate Taxation: **4.5**–Stable (very high tax rates)
Score—Change in Government Expenditures: **3**–Better (very low decrease)
Final Score: **3.9**–Better (high cost of government)

According to Deloitte, the United States' top federal income tax rate is 35 percent. The top corporate tax rate is also 35 percent. In 2004, government expenditures as a share of GDP decreased 0.5 percentage point to 36 percent, compared to a 0.2 percentage point increase in 2003. On net, the United States' fiscal burden of government score is 0.1 point better this year.

GOVERNMENT INTERVENTION IN THE ECONOMY
Score: **2**–Stable (low level)

Based on data from the *Economic Report of the President*, the government consumed 15.4 percent of GDP in 2004. In 2003, based on data from the International Monetary Fund's Government

Financial Statistics CD–ROM, the United States received 3.03 percent of its total revenues from state-owned enterprises and government ownership of property.

MONETARY POLICY
Score: 1–Stable (very low level of inflation)

From 1995 to 2004, the United States' weighted average annual rate of inflation was 2.50 percent.

CAPITAL FLOWS AND FOREIGN INVESTMENT
Score: 2–Stable (low barriers)

The United States welcomes foreign investment. Foreign and domestic enterprises are treated equally under the law, and foreign investors are not required to register with or seek approval from the federal government. According to the Economist Intelligence Unit, however, "Foreign investments face restrictions in banking, mining, defence contracting, certain energy-related industries, fishing, shipping, communications and aviation." The government also restricts foreign acquisitions that threaten to impair national security. The U.S. imposes a general embargo against Cuba, Burma, Iran, and Sudan and limited sanctions against Iraq, Libya, North Korea, and Syria. The U.S. also has sanctions targeting specific individuals in the Balkans, the Taliban, Liberia, and Zimbabwe and those involved in terrorism and drug trafficking. There are no controls or requirements on current transfers, access to foreign exchange, or repatriation of profits. Purchase of real estate is unrestricted on a national level, although purchase of agricultural land by foreign nationals or companies with at least 10 percent foreign ownership must be reported to the U.S. Department of Agriculture. Some states impose restrictions on purchases of land and other types of investments by foreign companies.

BANKING AND FINANCE
Score: 1–Stable (very low level of restrictions)

According to the Economist Intelligence Unit, "The United States has the most dynamic and developed financial markets in the world…. A large network of national and regional banks…provides companies with capital and a broad array of financial services. Large multi-purpose money-centre banks with international reach manage corporate needs both at home and abroad. Legislation breaking down previously existing barriers between commercial banks, insurance companies and securities firms should spur cross-industry tie-ups…. Foreign financial institutions face few restrictions, and the largest among them are increasingly visible in the US marketplace. The US economy is very open and liberal, and offers a favourable operating environment." Federal and state governments share regulatory responsibility for banks. Reform in 1999 eliminated barriers to entry into U.S. financial markets and removed prohibitions against the purchase of banks by insurance and securities companies. However, concerns have been raised about the costs associated with complying with Sar-

banes–Oxley regulations. This has facilitated both the creation of universal financial services companies and the competitiveness of U.S. banking, as well as further consolidation of the financial services industry, enabling U.S. firms to compete more effectively in global markets. Two government sponsored enterprises—the Federal National Mortgage Association (Fannie Mae) and Federal Home Mortgage Loan Corporation (Freddie Mac)—account for almost half of the $8 trillion outstanding on U.S. home mortgages. While both enterprises are shareholder-owned and listed on the stock market, they enjoy privileged treatment under congressional mandates. The overall trend in financial services is toward more competition and continued product innovation. From 1993 to 2003, the number of banking institutions fell by 29 percent to about 9,000, notes the EIU, which also reports that there were 276 banking mergers in 2003 and 180 in the first eight months of 2004.

WAGES AND PRICES
Score: 2–Stable (low level of intervention)

The market sets most wages and prices. According to the Economist Intelligence Unit, "Price controls apply to some regulated monopolies in the United States (like utilities and the postal service), and certain states and localities control residential rents." Hawaii imposes caps on gasoline prices. The government also influences prices through subsidies, particularly for the agricultural sector, dairy products, and some forms of transportation. The federal government imposes a minimum wage.

PROPERTY RIGHTS
Score: 1–Stable (very high level of protection)

The United States still does very well in most measures of property rights protection, including an honest and independent judiciary, a sound commercial code and other laws for the resolution of contract and property disputes between private parties, and the recognition of foreign arbitration and court rulings. However, the concerns outlined in recent years have worsened. Uncompensated government expropriations of property remain highly unlikely, but it is likely that local governments' abuse of eminent domain power with the seizure of private land (with some compensation) and its transfer to another party for a non-public or quasi-public use will accelerate with the U.S. Supreme Court's June 2005 *Kelo v. City of New London* ruling. By ruling that governments may take even non-blighted property and transfer it to another owner for the purpose of increasing the tax base, the Court's *Kelo* decision seriously undermines, or effectively eliminates, the U.S. Constitution's requirement that private property may be taken only for a "public use." Unless the decision is reversed or countered with legislative protections that stop the abuse of eminent domain, the practice will be difficult to isolate, and evidence of extensive use of this decision could be grounds for downgrading this factor in future editions of the *Index*. An even more serious problem is that governments at all levels impose numerous regulatory and land-use controls that diminish the value and enjoyment of private property. Examples include extensive "growth controls"; unreasonable zoning hurdles; facility permitting regimes; and far-reaching environmental, wetlands, and habitat restrictions on the use and development of real estate. Thus, the protections for private property are undermined by a vast bureaucracy that has the power to interfere substantially with many property rights. The level of protection for property in the United States will depend eventually on whether the courts and legislative bodies place clear limits on bureaucratic power or require cost-effective remedies for property owners whose rights have been affected. The Supreme Court's performance in such government "takings" cases has been decidedly mixed in recent years, and 2005 was worse than usual. Besides *Kelo*, two rent control decisions denying the recovery of any compensation further burden the owners of private property. Although the climate for judicial and legislative reform is improving, that is largely a reaction to these decisions, which are increasingly less favorable to property rights protections.

 ## REGULATION
Score: **2**–Stable (low level)

It is easy to establish a business. "Through a fairly simple procedure," reports the Economist Intelligence Unit, a firm "can then set up offices, plants or other permanent establishments under the corporation laws of other states.... Firms may choose a location on the basis of which state's laws offer greater flexibility." The U.S. labor market is one of the world's most flexible. Regulations are applied evenly and consistently. However, many regulations—for example, the Americans with Disabilities Act, various civil rights regulations, environmental laws, health and product safety standards, food and drug labeling requirements, and Sarbanes–Oxley—although well-intentioned, can be onerous. In February 2005, the government approved the Class Action Fairness Act, a bill aimed at reducing the costs that businesses face from class-action lawsuits. Electronic commerce is minimally regulated. Corruption in the bureaucracy is rare.

 ## INFORMAL MARKET
Score: **1.5**–Stable (low level of activity)

Transparency International's 2004 score for the United States is 7.5. Therefore, the United States' informal market score is 1.5 this year.

The United States qualifies for the Global Free Trade Alliance.

URUGUAY

Rank: 46

Score: 2.69

Category: Mostly Free

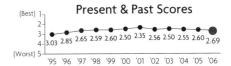

Present & Past Scores

(Best) 1-
2-
3-
4- 3.03 2.85 2.65 2.59 2.60 2.50 2.35 2.56 2.50 2.55 2.60 2.69
(Worst) 5-

'95 '96 '97 '98 '99 '00 '01 '02 '03 '04 '05 '06

QUICK STUDY

SCORES

Trade Policy	2.5
Fiscal Burden	3.4
Government Intervention	2.5
Monetary Policy	3
Foreign Investment	2
Banking and Finance	4
Wages and Prices	2
Property Rights	2
Regulation	3
Informal Market	2.5

Population: 3,380,000

Total area: 176,220 sq. km

GDP: $17.7 billion

GDP growth rate: 2.5%

GDP per capita: $5,235

Major exports: meat, leather products, rice products, wool, dairy products

Exports of goods and services: $3.3 billion

Major export trading partners: Brazil 21.4%, US 11.4%, Argentina 7.1%, Germany 6.6%, Italy 4.0%

Major imports: machinery and equipment, oil, food and beverages, transport equipment

Imports of goods and services: $2.9 billion

Major import trading partners: Argentina 26.1%, Brazil 21.0%, Russia 11.7%, US 7.6%

Foreign direct investment (net): $245.2 million

2003 Data (in constant 2000 US dollars)

Despite a tradition of democracy and free enterprise, socialist dreams are part of Uruguay's history. In October 2004, Broad Front candidate Tabaré Vázquez made his third run for president and won what many Uruguayans called the "other side's turn" in office, ending 170 years of National and Colorado party dominance. Rather than make a hard lurch to the left, he named pragmatic accountant Danilo Astori as finance minister. Despite restoring diplomatic relations with Cuba, his government rebuffed Cuban efforts to join MERCOSUR. Argentina's 2001 debt default contributed to a run on banks and a 12 percent economic contraction in Uruguay. Aided by free-market policies championed by the previous administration, the government averted a crisis by increasing exports of beef and other commodities. In 2003, Uruguay's $17.7 billion economy grew by 2.5 percent, but estimates for 2004 indicated more vigorous growth. Despite a commitment to more orthodox economics, however, Vázquez presides over an economy in which state enterprises account for up to 25 percent of GDP, and hard-liners will demand more government intervention. He has already created a $100 million Social Emergency Plan to offer monthly subsidies to families affected by the 2001 recession. Uruguay's monetary policy score is 1 point better this year; however, its trade policy score is 0.5 point worse, its fiscal burden of government score is 0.4 point worse, and its banking and finance score is 1 point worse. As a result, Uruguay's overall score is 0.09 point worse this year.

TRADE POLICY
Score: **2.5**–Worse (moderate level of protectionism)

As a member of the Southern Cone Common Market (MERCOSUR), Uruguay adheres to a common external tariff that ranges from 0 percent to 25 percent. According to the World Bank, Uruguay's weighted average tariff rate in 2004 was 4.3 percent, down from the 6.5 percent for 2001 reported in the 2005 *Index*, based on World Bank data. According to the U.S. Department of Commerce, however, "Certain imports (e.g. firearms, radioactive materials, fertilizers, vegetable products and frozen embryos) require special licenses or customs documents. Bureaucratic delays may also add to the cost of imports." Based on increased evidence of non-tariff barriers, as well as a revision of the trade factor methodology, Uruguay's trade policy score is 0.5 point worse this year.

FISCAL BURDEN OF GOVERNMENT
Score—Income Taxation: **1**–Stable (very low tax rates)
Score—Corporate Taxation: **4**–Stable (high tax rates)
Score—Change in Government Expenditures: **4.5**–Worse (high increase)
Final Score: **3.4**–Worse (moderate cost of government)

According to Deloitte, Uruguay imposes no income tax. The top corporate tax rate is 30 percent. In 2003, based on data from the central bank, government expenditures as a share of GDP increased 2.2 percentage points to 42.5 percent, compared to the 1.5 percentage point increase in 2002. On net, Uruguay's fiscal burden of government score is 0.4 point worse this year.

GOVERNMENT INTERVENTION IN THE ECONOMY
Score: **2.5**–Stable (moderate level)

The World Bank reports that the government consumed 11.7 percent of GDP in 2003. In 2004, based on data from the Ministry of Economy and Finance, Uruguay received 6.59 percent of its

397

total revenues from state-owned enterprises and government ownership of property.

MONETARY POLICY
Score: 3–Better (moderate level of inflation)

From 1995 to 2004, Uruguay's weighted average annual rate of inflation was 11.75 percent, down from the 16.20 percent from 1994 to 2003 reported in the 2005 *Index*. As a result, Uruguay's monetary policy score is 1 point better this year.

CAPITAL FLOWS AND FOREIGN INVESTMENT
Score: 2–Stable (low barriers)

The Economist Intelligence Unit reports that "Uruguay places few restrictions on the activities of foreign investors outside of state-monopoly sectors and has traditionally met all its commitments to foreign investors. Moreover, it has never confiscated any foreign capital—a claim few Latin American countries can make…. There is no discrimination against foreign investors per se. A foreign-owned company may locate anywhere in the country and is treated like a national firm." State monopolies include electricity, hydrocarbons, railroads, some minerals, port administration, and telecommunications, although the government permits some of these monopolies to forge private partnerships. According to the International Monetary Fund, both residents and non-residents may hold foreign exchange accounts; there are no restrictions or controls on payments, transactions, transfers, or repatriation of profits; and non-residents may purchase real estate.

BANKING AND FINANCE
Score: 4–Worse (high level of restrictions)

Rapid withdrawal of non-resident deposits from Uruguay's banks in 2001, spurred by economic crises in Argentina and Brazil, led to the closing of four major banks. The assets of those banks were grouped into a new state-owned (but privately managed) bank—Nuevo Banco Comercial—in 2003. Uruguay has adopted financial and banking reforms, including a deposit insurance system. According to First Initiative, "the banking system is highly fragmented and dominated by the two state-owned banks. There are also 23 private banks, nine investment banks and six savings and loans co-operatives as of 2004…. The insurance sector…is heavily dominated by the state-owned Banco de Seguros del Estado (BSE)." The Economist Intelligence Unit reports that "Banco de la República Oriental del Uruguay (BROU), by far the country's largest bank, performs all sorts of commercial activities. It also provides certain soft loans, mostly for agriculture. Uruguayan Mortgage Bank (Banco Hipotecario del Uruguay—BHU), the second-largest bank in the country, provides financing for housing construction and purchasing for individuals only." The U.S. Department of Commerce

reports that the BROU accounted for 40 percent of all banking assets. Based on evidence of heavy government involvement, Uruguay's banking and finance score is 1 point worse this year.

WAGES AND PRICES
Score: 2–Stable (low level of intervention)

"Although Uruguay has eliminated most price controls," reports the Economist Intelligence Unit, "the executive branch continues to fix prices on certain basics, including milk, fuels, electricity, water supply and telephone services. It also adjusts the monthly fees of collective medical-care institutions…and the annual increase of housing and office rents." The government mandates a minimum wage.

PROPERTY RIGHTS
Score: 2–Stable (high level of protection)

Private property is generally secure, and expropriation is unlikely. According to the Economist Intelligence Unit, "Contractual arrangements are generally secure in Uruguay. Judiciary proceedings tend to be slow, but verdicts are usually based on sound legal grounds. However, the lack of a large staff of judges and prosecutors, well trained in financial matters, often jeopardises the protection and timely exercise of property rights. The country's maze of laws, decrees, regulations and ordinances lends itself to varying interpretations. Hence, appeal is the rule rather than the exception in Uruguay." As an alternative to civil suits, the government has established a Settlement and Arbitration Center to improve investment relations.

REGULATION
Score: 3–Stable (moderate level)

The process for establishing a business can be lengthy because of the number of applicable regulations. According to the U.S. Department of Commerce, although firms "have not encountered major obstacles in Uruguay's investment climate, some have been frustrated by the length of time it takes to complete bureaucratic procedures and by the numerous changes in rules or…taxes." The Economist Intelligence Unit reports that "employer–employee relations are governed by hundreds of regulations scattered among various laws and decrees…." Corruption has been investigated but is not considered a serious impediment to business.

INFORMAL MARKET
Score: 2.5–Stable (moderate level of activity)

Transparency International's 2004 score for Uruguay is 6.2. Therefore, Uruguay's informal market score is 2.5 this year.

UZBEKISTAN

Rank: 144

Score: 3.91

Category: Mostly Unfree

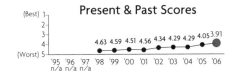

Present & Past Scores

(Best) 1 —
2 —
3 — 4.63 4.59 4.51 4.56 4.34 4.29 4.29 4.05 **3.91**
4 —
(Worst) 5 —

'95 '96 '97 '98 '99 '00 '01 '02 '03 '04 '05 '06
n/a n/a n/a

QUICK STUDY

SCORES

Trade Policy	3
Fiscal Burden	2.6
Government Intervention	3.5
Monetary Policy	4
Foreign Investment	4
Banking and Finance	5
Wages and Prices	4
Property Rights	4
Regulation	5
Informal Market	4

Population: 25,590,000

Total area: 447,400 sq. km

GDP: $15.6 billion

GDP growth rate: 2%

GDP per capita: $610

Major exports: cotton and agricultural products, machinery and equipment, chemicals, food, beverages, fuel and energy

Exports of goods and services: $3.3 billion

Major export trading partners: Russia 22.0%, China 9.2%, Ukraine 7.4%, Tajikistan 6.1%

Major imports: fuel and energy, machinery and equipment, chemicals

Imports of goods and services: $3.0 billion

Major import trading partners: Russia 22.3%, US 11.4%, South Korea 10.9%, Germany 9.5%

Foreign direct investment (net): $66 million

2003 Data (in constant 2000 US dollars)

Uzbekistan's support for the U.S. in the war on terrorism has included permission to open a military base in Karshi Khanabad. However, on July 31, 2005, following U.S. denunciations of indiscriminate shootings of protestors by government troops in the city of Andijan on May 13, the government of President Islam Karimov notified the U.S. that it must leave the base within six months. The Karimov government routinely violates basic human rights and has an estimated 6,500 political and religious prisoners in custody. Growth in the membership of radical and Islamist terrorist organizations has led to an increasing number of terrorist attacks, which are likely to spur more forceful crackdowns. In 2005, following mass demonstrations in neighboring Kyrgyzstan that toppled the Kyrgyz government, political unrest was reported in Uzbekistan's Jizzakh Province and Ferghana Valley. Parliamentary elections in December 2004 and January 2005 replaced the unicameral parliament with a bicameral one. However, it comprised only pro-government parties, deliberately banning and excluding opposition democratic parties from running. Despite ample reserves of gold, natural gas, oil, coal, silver, and copper, Uzbekistan remains largely underdeveloped. The government's budget lacks transparency. Uzbekistan's trade policy score is 0.5 point worse this year; however, its fiscal burden of government score is 0.4 point better, its government intervention score is 0.5 point better, and its monetary policy score is 1 point better. As a result, its overall score is 0.14 point better this year, causing Uzbekistan to be classified as a "mostly unfree" country.

TRADE POLICY
Score: **3**–Worse (moderate level of protectionism)

The World Bank reports that Uzbekistan's weighted average tariff rate in 2001 (the most recent year for which World Bank data are available) was 5.9 percent. (The World Bank has revised the figure for 2001 upward from the 4.2 percent reported in the 2005 *Index*.) According to the U.S. Department of Commerce, "Since 1996, the Government has severely suppressed imports…. Customs clearance is a tedious and capricious bureaucratic process." Based on the higher tariff rate, as well as a revision of the trade factor methodology, Uzbekistan's trade policy score is 0.5 point worse this year.

FISCAL BURDEN OF GOVERNMENT
Score—Income Taxation: **3**–Stable (moderate tax rates)
Score—Corporate Taxation: **1.5**–Better (low tax rates)
Score—Change in Government Expenditures: **4.5**–Better (high increase)
Final Score: **2.6**–Better (moderate cost of government)

Uzbekistan's top income tax rate is 30 percent. According to the Economist Intelligence Unit, as of the beginning of 2005, the top corporate tax rate was cut to 15 percent from the 20 percent reported in the 2005 *Index*. In 2003, according to the European Bank for Reconstruction and Development, government expenditures as a share of GDP increased 2.7 percentage points to 39.9 percent, compared to the 1.2 percentage point increase in 2002. On net, Uzbekistan's fiscal burden of government score is 0.4 point better this year.

GOVERNMENT INTERVENTION IN THE ECONOMY
Score: **3.5**–Better (high level)

The World Bank reports that the government consumed 18.8 percent of GDP in 2003. In

399

2004, based on data from the Ministry of Finance, Uzbekistan received 28.61 percent of its total revenues from state-owned enterprises and government ownership of property. Based on newly available data for revenues from state-owned enterprises, Uzbekistan's government intervention score is 0.5 point better this year.

 MONETARY POLICY
Score: **4**–Better (high level of inflation)

From 1995 to 2004, based on data from the International Monetary Fund's *2005 World Economic Outlook*, Uzbekistan's weighted average annual rate of inflation was 15.16 percent, down from the 26.20 percent from 1994 to 2003 reported in the 2005 *Index*. As a result, Uzbekistan's monetary policy score is 1 point better this year.

 CAPITAL FLOWS AND FOREIGN INVESTMENT
Score: **4**–Stable (high barriers)

Officially, all sectors of the economy are open to foreign investment except industries the government deems "strategic" (mining, agriculture, and machinery manufacturing). In practice, however, investors face numerous unofficial barriers. "Direct foreign investors are granted a host of incentives on a case-by-case basis, including tax holidays, duty-free capital goods imports, and protection against expropriation," reports the U.S. Department of Commerce. "However, legislative requirements for these benefits are ambiguous, processes and procedures are cumbersome, and the regulatory environment is capricious.... [T]he Government has been known to expropriate property of joint ventures (with foreign investment partners) at lower than fair market value." The International Monetary Fund reports that residents and non-residents may hold foreign exchange accounts subject to some restrictions. Payments and transfers face quantitative limits and bona fide tests. Some capital transactions, including credit operations and real estate transactions, are subject to controls. According to the U.S. Department of Commerce, "Several major incidents of bribe solicitation have been reported.... [C]orruption [has been cited] as an obstacle to foreign direct investment in Uzbekistan."

 BANKING AND FINANCE
Score: **5**–Stable (very high level of restrictions)

First Initiative reports that Uzbekistan's "government exercises severe control over most of the financial sector, which is comprised primarily of banks. The banking sector consists of 35 banks but is dominated by the six largest banks, all of which are state-owned or state-controlled and hold 95% of total sector assets (2003). The largest state-owned bank is the National Bank for Foreign Economic Activity (NB). Banks have the power to confiscate savings, freeze accounts and channel funds to government-favored enterprises based on bureaucratic decisions.... The insurance industry...is at a nascent stage, with four state insurance companies and 27 other registered companies (2002)." According to the U.S. Department of Commerce, "the banking system remains the primary conduit for the [government's]

directed credits to state-owned enterprises at negative real interest rates. The large portfolio of such credits poses a serious threat to the soundness of the banking system given the financial distress and non-profitability of most of these enterprises." Deposits are extremely low, "thanks to years of negative real interest rates, a weak exchange rate and occasional confiscations of savings," reports the Economist Intelligence Unit, and the government has closed "the only viable private bank."

 WAGES AND PRICES
Score: **4**–Stable (high level of intervention)

According to the U.S. Department of State, "Historical domestic subsidies and price controls for utilities and food products have created market distortions.... Price controls are exercised primarily by declaring companies or certain products national or regional monopolies, which automatically requires review and approval of prices for such products by the Ministry of Finance. Currently, prices of over 300 monopoly products are being regulated." The government also subsidizes agricultural inputs and determines the price of the 50 percent of crops that it buys.

 PROPERTY RIGHTS
Score: **4**–Stable (low level of protection)

According to the Economist Intelligence Unit, "The judiciary is subordinate to the government, since it is appointed by the executive. Judicial procedures fall a long way short of international standards and corruption is widespread." The U.S. Department of Commerce reports that the government "has also been known to frequently take property from local businesses and individuals with inadequate compensation. Agricultural enterprises are particularly vulnerable to expropriation of land."

 REGULATION
Score: **5**–Stable (very high level)

The process for establishing a business is highly burdensome. "Ambiguous rules, legislation, and Presidential decrees often contradict each other," reports the U.S. Department of Commerce. "Sudden legislative and regulatory changes are common; many decrees have secret provisions.... Business people in Uzbekistan note that if they are engaged in a sector in which either the GOU [Government of Uzbekistan], or a GOU-controlled firm is a competitor, they face more than the usual amount of bureaucratic hurdles." According to the Economist Intelligence Unit, "Corruption is a serious and all-pervasive problem...that weakens the effectiveness of the state and creates considerable popular discontent. The political elite dominates business."

 INFORMAL MARKET
Score: **4**–Stable (high level of activity)

Transparency International's 2004 score for Uzbekistan is 2.3. Therefore, Uzbekistan's informal market score is 4 this year.

VENEZUELA

Rank: 152

Score: 4.16

Category: Repressed

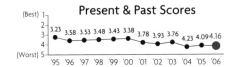

Present & Past Scores

(Best) 1
2
3
4
(Worst) 5

3.23 3.58 3.53 3.48 3.43 3.38 3.78 3.93 3.76 4.23 4.09 4.16

'95 '96 '97 '98 '99 '00 '01 '02 '03 '04 '05 '06

QUICK STUDY

SCORES

Trade Policy	4
Fiscal Burden	4.1
Government Intervention	3.5
Monetary Policy	5
Foreign Investment	5
Banking and Finance	4
Wages and Prices	4
Property Rights	4
Regulation	4
Informal Market	4

Population: 25,674,000

Total area: 912,050 sq. km

GDP: $102.9 billion

GDP growth rate: −9.4%

GDP per capita: $4,009

Major exports: petroleum, chemicals, basic manufactures

Exports of goods and services: $27.7 billion

Major export trading partners: US 52.7%, Colombia 3.2%, Brazil 3.1%, Germany 2.5%

Major imports: transport equipment, machinery, construction materials

Imports of goods and services: $12.9 billion

Major import trading partners: US 29.2%, Colombia 7.1%, Brazil 6.2%, Mexico 4.3%

Foreign direct investment (net): $1.3 billion

2003 Data (in constant 2000 US dollars)

I n the wake of a failed—and hotly contested—2004 recall attempt, Venezuelan President Hugo Chávez Frías has clamped down on civil liberties, property rights, and Western foreign oil companies that are still operating in this impoverished South American country. He has decreed new laws that define public protest as a crime, has imposed media restrictions that encourage substantial self-censorship under threat of operating license confiscation, and has begun to seize large rural farms and ranches that he claims are not sufficiently productive. Energy and Petroleum Minister Rafael Ramírez announced in May 2005 that income taxes on the handful of foreign firms pumping oil in Venezuela would be raised to 50 percent from 34 percent, retroactive to 2001. Energy experts reportedly believe that Venezuela is shipping less oil than it claims as a result of lagging maintenance at the state-owned Petróleos de Venezuela S.A., the internal resources of which allegedly have been sapped by corruption, mismanagement, and the diversion of profits to social programs and government officials. To the alarm of neighbors and internal opponents, the government has announced the purchase of 100,000 assault rifles, a number of Russian combat helicopters, and possibly MiG-29 jet fighters, as well as a reserve-force buildup to some 1.5 million cadres. Venezuela's fiscal burden of government is 0.7 point worse this year. As a result, its overall score is 0.07 point worse this year.

 TRADE POLICY
Score: **4**–Stable (high level of protectionism)

The World Bank reports that Venezuela's weighted average tariff rate in 2004 was 11 percent, down from the 11.3 percent for 2000 reported in the 2005 *Index*. According to the U.S. Trade Representative, "exchange controls have put a significant constraint on imports"; the government applies sanitary and phytosanitary standards to constrain imports; imports of used cars, buses, trucks, tires, and clothing are banned; and some goods can be imported only by government agencies. Based on the revised trade factor methodology, Venezuela's trade policy score is unchanged.

 FISCAL BURDEN OF GOVERNMENT
Score—Income Taxation: **3**–Stable (moderate tax rates)
Score—Corporate Taxation: **4.5**–Stable (very high tax rates)
Score—Change in Government Expenditures: **4.5**–Worse (high increase)
Final Score: **4.1**–Worse (high cost of government)

Venezuela's top income tax rate is 34 percent. The top corporate tax rate is also 34 percent. In 2003, according to the Economist Intelligence Unit, government expenditures as a share of GDP increased by 2.1 percentage points to 27.8 percent, compared to the 0.6 percentage point increase in 2002. On net, Venezuela's fiscal burden of government score is 0.7 point worse this year.

 GOVERNMENT INTERVENTION IN THE ECONOMY
Score: **3.5**–Stable (high level)

The World Bank reports that the government consumed 7.5 percent of GDP in 2003. In the same year, according to the International Monetary Fund's Government Financial Statistics CD–ROM, Venezuela received 49.36 percent of its total revenues from state-owned enterprises and government ownership of property.

MONETARY POLICY
Score: **5**–Stable (very high level of inflation)

From 1995 to 2004, Venezuela's weighted average annual rate of inflation was 23.69 percent.

CAPITAL FLOWS AND FOREIGN INVESTMENT
Score: **5**–Stable (very high barriers)

The political and economic changes that have marked the Chávez administration generate uncertainty among prospective investors. New investments must be registered with the government. The U.S. Trade Representative reports that the government "maintains restrictions on a number of service sectors…requires that certain professions be licensed in Venezuela (e.g., engineers, architects, economists, business consultants, accountants, lawyers, doctors, veterinarians and journalists)…[and]…limits foreign equity participation (except from other Andean Community countries) to 20 percent in enterprises engaged in television broadcasting, radio broadcasting and Spanish language newspapers…. [I]n any enterprise with more than 10 workers, foreign employees are restricted to 10 percent of the work force, and Venezuelan law limits foreign employee salaries to 20 percent of the payroll…. The government continues to control key sectors of the economy, including oil, petrochemicals and much of the mining and aluminum industries." The government has recently seized land, including that owned by foreign investors, citing irregularities in their ownership status and claiming that they were not being used productively enough. It has also ordered privately managed oil fields to become joint ventures with the state-owned oil company. According to the U.S. Department of Commerce, "Venezuela remains subject to comprehensive foreign exchange controls and a fixed exchange rate. Special regulations ('providencias') exist for a range of transactions including for foreign investment, remittances, foreign private debt, imports, exports, insurance and reinsurance, and the airline industry."

BANKING AND FINANCE
Score: **4**–Stable (high level of restrictions)

Banking has undergone substantial change since the financial crisis of the mid-1990s, experiencing greater foreign participation and consolidation. According to First Initiative, "The banking sector is the most substantial part of Venezuela's financial system, consisting of 50 commercial banks, with foreign banks controlling about half of the banking sector's assets (2003). It is highly consolidated, with 60% of deposits held by the six largest banks in the country…. [T]he insurance sector [also] has seen increased levels of foreign participation and consolidation, with the top 20 companies holding approximately 95% of all premiums in 2003." The government permits 100 percent foreign ownership in banking and financial services. The U.S. Department of Commerce reports that there were seven state-owned banks as of May 2004. According to the Economist Intelligence Unit, government borrowing accounts for half of all lending, and "the government continues to exercise increasing control over the allocation of credit.

This was most recently evidenced by the implementation of the mortgage law in early 2005, which sets below-market rates on low-income housing loans and sets a minimum percentage of the overall loan portfolio that must be directed to mortgage lending." The U.S. Department of Commerce reports that "the current economic crisis, foreign exchange controls, and heavy government debt burden with [banks] may limit their ability to lend to prospective investors and project developers."

WAGES AND PRICES
Score: **4**–Stable (high level of intervention)

The government has the authority to control most prices. "Shortly after foreign-exchange controls were introduced in February 2003," reports the Economist Intelligence Unit, "the government established maximum prices for some 169 basic goods and services, of which 106 were food products and the rest cleaning and personal-hygiene products. Officials have been emphatic in their insistence that price controls on these basic items will not be lifted. The prices of the inputs for manufacturing these goods were frozen soon after. In addition, telephone rates, school and health-service fees, public-transport fares, rubbish-collection charges and funeral-service costs were frozen indefinitely." Venezuela maintains a minimum wage.

PROPERTY RIGHTS
Score: **4**–Stable (low level of protection)

According to the Economist Intelligence Unit, "The overall quality of the judiciary remains poor, and corruption is a serious problem…. [T]he government still appears prone to back away from inconvenient contractual agreements on populist grounds or to seek more favorable terms, particularly in the oil sector." In addition, the "Supreme Court Law [allows] the government to add up to 12 new judges to the Supreme Court and to sack existing magistrates by a simple majority vote in the National Assembly. These powers grant the government effective control over the entire judicial system, thus worsening a situation already marked by corruption and arbitrary rulings."

REGULATION
Score: **4**–Stable (high level)

According to the Economist Intelligence Unit, "investors complain that regulators are often poorly equipped, trained and staffed and that decisions are based on political rather than technical criteria." The U.S. Department of Commerce reports that "Venezuelan laws are complicated, even more so since many activities are regulated, not only by laws, but also by presidential decrees or specific regulations. The bureaucracy and paperwork are often complicated." Labor laws are burdensome, and bureaucratic corruption is extensive.

INFORMAL MARKET
Score: **4**–Stable (high level of activity)

Transparency International's 2004 score for Venezuela is 2.3. Therefore, Venezuela's informal market score is 4 this year.

VIETNAM

Rank: 142

Score: 3.89

Category: Mostly Unfree

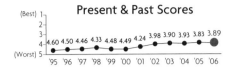

Present & Past Scores

(Best) 1
2
3
4
(Worst) 5

4.60 4.50 4.46 4.33 4.48 4.49 4.24 3.98 3.90 3.93 3.83 **3.89**

'95 '96 '97 '98 '99 '00 '01 '02 '03 '04 '05 '06

QUICK STUDY

SCORES

Trade Policy	4.5
Fiscal Burden	3.9
Government Intervention	3.5
Monetary Policy	2
Foreign Investment	4
Banking and Finance	4
Wages and Prices	3
Property Rights	5
Regulation	5
Informal Market	4

Population: 81,314,000

Total area: 329,560 sq. km

GDP: $38.3 billion

GDP growth rate: 7.2%

GDP per capita: $470

Major exports: crude oil, fisheries products, textiles and garments, rice, coffee, tea, footwear

Exports of goods and services: $23.9 billion

Major export trading partners: US 21.8%, Japan 13.7%, Australia 7.2%, China 6.5%

Major imports: refined petroleum, steel, cloth, computer and electronic goods

Imports of goods and services: $28.6 billion

Major import trading partners: China 13.6%, Taiwan 11.4%, Japan 11.2%, South Korea 11.0%, Singapore 10.3%

Foreign direct investment (net): $1.4 billion

2003 Data (in constant 2000 US dollars)

The Communist Party of Vietnam continues to balance one-party political rule with economic decentralization. Graft remains rampant, but government officials have been increasingly vigilant in investigating bribery and corruption cases to maintain legitimacy. Vietnam's human rights record remains poor, and the rule of law needs to be strengthened. Because of the judicial system's lack of transparency, arbitration is becoming more popular among local and foreign firms. The 11th Plenum of the Central Committee, held in January 2005, continued to affirm Vietnam's "socialist-oriented market economy" on its path to join the World Trade Organization (WTO). As of June 2005, Vietnam had reached bilateral agreements with Japan and South Korea concerning trade deregulation of industrial goods. Although Vietnam had concluded negotiations with European Union and Latin American countries, it still needed to reach agreement with the United States, China, Canada, and Australia—among other countries—before joining the WTO. The government continues to experiment with different forms of private ownership and equitization schemes with its state-owned enterprises. It also is pushing forward enterprise laws that would subject state and private firms to uniform regulation in an effort to attract foreign investment and meet conditions for accession to the WTO. Vietnam's trade policy score is 0.5 point better this year; however, its fiscal burden of government score is 0.1 point worse, and its monetary policy score is 1 point worse. As a result, Vietnam's overall score is 0.06 point worse this year.

TRADE POLICY
Score: **4.5**–Better (very high level of protectionism)

According to the World Bank, Vietnam's weighted average tariff rate in 2004 was 13.7 percent, down from the 17.4 percent for 2001 reported in the 2005 *Index,* based on World Bank data. The U.S. Trade Representative reports that "Vietnam has made significant progress in reducing the use of [non-tariff barriers]" but continues to prohibit numerous goods and apply quantitative restrictions and licensing requirements to others. Based on the lower tariff rate, as well as a revision of the trade factor methodology, Vietnam's trade policy score is 0.5 point better this year.

FISCAL BURDEN OF GOVERNMENT
Score—Income Taxation: **4**–Stable (high tax rates)
Score—Corporate Taxation: **3.5**–Stable (high tax rates)
Score—Change in Government Expenditures: **4.5**–Worse (high increase)
Final Score: **3.9**–Worse (high cost of government)

Vietnam's top income tax rate is 40 percent. The top corporate tax rate is 28 percent. In 2003, according to the Asian Development Bank, government expenditures as a share of GDP increased 2.6 percentage points to 29 percent, compared to a 2 percentage point increase in 2002. On net, Vietnam's fiscal burden of government score is 0.1 point worse this year.

GOVERNMENT INTERVENTION IN THE ECONOMY
Score: **3.5**–Stable (high level)

The World Bank reports that the government consumed 6.9 percent of GDP in 2003. In the same year, based on data from the International Monetary Fund, Vietnam received 12.12 percent of its total revenues from state-owned enterprises and government ownership of property. According to the Economist Intelligence Unit, however, Vietnam has over 5,000 state-owned enterprises, and the "state-owned sector generates 41% of industrial output...." The state is involved in finance, telecommunications, energy, and manufacturing. Based on the apparent unreliability of the figure for government consumption, 1 point has been added to Vietnam's government intervention score.

MONETARY POLICY
Score: 2–Worse (low level of inflation)

From 1995 to 2004, Vietnam's weighted average annual rate of inflation was 5.98 percent, up from the 2.96 percent from 1994 to 2003 reported in the 2005 *Index*. As a result, Vietnam's monetary policy score is 1 point worse this year.

CAPITAL FLOWS AND FOREIGN INVESTMENT
Score: 4–Stable (high barriers)

"Despite two decades of market reforms," reports the Economist Intelligence Unit, "Vietnam remains a difficult business environment. Relative political and economic stability must be weighed against poor physical infrastructure, government red tape and corruption, unevenness of skills and other obstacles to foreign investment." According to the U.S. Trade Representative, "the ...extensive investment licensing process...is characterized by stringent and time-consuming requirements that are frequently used to protect domestic interests, limit competition, and allocate foreign investment rights among various countries.... [A]ll enterprises operating in Vietnam [are limited] to employing foreign nationals at the lesser of: (1) a maximum rate of 3 percent of their total work force; or (2) 50 persons." The International Monetary Fund reports that both residents and non-residents may hold foreign exchange accounts, subject to restrictions and government approval for resident accounts held abroad. Payments and transfers face restrictions, including requirements for government approval over established amounts. Most transactions in money market and capital instruments, derivatives, commercial credits, and direct investments either are prohibited or require government approval. Foreigners may not own land but can lease it from the government.

BANKING AND FINANCE
Score: 4–Stable (high level of restrictions)

According to the Economist Intelligence Unit, "As of March 2005, there were five state-run commercial banks, 38 joint stock commercial banks, four joint-venture banks, 29 foreign bank branches and 46 foreign bank representative offices.... Vietnam's 'big four' state commercial banks are the Vietnam Bank for Agriculture and Rural Development (BARD), Vietcombank (VCB), Incombank (ICB) and the Bank for Investment and Development of Vietnam (BIDV).... [These four banks] plus the Bank for Housing Development of Cuu Long River Delta together accounted for nearly 75% of the financial system's total assets." The same source reports that "Vietnam has allowed 100%-foreign-owned banks since October 1st 2004." The government still affects the allocation of credit. "[State bank] lending practices frequently favour state-owned

firms over private companies," reports the EIU. "Bank lending is still treated in some ways as an arm of government policy, with banks directed to offer preferential interest rates and debt relief to farmers, and still often enjoying a cosy relationship with large state-owned enterprises." According to First Initiative, "Foreign competitors have spurred local firms, particularly the state-owned market leader, which controls close to half of the insurance market, to become more competitive."

WAGES AND PRICES
Score: 3–Stable (moderate level of intervention)

The government controls prices to stem inflation. "The government continues to set rates for electricity, telecommunications, petrol, water, and fares for train and air travel," reports the Economist Intelligence Unit. "In most of these areas, the rates have traditionally been higher for foreigners, although harmonization is underway." In addition, "The government made significant adjustments to price controls in the telecoms sector effective January 6th 2003.... In March 2005, the government began to implement procedures to limit the price of pharmaceuticals." Vietnam has a minimum wage.

PROPERTY RIGHTS
Score: 5–Stable (very low level of protection)

"Interference in the legal process and the bribing of judges to serve particular interests is common," reports the Economist Intelligence Unit. "Contractual arrangements are backed by the force of law but the legal system is complicated. Contractual disputes often involve a prolonged period of negotiation preceding any attempt to resolve the matter in court." Moreover, "Because of the lack of faith in the Vietnamese legal system, many foreign investors include clauses in their contracts allowing disputes to be dealt with by the Singapore Court of Arbitration." *The Economist* reports that the state owns all the land and grants land-use rights to farmers, businesses, and homeowners.

REGULATION
Score: 5–Stable (very high level)

The U.S. Department of Commerce reports that "The evolving nature of regulatory regimes and commercial law, combined with overlapping jurisdiction among government ministries, often result in a lack of transparency, uniformity and consistency in government policies and decisions on commercial projects. Many firms operating in Vietnam, foreign and domestic, find corruption to be a major source of difficulty." According to *The Economist*, the government "passed a law in 2000 making it easier to set [small businesses] up." However, medium-size businesses find it hard to grow because they "cannot readily get access to land or capital."

INFORMAL MARKET
Score: 4–Stable (high level of activity)

Transparency International's 2004 score for Vietnam is 2.6. Therefore, Vietnam's informal market score is 4 this year.

YEMEN

Rank: 139
Score: 3.84
Category: Mostly Unfree

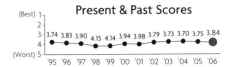

Present & Past Scores

(Best) 1
2
3 3.74 3.83 3.90 4.15 4.14 3.94 3.98 3.79 3.73 3.70 3.75 3.84
4
(Worst) 5
'95 '96 '97 '98 '99 '00 '01 '02 '03 '04 '05 '06

QUICK STUDY

SCORES

Trade Policy	4
Fiscal Burden	4.4
Government Intervention	4
Monetary Policy	4
Foreign Investment	3
Banking and Finance	4
Wages and Prices	3
Property Rights	4
Regulation	4
Informal Market	4

Population: 19,173,000

Total area: 527,970 sq. km

GDP: $10.6 billion

GDP growth rate: 3.8%

GDP per capita: $553

Major exports: minerals, crude oil, food and livestock, machines and transport equipment

Exports of goods and services: $3.3 billion

Major export trading partners: China 37.2%, Thailand 23.8%, South Korea 5.7%, Malaysia 5.1%

Major imports: food and livestock, machinery and transport equipment, chemicals, minerals, fuels and lubricants

Imports of goods and services: $3.9 billion

Major import trading partners: United Arab Emirates 12.7%, Saudi Arabia 10.1%, China 8.8%, US 4.9%

Foreign direct investment (net): $84.1 million

2003 Data (in constant 2000 US dollars)

Yemen, a poor Arab country with few natural resources, was divided into two spheres of influence in the 19th century by the Ottoman Empire in the north and the British Empire in the south. In 1990, North and South Yemen united after two decades of political tension and turmoil. A southern secessionist movement that erupted again in 1994 was quickly subdued, but President Ali Abdallah Saleh's government continues to face intermittent challenges from some of Yemen's often unruly tribes. President Saleh, who led Northern Yemen before the merger, also faces strong opposition from Southern Yemeni political parties and Islamic radicals who oppose the government's economic reform program and seek to obstruct private-sector initiatives. Yemen accepted an International Monetary Fund structural adjustment program as part of a 2002 $2.3 billion donor aid package. Yet the government has placed economic reforms on the back burner while it has waged war against Islamic extremists, many of them affiliated with al-Qaeda. The IMF continues to push for civil service reform, improvements in tax administration, and a reduction of subsidies. In recent years, the economy has been hurt by declining oil production, terrorist attacks, and kidnappings, which have undermined tourism and foreign investment. Yemen's trade policy score is 0.5 point better this year; however, its fiscal burden of government score is 0.4 point worse, and its monetary policy score is 1 point worse. As a result, Yemen's overall score is 0.09 point worse this year.

TRADE POLICY
Score: **4**–Better (high level of protectionism)

According to the World Bank, Yemen's weighted average tariff rate in 2000 was 11.7 percent. The *Index* methodology places greater emphasis on weighted average tariff rates, so the weighted average tariff rate for 2000 is used instead of the 12.6 percent average tariff rate for 2003 reported in the 2005 *Index*. According to the U.S. Department of Commerce, "The government prohibits importation of seven items: pork and pork products, coffee, alcohol, narcotics, some types of fresh fruits and vegetables during their local production season…and rhinoceros horns." The Economist Intelligence Unit reports that "excessively complex customs procedures" act as a trade barrier. Based on the lower tariff rate, as well as a revision of the trade factor methodology, Yemen's trade policy score is 0.5 point better this year.

FISCAL BURDEN OF GOVERNMENT
Score—Income Taxation: **3.5**–Stable (high tax rates)
Score—Corporate Taxation: **4.5**–Stable (very high tax rates)
Score—Change in Government Expenditures: **5**–Worse (very high increase)
Final Score: **4.4**–Worse (high cost of government)

Yemen's top income tax rate is 35 percent. The top corporate tax rate is also 35 percent. In 2003, according to the Embassy of Yemen, government expenditures as a share of GDP increased 4.8 percentage points to 38.2 percent, compared to the 1.3 percentage point increase in 2002. On net, Yemen's fiscal burden of government score is 0.4 point worse this year.

GOVERNMENT INTERVENTION IN THE ECONOMY
Score: **4**–Stable (high level)

The World Bank reports that the government consumed 13.8 percent of GDP in 2003. In the same year, based on data from the central bank, Yemen received 71.88 percent of its total revenues from state-owned enterprises and government ownership of property in the hydrocarbon sector.

 ## MONETARY POLICY
Score: **4**–Worse (high level of inflation)

From 1995 to 2004, based on data from the International Monetary Fund's *2005 World Economic Outlook*, Yemen's weighted average annual rate of inflation was 12.03 percent, up from the 11.02 percent from 1994 to 2003 reported in the 2005 *Index*. As a result, Yemen's monetary policy score is 1 point worse this year.

 ## CAPITAL FLOWS AND FOREIGN INVESTMENT
Score: **3**–Stable (moderate barriers)

Yemen has streamlined its investment laws and procedures in an attempt to attract more foreign investment. The government officially permits foreign investment in most sectors and grants equal treatment to all investors, both domestic and foreign. Foreign investment in the exploration for and production of oil, gas, and minerals is subject to production-sharing agreements. Foreign investment is not permitted in the arms and explosive materials industries, industries that could cause environmental disasters, or wholesale and retail imports. "While Yemen has fundamentally sound investment laws, labor laws, customs tariff regulations and tax laws," reports the U.S. Department of Commerce, "transparency of implementation and enforcement is elusive…. Yemen has a significant and widely-acknowledged corruption problem." Other barriers to foreign investment are ongoing security concerns and the lack of infrastructure. The International Monetary Fund reports that foreign exchange accounts are permitted. There are no restrictions on payments and transfers, and capital transactions face few restrictions.

 ## BANKING AND FINANCE
Score: **4**–Stable (high level of restrictions)

Yemen's financial system is small and dominated by the state. According to First Initiative, "The banking sector is characterized by heavy state involvement, led by the Central Bank of Yemen (CBY) and the Yemen Bank for Reconstruction and Development (YBRD) and the National Bank of Yemen (NBY). As of late 2004 there were 15 commercial banks, nine of which are private domestic banks (including four Islamic banks), four of which are private foreign banks and two of which are state-owned banks…. The banking sector in general suffers from a large volume of non-performing loans, low capitalization, and weak enforcement of prudential standards." The Economist Intelligence Unit reports that privatization of the National Bank of Yemen has "foundered after concerns that the bank's net worth has been overstated." The Embassy of Yemen reports that the state is the majority shareholder in four

banks, including the central bank, and a minority shareholder in six others. According to the EIU, the state-owned Yemen Bank for Reconstruction and Development—the largest bank in terms of branches, according to the Yemeni embassy—was also targeted for privatization but suffers from non-performing loans and is undercapitalized. The embassy reports that capital adequacy of commercial banks increased from 10 percent in 2002 to 11 percent in 2003.

 ## WAGES AND PRICES
Score: **3**–Stable (moderate level of intervention)

According to the Embassy of Yemen, petroleum products and utilities are subject to price controls. The Economist Intelligence Unit reports that the government continues to subsidize diesel fuel generously. The government also affects wages and prices through state-owned enterprises. Yemen's labor law specifies that the minimum wage for a private-sector worker may not be less than the minimum wage for a civil servant.

 ## PROPERTY RIGHTS
Score: **4**–Stable (low level of protection)

According to the Economist Intelligence Unit, "The judiciary is generally under-trained, inefficient and seen as corrupt." In addition, "Investors will remain wary of sinking their money into Yemen while the judicial system lacks teeth and government ministries fail to address problems of corruption within their ranks." The U.S. Department of Commerce reports that enforcement of laws and contracts "remains problematic at best and nonexistent at worst" and that, "in cases involving interest, most judges use Shari'a (Islamic) law as the guideline, under which claims for interest payments due are almost always rejected."

 ## REGULATION
Score: **4**–Stable (high level)

Bureaucratic inefficiency and corruption present serious impediments to business. According to the World Bank, the cost of starting a business, hiring and firing, and registering property is high in terms of both time and money. Ministries are hugely overstaffed, and reforming the civil service remains a promise unfulfilled. Regulations are applied haphazardly. According to the U.S. Department of Commerce, "While Yemen has fundamentally sound investment laws…transparency of implementation and enforcement is elusive."

 ## INFORMAL MARKET
Score: **4**–Stable (high level of activity)

Transparency International's 2004 score for Yemen is 2.4. Therefore, Yemen's informal market score is 4 this year.

ZAMBIA

Rank: 111

Score: 3.34

Category: Mostly Unfree

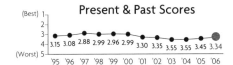

Present & Past Scores

(Best) 1—
2—
3—
4—
(Worst) 5—

3.15 3.08 2.88 2.99 2.96 2.99 3.30 3.35 3.55 3.55 3.45 3.34

'95 '96 '97 '98 '99 '00 '01 '02 '03 '04 '05 '06

QUICK STUDY

SCORES

Trade Policy   3.5
Fiscal Burden   3.9
Government Intervention   2
Monetary Policy   4
Foreign Investment   3
Banking and Finance   3
Wages and Prices   3
Property Rights   3
Regulation   4
Informal Market   4

Population: 10,403,000

Total area: 752,614 sq. km

GDP: $3.7 billion

GDP growth rate: 5.1%

GDP per capita: $354

Major exports: copper, cobalt, tobacco, cotton, electricity

Exports of goods and services: $1.0 billion

Major export trading partners: UK 26.6%, South Africa 21.6%, Tanzania 13.9%, Switzerland 8.1%

Major imports: transport equipment and machinery, petroleum products, electricity, clothing

Imports of goods and services: $1.3 billion

Major import trading partners: South Africa 48.3%, Zimbabwe 12.8%, UK 5.9%

Foreign direct investment (net): $94.3 million

2003 Data (in constant 2000 US dollars)

Zambia has been ruled by the Movement for Multi-Party Democracy since 1991. Levy Mwanawasa narrowly became president in 2001 in elections that, despite irregularities, were judged to be transparent and free. An anti-corruption effort begun in 2002 has resulted in the arrest and prosecution of numerous individuals, including the former vice president and former President Frederick Chiluba, but Mwanawasa and other members of the ruling party have also been accused of corruption and bribery. Drought, HIV/AIDS, and government mismanagement have hindered economic growth. Nearly three-quarters of the population lives below the poverty line. Agriculture accounts for only 15 percent of GDP but employs 60 percent of the country's workers. Copper and cobalt mining account for over 60 percent of total export earnings. Government wages and salaries comprise 8 percent of GDP. In 2005, Zambia qualified for debt relief under the International Monetary Fund and World Bank Heavily Indebted Poor Country initiative and secured a commitment by Paris Club donors to cancel three-quarters of its bilateral debt. The government has sporadically followed through on privatization plans initiated in 1991, but its support for further privatization has waned. Zambia is eligible for assistance as a threshold country for the U.S. Millennium Challenge Account. Zambia's fiscal burden of government score is 0.1 point better this year, and its monetary policy score is 1 point better. As a result, Zambia's overall score is 0.11 point better this year.

TRADE POLICY
Score: **3.5**–Stable (high level of protectionism)

According to the World Bank, Zambia's weighted average tariff rate in 2003 (the most recent year for which World Bank data are available) was 9.4 percent, up from the 8.4 percent for 2001 reported in the 2005 *Index,* based on World Bank data. The government requires "import certificates" for such items as meat, poultry, plants, pharmaceuticals, and firearms and ammunition. Export licenses are required for fertilizer, firearms, live animals, historical artifacts, and wildlife trophies. Based on the revised trade factor methodology, Zambia's trade policy score is unchanged.

FISCAL BURDEN OF GOVERNMENT
Score—Income Taxation: **3.5**–Better (high tax rates)
Score—Corporate Taxation: **4.5**–Stable (very high tax rates)
Score—Change in Government Expenditures: **3**–Stable (very low decrease)
Final Score: **3.9**–Better (high cost of government)

Effective April 2005, Zambia's top income tax rate was cut to 37.5 percent, down from the 40 percent reported in the 2005 *Index.* The top corporate tax rate is 35 percent. In 2003, according to the African Development Bank, government expenditures as a share of GDP decreased by 0.7 percentage point to 31.1 percent, compared to the 0.1 percentage point decrease in 2002. On net, Zambia's fiscal burden of government score is 0.1 point better this year.

GOVERNMENT INTERVENTION IN THE ECONOMY
Score: **2**–Stable (low level)

The World Bank reports that the government consumed 14.6 percent of GDP in 2003. In the same year, based on data from the International Monetary Fund, Zambia received 0.58 percent of its total revenues from state-owned enterprises and government ownership of property.

407

MONETARY POLICY
Score: **4**–Better (high level of inflation)

From 1995 to 2004, Zambia's weighted average annual rate of inflation was 19.44 percent, down from the 21.92 percent from 1994 to 2003 reported in the 2005 *Index*. As a result, Zambia's monetary policy score is 1 point better this year.

CAPITAL FLOWS AND FOREIGN INVESTMENT
Score: **3**–Stable (moderate barriers)

The U.S. Department of State reports that the government "actively seeks foreign investment through the Zambian Investment Center (ZIC), intended to be a one-stop resource for international investors interested in Zambia…. An investment board screens all investments for which incentives are requested, and usually makes its decision within thirty days. The reviews appear routine and non-discriminatory…. There is no distinction in law between foreign and domestic investors, with the exception of the retail sector, which is closed to foreigners. The privatization process is open to foreign bidders from the point at which companies are advertised." In practice, however, "red tape associated with licenses and permits presents problems. In some sectors, scores of licenses are required to run a business." There are no local content, equity, financing, employment, or technology transfer requirements. Investments may be expropriated only by an act of parliament, and compensation at a fair market value is required. According to the U.S. Department of State, however, "the method for determining fair market value is ill-defined." In addition, "Land, which is held under 99-year leases, may 'revert' to the government if it is ruled to be undeveloped." Corruption remains common despite government efforts to clamp down on it. The International Monetary Fund reports that both residents and non-residents may hold foreign exchange accounts. There are no controls on payments, transfers, capital transactions, or repatriation of profits.

BANKING AND FINANCE
Score: **3**–Stable (moderate level of restrictions)

Zambia's financial sector is small and dominated by banking. According to First Initiative, "Zambia's banking sector, which is one of the more liberally regulated in Africa, consisted of 15 operational commercial banks in 2004, including four international banks. Concentration is high, with the five largest banks controlling the vast majority of assets…. The Zambia National Commercial Bank (Zanaco), Zambia's only state bank and the country's largest domestic bank, is in the process of being privatized…. Zambia's insurance sector made moves toward privatization in 2003 with the restructuring of Zambia State Insurance Company (ZSIC) and the emergence of five private insurance firms. In 2004, however, the government removed ZSIC from the list of state firms to be privatized." The Economist Intelligence Unit reports that the sale of the state-owned Zambia National Commercial Bank has been delayed since the government terminated negotiations with bidders in March

2005. There are no restrictions on foreign investment in the stock exchange.

WAGES AND PRICES
Score: **3**–Stable (moderate level of intervention)

The government affects prices in the agricultural sector through the Food Reserve Agency (FRA), which buys and sells agricultural input products and crops from the private sector. The Economist Intelligence Unit reports that "over time the FRA became used for a host of very different functions, including purchasing large stocks of maize or fertiliser and distributing it at subsidised prices, and thus undercutting the private sector." Since agriculture is one of the most important sectors, influencing its prices significantly distorts the economy. Zambia also influences prices through its state-owned enterprises, which include (but are not limited to) state-owned enterprises in the railway, hydroelectric, and telecommunications sectors. There is a minimum wage for non-unionized workers.

PROPERTY RIGHTS
Score: **3**–Stable (moderate level of protection)

Zambia's judicial system suffers from inefficiency, government influence, and a lack of resources. The U.S. Department of Commerce reports that "contractual and property rights are weak and final court decisions can take a long time. There is no bankruptcy law…. Secured interests in property are possible and recognized, but fairly rare." In addition, "Zambian courts are relatively inexperienced in the area of commercial litigation. This, coupled with the large number of pending commercial cases in the system, impedes the regulatory system from being prompt and transparent. Some measures, mainly incentives to solve disputes by mediation, have been implemented in an attempt to clear the backlog, but have so far found limited success."

REGULATION
Score: **4**–Stable (high level)

Business in Zambia is hampered by outdated laws. According to the U.S. Department of Commerce, the business community questions "the enforceability of existing development agreements, and the fairness of competition between parastatals and private firms. Labor laws provide extremely generous severance benefits to workers, and slow investment. Although the Zambia Investment Center seeks to serve as a 'one stop shop' for investors, in practice red tape associated with licenses and permits presents problems. In some sectors, scores of licenses are required to run a business. Proposed laws and comments are not published in draft form for public comment."

INFORMAL MARKET
Score: **4**–Stable (high level of activity)

Transparency International's 2004 score for Zambia is 2.6. Therefore, Zambia's informal market score is 4 this year.

ZIMBABWE

Rank: 154

Score: 4.23

Category: Repressed

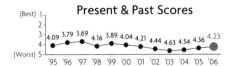

Present & Past Scores

(Best) 1
2
3 4.09 3.79 3.69 4.16 3.89 4.04 4.21 4.44 4.63 4.54 4.36 4.23
4
(Worst) 5
'95 '96 '97 '98 '99 '00 '01 '02 '03 '04 '05 '06

Zimbabwe has suffered economic collapse and political repression under President Robert Mugabe. In the March 2005 election, Mugabe and his Zimbabwe African National Union–Patriotic Front (ZANU–PF) used intimidation and violence to win a two-thirds majority in parliament, giving ZANU–PF the votes it needs to change the constitution. Corruption is endemic. Many people have fled, and many who remain are engaged in subsistence agriculture. Zimbabwe, once the breadbasket of Africa, cannot feed its own population and requires food assistance. Heavy regulation, price controls, expropriation of land and businesses, government spending equal to a quarter of GDP, inflationary monetary policy, and government-sanctioned violence have discouraged foreign investment and hindered economic production. Unemployment is estimated to be 80 percent, and most economic activity has been forced into the informal sector. Following the 2005 parliamentary elections, Mugabe sanctioned a crackdown on supporters of the opposition Movement for Democratic Change through arrests in urban areas, closure of informal markets, seizure of goods market stalls, and evictions that have left at least 300,000 people homeless. The campaign is especially pernicious given that disastrous economic policies have forced most of the population to rely on the informal sector for food and livelihood. Zimbabwe's trade policy score is 1 point worse this year; however, its fiscal burden of government score is 0.8 point better, its government intervention score is 0.5 point better, and its wages and prices score is 1 point better. As a result, Zimbabwe's overall score is 0.13 point better this year.

TRADE POLICY

Score: **5**–Worse (very high level of protectionism)

The World Bank reports that Zimbabwe's weighted average tariff rate in 2002 (the most recent year for which World Bank data are available) was 18.9 percent, up from the 12 percent for 2001 reported in the 2005 *Index*, based on World Bank data. According to the U.S. Department of Commerce, the government "maintains a 'negative list' of prohibited items that require special permission from the government to import." The same source reports that customs corruption acts as a non-tariff barrier. Based on the higher tariff rate, as well as a revision of the trade factor methodology, Zimbabwe's trade policy score is 1 point worse this year.

FISCAL BURDEN OF GOVERNMENT

Score—Income Taxation: **4**–Better (high tax rates)
Score—Corporate Taxation: **4**–Stable (high tax rates)
Score—Change in Government Expenditures: **1**–Better (very high decrease)
Final Score: **3.3**–Better (moderate cost of government)

Zimbabwe's top income tax rate is 41.2 percent, down from the 46.4 percent reported in the 2005 *Index*. The top corporate income tax rate is 30.9 percent. In 2003, according to the African Development Bank, government expenditures as a share of GDP decreased 5.2 percentage points to 24 percent, compared to the 1.6 percentage point increase in 2002. On net, Zimbabwe's fiscal burden of government score is 0.8 point better this year.

GOVERNMENT INTERVENTION IN THE ECONOMY

Score: **2**–Better (low level)

The African Development Bank reports that the government consumed 17.1 percent of GDP

QUICK STUDY

SCORES
Trade Policy 5
Fiscal Burden 3.3
Government Intervention ... 2
Monetary Policy 5
Foreign Investment 5
Banking and Finance 5
Wages and Prices 4
Property Rights 5
Regulation 4
Informal Market 4

Population: 13,102,000

Total area: 390,580 sq. km

GDP: $4.6 billion

GDP growth rate: −13.2%

GDP per capita: $351

Major exports: tobacco, gold, textiles and clothing

Exports of goods and services: $1.3 billion

Major export trading partners: Zambia 6.2%, South Africa 6.0%, China 5.3%, Germany 4.6%, Japan 4.4%

Major imports: transport equipment and machinery, chemicals, manufactures, petroleum products

Imports of goods and services: $1.6 billion

Major import trading partners: South Africa 51.1%, Germany 2.7%

Foreign direct investment (net): $14.2 million

2003 Data (in constant 2000 US dollars)

in 2003. In the same year, based on data from the International Monetary Fund, Zimbabwe received 3.38 percent of its total revenues from state-owned enterprises and government ownership of property, down from the 6.36 percent reported in the *2005 Index*. As a result, Zimbabwe's government intervention score is 0.5 point better this year.

 ## MONETARY POLICY
Score: 5–Stable (very high level of inflation)

From 1995 to 2004, Zimbabwe's weighted average annual rate of inflation was 294.30 percent.

 ## CAPITAL FLOWS AND FOREIGN INVESTMENT
Score: 5–Stable (very high barriers)

The government will consider foreign investment up to 100 percent in high-priority projects but applies pressure for eventual majority ownership by Zimbabweans. The U.S. Department of Commerce reports that "Zimbabwe is generally unwelcoming to foreign investment…. [T]he Government prefers majority Zimbabwean participation in new investment projects and specifies that the degree of local ownership will be a prime criterion in the evaluation of investment proposals…. Zimbabwe's constitution prohibits the acquisition of private property without compensation. Nonetheless, the Government has sanctioned land invasions…. [O]ver the past few years the President and other officials have made periodic statements indicating that the Government may next target the mining sector and/or manufacturing sector for similarly forced indigenization." The government re-imposed exchange controls in November 2002. According to the Economist Intelligence Unit, the government has "used various combinations of foreign-exchange controls and complicated multiple exchange-rate regimes to try to keep exporters in business while still allowing the government to capture a major share of the foreign exchange that they earn." The official exchange rate as of December 2004 was Z$5,700 to $1, but the parallel exchange rate is Z$8,600 to $1. The International Monetary Fund reports that foreign exchange accounts are subject to government approval and restrictions. Payments and transfers are subject to government approval and numerous restrictions, and all outward capital transactions are controlled.

 ## BANKING AND FINANCE
Score: 5–Stable (very high level of restrictions)

Zimbabwe's relatively sophisticated financial system has deteriorated from government intervention, lack of adequate supervision, and repeated crises ever since the 1997 economic downturn. The government has used the Reserve Bank of Zimbabwe to finance deficit spending and direct loans to state-owned enterprises. "The most recent crisis among locally owned banks came in early 2004, after nominal interest rates were raised sharply, temporarily, in late 2003," reports the Economist Intelligence Unit. "Since early 2001 economic policy has resulted in highly negative real interest rates, leading many banks to become involved in speculative investments,

most notably in property and the stock market, but also on the foreign-exchange market. The collapse of these markets as interest rates rose in late 2003 caused a major liquidity crisis. During the last year ten financial institutions were placed under RBZ curatorship…. The government merged three banks into a single financial institution, Zimbabwe Allied Banking Group (ZABG), and reopened them to the public in January 2005." The government indirectly owns this new bank. According to First Initiative, "Zimbabwe has been increasingly isolated from the international community and its financial sector has diminished greatly…. In 2004, the banking sector was comprised of 17 commercial banks. Three commercial banks, including the largest bank, had some degree of state-ownership, and all other commercial banks are privately owned. Four of Zimbabwe's private commercial banks are foreign owned."

 ## WAGES AND PRICES
Score: 4–Better (high level of intervention)

According to the U.S. Department of Commerce, "maximum prices are set for essential commodities such as agricultural seeds, bread, maize meal, sugar, beef, stock feeds, and fertilizer. The Government monitors all prices, but has not imposed across-the-board price controls since 2003." Zimbabwe maintains a minimum wage. Based on new evidence of a lower level of price controls, Zimbabwe's wages and prices score is 1 point better this year.

 ## PROPERTY RIGHTS
Score: 5–Stable (very low level of protection)

The U.S. Department of Commerce reports that "recent Government efforts to intimidate the judiciary and suspect new appointments to the bench have raised serious concerns in this area. Additionally, during 2002 many political heavyweights—including the Zimbabwean president—have publicly announced that they have no intention of honoring court orders if they are not politically acceptable to the ruling party." In May 2005, according to BBC News, the government announced that it would "amend the constitution so as to abolish rights to private ownership of land." All land would be state land, and farmers could lease it for 99 years.

 ## REGULATION
Score: 4–Stable (high level)

Businesses face considerable impediments in Zimbabwe. The bureaucracy is extremely arbitrary and not transparent. The U.S. Department of Commerce reports that "many bureaucratic functions in this still heavily controlled economy are not transparent and corruption within the regulatory system is increasingly worrisome."

 ## INFORMAL MARKET
Score: 4–Stable (high level of activity)

Transparency International's 2004 score for Zimbabwe is 2.3. Therefore, Zimbabwe's informal market score is 4 this year.

Appendix

2006 Index of Economic Freedom Rankings and Scores

2006 Rank	Country	2006	Trade Policy	Fiscal Burden	Govt. Intervention	Monetary Policy	Foreign Investment	Banking & Finance	Wages & Prices	Property Rights	Regulation	Informal Market
1	Hong Kong	1.28	1.0	1.8	1.5	1.0	1.0	1.0	2.0	1.0	1.0	1.5
2	Singapore	1.56	1.0	2.1	3.5	1.0	1.0	2.0	2.0	1.0	1.0	1.0
3	Ireland	1.58	2.0	2.3	2.0	1.0	1.0	1.0	2.0	1.0	2.0	1.5
4	Luxembourg	1.60	2.0	3.0	2.0	1.0	1.0	1.0	2.0	1.0	2.0	1.0
5	Iceland	1.74	2.5	2.4	2.5	1.0	3.0	1.0	1.0	1.0	2.0	1.0
5	United Kingdom	1.74	2.0	3.9	2.5	1.0	1.0	1.0	2.0	1.0	2.0	1.0
7	Estonia	1.75	2.0	2.0	2.0	1.0	1.0	1.0	2.0	2.0	2.0	2.5
8	Denmark	1.78	2.0	3.8	3.0	1.0	2.0	1.0	2.0	1.0	1.0	1.0
9	Australia	1.84	2.5	3.9	2.0	1.0	2.0	1.0	2.0	1.0	2.0	1.0
9	New Zealand	1.84	2.5	3.9	2.0	1.0	2.0	1.0	2.0	1.0	2.0	1.0
9	United States	1.84	2.0	3.9	2.0	1.0	2.0	1.0	2.0	1.0	2.0	1.5
12	Canada	1.85	2.0	2.5	2.0	1.0	3.0	2.0	2.0	1.0	2.0	1.0
12	Finland	1.85	2.0	3.0	2.5	1.0	2.0	2.0	2.0	1.0	2.0	1.0
14	Chile	1.88	1.5	2.3	2.5	1.0	2.0	2.0	2.0	1.0	3.0	1.5
15	Switzerland	1.89	2.0	2.9	2.0	1.0	2.0	2.0	2.0	1.0	3.0	1.0
16	Cyprus	1.90	2.0	2.5	2.0	1.0	2.0	2.0	2.0	1.0	2.0	2.5
16	Netherlands, The	1.90	2.0	4.0	3.0	1.0	1.0	1.0	2.0	1.0	3.0	1.0
18	Austria	1.95	2.0	3.5	2.0	1.0	2.0	2.0	2.0	1.0	3.0	1.0
19	Germany	1.96	2.0	3.1	2.0	1.0	1.0	3.0	2.0	1.0	3.0	1.5
19	Sweden	1.96	2.0	3.6	3.0	1.0	1.0	2.0	2.0	1.0	3.0	1.0
21	Czech Republic	2.10	2.0	2.5	2.5	1.0	2.0	1.0	2.0	2.0	3.0	3.0
22	Belgium	2.11	2.0	4.1	2.5	1.0	1.0	2.0	3.0	1.0	3.0	1.5
23	Lithuania	2.14	2.0	2.4	2.0	1.0	2.0	1.0	2.0	3.0	3.0	3.0
24	Malta	2.16	2.0	4.1	2.5	1.0	3.0	2.0	2.0	1.0	2.0	2.0
25	Bahrain	2.23	3.5	1.3	4.0	2.0	2.0	1.0	2.0	2.0	2.0	2.5
26	Barbados	2.25	4.0	3.5	2.5	1.0	3.0	2.0	2.0	1.0	2.0	1.5
27	Armenia	2.26	2.0	2.1	2.0	2.0	1.0	1.0	2.0	3.0	4.0	3.5
27	Bahamas, The	2.26	5.0	1.6	2.0	1.0	3.0	2.0	3.0	1.0	2.0	2.0
27	Japan	2.26	2.0	3.6	2.0	1.0	2.0	3.0	2.0	2.0	3.0	2.0
30	Botswana	2.29	1.5	2.9	3.0	3.0	2.0	2.0	2.0	2.0	2.0	2.5
30	Norway	2.29	2.0	3.4	3.5	1.0	3.0	3.0	2.0	1.0	3.0	1.0
30	Portugal	2.29	2.0	3.4	2.5	1.0	2.0	3.0	2.0	2.0	3.0	2.0
33	Spain	2.33	2.0	4.3	2.0	2.0	2.0	2.0	2.0	2.0	3.0	2.0
34	El Salvador	2.35	2.5	3.0	2.0	2.0	2.0	2.0	2.0	3.0	2.0	3.0
34	Slovak Republic	2.35	2.0	2.0	2.0	3.0	2.0	1.0	2.0	3.0	3.0	3.5
36	Israel	2.36	2.0	4.1	2.5	1.0	2.0	3.0	2.0	2.0	3.0	2.0
37	Taiwan	2.38	2.0	3.3	3.0	1.0	2.0	3.0	2.0	2.0	3.0	2.5
38	Slovenia	2.41	2.0	3.6	2.0	2.0	2.0	3.0	2.0	3.0	2.0	2.5
39	Latvia	2.43	2.0	2.3	2.5	2.0	2.0	2.0	2.0	3.0	3.0	3.5
40	Hungary	2.44	2.0	2.4	2.0	3.0	2.0	2.0	3.0	2.0	3.0	3.0
41	Poland	2.49	2.0	2.4	2.0	1.0	3.0	2.0	3.0	3.0	3.0	3.5
42	Italy	2.50	2.0	4.0	2.0	1.0	2.0	3.0	2.0	3.0	3.0	3.0
42	Trinidad and Tobago	2.50	2.5	3.5	2.0	2.0	2.0	2.0	3.0	2.0	3.0	3.0
44	France	2.51	2.0	4.1	3.0	1.0	3.0	3.0	2.0	2.0	3.0	2.0
45	Korea, Republic of (South Korea)	2.63	3.5	3.3	2.5	2.0	2.0	3.0	2.0	2.0	3.0	3.0
46	Cape Verde	2.69	5.0	2.9	2.0	1.0	3.0	3.0	2.0	2.0	2.0	4.0
46	Costa Rica	2.69	2.5	3.4	2.0	3.0	2.0	3.0	2.0	3.0	3.0	3.0
46	Uruguay	2.69	2.5	3.4	2.5	3.0	2.0	4.0	2.0	2.0	3.0	2.5
49	Panama	2.70	3.0	3.5	3.0	1.0	2.0	2.0	2.0	4.0	3.0	3.5
50	Kuwait	2.74	2.5	1.4	4.5	1.0	3.0	3.0	3.0	3.0	3.0	3.0
50	South Africa	2.74	2.5	3.9	2.0	2.0	3.0	3.0	2.0	3.0	3.0	3.0
52	Albania	2.75	4.0	2.5	2.0	1.0	2.0	2.0	2.0	4.0	4.0	4.0
52	Madagascar	2.75	2.5	4.0	1.5	3.0	2.0	3.0	2.0	3.0	3.0	3.5
54	Jamaica	2.76	3.5	4.1	2.5	3.0	1.0	2.0	2.0	3.0	3.0	3.5
55	Belize	2.78	4.5	2.8	2.0	1.0	3.0	3.0	2.0	3.0	3.0	3.5
55	Croatia	2.78	2.5	2.8	2.0	1.0	3.0	2.0	3.0	4.0	4.0	3.5
57	Greece	2.80	2.0	4.0	2.0	2.0	2.0	3.0	3.0	3.0	3.0	3.0
57	Jordan	2.80	4.0	4.0	3.5	1.0	3.0	2.0	2.0	3.0	3.0	2.5
57	Macedonia	2.80	3.5	1.5	3.0	1.0	3.0	2.0	2.0	4.0	4.0	4.0
60	Mexico	2.83	2.5	3.8	3.5	2.0	3.0	2.0	2.0	3.0	3.0	3.5
60	Mongolia	2.83	2.5	3.3	2.5	2.0	2.0	2.0	2.0	4.0	4.0	4.0
62	Saudi Arabia	2.84	3.0	1.4	4.5	1.0	4.0	3.0	2.0	3.0	3.0	3.5
63	Peru	2.86	3.5	3.6	2.0	1.0	3.0	2.0	2.0	4.0	4.0	3.5
64	Bulgaria	2.88	3.5	2.3	2.5	3.0	2.0	2.0	2.0	4.0	4.0	3.5
65	United Arab Emirates	2.93	2.5	1.3	4.0	2.0	4.0	4.0	3.0	3.0	3.0	2.5

2006 Index of Economic Freedom Rankings and Scores

2006 Rank	Country	2006	Trade Policy	Fiscal Burden	Govt. Intervention	Monetary Policy	Foreign Investment	Banking & Finance	Wages & Prices	Property Rights	Regulation	Informal Market
66	Uganda	2.95	3.0	3.5	2.0	2.0	3.0	2.0	2.0	4.0	4.0	4.0
67	Bolivia	2.96	3.0	2.6	2.0	2.0	4.0	2.0	2.0	4.0	4.0	4.0
68	Cambodia	2.98	4.0	2.3	2.5	1.0	3.0	2.0	2.0	4.0	4.0	5.0
68	Georgia	2.98	3.5	2.3	1.5	2.0	3.0	2.0	3.0	4.0	4.0	4.5
68	Malaysia	2.98	2.5	3.3	3.0	1.0	4.0	4.0	3.0	3.0	3.0	3.0
71	Kyrgyz Republic	2.99	2.5	2.4	2.0	2.0	3.0	3.0	3.0	4.0	4.0	4.0
71	Thailand	2.99	3.5	3.4	2.5	1.0	4.0	3.0	3.0	3.0	3.0	3.5
73	Lebanon	3.00	3.0	2.0	3.0	1.0	4.0	2.0	3.0	4.0	4.0	4.0
74	Bosnia and Herzegovina	3.01	2.5	2.6	2.5	1.0	3.0	2.0	3.0	5.0	5.0	3.5
74	Guatemala	3.01	2.5	3.6	1.0	3.0	3.0	3.0	2.0	4.0	4.0	4.0
74	Oman	3.01	4.5	1.6	4.5	1.0	3.0	3.0	4.0	3.0	3.0	2.5
77	Mauritius	3.03	4.5	3.3	3.0	2.0	2.0	3.0	4.0	2.0	3.0	3.5
78	Qatar	3.04	3.0	1.9	4.0	2.0	4.0	3.0	3.0	3.0	4.0	2.5
78	Swaziland	3.04	2.5	3.9	3.0	2.0	3.0	3.0	3.0	3.0	3.0	4.0
80	Nicaragua	3.05	2.5	4.0	2.0	3.0	2.0	2.0	3.0	4.0	4.0	4.0
81	Brazil	3.08	3.5	2.8	4.0	3.0	3.0	3.0	2.0	3.0	3.0	3.5
81	Mauritania	3.08	4.0	2.8	2.0	3.0	2.0	3.0	2.0	4.0	4.0	4.0
83	Moldova	3.10	2.5	2.5	2.0	3.0	4.0	3.0	3.0	3.0	4.0	4.0
83	Senegal	3.10	3.5	4.5	2.0	1.0	3.0	4.0	2.0	3.0	4.0	4.0
85	Guyana	3.11	4.0	4.1	3.0	2.0	3.0	2.0	2.0	3.0	4.0	4.0
85	Namibia	3.11	2.5	4.1	3.0	2.0	3.0	3.0	3.0	4.0	3.0	3.5
85	Turkey	3.11	2.0	3.1	2.5	4.0	3.0	3.0	3.0	3.0	4.0	3.5
88	Ivory Coast	3.14	4.0	4.4	1.5	1.0	3.0	2.0	3.0	4.0	4.0	4.5
88	Mali	3.14	4.0	3.9	2.0	1.0	3.0	4.0	3.0	4.0	3.0	3.5
90	Fiji	3.15	4.0	3.5	2.0	1.0	4.0	3.0	3.0	4.0	3.0	4.0
91	Colombia	3.16	3.5	4.1	3.5	3.0	3.0	2.0	2.0	4.0	3.0	3.5
92	Romania	3.19	3.5	1.9	1.5	4.0	3.0	3.0	3.0	4.0	4.0	4.0
92	Sri Lanka	3.19	3.0	3.4	2.0	3.0	4.0	4.0	3.0	3.0	3.0	3.5
94	Djibouti	3.20	5.0	3.5	3.5	1.0	3.0	2.0	2.0	4.0	4.0	4.0
94	Kenya	3.20	4.0	3.5	2.5	3.0	3.0	3.0	2.0	3.0	4.0	4.0
94	Tanzania	3.20	3.5	4.0	2.5	2.0	3.0	2.0	3.0	4.0	4.0	4.0
97	Morocco	3.21	5.0	4.1	2.5	1.0	2.0	4.0	3.0	4.0	3.0	3.5
98	Philippines, The	3.23	2.5	3.8	2.0	2.0	4.0	3.0	3.0	4.0	4.0	4.0
99	Lesotho	3.24	2.5	3.4	2.5	3.0	4.0	3.0	3.0	3.0	4.0	4.0
99	Tunisia	3.24	5.0	3.9	2.5	2.0	4.0	4.0	2.0	3.0	3.0	3.0
99	Ukraine	3.24	2.5	2.9	2.0	3.0	4.0	3.0	3.0	4.0	4.0	4.0
102	Burkina Faso	3.28	4.0	3.8	3.0	1.0	3.0	3.0	3.0	4.0	4.0	4.0
102	Gabon	3.28	4.5	3.8	3.0	1.0	3.0	4.0	3.0	3.0	4.0	3.5
102	Honduras	3.28	3.5	3.3	3.0	3.0	3.0	2.0	3.0	4.0	4.0	4.0
105	Chad	3.29	4.5	4.9	2.0	1.0	3.0	3.0	2.0	4.0	4.0	4.5
105	Ghana	3.29	4.5	3.9	2.0	4.0	3.0	3.0	3.0	3.0	3.0	3.5
107	Argentina	3.30	3.0	4.0	2.0	3.0	3.0	4.0	3.0	4.0	3.0	4.0
107	Ecuador	3.30	3.5	3.0	1.5	3.0	4.0	3.0	3.0	4.0	4.0	4.0
109	Paraguay	3.31	3.0	2.6	3.0	3.0	3.0	3.0	3.0	4.0	4.0	4.5
110	Pakistan	3.33	4.5	4.3	2.5	2.0	3.0	3.0	3.0	4.0	3.0	4.0
111	China, People's Republic of	3.34	3.0	3.9	3.0	1.0	4.0	4.0	3.0	4.0	4.0	3.5
111	Zambia	3.34	3.5	3.9	2.0	4.0	3.0	3.0	3.0	3.0	4.0	4.0
113	Kazakhstan	3.35	3.5	3.5	2.5	3.0	4.0	2.0	3.0	4.0	4.0	4.0
113	Mozambique	3.35	3.5	3.0	2.0	4.0	3.0	3.0	3.0	4.0	4.0	4.0
115	Niger	3.38	4.5	4.3	3.0	1.0	3.0	3.0	3.0	4.0	4.0	4.0
116	Dominican Republic	3.39	3.5	2.9	1.5	5.0	3.0	3.0	3.0	4.0	4.0	4.0
117	Benin	3.40	4.5	4.5	2.5	1.0	4.0	3.0	3.0	4.0	4.0	3.5
118	Central African Republic	3.41	5.0	4.1	3.0	1.0	3.0	3.0	3.0	4.0	4.0	4.0
119	Algeria	3.46	4.0	3.6	4.0	2.0	3.0	4.0	3.0	4.0	3.0	4.0
119	Cameroon	3.46	5.0	4.1	3.5	1.0	3.0	3.0	3.0	4.0	4.0	4.0
121	India	3.49	5.0	3.9	3.0	2.0	3.0	4.0	3.0	3.0	4.0	4.0
122	Russia	3.50	3.5	2.5	2.0	4.0	4.0	4.0	3.0	4.0	4.0	4.0
123	Azerbaijan	3.51	3.0	3.6	3.0	2.0	4.0	4.0	3.0	4.0	4.0	4.5
123	Gambia, The	3.51	4.5	3.6	2.0	4.0	3.0	3.0	3.0	4.0	4.0	4.0
125	Nepal	3.53	5.0	2.8	2.5	2.0	4.0	4.0	3.0	4.0	4.0	4.0
125	Rwanda	3.53	3.0	4.3	2.0	3.0	4.0	3.0	3.0	4.0	4.0	5.0
127	Guinea	3.55	5.0	4.0	1.5	4.0	4.0	3.0	2.0	4.0	4.0	4.0
128	Egypt	3.59	4.5	4.4	3.5	3.0	3.0	4.0	3.0	3.0	4.0	3.5

2006 Index of Economic Freedom Rankings and Scores

2006 Rank	Country	2006	Trade Policy	Fiscal Burden	Govt. Intervention	Monetary Policy	Foreign Investment	Banking & Finance	Wages & Prices	Property Rights	Regulation	Informal Market
129	Suriname	3.60	4.0	4.0	3.0	4.0	4.0	4.0	3.0	3.0	4.0	3.0
130	Malawi	3.63	4.0	4.3	4.0	4.0	3.0	3.0	3.0	3.0	4.0	4.0
131	Guinea-Bissau	3.65	4.5	4.0	2.0	1.0	3.0	4.0	3.0	5.0	5.0	5.0
132	Burundi	3.69	4.5	4.4	2.0	3.0	3.0	4.0	4.0	4.0	4.0	4.0
133	Ethiopia	3.70	4.5	4.0	3.5	3.0	3.0	4.0	3.0	4.0	4.0	4.0
134	Indonesia	3.71	3.0	4.1	3.5	3.0	4.0	4.0	3.0	4.0	4.0	4.5
134	Togo	3.71	3.5	4.6	3.0	1.0	4.0	4.0	3.0	4.0	5.0	5.0
136	Equatorial Guinea	3.74	4.5	3.4	2.5	3.0	4.0	3.0	4.0	4.0	4.0	5.0
137	Sierra Leone	3.76	4.5	4.1	2.0	3.0	4.0	4.0	2.0	5.0	5.0	4.0
137	Tajikistan	3.76	3.0	2.6	4.5	3.0	4.0	4.0	4.0	4.0	4.0	4.5
139	Angola	3.84	3.5	2.9	4.5	5.0	4.0	3.0	3.0	4.0	4.0	4.5
139	Yemen	3.84	4.0	4.4	4.0	4.0	3.0	4.0	3.0	4.0	4.0	4.0
141	Bangladesh	3.88	5.0	3.3	4.0	2.0	4.0	4.0	3.0	4.0	5.0	4.5
142	Vietnam	3.89	4.5	3.9	3.5	2.0	4.0	4.0	3.0	5.0	5.0	4.0
143	Congo, Republic of	3.90	5.00	4.0	4.0	1.0	4.0	4.0	3.0	5.0	5.0	4.0
144	Uzbekistan	3.91	3.0	2.6	3.5	4.0	4.0	5.0	4.0	4.0	5.0	4.0
145	Syria	3.93	5.0	3.8	5.0	2.0	4.0	4.0	4.0	4.0	4.0	3.5
146	Nigeria	4.00	5.0	3.0	4.5	4.0	4.0	4.0	3.0	4.0	4.0	4.5
147	Haiti	4.03	2.5	4.3	3.0	5.0	4.0	4.0	3.0	5.0	5.0	4.5
148	Turkmenistan	4.04	2.5	2.4	5.0	3.0	5.0	5.0	4.0	5.0	4.0	4.5
149	Laos	4.08	4.5	3.8	1.5	4.0	4.0	4.0	4.0	5.0	5.0	5.0
150	Cuba	4.10	3.5	4.5	4.5	1.0	4.0	5.0	5.0	5.0	5.0	3.5
151	Belarus	4.11	3.5	3.6	3.5	5.0	4.0	4.0	5.0	4.0	5.0	3.5
152	Libya	4.16	5.0	4.6	4.0	1.0	4.0	4.0	5.0	5.0	5.0	4.0
152	Venezuela	4.16	4.0	4.1	3.5	5.0	5.0	4.0	4.0	4.0	4.0	4.0
154	Zimbabwe	4.23	5.0	3.3	2.0	5.0	5.0	5.0	4.0	5.0	4.0	4.0
155	Burma (Myanmar)	4.46	5.0	3.6	3.5	4.0	5.0	5.0	4.0	5.0	5.0	4.5
156	Iran	4.51	4.5	3.6	5.0	4.0	5.0	5.0	4.0	5.0	5.0	4.0
157	Korea, Democratic Republic of (North Korea)	5.00	5.0	5.0	5.0	5.0	5.0	5.0	5.0	5.0	5.0	5.0
n/a	Congo, (Democratic Republic of)	n/a	n/a	n/a	n/a	n/a	n/a	n/a	n/a	n/a	n/a	n/a
n/a	Iraq	n/a	n/a	n/a	n/a	n/a	n/a	n/a	n/a	n/a	n/a	n/a
n/a	Serbia and Montenegro	n/a	n/a	n/a	n/a	n/a	n/a	n/a	n/a	n/a	n/a	n/a
n/a	Sudan	n/a	n/a	n/a	n/a	n/a	n/a	n/a	n/a	n/a	n/a	n/a

Per Capita Income Throughout the World
(Expressed in Purchasing Power Parity and in Constant 2000 U.S. Dollars)

This table is provided for those readers interested in per capita income measured in terms of purchasing power parity compared to per capita income measured in constant U.S. dollars.

Country	2003 per capita GDP (measured in purchasing power parity*)	2003 per capita GDP (measured in 2000 constant U.S. dollars**)	Country	2003 per capita GDP (measured in purchasing power parity*)	2003 per capita GDP (measured in 2000 constant U.S. dollars**)
Albania	$4,575	$1,392	Ethiopia	716	102
Algeria	6,175	1,916	Fiji	5,765	2,328
Angola	2,141	814	Finland	28,106	24,225
Argentina	11,560	7,165	France	28,231	22,723
Armenia	3,671	884	Gabon	6,397	3,865
Australia	28,939	21,688	The Gambia	1,855	324
Austria	30,938	24,217	Georgia	2,666	777
Azerbaijan	3,617	865	Germany	27,124	22,868
The Bahamas	17,700	16,067	Ghana	2,206	276
Bahrain	19,109	10,889	Greece	20,818	11,449
Bangladesh	1,770	395	Guatemala	4,109	1,675
Barbados	15,720	9,256	Guinea	2,097	431
Belarus	6,065	1,513	Guinea–Bissau	701	135
Belgium	28,331	22,544	Guyana	4,267	942
Belize	6,471	3,635	Haiti	1,750	467
Benin	1,105	392	Honduras	2,709	927
Bolivia	2,594	1,017	Hong Kong, China	27,881	25,627
Bosnia and Herzegovina	6,646	1,225	Hungary	15,405	5,333
Botswana	8,714	3,532	Iceland	30,906	30,952
Brazil	7,838	3,510	India	2,893	511
Bulgaria	7,501	1,835	Indonesia	3,401	781
Burkina Faso	1,174	253	Iran	6,995	1,715
Burma (Myanmar)	1,700	154	Iraq	2,100	n/a
Burundi	647	100	Ireland	38,059	27,932
Cambodia	2,145	313	Israel	23,132	17,298
Cameroon	2,077	634	Italy	27,228	19,090
Canada	30,065	24,222	Ivory Coast	1,500	597
Cape Verde	5,456	1,290	Jamaica	3,789	3,156
Central African Republic	1,105	229	Japan	28,220	38,222
Chad	1,215	218	Jordan	4,282	1,819
Chile	10,274	5,196	Kazakhstan	6,663	1,673
China, People's Republic of	5,003	1,067	Kenya	1,041	341.
Colombia	6,490	2,017	Korea, Democratic Republic of (North Korea)	1,700	n/a
Congo, Democratic Republic of	665	87	Korea, Republic of (South Korea)	19,168	12,236
Congo, Republic of	965	943	Kuwait	18,073	16,738
Costa Rica	9,550	4,410	Kyrgyz Republic	1,755	305
Croatia	11,671	4,751	Laos	1,818	352
Cuba	3,000	2,516	Latvia	10,635	4,116
Cyprus	21,896	12,647	Lebanon	5,034	3,925
Czech Republic	18,154	5,899	Lesotho	2,505	530
Denmark	30,646	30,262	Libya	6,700	4,083
Djibouti	2,058	848	Lithuania	11,846	4,078
Dominican Republic	7,108	2,413	Luxembourg	64,710	46,067
Ecuador	3,641	1,368	Macedonia	6,275	1,740
Egypt	3,950	1,622	Madagascar	809	233
El Salvador	5,028	2,129	Malawi	609	157
Equatorial Guinea	2,700	3,716	Malaysia	9,512	4,011
Estonia	12,913	7,475			

Per Capita Income Throughout the World
(Expressed in Purchasing Power Parity and in Constant 2000 U.S. Dollars)

This table is provided for those readers interested in per capita income measured in terms of purchasing power parity compared to per capita income measured in constant U.S. dollars.

Country	2003 per capita GDP (measured in purchasing power parity*)	2003 per capita GDP (measured in 2000 constant U.S. dollars**)	Country	2003 per capita GDP (measured in purchasing power parity*)	2003 per capita GDP (measured in 2000 constant U.S. dollars**)
Mali	1,002	258	Singapore	24,894	22,238
Malta	18,017	9,568	Slovak Republic	13,400	4,254
Mauritania	1,958	372	Slovenia	19,555	10,396
Mauritius	11,276	4,167	South Africa	10,594	3,026
Mexico	9,313	5,803	Spain	24,188	14,691
Moldova	1,512	370	Sri Lanka	3,751	921
Mongolia	1,835	424	Sudan	1,922	433
Morocco	4,010	1,278	Suriname	4,300	2,257
Mozambique	1,120	255	Swaziland	4,856	1,358
Namibia	6,132	1,845	Sweden	28,289	27,998
Nepal	1,420	241	Switzerland	32,451	34,369
The Netherlands	31,073	22,973	Syria	3,721	1,135
New Zealand	22,257	14,538	Taiwan	25,300	13,569
Nicaragua	3,271	767	Tajikistan	1,091	208
Niger	837	178	Tanzania	621	309
Nigeria	1,045	357	Thailand	7,595	2,276
Norway	36,633	38,260	Togo	1,699	292
Oman	13,795	7,876	Trinidad and Tobago	10,766	7,520
Pakistan	2,093	546	Tunisia	7,161	2,214
Panama	6,868	4,167	Turkey	7,068	2,977
Paraguay	4,746	1,407	Turkmenistan	5,943	989
Peru	5,260	2,131	Uganda	1,478	277
The Philippines	4,278	1,047	Ukraine	5,490	812
Poland	11,924	4,885	United Arab Emirates	25,200	19,717
Portugal	19,097	10,284	United Kingdom	29,345	25,742
Qatar	23,200	30,013	United States	37,425	35,566
Romania	7,596	1,963	Uruguay	8,336	5,235
Russia	9,033	2,138	Uzbekistan	1,737	610
Rwanda	1,257	260	Venezuela	5,043	4,009
Saudi Arabia	13,520	9,038	Vietnam	2,490	470
Senegal	1,648	485	Yemen	869	553
Serbia and Montenegro	2,400	1,200	Zambia	877	354
Sierra Leone	758	141	Zimbabwe	1,900	351

Note: * Purchasing power parity (PPP) GDP is adjusted for inflation (real GDP) and converted to U.S. dollars using current PPP exchange rates. PPP exchange rates are a ratio of the current year's price levels in two countries.

** GDP in constant U.S. dollars is adjusted for inflation and exchange rate changes. GDP in constant 2000 U.S. dollars is converted from real GDP in national currencies using 2000 official market exchange rates.

Sources: World Bank, *World Development Indicators Online*, available at www.worldbank.org/data by subscription, and U.S. Central Intelligence Agency, *World Factbook 2005*, available at www.cia.gov/cia/publications/factbook/fields/2004.html.

Foreign Aid*

Country	**USAID		World Bank (***IDA: International Development Association)	
		(in millions of US dollars)		
	Aid in 2004	Cumulative Aid (since 1997)	Loans in 2004	Cumulative Loans (since 1997)
Albania	$24.1	$267.8	$58.0	$485.3
Algeria	0.9	3.6	0.0	0.0
Angola	91.4	542.7	55.0	142.6
Armenia	64.9	650.1	84.8	572.3
Azerbaijan	34.8	253.7	25.0	457.3
Bangladesh	83.1	699.2	526.5	3841.7
Belarus	2.9	51.7	n/a	n/a
Benin	21.0	159.9	20.0	204.4
Bolivia	57.0	583.9	54.0	714.7
Bosnia and Herzegovina	32.1	1,038.5	97.0	920.9
Brazil	19.0	121.6	0.0	0.0
Bulgaria	23.0	251.4	0.0	0.0
Burkina Faso	8.8	95.9	120.0	672.3
Burma (Myanmar)	5.3	33.7	n/a	n/a
Burundi	28.2	98.0	110.4	318.6
Cambodia	57.3	244.0	60.0	427.5
Cameroon	0.0	7.2	20.0	458.5
Cape Verde	4.4	26.2	4.0	130.1
Central African Republic	1.0	2.1	0.0	45
Chad	18.1	32.5	20.0	442.6
China, People's Republic of	6.8	7.8	0.0	1041
Colombia	0.0	19.2	0.0	0.0
Congo, Democratic Republic of	77.4	271.7	736.0	1690
Congo, Republic of	n/a	n/a	19.0	149.7
Croatia	19.9	213.1	0.0	0.0
Cuba	8.2	8.2	n/a	n/a
Cyprus	7.3	84.8	n/a	n/a
Djibouti	26.0	36.5	0.0	97
Dominican Republic	28.6	153.0	0.0	2.2
Ecuador	18.3	146.8	0.0	0.0
Egypt	650.8	5,585.0	0.0	452
El Salvador	34.4	382.0	0.0	0.0
Ethiopia	332.7	1,397.6	320.0	1600.8
The Gambia	0.5	11.3	0.0	46
Georgia	64.6	597.8	47.6	578.9
Ghana	68.3	445.6	160.5	1326.5
Guatemala	43.7	446.6	0.0	0.0
Guinea	30.8	204.2	0.0	344.7
Guinea–Bissau	0.0	7.3	7.0	203
Guyana	5.3	32.3	10.0	44.3
Haiti	116.6	693.5	n/a	n/a
Honduras	42.3	317.1	154.9	808.7
Hungary	0.0	28.3	n/a	n/a
India	148.7	1,154.3	1,033.0	7034
Indonesia	109.6	862.8	55.8	736.7
Iraq	0.0	8.1	n/a	n/a
Israel	477.2	7,060.5	n/a	n/a

Foreign Aid (continued)

Country	**USAID** Aid in 2004	Cumulative Aid (since 1997)	World Bank (***IDA: International Development Association) Loans in 2004	Cumulative Loans (since 1997)
	(in millions of US dollars)			
Ivory Coast	7.6	15.2	0.0	753.3
Jamaica	20.1	110.8	0.0	0.0
Jordan	350.8	2,137.6	0.0	0.0
Kazakhstan	27.7	305.9	0.0	0.0
Kenya	101.3	521.5	264.7	741.9
Korea, Democratic Republic of (North Korea)	94.5	241.7	n/a	n/a
Kyrgyz Republic	29.7	262.8	31.0	366.7
Laos	1.7	9.2	35.7	146.9
Latvia	0.0	6.9	0.0	0.0
Lebanon	33.3	183.8	0.0	0.0
Lesotho	1.3	3.7	21.0	67.6
Lithuania	0.0	16.9	n/a	n/a
Macedonia	35.1	288.5	0.0	84.9
Madagascar	32.8	207.2	230.0	1232.5
Malawi	39.9	274.7	116.0	614.8
Mali	41.2	302.7	127.4	614
Malta	0.0	0.0	n/a	n/a
Mauritania	41.2	71.8	84.0	392.8
Mexico	32.4	161.3	0.0	0.0
Moldova	29.3	297.5	63.0	143.2
Mongolia	9.9	87.9	18.0	195.9
Morocco	13.8	13.8	0.0	0.0
Mozambique	68.3	522.3	97.3	1060
Namibia	6.6	75.5	n/a	n/a
Nepal	39.4	212.3	185.8	522.9
Nicaragua	40.4	302.1	100.5	753.2
Niger	12.8	54.6	109.8	584.7
Nigeria	111.0	412.0	322.0	1233.3
Pakistan	62.5	769.0	731.2	2202.7
Panama	6.6	43.9	n/a	n/a
Paraguay	10.1	63.0	n/a	n/a
Peru	60.1	725.2	0.0	0.0
The Philippines	73.2	387.7	0.0	0.0
Poland	0.0	95.4	n/a	n/a
Romania	26.7	293.1	0.0	0.0
Russia	93.7	1,112.0	0.0	0.0
Rwanda	36.6	319.5	20.0	514.1
Senegal	29.1	204.4	45.0	940.9
Serbia and Montenegro***	140.4	454.6	125.0	522.1
Sierra Leone	24.6	210.0	25.1	263.7
Slovakia	0.0	29.9	0.0	0.0
South Africa	65.9	491.6	0.0	0.0
Sri Lanka	16.4	60.0	175.7	780
Sudan	334.5	789.0	n/a	n/a
Tajikistan	30.5	215.7	10.8	327.9
Tanzania	52.7	328.8	451.0	1790.7

Foreign Aid (continued)

Country	**USAID Aid in 2004	Cumulative Aid (since 1997)	World Bank (***IDA: International Development Association) (in millions of US dollars) Loans in 2004	Cumulative Loans (since 1997)
Thailand	4.1	13.7	n/a	n/a
Turkey	0.0	1,238.6	0.0	0.0
Turkmenistan	4.0	49.9	n/a	n/a
Uganda	138.3	712.6	189.6	1756.6
Ukraine	96.5	1,273.9	0.0	0.0
Uzbekistan	26.8	259.7	0.0	45
Venezuela	0.0	0.5	n/a	n/a
Vietnam	6.3	48.4	705.5	3559.3
Yemen	18.8	29.1	145.0	1063.4
Zambia	56.1	298.2	50.0	1089.5
Zimbabwe	19.0	134.4	0.0	148.6
Total	5,551.2	43,091.4	8,278.6	50,502.4

Note: * 104 countries that are covered by the Index and for which aid data (either USAID or IDA) are available.

** Economic assistance only. Selection of recipients of USAID economic assistance reflects the priorities and interests of United States foreign policy.

*** The International Development Association (IDA) provides the world's poorest countries with credits, which are loans at zero interest with a 10-year grace period and maturities of 35 to 40 years. The operational cutoff for IDA eligibility for FY 2005 is $965 in GNI per capita. Currently, 81 countries are eligible for IDA credits.

****Data include U.S. aid to Kosovo.

Sources: USAID, Congressional Budget Presentation FY 2006, FY 2005, FY 2004, FY 2002, FY 2000, and FY 1998, at *http://www.usaid.gov/policy/budget/*; World Bank, *Annual Report*, 2004, 2003, 2002, 2001, 2000, 1999, 1998, and 1997, at *http://web.worldbank.org/WBSITE/EXTERNAL/EXTABOUTUS/0,,contentMDK:20042527 ~menuPK:34633~pagePK:43912~piPK:44037,00.html*

Major Works Cited

The following sources provided the basis for the country factor analyses in the 2006 *Index of Economic Freedom*. In addition, the authors and analysts of the various elements of the *Index* relied on supporting documentation and information from various government agencies and sites on the Internet, news reports and journal articles, and official responses to inquiries. These sources are cited in each chapter where appropriate. All statistical and other information received from government sources was verified with independent, internationally recognized nongovernmental sources as well.

African Development Bank, *ADB Statistics Pocketbook 2005*; available at *www.afdb.org/pls/portal/docs/PAGE/ADB_ADMIN_PG/DOCUMENTS/STATISTICS/POCKETBOOK%202005_WEB.PDF*.

Asian Development Bank, *Key Indicators of Developing Asian and Pacific Countries 2004*, Vol. XXXIV; available at *www.adb.org/Documents/Books/Key_Indicators/2004/default.asp*.

Country statistical agencies, central banks, and ministries of finance, economy, and trade; available at *www.un.org/Depts/unsd/gs_natstat.htm*; *www.census.gov/main/www/stat_int.html*; *www.centralbanking.co.uk/links/mof.htm*; *www.bis.org/cbanks.htm*; and *http://dir.yahoo.com/Government/Statistics/*.

Deloitte, *Country Snapshots*; available at *www.deloitte.com/dtt/section_node/0,1042,sid%253D11410,00.html*.

Economist Intelligence Unit Limited, *Country Profile*, London, U.K., 2004 and 2005.

———, *EIU Country Report*, London, U.K., 1996 through 2005.

———, *Country Commerce*, London, U.K., 2004 and 2005.

Ernst & Young International, Ltd., *The Global Executive*, New York, N.Y., 2005.

———, *Worldwide Corporate Tax Guide*, New York, N.Y., 2005.

———, direct correspondence with Country Office.

European Bank for Reconstruction and Development, *Country Strategies*, 2004 and 2005; available at *www.ebrd.org/about/strategy/index.htm*.

First Initiative, *Information Exchange*; available at *www.firstinitiative.org/informationExchange/countries/index.cfm*.

Inter-American Development Bank; available at *www.iadb.org*.

International Monetary Fund, *Annual Report on Exchange Arrangements and Exchange Restrictions 2004*, Washington, D.C., 2004.

————, *Article IV Staff Reports*, various countries, Washington, D.C., 2002 through 2005; available at *www.imf.org/external/ns/cs.aspx?id=51*.

————, *Government Finance Statistics* CD–ROM 2005, Washington, D.C., 2005.

————, *International Financial Statistics Online*, Washington, D.C., 2005; available by subscription at *http://ifs.apdi.net/imf/logon.aspx*.

————, *Selected Issues and Statistical Appendix*, various countries, Washington, D.C., 2001 through 2005.

————, *World Economic Outlook: Advancing Structural Reforms*, Washington, D.C., April 2005; available at *www.imf.org/external/pubs/ft/weo/2005/01/index.htm*.

————, *Country Information*; available at *www.imf.org/external/country/index.htm*.

Miles, Marc A., Edwin J. Feulner, and Mary Anastasia O'Grady, *2005 Index of Economic Freedom* (Washington, D.C.: The Heritage Foundation and Dow Jones & Company, Inc., 2005).

Organisation for Economic Co-operation and Development, *OECD Economic Outlook*, No. 76 (December 2004) and No. 77 (May 2005).

————, *OECD Statistics*; available at *http://cs4hq.oecd.org/oecd/*.

————, OECD Web site; available at *www.oecd.org/statsportal/0,2639,en_2825_293564_1_1_1_1_1,00.html*.

Standard & Poor's, *Sovereigns Ratings Analysis*, New York, N.Y., 2005; available at *www2.standardandpoors.com/NASApp/cs/ContentServer?pagename=sp/Page/FixedIncomeBrowsePg&r=1&l=EN&b=2&s=17&f=3*.

Transparency International, *The Corruption Perceptions Index*, Berlin, Germany, 2004, 2003, 2002, 2001, 2000, and 1999; available at *www.transparency.org/cpi/index.html#cpi*.

United Nations, *National Account Statistics Databases*; available at *http://unstats.un.org/unsd/snaama/Introduction.asp*.

United States Department of Commerce, *Country Commercial Guides*, Washington, D.C., 2002, 2003, 2004, and 2005; available at *www.buyusainfo.net/adsearch.cfm?search_type=int&loadnav=no*.

United States Department of State, *Country Reports on Human Rights Practices for 2003*, released by the Bureau of Democracy, Human Rights, and Labor, February 2005; available at *www.state.gov/g/drl/rls/hrrpt/2004/index.htm*.

United States Department of State, *Investment Climate Statements: 2005*, released by the Bureau of Economic and Business Affairs, February 2005; available at *www.state.gov/e/eb/ifd/2005/*.

United States Trade Representative, Office of the, *2005 National Trade Estimate Report on Foreign Trade Barriers*, 2004; available at *www.ustr.gov/Document_Library/Reports_Publications/2005/2005_NTE_Report/Section_Index.html*.

World Bank, *World Bank World Development Indicators Online*, Washington, D.C., 2005; available by subscription at *http://publications.worldbank.org/WDI/*.

World Trade Organization, *Trade Policy Reviews*, 1995 through 2005; available at *www.wto.org/english/tratop_e/tpr_e/tpr_e.htm*.